THE
BILL JAMES
BASEBALL
ABSTRACT
1988

THE
BILL JAMES
BASEBALL
ABSTRACT
1988

Bill James

Ballantine Books • New York

Library of Congress Catalog Card Number: 87-91554
ISBN 0-345-35171-1

Cover design by James R. Harris
Photo by Don Banks

Manufactured in the United States of America

First Edition: April 1988

10 9 8 7 6 5 4 3 2 1

DEDICATION

I used to be in a table-game league. This was ten, twelve years ago. We played a local game called *Ballpark,* which was never marketed in a very professional way but which was ahead of its time: complex, layered, intricate. We were replaying the seasons of the American League in the 1930s; I had a roster made up of players like Bill Dickey, Hank Greenberg, and Earl Whitehill, not to mention Frank Doljack, Larry Rosenthal, and Milt Galatzer.

As you reach the end of things, you look back to the beginnings. It was during this period, in trying to win that league, that I became obsessed with how an offense works and why it doesn't work sometimes, with how you could evaluate a trade and understand whether you had won or lost, with finding what information you would need to have to simulate baseball in a more accurate way. I had

thought about these things before, of course, but to win that damn little league I had to know. That focused my interest in the game onto analytical questions; and then there was an economic accident, and there I was on the bestseller list.

So I dedicate this, my last *Baseball Abstract,* to those guys who, in an odd way, helped to get it started: Collin Gage, Jim Johnson, Chris Ketzel, John Rinkenbaugh, Jack Turcotte, Phil Wedge, Paul Worth. I can't remember the name of the guy who used to own the Cleveland franchise; sorry. I'll mention Robert Weisman, who took it over, and Jim Carothers, and my nephew Jim West. I miss those days, but then I guess you always miss being young and thinking that you are doing nothing.

ACKNOWLEDGMENTS

All of the people who have helped me in the past to do this book have helped me again this year. Well, maybe not all of them, but most of them. I am still married to Susie McCarthy, who remains (you will be happy to hear the yearly update on this), who remains the best wife in the world. Yes, it's true; the computerized rankings were just released on Tuesday by WWRS (World Wife-Rating Service), and Susie is ranked first again, edging out a Polynesian woman named Baktal, a Sepatoli, whose husband was attacked by a shark while he was swimming, and who dived into the water and gave that shark wherefore and whathaveyou until the terrified fish gave back her husband's hand and agreed to pay all of his medical bills. This service is nothing compared to what Susie does for me— figures the catchers' stats, for example, and reads all the articles and makes corrections, and takes care of all the details of life for the months known (we will not miss this expression) as the Abstract Crunch. Among husbands, by the way, I rated 912,474,384th, between a Yugoslavian alcoholic and a Jamaican guy who's been dead for several years. I think it was a misprint.

My agent remains Liz Darhansoff. My editor remains Peter Gethers. Your help is much appreciated. My daughter remains Rachel; going to have another one in May. Don't know yet if it's a girl or a porcupine.

I haven't talked to Dan Okrent for a couple of years now, which is one of my great regrets, but in drawing the circle to a close I would like to thank Dan again for introducing me to the people who had the professional skills to make the *Baseball Abstract,* after five years of anonymity, into a paying proposition. There are other people who were important early that I should also like to thank here, one last time: Dallas Adams, Walt Campbell, Pete Palmer.

Various people helped in getting the data together this year: John Dewan, Ron Blake, Gary Skoog, Dave Nichols, Don Zminda. Some other people didn't help, but what the hell; this isn't the place to talk about that. For all you do. This book's for you.

CONTENTS

SECTION
I

ESSAYS

RAIN DELAY

You think he's the best player in baseball?

Who?

First Base.

Mattingly? I don't know. Seems to be what everybody thinks.

Well, not really.

Why? Wasn't there a poll of the players that chose Mattingly as the best player in the game?

A couple of years ago, yeah. Mattingly won about 15 percent of the vote, and at that did better in the voting among National League players than among the guys he plays against. Nobody else got more than 11 percent of the vote, but I can't see that that amounts to much evidence.

Well, what's good evidence?

What's the player do? His job is to help his team win. Any evidence about what the player does to help his team win is good evidence.

Who do you think is the best, if it's not Mattingly?

I didn't say it wasn't Mattingly. There's just a lot of other candidates.

Such as?

Andre Dawson. Roger Clemens, I suppose. Kirby Puckett. George Brett. Dale Murphy. You could probably take almost any position and make an argument for somebody.

Looks like it's going to rain awhile.

OK.

Let's start with catcher.

Well, Terry Kennedy started the All-Star Game for the American League last year, so I'd say you can eliminate 14 teams right away.

I'd say so. I guess Carter remains the best catcher in the game?

I suppose.

He's never won an MVP, either.

Nope. Two or three years ago you could argue for Carter as the best player in the game. But with the knees, the .235 batting average, with all the games he's caught and all the bases stolen against him, not anymore . . . I'd have to say nobody now would trade Mattingly for Carter.

That seems pretty safe. OK, we'll eliminate the catchers. Any other first basemen we ought to mention?

Hernandez is a hell of a player, but I don't know that he's better than Mattingly.

Mattingly has more power and hits for a better average. Mattingly runs better.

Everybody in the league runs better.

Just about.

Hernandez has his points.

A lot of people feel he's the best defensive first baseman ever, although Mattingly's got a good glove, too.

Hernandez is a more patient hitter than Mattingly, but their on-base percentages are just the same. I don't think too many people would rather have Hernandez.

Any other first basemen we ought to consider? Eddie Murray doesn't have any big positives that Mattingly doesn't have. Mark McGwire?

Too early. I'd say Pete O'Brien is 99 percent of the player that Hernandez is, but he isn't any better. I guess we can clear first.

Second base. Sandberg?

No way.

No way? Here's a Gold Glove second baseman, terrific baserunner who in his best years has the stats of an outfielder.

In Wrigley Field. But you take him out of Wrigley and he'll hit .285 with 12 to 15 homers a year.

With a lot of other markers.

Sure, but not enough to turn that kind of a hitter into the best player in baseball.

All right, I'll buy. What about Samuel?

He's gettin' there.

Gettin' there? He drives in a hundred, scores 113, steals bases, hits for power. Where's he supposed to be going?

Somewhere where they don't strike out once a game.

Well, yeah, but his strikeout and walk data was a lot better last year. Didn't he draw 60 walks or something? Sixty walks, decent average despite the strikeouts, 80 extra base hits, steals up to 70 bases in a year, has improved a bunch at second base.

You're giving him credit for all of the things he does in all of his best years. He stole 35 bases last year, not 70, and was caught 15 times, which has a net value of about two runs. He made 510 outs, 99 more than Mattingly. His batting average is just average for a second baseman, and his on-base percentage is less than average. That's half of offense—an offense is half getting people on base, and half scoring them once they are on there. His defense is the same, a combination of brilliant plays and real short-comings.

You're not saying he's an average player?

No, but he's half superstar and half average player. In another three years he may be all superstar or at least 70 percent superstar, but not now.

Nobody's all superstar.

We're talking about the best player in baseball here. You've got to expect to come pretty close.

What's the biggest thing that bothers you about him?

The outs. Samuel made 510 outs. Given that many outs, just an average NL second baseman would put about 90 runs on the scoreboard. Samuel created 109 runs, but that's just 19 better than average—in his best season. Mattingly was 22 runs better than an average AL first baseman, not having his best season. And Mattingly is a better defensive player, for his position, than Samuel.

OK, we'll pass on Samuel. Third base is Boggs.

Here's the first serious argument.

I suppose. He's never won an MVP, either. Do you really think he could be better than Mattingly?

Not only could be. He is. Remember I said Mattingly was 22 runs better than an average American League first baseman, given the same number of outs? Well, Boggs was 82 runs better than an average AL third baseman, given the same number of outs. Eighty-two runs.

There's got to be a "but" there somewhere.

Sure. I'll give you four. Boggs was having his best year, hit three times as many homers as ever before. Mattingly wasn't having an especially good year by his own standards. Boggs hits in Fenway Park; Mattingly hits in Yankee Stadium, which is not a good park for a hitter. The American League has eight terrific first basemen, so the average performance for an American League first baseman is a little misleading. And the runs created formula may overestimate a player who has both a high on-base percentage and a high slugging percentage, like Boggs, meaning that maybe he created 144 runs rather than 154.

Can you adjust for all those?

Not very well, no. You can hang numbers on them, but we don't have enough ways to double-check that we can be really sure if the numbers fit or not.

But then there are other things you can say for Boggs, too.

That's right. Boggs announced in spring training that he was going to hit more home runs, so I don't think that's a fluke. I think it's a real level of ability, albeit a new one. If you cut Boggs down ten runs for playing in Fenway and ten runs because the runs created formula isn't perfect, he's still +62—that's 62 runs better than the average guy at his position. If you give Mattingly a bonus because it wasn't his best year, give him a few runs for playing in Yankee Stadium and make an adjustment against average first basemen, rather than who happens to be in the American League right now, he still don't get there.

So even making what seem like larger-than-reasonable adjustments, you still don't think Mattingly means as much to the Yankee offense as Boggs does to the Red Sox.

Exactly.

OK. But when push comes to shove, who would you rather have? Mattingly is an RBI man.

Put Boggs hitting third behind Rickey Henderson, and he'll be an RBI man, too. Who would you take?

I'd take a beer vendor if you can catch one. You need a beer?

Please.

That's one of those expressions.

What?

Need a beer. It works its way into the language because we don't want to say what we mean. I told my wife last week that one of my jackets had gotten too small for me.

All by itself.

Right.

You gonna choose?

Bud or Busch?

Boggs or Mattingly.

Boggs, I guess. It's real hard to pass up a .355 hitter, even if he was just a singles hitter. Boggs hits doubles, some homers now, draws a hundred walks a year. I think I'd have to take him over Mattingly.

Agreed. Boggs is number one, then. Who else should we think about at third base.

Brett?

His durability is too big a negative.

A friend of mine who's a Kansas City fan told me last year that Brett would be the best 120-game player in baseball if he could just play 120 games a year. How about Schmidt?

He's hard to dismiss, even at 38.

How would you compare them defensively?

Schmidt and Boggs?

Yeah.

I don't get to see Schmidt that much. He's hard to figure.

What are his defensive stats like?

Four years ago—he was 34 then—they started to slip. Three years ago it looked like he'd never play third again. Two years ago he made only six errors, and they gave him the Gold Glove in one of the worst votes ever, 'cause he just didn't make enough plays to justify comparing him to Terry Pendleton or Tim Wallach. And then last year he didn't win the Gold Glove, but he had his best all-around defensive stats in five years. I don't know what to make of him anymore.

Maybe he's made a deal with the Devil.

Maybe he's been working out with José Cruz and Darrell Evans.

Didn't Brooks Robinson go on forever, too?

They talked a lot about him lasting forever, but when Brooksie was 38 he hit .201 with six homers in 144 games. That ain't exactly Mike Schmidt.

Schmidt's still a monster in the batter's box.

But Boggs is a bigger monster.

And a good, consistent third baseman.

You agree on Boggs, then?

I do, yeah.

Shortstops.

Ozzie?

Ozzie and Trammell, the number-two men in the MVP voting.

It sure is hard to compare him to guys like Boggs and Mattingly. Does different things.

Right. How can you know if Ozzie saves the Cardinals as many runs as Boggs creates?

What would you get if you just crunched numbers?

It would all depend on the assumptions you made. If you made one set of assumptions, you could prove logically that Ozzie saved the Cardinals 70, 80 runs a year as opposed to an average shortstop. If you made another set of assumptions you could prove logically that he couldn't possibly save them that many.

How would you resolve it?

We can't. We don't know enough.

What do you need to know?

A whole lot of things. How many ground ball hits go through the third base hole against St. Louis, as opposed to how many go through there—or go up the middle, or wherever—against another team. It would be nice to know how many runs per game the Cardinals allow when Ozzie is in the lineup and out of the lineup, and whether there are any other differences that might explain that. We need to be able to adjust for everything that might distort the defensive stats—ground ball tendencies of the staff, right-handed/left-handed bias of the pitching staff, the fielders surrounding him.

Why hasn't all that been done?

It's just too much work. Sabermetricians are like anybody else; we want to get to the payoff. It's a lot easier to take a set of assumptions, construct an argument for the validity of the assumptions, and then zoom directly to a conclusion as to how many runs Ozzie is saving.

Well, what's your gut instinct?

My instinct is that Ozzie is as valuable, year in and year out, as anybody in the game. Maybe not number one, but right up there, right up in the top five.

For one thing, he's a hell of an offensive player.

He's a hell of hitter. It's just amazing how hard it is to get people to understand that.

Images. People get it in their heads that he's a light-hitting glove man, you can't get it out. He's got everything except power.

He doesn't hit 'em out. But he hits for a good average, hit 40 doubles last year. He and Mike Scioscia have the best strikeout/walk ratios in the league every year. He's a base stealer and a good percentage runner. And he's better every year than he was the year before. One amazing player—by far the best hitter at his position in his league, and the best defensive player in baseball at any position.

That's hard to beat. But would you really take him over Boggs?

I just don't know.

If you were in an APBA league, who would you take?

Boggs, obviously. But that's because offense is easy to measure, so they know exactly how good to make Boggs' card. Nobody knows exactly how good to make Ozzie on defense, how many hits he should be allowed to take away from somebody. So they make conservative assumptions.

If you could have either one in a trade, who would you take?

It would depend on my team. If I was losing 7–5, I'd take Ozzie. If I was losing 3–2, I'd take Boggs.

Fair enough. But if a shortstop is the best player, why Ozzie rather than a guy like Trammell who can hit cleanup, too?

Ozzie isn't the player he is because he plays shortstop. He's the player he is because of the way he plays shortstop.

Well, yeah, but Trammell isn't exactly Wayne Tolleson out there, and just look at the numbers.

If he has the same numbers again next year, I'll put him at the top of the list.

He's always been a good hitter.

But the year is out of the context of his career. He hit 21 homers in '86 but he hit .277. In '85 he hit .258. I'm real reluctant to say he's the best player in baseball on the basis of one year that's 60 points over his lifetime average with more than the usual power.

It's like Yount's year in '82.

It's exactly like Yount's year in '82, kind of like Ripken's in '83. A lot of us got fooled then, started saying that Yount was the best player in baseball—which he was, for a year or so. And Ripken—he's not even close anymore—should be in his prime.

OK. We ready for the outfield?

Has the rain slacked off?

Maybe a little.

Pick three to argue for.

Tony Gwynn and Tim Raines are the first two. Dale Murphy, Andre Dawson, Rickey Henderson. I guess I can't pick three. Darryl Strawberry's an awesome player. Eric Davis last summer was Willie Mays for about a month and a half. George Bell is up there in the MVP voting pretty regular. Kirby Puckett has a bunch of strengths and no real weakness.

Kirby—I wanted to make an argument here that might sound a little off the wall.

Shoot.

Phil Bradley.

Phil Bradley what?

As good as Kirby.

Give me a break.

No, I'm serious.

What does Phil Bradley do as well as Kirby?

What doesn't he do as well as Kirby? Compare them.

OK. Kirby's a .330 hitter.

Through their first three years Kirby's average was .304. Bradley's was .302. Kirby pulled a few points ahead last year (.311 to .301 lifetime), but that's no big deal. You can't put Kirby way ahead on that basis unless you put such a weight on batting average that you give the whole ballgame to Wade Boggs.

OK, but Puckett's ahead. Power.

Kirby's career slugging percentage is .456. Bradley's is .449.

Puckett is still ahead.

He's seven points ahead. What's the other major offensive indicator?

On-base percentage.

You got it. And . . .

Bradley's ahead.

Bradley's way ahead. Puckett's career on-base percentage is .347. Bradley's is .382.

And you put a lot of weight on that?

Well, I put a lot of weight on this: Teams that get people on base score runs and win games. You look up almost any team, almost any year. If they get more people on base than their opponents, they'll have a winning record. If they don't, they'll have a losing record. Almost nothing else you can name has as close a connection to winning. So given two basic offensive indicators, on-base percentage and slugging percentage, Puckett is seven points ahead on one and Bradley is 35 points ahead on the other. Now tell me why Puckett is a superstar and Bradley isn't.

I don't know. Speed?

Bradley stole 40 bases last year, Puckett 12. Bradley in his career has 107 stolen bases and a 73 percent success rate. Puckett has 67 steals and has been successful 64 percent of the time.

There are other speed indicators.

They're even in triples. Puckett has a few more, Bradley more per at bat. They're even (the other way around) in grounding into double plays.

What about the parks they play in? Bradley played in the Kingdome.

And Puckett plays in the Metrodome. That one goes nowhere.

Puckett's an RBI man.

And Bradley is a run scorer. Throughout their careers, Puckett has driven in or scored 9.5 runs per 27 outs. Bradley has driven in or scored 9.6. I don't see the edge.

But is a run scorer really as valuable as an RBI man? Is a number-two hitter as valuable as a number-three hitter?

Give me a logical reason why he isn't. It's real hard to drive in a run if nobody is on there to score it, unless you hit a home run in which case you're in both columns. Hitting second a lot of his career really hurts Bradley's run and RBI totals, because it isn't either an RBI slot or a place where you can lead the league in runs scored. But put Bradley leading off, like Puckett did for three years, and he'd lead the league in runs scored. If Rickey Henderson didn't.

Didn't Bradley have some trouble hitting in the clutch last year?

Well, yeah. Early last year he was taking too many pitches to let Reynolds steal second. Then he'd be hitting with Reynolds on second and an 0–2 count. But through their first three years up Bradley hit .291 with runners in scoring position. Puckett hit .312 with men in scoring position, but in the late innings of close games, Bradley hit .319 to Puckett's .297. So the clutch stats are as even as anything else.

OK, you give me 120 reasons why Bradley and Puckett are even, but the fact remains that Puckett is a big star and Bradley isn't. There's got to be some reason for it. The Mariners traded Bradley for an arm. Nobody in Minnesota wants to get rid of Puckett. There's got to be a reason for it.

I'll buy that. I don't know who the people are up there who were unhappy with Bradley—probably the same Yahoos who wanted to get rid of Danny Tartabull and Ivan Calderon. Seattle is the dead zone as far as the baseball media is concerned; you put Darryl Strawberry up there and you'd never hear of him, either. But there are a couple of legitimate edges that Puckett has. Puckett has a center fielder's arm. Bradley is an excellent outfielder, probably the best defensive left fielder in the American League, but he doesn't have a center fielder's arm. That's an edge for Kirby, who has one of the best arms going. Kirby is two years younger than Bradley, and maybe he is developing more as a hitter. I'm not saying that Bradley is ahead of Puckett. I'm just saying that if you're going to list one of them among the best players in baseball, you're going to have to list both of them. Or give me a logical reason why not.

You don't think Kirby could be considered the best? The way he hits, he's kind of like Don Mattingly playing center field.

Well, you said he didn't have a weakness. He does have a weakness, a big one. He doesn't have control of the strike zone. He's never driven in a hundred runs, which kind of messes up the Mattingly comparison. Maybe he will be the best player in baseball someday, but I don't think he is now.

Any other outfielders we can eliminate pretty easily?

Dawson, I think. In a competition this tough, something as important as a below-average on-base percentage is just too big a negative.

Could you eliminate George Bell on the same basis?

Maybe. They're similar. Bell is a more consistent hitter year in and year out, probably a better hitter if you put the two in the same park. His on-base percentage is better because he's a .300 hitter.

But he doesn't have the arm.

No, he does.

He plays left.

He has a good arm, though. Well, OK, he doesn't have Dawson's arm, but he has a right fielder's arm. He just plays left because of Barfield. He could play right if they needed him there.

Would you take him over Boggs, though?

I don't know. Would you?

I don't think so. It's hard to evaluate a player when he is right in the center of his prime, having the year of his life. Bell is a great player, but in three years Wade Boggs is still going to be hitting .350. I'm not as certain that George is going to be having those Hall of Fame seasons.

Well, I don't disagree with you, but I'd want to point out a couple of things. Bell is about Boggs' age, a year younger. He's faster and stronger. He's had four straight excellent offensive seasons. Boston is more of a media hub than Toronto is. Boggs is a better interview than Bell is, which is like being faster than Keith Hernandez. The game revolves around control of the strike zone, and on that basis I'll give the nod to Boggs, but I'm not 100 percent certain I'd still feel that way if I watched them both play for a year.

Agreed. Tony Gwynn?

Now there's a guy who is really under-publicized compared to Boggs.

Kirby Puckett's body and Wade Boggs' batting average.

His whole batting record, except that Boggs added the power last year. He's much faster than Boggs, has great command of the strike zone.

He's a super outfielder.

And hits for the same kind of averages Boggs does without the benefit of Fenway Park. And did you ever hear anybody wondering whether Tony Gwynn would ever hit .400?

Maybe we will now. .370—wow. Even Boggs never hit .370.

Or stole 56 bases.

Is Boggs still our standard here?

I think so.

OK, what does Boggs have that Gwynn doesn't?

The power, of course. Plus he has been more consistent at the .350 + level than Gwynn.

Right. Poor Tony has only hit over .350 twice and has a lifetime average of just .336.

He doesn't hit homers, but he hits triples.

You sound a little reserved.

He's one of the top ten, for sure. But at this level, you know, almost anything the player lacks is a disqualification. Mattingly is great, but he lacks speed and is a first baseman. Puckett and Bell are great, but they don't get on base as much as they might. To be the best you've got to do almost everything and be durable and consistent. Gwynn doesn't have power and Boggs doesn't have speed, but given the choice, I'll have to take the power and consistency of Boggs.

In a way an equally good comparison for Gwynn is Ozzie Smith.

How so?

Ozzie and Gwynn are even in a lot of areas. Their strikeout and walk data are almost the same. They're even as base stealers, really. Gwynn has a little more power, but they're both singles hitters. If you compare the two, there's an awful lot of things you can throw out because they're even. Gwynn gets an extra 35, 40 hits a year—and Smith takes probably the same number away from somebody else. It's hard to say who you'd take.

Interesting thought. But I'd take Ozzie because he's in the middle of the field. He stabilizes the whole team defensively. Gwynn's just one bat. Who have we got left in the outfield?

Eric Davis?

Not enough time. He hasn't hit .300 yet, maybe never will as much as he strikes out. He hasn't been durable. Maybe next year.

What is that woman doing?

I don't know. I just hope she doesn't sit near here.

They look like upper-deck people, just down here under the over-hang. Where were we?

Strawberry, I guess.

The only player in baseball who simultaneously manages to be overrated and underrated.

What a season he had, though. Thirty-nine homers, 36 steals, 97 walks, .284 average in a tough park. What kind of stats would he have had in Wrigley Field or Atlanta? What do you think of his defense?

I'm damned if I know what to think. You know, in the '86 World Series and Championship series, he just played terrific ball in the outfield—ran down several drives in the gap that could have been triples. Cut off balls down the line and drilled them back into the infield. Climbed a fence to take away a home run. The announcers—NBC and ABC both—hardly noticed he was out there. I don't know what to think. The only time you hear about him in the outfield is when he makes a mistake, which makes you think he must be OK most of the time.

He makes the All-Star team every year, and every year media people bitch about his making the All-Star team rather than Candy Maldonado or Billy Hatcher or whoever is on a hot streak. He's 25 years old and a month away from his team record for career home runs. He may hit more home runs than any other player of our generation, despite playing in a park that just murders his statistics. His on-base percentage last year was one of the best in the league. He's fast and strong and graceful. He's never really had an off year. I just don't know what is missing for him. Sometimes I feel like he could be the best player in baseball, and we'd still be arguing about his potential. He did not have good defensive stats last year, though. Had more errors than assists.

I see your point, but in some ways it's almost like the Phil Bradley argument. Logically, he's a hell of a player. But we're talking about who is the BEST player here. If he's the best, isn't it up to the New York media to nominate him for the honor? And if they won't do it, then doesn't that suggest that something is missing?

Yes. Yes, it does.

They've never been shy about telling us that Don Mattingly was the best player in baseball, or Dwight Gooden when he was on top.

I agree with that. You've got to respect what the local people see, or think they see. I'll agree that Darryl still has something to prove on this level. But I'm just a little bit afraid, somehow, that what is missing may not be missing from Darryl, but from the people who are watching him. Most people's perceptions of ballplayers are based on statistics, particularly the perceptions of people who don't believe in statistics. I just can't shake the suspicion that if Shea Stadium was Wrigley Field, Dwight Gooden would have ERAs a run higher and Strawberry would be a .300 hitter with 35 to 50 homers a year, and then Dwight would be the star who somehow never reached his potential, and Strawberry would be the second coming of Babe Ruth. But I'm not prepared to tell the New York writers that they're watching the best player in baseball and don't recognize him.

An argument which a year ago could have been applied to Rickey Henderson.

Right. Rickey and Tim Raines—Raines has now clearly pulled ahead of him, don't you think?

For the moment. Like you said, one negative is all it takes. Rickey's not durable, not a .300 hitter. At this level, that's enough.

Now, Tim Raines.

Tim Raines and Wade Boggs.

Tough one.

Let's do it point by point. Hitting for average.

Boggs, but it's not a mismatch. Raines has got back to back .330 seasons, .320 the year before that. I don't have '87 home/road stats, but for the three years before that they were even in neutral parks, both at .325 each.

Hitting for power . . . about even I guess.

I'd lean to Raines, but it's even, really.

Strike zone judgment?

Edge to Boggs. Slim edge. Two-nothing, Boggs.

Speed?

Big difference. Fifty, 70 stolen bases a year for Raines, with almost no cost in caught stealing.

Overall offense?

Got to go with Boggs. But it's close.

Hey, an umpire.

That's a good sign.

Defensive position . . . I guess a third baseman is harder to find than a left fielder.

Right. But Raines is a hell of a left fielder. Defensive range, obviously, edge to Raines. Arm, edge to Boggs. Reliability, probably an edge to Raines. He don't make many mistakes.

Overall defensive value?

Even, I guess.

OK. Consistency?

Have to grade them both A, I think.

Durability?

About the same.

So you still go with Boggs.

I wish I knew. I'll say this: If Raines had the arm to play center field, he would be more valuable than Boggs, which at this point would make him probably the best player in baseball. But he didn't, so I guess I'll have to stick with Boggs.

You said that Boggs was 82 runs better than an average third baseman. What's the same stat for Raines.

Fifty-one. Raines was 51 runs better than average.

That seems like a fair difference.

It's just one year. And there's a lot of other things that go into that. But I think there's a presumption that Boggs is a better hitter than Raines, and as long as the stats show the same thing you have to go with it.

OK, coming down the stretch and Boggs is still ahead.

Dale Murphy.

A fine candidate.

Indeed.

OK, let's start with the 1987 season. Who created more runs?

Boggs.

Close?

Fairly. About 18 runs, but Murphy also made more outs than Boggs.

Both in hitter's parks, Atlanta may be better at this time.

Right. 1987 defense?

No difference to speak of. A good right fielder versus a good third baseman. Let's go back to 1986. Who created more runs?

Boggs, easily. Murphy was playing center field that year, but his range really wasn't very good for a center fielder. Also Boggs' team won their league.

OK, two straight years for Boggs. Still . . . 44 homers, 118 walks, .295 average, good speed and defense. Murphy's got to be top ten, don't you think?

Well, I'd pick him ahead of Phil Bradley, let's just say. One more outfielder.

Who's that?

Pedro.

Guerrero?

The best hitter in baseball. Period. The best.

You really think so.

I do. What'd he hit last year . . . .338? .338 in Dodger Stadium has got to be equivalent to .380 in Fenway Park. Power. Draws a few walks. You put all the best hitters in baseball in the same park year-round, and at the end of the year Pedro would have the best stats, counting average, power, walks, everything.

Which doesn't make him the best player in the game.

No, it doesn't.

He gets hurt.

And they farted around with him defensively until he's not very good anywhere. His speed is just fair. I see some umbrellas going down. What's left?

Pitchers.

Pitchers. Fortunately, there's no Bruce Sutter right now. That saves us an argument.

And little doubt about who the top starter is.

Rocket man.

Teammates.

Wonder who they'd give up.

Roger won the MVP Award.

And deserved it, I think. Still, you know, there's a funny thing operating there. If you come out of nowhere and have a great year and your team wins the pennant, they'll give you the MVP Award every time because you were the difference between first and fourth. But if you have a great year every year, then it removes an argument for your value.

Witness?

Ozzie Smith, I guess. If he did all those things coming out of nowhere, can you imagine what people would write about him? Or Boggs. Clemens gave the Red Sox a big boost in '86, but Boggs is in there every year. Or Eddie Murray in '83. Ripken was seen as being more valuable in part because Eddie was just doing what he did every year.

Clemens is a great pitcher.

He is, but what did we figure Boggs was last year—82 runs better than average? Clemens was 50 to 60 runs better than an average pitcher—about the same as in 1986, actually.

It would be interesting to ask John McNamara who he would rather give up.

Oh, I'm sure it would be fascinating. I'm sure his analysis would be thorough, but a better question is who you or I would rather acquire?

Boggs?

Got to be. He adds more runs than Roger subtracts, and a pitcher is iffy from year to year.

We got it, then?

I got mine. You got yours?

OK. Let's put them together.

OK. Here it is. The best players in baseball are:

1. Wade Boggs
2. Tim Raines
3. Ozzie Smith
4. Don Mattingly
5. Tony Gwynn
6. Darryl Strawberry
7. Dale Murphy
8. Roger Clemens
9. Rickey Henderson
10. Kirby Puckett
11. Mike Schmidt
12. George Bell
13. Jack Morris
14. Pedro Guerrero
15. Alan Trammell
16. Eric Davis
17. Ryne Sandberg
18. Phil Bradley
19. Dwight Gooden
20. Dwight Evans

PLATOONING

It is an old strategy, dating back at least to 1906. It plays a part in every game. It defines careers, it directs strategy. Every manager uses it to a greater or lesser extent. It helps decide who is in the starting lineup, when pitching changes are made, when intentional walks occur. It virtually dictates which pinch hitters can be used and when they can be used. And yet, remarkably, we know almost nothing about it. We don't know who invented it. Ten years ago there were no reference sources for information about platoon differentials, so that we couldn't find out who hit what against left-handed and right-handed pitching. How many players actually hit better the way they are supposed to, and how many hit better the other way? How large are the differences? Is there a "standard margin," or is it widely variable? What is the league average for left-handed hitters against left-handed pitchers, for right-handed hitters against right-handed pitchers, etc? What players have the largest platoon differences, and what players hit better the other way?

What type of players have large platoon differentials? Is the platoon advantage peculiar to power hitters, or is a singles hitter just as likely to hit better when he has the platoon advantage? Is a young player more likely to suffer when facing his own type than when facing a veteran player? Is a good hitter less likely to have a platoon differential than a poor hitter? Is a player who strikes out a lot more vulnerable than a player who rarely strikes out? Does a player who has good strike-zone judgment tend to have a smaller platoon differential than a free swinger?

Related to these questions is a set of parallel issues: Where does the platoon differential come from? Why do left-handed hitters hit better against right-handed pitchers than against left-handers? Is it just a self-fulfilling prophecy—that is, left-handers don't hit left-handed pitchers because when they are young they are not exposed to them? Is it because of the break of the pitch, because of the fact that a left-hander's ball breaks toward a right-handed hitter but away from a left-hander? Is it that you see the ball better when it starts out away from you? Is it the fear factor, the tendency of right-handers to bail out on inside pitches from right-handed pitchers, that causes them to do less well when right-handers are on the mound? Is it learned or innate? Is platooning really justified by the margins that can be gained?

How can we know so little about something that is so central to the game? Every time we go to a game, this animal plays–and yet we don't know what size he is, or what shape, or what color. Remarkable, isn't it?

My place in the baseball world is to worry about these sorts of gaps in our knowledge, and to stretch a net over them as best I can. I have been collecting and publishing platoon data for about ten years now, hoping to develop a library with which to study the issue. What became apparent after a couple of years of collecting this data, though, is that platoon differentials are extremely variable from year to year. In 1985, for example, Gary Matthews hit .236 against right-handed pitchers, but just .232 against left-handers, apparent evidence that it doesn't make any difference to Matthews whether the pitcher is left- or right-handed—until you realize that Mathews hit .326 against left-handed pitchers in 1984 and .352 against them in 1986, while hitting .277 and .223 against right-handers. When you consider that a player normally bats 100 to 200 times a year against left-handed pitching, this variability is not surprising. The data samples in each year are too small to get a valid reading on the player's ability in this respect.

With the publication of *The Great American Baseball Stat Book*, however, I no longer had a good excuse not to do a study of the issue. The *Stat Book* contains data on the performance of several hundred players over a period of three years (1984–1986). I defined the initial study group as

all players
who have a minimum of 400 at bats plus walks
against left-handed pitching AND
against right-handed pitching
over the three-year period 1984–1986
and who were not switch hitters.

That is, you have to have 400 plate appearances each way—not 400 total. There were 119 qualifying players.

For each player, I entered 14 pieces of information in the data base:

1) Whether the player batted left- or right-handed;

2–4) His batting average, slugging percentage, and on-base percentage;

5–7) His total at bats, strikeouts, and walks;

8–10) His batting, slugging, and on-base averages against left-handed pitching;

11–13) His batting, slugging, and on-base averages against right-handed pitching; and

14) His year of birth.

With that information, I attempted to answer some of the questions outlined above. The basic unit of measurement was on-base + slugging, which is an excellent measure of a player's productivity, including information on power and walks drawn as well as hitting for average. For example, Harold Baines versus left-handed pitchers over the three years had an on-base percentage of .328 and a slugging percentage of .444, a total of 772; against right-handers (against whom he should be better) he had an on-base percentage of .359 and a slugging percentage of .515, a total of 874. So Baines versus right-handed pitching was +102—874 − 772. I don't use the decimal points for OB + SLG because when the two are added together the sum no longer represents a percentage; Baines doesn't have 87.4 percent or .874 of anything, so the decimal point is meaningless.

HOW MANY PLAYERS ACTUALLY HIT BETTER THE WAY THEY SHOULD?

Of the 119 players in the study, 103 (or 87 percent) were more effective offensively when they had the platoon advantage. Only 16 players (or 13 percent) were more effective going the other way.

Of the 90 right-handed batters, 76 (or 84 percent) hit better against left-handed pitchers than they did against right-handers. Of the 29 left-handed hitters, 27 (or 93 percent) hit better against right-handed pitchers than they did against their own kind.

HOW LARGE ARE THE DIFFERENCES?

As a whole, the 119 players hit .284 with the platoon advantage, .260 without it.

The differences in power were larger than the differences in batting average. With the platoon advantage, the average slugging percentage was .455. Without the advantage, the slugging percentage was .402—a difference of 53 points. So if you break slugging percentage down into its two parts (hitting for average and isolated power) the difference in average is 24 points (.284 − .260), while the difference in isolated power is 29 points (.171 − .142).

The average on-base percentage with the advantage was .356. Without the advantage, the on-base percentage was .322. So the "average" platoon advantage in terms of on-base + slugging was 87 points (811 vs. 724).

The right-handed hitters in the study hit .266 overall, .258 when facing right-handed pitchers and .281 with the platoon advantage. The left-handed hitters hit .284 overall (18 points better than the right-handers). The .284 breaks down as .266 against left-handers, but .292 with the platoon edge.

WHAT PLAYERS HAD THE LARGEST PLATOON DIFFERENTIALS?

The largest platoon differential of any player in the study was for Rick Dempsey. Over the three years studied, Dempsey hit .284 against left-handed pitchers with 18 homers, 61 RBI in 380 at bats. His slugging percentage against lefties was .500, his on-base percentage .384 (total

884). Against right-handed pitching, Dempsey hit just .197 with the same number of homers in many more at bats (640 vs. 380). His slugging percentage against right-handers was .314, his on-base percentage .285 (total 599). Now you know why Dempsey is always talking about trying to switch hit. In his case, it can't hurt.

The ten players with the largest platoon differentials over the three-year period:

1. Dempsey (285)

	AB	H	2B	3B	HR	RBI	Avg.	OBP	SLG
vs. LHP	380	110	24	1	18	61	.289	.384	.500
vs. RHP	640	126	21	0	18	54	.197	.285	.314

2. Chet Lemon (271)

	AB	H	2B	3B	HR	RBI	Avg.	OBP	SLG
vs. LHP	509	170	39	5	24	84	.334	.393	.572
vs. RHP	920	214	44	8	26	113	.233	.311	.383

3. Darryl Strawberry (249)

	AB	H	2B	3B	HR	RBI	Avg.	OBP	SLG
vs. LHP	510	116	15	4	22	78	.227	.307	.402
vs. RHP	880	247	54	9	60	191	.281	.391	.567

4. Ray Knight (245)

	AB	H	2B	3B	HR	RBI	Avg.	OBP	SLG
vs. LHP	503	153	30	1	17	78	.304	.331	.469
vs. RHP	625	139	20	1	3	69	.222	.283	.272

5. Von Hayes (241)

	AB	H	2B	3B	HR	RBI	Avg.	OBP	SLG
vs. LHP	463	107	18	1	9	62	.231	.290	.333
vs. RHP	1278	393	85	11	39	173	.308	.381	.483

6. Lou Whitaker (235)

	AB	H	2B	3B	HR	RBI	Avg.	OBP	SLG
vs. LHP	482	109	15	4	7	52	.226	.299	.317
vs. RHP	1269	379	65	11	47	150	.299	.373	.478

7. Jeff Leonard (228)

	AB	H	2B	3B	HR	RBI	Avg.	OBP	SLG
vs. LHP	426	138	21	3	23	69	.324	.351	.549
vs. RHP	936	234	38	5	21	121	.250	.303	.369

8. Pete O'Brien (207)

	AB	H	2B	3B	HR	RBI	Avg.	OBP	SLG
vs. LHP	484	121	23	0	8	65	.250	.322	.347
vs. RHP	1160	341	60	8	55	197	.294	.374	.502

9 tie. Mike Easler (191)

	AB	H	2B	3B	HR	RBI	Avg.	OBP	SLG
vs. LHP	458	115	20	3	10	47	.251	.303	.373
vs. RHP	1201	370	66	8	47	196	.308	.373	.494

Tom Brookens (191)

	AB	H	2B	3B	HR	RBI	Avg.	OBP	SLG
vs. LHP	471	134	28	8	9	45	.285	.336	.435
vs. RHP	519	112	28	4	6	53	.216	.260	.320

WHO WERE THE PLAYERS WHO HIT BEST AGAINST THEIR OWN KIND?

Alphabetically, the "reverse platoon players" were Jesse Barfield, Bob Boone, Phil Bradley, Brett Butler, Cecil Cooper, Carlton Fisk, Gary Gaetti, Glenn Hubbard, Ron Kittle, Jim Morrison, Rafael Ramirez, Juan Samuel,

Ryne Sandberg, Tim Teufel, Ozzie Virgil, and Robin Yount.

Most of the platoon differentials of these 16 players were small to microscopic (for example, Carlton Fisk versus left-handed pitching had a .294 on-base percentage and a .430 slugging percentage; against right-handers his figures were .293 and .433). The largest platoon differentials going in the wrong direction belonged to Bradley, Samuel, and Cecil Cooper:

1. Bradley (108)

	AB	H	2B	3B	HR	RBI	Avg.	OBP	SLG
vs. LHP	414	111	15	5	11	41	.268	.345	.408
vs. RHP	1075	341	57	11	27	121	.317	.395	.466

2. Samuel (87)

	AB	H	2B	3B	HR	RBI	Avg.	OBP	SLG
vs. LHP	569	146	32	10	11	59	.257	.278	.406
vs. RHP	1386	377	71	34	39	162	.272	.314	.457

3. Cooper (69)

	AB	H	2B	3B	HR	RBI	Avg.	OBP	SLG
vs. LHP	561	170	26	5	10	94	.303	.347	.421
vs. RHP	1215	321	65	7	29	147	.264	.298	.401

The platoon differentials of Bradley and Samuel, were they directed the other way, would be considered of normal range. All the other "wrong way" differentials would be considered small or insignificant.

HOW MANY PLAYERS HAVE LARGE PLATOON ADVANTAGES?

Measured (as always) by on base + slugging, we'll use the following terms:

+176 or more	Extremely Large Advantage
+126 to 175	Large Platoon Advantage
+76 to 125	Normal Platoon Advantage
+26 to 75	Small Platoon Advantage
-25 to +25	No Real Platoon Differential
-26 to -75	Reverse Platoon Advantage
-76 or more	Significant Reverse Platoon Advantage

This chart will define the descriptions used for platoon differentials throughout this article.

Of the 119 players, 13 had extremely large platoon differentials (the ten listed above, plus Cliff Johnson, Gary Carter, and Juan Beniquez.) Twenty players had large platoon differentials, 40 had normal platoon differentials, and 23 had small platoon differentials. There were 14 players to whom the orientation of the pitcher was no apparent factor, 7 players had small reverse platoon advantages, and 2 players (Bradley and Samuel) had significant reverse platoon advantages. Let's chart that:

Extremely Large Advantage	13
Large Platoon Advantage	20
Normal Platoon Advantage	40
Small Platoon Advantage	23
No Real Platoon Differential	14
Reverse Platoon Advantage	7
Significant Reverse Platoon Advantage	2

The distribution of these differentials by left-handed and right-handed batters is similar, although a larger percentage of left-handed than right-handed hitters had extremely large platoon differentials (8 of 90 right-handers, or 9 percent, and 5 of 29 left-handers, or 17 percent).

DO POWER HITTERS TEND TO HAVE LARGE PLATOON DIFFERENTIALS?

No, they definitely do not.

I divided the players into four groups by isolated power. The true power hitters were those with isolated power of .200 or greater (20 of 119 players); the other groups we could call players with some power (isolated power of .156 to .199), players with a little power (isolated power .120 to .155) and players with very little power (isolated power less than .120).

Among the four groups, the true power hitters had the smallest platoon advantage, an average 75 points of OB + SLG. However, there is no apparent pattern, and the platoon advantage of power hitters in the main is probably neither larger nor smaller than that of other players. The advantages were:

GROUP	Platoon Advantage
True power hitters	+77
Players with some power	+95
Players with little power	+87
Players with very little power	+85

At least 85 percent and no more than 90 percent of the players in each group had platoon differentials running in the normal direction.

DO POOR HITTERS TEND TO HAVE LARGER PLATOON DIFFERENTIALS THAN GOOD HITTERS?

No, they do not. It appears that the platoon differential tends to be proportional to productivity—that is, that good hitters have slightly larger platoon differentials than poor hitters in absolute terms, but about the same in percentage terms.

Again, I divided the players into four groups:

GROUP	Platoon Advantage
Outstanding hitters	+93
Good hitters	+107
Fair hitters	+69
Poor hitters	+92

No clear pattern, but if you just split them in the middle (which happens to be an OBP + SLG of 763.5) then 52 of the 57 best hitters (91 percent) had platoon differentials going in the normal direction, while 51 of the 62 poorer hitters (or 82 percent) had differentials going in the normal direction.

The better hitters had an on-base percentage of .334 and a slugging percentage of .433 without the platoon advantage; with the advantage the figures were .375 and .494. Thus, the better hitters were +102 or +13% (869/767) when they had the edge.

The poorer hitters had an on-base percentage of .310 and a slugging percentage of .373 without the platoon advantage; with the advantage the figures were .339 and .420. Thus, the poorer hitters were +76 or +11 percent (759/683) when they had the edge.

DO HIGH-AVERAGE HITTERS HAVE SMALLER PLATOON DIFFERENTIALS THAN LOW-AVERAGE HITTERS?

The pattern is pretty much the same as for power hitters, which is to say indecisive. One cannot say for sure whether platoon advantage does or does not increase (or decrease) at higher averages:

GROUP	Platoon Advantage
Hitting .290 or better	+80
Hitting .270–.289	+104
Hitting .250–.269	+82
Hitting less than .250	+81

DO PLAYERS WHO STRIKE OUT A LOT HAVE LARGE PLATOON ADVANTAGES?

No, they do not.

Surprisingly, the platoon differential seems to decrease as strikeouts increase. I used three groups this time:

GROUP	Platoon Advantage
Strikes out a lot	+80
Average range strikeouts	+89
Strikes out little	+94

This pattern emerged despite the fact that the players who struck out most were slightly better hitters than the other players. So proportionally the platoon advantage was 11 percent for the players who struck out most (822/742), 12 percent for the middle group (815/726), and 13 percent for those who struck out least (796/702).

Since this conclusion is rather surprising—one would expect free-swinging power hitters to be vulnerable to pitchers who can jam them—let's look at some specific examples. Ron Kittle, as mentioned, was one of the 16 reverse-platoon players. Kittle, a right-handed hitter, hit .217 against left-handed pitching over the three-year period, .222 against right-handers. His home-run percentage was markedly better against right-handers than against left-handers (1/14.3 at bats against right-handers, 1/17.4 against lefties), offsetting the fact that he walked much more often against the left-handers. His strikeout frequency was about the same, 27 percent against lefties, 28 percent against right-handers.

Dave Kingman, a similar hitter, had a normal platoon advantage, hitting .245 against lefties versus .236 against right-handers, walking a little more and homering somewhat more often against left-handed hitters. Steve Balboni, the token bald person on this motley crew, had similar stats to Kingman's—.253 against left-handers, .233 against right-handers, a few more homers and walks against lefties. Jesse Barfield, a better player but another strikeout king, hit for a better average against lefties (.303 vs. .279) but with less power, and thus joined Kittle in the reverse-platoon group. There just isn't any evidence, not even a hint, that these types of "full-rip" hitters have larger-than-normal platoon differentials.

DO PLAYERS WHO WALK A LOT HAVE LARGE PLATOON ADVANTAGES?

Probably.

In my studies, the platoon advantage did increase as players walked more, although this could have been a chance pattern.

GROUP	Platoon Advantage
Walks a lot	+97
Average walk frequency	+91
Walks little	+76

The percentage differential is 10 percent for the players who walk little, 13 percent for the players who walk most.

DO YOUNG PLAYERS HAVE LARGER PLATOON ADVANTAGES THAN OLDER PLAYERS?

No; in fact, older players may have larger platoon advantages than younger players.

GROUP	Platoon Advantage
Born 1959–1962	+77
Born 1956–1958	+75
Born 1951–1955	+109
Born 1946–1950	+91

That concludes the factual summary of the data drawn from the original 119-man database. Some additional conclusions or inferences can be made from this information. Most importantly, the percentage of players who have platoon differentials running in the normal direction is probably markedly higher than is measured in this study. There are two reasons to think that this would be so. First, the standards for inclusion in the study contain a bias that would probably tend to exclude players with larger-than-average platoon differentials. And second, the frequency of aberrant data points in a short-run data sample is always larger than in a long-run data sample, and the data sample here did not run long enough (400 plate appearances each way) for the material to reach full maturity.

The bias, the first point above, probably isn't a big issue. The 400 plate appearance standard, while necessary to drive out random aberrations, biases the study in a way that would tend to increase the percentage of players showing abnormal differentials. Why? Because it cuts out most of the players who are platooned. Take Wally Backman, for example. Backman over the three-year period batted 1,122 times against right-handed pitchers and hit .316 against them. Because he hits so well against right-handers, the Mets tried in 1985 to make a regular out of him, but he's just hopeless against left-handed pitching. Over the three seasons he batted 221 times against left-handed pitchers and hit a robust .149 against them, with a .190 slugging percentage. Because he can't hit left-handers at all, he doesn't play against them except on rare occasions, such as when every other infielder in the Mets system has to appear in court or something. So he doesn't have 400 plate appearances against lefties, so he doesn't make the study—precisely because he has a large platoon differential.

The same is true of guys like Pat Sheridan, Rance Mulliniks, Garth Iorg, Reggie Jackson, Denny Walling,

Jerry Royster, Jorge Orta, and others: because they are platooned, they are excluded from the study even though they play a hundred games a year. This no doubt causes the platoon differential in the study to be undermeasured, but probably not to a huge extent. Most platoon players are platooned not because they have enormous platoon differentials, like Backman, but because they are marginal talents, players who are within the range where the 25- or 30-point platoon differential is larger than the difference between them and the next best available player. There aren't a huge number of platoon players around, and some of those who are platooned make the study anyway.

A more serious problem is the second one above. To put it in simple English, if you did this study using a cutoff for inclusion of 10 at bats each way, you would probably find that it was almost a 50–50 proposition as to whether a player would hit better or worse when he had the platoon advantage, since the dominant factor in determining his splits would be random chance. If you moved the standard for inclusion up to 50 at bats, the percentage of players who conformed to the group expectation would increase to perhaps 55, 58 percent; at 150 at bats, it might be 70 percent.

The 400 plate appearance standard is the most rigorous that it was feasible to use given the available data, but by no means is this process of driving out random aberrations complete at 400 PA. Many, perhaps most, of the players who are shown as reverse-platoon players have differentials so small that they could move to the other side of the fence just by having one big game when they had the platoon advantage.

I did a quick study to examine the extent to which the "reverse-platoon" players could be expected to conform to norms if a larger data sample were available. If these 16 reverse-platoon players truly hit better the opposite way, then if we looked at another year, outside the study, they should continue to hit better the opposite way in that season. If, in the "extra" season, these players tended to show normal platoon effects, that would suggest that their performance in the study period was just a somewhat sustained aberration, which would disappear with more time.

The obvious "extra year" is 1983, since this study was done early in the 1987 season so that 1987 data was not available. For the 1983 season there is no complete data reference, as there is from 1984 to the present, but the 1984 *Baseball Abstract* contains platoon data for most players.

Of the 16 players who bucked the trend in the 1984–1986 period, 1983 data was unavailable for six players, either because they were in the minor leagues at that time, played little during the 1983 season or (in one case) because I just couldn't get the data at the time. The other ten players, however, showed almost 100 percent normal platoon effects during the 1983 season. Seven of the ten players were more effective offensively with the platoon edge going for them, the exceptions being Barfield, Boone and Yount. As a group, the ten players in the extra year had an on-base + slugging of 821 with the platoon advantage, 736 without it, making them +85.

Cecil Cooper, who had the largest reverse-platoon differential of any player who had an extra year to look at (Bradley and Samuel being 1984 rookies), in 1983 hit just .258 against left-handers, but .323 with the platoon advantage. His OB + SLG was 934 with the platoon advantage, 662 without it, making him +272. Thus, if the study had covered four years rather than three, Cooper would have shown a platoon differential running in the normal direction.

Over the three years of the original study Rafael Ramirez performed substantially better the wrong way (−56); in the extra year, however, he hit .358 against left-handers, .276 against right-handers, totalling +238. Carlton Fisk, who was −2 over the three year period, was +53 in the extra year. Gary Gaetti, who was −8 over the three year period, was +87 in the extra year. Glenn Hubbard, who was −24 over the three year period, switched to +130 in the extra year. Ron Kittle, who was −22 over the three year period, was +64 in the extra year. All of these players would have shown normal platoon differentials had the study covered four years rather than three, thus leaving little doubt that in a longer-term study the 13-percent figure for players hitting better the wrong way would shrink very substantially.

There are two basic measures of the size of the platoon differential that we are using here—the percentage of players who have a positive platoon differential, which we have measured at 87 percent, and the average platoon differential in terms of OB + SLG, which we have measured at 87 points. The "exclusion bias," the first problem, would have an impact on the average differential, 87 points, and would have a small impact on the percentage of players showing the normal advantage. The "400 plate appearances is not enough" problem would affect the percentage of players with a normal advantage, but would not affect the average size of the platoon advantage at all, since a longer study would fold both extremes back toward the middle. So the true platoon differential is probably somewhat larger and even more consistent than it is measured as being in this study.

But there can be no doubt that the percentage of players who actually hit better when facing their own kind is much smaller than 13 percent, and that this study, if repeated two years from now and using a standard something like "600 plate appearances each way or 1500 plate appearances total and at least 300 each way" would show less than 13 percent of players with negative or abnormal platoon effects. The true figure may not be zero percent—but it probably is very close to zero.

(NOTE: This study was done during the summer of 1987. However, after the 1987 season I also checked the platoon records of these 16 players in 1987.

The conclusion is the same: Obviously, the reverse-platoon performance over the three year period 1984–1986 was an anomaly created by limited data. Phil Bradley over the three seasons was the most out of line of any major-league player—but in 1987, he had an enormous platoon differential going in the normal direction. In 1987 Bradley, a right-hander, hit .337 against left-handers, .279 against righties, and with 11 of his 14 home runs coming in 178 at bats against left-handers. He homered more than eight times as frequently against left-handed pitchers.

Brett Butler, Ron Kittle, Jesse Barfield, and Rafael Ramirez also hit much better in 1987 with the platoon advantage than without it. Bob Boone and Ryne Sandberg hit somewhat better with the advantage. Gary Gaetti, Ozzie Virgil, and Carlton Fisk continued to perform as reverse-platoon players. Glenn Hubbard's performance was almost the same against either; without more detailed stats I can't tell where his advantage was. Juan Samuel apparently continued to hit better against right-handers, although without more complete stats I can't be sure. I haven't seen data yet on the other four players. The data as a whole leaves little doubt but that almost every player, if studied over a long enough period of time, would hit better with than without the platoon advantage. End of Note.)

And that is by far the most important conclusion of this study: Almost every player, if not actually every player, probably has a platoon direction running in the normal direction. That fact, in and of itself, effectively answers several of the questions that we posed at the beginning of this article.

Is the platoon differential acquired or innate? If the platoon advantage is virtually a universal phenomenon, then that would rather powerfully suggest that it is innate, unavoidable, that if you studied high-school kids or Japanese baseball or the Italian League you would probably find that the right-handers hit best against the left-handers and vice versa.

Some left-handed hitters will tell you that the only reason they don't hit left-handed pitchers as well is that they don't get to see them as often and are not as familiar with them. Clearly, this is not true. Batters of both kinds are more familiar with right-handed pitching than left-handed pitching. All but five players in the study had more at bats against right-handed pitchers than against left-handers. So if the platoon differential was due to the familiarity factor, or even if some small part of the platoon differential was due to the familiarity factor, then obviously the average platoon advantage of left-handed hitters would be much larger than that of right-handed hitters. Suppose that you have two factors at work, an "innate platoon edge," which is 25 points of batting average, and a "familiarity edge," which is just 10 points of batting average. That being the case, the platoon advantage of right-handed hitters would be 15 points (25 − 10), and that of left-handed hitters would be 35 points (25 + 10), or more than twice as large. The fact that the platoon margins are essentially the same for hitters of both kinds shows that familiarity has almost nothing to do with creating normal platoon differentials.

It is just a self-fulfilling prophecy? Obviously, it is not. Few players are platooned. Almost all players have platoon differentials. If it was just a self-fulfilling prophecy, then why would it apply to Dale Murphy and Jim Rice and Cal Ripken and George Brett and Jack Clark? Nobody tells these guys they can't hit left-handers or right-handers.

Is platooning justified by the margins that can be gained? Quite certainly, yes. In this study, the players who hit .290 or better had an overall batting average of .304 and an OB + SLG of 823. The players who hit .250–.269 hit .260 overall and had an OB + SLG of 744. But with the platoon advantage, the .260 hitters were better offensive players than the .304 hitters were without it (791 vs. 781). No manager could responsibly ignore an advantage

like that—and there probably should be more position platooning than there is.

What I am struck by most of all in this study is the consistency of the platoon differential among players of different types. If you had asked me before I started the study, I would have bet you dollars to doughnuts—that's about 3–2 odds in today's market—that I would be able to isolate the kinds of players who tend to have large platoon differentials, and the kind to whom it doesn't make much difference. I expected to find charts that looked like this:

Type 1	+113
Type 2	+ 84
Type 3	+ 71
Type 4	+ 30

Instead, they all looked like this:

Type 1	+ 80
Type 2	+ 84
Type 3	+ 68
Type 4	+ 82

If I had found what I expected, then by combining characteristics I could give you a profile of the type of hitter with whom the platoon game just had to be played, and the type for whom it could be ignored. Suppose that I had found, in those studies, that right-handed hitters have smaller differentials than left-handers, that players who strike out a lot have larger differentials than those who don't, that young players have larger differentials than older players, that power hitters have larger differentials than high-average hitters. If that had happened, then we could combine those characteristics and I could show you a group of players—a cluster, like Steve Balboni, Ron Kittle, and Dave Kingman—and tell you what the platoon differential should be for such a cluster. But you can't do it. Brett Butler has a lot of things in common with Wally Backman—but Backman has an enormous platoon differential, and Butler is a reverse-platoon player.

To me, that reinforces the point I was making before: that it's just there. It's innate. You can't get away from it. The fact that every identifiable group of players has a platoon advantage of roughly the same magnitude reinforces the conclusion that if a longer-run study were possible, the 13 percent of individual players who hit better the wrong way would probably all but disappear.

The platoon differential is not a weakness peculiar to some players. It is a condition of the game, shared by everybody. Early last year Gary Ward was platooned for about a week before he got hot and got back in the lineup. Ward objected to this, saying that he had hit better against right-handers than left-handers every year since he came up. Why does he say this? Obviously, because he doesn't want to get a platoon label hung on him. "I don't have that weakness," he is saying in effect; "I'm one of those players who can hit both ways." Whenever a superstar comes to the plate in a situation in which a pitching change is anticipated, you know what the announcer is going to say. "To a hitter like Dale Murphy (or Kirby Puckett, or Pedro Guerrero, or Don Mattingly) it doesn't make any difference who's out there," the announcer's going to say, "he can hit anybody." The comment is intended as a compliment to the superstar. A hitter this good, the announcer assumes, doesn't have that kind of weakness. He's not vulnerable to the platoon effect.

In fact, though, Gary Ward does hit better against left-handed than right-handed pitching, though not a lot. Over the three-year period of the study he hit .293 each way, but had a .468 slugging percentage against left-handers, just .416 against right-handers. In 1983, the "extra" season, he hit .267 and slugged .366 against right-handers, while hitting .303 and slugging .567 against left-handers. (In 1987, Ward again hit substantially better against left-handed pitchers.) It makes a difference to Gary Ward, and it matters to Dale Murphy, and Kirby Puckett, and George Brett, and Gary Carter, and just about anybody else you can name. Hitting better when you have the platoon advantage is not a weakness peculiar to some players. It is ingrained in the game.

REVOLUTION

I am writing this in the fall of 1987, and there is a football strike. At this moment the strike is not over, but the outcome has pulled into view like a dragon along the roadside. As each week of the strike passes, more players cross the picket lines to go back to work. The attendance in the second week of the strike was up substantially from the first week. The television ratings, though low, will head up as soon as the World Series is over. In one of the most crucial variables, the news media, which absolutely has to have something to write and talk about, has begun to write and talk about the players who are on the field as well as those who are on the picket lines. As time passes they will have more to say about those players who are playing, and less to say about those who are not. The public interest in those who are playing will grow; the interest in those who are not will wane.

In short, then, the players, having sacrificed several very nice paychecks, are as a reward going to gain absolutely nothing, and will lose a great deal of bargaining strength as well. The owners' tactic of filling up the uniforms with available bodies and carrying on as if nothing really had happened has succeeded, which brings up an obvious question of why this has never been tried or really even been discussed in our own sport. Why it is that what works in one sport cannot work in another?

In the baseball strikes, the very short strike we had in 1985 and the much longer strike we had in 1981, there were no strike-breakers used, and there was no serious talk about doing it. If there is another strike next year there will be no talk about it again. The crucial difference between football and baseball in this respect is what I am going to call the players' insulation: the minor leagues. In football, there is only a fine line distinguishing those who are good enough to have jobs from those who are out scrounging for regular work. Players come out of college trained, ready to play, many of them good enough to leap right into the league and contribute. Others are not quite good enough, barely, and so they are let go—free. Sometimes teams make mistakes in judging, and those who are really good enough to play are let go. Sometimes a player who is let go by one team in August will be a star by December.

In baseball, this doesn't happen. Occasionally, a player will be released by one team and turn out to be a good player, but even so, generally there is an interim of several years between the time of the release and the time of stardom.

The difference, of course, is the minor leagues. The raw talent distribution of the two sports is exactly the same: talent in all sports is a pyramid. For every player who is this good, there are several times as many who are half as good, and hundreds who are half as good as that. In baseball those players are playing minor-league baseball. Because they are playing in the minor leagues, they see themselves as standing in line, waiting for a chance which they know will come if they play well enough. They are within the structure that contains their eventual success. They will not violate that structure. The free football players know that their chance will never come within the existing structure.

So the second-level baseball players are not going to cross the picket lines, nor the third-level players either. That means that in order to play replacement games, you would have to dip way, way down into the talent pool, and what you would lose is what we might call The Prospect of Eventual Credibility. What replacement players have in football is the prospect of eventual credibility. In the first week of the replacement-level games, there were some players who played so well that they established pretty clearly that they should have been there all along. As each week passes, another one or two players per team is going to establish that he is better than one of the 45 guys who isn't there. Further, as each week passes the players who are playing, competing as they are at the best level of football available, benefiting from the level of training, benefiting from the coaching and the weight rooms, benefiting from the experience, get a little bit better—while the players who aren't playing, week after week, get a little bit worse, their skills deteriorating from age, from the lack of training, from the lack of competition, until after a period of time that fine line that distinguished those who were in from those who were out just disappears.

Suppose that the players were to stay on strike for, let us say, two years. At the end of that time, if the Union were to say "OK, we give up, go back to work," there wouldn't be any jobs for them to go back to, simply because they would, for the most part, no longer be good enough to play.

In baseball, that can't happen. In baseball, there is that gap, that insulation provided by the players in the minor leagues, which separates the best players from those who are out of work by a gap so great that there is no prospect that the players who could be called in to replace the strikers would ever rise to the level represented by the Mark McGwires, the Ryne Sandbergs, the best young players around today.

So then, if the baseball owners were even to hint that they were thinking of using scabs, what do you think would happen? In a flash, the baseball players would start talking about forming a new league. We would see a repeat of what happened almost a century ago with the Players League of 1890, although most likely the players would not now attempt to finance the league themselves. It would take a year to organize it, but after that year the critical question would be "Who has the credibility here: the established leagues or the players' league?" And the answer is obvious. Unlike in football, where the uniforms and the names recognized from college stardom provide a measure of instant credibility, in baseball all of the credibility would belong to the players.

And that is why, no matter what the situation is, you will never hear baseball owners whispering about using scabs to break a strike—because to do so would invite the possibility of a rival league, and a rival league could cause a $50-million investment to crumble in the owner's hand. No other outcome of a strike could be as disastrous for ownership, no matter what they have to surrender.

In football, you see, the owners have options because there exists a form of live football outside the existing structure, outside of their control. In baseball, THE EXISTENCE OF THE MINOR LEAGUES forces the owners to deal with the players on generous terms, and forces them to pass on to the players a great deal of the income that in football the owners are able to keep for themselves.

Now, let's back off and run at this from a completely different direction.

The minor leagues were not created by the major leagues. The minor leagues originally formed on the same basis as the major leagues, only in smaller cities and even that distinction is limited, since there were moments in the early history of what is now the National League at which it played in places like Troy, New York, and Fort Wayne, Indiana, while minor leagues were left to thrash around in places like New York City and Detroit. In any case, the National League successfully established itself in the nation's largest cities, while other leagues, competitor leagues, foraged for what was left.

At first there was no reserve clause. This was a sort of primordial soup for baseball, an original chaos in which the land itself was liquid, and the players would just drift from team to team as suited themselves. So the owners said "We've got to get organized here. We can have competition between different leagues, yes, but we can't let these players move around from team to team just however they want. Let's construct a reserve arrangement." Organized baseball began, then, in an attempt to deprive the players of negotiating power.

In a few years the National League and the American Association began to pull ahead of the other leagues, and the best players began to become concentrated in these leagues. The owners of these major-league teams would go to the owners of the minor-league teams and say, "Hey,

you've got a player there that we think is pretty good. I'll tell you what: we'll respect your reserve clause, but why don't you sell us this player for, say, $1,000." The minor-league team owner, who might be making $800 on the year (this was a century ago), would sell the player to the big city team, and so the gap between the minor-league and the major-league teams would grow wider.

Well, it didn't take too long until the owners of some of the minor-league teams began to realize that it was in their interest, when they had a player of quality, to hold onto him awhile and let the interest grow, and then sell him to the highest bidder. So the major-league owners got together and said, "Hey, we need to get more organized here. This situation is too . . . chaotic. We need to establish some arrangements whereby, when there is a player for sale, we'll have a way of claiming him, so we won't have this wild bidding for minor-league players anymore. We'll meet with the minor-league owners, and we'll establish a system where if they have a player to sell they can just list him, and then we'll see who picks up the option. To get them to go along with it, we'll fix a good price that they'll be happy to get for the player." And so they did, and then even more of the best players were all concentrated in the major leagues, and the gap was wider than before, and as inflation came along, the amount of money that they actually had to pay for these young players began to reduce the cost of the talent.

Generous as this system was, there were some minor-league owners who weren't happy with it. Early in the twentieth century some minor-league teams still refused to list their best players on waivers and sell them to the major leagues. You would have owners like Jack Dunn in Baltimore who would figure that "I'm in a pretty good sized city here. I can draw as many fans here as the Browns can in St. Louis. Why should I sell my best players to anybody?"

So the major-league teams came back to the minor-league teams and said "We've got to get better organized here. Let's set up a structure with different levels of minor-league teams, and each level can buy whoever they want from the lower levels. We'll fix a good price, and we'll even let you keep the player for two or three years before you have to move him on up the line, and that way everybody will have a steady supply of talent—the major-league teams from the top minors, the top minors from the B Leagues, the B Leagues from the C Leagues, etc. When the player is sold from a C League to a B League it'll be one price, and when he goes from a B League to an A League it will be more, so as you buy a player and pass him along you'll always make a profit. It's more fair to the player that way, if he has a structure that he can move up through. If we don't do this, you see, then the teams that keep all their best players are going to get so strong that they'll walk all over the rest of the league."

Well, that seemed fair enough to the minor-league owners, and indeed the Baltimore team did walk all over the other teams, and so in time the minor-league owners went along with it, and forced everyone in their leagues to go along with it, and by the early 1920s every minor-league team was required, by the rules of organized baseball, to sell its best players to the major leagues. As part of the deal, the major leagues agreed not to sign players straight out of high school. That way, the minor-league teams would each have their own territory, and they could sign the players out of high school and make a profit by selling them up the line.

So the gap between the major leagues and the minor leagues got a little wider, and in a few years the major leagues kind of forgot about their guarantees not to sign players out of high school. The minor-league teams, mind you, are still at this point in the business of running baseball teams. They're not in business to develop ballplayers. They're in business to develop teams, get into pennant races, draw crowds, and make money. Selling ballplayers is just one of the ways that they make money. So then the major-league owners begin to pick out some of the weaker minor-league teams and say, "Hey, why don't you go to work for us? Rather than just selling ballplayers to whoever claims them on waivers or negotiating a deal to sell them before the waiver claim hits, why don't you have an arrangement just with us? We'll pay you money up front—I'll tell you what, we'll pay you so much money up front that we'll guarantee you a profit for the season. Besides that, we'll provide players for you, guys we've got from other teams. You'll be like a farm, growing players for us and growing money for yourself."

Well, to a guy struggling to make ends meet in Mt. Vernon, Illinois, or Decatur, Georgia, that sounded like a pretty good deal, so they'd go along with it. Those minor-league teams, then, would get stronger and their opponents would get weaker, so then the major-league teams would make arrangements with their opponents, too, or sometimes they would just flat buy them out. This went on for about thirty years or so, and then there weren't any free minor leagues left. Everybody worked for somebody.

Once everybody worked for somebody, the major-league teams had the minor-league teams over a barrel. There wasn't any negotiating, now; the major-league teams just wrote the rules, and if the minor-league teams didn't like it they could suck eggs. If the minor-league team was in a pennant race and the major-league team needed their best ballplayer, they'd just take him; hey, we don't care about your damned little pennant race. At first they were apologetic about this, and they would try not to do too much of it; when they took a star player off a contending team they would make every effort to replace him with a player off the major-league roster or a potential star from a lower level, and they would try not to lift a player unless he really made a difference to them. In about ten years, however, that too went by the boards, and if a player was hitting .385 at AAA ball and the minor-league team was a half game ahead with two weeks to play and the major-league team needed him to pinch run once a week, they'd just take him anyway.

Historian Dee Brown has written that probably at no point in our history did white Americans intend to do to American Indians what they actually did. It was a process, extending over a couple of centuries: One generation would make treaties, and the next generation would amend them, cut them back a little bit, claim a little more land, and the generation after that would forget about the treaties altogether, so that, looking at the entire pattern over a period of generations, one would swear that there was a conscious decision to drive the American Indian into the ground. The history of the relationship between the minors and the majors is very similar: One generation would make agreements, and the next generation would amend those agreements, and the third generation would renege on them entirely or forget that they had ever been made. The minor leagues, originally independent competitors of the major leagues, were by tiny degrees and yearly increments reduced into mere servants, living on crumbs, sustained by the major leagues for their own uses like a farmer keeps chickens, just for the eggs.

This process of driving down the minor leagues continues to this day. Just a couple of years ago, the owner of a minor-league team told me that "Every year, they do something that makes it more impossible for us to operate. Every year, the major-league teams change the rules a little bit to make it harder for us."

The minor-league system as it exists today is an abomination in the sight of the Lord. Players are assigned to the minor-league team at the last minute without the team having any say in who wears their uniform, players spend two weeks at a city and then are moved around like checkers, anonymous young men playing to develop skills rather than playing to win, teams in great cities drawing a couple of hundred fans a game, pennant races with no meaning, no connection between city and player, player and fan, fan and city. They have really, truly reached the point at which they don't care about winning.

If you're selling a sport and the players don't care about winning, that's not a sport. That's a fraud. Minor-league baseball today is exactly what the 1919 World Series was: a charade, a rip-off, an exhibition masquerading as a contest. In one of his books Earl Weaver tells about one time when he was managing in the minor leagues he had a sluggish first baseman that the major-league team was trying to make into a third baseman. The guy couldn't play third base, and Weaver knew if he put him there he would cost him the pennant race. Earl wanted to WIN. In desperation, he finally started sending the major-league team phony box scores, showing the guy playing third base when he was actually playing first, living in terror that a scout would catch him and he would get fired—for trying to win.

That's a disgraceful situation. Baseball, for most of the cities in the nation, has been reduced to the level of professional wrestling. By this horrible system, then, most of the nation is deprived of having real baseball. Look at a map—how many great cities do we have in this country? We've got 23 cities that have "real" teams; everything else is an imitation. Miami, Washington, Memphis, Phoenix, San Antonio, Indianapolis, New Orleans, Denver, Nashville, Oklahoma City, Portland—why do these cities have no real baseball? The Memphis team works for my team, the Kansas City Royals—but why should Memphis have nothing, so that Kansas City can have everything? Why should Memphis not be allowed to keep a good ballplayer, so that Kansas City can have them all? It's not right. It's unethical, it's immoral, it is corrupt. We have no right, as Kansas City fans, to use Omaha, Memphis, and Fort Myers as our servants. Every city, whether a great city like those listed above or a small city like Mobile or Bakersfield, should have its own proud team, the best team that it can support. There should be leagues, and there should be pennant races, and there should be civic pride invested in them. And they should serve no master except the urgency of competition.

And yet you see the wonderful irony of the situation: For whose benefit was this greedy system established and for whom is it maintained? For the major-league owners, of course; they've got the whole $80 million-dollar TV contract to themselves (or is it more than that now?), and they don't want to split it 80 ways, they want to split it 26 ways. And yet, they can't really keep the TV money, being essentially merely caretakers who pass it on to the players, and why is that? Because of the minor leagues! If the system existed that should exist, there would be dozens of leagues, hundreds of teams, and, in one way or another, an inevitable supply of talent as there is in football, inasmuch as it would be impossible for the union to lock up the entire sprawling independent system.

Having struggled for a century to create this system, having tightened the organization of baseball tighter and tauter and sounder, having wrestled all of professional baseball into their ironclad structure, the owners now find themselves the victim of that system, their options eliminated by the fact that nothing exists for them to draw from outside their own ironclad structure. Like a tyrant suffocated in bed by his own hired thugs, major-league baseball has choked nearly to death all of the other leagues, and now finds itself kneeling before its own hired help. It is, like the sorry life of Howard Hughes, a marvelous lesson on the end products of greed.

Another of the ugly features of the current system is the abuse by club owners of their monopolistic position in negotiations with cities. Although major-league baseball has a relatively good record on this point in the last fifteen years, a good example of what can happen is what has happened to the football St. Louis Cardinals. The Cardinals, who may be the Phoenix Assholes or something by the time you read this, are owned by an oversized wart named Bidwell. The Cardinals have a perfectly good stadium, Busch Stadium, a major-league facility in every way; nonetheless, Mr. Bidwell is not satisfied. He wants a new stadium, all his own, and he wants the city of St. Louis to tax its $18,000-a-year citizens to build it for him, and if he can't have that at the very least he feels he is entitled to have several hundred luxury boxes constructed for him at taxpayer expense so he can sell them to rich people for $150 a game. In effect, Bidwell is telling the people of St. Louis that if they don't give him millions of dollars he will deprive them of their status as a major-league football city—while Phoenix stands by, anxious to give him millions of dollars to acquire that status. It's an appalling situation, the most blatant abuse of monopolistic power.

In a situation of competing leagues, you see, the city of St. Louis would not have a great deal of interest in whether or not Mr. Bidwell threatened to move to Phoenix. St. Louis has proven itself to be a viable major-league market. In a competitive environment, if one league abandoned the city, another league would immediately move in. The "owner" would have no power to force the city to dance to his tune. Building and maintaining a stadium would be strictly a matter of civic pride, as it should be.

It is all well to say that Lincoln, Nebraska, should have the best baseball team that Lincoln, Nebraska, can support, you might ask, but is baseball really viable there? Would Lincoln, Nebraska, really support a team, at all?

Answer: You bet your ass. A well-managed, free minor-league team in Lincoln, Nebraska, would draw 200,000 to 300,000 fans in a season. In 1949, in a system that wasn't very good but wasn't as oppressive as the one existing now, the team in Lincoln drew 149,000 fans. That's plenty to support an 18-man roster. The Nebraska Cornhuskers football team plays six home games a year in Lincoln and draws more than that, about 70,000 a game. We all understand that they're "minor league," that although they represent the best at their level of competition they couldn't stay on the field with the Kansas City Chiefs, a poor professional team. People will try to tell you that that's different because they're a college so the alumni support them, but anybody who has lived around here knows that's not the way it is. At least half the people who support the Cornhuskers never had any connection with the University of Nebraska. When you're growing up around here you just pick out a college team and root for them; whether or not you wind up going to that college is a completely unrelated issue. People will root for that team, and will invest their regional pride in that team BECAUSE THAT TEAM IS FREE TO TRY TO WIN. They would do the same for a baseball team if that team was really trying to win. A Lincoln baseball team wouldn't get quite the same size crowds because they'd have to split the audience with Omaha and Council Bluffs, Iowa, but they'd still draw real well.

People will tell you that television killed the minor leagues, but that brings us back to the same issue: if television killed minor league baseball, why did college football and college basketball boom at the same time? If the Boston Celtics and the Kansas Jayhawks are on television in this area on the same night, virtually nobody will watch the Celtics, although they are a vastly better team. Why? Television temporarily gripped the interest of the public and had a temporary effect on minor-league attendance, just as it had a temporary effect on attendance at the movies, but those periodic recessions will happen. The problem here was that after this periodic recession passed there were no free minor leagues left to recover.

What would be the economic effects of freeing the minors? First of all, total attendance at professional baseball games nationwide would increase tremendously. Total professional attendance in 1987 will be around 70 million fans—a little over 50 million for the majors, but less than 20 million for the rest of the country. That figure would increase probably to the range of 170 to 200 million fans. There would be a great deal more interest in local teams. At present, most of the people in this nation do not live within easy driving range of real baseball. The Kansas City area has about 1.5 million people, yet it regularly draws 2.2 million fans or more—one and a half fans per person. If competitive teams were accessible to the fans, a figure of 200 million attendance for a nation of more than 240 million people is extremely realistic.

The TV money, however, probably would not increase. The national networks, rather than dealing with a monopoly, would have options; if the National League tried to hold them up, they'd start dickering with the Continental League, or the Pacific Coast League, or the Southwest Conference. The result: the same amount of TV money, cut up many more ways, meaning less TV and radio income per team.

Which would mean, of course, the end of the $2 million salaries. Many more baseball players would make a living, but none would reach the levels of tremendous wealth attained today.

"But what about the quality of play," you might ask; "Aren't you really talking about an expansion of the current 26 teams to maybe 80 or a hundred teams, and isn't the talent already thinned out something terrible by expansion?"

Now there is a truly preposterous argument. This nation could support, without any detectable loss of player quality, at a very, very minimum, 200 major-league teams.

Think about it. If we had 240 major-league teams, each team would represent about a million people. Do you have any idea how many people a million people are? Start counting people that you meet on the street sometime. If you live in New York and ride the subway, start counting the people on the subway. It will take you years and years of counting people that you meet on the street and in the subway to reach a million. You trying to tell me that's not enough people to pick 25 ballplayers out of?

Or look at it this way: start with a group of 250 people, and choose a baseball team from them. Let's see, with 250 people you should have about 60 men between the ages of 18 and 45, at a guess, so choose the best 18 athletes out of those 60 and make them a baseball team. (At this level, obviously some of the best athletes would be women, but never mind.)

Then put that team in a four-team league of such teams, and at the end of the year choose an All-Star team, the best player at each position. This will be the first generation All-Star team.

Put the All-Star team in a league of four All-Star teams, and at the end of the year choose an All-Star team of the All-Star teams; this will be the second-generation All-Star team.

Put that team in a league of four such teams and play a season and choose the best player at each position. At this point I'd say you should have a pretty fair team, wouldn't you? That would be the third-generation All-Star team.

Put four of those pretty fair teams in a league, and play a season with them, and choose the best players. That would be the fourth-generation All-Star team.

Put four of those together and play a season and choose a team of the best of them.

That team, the fifth-generation All-Star team, would represent about 250,000 people.

The team representing a million people would be the All-Star team that you would get if you repeated the process again, again choosing the best players. With 240 million people we'd have 240 teams, not counting the players imported from Puerto Rico, Jamaica, the Dominican Republic, Canada, Venezuela, Mexico, or wherever. I'm not suggesting that we should have anything like 240 major-league teams; I'm suggesting something like 60 major-league and 150 free minor-league teams.

To say that that level of talent, the seventh-generation

All-Star team, is not good enough to be called major-league talent, that we have to move another half-generation beyond that, so that each major-league team represents 8 million fans rather than 4 million . . . well, it's absurd. It's making a distinction in talent which is unimaginably trivial. If you timed every man in the country in a hundred yard dash, the difference between the 650th-fastest man (completing the 26th team) and the 2000th-fastest probably would not be a hundredth of a second. It certainly would not be a tenth of a second.

Of course, if you instantly expanded from 26 teams to the number that should exist you would have a decline in the talent level. You'd have inexperienced players, a great loss in knowledge along with a minimal loss in athletic ability. It would take time for the knowledge of how to play the game and the acquisition of the developed skills to spread throughout the enlarged baseball population. But a gradual expansion of the number of teams? It wouldn't do a thing to the talent.

I'm not saying that we should not allow the best players to be concentrated in the best leagues. That will happen naturally. In college football or basketball, there is no rule that automatically, inflexibly railroads all of the best players to the biggest and best leagues—and yet that's where they are. You don't get too many NBA stars coming out of small colleges in Arizona. The best players will gravitate toward the biggest cities and the best leagues because that's where the money is. The small teams should be able to sell the rights to players while they are under contract, and the contracts should run out at regular intervals because men are not chattel to be moved around without their consent. It's one thing if it happens naturally, and quite another if it happens by force—the difference between rape and chemistry.

But is it really possible for this world to exist? Is this just an air-castle article?

It is, in theory, quite simple to see how the sports world could be changed to get rid of this peculiar closed structure in which we have lived all of our lives. It requires only one action. It requires the antitrust division of the Justice Department to order major-league baseball (and football, and basketball) to stop acting as a monopoly. That given, everything else I have outlined here will follow in time. It could be done either by the Justice Department or by Congress, or by the one at the behest of the other. As a practical matter, they could do this in either of two ways. They could order the existing major leagues to split into four competing entities (six to eight teams each), and instruct those four leagues that they must compete; they must not coordinate their activities in any way whatsoever except to organize a National Championship. They can't get together to negotiate a TV contract. They can't get together to form reserve arrangements and inhibit the movement of players. They especially can't make collective decisions about which cities will have teams and which won't. Very quickly, at least one of those leagues would become aggressive, would expand to perhaps ten or twelve teams, and there would be a team in Washington and a team in Phoenix and a team in Miami within a few years.

The other alternative would be much slower and somewhat less certain, but is probably sounder in the long run: order major-league baseball teams to divest themselves of their minor-league affiliates, and prohibit them from continuing to engage in predatory and monopolistic practices with regard to teams in other leagues—as they have done for a hundred years. Prohibit teams from forming alliances with teams in other leagues.

In time, since leagues would not be able to enter into the kind of unequal agreements with stronger teams that they have so long lived with—agreements which forced them to act in the interest of other teams—what would they do? The leagues would act in their selfish interest. It would be in the best interests of each league to move into the biggest cities that it could control. You would get a league, like maybe the Pacific Coast League, which might put a team in Los Angeles, snarf up San Jose and Sacramento, and move in the direction of being a West Coast major league. The Los Angeles team, trying to compete with the two established teams, might blow its wad on George Brett or Eric Davis.

If the first approach was selected, the major leagues should also be required to divest themselves of their minor-league affiliates, or at least most of them. If the second approach was selected, the regulation should prohibit the existing majors from expanding for a period of 15 to 20 years. At first, some minor-league owners would complain that they were being cut off from their main source of support, which was their major-league "partner." In the short run, of course, that's exactly what it would do: it would snip the lifeline, and force the team to scramble for survival on its own, by doing novel things like promoting,

putting together a good ballteam, getting into a pennant race, and trying to win. Looking at the Phoenix team, for example, somebody would have to invest some money to build that team up toward a more competitive level. If there was the danger that an established league would expand into the Phoenix area, it would be difficult to get anybody interested in investing in the upstart team. But if the Phoenix prospects could be assured that there would be no expansion for the next 15 years, then the Phoenix people could turn their attention toward building the best team that they could put together.

Well, I hope I've made you think, anyway. I hope I have made you realize that the world in which we live is not the only possible world, nor even the best of all possible worlds. I am not arguing for these changes because I want to be provocative; I am arguing for these changes because I believe they would make baseball healthier, more exciting, and more fun.

Competition isn't always pretty. Teams would fold, go bankrupt sometimes, use nearly naked usherettes in a cheap attempt to boost attendance, pull out in the middle of the night without paying their debts—all of the things that businesses do. Baseball would be less stable. It would change more rapidly than it ever has, in part because each league would be learning from the experiences of the other leagues. But it would be changing because it would be growing, and it would be growing toward a baseball world which is larger, stronger, smarter, richer, more diverse, and more fair to the fans. It can happen.

Hey, buddy, I love tradition, too.

THE NEW STRIKE ZONE

I had 20-10 vision. A lot of guys can see that well. I sure couldn't read labels on revolving phonograph records as people wrote I did. I couldn't "see" the bat hit the ball, another thing they wrote. . . . What I had more of wasn't eyesight, it was discipline. . . . Giving the pitcher an extra two inches around the strike zone increases the area of the strike zone 35 percent. . . . Give a major-league pitcher that kind of advantage and he'll murder you."

Ted Williams
The Science of Hitting

Fooling around with the strike zone is playing with dynamite. At the winter meetings last December in Dallas, it was announced that the strike zone for 1988 would be larger and smaller. The 1988 strike zone will be smaller in law, but larger in fact, there being an attempt made to reconcile the *de fatso* strike zone, the one called by the umpires, with the strike zone as laid out in the book. What really counts, we are told, is the instructions that will be given to the umpires by the league offices at the start of the 1988 season. Why the umpires can't simply be told to enforce the rules is a matter too subtle for most of us, but anyway, we are assured that the situation is being brought under control, and there will be no more strike zone A and strike zone B.

The strike zone is the very heart of a baseball game. An inch in the strike zone means far more than ten yards in the outfield. Nonetheless, cautious as one must be in dealing with the heart, there are times when heart surgery cannot be avoided, and in 1987 it was perceived that such an occasion had arrived. The strike zone had gotten too small. It was crimping the pitcher's style, making work too easy for the hitters.

We have, of course, been here before. In 1963, reacting to a perception that home runs had become too cheap, the same rules committee expanded the strike zone. The expansion in that case was not a reduction in disguise; it was a real expansion. The effect was dramatic: the pitchers took over. In the 15 years prior to the new strike zone, only one major-league pitcher, qualifying for the ERA title, had posted an earned run average under 2.00. In the next six years, 14 pitchers posted ERAs under 2.00, and the undertow seemed soon likely to pull the league leaders under 1.00. The National League batting average plum-

meted 16 points in a single year. In 1962 the National League batting average was .261. In 1963 only one National League team hit as high as .261.

The rules committee had overshot its mark. No one had anticipated such a drastic change in the game. The change was so great that few people could believe that a little alteration of the strike zone had caused offenses to contract so sharply. By the time baseball got around to undoing the act six years had passed, and the game had grown stagnant. A year from now, a quarter-century later, we will know to what extent we have repeated history.

The new rule was no more promulgated than the players began to wonder, sometimes aloud, "How is this going to effect *me*?" Frank White was not pleased, whining in the KC papers that the umpires were not going to take strikes away from Wade Boggs, and that the costs of the new rule would fall disproportionately upon hitters such as himself. Pitchers, of course, were more pleased, and the thought was expressed that it was high time that an effort be made to improve the pitcher's lot in life.

The recurrence of this debate has prompted me to finally undertake a study which I have contemplated doing for at least ten years. The question that has long troubled me is, "When the strike zone is redefined, what type of player is most disadvantaged, and what type of player is helped?" This question has intrigued me because it exposes, in a sense, the heart of the game. The question of how a player is affected by a change in the strike zone is related to the question of how a given player is affected by his own use of the strike zone. If Alfredo Griffin didn't swing at everything, what would he hit? That is not the same question, obviously, but it is a related question, and related to a question which offers few other avenues of approach. Who will be hurt by the new strike zone? Will it be the Alfredo Griffins, who have a large strike zone anyway, or will it be the Wade Boggses (there is only one Wade Boggs, James) who use the strike zone as a weapon to force the pitcher to throw the pitch they want? If you make the strike zone larger, does plate discipline become more important or less important?

Of course, studying the past is not predicting the future. We do not know to what extent 1988 will repeat the experience of 1963. I'm just saying that the experience of 1963 is more likely to be a guide to what happens in 1988 than, let's say, the experience of 1974 or the experience of 1913.

I began this study by entering into a data base the basic hitting statistics for 1962 and 1963 of eight players for each major-league team, the eight regulars of 1962 (160 players total.) Six of those players (four of them New York Mets) did not play or played almost not at all in 1963, so their performance under the new rules could tell us nothing about how they were affected by the change. Those six players I replaced with the six players from 1962 who had the most playing time but were not already included.

Overall, 124 of the 160 players (77.5 percent) declined offensively from 1962 to 1963, as measured by runs created per out made. Only 36 players had better seasons in 1963 than in 1962. As a group, the players created 4.998 runs per game in 1962, and 4.327 runs per game in 1963, a decline of 13.4 percent. A sudden 13 percent decline in offensive production for a player from one season to the next would be substantial but not alarming. A sudden 13 percent decline for a group of 160 players, all of the regulars in baseball, is startling. The 13 percent decline is essentially consistent with the league data for the two seasons, which shows a 12 percent decline in runs scored between the two seasons, and a 12.5 percent decline in Earned Run Average.

It was not simply that the players walked less and struck out more, nor was it even that they declined especially in these respects.

• 70 percent of the 160 players, or 112 of them, declined in batting average.

• 76 percent of the players, or 121 of 160, declined in slugging percentage.

By contrast:

• Only 59 percent of the players—more than half, but not a lot more than half—struck out more often.

• 63 percent of the players, or 101 of 160, walked less often.

The increase in strikeouts was relatively modest, from 74 per 550 at bats to 77. The decrease in walks was relatively modest, from 55 per 550 at bats to 50. The differences are five walks and three strikeouts for a typical player during the season.

But their overall slugging percentage decreased from .426 to .396, and their batting average from .274 to .261. The differences here are 7 hits and 16 total bases per 550 at bats.

That outlines the normal declines for all players within the study. Then I proceeded to sort the 160 players into groups of players, trying to find the effect on each group. The first thing that I looked at was the height of the player. The shortest player of 1963 was Albie Pearson, a 5'5" center fielder who had the best year of his career in that season. Pearson was one of no more than half a dozen hitters who had their best seasons in 1963. The tallest player of the time was Frank Howard, a 6'7" slugger who, after hitting .296 in 1961 and 1962, driving in 119 runs the second year, saw his career go into a precipitous decline under the new strike zone. Though he finished the season hitting a respectable .273, Howard struggled terribly most of the season and was benched in early July, escaping the bench and salvaging his average with a tremendous late-season hot streak. He finished with only 64 RBI. Howard hit .296 in 1961, .296 in 1962 and .296 in 1969—but .267 under the expanded strike zone.

Howard's strike zone, of course, was a lot bigger than Albie Pearson's. When you expand their strike zones, you magnify Frank Howard's problems more than Albie Pearson's. But was this, in fact, a generalized phenomenon? Did the taller players actually suffer with the larger strike zone?

Yes. Well, at least I can give you a good, loud "maybe." In 1962, there was no correlation between height and batting average. The taller players, as one might expect, had more power, but their batting averages were almost the same, as the chart below shows:

Height	Batting	Slugging
5'7" to 5'10"	.273	.402
5'8" to 5'11"	.274	.407
5'9" to 6'0"	.274	.414
5'10" to 6'1"	.274	.423
5'11" to 6'2"	.276	.428
6'0" to 6'3"	.274	.436
6'1" to 6'4"	.274	.442
6'2" to 6'5"	.273	.443
ALL PLAYERS	.274	.426

I used overlapping ranges to get groups large enough for meaningful data. Note that even so Pearson is too short, and Howard too tall, to be a part of a meaningful group. There were 31 players in the 5'7" to 5'10" group, increasing to 114 players in the 5'10" to 6'1" group (the largest), back down to 34 players in the 6'2" to 6'5" group.

Anyway, in 1963 a definite pattern emerged in these same groupings:

Height	1962 Batting	1962 Slugging	1963 Batting	1963 Slugging
5'7" to 5'10"	.273	.402	.267	.382
5'8" to 5'11"	.274	.407	.264	.378
5'9" to 6'0"	.274	.414	.263	.388
5'10" to 6'1"	.274	.423	.261	.395
5'11" to 6'2"	.276	.428	.260	.396
6'0" to 6'3"	.274	.436	.259	.405
6'1" to 6'4"	.274	.442	.258	.406
6'2" to 6'5"	.273	.443	.258	.408

All of the groups of players declined as hitters. Everyone lost, but whereas the shortest group of players lost only 6 points in their batting average and 20 points in slugging percentage, the tallest players lost 15 points in batting average and 35 points in slugging percentage.

This was a result which was, to some degree, anticipated. It was, however, largely offset by a completely unanticipated result. There are two basic offensive measurements, slugging percentage and on-base percentage. For some unknown reason, the shortest players lost a lot more walks than the taller players, and thus lost more in on-base percentage, despite hitting for higher averages. The chart below gives the percentage of the players in each group who walked less often in 1963 than in 1962:

Height	Walked Less Often
5'7" to 5'10"	74%
5'8" to 5'11"	76%
5'9" to 6'0"	76%

Height	Walked Less Often
5'10" to 6'1"	70%
5'11" to 6'2"	61%
6'0" to 6'3"	55%
6'1" to 6'4"	49%
6'2" to 6'5"	47%
ALL PLAYERS	59%

The shortest group of players declined from 54 walks per season to 44. The tallest group of players declined only from 55 to 53.

Let us speculate briefly about why this happened. The most important impact of the 1963 strike zone redefinition was to give the pitchers a LOW strike. The bottom of the strike zone was changed from the knees to the BOTTOM of the knees. At that time it was believed, and for all I know it was true, that most home runs were hit off of high pitches, above the belt. It was thought that if you gave the pitcher the low strike, it would eliminate some of the cheap home runs. Although they also moved the top of the strike zone up (in theory), it was not believed that this had as much impact on the game.

The tall players, the Frank Howards, may have just let the pitch at the knees go by because they couldn't hit it anyway. This put them behind in the count more often, reducing their batting and slugging averages, but it also led sometimes to walks. The shorter players, who could hit that pitch, didn't let it go by when there was a chance it would be a strike—consequently, fewer walks, but less decline in batting and slugging.

If that is true, then we should remember that in 1988 we will be adding *high* strikes, not low strikes. It might be a totally different effect. Even so, I think it is a fair guess that the tallest players (the Mark McGwires, the Mike Marshalls) will (as a group) suffer more than the shortest players.

In any case, the import of it is that, while their batting averages declined disproportionately in 1963, the tallest players remained essentially as productive relative to the league as did the shortest players, with the exception of the fact that the *very* shortest group, the 5'7" to 5'10" group, did retain a higher percentage of their offensive ability (90 percent) than did any other group.

This tendency of the most extreme groups to show an effect which was not visible anywhere else along the spectrum came up again and again later in the study, often complicating the issue of whether or not a real effect could be observed. Observing that the taller players, who had the highest slugging percentages, lost more in average and power than the shorter players, I wondered if perhaps this might be not because they were taller, but because they were power hitters. To examine this, I broke the 160 players down into groups by isolated power (slugging percentage minus batting average).

Decreases in power, I found, were directly proportional to power itself. Players in all power ranges except the lowest retained 82 to 87 percent of their isolated power, and 82 to 86 percent of their overall offensive ability. As had happened before, the extreme group, the players with NO power, did retain a higher percentage of their offensive ability (96 percent) than any other power group. (To be precise, that figure applies to the 29 players with

isolated power between .050 and .100.) Walks and strikeouts showed no distinct patterns of change.

Most interesting, however, was the fact that losses in batting average were consistent along the spectrum except for the lowest range. The players with isolated power over .200 slipped in batting average from .281 to .269 (12 points). The players with isolated power of .100 to .150 slipped in batting average from .270 to .256, about the same amount. That means that the slippage in batting average that occurred among the taller players did NOT occur because they were power hitters, but (presumably) simply because they were taller.

The third study of the data focused on how players in different ranges of batting average were affected by the new strike zone. Let me give a chart first:

'62 Batting Range	1962 Avg.	1963 Avg.	Decline
.300 and up	.313	.284	29 points
.275-.300	.287	.268	19 points
.250-.275	.264	.253	11 points
.225-.249	.240	.244	UP 4 points

What we have here, unfortunately, canNOT be interpreted as evidence that the new strike zone will work against the Tony Gwynn–Wade Boggs class, and in favor of the Frank White class. The problem is what I call the law of competitive balance. In any season-to-season study, the best players would tend to return toward league norms, while the worst hitters (actually, the hitters who had had the worst seasons) would tend to improve. Without doing a parallel study of season-to-season movement under normal conditions, which I don't have time to do, I can't really say whether this particular chart shows anything meaningful or not, but I suspect that it doesn't. I would expect that this is a completely normal chart, simply adjusted downward by about 12 to 15 points, and that it doesn't really show anything.

There is, however, another odd phenomenon which turns up in the strikeout and walk data. Remember, the averages were *down* in walks and *up* in strikeouts. Among the best hitters, the .300 hitters, 79 percent of the players were up in strikeouts, but only 54 percent were down in walks. Look what happened after that:

'62 Batting Range	1963 Up in Strikeouts	1963 Down in Walks
.300 and up	79%	54%
.275-.300	60%	58%
.250-.275	53%	65%
.225-.249	51%	74%

The .300 hitters, as a group, struck out much more in 1963, but did not decline much in walks. The low-average hitters, however, did not strike out much more often in 1963, but declined sharply in walks drawn.

The strikeout effect could be caused by the law of competitive balance, but then what about the walks? It doesn't seem to make any sense, but given groups of 28 to 51 players and a clear pattern in the data, there is probably some real reason for it. I could speculate on what this is, but then so could you, and I'll leave it to you.

The fourth study grouped the players in order of their

productivity as hitters in 1962, the highest group of meaningful size being those who created six to eight runs per game, the second group five to seven, the third group four to six, etc. This grouping, again, shows the law of competitive balance or something similar. The players who in 1962 created six to eight runs per game declined in 1963 by 18 percent. The players who in 1962 created only two to four runs per game declined in 1963 by only 2 percent. Of the most productive players, 86 percent declined in 1963; of the least productive, only 64 percent declined. I can't draw any conclusion from this.

The fifth study grouped the players according to strikeout range. Before doing this study, I talked to Craig Wright, and asked him what players he thought would be most hurt by the new strike zone. Craig suggested that power hitters would be particularly hurt (not true in 1963), and that players who strike out a lot would suffer. This was true in 1963. The players who in 1962 struck out in 19 to 22 percent of their at bats—struck out a lot, let's say—lost 19 percent of their offensive productivity in 1963. The players who struck out in only 7 to 10 percent of their at bats (struck out little) lost only 5 percent of their offensive productivity.

Oddly, however, the players who struck out a lot showed *no* increase in strikeouts in 1963. All of the players who struck out in 14 percent of their at bats or more, a total of 62 players, showed, as a group, a slight *decrease* in the frequency of their strikeouts in 1963. Their batting averages dropped a lot, their slugging percentages dropped, their walks dropped—but their strikeouts did not increase. One draws the conclusion that they were hitting 0-2 rather than 2-2. The low-strikeout group lost less in batting average and slugging percentage, but did strikeout more.

In this case again, the extreme groups went contrary to the general pattern. The players who struck out the *very* most did well in 1963; the players who struck out the *very* least did poorly. The players who struck out the very least happened to be (coincidence, probably) much older than average, which probably explains that. The group of players who struck out the very most included Harmon Killebrew, Dick Stuart, Joe Adcock, Jim Hickman, Bob Allison, Woody Held, Lou Brock, and a few others. These players essentially did as well in 1963 as in 1962. I couldn't tell you why, other than to suggest that in some cases the strike zone was just irrelevant to them. If you swing at *anything* then you're making your own strike zone. It was a small group.

I have several more studies, but at this point I sense that I am reaching a saturation point in terms of your ability to assimilate this material, so I'll pause and talk in more general terms for a moment. In the first study, the study of batting by height, I found a predictable, sensible effect: the taller players suffered in batting and slugging. That was the last time that happened. Well, not completely, maybe, but the patterned, predictable effects that I had hoped for by and large did not materialize. Instead, I found real effects and real patterns, but patterns that don't always make sense, don't seem to fit together one with another very well. Players who strike out a lot seem to be hurt, probably, unless they strike out a *whole* lot. Power hitters lose power but compensate by drawing more walks and so make out just as well as singles batters except for

the players who don't have ANY power. What kind of use is this? Very little, frankly, unless you can develop a coherent theory which ties it all together and gives it some predictive significance.

This continued when I studied groups of players aligned according to the frequency of walks; I found patterns, but not always patterns that make any sense. The clearest pattern is that the more a player walks, the more likely he is to suffer a sharp decline in walks. Of the 13 players who walked the most, all suffered 1963 declines in productivity, in large part because they lost a great deal of power and a good many walks. Per 550 at bats, this group of players walked 107 times in 1962, but only 79 times in 1963. Their slugging percentage dropped from .460 to .430. That might seem to be a sensible pattern. The players who tried to work the strike zone, force the pitcher to give them a pitch they could drive—found themselves behind in the count more often than they had in the past—consequently drawing fewer walks and getting fewer pitches that they could hit hard.

Of the eleven players who walked the least often in 1962—the players who hit the first pitch they took a shine to—nine actually *increased* their walk frequency in 1963, and as a group they increased from 23 walks/550 plate appearances to 31. This group of players, by the way, was *not* particularly young; their average age in 1962 was 27.4, while the group average for all 160 players was 27.6, which shoots down the most obvious explanation for why this would happen, other than simply ascribing it to the Law of Competitive Balance.

And just when you're beginning to think that the data might make some sense, you start trying to assemble more data and realize that it doesn't. This last group, the free swingers, actually lost *more* in slugging percentage than did the disciplined hitter mentioned before, dropping from an aggregate .414 to .380. Both extreme groups of players, really, lost about the same number of points in slugging percentage as did the entire group of 160 players, which declined from .426 to .396. And the data which stretches the spectrum between these extremes (with the exception of the walks column, which behaves rationally) is just all over the place—up and then down and then up and then down again, in almost every category. Perhaps the only safe conclusions from this study are that:

1) The players who walked the most dropped sharply in walks. The players who walked the least walked more often than before.

2) The players who walked the least often lost more points in batting average than the players who walked most often. The high-walk group declined in batting average by 8 points. The low-walk group declined by 18 points, and there is a clearly (if irregularly) ascending pattern between the extremes.

3) The walks and the singles are essentially traded off, and there is no clear pattern of either extreme group or any portion of the spectrum being hurt, overall, more than any other.

Next I tried grouping together players who struck out *and* walked little, or a lot. If your eyes start to glaze over here just skip ahead about a page, but I'm going to report on the studies for the benefit of the small number of people who will take the time to straighten them out. There are players who strike out a lot because they swing with more force than they can quite control, like Rob Deer and Steve Balboni. There are other players who strike out a lot as a cost of trying to work the count, taking a lot of pitches, like Phil Bradley and Dale Murphy, who both strikeout and walk a lot. The earlier study of strikeouts grouped all of the high-strikeout hitters together. This study focuses on total strikeouts and walks.

This study, at least, clearly found something. Of the players who struck out or walked most often, only 33 percent struck out more often in 1963, but 78 percent walked less often. Going down from there, the paths crossed:

Strikeouts and walks as a % of Plate Appearances	% of players striking out more often	% of players drawing walks less often
.29 or higher	33	78
.26-.29	58	68
.23-.26	48	87
.20-.23	68	59
.17-.20	54	60
.14-.17	79	36
.11-.14	82	36

We have seen a similar pattern before, and frankly I didn't understand it then, either. The strikeout/walk ratios of all players deteriorated, but in opposite directions. The players who struck out and walked a lot, like Dale Murphy, struck out no more but walked less. The players who struck out and walked little, like Johnny Ray, walked no less but struck out more. Each group lost from its strength; the players who walked a lot walked less, and the players who struck out little struck out more.

This data shows a clear pattern if not necessarily an understandable one. The rest of the data in this study shows no clear patterns. The players who were least effected by the change were the players in the top strikeout/walk group, who lost only 8 percent of their offensive productivity; however, the players who were *most* effected by the change were the players in the next group, those who struck out or walked almost as often, who lost 20 percent of their productivity. Again, the extreme group shows a tendency which is not necessarily supported by the rest of the study.

The final study (Whew! Chorley, I didn't think he was *eveh* gonna git to the final study, did you?) sorted players according to their strikeout to walk ratios. This study, again, showed a clear pattern in the strikeout and walk categories, but no clear pattern anywhere else.

Strikeouts as a % of strikeouts and walks	% of players striking out more often	% of players drawing walks less often
.7 or higher	45	40
.60-.70	56	56
.50-.60	61	71
.40-.50	67	73
up to .40	67	75

The players at the top of the chart have the worst strikeout/walk ratios; those at the bottom have the best.

The players with the best strikeout/walk ratios, the bottom two groups, struck out more often and walked less

often in 1963. The players with the worst ratios, the top two groups, had essentially the same strikeout/walk data in 1963 as in 1962. Again, remember the Law of Competitive Balance: the best players always tend to be drawn back toward the league norms.

The players with the best strikeout/walk ratios did tend to decline in 1963 somewhat more than the other players, but not dramatically so; they retained 82 percent of their offensive ability, as opposed to 88 percent of the other three groups.

I checked a few other things (Dang. Elbert, I coulda swo' he said that otha study was gonna be the last one) which didn't go anywhere. I separated left-handed from right-handed batters. The differences are there, but may not be significant: right-handed hitters retained 86.9 percent of their 1962 productivity, left-handers 85.2 percent. In a revealing note about changes in the game, in 1962 there were only five major-league regulars who were switch hitters—Mickey Mantle, Jim Gilliam, Maury Wills, Buck Rodgers, and Tom Tresh.

On a hunch that the catchers might have adapted to the new strike zone more quickly than other players, I sorted players by position. That showed no significant effects.

I sorted players according to age, which of course showed that the older players declined more than the younger players, but without a comparison chart from another season, this information cannot be interpreted.

That completes the studies.

We now face the question of what, in general, the 1963 season has to tell us about the 1988 season.

I didn't study the pitchers. I didn't study the pitchers in part because of time constraints, but also because part of what I would conclude seems to me too obvious to require study.

What type of pitcher will be helped by the new strike zone? Power pitchers. Power pitchers, power pitchers, and more power pitchers.

The problem that young, hard-throwing pitchers have, of course, is that they have trouble hitting that little tiny strike zone. When you make the target larger, you minimize their troubles—and they will take advantage of it. Consider a few examples:

In 1962 Jim Maloney, a 22-year-old right-hander with a monster of a fastball, walked 66 men in 115 innings, finishing 9–7 with a 3.52 ERA. An article in *Sport* magazine that winter said that skeptics wondered if he was capable of doing much more. In 1963 he won 23 games, (23–7), and struck out 265 men in 250 innings with only 88 walks.

In 1962 Bob Veale, a 6′5″ left-hander, walked 25 men in 46 innings, pitching his way off the roster and back to Columbus early in the year, although his record was decent (2–2, 3.72 ERA). In 1963, overcoming early-season arm troubles, he pitched 78 innings with a 1.04 ERA. Over the following four years he won 67 games as a starting pitcher.

In 1961 Bob Gibson was 13–12, walking 119 men in 211 games. In 1962 he was 15–13, walking 95 in 234 innings. But in 1963, given the new strike zone, Gibson was 18–9 and headed higher.

Sandy Koufax had his first great season in 1963.

Juan Pizzaro, another left-hander with a fearsome fastball, had been in the major leagues since 1957, always regarded as a potential star. In 1960 Milwaukee gave up on him after he walked 72 men in 115 innings. In 1962, walking 97 men in 203 innings, he finished 12–14 with a 3.81 ERA. With the new strike zone in 1963, he cut his walks by a third, cut his ERA to 2.39 and finished 16–8.

Al Downing in 1962 was 9–13 at Richmond, walking 113 men in 169 innings, 4.10 ERA although striking out 9.6 men per game. In 1963 he was 13–5 in the American League, 2.56 ERA.

Dick Radatz, though an effective pitcher as a rookie in 1962, turned into The Monster in 1963, striking out 162 men in 132 innings with a 1.98 ERA.

Of course, there were hard-throwing youngsters who did not come into their own in 1963, and there were finesse pitchers who had outstanding years in 1963, like the 42-year-old Warren Spahn. But unless somebody studies it and says it ain't so, the pattern seems clear to me: 1963 was the year the power pitchers took over.

This, in part, explains some of the patterns in data which we observed before. Why did the league strikeout and walk data not change as much as the batting average and slugging percentage? Because there was a change in the composition of the league pitching staff, a shift to more hard-throwers without pinpoint control. If the same pitchers had continued to pitch, what would probably have happened is that league walk totals would have dropped sharply, but the impact on the league batting and slugging averages would have been small. Total strikeouts probably also would have declined, as the hitters learned to jump on an earlier pitch to avoid getting behind in the count. The larger strike zone enabled pitchers like Jim Maloney and Al Downing to take innings away from guys like Bob Purkey and Bill Stafford, thus offsetting most of the decrease in walks and replacing it (since power pitchers give up few hits and fewer home runs) with lowered batting averages and slugging percentages.

I've already spent enough time on those studies, so I'm not going to go back and discuss them some more, but it is possible that some of the puzzling effects observed in the earlier studies, having to do with who struck out more and who walked less, could be explained by this "compensation," this shift in the makeup of the league's pitchers dictated by the change in strike zones.

The more interesting question is, will this happen again in 1988? I'm betting that it will—in fact, I'm betting that the effect with respect to the power pitchers will be more dramatic this time than in 1963. We have, you know, kind of been at the end of an era of outstanding pitchers. The Seavers, Palmers, Carltons, Niekros, and Vida Blues are gone, and the new generation of star pitchers has been slow to step into their shoes. That began to change in 1985. Pitchers like Gooden, Clemens, Higuera, Jack Morris, and Mike Witt can pretty much be counted on to have good seasons every year—and with the new strike zone, I'll bet they're a little bit better.

But they're not the pitchers who will be helped the most. Those guys are ahead of the game already. The pitchers who will be helped most are the young, wild hard-throwers, in the class of Jamie Moyer, Tim Conroy, Mark Gubicza, Mitch Williams, Bobby Witt, Juan Nieves, Mark Davis, Danny Jackson, Eric Plunk, and José Rijo. Ron

Darling and Fernando Valenzuela, though better pitchers, could also be helped; they fight the strike zone sometimes. These pitchers unquestionably have major-league stuff. Their problem is that they miss with that first pitch, and wind up pitching behind in the count. You give them a high strike once in awhile, and they'll find themselves ahead in the count 45 percent of the time rather than 35 percent of the time. That's all it takes. They get their feet on the ground, get some confidence, and in two months you've got a completely different pitcher.

In any season, maybe 10 percent of the pitchers in that class will find themselves and turn in good seasons. The difference in 1988 is that it's going to be 30 percent, rather than 10 percent—and "good" is going to be "better." I don't make many predictions, but I'm predicting this. A couple of the pitchers in that class, those I mentioned or somebody I forgot just like them, are going to go 22–5 and 24–7 or something. A guy like Mark Langston—man, could he have a year. The critical difference between 1963 and 1988 is that in 1988 we're going to be giving these guys a *high* strike. That's the pitch they need; these guys don't throw for the knees. They're wild high. You give Danny Jackson that slider above the belt, and I'm telling you the batter is going to have has hands full. Giving Danny Jackson the high strike is like giving a grizzly bear the first swat.

As to what class of hitters will be effected how, I studied that for several pages and didn't reach any definitive conclusions. However, just on the off chance that 1988 might in fact resemble 1963, let us make a few guesses, without any guarantees:

CLASS ONE: Good hitters with power who hit for average but have poor K/W ratios. Includes Larry Sheets, George Bell, Kirby Puckett, Andre Dawson, Will Clark, and Tim Wallach. These players will probably lose less power, as a group, than most others (understanding, of course, that Dawson and Bell are unlikely to push 50 homers again simply because that is not their normal performance level). They probably won't (as a group) strike out more or walk less, but they will lose some power and some in batting average due to hitting more often behind in the count.

CLASS TWO: Power hitters who work the strike zone to get a pitch they can drive. Includes players like Eddie Murray, Dwight Evans, Kent Hrbek, George Brett, Wally Joyner, Jack Clark, Danny Tartabull, and Darryl Strawberry. These guys, as a group, may be hurt more. Taking more pitches than other players, they will find themselves behind in the count more often. Look for a significant loss of power, significant decline in walks drawn, although there will be some exceptions within the group. Darryl Strawberry strikes me as the most likely player to buck the trend. Howard Johnson and Mike Schmidt are in this group.

CLASS THREE: Oversized power hitters. Includes players like Mark McGwire, Dale Murphy, and Mike Marshall. These guys may lose 15 to 20 points, as a group, in batting average—more than almost any other group of players. They will lose homers.

CLASS FOUR: The pure hitters who work the strike zone. Includes players like Wade Boggs, Tony Gwynn,

Paul Molitor, Kevin Seitzer, and Tim Raines. These gentlemen will probably not lose a lot in batting average—maybe 5 to 10 points off their career norms. They will walk a lot less often, and they will lose some power, but they'll still be able to cover their strike zones.

CLASS FIVE: Don Mattingly. Isn't really like anybody else. Aren't enough players like him to generalize.

CLASS SIX: The true singles hitters who work the strike zone. Includes Ozzie Smith, Scott Fletcher, Willie Randolph, and Tommie Herr. I suspect that early in the season, many of these guys will have trouble adjusting to the new strike zone and will be in slumps. Later on, once they begin to feel comfortable, the slap-hitting style may be just the thing to deal with the new generation of power pitchers.

CLASS SEVEN: The singles hitters who don't work the strike zone. Includes Willie McGee, Willie Wilson, Vince Coleman, Mookie Wilson, Milt Thompson. These guys may carry on as if not much had happened. They may walk more often than they did before, losing a few points in batting average. With no power to lose and loosely defined strike zones anyway, they're not too vulnerable.

CLASS EIGHT: Low-average power hitters who strike out a lot. Includes guys like Rob Deer, Jose Canseco, Lance Parrish, Larry Parrish, Ruben Sierra, Steve Balboni, Ozzie Virgil, Dave Parker—primarily American League players. These guys will split, I think. Some of them will be devasted, lose 30 points off their batting average and slip out of the league. Others will adjust and keep hitting the ball out of the park.

CLASS NINE: The tweeners. The guys who hit for average, but aren't batting champions, the guys who hit 15 to 20 homers a year with averages of .275 to .310. Includes players like Bobby Bonilla, Ryne Sandberg, Keith Hernandez, Terry Pendleton, Phil Bradley, Carney Lansford, and Pete O'Brien.

This is an interesting class. In 1963, this group just got killed. I mean, they drove off the bridge. Tito Francona, a fine line-drive hitter with a little power, hit .228 in 1963. Vic Power's career reached an abrupt, and premature, end. Bob Skinner hit .302 with 20 homers in 1962; in 1963 he hit .259 with three homers. Willie Davis dropped from .285 with 21 homers to .245 with nine homers. George Altman dropped from .318 with 22 homers to .274 with nine homers. Brooks Robinson, who hit .303 with 23 homers in 1962, dropped to .251 with 11 homers in 1963, although Brooksie came back to be the MVP in 1964.

Since I couldn't really say why this happened to this group of players, I have no idea whether it will happen again. The only two of these players who survived until the strike zone was restored in 1969 were Willie Davis and Brooks Robinson. Davis struggled through 1968 and then hit .311, .305 and .309 from 1969 to 1971, suggesting that some of his problems were caused by the strike zone. Robinson had his best years under the constricted K range, but then those were his prime years. After hitting .253 in 1967 and .234 in 1968, Robinson hit .276 in 1969 and .272 in 1970, a 30-point jump, suggesting that he too lost quite a few hits to the 1963 rules change.

CLASS TEN: The non-hitters. The Spike Owens, Lombardozzis, Garry Templetons, and Rafael Santanas. These guys will never know that the strike zone has been fiddled with.

CLASS ELEVEN: The contact hitters. Johnny Ray, Harold Reynolds, Mike Scioscia—players who don't strike out but also don't hit a whole lot. These guys will strike out more in 1988 and consequently lose 8 to 10 points off their averages, but there probably won't be any dramatic effects, and you'd have to look at the whole group to realize that they were off at all.

Well, don't take those predictions too seriously; they're just something to add a little bit of interest to the 1988 season, wondering where James was right and where he was wrong. Some hitters don't fit in any class. I will, however, make one more serious prediction before I shut up.

Major-league attendance in 1988 will be down by 600,000 fans or more. Attendance has been going up year after year after year. In 1988 it will be down, and it will be down enough that people will notice.

Why? Because fans like hitting. In the history of baseball, whenever runs scored go down, attendance goes down. When runs scored go up, attendance goes up. Election years don't tend to be very good attendance years anyway. Runs scored are going to be down this year—and attendance will be down right with them.

GAME SCORES

When Roger Clemens struck out 20 early in the '86 season, a friend of mine said, "Now *that* is a quality start." The concept of game scores is an extension, in a sense, of the concept of the quality start. It's a phrase you hear regularly during the season, in a hundred variations: That was the best pitched game we've had in a week. . . . I think that may have been Bobby's finest outing of the season. . . . Carl pitched perhaps his best game of the season last Thursday in Houston, but a ninth-inning error pulled the rug out from under him. . . . Hershiser's last start was his best start in a month. . . . That was probably the Red Sox' best pitching performance all season, etc. Whereas the concept of the quality start creates a black/white division, the things people say reflect a continuum from the best starts down to the ones that we don't talk about after a few days.

This is my annual fun stat, a kind of garbage stat that I present not because it helps us understand anything in particular but because it is fun to play around with. The general goal here was to create a way to scan a pitcher's line from a game, like Roger Clemens' game of April 29, 1986 (9 3 1 1 0 20), and give it its proper rank along the continuum. I decided to evaluate games on a scale of zero to a hundred, with the idea being that I would try to develop a system that evaluated the games as much as possible the same way baseball people evaluate them in conversation. If a manager said that Carl took a tough loss last time out but may have pitched his best game of the season, I wanted to scan the game and see that it was, indeed, as good as any game he had pitched all season. I wanted a great game to approach 100, an average game to be about 50, and a terrible game to approach 0. And I wanted the system to be as simple as possible.

Here's how the game scores are figured:

1) Start with 50.

2) Add one point for every hitter the batter retires.

3) Add two points for each inning the pitcher completes after the fourth inning (that is, two points for five innings, four to six complete innings, ten points for a nine-inning complete game, etc.)

4) Add one point for each strikeout.

5) Subtract one point for each walk.

6) Subtract two points for each hit.

7) Subtract four points for each earned run he gives up.

8) Subtract two points for an unearned run.

After you get the point values in mind you can glance at a line in the morning paper and sum it up in your head in a few seconds. I said four points for an earned run/two for an unearned run, but actually you can just add up the hits, runs and earned runs and multiply them all by two; that way the earned runs will be counted twice and the unearned only once.

Let's do Clemens' 20K game. Fifty points to start with; one for each out pushes him up to 77. Add ten for the complete game and one for each strikeout and he's at 107. Subtract six for the hits and four for the one run and he's at 97. He didn't walk anybody, so that's it: 97. After you do a couple you realize that the positive total for a complete game is just 87 plus the strikeouts.

As you see, it is theoretically possible to exceed a hundred. It's possible, but I don't think it's happened in the last thirteen years. Clemens' game was the best game in the American League in 1986, and in most years I think would be the best of the year. In 1986 it was beaten out as best by Mike Scott's pennant-clinching no hitter (9 0 0 0 2 13; game score of 98). To get a hundred without extra innings you'd have to pitch a perfect game and strike out 13 men, or if you walked one strike out 14, etc.

I figured game scores for every major-league game in 1987. Clemens, again, was at the top of the list with his 2-hit, 12-strikeout, no-walk shutout on the last day of the season, which scores at 95. Floyd Bannister also posted a 95, throwing a one-hitter at Seattle in which he struck out 10 and also walked nobody. There were fifteen 90 or 90 + game scores in 1987:

	IP	H	R	ER	BB	SO		
Clemens vs. Mil, Oct 4	9	2	0	0	0	12	Win	95
Bannister at Sea, Sep 13	9	1	0	0	0	10	Win	95
Higuera vs. Cle, Aug 26	10	3	0	0	2	10	Win	94
Scott at LA, Apr 15	9	1	0	0	1	10	Win	94
Scott at Mon, May 8	9	2	0	0	2	12	Win	93
Higuera at KC, Sep 1	9	1	0	0	2	9	Win	92
Saberhagen at Cle, May 9	9	2	0	0	0	9	Win	92
Welch vs. SF, Oct 1	9	1	0	0	1	7	Win	91
Clancy at Cal, May 18	9	2	0	0	1	9	Win	91
Langston vs. Tex, June 8	9	2	0	0	1	9	Win	91
Leibrandt vs. Mil, May 16	9	1	0	0	1	6	Win	90
Schmidt vs. Minn, July 12	9	2	0	0	0	7	Win	90
Sebra vs. Chi, July 1	9	3	1	1	1	14	Loss	90
Gooden at Mon, Sep 16	9	3	0	0	2	11	Win	90
Carman vs. NY, Sep 29	9	1	0	0	0	5	Win	90

Those 15 games account for one-third of one percent of the major-league starts in 1987. If you saw every home game, you'd see a game like that about once every two years.

One way I get into a lot of trouble is by carefully balancing the positives and the negatives, and I'm going to do that here again. There were 14 truly outstanding starts in 1987, scoring in the nineties; there were 13 that scored under ten, including one which managed the difficult feat of clearing zero. Kevin Gross, at New York on August 5th, last four innings, during which he gave up eleven hits and ten runs, all earned. He struck out one man. Game score: −1. It was the worst start of the 1987 season:

	IP	H	R	ER	BB	SO		
Gross at NY, Aug 5	4 *	11	10	10	2	1	Loss	−1
Knepper at Chi, June 3	1	7	9	9	2	1	Loss	2
Nipper at Chi, May 31	1⅓	7	9	9	2	1	—	3
Carlton at Cal, Aug 4	4⅔	11	9	9	4	1	Loss	3
Moore at Bos, July 26	3⅓	11	9	7	2	0	Loss	4
Moyer at Atl, Aug 20	5⅓	10	10	10	4	1	Loss	5
Bannister at Tex, June 3	3	11	8	8	1	2	Loss	6
Clemens at NY, June 26	2⅓	9	8	8	2	3	—	8
John vs. Bos, June 26	1⅓	6	8	8	2	0	—	8
Carlton at Det, Aug 18	3	11	9	6	1	2	Loss	8
Moyer vs. SD, July 8	3	10	7	7	4	2	Loss	9
Cerutti vs. NY, June 29	1⅓	5	8	8	3	0	—	9
Morgan vs. Cle, Sep 14	3⅔	11	7	7	2	0	Loss	9

Those 13 pitchers (actually 12 pitchers with Steve Carlton twice) pitched a total of 37⅓ innings, during which they allowed 120 hits and 106 earned runs, an ERA of 25.55. They struck out 14 men and walked 31. With each team, I presented lists of their ten best and ten worst starts of the season.

I wanted the average game to be 50, and I think in another year it might have been. The actual average in 1987 was 49.2 (National League: 49.4; American League: 48.9). This is the complete distribution of game scores:

Range	Games
90–99	15
80–89	149
70–79	360
60–69	712
50–59	860
40–49	817
30–39	697
20–29	472
10–19	115
Up to 9	13

Of the 149 games in which a pitcher posted a game score in the 80s, 139 were wins for the pitcher's team, a .933 winning percentage. Of the 115 games in the teens, 104 were losses, an .096 winning percentage. The full spectrum of such information:

Range	Games	W–L	Pct.
90–99	15	14–1	.933
80–89	149	139–10	.933
70–79	360	302–58	.839
60–69	712	518–194	.728
50–59	860	499–361	.580
40–49	817	344–473	.421
30–39	697	180–517	.258
20–29	472	95–377	.201
10–19	115	11–104	.096
Up to 9	13	3–10	.231

It would have been nice if a game score of 55 meant that the pitcher would win about 55 percent of the time. In fact, although a pitcher with a game score of 50 does win 50 percent of the time, or very nearly, the data decentralizes after that; with a game score of 55, a pitcher's team will win 58 to 59 percent of the time, and at 70 his team will win almost 80 percent of the time. The winning percentage of the starting pitcher himself decentralizes even more rapidly than that. Whereas the winning percentage of teams when the pitcher posts a game score in the sixties is .728, the winning percentage of starting pitchers is .785. This is because when those games are lost they are often lost by the bullpen. Conversely, when the game score is low but the game is won, it is almost always won by the bullpen. Whereas the winning percentage of teams with a game score in the twenties is .201, the winning percentage of starting pitchers in such games is .020.

I believe that the last pitcher to post a game score over 100 was Tom Seaver on May 1, 1974. Seaver pitched 12 innings that day, giving up only three hits and one run; he struck out 16 and walked 2 for a game score of 106. To exceed 100 almost requires extra innings—but even an exceptional extra-inning performance still very rarely puts the pitcher over a hundred. I think that the last pitcher to have reached 100 in nine innings was Nolan Ryan, in his 17-strikeout no-hitter of July 15, 1973. Using Ryan's 1987 starts, his no-hitters, his one-hitters and two-hitters, his 15-strikeout performances and his 1–0 victories, I came up with this rather awesome list of Nolan Ryan performances:

	IP	H	R	ER	BB	SO		
July 9, 1972	9	1	0	0	1	16	Win	100
July 15, 1973	9	0	0	0	4	17	Win	100
Aug 20, 1974	11	4	1	1	5	19	Loss	99
May 15, 1973	9	0	0	0	3	12	Win	96
July 22, 1986	9⅓	1	0	0	4	14	—	96
Sep 26, 1981	9	0	0	0	3	11	Win	95
Apr 18, 1970	9	1	0	0	6	15	Win	94
Sep 28, 1974	9	0	0	0	8	15	Win	94
May 20, 1979	9	2	0	0	1	11	Win	93
June 8, 1977	10	6	1	0	5	19	Win	92

Ryan, in his epic career, has put in the books at least 15 games of 90 or better—15 that I know of, and probably several more.

I think that the last pitcher (and for all I know, maybe the only pitcher) to get over 100 in a nine-inning game was Sandy Koufax in his fourth no-hitter on August 9, 1965, a perfect game in which he struck out 14 men (game score: 101). The book *Koufax*, by Sandy with Ed Linn, contains Allan Roth's list of every regular-season start of Koufax's career through 1965, and just for the heck of it I entered them all into the computer, along with his World Series performance and one start from his final season (1966) which is recorded in the 1967 Guide. Altogether I have 365 of his 405 career appearances.

To my knowledge, that was the only time Sandy posted a game score over 100, although he too had any number of astonishing extra-inning performances, no-hitters and 15- to 18-strikeout games. In my data base there were 18 game scores over 90; a good guess would be that he probably had four or five more in 1966 that I am missing. Koufax's best games that I found record of:

	IP	H	R	ER	BB	SO		
Aug 9, 1965	9	0	0	0	0	14	Win	101
June 4, 1964	9	0	0	0	1	12	Win	98
July 26, 1966	11	4	1	1	3	16	—	98
Sep 20, 1961	13	7	2	2	3	15	Win	97
Aug 11, 1960	9	2	0	0	1	13	Win	95
June 20, 1961	9	2	0	0	2	14	Win	95
June 30, 1962	9	0	0	0	5	13	Win	95
Apr 19, 1963	9	2	0	0	2	14	Win	95
Sep 29, 1965	9	2	0	0	1	13	Win	95

Clemens and Scott are not yet in the same class with these guys, but they're gaining on them. Gooden, for some reason, hasn't really had any towering single-game performances; he's struck out 16 several times, but it seems like he's always given up 6 or 7 hits when he has. There is one respect in which none of these guys will ever match Sandy, though. Clemens last year posted a game score of 8 in that amazing June 26 game, and Scott also was below 20 a couple of times. Koufax never in his career, unless he did it in 1966, posted a game score below 20, not even in all the years when he was struggling to find himself. The split of his 281 starts that I have:

100	90s	80s	70s	60s	50s	40s	30s	20s	10s	−9
1	17	52	53	34	42	36	31	15	0	0

One-fourth of his career starts were games in the eighties or better. To give you an idea of what that means, look up game scores of 80 on the team pages. Some teams last year only had a couple of games that good. Actually, if you added in 1966 Koufax would have been over 80 in *over* a fourth of his games.

At this point I suppose that I am running so many eye-popping games at you that they're losing their impact. You have to remember how you would react if you saw one of these in the morning paper. Remember: average 50, one game in 300 reaches 90, best in majors last year was 95, hasn't been a 100 in 13 years. Ordinary pitchers virtually never reach these levels; these are the greatest games of the best pitchers. As to the highest game score of all time, I don't really know but I assume that the highest game score ever belongs to Joe Oescheger in a game pitched on May 1, 1920. You know the game, I'm sure. Oescheger's line: 26 9 1 1 3 4—a game score of 151. It's cheap, at that, because if you divided that into three games they would score about 84 apiece.

As to the highest game score in World Series play, I

believe that also was an extraordinary extra-inning performance. On October 9, 1916, an obscure pitcher by the name of George Ruth pitched a 14-inning complete game for a 2–1 win over Brooklyn, game line 14 6 1 1 3 4. His game score: 97. The highest ever for a nine-inning game was by Larsen in his perfect game, which scores at 94, and also by Ed Walsh in a forgotten gem of October 11, 1906, (9 2 0 0 1 12, game score 94). Gibson in his 17-strikeout performance in 1968 gave up five hits and walked one man, which puts him at 93.

Another noteworthy pitching performance by a contemporary of Gibson and Koufax occurred on July 2, 1963, when Juan Marichal beat Warren Spahn 1–0. In 16 innings. I don't seem to have a box score of the game in my library, but at a guess Marichal's performance must have scored in the range of 120, possibly higher. Warren Spahn's 16-inning performance giving up one run wasn't too shabby for a 42-year-old, either. Spahn had beaten Don Drysdale 1–0 just four days earlier. Guy didn't even throw a knuckle ball.

As to the worst games ever pitched, I'm just guessing but I'll give you a couple of championship-level washouts to consider. When the Tigers went on a one-game strike on May 18, 1912, they hired a sandlot pitcher named Allen Travers to work for them against the powerful Philadelphia Athletics. Travers was rudely separated from his dreams, allowing 26 hits and 24 runs in 8 innings: 8 26 24 14 7 1, a game score of −54.

This level of comic ineptitude is probably unparalleled in the twentieth century, but on July 24, 1882, an outfielder named Dave Rowe took the mound for the Cleveland team in the National League, and did not surrender it until the opposition had scratched out 29 hits and 35 runs in nine innings. According to the *Macmillan Encyclopedia,* the editors of whom must have had the Devil's own time figuring it out, 12 of the runs were earned, creating 9 29 35 12 7 0, a game score of −68. It seems a pretty safe guess that this performance will not be outdone in 1988, unless somebody calls Randy Lerch out of retirement or something.

Well, enough about game scores. You'll be seeing them often throughout the book. There are a couple of spinoff concepts of game scores here which will be dealt with more quickly and then dismissed. Those are "Cheap Wins" and "Tough Losses." A cheap win is any game in which a starting pitcher is credited with a victory despite a game score below 50; a tough loss is any game in which a starter is charged with a defeat despite a game score of 50 or better. I'll write about them later.

WAKE-UP CALL

Hey, American League. Wake up! You're being taken. For as long as I have been doing this stuff for a living (beginning in 1976), the American League statistics have been prepared by a Boston-area company named the Sports Information Center. The National League statistics have always been done by the Elias Bureau. The American League product was supervised and directed by Pete Palmer, a fine and generous man whose goal in putting together the book was to get out as much interesting and meaningful information as possible in the limited space of a 32-page booklet. The National League product was supervised by Seymour Siwoff. The American League booklet was better in 1976, and over the years it became *a lot* better, as Pete found ways to get out more material.

Now, I've never really understood or participated in the politics of the world of baseball statistics. There are always these companies being formed with acronyms in place of names and shadowy game plans in place of investors. The Commissioner's Office apparently is trying to centralize (i.e., gain control of) the accumulation and processing of data, but has trouble gathering the technical expertise to accomplish this, and other folks are always trying to sidle into the vacuum. There are six potential markets: the leagues, the teams, the players and agents, the public through print, the public through computer access, and the "special needs" people like APBA and Topps baseball cards. Three or four times a year I'll sit down with one of the players in the game and get an hour-long briefing, for free, on how the fight for control of the field is going. I am brought up to date on what the Commissioner's Office is doing and what Pete Palmer is doing and what Steve Mann is doing and what Dick Cramer is doing and what Floyd Kephardt is doing through SNN and STATS and the Baseball Analysis Company and the Elias Bureau and the Howe News Bureau and Project Scoresheet and the Sports Information Center and the Macmillan Publishing Company and the Players Association and AP and UPI and some guy named Rodriguez and God knows who all; there's a lot of loose talk about the participation of IBM and *USA Today* and *The Sporting News* and the Hall of Fame and this or that or the other General Manager or former General Manager and college professor and businessman and would-be businessman in a project which is being planned or attempted or financed or refinanced or bought or sold or reorganized or redirected toward a different market.

Alliances are formed and alliances dissolve, often bitterly, sometimes in bankruptcy. I find almost all of these people likable, some more than others, I suppose because it is my nature to like anybody unless I have a reason not to. Among the participants there are an infinite number of permutations in the combinations of markets, companies, businessmen, computer experts, and money. These battles have raged for at least eight years, during which, as nearly as I can tell, damned near nothing has happened, and certainly nothing has happened compared to all of what was supposed to happen. I am told what all of these people are doing to take control of the field and in place I am supposed to tell what it is that I am doing to take control of the field, which is nothing. I am not doing anything first of all because I am not a businessman and second because I am not a baseball statistician, either. I have my own alliances, I suppose, but I have no dreams in this field and very few investments.

Anyway, as a result of some of these Byzantine comings and goings, a year ago it became known that the Sports Information Center had been elbowed aside as the official statistician of the American League. At first the leagues were going to do the stats "themselves"; then it came out that the Elias Bureau was going to do the stats for both leagues. Now, the problem with the Elias Bureau is that the Elias Bureau never turns loose of a statistic unless they get a dollar for it. Their overarching concern in life is to get every dollar they can from you and give you as little as possible in return for it—like a lot of other businesses, I suppose, only with a more naked display of greed than is really usual. It was apparent to me, then, that this change would mean only one thing to the public: less information available for free.

Early last season I called the American League Office to ask whether the fact that the Elias Bureau was now doing their stats would mean that information would be disappearing from the official stat books. They assured me that the Elias Bureau had promised them that no information would be deleted from the official statistics, which would be better than ever. I knew that was bullshit, and sure enough it was. When the American League stats came out, hundreds of bits of information (well, thousands, I guess, if you want to be technical about it) had disappeared.

A list of the top consecutive game hitting streaks, a feature of the American League stats which was not in the NL, had disappeared.

A chart of records in games decided by two-runs—

gone. The NL had presented records in one-run games, the AL in one-run and two-runs games. Now they had been standardized—by eliminating the extra information.

A chart of the leading hitters in road games, added to the AL stats by Pete Palmer about five years ago—gone.

A chart of opponents' records, a delightful little thing from which I picked up and passed on to you a lot of miscellaneous information like how many balks and wild pitches each team had benefited from, official counts of opposition stolen bases and caught stealing, how many errors had been committed against each team and how many opponents had been left on base—all of that was gone, no longer a part of the official record of the season.

A list of the league slugging leaders, with full stats in order of slugging percentage—out. A chart of the home runs hit by each team against each other team—gone.

When the Sports Information Center prepared the American League statistics, they gave you a list of the league leaders in each category. Like this:

EXTRA BASE HITS: 86, Mattingly, NY; 77, Barfield, Tor; 75, Bell, Tor; 74, Puckett, Minn; 74, Carter, Clev; 69, Gaetti, Minn; 64, Presley, Sea; 64, Henderson, NY; 63, Canseco, Oak; 62, White, KC.

It's not a big item, but once in a while you want to know whether Bobby Witt with 160 strikeouts was one of the top ten men in the league, and you don't really want to stop and count everybody. The National League statistics never gave this, merely listing instead the number-one man in each category. When the 1987 statistics came out, these had been standardized—in the inferior manner. They had been standardized merely by eliminating the lists of league leaders, and listing only one man. Well, they listed only one man in most areas. In minor stuff like the one above, extra base hits, they just didn't mention it.

Whereas the Sports Information Center, when listing records in night games and day games, would give a full chart of performance by each team against each other team, the Elias Bureau saved themselves $1.75 by just presenting the summaries, the total games won and lost against all teams at day and night. The stats used to tell you that California shut out Seattle three times; now they just tell you that California had seven shutouts on the season.

To disguise the fact that thousands of pieces of information had been eliminated, the Elias Bureau switched to a slightly larger type and put more space on the charts, so that they still have the same 32-page booklet as before (clever bastards, you have to admit). If you don't need the information and you don't use it, you'll never know it's gone. If you need it, I'm sure the Elias Bureau will be happy to sell it to you at the right price.

As a special bonus for doing such a good job, they were able to get the American League statistics out just a month later than they have been out before.

Hey! American League, wake up. The Elias Bureau is ripping you off. Now, I don't want to do it, and I don't want to make any money off of it, but the world is just teeming with people who would love to be your official statisticians. How about showing a little consideration for the public here, huh? How about setting up some standards, laying out some guidelines to see that the job gets done right? I mean, I know it's important that Seymour Siwoff die a wealthy man, but I don't really think that is supposed to be your primary objective.

If you don't watch the product that's being put out with your name on it, I will guarantee you that that product is going to deteriorate. Every year or every couple of years, the Elias Bureau is going to find a corner to cut, a stat that can be eliminated without hardly anybody noticing. In five years, you'll look at the booklet one day and say, "Hey, whatever happened to that record of the Grand Slam Home Runs that we used to have in our stat summary, or that Club Pinch Hitting chart or that chart of Average Game Times?" And you'll call the stat bureau, and they will tell you that it wasn't specified in the contract. That is not a generous woman that you are in bed with, Dr. Brown. Keep an eye on your pockets.

TWILIGHT (STRIKE) ZONE

The rhubarb over the nomination of Robert Bork for the Supreme Court set me to thinking about the strike zone. Not the one described in the rule book (Baseball's equivalent of the Constitution) that stretches from the armpits to the top of the knees, but rather the new, improved strike zone that runs from the waist to the bottom of the knees, and maybe a tad past the outside corner. The reason I think of this in relation to the Bork controversy is that in both instances a fundamental principle is involved, a principle which Bork believes has been consistently violated with regard to the law, and which I believe is being blatantly violated with regard to the rules of baseball. Simply put, the question is: in government, who makes the laws, and in baseball, who makes the rules? Bork's basic argument is that the judiciary has subverted the legislative branch's law-making function, and it now seems apparent to me that the umpires have subverted the function of the Rules Committee.

In baseball, at least, this subversion is not exactly a sudden development. The phantom double play probably goes back as far as Alexander Cartwright, and has become a universally accepted part of the game (the last man to abjure it, apparently, was umpire Steve Fields, who endured assault from Dallas Green, and summary dismissal at the end of the season for his pains), but some of the excuses trotted out to justify it still rub me the wrong way. According to Ron Luciano, the phantom double play is called to protect middle infielders from unnecessary collisions. Aside from the fact that Tony Fernandez might argue for enforcement of the interference rule as a more direct solution to the problem, it seems disgustingly hypocritical for umpires to voice such solicitude for double play combos, and then shrug their shoulders when Ruppert Jones is leveled by Joaquin Andujar after homering in his previous at-bat.

And if the arbiters are so concerned with the health and well-being of the players, how to explain their more recent disdain for another rule: the one prohibiting catchers from blocking home plate without the ball. Bill James argued in the *Historical Abstract* that, unlike the phantom double play, this rule was once enforced, and only gradually fell into disuse, like the still-existing laws forbidding the teaching of evolution. Why did this come about? I'm sure Bill is right when he says they didn't wake up one morning and invent it, but all the same, didn't some umpires' supervisor or league president figure out somewhere

along the way what was happening? Wasn't this trend toward blocking the plate sans ball considered significant enough to discuss at the highest levels? And if it was discussed, did they really decide to give the umpires a blank check to enact an important de facto rules change? Curious.

But if that is indeed what happened, then it's not surprising that it would happen again. I'm referring, of course, to the revised and edited strike zone, which, everyone now concedes, differs considerably from the rule-book definition. I don't know what umpires say when asked—if they're asked—why they blithely accept illegal blocking of the plate, but when it comes to their own illicit strike zone, they're not exactly blushing with shame. If you read Peter Gammons' excellent article on the bowdlerized strike zone, you may recall umpire Dick Stello saying, "If we called strikes up around the letters, the hitters wouldn't hit." Why should he dissemble when no less an authority than Marty Springstead, chief supervisor of AL umpires, argues that "The rule book doesn't really have any touch with reality." A truly remarkable statement, that; suppose a Supreme Court Justice said the same with respect to the Constitution?

Which brings me back to the Bork nomination, and the question of who makes the law. Bork and his adherents concede that on occasion the law is out of touch with reality. Where they beg to differ is in the method of redress. They believe that if a law is faulty, rather than ignore it or promulgate a new constitutional right to overturn it, the legislative branch—after all, the branch most directly responsive to the people—should amend or repeal it. But the legislative process is manifestly no longer acceptable to many members of the judiciary; they cannot resist the temptation to rule by fiat.

And as with the judiciary, so, it appears, with the umpires. They perceived—for all I know, correctly—that the rule book armpits-to-top-of-knees strike zone was tilting the balance of power inevitably toward the pitcher. Undoubtedly they remembered baseball's most recent nadir, the '68 season, featuring Gibson's 1.12 ERA and Yaz's .301 batting title. Can we assume they were determined not to see that happen again? That, not trusting the Rules Committee to make the proper adjustments at the proper time, they gradually, almost imperceptibly, rearranged the strike zone to meet the needs of the ever evolving game, to bring it "in touch with reality"? Have they in fact already spared us another 1968, with its preponderance of goose eggs on the scoreboard? If so, perhaps we should be grateful, but I for one am not, because the fact remains that baseball, like the nation, is governed by laws rather than men, and in both cases, whenever we allow the laws and the men to get seriously out of synch, we're asking for trouble. In bypassing the Rules Committee, the umpires have staged a power play that is in many ways more deplorable than those of the Supreme Court; at least when the justices hand down a judicial bull, it becomes, for better or worse, the law of the land. But the umpire's rejuvenated strike zone exists only de facto, not de jure: it is, to paraphrase Samuel Goldwyn on oral agreements, not worth the paper it's not printed on.

So we've come to this: The infielder must touch second on the front end of a double play, only he needn't. The catcher is prohibited from blocking the plate without the ball, only he can. And the strike zone is from the armpits to the top of the knees, only it isn't. None of this, of course, is ruining the game; but you have to wonder which rule are the men in blue going to diddle with next in the name of "reality," and how long before one of their fraternity, in a momentary lapse, rules de jure instead of de facto, and creates an eminently avoidable brouhaha, witnessed by millions on TV, with replays from every possible angle, that will make the Merkle Boner seem like a donnybrook pitting Mister Rogers against Pee-Wee Herman?

—Mike Kopf

SECTION
II

TEAM COMMENTS

AMERICAN LEAGUE WEST

MINNESOTA TWINS

Just good enough, gentlemen, just barely good enough. The doorbell rang, and the Twins answered. With nine days left in the 1987 season, Minnesota had whittled the magic number to three. On Friday and Saturday, however, Kansas City beat the Twins, in the dome. A third loss would send them into a six-game, season-ending road trip still needing those three wins. They would be carrying a three-game losing streak onto the road, where they had had little success. In all likelihood, another loss would put the Twins in Kansas City for the last series of the year, still needing at least one win.

Anybody who saw the Twins play that Sunday had to know that they had a chance to win it all. The Twins came out with pepper in their jock straps, attacking Royals starter Charlie Leibrandt as if he were an amateur. After two innings it was 6–0, Twins, and looked worse.

There has always been a lot of talent here. My summation of the Minnesota Twins a year ago was that "the Twins should play better this year, but then they should have played better last year and the year before, too. I think they should play .500 or better ball . . . but I'm not optimistic about their chances of winning." The Twins finished only four full games over .500, but they were just as good as they needed to be.

To start the 1987 season, Al Campanis kicked up a rumpus by his inability to give an appropriately dodgy answer to the unanswerable question of why baseball had not yet given blacks a key to the executive washroom. (I hear that Al has been invited to the Democratic Convention to throw out the first ethnic slur.) The Twins, as baseball's whitest team and the team with the most egregious record of nepotism and cronyism in the front office, came under renewed fire. Reggie Jackson, for the second time in two years, ripped the Twins for their lack of black players, telling the St. Paul *Pioneer Press-Dispatch* that it was "a sad commentary on all of us" that nothing had changed since the previous year.

Although the numbers had not changed dramatically, something had indeed changed in Minnesota. A year ago, in my estimate of team speed scores, the Twins scored at 4.41, one of the slowest teams in baseball (22nd of 26, see page 95, 1987 *Abstract*.) Last year the Twins speed score moved up to 5.05, still below the median 5.2, but a big improvement. Two personnel changes contributed to that, the switch from Mickey Hatcher to Dan Gladden in left field and the use of Al Newman at second base. The Twins became faster, more alert and more aggressive on the bases, particularly in their home park.

Fans often complain that the players now always play it halfway on a deep fly, not tagging up and advancing when they have the opportunity. It does seem curious that players choose to pass up a free base on the remote chance that a fly will be dropped at the wall. The Twins of past seasons were one of the most passive, by-the-numbers teams you will ever see. The Twins of 1987 routinely took advantage of that free base. Twice last year, I saw Kent Hrbek tag up at first and take second on a fly ball. I haven't got a stat to give you about it, but the Twins just made a tremendous improvement in offensive and defensive alertness and aggressiveness.

Obviously, Tom Kelly was primarily responsible for that. Al Newman, one of the new Twins, is a very sharp cookie in the field. Greg Gagne, in his second year as a regular, substitutes intelligence for agility, baseball instincts for native talent. Kelly and coaches ran counter plays, daylight plays, time plays, an assortment of dekes and dives like the play which saved their bacon in the sixth inning of Game Four in Detroit, when Laudner caught Darrell Evans off third base. This is a fine defensive team. The Twins had only two games all year in which they committed more than two errors (Toronto also had two; every other major-league team had more). Aside from their inability to stop the running game, all elements of the Twin defense were strong. Their ratio of double plays to errors was the third-best in baseball. The team defensive efficiency record was above average. Two outfielders can run (Puckett and Hatcher) and two can throw (Puckett and Brunansky). All four defensive infielders are above average, the best being Gaetti and the weakest (in my opinion) being Hrbek. Only one other American League team (Toronto) is strong defensively both inside and outside. The addition of Gladden to the outfield improved the defense considerably, particularly in Minnesota where the left field area is huge.

Which made them even better at home. Over the last five years the Twins record is 77 games better at home than on the road, a home/road differential of more than 15 games a year. No other major-league team has a comparable split (see chart). The Twins over those years are 232–176 at home (.569), but 152–250 on the road (.378). Their record on the road is the worst in baseball; their record at home, the seventh best among 26 teams. To me, the puzzle is not why they win at home, but why they can't win on the road. There are a lot of fine players here—Puckett, Brunansky, Hrbek, Gaetti, Viola, Blyleven. Supplemented by some quality fringe players and well coached, these guys should be able to go anywhere and compete.

I think that a team's home field advantage is determined by three essential factors: the stability of the personnel, the uniqueness of the park, and the suitability of the park to the personnel. The third factor draws all the analysis—the speed of the Cardinals on artificial turf, the left-handed power of the Yankees in Yankee Stadium, the right-handed power of the Red Sox, etc.—but as I have written before, it is questionable how much we really know about what kind of players do best in any park, and how much of what we think we know holds any water.

The Twins' personnel over the last five years has been extremely stable, and the park is one of the most unique in baseball, so those two factors certainly help explain the phenomenon. (Did you ever notice that the people who complain about all the parks now looking alike are the same people who hate the Metrodome, which is not at all like anyplace else?) Anyway, given that the Twins' home-field advantage is so large, it must be assumed that all three factors are operating in that direction, meaning that the personnel is well suited to this park; either that, or they really are playing tricks with the air conditioning.

Some part of the park/team symbiosis, I suspect, is due to the fact that most of the Twins players grew up here. They learned to play major-league ball in this park; in the pivotal struggle of their professional lives, the struggle to prove that they could play major-league ball, this park was the element with which they contended. They know the park, perhaps, in ways that even they don't fully understand; their knowledge of it has become instinctive, using the term instinct in the way that sports people use it, which is different from the way that psychologists use it. If you import a lot of players in mid-career, like the Baltimore Orioles have, that can't happen to you. You can't develop a second set of instincts which is equal to the first.

It has been suggested that the noise is a contributing factor in the success of the Twins at home. The Dome is a deafening place; at a day game in August last year the noise was such that I had to communicate with Susie with shouts and gestures. The public address system is set way too loud, and echoes boom off of everything, creating a muddy sound (who is that in right field? Comrade Nubo-kowsky? Is he a rookie?). The crowd screams every time Kirby Puckett scratches his nose, and the overpowering racket could cause problems for the opposition. Another observation from the World Series was that when the Metrodome is nearly empty, the ball doesn't travel very well, but when there is a large crowd it heats the place up and the ball jumps.

Because of these suggestions, I decided to check the performance of the team with different levels of attendance. The theory that the ball travels better when there is a big crowd here can be put in the category of "some evidence to support—no clear pattern." It probably is no big deal, but the average runs scored per game in the 27 games (one third of the home games) with the largest crowds was 10.1, higher than either the average with a small crowd (9.4) or with a medium-sized crowd (8.6). Maybe whoever does this book next year will want to look more closely at that.

Almost all of the variation in offensive levels was in runs allowed. The number of runs scored by the Twins was almost the same in each group, but the number of runs scored by the opposition nose-dived in the middle, resulting in an intriguing split of wins and losses. With crowds of less than 17,000, the Twins' record at home was 8–10.

With crowds of 17,000 to 29,000, their record was 33–3, and the Twins outscored their opponents by almost two runs a game. With crowds of more than 29,000, their record was just 15-12.

The paranoid interpretation of this pattern would begin with the assumption that with a small crowd in a big park, the air conditioning probably is hardly used, and the Twins have a normal home-park advantage. With a large crowd, the air conditioning has to run constantly, and is a minimal factor in the games. With a medium-sized crowd, the Twins are able to manipulate the air conditioning to only blow while the Twins are at bat.

That, as I say, is the conspiracy-theory interpretation; as a practical matter, there are any number of nonrandom factors among these games which could contribute to the splits, not to mention that tremendous splits often can be found in random data if studied carefully enough. The schedule for these groups was nonrandom. Games attended by crowds numbering under 17,000 included no games in July or August; the largest crowds were mostly (17 of 27) in those two months. If the schedule was nonrandom, then the external heat, a primary determinant of how much heat or air conditioning was used, was not constant in the groups. The opposition can be presumed to have been nonrandom. The only safe statement about the pattern is that it is odd.

For whatever reason, the Twins couldn't keep the opposition off the scoreboard on the road. At home, in what is erroneously believed to be a great home-run park, the Twins allowed only 348 runs, a better-than-average number. On the road, they allowed 458 runs, the most of any major-league team. Not only did they not win on the road, but often they were not even in the game. They lost 31 games by five or more runs. Only one major-league team, Cleveland, was blown out more often. In their losses, the Twins allowed an average of seven runs a game, a figure exceeded only by Cleveland.

But as long as the game was under control, the Twins had a very good chance to win. The Twins had a tremendous 20–9 record in pitcher's duels (games in which no more than five runs were scored), the best of any major-league team (see chart). In the Metrodome, they won 14 of 15 pitcher's duels. The Twins scored only 42 runs in those 15 games; 2.8 runs scored per game, and they won 14 out of 15. In those 15 games they out-homered their opponents 17-7—but they also committed only 5 errors, while the bad guys committed 13. Frank Viola started 9 of those 15 games. Viola won games in the dome by scores of 3–2, 3–2, 3–1, 2–1, 2–1, and 3–1.

Viola is no secret anymore. If the Twins had a secret weapon and it wasn't the air conditioning, then it was a large Panamanian secret named Juan Berenguer. Berenguer won 11 games for the 1984 World Champion Tigers but did not pitch in the playoffs or World Series, and was released by San Francisco following the 1986 season despite a 2.70 ERA and 72 strikeouts in 73 innings. Early in the season, with Mike Smithson struggling and the starting rotation in danger of pulling apart, Berenguer stepped into the rotation to post a 2.92 ERA in six starts, four of which the Twins won. During the period in which Berenguer was primarily a starter, the Twins moved from 17–17 to 42–32, nearly as far over .500 as they would ever get. When Tom Kelly chose to return him to the bullpen, Berenguer performed the setup role the rest of the year, winding up with eight wins, four saves and 110 strikeouts in 112 innings. He was in position to lose a lot of games; he lost only once. If there is any player who deserves more credit than he got for the Twins' surprising World Championship, Berenguer is the man. He did almost as much as Reardon to improve the bullpen.

Kelly does a lot of things that I understand but don't necessarily agree with. The Twins had two good starting pitchers at Portland, Roy Smith (3.79 ERA, excellent K/W ratio) and Jeff Bittiger (12–10, 3.40 ERA). Called up late, Smith started once and pitched well (14–4 win over Seattle, game score 47), and Bittiger started once and pitched extremely well (8–1 win over Chicago, game score 66). Then they disappeared. With his starting pitchers getting battered from pillar to post, Kelly refused to start either rookie over the last three weeks. I see the logic of going with veterans in the pennant stretch, but the way Carlton and Niekro were pitching, it was a rather extreme application of the logic—almost, combined with the re-moval of Berenguer from the rotation, as if Kelly had a death wish for the starting rotation. I'll guarantee you that Whitey Herzog would have started them, and Whitey hasn't lost a lot of pennant races.

I am of two minds concerning the Twins in 1988. I use an index of six leading indicators to gauge the underlying strengths and weaknesses that might manifest themselves next season. For only three major-league teams do all indicators agree. All six indicators say that San Diego will be better, and all six say that Minnesota and St. Louis will be down. I know better than to ignore those indicators; I have been wrong that way too many times before, and so if forced to choose I would pick the Twins third or fourth in this rapidly improving division. But I am also certain that the wire-to-wire play of the Twins in 1987 does not represent the full potential of the team. They do a lot of things well beside hit home runs. I think that if Straker or one of the kids out of Triple A were to develop, this team is very capable of winning 90 games.

WINNING PERCENTAGE IN LOW-SCORING GAMES

Minnesota	.690
Detroit	.677
Montreal	.667
Yankees	.622
San Francisco	.588
Pittsburgh	.581
Baltimore	.552
Mets	.552
Seattle	.526
St. Louis	.526
Philadelphia	.513
Cleveland	.500
San Diego	.500
Oakland	.500
Cincinnati	.471
Cubs	.469
Houston	.465
California	.455
White Sox	.450
Boston	.433
Milwaukee	.417
Toronto	.415
Kansas City	.395
Texas	.385
Atlanta	.375
Los Angeles	.317

RUNS SCORED AND ALLOWED WINS AND LOSSES

Wins	544	267	85-0	1.000
Home Games	411	348	56-25	.691
Pitchers' Duels	65	40	20-9	.690
Blyleven	185	161	23-14	.622
Viola	155	135	22-14	.611
Smithson	120	123	11-9	.550
Slugfests	463	446	33-28	.541
All Games	786	806	85-77	.525
One-Run Games	177	175	24-22	.522
Blowouts	283	343	22-31	.415
Straker	114	139	10-16	.385
Road Games	375	458	29-52	.358
Niekro	74	112	6-12	.333
Losses	242	539	0-77	.000

HALL OF FAME WATCH

Fully qualified Steve Carlton, 238.5; **Could be elected on present accomplishments:** Blyleven 102.5; **Building credentials but not yet viable candidate:** Joe Niekro 53, Baylor 42.5, Puckett 36; **Working on it:** Reardon 28, Viola 24, Gaetti 16, Hrbek 15, Smalley 11, Tom Kelly 10; **Long way to go:** Brunansky 9, Gagne 6, Laudner 6, Lombardozzi 5, Frazier 5, Schatzeder 5, Straker 4, Smithson 4, Berenguer 3, Atherton 2, Gladden 2, and Bush 1.

TEN WORST STARTS

	IP	H	R	ER	BB	SO		
Carlton at Cal, Aug 4	4⅔	11	9	9	4	1	L	3
Carlton at Det, Aug 18	3*	11	9	6	1	2	L	8
Blyleven at Det, Aug 19	4⅓	9	7	7	2	2	L	17
Portugal vs. Tor, May 13	2⅓	7	6	6	1	1	L	19
Straker at Tor, July 25	3*	6	6	6	4	1	—	20
Niekro at KC, Oct 4	1⅓	3	6	6	3	1	L	22
Straker vs. Cal, Aug 12	3⅓	6	6	6	3	1	L	22
Smithson vs. Tor, July 19	2⅔	7	5	5	3	1	—	22
Blyleven at Bal, July 10	5	5	8	8	4	2	—	23
Straker at Det, May 29	3	5	6	6	3	1	L	23

TEN BEST STARTS

	IP	H	R	ER	BB	SO		
Blyleven at Mil, June 15	9	4	0	0	2	6	W	83
Viola vs. Tex, Sep 24	8	3	0	0	3	10	W	83
Viola at NY, July 6	9	5	0	0	4	7	W	80
Blyleven vs. KC, Sep 27	9	5	1	1	2	8	W	79
Blyleven vs. Bos, Sep 3	9	6	1	1	4	11	—	78
Viola vs. Chi, Sep 9	9	6	1	1	2	9	W	78
Berenguer vs. Bos, May 15	8	3	1	1	4	4	—	75
Berenguer vs. Mil, May 28	7	4	0	0	0	5	W	74
Viola vs. NY, July 22	8	4	1	1	2	6	W	74
Viola vs. Sea, Aug 16	8	5	1	0	1	5	W	74

PITCHERS WHEN SUPPORTED BY THREE TO FIVE RUNS

	G	IP	W-L	Pct	SO	BB	ERA
Straker	12	69	5-2	.714	30	25	4.17
Viola	16	109	9-4	.692	99	30	2.48
Blyleven	14	104	6-3	.667	71	41	3.28
Niekro	6	36	1-3	.250	21	18	5.30
Smithson	7	38	1-4	.200	24	10	7.17

HOME FIELD ADVANTAGE OVER LAST FIVE SEASONS

	(games)
Minnesota	77
Yankees	51½
Oakland	51
Texas	49
Kansas City	46
Cubs	45½
Milwaukee	45½
Houston	43
San Diego	43
Cleveland	42
White Sox	37
San Francisco	36
Seattle	34
Los Angeles	34
Philadelphia	32½
Toronto	31½
Mets	31
Pittsburgh	30½
Detroit	29½
Boston	29½
St. Louis	27½
Atlanta	23
Montreal	12½
California	11
Cincinnati	10½
Baltimore	8½

Tim LAUDNER, Catcher
Runs Created: 29

	G	AB	Hit	2B	3B	HR	Run	RBI	TBB	SO	SB	CS	Avg
3.19 years		446	97	21	1	18	50	57	40	125	1	1	.217
1987	113	288	55	7	1	16	30	43	23	80	1	0	.191
First Half	58	149	27	2	0	12	18	32	11	42	1	0	.181
Second Half	55	139	28	5	1	4	12	11	12	38	0	0	.201
Vs. RHP		190	36	5	0	9	13	24	11	58	1	0	.189
Vs. LHP		98	19	2	1	7	17	19	12	22	0	0	.194
Home	61	151	26	3	1	7	14	16	14	42	1	0	.172
Road	52	137	29	4	0	9	16	27	9	38	0	0	.212

Dan GLADDEN, Left Field
Runs Created: 50

	G	AB	Hit	2B	3B	HR	Run	RBI	TBB	SO	SB	CS	Avg
2.90 years		585	159	24	4	8	91	51	53	89	41	18	.272
1987	121	438	109	21	2	8	69	38	38	72	25	9	.249
First Half	72	269	76	16	1	5	44	26	21	38	14	7	.283
Second Half	49	169	33	5	1	3	25	12	17	34	11	2	.195
Vs. RHP		275	67	10	2	6	47	25	27	53	18	5	.244
Vs. LHP		163	42	11	0	2	22	13	11	19	7	4	.258
Home	58	203	55	11	2	4	35	15	21	23	18	3	.271
Road	63	235	54	10	0	4	34	23	17	49	7	6	.230

Kent HRBEK, First Base
Runs Created: 103

	G	AB	Hit	2B	3B	HR	Run	RBI	TBB	SO	SB	CS	Avg
5.58 years		590	170	32	3	27	88	101	72	85	3	2	.288
1987	143	477	136	20	1	34	85	90	84	60	5	2	.285
First Half	79	283	77	6	0	23	49	55	43	38	4	1	.272
Second Half	64	194	59	14	1	11	36	35	41	22	1	1	.304
Vs. RHP		339	105	18	1	28	72	69	70	37	4	1	.310
Vs. LHP		138	31	2	0	6	13	21	14	23	1	1	.225
Home	72	234	69	8	1	20	47	51	48	30	5	1	.295
Road	71	243	67	12	0	14	38	39	36	30	0	1	.276

Kirby PUCKETT, Center Field
Runs Created: 116

	G	AB	Hit	2B	3B	HR	Run	RBI	TBB	SO	SB	CS	Avg
3.75 years		681	212	29	8	17	95	80	33	92	18	10	.311
1987	157	624	207	32	5	28	96	99	32	91	12	7	.332
First Half	86	344	116	16	3	14	55	55	21	53	8	6	.337
Second Half	71	280	91	16	2	14	41	44	11	38	4	1	.325
Vs. RHP		447	147	22	1	17	64	67	21	67	8	6	.329
Vs. LHP		177	60	10	4	11	32	32	11	24	4	1	.339
Home	79	309	93	15	2	18	50	59	19	44	6	2	.301
Road	78	315	114	17	3	10	46	40	13	47	6	5	.362

Steve LOMBARDOZZI, Second Base
Runs Created: 46

	G	AB	Hit	2B	3B	HR	Run	RBI	TBB	SO	SB	CS	Avg
1.98 years		474	114	22	5	8	58	39	46	75	6	2	.241
1987	136	432	103	19	3	8	51	38	33	66	5	1	.238
First Half	75	241	57	7	2	3	31	13	18	26	2	1	.237
Second Half	61	191	46	12	1	5	20	25	15	40	3	0	.241
Vs. RHP		293	63	9	2	6	32	28	24	49	4	1	.215
Vs. LHP		139	40	10	1	2	19	10	9	17	1	0	.288
Home	69	213	45	9	2	3	25	15	18	29	3	0	.211
Road	67	219	58	10	1	5	26	23	15	37	2	1	.265

Tom BRUNANSKY, Right Field
Runs Created: 90

	G	AB	Hit	2B	3B	HR	Run	RBI	TBB	SO	SB	CS	Avg
5.64 years		585	146	27	2	29	80	83	70	104	6	5	.250
1987	155	532	138	22	2	32	83	85	74	104	11	11	.259
First Half	85	286	75	10	1	18	51	47	44	59	8	6	.262
Second Half	70	246	63	12	1	14	32	38	30	45	3	5	.256
Vs. RHP		374	102	14	1	22	60	58	51	84	7	10	.273
Vs. LHP		158	36	8	1	10	23	27	23	20	4	1	.228
Home	80	277	83	15	2	19	45	50	37	57	7	4	.300
Road	75	255	55	7	0	13	38	35	37	47	4	7	.216

Gary GAETTI, Third Base
Runs Created: 75

	G	AB	Hit	2B	3B	HR	Run	RBI	TBB	SO	SB	CS	Avg
5.83 years		591	151	32	2	24	78	87	45	104	9	6	.255
1987	154	584	150	36	2	31	95	109	37	92	10	7	.257
First Half	82	311	78	15	1	16	50	51	24	54	5	5	.251
Second Half	72	273	72	21	1	15	45	58	13	38	5	2	.264
Vs. RHP		418	111	30	0	24	70	82	25	63	8	5	.266
Vs. LHP		166	39	6	2	7	25	27	12	29	2	2	.235
Home	80	301	92	23	2	18	59	57	20	47	7	5	.306
Road	74	283	58	13	0	13	36	52	17	45	3	2	.205

Roy SMALLEY, Utility
Runs Created: 46

	G	AB	Hit	2B	3B	HR	Run	RBI	TBB	SO	SB	CS	Avg
10.20 years		555	143	24	2	16	73	68	76	89	3	3	.258
1987	110	309	85	16	1	8	32	34	36	52	2	0	.275
First Half	67	213	66	16	1	5	27	30	22	32	2	0	.310
Second Half	43	96	19	0	0	3	5	4	14	20	0	0	.198
Vs. RHP		285	79	16	1	7	31	28	35	48	2	0	.277
Vs. LHP		24	6	0	0	1	1	6	1	4	0	0	.250
Home	50	140	38	8	0	5	14	17	14	26	0	0	.271
Road	60	169	47	8	1	3	18	17	22	26	2	0	.278

Greg GAGNE, Shortstop
Runs Created: 58

	G	AB	Hit	2B	3B	HR	Run	RBI	TBB	SO	SB	CS	Avg
2.59 years		475	117	25	6	9	66	46	29	98	11	8	.246
1987	137	437	116	28	7	10	68	40	25	84	6	6	.265
First Half	72	213	52	14	3	5	26	22	15	42	5	5	.244
Second Half	65	224	64	14	4	5	42	18	10	42	1	1	.286
Vs. RHP		309	82	21	4	10	50	30	19	56	3	6	.265
Vs. LHP		128	34	7	3	0	18	10	6	28	3	0	.266
Home	68	212	51	10	5	7	34	22	18	45	2	2	.241
Road	69	225	65	18	2	3	34	18	7	39	4	4	.289

Randy BUSH, Designated Hitter
Runs Created: 45

	G	AB	Hit	2B	3B	HR	Run	RBI	TBB	SO	SB	CS	Avg
3.96 years		426	105	22	4	14	57	60	45	71	5	2	.246
1987	122	293	74	10	2	11	46	46	43	49	10	3	.253
First Half	63	142	35	6	1	6	24	22	21	14	5	2	.246
Second Half	59	151	39	4	1	5	22	24	22	35	5	1	.258
Vs. RHP		284	72	10	2	11	45	44	40	47	9	3	.254
Vs. LHP		9	2	0	0	0	1	2	3	2	1	0	.222
Home	58	128	33	3	1	8	20	19	25	21	5	1	.258
Road	64	165	41	7	1	8	26	27	18	28	5	2	.248

THE GAP

During the 1987 World Series, the idea hit that the Minnesota Twins were a two-pitcher team, a very good team with their top two pitchers on the mound, and not a good team at all beyond that. "They've got two pitchers, that's it," said Whitey Herzog. "But you've got an advantage when you have two starting pitchers and two off days. They've won six [post-season games], and Viola and Blyleven won all six. I think it's ridiculous when you don't see the pitching staff and the true strengths of a baseball team." (Quote is taken from the *Kansas City Times*, October 20, 1987, article by Bob Nightengale.)

I was, in a way, very happy to hear these remarks and to see the attention that they received. I've been trying to tell people every World Series time for ten years that in a short, crucial series, *depth don't count*. That's an exaggeration, of course, it does count a little, but the World Series is usually decided by front-line talent. Maybe Whitey's comments will keep the announcers from talking about depth in the World Series teams for a few years.

This subject, however, came to the fore at what struck me as a perhaps inopportune moment. Are the Minnesota Twins, in fact, unusually dependent on their top two pitchers? Let's check.

What would be the characteristics of a team that had two pitchers but nothing else, as Whitey described the Minnesota Twins? One characteristic, obviously, would be a big gap between the winning percentage of those two pitchers and the winning percentage of the rest of the team. Let's look at the Twins in that respect:

Frank Viola	17-10,	.630
Bert Blyleven	15-12,	.556
Team Record	85-77,	.525
Total, Top Two	35-22,	.593
Rest of Team	53-55,	.491

The difference between Viola/Blyleven and the rest of the team is 102 points, 593–491.

Is this figure abnormally high? Is it one of the widest in history? I ran the same figures for all championship teams since 1901. The widest gap of all time between the top two pitchers and the rest of a championship team was by the 1940 Detroit Tigers.

Bobo Newsom	21-5,	.808
Schoolboy Rowe	16-3,	.842
Team Record	90-64,	.584
Total, Top Two	37-8,	.822
Rest of Team	53-56,	.486
GAP		.336

The rest of the top ten are given in the chart at the bottom of the page. The definition of the top two pitchers was simply the two pitchers who won the most games, with the pitcher who lost the fewest being used in case of a tie for the number-two spot.

As you can see, the gap between Viola/Blyleven and the rest of the Twins was nowhere near the greatest ever, less than half the gap required to make the list of leaders, less than a third of the all-time record. Where does it fit in? The 102-point gap between Viola/Blyleven and the rest of the Twin pitching is, in fact, *less* than the historical average, which is 106 points.

How else could we measure the dependence of a team on two pitchers? The other obvious way would be to look at the teams according to the percentage of games won by two pitchers:

1987   Twins   Viola and Blyleven   32/85 38%

This, again, is not quite the highest figure ever. The 1904 New York Giants got 35 wins from Joe McGinnity and 33 from Christy Mathewson. The rest of the team won 38. The mighty Mack and Matty won 64 percent of the Giants' victories.

In the first 20 years of the century, two pitchers frequently won over 50 percent of the games for championship teams. Other leaders to round out the top five were the 1919 Black Sox (59 percent), the 1915 Phillies (58 percent), the 1914 Braves (56 percent), and the 1920 Cleveland Indians (56 percent).

Since 1920 there have been only three cases in which two pitchers won over half of the wins for a championship team. Those were the 1934 Cardinals (Dizzy and Paul Dean), the 1939 Cincinnati Reds (Bucky Walters and Paul Derringer), and the 1965 Dodgers (Koufax and Drysdale).

Even in recent years, however, the 38 percent of the Twins' games won by Viola and Blyleven is not unusually

	Year	Team	Top Two Winners	W-L	Pct	Rest of Team		GAP
1.	1940	Detroit	Newsom and Rowe	37-8,	.822	53-56,	.486	.336
2.	1978	Yankees	Guidry and Figueroa	45-12,	.789	55-51,	.519	.270
3.	1914	Braves	Rudolph and James	53-17,	.757	41-42,	.494	.263
4.	1961	Yankees	Ford and Terry	41-7,	.854	68-46,	.596	.258
5.	1956	Dodgers	Newcombe and Maglie	40-12,	.769	53-49,	.520	.249
6.	1984	Cubs	Sutcliffe and Trout	29-8,	.784	67-57,	.540	.244
7.	1907	Tigers	Donovan and Killian	50-17,	.746	42-41,	.506	.240
8.	1919	W. Sox	Cicotte and Williams	52-18,	.743	36-34,	.514	.229
9.	1986	Red Sox	Clemens and Boyd	40-14,	.741	55-52,	.514	.227
10.	1908	Cubs	Brown and Reulbach	53-16,	.768	46-39,	.541	.227

high, nor even high, at all. In 1986 Clemens and Boyd won 42% of the Red Sox' victories, and Witt and Mc-Caskill also accounted for a larger share of California's wins than did the Twins' twins. In 1985 three of the four division champions got a larger share of their wins from two pitchers than did the 1987 Twins, led by Herzog's Cardinals, who got 42 of their 101 wins (42 percent) from Andujar and Tudor. The Royals were also over 40 percent from Leibrandt and Saberhagen, and the Dodgers were at a higher 38 percent from Hershiser and Valenzuela. As recently as 1983 Lamar Hoyt and Richard Dotson accounted for 46 percent of the wins for a division champion.

And for the history of baseball over the century, the 38 percent of wins accounted for by two Twin pitchers is, for a championship team, well below average, the average being 41 percent.

Well, what else could we say that would make Herzog's claim valid? "I didn't say that Viola and Blyleven were exceptionally good," Herzog might argue, "but just that they didn't have anything else. The rest of the team was bad."

This is perhaps closer to being true, but it's an unremarkable truth. The Twins' winning percentage, for the team as a whole, was .525, the lowest ever by a World Championship team, and the second-lowest for a team which was in the World Series, the 1973 Mets being worse. They were five full games worse than any other World Champion.

If you take away their top two pitchers, they of course remain one of the weaker champions, but their place among the weakest becomes less prominent. The Twins after their top two pitchers had a winning percentage of .491. There have been seven other championship teams, including three other World Champions, which had winning percentages below .500 after you got past their top two pitchers. Two other World Championship teams of the 1980s had winning percentages no better than the Twins after the top two pitchers. The 1980 Phillies had a 41–19 record from Carlton and Ruthven, but the rest of the team had a winning percentage of .490. The 1985 Royals had a 37–15 record from Saberhagen and Leibrandt, but a .491 percentage from the rest of the team. As you can see if you check the chart of the widest gaps, winning percentages of around .500 for championship teams after their top two pitchers are actually quite common.

If you'd rather look at raw numbers than percentages, the Twins had 53 victories that did not come from Viola or Blyleven. There have been dozens of championship teams that couldn't match that. The Oakland A's of 1972–1974, World Champions each year, never had more than 53 wins from pitchers other than their top two, and in 1974 had only 46 wins that didn't come from Catfish Hunter or Ken Holtzman.

It seems to me very strange to say that the Twins were a weak champion after their top two pitchers, when they were weaker overall than they were if you compare teams without their top two starters.

"Well," Herzog might argue, "I still say there was something funny about that team. I faced the 1985 Royals and they didn't deserve to beat me, either, but they had a good number-four starter, in Mark Gubicza, and a helluva

a number-three starter, in Danny Jackson. Your charts show that the 1986 Red Sox had a much bigger gap between the top two and the rest of the team and that Clemens and Boyd won a bigger percentage of the Sox wins, but that team definitely had three starters, with Bruce Hurst being probably better than Boyd."

At this point, I think we've reached a true statement: the specific position of number-three starter on the Twins was, in fact, unusually weak for a championship team. Not "everything behind the top two starters"; the number-three spot, specifically. Every team has weaknesses. The Royals in '85 had excellent depth in the starting corps, but they didn't have a winning record after the top two men because their offense was so weak that they had to have exceptional starting pitching to win. The Red Sox in '86 had a good number-three starter, but they were basically a .500 team after the top two men because they had no number-four starter and a poor bullpen most of the year. The Twins had a lot of weaknesses for a championship team, one of which was that they did not have a good number-three starter. But they had Jeff Reardon in the bullpen. They had Juan Berenguer. Les Straker pitched well at times. They had an offense that was good enough to have a chance with anybody they threw out there. They had 53 wins after Viola and Blyleven, a normal total for a champion. They simply didn't have a reliable number-three starter, just as the Cardinals don't have a number-five hitter.

And having located the specific point that Herzog and the others were making about the Twins, my reaction is "So what?" Since when did the World Series become a test of a team's number-three starter, in particular? The World Series has been played with two off days (or more) since 1956, and most of the time before that. I've never before heard the idea that this was a plot to deprive Whitey Herzog of the World Championship. The development of the seven-game playoffs obviously makes it more difficult for a team to win with two starters than it was before, since now a team must win two seven-game series in a row with those two starters. That's a tough job. If the Twins hadn't beaten the Tigers quickly, they wouldn't have been able to start their number-one pitcher three times, as teams have been doing since 1903. They would have had to start Straker or Niekro in the second game of the World Series. The Twins had a tough challenge, and they met it, and power to them.

Well, let's clean up some notes from the study. There have been eleven times in history (among 214 championship teams) when the winning percentage of the "rest of the team" was actually better than that of the top two starters. The most extreme case was in 1979 when the top starters for Baltimore were Mike Flanagan (23–9) and Dennis Martinez (15–16), a total of of 38–25, a .603 percentage. The rest of the team was 64–32, .667—64 points better than the top starters. The disappointing performance of Dennis Martinez and an injury to Scott McGregor were the keys to the oddity. Whitey Herzog's 1977 Royals team was 59 points better with the rest of the staff than with its number-one and -two starters, Dennis Leonard (20–12) and Jim Colborn (18–14). No other team had a similar reverse gap.

The strangest of the "reverse gaps" was that of the

1948 Braves, who had a .591 winning percentage with their top two starters and a .598 winning percentage with the rest of the team. You ever hear of "Spahn and Sain and pray for rain"? That's the team. Oddly enough, the one team in baseball history that is most famous for having only two starting pitchers was, in fact, one of the few championship teams that had a better winning percentage with the rest of the team than with the top two starters.

Another of the "reverse gap" teams was, you might have guessed, the 1987 Cardinals. The top two starters for the Cards (in terms of most wins) were Bob Forsch (11–7) and Danny Cox (11–9), a total of 22–16, .579. The rest of the team was at .589. The remarkable thing here, though, is that the Cardinals top two pitchers won only 22 games, or 23 percent of the St. Louis victories. This is by far the lowest percentage of wins accounted for by two pitchers on a championship team, ever. Nothing close.

There've been several championship teams that were below 30 percent, but they were all 29 percent or 28 percent. The norm, as we said before, is around 40 percent.

So it wasn't *Minnesota* that was the oddity, at all. It is normal for a championship team to have two or three starters much better than the rest of the team. The Twins top two starters bore an absolutely normal relationship to the rest of the team. It was *St. Louis* that was off the wall. The Cardinals, due to the injuries, went through the year without any solid rotation or without any number-one or -two starter. They were able to pull through it because they had exceptional depth. Herzog was, in a sense, much like a one-legged man in a footrace, complaining that it wasn't fair for the other guy to have two good legs. Maybe it's not fair, Whitey, but that's the world we live in. Their two legs were better than your one leg, and they deserved to win.

KANSAS CITY ROYALS

It is dangerous for a baseball team to have too many players with the same weakness, no matter what the weakness. To have two or three regulars who are bad defensive players may not cost much, but if you add one more you may be shoving a poor defensive player into a key defensive role. The ability of the good fielders to cover the mistakes of the bad ones will be overloaded, and the problem will blow up on you. To have three players who are slow may have a very minimal effect, but if you add one or two more who are slow, then you're going to be shoving people who are slow into offensive and defensive roles which require speed, and the incremental effect of the extra slow guy can be many times the effect of the first slow guy. The ability of the manager to adjust to situations in which speed is needed, such as a speed park or a running situation, diminishes greatly with each extra slow player; the ability to hide a slow player from the place where a slow player can't do the job is lost.

So in building a ballclub, you have to be aware of the weaknesses of your stalwart players, and avoid duplicating those weaknesses among the replaceable parts. Willie Wilson used to be a good player and still does some things well, but his on-base percentages have never been good and now are very poor. Frank White is a terrific player, but the ability to reach base is his weakest point. When you patch around those players with marginal talents like Larry Owen (on-base percentage: .260), Angel Salazar (on-base percentage: .219) and Steve Balboni (on-base percentage: .273), then you've got five guys in the lineup who don't get on base, and then you can't hide from it. Vincent Jackson, regular left fielder for much of the season, had an on-base percentage of .296.

No one can say why everything should revolve around Bo Jackson, but nonetheless it did. Kevin Seitzer is eight times the player that Bo is, but if Jackson and Seitzer collided in short left and Bo had a cut on his cheek and Seitzer a broken leg, the headline in *USA Today* would read "BO HAS TWO STITCHES, Third Baseman Also Hurt." Early in the season the Royals looked like worldbeaters. By May 26 the Royals were ten games over .500 at 26–16; they held their ground for a month after that. In late June, when Dick Howser was near death, the Royals, perhaps coincidentally, went into a slump. Just when they appeared ready to pull out of it, the Bo Jackson mess exploded.

While the underlying causes of the mid-season collapse were in the mismanagement of resources (see article on managers), the proximate cause was the Bo Jackson furor. There were many mistakes made here, which are dealt with in a separate article. In the early part of the season, Bo was the new Mickey Mantle. The Royals walked on eggshells around him. When the situation blew up there was an enormous three-week distraction, during which the team lost 18 of 22 games (from July 6 to July 31). The Royals rallied and staggered into the edges of the pennant race, but never again resembled the team that played the first two months of the season.

If baseball were 51 percent pitching or more, the Royals would have won this division easily. When they scored three to five runs, giving the pitchers a chance to win, the Royals record (28–20) was the best in the American League, second best in baseball behind the Cardinals. On this team, there were too many games in which they didn't get three runs. In 57 games, 11 more than any other AL team, the Royals scored 0 to 2 runs; the White Sox had 46 such games. Of those 57 games, 51 were losses, a normal percentage but a prohibitive total. The Royals scored only 715 runs, last in the American League.

Their essential offensive problem remains what it has been for five years: they don't have enough people on base. During the 1986 season, the Kansas City baseball community talked incessantly about the need to get someone who could "bat behind Brett and drive in runs." If I heard that once, I heard it every day between June 15 and the Tartabull trade. You try to tell them: Look, this team is last in the American League in men on base. You can't drive in runners who aren't there. You don't score 780 runs when you only have 1800 to 1900 runners on base. It can't be done.

So the Royals add Danny Tartabull, Tartabull is super, and what happens? The Royals are last in the league in runs scored. So what do people say? The Royals have to add more speed! No joke. The Royals have got to get back to "moving baserunners, like they did when Whitey Herzog was here." What baserunners? Look, the percentage of the Royal baserunners who scored last year, given that this is a poor home run park, was *not* low. It was good. The number of Royals on base and the number who scored was virtually identical in 1987 to Whitey Herzog's first championship team (1976); actually Herzog's team had nine more men on base and scored two fewer runs. That level of runs scored was good in 1976, poor in 1987, but the relevant point is that with a given number of baserunners, Herzog's team was no more successful than Gardner's.

In the June 18 broadcast from California, there occurred this exchange between broadcaster Denny Trease and Buddy Biancalana, sitting in the booth while on the Disabled List. Speaking of California rookie Mark McLemore:

TREASE: Very patient hitter. He takes a lot of pitches. Even in batting practice, he'll take pitches.

BIANCALANA: That doesn't go over too well with the veterans. Not on our ballclub, at least.

TREASE: Get in there and swing, uh?

That's the problem in a nutshell, guys. Sure, it helps if you can add a Danny Tartabull, and it will help if Gary Thurman is as good as he looked in September. But as long as you consider it a moral imperative to swing at bad pitches, you ain't going to score runs. The Royals have so many low on-base percentages that there are a lot of games where they get six to eight men on base the whole game, and really don't have a chance to do anything. The Royals scored only 180 runs in the games they lost, an average of 2.28 runs per game, both figures the lowest in the major leagues. Every other major-league team scored at least 2.5 runs per game in their losses.

At the same time, there are signs of long-term progress. Owen, Salazar, and Balboni are short-term Royals. In 1987 the Royals added Kevin Seitzer (on-base percentage: .399) and Danny Tartabull (on-base percentage: .390) to the lineup. They are long-term Royals. The Royals in '87 drew 523 walks, the most since 1979, Herzog's last year. The trade for Kurt Stillwell is another positive step in this direction.

Danny Jackson was one of my favorites, and his trade is difficult for me to accept emotionally. Despite disappointing won-lost records, Jackson pitched very well in Kansas City. There is a real chance he will be one of the best pitchers in the National League in 1988.

But the Jackson-for-Stillwell trade makes sense, and will probably help the Royals over a period of years. The trade is consistent with the trading philosophy that built the Royals in the years 1969–1975. It focuses on the right problem. Of what might be called the Royals agreed-upon problems (catcher, shortstop, and the bullpen), the one to address first was the shortstop problem. Although Quirk isn't an All Star, he's not a bad player—a .240 hitter with a few other offensive assets who throws well. (Royal opponents stole 124 bases, an average number, while the Royals threw out 66 runners, 11 more than average.) Given a better right-handed running mate, he's all right. Ed Hearn might come back and develop as the right-handed complement, or even the regular catcher. One of the Royals' top prospects, Mike Macfarlane, is a right-handed hitting catcher.

You could concentrate on solving the bullpen problem, but that's a speculative thing. Top relievers blaze and fade. They could have traded Danny Jackson for a relief ace and found themselves in two years without Danny and without a relief ace. The shortstop production was just inadequate, and there was no one in sight who was about to solve the problem. It made sense for them to invest their resources in acquiring a young shortstop who will probably solidify the position for several years. They accomplished that.

With respect to the trade of four kids for Floyd Bannister, I am less enthusiastic. Bannister, despite being a media whipping boy, is a durable and consistent starting pitcher. But the trade follows the pattern of the worst trades that you can make, the kind in which what you give up turns out to be worth 40 times what you acquire. Think about it: overlooking the minor-league player (Dave Cochrane), KC traded four full careers for probably 20 percent of one career, a ratio of 4.00 to .020, or 20–1, if all players involved perform at the same level. Of course, it is massively unlikely that all four of the young pitchers will develop to have full careers, so the 4.00 figure is unrealistic—but it is very possible that one or two of them up

will develop into stars, while Bannister might suddenly encounter the end of the road. Then you find that you've given up 20, 25 years of major-league play for nothing; that, in fact, is precisely how most of the worst trades in major-league history happened. The Royals built this team in the early seventies by being on the other end of those trades. This trade has the potential to be a disaster, and even if that is only a 10 percent risk, why take a 10 percent chance of losing your shirt, for a potential gain of maybe three years?

There's another reason I don't like the trade. In the Danny Jackson trade, the Royals acquired pitcher Ted Power, who was projected either to be a fifth starter or to be a reliever. With John Davis gone (2.27 ERA in 27 relief appearances) and Bannister acquired, Power is almost certainly shoved into the bullpen—and I feel strongly that that is a mistake. Power's successful 1985 season as a reliever was a fluke. His stuff is not that of a reliever, but that of a starter. The Bannister trade puts Power in the role where he is less likely to succeed.

The Bannister trade represents the bad side of John Schuerholz—the attempt to find a quick fix, fixing the engine with a used part so that it will have to be fixed again in a year or at best two or three years. The Bannister trade is consistent with the trading philosophy which nearly destroyed this team in the early eighties, filling up the roster with players like Jerry Martin and Vida Blue. The reason you make those trades is because you don't have the self-confidence to make a judgment about which of a group of kids will develop, and live with that judgment. Schuerholz sees the Bannister trade as a gamble, but what it really is is an attempt to duck a gamble, an attempt to put a "proven" player into a slot.

But the bad side of John Schuerholz is easier to live with when the good side is doing so well. In the last year the Royals have added to the roster four terrific young players, in Tartabull, Seitzer, Stillwell, and Thurman. It's been a long time since the organization has had such a good phase of talent acquisition. The organization is in a position not only to contend in 1988, but, if the Bannister-type stuff doesn't get out of hand, to contend for many years.

How will the Royals do in 1988? There is enough talent to win. In my opinion the biggest problem that the Royals face in 1988 is not at catcher or shortstop or even in the bullpen. It is Willie Wilson. The catching problem is naked and obvious, and they'll use all their options to resolve it. The Willie Wilson problem is disguised by a decent batting average, a league-leading fielding percentage and 59 stolen bases. But with a .320 on-base percentage, Wilson is an awful leadoff man, and his throwing arm is so bad that he really is not an asset in center field. There is little question but that Gary Thurman is a better player or that the Royals would be a better team with Thurman in center.

What makes this a particularly difficult problem is Wilson's personality and contract. Wilson is the type of person that if you ask for an interview there's a fifty percent chance you'll get an interview, and a 50 percent chance you'll get an obscenity. He carries a chip on his shoulder about his mistreatment by the law, and it is generally agreed that he was singled out for extraordinary punishment for the crime he committed. But Wilson uses his anger to manipulate. There is an implied threat that if you don't handle him the way he wants, then he's going to be real hard to live with. The unspoken message is that if you take him out of center field he's going to sulk and pout until he poisons the atmosphere in the clubhouse. His attitude is that if he wants to swing at bad pitches he'll swing at bad pitches, and if you take him out of the leadoff spot he'll hold his breath until he turns blue. His megabuck, live-forever contract gives him a big advantage in this war. He can't be traded, and he can't really be released.

Billy Gardner didn't have what it takes to stand up to that emotional blackmail. Different people will interpret Whitey Herzog's success in different ways, but I believe the foundation rock of Herzog's ability is that Herzog don't back away from nobody. Wilson wouldn't pull this crap on Whitey Herzog or Billy Martin or Earl Weaver or Leo Durocher or Walt Alston or Casey Stengel, not for very long anyway. If Herzog thought that the Royals would be a better team with Gary Thurman in center, then Thurman would play center.

With that in mind, what happened in a game in September was an awfully good sign. In the ninth inning, Wilson took a called third strike, and screamed at the umpire until he was ejected. Then he went up the runway leading from the dugout, and continued his tantrum by throwing bats and balls out onto the field. By this time John Wathan was managing the Royals. The Duke sprang to the end of the runway and told Wilson in clear language and gestures visible from the cheap seats to cut it out and get on up the runway. It happened so quickly that Wathan didn't have time to think about it; he just instinctively asserted his authority. If he does that consistently, he has a heck of a chance to manage this team to about a half-dozen division championships.

INNINGS PITCHED BY STARTING PITCHERS

Kansas City	1079
Los Angeles	1075.2
Detroit	1072.2
Boston	1067.2
Seattle	1058
White Sox	1020.1
Pittsburgh	1009.1
Houston	1009.1
Milwaukee	998.1
Minnesota	997.2
Mets	997
St. Louis	973.1
Toronto	970.1
Cubs	966
Atlanta	958.1
California	953
Philadelphia	952.1
Texas	947.1
Cleveland	945
Yankees	945
San Francisco	944.1
Montreal	941.2
Oakland	939
Cincinnati	938.1
San Diego	928.1
Baltimore	912

RUNS SCORED AND ALLOWED WINS AND LOSSES

Wins	535	222	83-0	1.000
Saberhagen	174	115	21-12	.636
Slugfests	367	326	30-19	.612
Black	98	90	11-7	.611
Leibrandt	162	129	21-14	.600
Home Games	375	349	46-35	.568
Blowouts	281	255	26-21	.553
All Games	715	691	83-79	.512
One Run Games	157	156	22-21	.512
Road Games	340	342	37-44	.457
Gubicza	143	151	15-20	.429
Pitchers' Duels	69	93	17-26	.395
Jackson	114	160	12-22	.352
Losses	180	469	0-79	.000

TEN BEST STARTS

	IP	H	R	ER	BB	SO		
Saberhagen at Cle, May 9	9	2	0	0	0	9	W	92
Leibrandt vs. Mil, May 16	9	1	0	0	1	6	W	90
Saberhagen vs. Cal, June 12	9	3	0	0	0	8	W	89
Gubicza at Oak, June 23	9	3	0	0	4	10	W	87
Leibrandt at Bal, June 26	9	2	0	0	3	7	W	87
Saberhagen at Tor, July 11	9	3	1	1	1	10	W	86
Gubicza at Sea, Sep 23	9	5	0	0	4	11	W	84
Saberhagen vs. Sea, June 27	9	3	0	0	2	4	W	83
Jackson vs. Tex, Aug 26	9	4	0	0	5	7	W	81
Saberhagen vs. NY, Apr 10	9	2	1	1	2	4	W	81

PITCHERS WHEN SUPPORTED BY THREE TO FIVE RUNS

	G	IP	W-L	Pct	SO	BB	ERA
Leibrandt	13	97	6-2	.750	59	33	2.41
Jackson	9	65	4-3	.571	57	23	4.02
Gubicza	9	54	4-3	.571	39	37	4.70
Saberhagen	9	68	3-4	.429	52	13	3.71
Black	6	34	1-3	.250	17	11	3.97

HALL OF FAME WATCH

Fully qualified: Brett 142.5; **Building credentials but not yet viable candidate:** Quisenberry 69, F White 61, W Wilson 52.5, McRae 50, Dick Howser 41; **Working on it:** Saberhagen 29, Garber 28, L Smith 23.5, Seitzer 15.5, Leibrandt 10; **Long way to go:** Orta 8, Tartabull 7.5, D Jackson 7, Wathan 5.5, Balboni 3, Bosley 2.5, B Black 2, and Gubicza 1. (Howser's totals include 30 points as a manager, 11 as a player. Gardner's totals include 11 points as a manager, 3 as a player. All of Wathan's points were as a player.)

TEN WORST STARTS

	IP	H	R	ER	BB	SO		
Gubicza at Bos, Aug 8	2⅔	7	7	7	3	3	L	16
Gubicza at Det, Apr 25	3⅔	8	7	7	1	1	L	17
Saberhagen vs. Cle, July 20	3⅓	10	6	6	0	2	L	18
Gabicza vs. Tex, May 29	2⅔	6	6	6	3	1	L	20
Black at Tex, Aug 19	2⅓	7	6	6	1	2	—	20
Leibrandt vs. Cal, Sep 17	2⅓	6	6	6	2	1	—	20
Perez vs. Oak, Sep 29	1⅓	6	6	4	1	1	L	21
Leibrandt at Minn, Sep 27	⅔	5	5	5	0	0	L	21
Jackson vs. Cal, June 14	4	7	6	6	6	5	L	23
Perez vs. Cal, Sep 14	2*	6	5	5	1	0	—	23

AVERAGE RUNS SCORED IN LOSSES

Boston	3.45
Cleveland	3.36
Texas	3.23
Detroit	3.22
Mets	3.17
Baltimore	3.17
California	3.17
Minnesota	3.14
Milwaukee	3.14
White Sox	3.12
San Francisco	3.11
Oakland	3.07
St. Louis	3.07
Seattle	3.05
Cincinnati	3.04
Pittsburgh	3.00
Montreal	2.94
San Diego	2.94
Atlanta	2.93
Toronto	2.89
Philadelphia	2.87
Cubs	2.78
Yankees	2.77
Los Angeles	2.52
Houston	2.50
Kansas City	2.28

Jamie QUIRK, Catcher
Runs Created: 32

	G	AB	Hit	2B	3B	HR	Run	RBI	TBB	SO	SB	CS	Avg
3.97 years		374	90	19	1	7	31	40	23	72	1	2	.241
1987	109	296	70	17	0	5	24	33	28	56	1	0	.236
First Half	57	152	35	8	0	2	16	11	12	19	0	0	.230
Second Half	52	144	35	9	0	3	8	22	16	37	1	0	.243
Vs. RHP		279	66	16	0	5	22	32	27	52	0	0	.237
Vs. LHP		17	4	1	0	0	2	1	1	4	1	0	.235
Home	58	147	32	11	0	0	7	11	14	24	0	0	.218
Road	51	149	38	6	0	5	17	22	14	32	1	0	.255

Bo JACKSON, Left Field
Runs Created: 55

	G	AB	Hit	2B	3B	HR	Run	RBI	TBB	SO	SB	CS	Avg
0.87 years		549	126	22	3	28	63	71	43	221	15	6	.230
1987	116	396	93	17	2	22	46	53	30	158	10	4	.235
First Half	81	284	72	13	1	18	38	45	20	115	6	2	.254
Second Half	35	112	21	4	1	4	8	8	10	43	4	2	.188
Vs. RHP		283	65	12	1	15	36	40	20	112	9	2	.230
Vs. LHP		113	28	5	1	7	10	13	10	46	1	2	.248
Home	57	197	56	14	1	14	23	39	18	59	3	2	.284
Road	59	199	37	3	1	8	23	14	12	99	7	2	.186

George BRETT, First Base
Runs Created: 85

	G	AB	Hit	2B	3B	HR	Run	RBI	TBB	SO	SB	CS	Avg
11.46 years		620	194	39	10	20	100	98	67	47	13	7	.313
1987	115	427	124	18	2	22	71	78	72	47	6	3	.290
First Half	42	152	46	10	0	7	30	30	26	18	1	0	.303
Second Half	73	275	78	8	2	15	41	48	46	29	5	3	.284
Vs. RHP		278	84	15	2	15	54	53	60	25	6	2	.302
Vs. LHP		149	40	3	0	7	17	25	12	22	0	1	.268
Home	62	231	62	6	2	14	37	48	36	26	3	0	.268
Road	53	196	62	12	0	8	34	30	36	21	3	3	.316

Willie WILSON, Center Field
Runs Created: 78

	G	AB	Hit	2B	3B	HR	Run	RBI	TBB	SO	SB	CS	Avg
8.72 years		633	187	22	13	4	100	44	32	86	61	11	.295
1987	146	610	170	18	15	4	97	30	32	88	59	11	.279
First Half	78	318	90	8	8	3	54	12	12	45	27	5	.283
Second Half	68	292	80	10	7	1	43	18	20	43	32	6	.274
Vs. RHP		440	129	13	13	3	79	19	25	53	53	9	.293
Vs. LHP		170	41	5	2	1	18	11	7	35	6	2	.241
Home	78	321	95	13	10	0	58	18	17	40	37	5	.296
Road	68	289	75	5	5	4	39	12	15	48	22	6	.260

Frank WHITE, Second Base
Runs Created: 67

	G	AB	Hit	2B	3B	HR	Run	RBI	TBB	SO	SB	CS	Avg
12.08 years		552	142	29	5	12	67	64	29	73	14	6	.257
1987	154	563	138	32	2	17	67	78	51	86	1	3	.245
First Half	83	301	70	15	1	7	34	44	29	51	0	2	.233
Second Half	71	262	68	17	1	10	33	34	22	35	1	1	.260
Vs. RHP		415	96	22	2	12	53	56	36	68	1	3	.231
Vs. LHP		148	42	10	0	5	14	22	15	18	0	0	.284
Home	76	256	70	19	0	6	32	40	33	33	0	1	.273
Road	78	307	68	13	2	11	35	38	18	53	1	2	.221

Danny TARTABULL, Right Field
Runs Created: 124

	G	AB	Hit	2B	3B	HR	Run	RBI	TBB	SO	SB	CS	Avg
2.00 years		587	172	30	5	31	91	106	75	155	7	6	.293
1987	158	582	180	27	3	34	95	101	79	136	9	4	.309
First Half	83	304	92	9	2	14	45	45	35	65	1	2	.303
Second Half	75	278	88	18	1	20	50	56	44	71	8	2	.317
Vs. RHP		433	137	20	1	27	68	78	54	97	7	3	.316
Vs. LHP		149	43	7	2	7	27	23	25	39	2	1	.289
Home	78	282	82	13	2	15	48	43	42	57	5	1	.291
Road	80	300	98	14	1	19	47	58	37	79	4	3	.327

Kevin SEITZER, Third Base
Runs Created: 120

	G	AB	Hit	2B	3B	HR	Run	RBI	TBB	SO	SB	CS	Avg
1.17 years		630	203	32	8	15	103	80	85	85	10	6	.322
1987	161	641	207	33	8	15	105	83	80	85	12	7	.323
First Half	87	344	105	17	5	4	53	38	45	49	6	4	.305
Second Half	74	297	102	16	3	11	52	45	35	36	6	3	.343
Vs. RHP		466	153	27	3	13	76	70	58	65	9	4	.328
Vs. LHP		175	54	6	5	2	29	13	22	20	3	3	.309
Home	81	319	107	21	7	7	55	47	42	33	5	3	.335
Road	80	322	100	12	1	8	50	36	38	52	7	4	.311

Steve BALBONI, Designated Hitter
Runs Created: 43

	G	AB	Hit	2B	3B	HR	Run	RBI	TBB	SO	SB	CS	Avg
3.79 years		564	130	24	2	33	65	89	50	161	0	0	.230
1987	121	386	80	11	1	24	44	60	34	97	0	0	.207
First Half	73	237	50	7	0	12	23	32	21	50	0	0	.211
Second Half	48	149	30	4	1	12	21	28	13	47	0	0	.201
Vs. RHP		283	60	10	1	18	32	50	24	70	0	0	.212
Vs. LHP		103	20	1	0	6	12	10	10	27	0	0	.194
Home	58	190	36	6	0	8	17	22	16	49	0	0	.189
Road	63	196	44	5	1	16	27	38	18	48	0	0	.224

Angel SALAZAR, Shortstop
Runs Created: 16

	G	AB	Hit	2B	3B	HR	Run	RBI	TBB	SO	SB	CS	Avg
2.15 years		384	80	15	2	1	30	27	8	65	3	3	.208
1987	116	317	65	7	0	2	24	21	6	46	4	4	.205
First Half	85	274	57	7	0	2	21	18	6	36	4	3	.208
Second Half	31	43	8	0	0	0	3	3	0	10	0	1	.186
Vs. RHP		226	47	5	0	1	17	14	5	31	4	1	.208
Vs. LHP		91	18	2	0	2	7	7	1	15	0	3	.198
Home	53	132	24	3	0	1	14	10	3	12	2	1	.182
Road	63	185	41	4	0	1	10	11	3	34	2	3	.222

Juan BENIQUEZ, Utility
Runs Created: 27

	G	AB	Hit	2B	3B	HR	Run	RBI	TBB	SO	SB	CS	Avg
9.09 years		505	138	21	3	9	66	51	38	60	11	8	.273
1987	96	255	64	12	1	8	20	47	16	39	0	0	.251
First Half	57	174	41	7	0	3	14	26	11	26	0	0	.236
Second Half	39	81	23	5	1	5	6	21	5	13	0	0	.284
Vs. RHP		139	33	4	1	2	10	21	10	23	0	0	.237
Vs. LHP		116	31	8	0	6	10	26	6	16	0	0	.267
Home	50	112	26	6	1	2	10	21	7	16	0	0	.232
Road	46	143	38	6	0	6	10	26	9	23	0	0	.266

THE HOBBY

We didn't handle it very well, guys. None of us—fans, players, manager, front office, ownership, media. Bo Jackson represents, to an organization, a unique collection of possibilities and problems. As of July 2, the athlete of the decade was hitting .269 with 16 homers and 42 RBI, figures which project for the season to 34 homers and 90 RBI. He was playing fairly well in left field, with his tremendous throwing arm and speed compensating for his predictable mistakes. A whale of a rookie year, let's say.

How we got from there to Jackson winding up as the scapegoat for the season is a long story with no heroes. We all made mistakes. The ownership, to begin with. Jackson in the fall of 1986 didn't look anything like a major-league player, and it was assumed that he would most likely open 1987 at Omaha. Jackson worked hard during the off-season, however, and showed well in spring training. The front office still thought he would benefit from AAA experience, and announced the intention of sending him down.

Royals co-owner Avron Fogelman, however, decided not to let that happen. He was, he said, afraid that it would break Bo's spirit to send him down after he had worked so hard all winter and played so well in the spring. He talked to John Schuerholz, and the decision was made that Jackson would stay in the major leagues.

That, looking backward, was the first mistake, or at least the first one we'll count. The subsequent story became a case history to teach owners why they should not intervene publicly in personnel decisions: because if you do, it undermines the authority of everyone between the owner and the player on the club's organizational chart.

Jackson is a difficult personality, a man whose ego is as well developed as his thighs. When former manager Mike Ferraro introduced himself to Jackson, Bo reportedly turned his back and walked away without speaking or shaking hands. I have asked myself many times why a man would do a thing like that, and I can't come up with a credible answer. Whatever the reason, the gesture was interpreted on the level of appearances, and it certainly didn't look very good.

So Jackson was playing well, early in the year, but in the back of his mind he had to have figured out that he had the upper hand on his manager. He knew that his manager couldn't send him down. He knew that even the owners couldn't really hurt him, because he could always go play football. In early July he went through a minor slump, losing about 15 points in batting average in a week. It was reported as a major slump, but that was just more Bo stuff; everything gets blown out of proportion. Anyway, he was frustrated.

On July 10 in Toronto, Thad Bosley pinch hit for Jackson. Jackson cleaned out his locker, perhaps intending to quit baseball, perhaps intending only to threaten to quit so as to obtain the right to play football in the off-season, which was prohibited under his contract. Perhaps he

wanted a guarantee that he wouldn't be pinch hit for anymore; who knows. Avron Fogelman flew to Toronto. A deal was negotiated: Jackson would stay for the season, but would be allowed to play for the Raiders after the season ended.

At the time, I thought the club had done the right thing. If I had known how it was going to turn out, obviously I wouldn't have thought that. What I had not anticipated, and what made this the second mistake, was that the reaction of so many people would be so immature. George Brett had two quotes about the subject, both of which were so restrained that no one bothered to requote them, but which I thought summed up perfectly what the mature reaction would have been. The two quotes were "Life's too short to choose up sides," and "I can't decide what he ought to do. It's his life."

Brett's reaction was, like Brett himself, restrained, intelligent, and mature. Willie Wilson's reaction was, like Wilson, loud, opinionated, and childish. "I guess he got the last laugh, didn't he?" said Wilson. "He got us to believe him, and now we're fools." Other Royals were reported upset, but Wilson, who himself was a spectacular football player in high school, but was told by the Royals that he would have to give up football to take the money, was the loudest.

Unfortunately for everybody, the community chose to follow Willie Wilson, rather than following George Brett. That was the third mistake. Jackson was booed every time he moved. The fans hooted when he took the field, howled when he came to bat, screamed when he struck out. Fans threw toy footballs on the field. New York fans held up a sign: LT'S NEW HOBBY: TYING BO INTO KNOTS. The local fans were no kinder.

Somewhere in there, trying to explain the decision, Jackson had described his football playing as "just another hobby, like hunting or fishing." I'm not sure if this word was used only once or was used a few times. Jackson is not an articulate speaker. He stutters badly, and just doing an interview is an obvious effort for him. He refers to himself as "Bo," in the third person, as people with speech impediments are sometimes taught to do to avoid saying "I." He often doesn't say things exactly as he wants.

In any case, this word "hobby," was picked up by the media and repeated and repeated and rephrased and requoted and reframed again and again and again; from a quiet utterance, it found its way into a thousand headlines. Network commentators who deal with sports only in passing would pick up this word, hobby, and cast a snide remark toward anyone who would be so impertinent as to describe playing professional football as a hobby. Talk-show hosts and minor-league broadcasters and editorial writers all gave us their opinions of professional football as a hobby; their opinion, perhaps I should say, since there was only one opinion, signed by ten thousand claimants. Jackson was treated as if wanting to play both professional baseball and professional football were criminal as well as stupid beyond any description. The cartoonist for the local newspaper, a mean-spirited bush leaguer who has never drawn a funny cartoon in his life, drew a "cartoon" which consisted of three pictures with the headlines: baseball, football, screwball.

Maybe I don't understand something here, folks, but I don't how you all can live with yourselves. I mean, I know I've got a mean streak. I've written some awful things about ballplayers over the years, for sins no more heinous than falling down chasing a fly ball or running the bases with one's head down. But Lord help me, I never abused a man this way for searching his vocabulary and choosing the wrong word. All right, it was a poor choice of words, by a young man under tremendous pressure who isn't famous for his ability to choose words. But to pick up that word and hammer him with it and hammer him with it until the pain is tatooed on his forehead . . . well, I just don't understand it. I know that Bo is awfully well paid for being a public figure, and in that case there is an argument that anything which is true is fair. But is it true, or is it a distortion, to rip a word out of a man's sentence and blast it out of the headlines as if it were his philosophy?

What was lost in the rush to judge Bo is that the man never stopped hustling. I have always thought, as a baseball fan, that if a player works hard on the field, he's entitled to a break on anything else. If a player doesn't hustle and pulls a rock, boo him, but if a player gives you everything he has and makes the same mistake, maybe you ought to give him a break. I don't mean that Bo does what is expected of him, but that I see a lot of Royals games, and if you asked me which Royal gives the best effort, start to finish, every ground ball, I'd have to tell you it was Bo Jackson. When the booing started, when the toy footballs started coming out of the stands, I couldn't understand, and I still can't understand, why that didn't count.

Can Jackson excel, over a period of years, in two sports? Probably not. If he were to play two sports year round for several years, there would certainly be a price to pay in terms of performance in either sport. But what puzzles the hell out of me about all of these people is the presumption that they know more than Bo Jackson does about what that price would be. Let's take that sign: LT'S NEW HOBBY: TYING BO IN KNOTS. Now, who knows more about what it is like to be hit by Lawrence Taylor: Bo Jackson, or the guy who held up the sign? The same idea showed up in about 30 letters to the editor in the *Star and Times* sports pages: I wonder how Mike Singletary is going to react to a guy who talks about playing pro football as a hobby. Well, who knows more about tangling with Mike Singletary: Bo Jackson, or the guy who wrote the letter? Who understands better the price of trying to play both sports: Bo Jackson, or the morning disc jockey? It's obvious, isn't it? How can these people be so arrogant as to assume that they know more than Bo does about the costs of his decision?

This is not to say that the Royals organization doesn't have the right to tell Bo to make a choice. If they want to say "We'd love to have all of Bo Jackson, but we don't want half of him," that's their option. In retrospect, it couldn't have worked out much worse—understanding that Bo's option is not only to go play football, but to talk to the other 25 baseball teams as well.

Sports fans, as a group, have an inordinate amount of trouble coming to grips with a fundamental principle of satisfactory relationships: that I don't own anyone's talents except my own. A hundred times a year, someone will ask me, about one aging ballplayer or another, "Don't you think he should retire now? Isn't he hurting his reputation and his image by trying to hang on this way?" My answer is always the same: "Hell, I don't know what he should do. It's his life. It's his talent. It's his reputation. It's none of my business what he does with it." I'm damned if I'm going to let anybody else make those decisions for me, and because of that I recognize that I don't get to make those decisions for anybody else.

About the time that Bo signed with the Raiders, I was reading the biography of Moe Berg, a major-league catcher in the twenties and thirties. In addition to being a baseball player, Berg was a scholar. He graduated from Princeton and the Sorbonne with degrees in languages, of which he spoke somewhere between 15 and 20. He was a leading authority in his day on Sanskrit literature, which was one of his main passions, another being Medieval French. Berg read about 20 newspapers a day, in a wide variety of languages, and seemingly remembered everything in them. On a radio quiz show in the late thirties, experts attempted to stump Berg by asking questions like "Who was Poppea Sabina?," "Who was Calamity Jane?," "Who was the Black Napoleon?," and "Who or what are the Seven Sleepers, the Seven Wise Masters, the Seven Wise Men, the Seven Wonders of the World, and the Seven Stars?" Berg answered these questions in great detail, giving the astrological reference points of the Seven Stars, the real name of Calamity Jane and throwing in where she died and where she was buried. Berg wrote articles for publications like the *Atlantic Monthly*, and also took advantage of his facility with languages to do serious high-level espionage prior to and during World War II.

Now, if you were to ask, "Is it possible to be, at the same time, a linguist, a scholar of repute, a spy, a compendium of limitless miscellaneous information, and a major-league baseball player?"—if you were to ask this, I say, in the same way that we now ask "Is it possible for a man to compete successfully in both major-league baseball and major-league football, one would ordinarily have to answer, "No, it isn't possible." It wouldn't be possible for any ordinary athlete. It was possible for him. Certainly, Berg's decision to play baseball hurt his career as a scholar enormously, and the time he spent in the off-season learning Japanese and sneaking around Tokyo in a kimono taking pictures of military installations no doubt cut into his success as a ballplayer. But what the hell, it was his life, wasn't it? It didn't cost us anything, did it? If Bo wants to have half of a baseball career and half of a football career, what do we as fans have to lose by letting him take his shot?

Jackson stayed with the Royals, but it would have been far better had he not. The furor over Jackson became the center of the season. Facing intense hostility from fans, his manager and some teammates, Jackson stopped hitting. He started dropping fly balls in the outfield. On July 28 in New York, Jackson beat out a bunt single with two out, nobody on and the Royals trailing 2–1, top of the sixth inning. Gardner, under pressure from the front office to be tougher in his handling of players and unhappy with Bo anyway, was furious. He felt that Jackson was playing for his own stats, not interested in the team. He told reporters after the game that "we" had talked to Jackson about this before, presumably meaning that he had asked Hal McRae to talk to Jackson about it. He threw in a gratuitous insult for the two hitters coming up after Jackson (Salazar and Macfarlane) describing them as "Lou Gehrig and Babe Ruth." But two days later, Gardner acknowledged that he still had not talked to Jackson about the incident. Somehow, I don't think this is the recommended way to handle this, is it, Billy?

After that Jackson's play deteriorated to such a point that there was simply no issue as to whether or not to play him. He disappeared. Billy Gardner got fired.

None of us understands Bo very well or probably ever will, but I think a key toward understanding is to remember that every unusual strength that we develop in life, in my experience, we develop as a way of covering a weakness, much as a blind man learns to use his ears. Bo didn't develop the ego he has because he wanted to have an outsized ego. He developed that ego, I suspect, to cover a center of self-doubt. Another key, I think, is the stuttering. Stuttering, as I understand it, is in many cases a manifestation of a deep-rooted psychic scar; that's why stutterers may have trouble saying "I." What seems to be arrogance in Bo may be, I suspect, in fact a manifestation of insecurity. Or perhaps that is redundant, for perhaps arrogance is always a manifestation of insecurity.

My sister Rosalie, who is not a baseball fan, asked me a simple question: Why is it that everybody is mad at this man who wants to play both baseball and football? It seemed to her, as it does to me, that there was something rather magnificent about a man's trying to do something that nobody else can do. Why were people so mad?

I told her that I thought there were two reasons: 1) That people thought they had been lied to when Jackson seemed to speak definitively about playing baseball; and 2) that Jackson signed with the Los Angeles Raiders, the most hated rivals of the Kansas City football team. If he had signed with the Chiefs, the reaction would have been positive; if with a neutral team like the Cleveland Browns, a less intense reaction. A third answer would be that that is the way people react to arrogance: they feel the need to poke a hole through it, and to expose the raging self-doubt underneath.

That's what happened, but it's a pretty sorry excuse, isn't it? Look what we did: We destroyed the player, at least temporarily, and we destroyed the season. The fans, the owner, the front office, the manager, the teammates, the media—we all behaved badly. Bo made mistakes, but we didn't deal with his mistakes in a way that was mature or intelligent or that did anything positive for anybody. I say, let's face up to that. We had a unique and wonderful talent out there busting his butt for us, and we booed him and ridiculed him until he broke. What good did that do? If Bo is back with the team this year, let's try to do right by him.

THE KANSAS CITY MANAGERS

When condemned prisoners are being moved through the inmate population at San Quentin, the accompanying guards shout "Dead man coming through" to clear the walkways. The Kansas City Royals opened spring training with a dead man managing the team. One of the ways that sports contribute to society is by the creation of a community of interest, which can be a wonderful teaching vehicle. Through Len Bias and others, we have all learned something about the dangers of cocaine that we might never have learned through public education projects throwing out statistics and studies.

Through the experience of Dick Howser, we in the Kansas City area learned a great deal about brain tumors. There was no good news along the way. At first we were told that the big difference was between benign and malignant tumors. Dick's was malignant. Then we were told that even among malignant tumors, there were four different grades of malignancy, from those which grew rapidly to those which hardly grew at all. There was no announcement about the grade of Howser's malignancy. They said there would be an announcement the next day, and then they said they'd decided not to divulge it. Anyone could interpret that. Although the Royals carried out a charade of hope for Howser's benefit, an experienced manager was on hand to step into the role when the inevitable could no longer be denied.

I have seen worse managers than Billy Gardner, but I have never seen a manager who made mistakes which were quite so obvious. Juan Beniquez in 1983 hit .305 for John McNamara. Then he hit .336 for McNamara in 1984, .304 for Gene Mauch in 1985, .300 for Earl Weaver in 1986, and .284 for Jimy Williams in 1987. In between, to start the 1987 season, he played for Billy Gardner. He hit .236 for Gardner. Why?

Well, if you look at the way he was handled, it ain't hard to figure. In the first three weeks of the season, Beniquez hardly played. Then Brett was out for a couple of days, and Beniquez stepped in at third base. He got a few hits quickly, so he got a chance to play the outfield when Willie Wilson was out. By mid-May he was a regular, with 71 at bats by May 14 and a .310 batting average; he was also shining defensively in the outfield. Then all of a sudden Gardner decided that Beniquez was Honus Wagner; he was playing third base, left field, center field, right field, first base, designated hitter, playing every day against right-handers or left-handers, day game after a night game, everything. By May 28 his batting average was down to .269, but he was still among the team leaders in RBI. By June 18 he was down to .247.

Then he disappeared. Left-handers, right-handers, day game after a night game, injury, anything; he'd have maybe two at-bats a week. Gardner had decided he couldn't play after all.

The loss of Juan Beniquez was something the Royals could live with. The effective loss of Bret Saberhagen was another matter. In the first half of the season, Saberhagen pitched as well as a man can pitch. Saberhagen in early 1987 was throwing the ball not only harder than he had when he won the Cy Young Award in 1985, but much harder. He had the big year in 1985 throwing 89 to 92 miles an hour. In early 1987 he was throwing 93 to 95. After 18 starts he seemed to have the Cy Young Award locked up. Any time he took the mound you thought he had a chance to pitch a no-hitter if things broke right. By the All-Star break he had 15 wins, including five games (complete games) in which Saberhagen had given up only two or three hits.

With Saberhagen's leadership and three other good starting pitchers (Leibrandt, Jackson, and Gubicza), the Royals starting pitching had them in the race despite the manifest weaknesses of the team. Through 42 games the Royals were 26–16; their starting pitchers had an ERA of 2.92. Through 80 games they were still ten over at 45–35, with the ERA of their starting pitchers still at 3.33, a fairly remarkable figure for a group of pitchers in the DH league in a hitter's year.

The problem is, Saberhagen was pitching too much. Now, I don't mean that pitching 161 innings in a half-season is necessarily destructive. Working in a four-man rotation, seven innings a start and occasionally eight or nine, for some pitchers, might be all right. The critical factor isn't the number of innings pitched, but the number of innings pitched when tired. You can destroy a pitcher's arm with 30 innings if that means two games of 15 innings each. But Saberhagen is still awfully young—he turned 23 after the season started—he is small, and he has a history of arm trouble.

Under those circumstances, to allow Saberhagen to pitch eight or nine innings a start, start after start, in the early part of the season, was an awful gamble. Saberhagen's innings pitched for his first 18 starts of the year read, 9, 8, 8, 9, 8, 9, 7, 9, 9, 5, 9, 9, 9, 7⅔, 9, 9, 7, and 9. In the game that he pitched 7⅔ he threw 142 pitches. What makes this so irritating, in retrospect, is that it was so unnecessary. Those games include wins by the scored of 13–1, 10–2, 6–1, 4–0, 4–1, 6–1, 6–1, 10–5, 6–0, and 10–3. In Saberhagen's first 16 starts the Royals outscored the opposition 99 to 35. In game after game, the risks involved in letting somebody else finish up would have been minimal; the worst reliever in baseball couldn't have lost more than a couple of those games. For the season as a whole, Royals starters still led the league ERA at 3.80 and led the majors in innings pitched with 1,079 (see chart), but it was really a quarter of a season of magnificent starting pitching and three-quarters of a season of average starting pitching.

While Saberhagen was working like a dray horse, Quisenberry was going to rot in the bullpen. Through August 13 Quisenberry had a 2.01 ERA, with 39 hits allowed and 9 walks in 40⅓ innings. That comes to a little under ten innings a month, for a guy making $2.5 million a year or something and pitching fine. Gardner couldn't find a role for a man with a 2.01 ERA, not an inning here and an inning there, not long relief, not finishing up some of those 6–1 games. This was wunnerful for Quisenberry's confidence.

In the second half of the season, Saberhagen wasn't the same pitcher. The workload had been maybe 2 percent too heavy, just enough to break the camel's back. These are team-level mistakes; Gardner handled Beniquez, Saberhagen, and Quisenberry in such a way that each was essentially destroyed, of no value to the team during the formative stages of the pennant race.

Gardner wanted to handle every player the way he himself was handled when he had his best year with Baltimore in 1957. He played every game that year, led the league in at bats. He wanted to put players in the lineup and forget about them, or put them on the bench and forget about them. He wanted to sort the roster into 13 guys who would play and 12 who would watch. He refused to disturb the team by making day to day decisions about which player was better against this pitcher in this park on this day; he thought that either this player was better or that one was, and that was all there was to it. This approach destroyed the bench, let the bullpen atrophy, and overloaded the starting pitching. Looking backward, I understand much better the failure of the Twins to develop beyond a point in Gardner's hands.

A WHOLE NEW BALLGAME

I take baseball seriously. Arrive slightly late at the ballpark? Unthinkable. Miss an at-bat to visit the concession stand? Intolerable. Leave before the game is over, even if the score is 15–0? Unpardonable. Work a respectable 8-to-5 job and miss afternoon league championship games? Unacceptable, I quit. Even desire, it must be admitted, has usually played second fiddle to my romance with baseball, a fact driven home to me most conspicuously one freezing April night at Royals Stadium as gale force winds ripped through a lady and me while the home nine struggled to defeat the visiting Mauchingbirds. The lady, possessor of those most desirable of female characteristics, high physical attractiveness and low moral standards, was ready to leave after the third, but neither her implied promise of ever-lowering moral standards if only we would depart for someplace warm, nor the 11–2 California rout taking place on the field could sway me: the game must be seen through to its conclusion. Unfortunately, by the time it was over, so was my relationship with the lady—such is the price I pay for taking baseball seriously.

But that is merely by way of prologue to some momentous events that occurred in my life on the last day of the '87 season. Early that morning my friend Jane called and said, "I hear you have an extra ticket for the ballgame."

"Yeah, I do, but I can't find anyone who wants to go. You interested?"

"No, I'm not," she replied. "But Molly is. And we could use a babysitter for this afternoon. Can you help us out?"

Help them out? Take a four-year-girl—even a sweetie, as Molly unquestionably is—to a major-league baseball game? Let's be clear about something: I most assuredly do not share W. C. Fields attitudes toward children. When I visit my friends who have kids, I often end up on the floor with them, ignoring the friends, and not always because I have drunk too deeply. After all, kids and I are natural allies—we have the same level of maturity. But still, take a four-year-old to the ballpark? Do you take a four-year-old to hear *The Messiah?* To see the Louvre? This would be an act unprecedented in my experience. Could I steel myself to do it? After all, Jane and Dan are my closest friends, and I owe them a lot. And yet . . . a four-year-old at the ballpark—with me?

I arrived at Jane and Dan's an hour before game time. The insouciant Molly, wearing Royals T-shirt and waving world championship pennant, greeted me with her usual "Hi, Mike Kopf." (It is her habit, derivation unknown, to call me by my full name. I've told her time and again that "Mr. Kopf" will suffice.) Immediately I had a sense that this baseball outing was going to be different. Usually the last thing I do before heading for the stadium is double check my beer cooler. This time my last act was to carefully strap Molly into her car seat.

"I'm not sure I trust you with my daughter, Kopf," Dan hollered as we backed out of the driveway.

"Not to worry," I yelled back. "She's as safe as if she was with Ted Kennedy."

"Who is Ted Kennedy?" Molly asked.

"He plays left field for the Twins. Good hitter, but he runs the bases like he's under water."

We arrived at Royals Stadium without incident, and once again I could see that things would be different. Generally I race from parking lot to gate clutching binoculars, scoresheet, and one last can of beer. Today I took a leisurely stroll, holding a little girl's hand. Invariably, once inside the park, my first act is to scribble down the lineups. On this day our first act was to seek a cotton-candy vendor. Jane had alerted me in advance, so it wasn't too great a shock.

"Cotton candy is my favorite, Mike Kopf," Molly said between nibbles as we took our seats in the upper deck.

"I know just what you mean, Molly," I replied. "I remember when cotton candy was my favorite, too," and strangely, I did have a sudden sense of those long-past days, over thirty years ago, when a stick of cotton candy seemed more desirable than a Sunday doubleheader. Long before alcohol had subverted my tastebuds, it had been sweet stuff all the way, and cotton candy is the sweetest of the sweet. Why had I forgotten for so long?

My reveries were interrupted by the appearance of some Twins in front of their dugout, including the one player who is a particular object of my disapproval. "Hrbek, you fat pig!" I screamed. "Back to the slaughterhouse where you belong." This was cleverly stated, I thought, but resulted only in growls and snarls from adjacent fans. Too late I noted the insignia on caps and jackets—Molly and I had washed up on an island of Twins fans, down from Minnesota for the grand finale, and naturally many of them were males of Paul Bunyanesque stature. If looks could kill, I would now be communicating from the spirit world. Sensing that I had been warned, I subsided into tactful silence, and just as the tension seemed to be dissolving, Molly shouted, "Hrbek, you fat pig!"

"No, Molly, no," I spluttered, panic-stricken. "He's not a fat pig. I was just fooling. He's really the salt of the earth, Molly, the salt of the earth!" I said this loudly enough, I hoped, for everyone in the vicinity to hear. Then, in a desperate attempt to distract her, I asked if I might sample a bit of her cotton candy. "It tastes great, Mike Kopf," she remarked as I tore off a small piece. "Less filling, Molly," I chortled, though the witticism was lost on her, no connoisseur of Lite beer commercials. But there was no doubt as to who won the argument—cotton candy definitely still tasted great. Before long, being, like Oscar Wilde, able to resist anything except temptation, I began to contemplate purchasing a whole stick for myself, and only the thought of being mistaken for a punk rocker with a pinkish-gray beard dissuaded me. Eventually I remembered that I had come to watch a ballgame, and managed to copy the lineups onto my scoresheet.

The game began and I focused my attention, carefully noting all of the plays. The Royals took control early. Molly followed the action sporadically, and applauded wildly when cued by the crowd. Soon her cotton candy was gone and she sat pink-faced and beaming. "Will you wipe my face, Mike Kopf?" she asked amiably. Wipe her face? With two on and only one out? I set down my score sheet and groped for my handkerchief, hoping it was not too snot-encrusted. I think I did a middling fair job of cleaning her, all things considered, and was congratulating myself on my success as a surrogate mother when the roar of the crowd brought me back to reality and I looked up in time to see Seitzer's gapper carom off the wall. Runners sped around the bases, and I grabbed for my scoresheet, only to discover that, according to my calculations, the number nine hitter was still at bat. What happened to Pecota? How had Wilson reached base? It was only the third inning, and my scoresheet was a shambles. It was all the fault of the imp sitting beside me. She turned to me and the most virulent recriminations balanced on the tip of my tongue. "Can I have a coke, Mike Kopf?"

I hesitated. Perhaps my scoresheet could yet be salvaged—surely one of the adjacent Twins fans could fill me in. And Molly, after all, was only a four-year-old girl. It was difficult to imagine, but rumor was rife that I had once been four. "Of course you can, Molly," and a vendor was summoned. She took her first sip as the inning ended and I busied myself repairing my scoresheet.

The innings slipped past, and the Royals turned the game into a rout. Hrbek, the fat pig, fanned twice, but I maintained a discreet silence. Molly finished her coke, and shifted her attention to the fans, studying intently the variety of their hats. The sun washed down upon us; a perfect Indian summer day. The Royals were mounting yet another threat when Molly asked, "Could I please have some peanuts, Mike Kopf?"

"Sure thing, Molly," I smiled. "I think I'm ready for some myself." Then I realized that I hadn't seen a peanut vendor since the second inning. That meant only one

thing—a trip to the concession stand. Even if I waited for the inning to end (and a long wait it might be; the Royals had two on with none out) I was certain to miss at least two at-bats, probably more. What would become of my scoresheet? I hadn't left a ballpark with an imperfect scoresheet in years; it was unthinkable. I could easily tell Molly that I was out of money, or that she would just have to wait. After all, four-year-old girls have no divine right to peanuts, do they? "I'll be right back, Molly," I heard myself saying. "I'm going to get us some peanuts."

The concession line was even longer than I had feared. By the time I returned with the peanuts, the Twins had already come to bat. There was no hope of reconstructing my scoresheet. It suddenly didn't seem so important after all. I set it aside with a shrug and concentrated on my peanuts. After awhile, Molly took it in hand and began to obliterate the home runs and stolen bases with her impressions of the physiognomy of the spectators. "That's a good one, Molly," I nodded, as she ruthlessly caricatured an elderly Twins fans sitting in front of us. "Next time I think I'll take you to the Louvre."

Before long, with the cotton candy, coke, and peanuts consumed, and the score steadily mounting in the Royals favor, Molly was ready to go home. Seven innings had been played. As we started down the ramp, Molly said she wanted one more stick of cotton candy, to share at home with her brother Isaac. Fair enough; I accosted a vendor, and then made the mistake of pulling two dollars out of my pocket—enough for two cotton candies. After thirty-plus years of cold turkey, did I dare? "Give me two," I said. I figured in the parking lot, almost devoid at this time of fans, no one would notice a middle-aged child.

When we reached the car Molly said, "You sure look funny with a pink-and-gray beard, Mike Kopf."

"I'm going to be playing in a punk rock band, Molly. Did you have a nice time?"

"Yes, I had a nice time. I just go for the fun."

"That's a pretty good reason to go, Molly," I said. "And it was nice of you to remind me."

—Mike Kopf

OAKLAND ATHLETICS

The lesson of the Oakland A's is that you can, too, have too much pitching. I wrote a year ago that "the most serious question is whether or not LaRussa can identify in spring training a group of pitchers who not only will pitch well for a time, but who have a shot at staying in the rotation and carrying the ball all the way. . . . If LaRussa can identify those five pitchers (from among Young, Haas, Stewart, Andujar, Codiroli, Mooneyham, Rijo, Plunk, Birtsas, Nelson, and Krueger), the A's will win this division."

Maybe the five men just weren't there, but in any case LaRussa didn't find them, and that was the story of the season. The A's opened April with a rotation of Young, Plunk, Codiroli, Stewart, and Rijo. Two of them were terrific. Three were terrible. Four hundred as a hitter is great; two for five in choosing pitchers won't get it done. Stewart and Young had a .623 winning percentage; the rest of the team was at .440. It was the second-largest such gap in the majors (see Cincinnati).

The A's rolled to a 2–9 start. They righted the rotation by inserting Moose Haas (May 1) and Steve Ontiveros (May 19) and scrambled back into the race. By June 28 they were seven games over .500 at 40–33. Then the rotation began to degenerate. Haas couldn't continue. Curt Young was out of action for three weeks, and struggled upon his return. When Andujar was ready to pitch (or was coerced into pitching, depending on who you believe), he wasn't effective. It was back to square one: Who do we try next?

If a team has only five candidates for starting jobs, that's trouble, because a couple won't come through. If a team has seven candidates they have protection. If they have eleven candidates, they have confusion. All pitchers go up and down during the season. Having pitchers waiting in the wings undermines the commitment to work out the problems of the pitchers on the downswing. If a pitcher is struggling and Joaquin Andujar or Moose Haas is ready to come off the disabled list, the manager has to jerk the guy who is struggling out of the rotation and try Andujar or Haas. If he doesn't work out you try the next guy. It's real easy for the season to turn into a running experiment with the starting rotation. The ultimate example was Gene Nelson. Nelson didn't start until August 12, but when he pitched well his first three outings LaRussa was talking about his being a 20-game winner in 1988. Then he had three more starts and it was back to the bullpen; his stint in the starting rotation lasted a little less than a month. If the guy happens to pitch well, like Dave Stewart, great, but if he doesn't you just try somebody else. It's unhealthy for the staff, I think, for there to be such a weak commitment to the rotation.

This is still a pitcher's park. You might lose track of that, because the A's score and allow so many runs. In 81 home games, the A's scored 363 runs and allowed 351. On the road, they scored 443 and allowed 438. On the road, they were second in the majors in runs scored, be-

hind Detroit, but third in the majors in most runs allowed. The park kept McGwire, Canseco et al. from possibly leading the league in runs scored. It also kept Plunk, Rijo et al. from leading the league in runs allowed.

In any park, it is tough to win by battering the opposition 7–5 and 11–10. In a pitcher's park, it's impossible. In an extreme hitters' park, to win 90 games you have to be near the league lead in runs scored. In an extreme pitcher's park, to win 90 games you have to be near the league lead in ERA. If your pitching is truly just average and the park knocks 40 to 50 points off your ERA, that will put you near the league lead. If your pitching staff or your offense is truly below average, you don't have much chance of winning 90 games. It'll happen once in a while, but not often.

The Oakland staff ERA was 4.32, better than the American League average, but not nearly good enough in this park. When scoring three to five runs, the A's record was 23–38, one of the worse in baseball (see Cleveland chart). The A's had only 67 quality starts, about 20 less than they need (KC and Minnesota, in better hitting parks, had 84 and 80, respectively.) The A's won a lot of poorly pitched games, including 38 games in which they didn't get a quality start (most in the majors except for Milwaukee).

OK, the quality start count is misleading, because LaRussa often removes a starting pitcher an out or two away from a quality start. The A's had 67 quality starts, but 77 starts with game scores of 50 or better. Thirty-one times, most in the American League, LaRussa removed the starting pitcher before he had pitched six innings or allowed four runs, (see San Francisco charts). The A's won 20 of those 31 games. Although Jay Howell started the season as the closer and wasn't good, the A's long relief was very good, with Dennis Eckersley (early season), Dave Leiper (all year), Ontiveros (very early), and Gene Nelson (almost all year). All four had good ERAs, with composite strikeout/walk totals of 233/71, not counting performance as a starter.

Maybe I shouldn't spend much time on this right here, but who the hell decided to put Jay Howell on the All-Star team? Howell hasn't pitched well consistently since the first half of the 1985 season. After making the All-Star team (legitimately) in 1985, Howell had a second-half ERA about 5.00. In 1986 he spent two spans on the disabled list and pitched well at times but poorly at other times, finishing 3–6 with a 3.38 ERA. As of July 9, 1987, about the day he was selected to the All-Star game, he had an ERA of 4.41. He had lost his job as the bullpen closer to Dennis Eckersley, and had pitched only 33 innings.

But John McNamara, or some other nitwit, decided to put Howell on the All-Star team. Here's your choice: Jay Howell, Frank Viola (131 innings, 3.09 ERA and 7–6 record), Jimmie Key (138 innings, 2.93 ERA, 9–5 record), Charlie Leibrandt (127 innings with a 2.70 ERA, 8–6 record), or Dennis Eckersley (70 innings with 2.84

ERA, 5–4 record and 59–12 K/W ratio). There are other options, of course—Roger Clemens, Curt Young, Bert Blyleven, Rick Rhoden, Dave Stewart, Jeff Reardon. The only one who made the All-Star team is the guy with the 4.41 ERA in 33 innings who has pitched himself out of the closer role. Who is responsible for this, and why hasn't he been brought up on charges? I know I'm over-reacting, but I was furious about this before the game was played. When Howell actually had to pitch and immediately lost the game, bringing to an end a 15-inning scoreless match, I was fit to be tied. How about we name an All-Stupid team next year, instead? I know where we can find a hell of a manager.

Anyway, back to the A's. LaRussa went to the bullpen early because the long relievers were good and the starters weren't, but I think this also undermines the development of a solid starting rotation. Starting pitchers who come out of the game at the first sign of trouble frequently lose their confidence. Oakland starting pitchers pitched only 939 innings, fewest in the league except for Baltimore. It should be noted that LaRussa was very successful at building a rotation in Chicago.

Despite finishing eleventh in the league in batting average, .260, the A's scored 806 runs (sixth in the league) because of a secondary average of .301, second best in baseball. They were the only American League team that was above average in all the primary elements of secondary average—home runs (199, league average 188), walks (593, average 588), and stolen bases (140, average 124). A lot of people thought the injury to Dwayne Murphy improved the offense, pushing Luis Polonia into the outfield. It didn't (Polonia hit .287 but had an on base percentage of .335; Murphy hit 54 points lower but had an on base percentage 53 points higher), but the development of McGwire and Steinbach obviously did. The profile of a championship team in a pitcher's park: average number of runs scored, lead the league in ERA. The A's had the offense.

The A's appear to be the preseason favorite in this division. I would not want to spend much time trying to look ahead; if you put too much effort into trying to foresee the future, you begin to kid yourself that you can, and then as an analyst you are lost. Obviously the Bob Welch trade strengthens the A's. Walt Weiss, projected to start at shortstop, was regarded in the Southern League as a major-league defensive player, while as an offensive player he is likely to be within ten runs of contributing as much as Alfredo. (It will improve the offense, for one thing, just to get the shortstop out of the middle of the batting order.) While Weiss at short is a gamble because of his limited professional experience, one ordinarily assumes that the primary responsibility for keeping the other side from scoring belongs to the pitching staff.

That trade addresses a real need in an intelligent way. But like the Royals, the A's made one trade which will help them, and one trade which won't. My view of the Dave Parker trade is that it is the same song, third verse. A few years ago the A's thought they had improved the team when Dave Kingman started hitting home runs for them. A year ago, we heard how Reggie Jackson was going to make this team a winner just like he did all of his

other teams. Now it's Dave Parker—another old power hitter with a big rep and a big swing who is going to strike out 120 times and give the press something to write about.

In 1987 McGwire, Canseco, and Parker hit 106 homers and drove in 328 runs. In 1988 I'll bet they're down, collectively, 20 homers and 80 RBI. With the new strike zone, the big players will suffer most. This is probably the biggest lineup in baseball. McGwire is almost sure to be down. Parker turns 37 in June and is moving to a tougher park. Last year all three were in the lineup virtually every day; this year all three of them might be hurt. With fewer walks, there will be fewer people on base when you start through the three of them, and God knows there won't be many people left on base by the time you get to the number five spot.

The A's had a good offense anyway. The strength of the offense was in power; now they have another power hitter. It seems to me that when you have two oversized, free-swinging sluggers, there is not a great incremental value in adding a third. The A's had a poor defense last year; the trade of Griffin and the addition of Parker makes it weaker on the one hand and more suspect on the other. I'm not a big fan of Mike Davis, but I'd rather have Davis in right field than Dave Parker. A year from now 70 percent of Oakland fans will agree with me.

Pitching and defense interact. A great deal of what people think is pitching is in fact defense, which is one reason people think that baseball is 75 percent pitching or something. The A's of '87 were one of the poorest defensive teams in the American League. Their ratio of errors to double plays (122 to 142) was one of the worst in baseball. Their Defensive Efficiency Record, which is usually high because of the ballpark, was below average. The A's had 14 games in which they committed more than two errors (only Cleveland had more), and they lost 11 of the 14 games.

Tony Bernazard, though he is a player that I like, is not a glove wizard. He doesn't turn the double play very well, isn't lightning quick, doesn't cover a lot of ground. Glenn Hubbard is a player I like even more, for his hustle, ability to get on base and ability to turn the double play; even so, he's 30, and not the calibre of player who lasts much past 30. He might hit .190 in this park. Adding Hubbard and losing Tony Phillips is an even trade. Lansford at third has limited range, particularly damaging in view of the large foul territory in the Coliseum. The Oakland outfield, a few years ago the best in the majors, had only 21 assists last year, tying Milwaukee for the fewest of any team. If Parker is in the outfield this year, they may have more assists but they won't have a better defensive outfield. Steinbach seems to have good tools, but he's been catching only about two and a half years. Canseco is decent but episodic, Polonia can't throw long and Parker should be a DH.

You know that old saw about championship teams being strong up the middle? How many proven, quality players do the A's have up the middle? If you can find one, you can count higher than I can. Opening the season, the Seattle Mariners are stronger at all four up-the-middle positions. The A's will improve defensively in 1988 if Weiss turns out to be a Gold Glove candidate and Stan Javier develops as a hitter, but counting on rookies and unproven player to take care of your defense is like counting on TV evangelists to take care of the poor.

I think there are still too many pitchers here. There are almost as many candidates for starting jobs as there were last year: Young, Stewart, Welch, Storm Davis, Honeycutt, Ontiveros, Nelson, Codiroli, Tom Dozier, Tim Meeks. I'm not sure that all of these people are still on the roster, but as far as I know they are. Adding Bob Welch obviously improves LaRussa's chance of finding the five men he needs, but in April 1987, Andujar's credentials were as good as Welch's are now (53 wins in three years), and Codiroli's were as good as Ontiveros'.

If I was forced to pick this division, I guess I might pick the A's, but without much enthusiasm. Seattle is trying to build a team which is really *good*. The A's are trying to rush the process, get an instant winner even if, like the 1983 White Sox, the whole thing falls apart in a season. It is possible that the new DP combination of Hubbard and Weiss will improve the Oakland defense dramatically. Even so, they might not win. I foresee two scenarios for the A's, one in which the defense continues to plague them, and one in which they pay such a price to solidify the defense that the offense doesn't click. The A's won 81 last year, and they should be better—but not much better. I expect them to win 84 to 88 games. The real question is whether that will be enough.

SECONDARY AVERAGE

Detroit	.314
Oakland	.301
Mets	.300
Toronto	.298
Milwaukee	.289
Atlanta	.288
Texas	.288
Yankees	.285
Minnesota	.285
San Francisco	.284
Philadelphia	.284
Cincinnati	.284
Seattle	.279
Cubs	.278
St. Louis	.277
California	.276
Boston	.274
Chicago	.271
Cleveland	.271
Kansas City	.268
Baltimore	.266
Pittsburgh	.260
San Diego	.260
Montreal	.256
Houston	.246
Los Angeles	.223

RUNS SCORED AND ALLOWED WINS AND LOSSES

Wins	557	259	81-0	1.000
Young	171	129	20-11	.645
Ontiveros	119	100	12-10	.545
Stewart	175	159	20-17	.541
Blowouts	281	268	25-21	.543
Home Games	363	351	42-39	.519
Slugfests	470	479	35-34	.507
Pitchers' Duels	58	58	14-14	.500
All Games	806	789	81-81	.500
Road Games	443	438	39-42	.481
One Run Games	199	206	20-27	.426
Losses	249	530	0-81	.000

TEN BEST STARTS

	IP	H	R	ER	BB	SO		
Ontiveros at Cle, June 28	9	2	0	0	6	W	89
Stewart vs. Tor, May 17	9	4	0	0	3	7	W	83
Stewart at Tex, June 12	9	4	1	1	3	9	W	81
Stewart vs. Cal, July 27	9	5	1	1	0	6	W	79
Young vs. Chi, June 9	9	1	3	2	3	7	W	79
Stewart vs. Min, Aug 1	9	8	2	2	1	14	W	76
Young vs. Cal, Apr 12	9	5	1	1	2	5	W	76
Stewart vs. Chi, Sep 25	9	6	1	1	2	6	—	75
Plunk vs. Det, May 3	8⅓	6	0	0	3	5	W	73
Stewart vs. Mil, Apr 30	7⅓	3	1	1	3	8	W	73

PITCHERS WHEN SUPPORTED BY THREE TO FIVE RUNS

	G	IP	W-L	Pct	SO	BB	ERA
Young	8	57	2-1	.667	43	14	2.67
Stewart	14	100	17-5	.583	85	46	3.52
Ontiveros	10	60	3-3	.500	35	17	3.90

HALL OF FAME WATCH

Fully qualified: Reggie Jackson, 165; **Building credentials but not yet viable candidate:** Ron Cey 55, Andujar 33; **Working on it:** Eckersley 27, Lavelle 26, LaRussa 25, Lansford 17.5, Caudill 16, McGuire 15, Canseco 12, Griffin 10; **Long way to go:** Stewart 8, Murphy 9, Honeycutt 7, Howell 7, Haas 6, Bernazard 5.5, S. Davis 4, Steinbach 1.

ASSISTS BY OUTFIELDERS

Boston	47
Seattle	41
Houston	41
Toronto	40
Philadelphia	39
Pittsburgh	38
St. Louis	37
Texas	33
San Diego	33
White Sox	32
Cincinnati	32
Cubs	32
Minnesota	31
Los Angeles	31
Montreal	30
Atlanta	30
Kansas City	30
Cleveland	29
Yankees	29
San Francisco	26
California	26
Baltimore	24
Detroit	23
Mets	22
Oakland	21
Milwaukee	21

TEN WORST STARTS

	IP	H	R	ER	BB	SO		
Andujar at Mil, July 23	3⅓	8	8	8	1	3	L	14
Stewart vs. KC, Sep 12	4⅓	8	8	7	3	2	L	16
Rijo at Chi, June 30	4⅓	9	7	7	3	3	L	17
Young vs. Tex, June 20	4*	8	7	7	1	3	L	20
Rijo at Sea, Apr 16	3⅔	8	6	5	3	3	L	23
Ontiveros at Cle, Sep 23	3*	8	5	4	1	1	—	25
Ontiveros vs. Det, July 8	3*	6	7	3	3	1	L	25
Plunk vs. Tex, June 21	1⅔	1	6	6	6	3	L	26
Stewart at Bos, May 5	4⅓	6	6	6	4	3	L	26
Haas at Det, May 10	4⅓	8	5	5	1	0	—	26

Terry STEINBACH, Catcher
Runs Created: 62

	G	AB	Hit	2B	3B	HR	Run	RBI	TBB	SO	SB	CS	Avg
0.79 years		514	147	20	4	23	87	76	42	84	1	3	.286
1987	122	391	111	16	3	16	66	56	32	66	1	2	.284
First Half	55	186	49	8	2	7	29	29	19	31	0	1	.263
Second Half	67	205	62	8	1	9	37	27	13	35	1	1	.302
Vs. RHP		254	71	8	0	11	43	41	20	44	1	1	.280
Vs. LHP		137	40	8	3	5	23	15	12	22	0	1	.292
Home	57	175	41	4	0	6	24	22	17	24	0	0	.234
Road	65	216	70	12	3	10	42	34	15	42	1	2	.324

José CANSECO, Left Field
Runs Created: 91

	G	AB	Hit	2B	3B	HR	Run	RBI	TBB	SO	SB	CS	Avg
2.13 years		623	157	31	2	32	85	114	56	170	15	5	.252
1987	159	630	162	35	3	31	81	113	50	157	15	3	.257
First Half	85	338	93	17	1	18	44	55	20	81	9	1	.275
Second Half	74	292	69	18	2	13	37	58	30	76	6	2	.236
Vs. RHP		426	99	23	0	16	45	67	34	111	10	2	.232
Vs. LHP		204	63	12	3	15	36	46	16	46	5	1	.309
Home	79	298	82	17	2	16	41	59	28	66	7	1	.275
Road	80	332	80	18	1	15	40	54	22	91	8	2	.241

Mark MCGWIRE, First Base
Runs Created: 131

	G	AB	Hit	2B	3B	HR	Run	RBI	TBB	SO	SB	CS	Avg
1.04 years		587	164	28	4	50	103	122	72	143	1	2	.279
1987	151	557	161	28	4	49	97	118	71	131	1	1	.289
First Half	80	289	85	10	3	33	59	68	39	68	0	0	.294
Second Half	71	268	76	18	1	16	38	50	32	63	1	1	.284
Vs. RHP		386	112	18	4	33	63	80	36	91	1	0	.290
Vs. LHP		171	49	10	0	16	34	38	35	40	0	1	.287
Home	78	278	77	15	2	21	43	49	38	67	0	0	.277
Road	73	279	84	13	2	28	54	69	33	64	1	1	.301

Luis POLONIA, Center Field
Runs Created: 61

	G	AB	Hit	2B	3B	HR	Run	RBI	TBB	SO	SB	CS	Avg
0.77 years		565	162	21	13	5	101	64	42	83	38	9	.287
1987	125	435	125	16	10	4	78	49	32	64	29	7	.287
First Half	59	213	68	9	5	3	40	26	16	28	18	2	.319
Second Half	66	222	57	7	5	1	38	23	16	36	11	5	.257
Vs. RHP		346	104	14	7	4	64	41	25	47	28	5	.301
Vs. LHP		89	21	2	3	0	14	8	7	17	1	2	.236
Home	53	184	51	12	4	1	30	21	14	27	14	4	.277
Road	72	251	74	4	6	3	48	28	18	37	15	3	.295

Tony BERNAZARD, Second Base
Runs Created: 64

	G	AB	Hit	2B	3B	HR	Run	RBI	TBB	SO	SB	CS	Avg
6.57 years		561	147	25	5	11	80	60	65	92	17	8	.262
1987	140	507	127	26	2	14	73	49	55	79	11	8	.250
First Half	79	293	70	12	1	11	39	30	25	49	7	4	.239
Second Half	61	214	57	14	1	3	34	19	30	30	4	4	.266
Vs. RHP		368	95	19	1	10	53	33	36	57	8	6	.258
Vs. LHP		139	32	7	1	4	20	16	19	22	3	2	.230
Home	66	227	54	12	1	3	28	16	24	31	5	5	.238
Road	74	280	73	14	1	11	45	33	31	48	6	3	.261

Mike DAVIS, Right Field
Runs Created: 72

	G	AB	Hit	2B	3B	HR	Run	RBI	TBB	SO	SB	CS	Avg
4.86 years		524	140	29	3	17	76	69	40	93	25	10	.267
1987	139	494	131	32	1	22	69	72	42	94	19	7	.265
First Half	78	298	87	22	1	20	49	53	29	55	11	6	.292
Second Half	61	196	44	10	0	2	20	19	13	39	8	1	.224
Vs. RHP		368	96	24	0	16	53	44	32	63	19	4	.261
Vs. LHP		126	35	8	1	6	16	28	10	31	0	3	.278
Home	67	234	61	17	0	9	36	31	21	45	7	1	.261
Road	72	260	70	15	1	13	33	41	21	49	12	6	.269

Carney LANSFORD, Third Base
Runs Created: 96

	G	AB	Hit	2B	3B	HR	Run	RBI	TBB	SO	SB	CS	Avg
7.96 years		632	184	30	4	17	91	80	48	71	17	8	.291
1987	151	554	160	27	4	19	89	76	60	44	27	8	.289
First Half	79	288	81	16	1	9	47	36	40	31	19	3	.281
Second Half	72	266	79	11	3	10	42	40	20	13	8	5	.297
Vs. RHP		379	111	23	4	11	61	54	43	28	24	7	.293
Vs. LHP		175	49	4	0	8	28	22	17	16	3	1	.280
Home	75	271	78	16	3	9	39	31	31	25	12	5	.288
Road	76	283	82	11	1	10	50	45	29	19	15	3	.290

Reggie JACKSON, Designated Hitter
Runs Created: 42

	G	AB	Hit	2B	3B	HR	Run	RBI	TBB	SO	SB	CS	Avg
17.41 years		567	148	27	3	32	89	98	79	149	13	7	.261
1987	115	336	74	14	1	15	42	43	33	97	2	1	.220
First Half	72	234	47	9	1	11	33	32	24	65	2	1	.201
Second Half	43	102	27	5	0	4	9	11	9	32	0	0	.265
Vs. RHP		288	60	9	1	13	35	35	31	82	2	1	.208
Vs. LHP		48	14	5	0	2	7	8	2	15	0	0	.292
Home	57	165	36	8	0	7	23	24	17	57	0	0	.218
Road	58	171	38	6	1	8	19	19	16	40	2	1	.222

Alfredo GRIFFIN, Shortstop
Runs Created: 52

	G	AB	Hit	2B	3B	HR	Run	RBI	TBB	SO	SB	CS	Avg
8.47 years		579	149	22	8	3	67	47	26	51	19	13	.257
1987	144	494	130	23	5	3	69	60	28	41	26	13	.263
First Half	80	287	73	12	2	1	35	25	18	23	14	7	.254
Second Half	64	207	57	11	3	2	34	35	10	18	12	6	.275
Vs. RHP		306	84	16	4	2	49	41	17	28	18	7	.275
Vs. LHP		188	46	7	1	1	20	19	11	13	8	6	.245
Home	70	233	55	9	2	2	27	29	12	22	15	7	.236
Road	74	261	75	14	3	1	42	31	16	19	11	6	.287

Tony PHILLIPS, Second Base
Runs Created: 49

	G	AB	Hit	2B	3B	HR	Run	RBI	TBB	SO	SB	CS	Avg
3.78 years		509	129	22	4	7	72	52	66	99	14	8	.253
1987	111	379	91	20	0	10	48	46	57	76	7	6	.240
First Half	83	294	75	17	0	8	41	35	47	58	7	6	.255
Second Half	28	85	16	3	0	2	7	11	10	18	0	0	.188
Vs. RHP		251	54	17	0	7	30	30	32	59	6	5	.215
Vs. LHP		128	37	3	0	3	18	16	25	17	1	1	.289
Home	55	175	44	8	0	5	26	19	28	40	6	4	.251
Road	56	204	47	12	0	5	22	27	21	36	1	2	.230

SEATTLE MARINERS

The Seattle Mariners treat talent as if it were a free resource. About 5:00 one winter morn some 16 years ago I rolled out of bed with 130 equally disaffected strangers. We gathered in front of the barracks, made a formation, and marched over a mile. Spreading out, we meandered down a half-mile grass strip between the two lanes of a highway, "policing the area," which is military talk for picking up all the little bits of paper and trash. This took maybe 20 minutes, but with the formation and the march to and the march back it took well over an hour, every day. I estimated that the Army was spending about $1,800 a week ($7,800 a month) to keep the paper picked up on this little stretch of grass between the two lanes of a highway.

The problem was that the generals were in the habit of thinking of manpower as a free resource. Economists used to refer to things like air and water, which could be used by anyone without charge, as free resources. They were assumed to be available in unlimited supply. At one time grazing lands were a free resource. Probably at some point in the early history of man, the land was a free resource. Now it is realized that even air and water are limited, and I don't think economists even use the term anymore.

Military officers didn't use the term, either, but when I entered the Army I was paid something like $70 a month. If one man got killed or served his time or ran away, they just drafted another one; they didn't worry about what it cost. My monthly salary rose rapidly, however, not because I was a good soldier but because Congress was regularly raising the salaries of lower-ranked enlisted men. This was toward the end of the Vietnam era, and it no longer seemed viable to draft men and pay them nothing. The society would no longer accept it. With the draft discontinued, soldiers were being paid substantial sums of money to reenlist—and the generals, once those men had reenlisted, were ordering these expensive soldiers to march in circles about 80 hours a month, at a cost of billions of dollars.

Being treated for two years as if I were essentially worthless impressed a lesson upon me: the more talent available to you, the less respect you have for it. The Seattle Mariners' farm system over the last five years has been as good as any. Last year Danny Tartabull, a 1986 graduate of the Seattle farms, hit .309 with 34 homers and 101 RBI—for Kansas City. Ivan Calderon, a 1985 graduate, hit .293 with 28 homers and 83 RBI—for the White Sox. Both men are young, and one might think that the Mariners perhaps would project what their team would look like with those men in left and right fields over the next ten years, slap themselves in the forehead and say "we can't let that happen again."

The Mariners, however, still have all kinds of young talent, so they think it's a free resource, never going to run out. Not properly chastised for having disposed of Tartabull and Calderon, they went for the hat trick with Phil Bradley. The Mariners have by far the worst record in the majors during the 1980s, a .427 winning percentage. In a decade in which everyone else has been up and down, the Mariners have been down and down further. Their record over their first 11 years is the poorest of any expansion team except the Padres. They have intact a streak of 11 consecutive losing seasons, the longest streak in the majors since the Kansas City A's streak ended in 1967. The failure of the team to improve dramatically is in part due to the organization's failure to perceive a simple reality: that young men who can play baseball are precious to baseball teams. You shouldn't give one away unless you also acquire one.

My first reaction to the Phil Bradley trade was that it was another mistake, worse than the Tartabull fiasco. While I admire Dick Williams, I don't admire him blindly. His interaction with Bradley shows some of his bad side, focusing on personalities rather than productivity. Glenn Wilson isn't the player that Phil Bradley is. Wilson's 102 RBI in 1985 was a fluke; Bradley's 101 runs scored in 1987 is an ability.

Later, I found a videotape of a game Mike Jackson started, and got a look at his fastball. Jackson's basic numbers, aside from that ugly won-lost mark (3–10), aren't bad. He had a 4.20 ERA, near the league average (4.08), but in 109 innings he gave up only 88 hits and struck out 93. Then you take out Jackson's stats as a starter: seven games, 6.68 ERA, more walks than strikeouts. His ERA in relief was barely over 3.00, with more than twice as many strikeouts as walks. Them are pretty fair stats for a 22-year-old kid (now 23) who is capable of getting a lot better. In the minors Jackson was a reliever; he just didn't handle the starting role. Physically, he is built in the Bob Gibson mold, a six-foot, 185-pound right-hander, superb athlete. I realize now that this man definitely has the ability to save that trade.

If anybody really understands what the trouble between Bradley and Williams was about, he never wrote it up so I could understand it. Williams talked about Bradley being a cancer on the team, a cliché image which does absolutely nothing to explain what the problem was. All it says is "I don't like him." You wish that these people would go so far as to say that he's a cancer on the colon of the team, or a cancer in the breast of the team, or something. Give us a hint. A cancer on the wallet, perhaps.

Whatever he was, he wasn't a cancer in left field or a cancer on the batting order. The Mariners were unhappy with Bradley for not hitting with men in scoring position and not driving in runs, but as I think I explained earlier, that hasn't been a problem over a period of years, and wasn't the second half of 1987; it was just a temporary thing where he was taking pitches to allow Reynolds and Donell Nixon to steal second, and then was hitting behind in the count.

One suspects that essentially Bradley was traded because he didn't like Dick Williams and wouldn't pretend to. If you were unhappy with his RBI production, the logical move would be to put him in the leadoff spot. His normal on-base percentage is among the best in baseball, and in 1987 he swiped 40 bases in 50 attempts. For most of the year the Mariner leadoff men were hopeless. Donell Nixon opened the season leading off but was mailed to Calgary hitting .130. John Moses moved back into the center field/leadoff spot and was worse than ever, hitting .223 in 72 games as the leadoff man. When actually leading off the inning, Moses hit .197 (28/142) with a .260 on base percentage. When Bradley was leading off an inning he hit .375 (39/104) and had a .463 on base percentage. He was never used in the leadoff spot, not even once. Harold Reynolds, who led the league in stolen bases, also batted leadoff in only three games, presumably because Williams wanted to keep the pressure off of him.

Led by Bradley and Reynolds, Seattle had 247 stolen base attempts (just missing the league leading total, 250 by Milwaukee), but still lost 132 runners on double plays; altogether they lost more runners by caught stealing or the double-play ball than any other American League team. Official records show Bradley and Reynolds to be comparable base stealers, Reynolds 60 for 80 (75 percent) and Bradley 40 for 50 (80 percent). What the totals don't show is that Reynolds was picked off first without being charged with a caught stealing six times, making him actually 60–26 (70 percent), while Bradley wasn't caught off at all. Mickey Brantley, on the disabled list most of the first half, eventually moved in to solve the leadoff problem, hitting .366 in 44 games as mariner leadoff man.

Then the power went south. The Mariners had, in a sense, a surprising consistency. Broken down into six 27-game sets, their 1987 records were 14–13, 14–13, 12–15, 12–15, 11–17, and 15–12. Their runs scored in those six groups: 133, 126, 107, 132, 126, and 136. Broken down into 10-game sets, the records are almost all between 4–6 and 6–4. With the exception of a July swoon by the pitching staff, neither the offense nor the pitching staff was subject to wild swings.

The reason their offense was so consistent is that when one part started, another stopped. Early in the season, with no leadoff man and Bradley not hitting, they didn't have people on base but Ken Phelps and Jim Presley were hitting home runs and Scott Bradley was hitting .340. Then Phelps stopped hitting for two months, but Phil Bradley hit his stride, Alvin Davis popped 16 homers in July and August, and Rey Quinones and Harold Reynolds got hot. Then Brantley finally solved the leadoff problem, but Davis stopped hitting (.202 in September) and Quinones and Dave Valle tailed off.

After a 3–6 start the Mariners climbed to .500 by April 26. They stayed over .500 most of the first half, which was misleading, as they were being outscored by a substantial margin. The last day on which the Mariners were over .500 was July 16, when their record was 45–44 but they had been outscored by their opponents by 32 runs. Over the second half of the season their won-lost record and their ratio of runs to opposition runs drifted into synch.

On balance, it was not a great year, but it was a better year. My synopsis of this team a year ago was that "I see the Mariners as a much improved team, a team that should have the best record in the history of the organization." The Mariners did improve, from 67 wins to 78, and did post the best record in the history of the organization. Despite rumors circulating about the ownership of the team (a man named Martin Stone was interested in purchasing the Mariners and spiriting them away to Phoenix, while George Argyros talked openly of selling the Mariners and purchasing the San Diego Padres) the Mariners drew over a million fans for the third straight season, with their home attendance being their best since their first season (1977).

Seattle played only 34 one-run games, the fewest of any major-league team, and only 66 games decided by one or two runs, also the fewest of any major-league team. Seattle gave away only 19 intentional walks last year, also the fewest of any major-league team. Williams and I agree about that (see charts).

How do I see the 1988 Mariners? I wouldn't be shocked if they were World Champions. Not only is there some terrific front-line talent here, in Langston, Presley, and Davis, but there is also a lot of good second-line talent, in Harold Reynolds, Scott Bradley, Mike Moore, Mike Kingery, Ken Phelps, and Dave Valle. There are three youngsters who are capable of taking the league by storm, in Rey Quinones, Mickey Brantley, and Mike Campbell.

The Mariners were the youngest team in the division last year, with their regulars and top starters averaging 26.4 years.

The Mariners' outfield is probably the strongest defensively in the division. Mariner outfielders threw out 41 runners last year, second-highest total in baseball. With the addition of Glenn Wilson, the assist total may be even higher in 1988. Mike Kingery, an exceptional outfielder, gunned down 15 men in 114 games. I personally think Kingery could play center field, although Dick Williams has shown little eagerness for the idea. Mariner outfielders also were charged with only 14 errors (an average team is in the low twenties).

The Mariners up the middle are stronger than anyone else in this division. They have two good catchers and a fine double-play combination. The acquisition of Wilson may put Brantley in center. I'm convinced that Brantley as a hitter is very comparable to Calderon and Tartabull, although his ability to play center is unproven.

The Mariners at the corners have two power hitters (Presley and Davis) and three fine defensive players (Presley, Kingery and Wilson).

What, then, do they have to do to win the pennant?

First, they have to solidify the starting pitching. Their chances of doing that are excellent. Mike Moore probably will not go 9–19 again. In his last 12 starts he was 6–5 with a 3.76 ERA in 96 innings. The top prospect at AAA was starting pitcher Mike Campbell, who was 15–2 with a 2.77 ERA in the Pacific Coast League, regarded by *Baseball America* as the number one prospect in the PCL. Ken Dixon, acquired from the Orioles, is just an arm, but it is unusual for a pitcher with a terrific strikeout/walk ratio (Dixon's was 91–27) to be so completely ineffective as Dixon was, so the M's may have spotted a tipoff in his delivery that is causing him to give up all the home runs, or perhaps Williams thinks he can win if he will junk one of his pitches or something.

Steve Trout is on hand. Trout needs a good double-play combination to be effective. He has that here.

Second, they need to improve the bullpen. That may have been accomplished with the acquisition of Jackson. Bill Wilkinson, left-hander, was good last year.

Third, they have to get more out of the offense. They can't go through another four-month period without a leadoff man.

You know that in the last few years there have sprung up a number of statistical reports about teams. Ordinarily I recommend these only once, but one of the very best is *The Seattle Baseball Bulletin*, edited by Steve Russell; several items in this section are taken from it (P.O. Box 221, Redmond, Washington 98073). Russell feels that an essential step in improving the team is to keep Ken Phelps, probably the Mariners best offensive player, in the lineup every day. There is something to be said for this. Phelps

was the Mariner pinch hit for most often in 1987, 26 times. Phelps was lifted against left-handed pitchers, but when he did face left-handed pitchers (51 times) he was quite effective, with a .622 slugging percentage and .451 on-base percentage. Mariner pinch hitters hit .213. Over a period of four years Phelps has been somewhat more effective against right-handed pitchers than lefties, and (as the breakdowns in the 1987 *Great American Baseball Stat Book* show) a power pitcher can really turn off his faucet. But pinch hitting is a tough job, and it is pretty hard to believe that Phelps wouldn't have produced more than the men who pinched him. Phelps as a designated hitter hit 26 homers in 325 at bats; other Mariner DHs hit 8 homers in 248 at bats.

But I remain high on this team. I'll say the same thing I said a year ago: I think this will be the best season the Seattle Mariners have ever had.

INTENTIONAL WALKS ISSUED

San Francisco	86
Philadelphia	86
St. Louis	79
Cincinnati	68
Cubs	67
Toronto	65
Los Angeles	62
San Diego	62
Houston	61
Detroit	61
Pittsburgh	60
Atlanta	55
Mets	51
Baltimore	50
Montreal	45
Minnesota	40
Boston	38
Texas	34
Milwaukee	33
Yankees	31
California	30
White Sox	28
Cleveland	28
Kansas City	27
Oakland	21
Seattle	19

RUNS SCORED AND ALLOWED WINS AND LOSSES

Wins	504	218	78-0	1.000
Langston	160	147	21-14	.600
Guetterman	94	85	10-7	.588
One Run Games	131	127	19-15	.559
Pitchers' Duels	36	34	10-9	.526
Home Games	403	400	40-41	.494
All Games	760	801	78-84	.481
Bankhead	127	133	12-13	.480
Blowouts	273	294	24-27	.471
Road Games	357	401	38-43	.469
Slugfests	391	406	25-31	.446
Morgan	148	166	13-18	.419
Moore	134	165	12-21	.364
Losses	256	583	0-69	.000

TEN BEST STARTS

	IP	H	R	ER	BB	SO		
Langston vs. Tex, June 8	9	2	0	0	1	9	W	91
Langston vs. Tor, May 24	9	4	2	2	3	14	W	82
Bankhead vs. Chi, June 17	8⅔	4	0	0	1	7	W	82
Guetterman at Cle, June 21	9	3	0	0	1	2	W	82
Langston vs. Chi, Sep 13	9	2	2	2	3	9	L	81
Langston at Mil, July 22	9	4	1	1	4	7	W	78
Bankhead vs. Oak, Apr 19	9	5	1	1	3	8	W	78
Langston vs. Cal, Aug 7	9	7	0	0	6	11	W	78
Langston at Cal, Sep 18	9	6	0	0	4	6	W	77
Morgan at Bal, May 30	9	7	0	0	0	4	W	77

PITCHERS WHEN SUPPORTED BY THREE TO FIVE RUNS

	G	IP	W-L	Pct	SO	BB	ERA
Langston	15	118	7-5	.583	118	40	3.80
Guetterman	8	44	3-3	.500	13	10	2.84
Morgan	14	77	4-9	.308	30	24	5.99
Bankhead	10	51	2-5	.286	35	13	7.19
Moore	15	106	3-9	.250	60	36	4.60

HALL OF FAME WATCH

Could be elected on current accomplishments: Dick Williams 79;
Working on it: Phil Bradley 17.5, Langston 17, Mathews 15, A. Davis 11;
Long way to go: Reynolds 6, Presley 3, Moore 2, Quinones 1.

TEN WORST STARTS

	IP	H	R	ER	BB	SO		
Moore at Bos, July 26	3⅓	11	9	7	2	0	L	4
Morgan vs. Cle, Sep 14	3⅔	11	7	7	2	0	L	9
Bankhead at Cal, Sep 17	1	6	6	6	1	0	—	16
Morgan at Min, Apr 20	0*	4	6	6	1	0	L	17
Morgan vs. Bos, July 11	2*	7	6	6	1	0	L	17
Trujillo vs. Bal, May 19	2⅓	6	6	6	2	1	L	20
Moore vs. Bos, Apr 29	1*	6	6	2	3	0	L	22
Bankhead at Det, May 6	5	8	7	7	2	1	L	22
Bankhead at Chi, June 23	4	8	6	6	2	3	L	23
Bankhead at Oak, Apr 25	3*	9	5	5	1	3	L	23

WINNING PERCENTAGE DURING THE EIGHTIES

Yankees	.560
Detroit	.557
St. Louis	.536
Baltimore	.532
Kansas City	.525
Philadelphia	.525
Los Angeles	.525
Boston	.523
Montreal	.523
Houston	.522
Toronto	.517
Milwaukee	.512
Mets	.508
White Sox	.499
Cincinnati	.498
California	.496
Oakland	.482
Atlanta	.481
San Francisco	.480
San Diego	.474
Pittsburgh	.463
Texas	.458
Cubs	.458
Cleveland	.452
Minnesota	.452
Seattle	.427

Scott BRADLEY, Catcher
Runs Created: 36

	G	AB	Hit	2B	3B	HR	Run	RBI	TBB	SO	SB	CS	Avg
1.28 years		494	137	20	4	8	48	58	23	24	1	2	.277
1987	102	342	95	15	1	5	34	43	15	18	0	1	.278
First Half	62	213	62	8	1	2	20	25	7	10	0	1	.291
Second Half	40	129	33	7	0	3	14	18	8	8	0	0	.256
Vs. RHP		288	81	13	1	4	27	34	14	15	0	1	.281
Vs. LHP		54	14	2	0	1	7	9	1	3	0	0	.259
Home	46	145	42	6	1	5	16	24	9	4	0	1	.290
Road	56	197	53	9	0	0	18	19	6	14	0	0	.269

Phil BRADLEY, Left Field
Runs Created: 113

	G	AB	Hit	2B	3B	HR	Run	RBI	TBB	SO	SB	CS	Avg
3.75 years		576	173	30	7	14	92	62	69	119	29	11	.300
1987	158	603	179	38	10	14	101	67	84	119	40	10	.297
First Half	88	326	90	21	10	10	55	38	55	69	25	6	.276
Second Half	70	277	89	17	0	4	46	29	29	50	15	4	.321
Vs. RHP		427	118	23	8	3	68	41	59	89	31	8	.276
Vs. LHP		176	61	15	2	11	33	26	25	30	9	2	.347
Home	81	304	94	18	5	12	57	41	43	64	25	2	.309
Road	77	299	85	20	5	2	44	26	41	55	15	8	.284

Alvin DAVIS, First Base
Runs Created: 111

	G	AB	Hit	2B	3B	HR	Run	RBI	TBB	SO	SB	CS	Avg
3.70 years		596	170	33	2	25	84	99	91	81	2	2	.285
1987	157	580	171	37	2	29	86	100	72	84	0	0	.295
First Half	87	307	93	19	2	10	42	45	43	49	0	0	.303
Second Half	70	273	78	18	0	19	44	55	29	35	0	0	.286
Vs. RHP		372	121	23	2	24	63	74	53	46	0	0	.325
Vs. LHP		208	50	14	0	5	23	26	19	38	0	0	.240
Home	79	277	85	17	1	18	48	55	44	39	0	0	.307
Road	78	303	86	20	1	11	38	45	28	45	0	0	.284

Mickey BRANTLEY, Outfield
Runs Created: 62

	G	AB	Hit	2B	3B	HR	Run	RBI	TBB	SO	SB	CS	Avg
0.73 years		621	173	36	5	23	88	84	47	89	19	7	.279
1987	92	351	106	23	2	14	52	54	24	44	13	4	.302
First Half	40	138	40	8	1	4	22	20	10	15	4	3	.290
Second Half	52	213	66	15	1	10	30	34	14	29	9	1	.310
Vs. RHP		224	70	15	1	7	35	28	16	30	8	3	.313
Vs. LHP		127	36	8	1	7	17	26	8	14	5	1	.283
Home	45	159	51	8	2	11	24	30	8	17	6	4	.321
Road	47	192	55	15	0	3	28	24	16	27	7	0	.286

Harold REYNOLDS, Second Base
Runs Created: 67

	G	AB	Hit	2B	3B	HR	Run	RBI	TBB	SO	SB	CS	Avg
2.36 years		486	117	24	6	1	61	28	37	42	40	16	.241
1987	160	530	146	31	8	1	73	35	39	34	60	20	.275
First Half	87	282	76	16	4	0	38	18	22	16	32	9	.270
Second Half	73	248	70	15	4	1	35	17	17	18	28	11	.282
Vs. RHP		368	101	23	6	0	51	23	29	20	41	13	.274
Vs. LHP		162	45	8	2	1	22	12	10	14	19	7	.278
Home	80	257	60	11	4	1	39	11	22	15	29	9	.233
Road	80	273	86	20	4	0	34	24	17	19	31	11	.315

Mike KINGERY, Right Field
Runs Created: 51

	G	AB	Hit	2B	3B	HR	Run	RBI	TBB	SO	SB	CS	Avg
1.12 years		503	137	29	8	11	56	59	35	65	13	11	.272
1987	120	354	99	25	4	9	38	52	27	43	7	9	.280
First Half	67	182	48	7	4	5	16	30	12	26	6	7	.264
Second Half	53	172	51	18	0	4	22	22	15	17	1	2	.297
Vs. RHP		315	92	24	4	8	36	51	26	35	7	9	.292
Vs. LHP		39	7	1	0	1	2	1	1	8	0	0	.179
Home	61	174	53	17	3	5	23	26	12	22	5	3	.305
Road	59	180	46	8	1	4	15	26	15	21	2	6	.256

Jim PRESLEY, Third Base
Runs Created: 72

	G	AB	Hit	2B	3B	HR	Run	RBI	TBB	SO	SB	CS	Avg
3.28 years		613	158	31	4	27	79	96	37	150	2	2	.258
1987	152	575	142	23	6	24	78	88	38	157	2	0	.247
First Half	86	335	83	10	5	14	46	52	17	102	2	0	.248
Second Half	66	240	59	13	1	10	32	36	21	55	0	0	.246
Vs. RHP		385	91	10	5	19	52	65	26	116	1	0	.236
Vs. LHP		190	51	13	1	5	26	23	12	41	1	0	.268
Home	75	288	74	16	4	11	40	43	13	80	0	0	.257
Road	77	287	68	7	2	13	38	45	25	77	2	0	.237

Ken PHELPS, Designated Hitter
Runs Created: 81

	G	AB	Hit	2B	3B	HR	Run	RBI	TBB	SO	SB	CS	Avg
3.03 years		410	99	15	2	30	72	74	88	106	3	2	.241
1987	120	332	86	13	1	27	68	68	80	75	1	1	.259
First Half	67	199	47	5	0	14	36	36	40	46	0	1	.236
Second Half	53	133	39	8	1	13	32	32	40	29	1	0	.293
Vs. RHP		295	76	9	1	24	61	60	69	67	1	1	.258
Vs. LHP		37	10	4	0	3	7	8	11	8	0	0	.270
Home	61	164	38	6	1	15	33	36	42	34	0	0	.232
Road	59	168	48	7	0	12	35	32	38	41	1	1	.286

Rey QUINONES, Third Base
Runs Created: 57

	G	AB	Hit	2B	3B	HR	Run	RBI	TBB	SO	SB	CS	Avg
1.44 years		549	139	24	2	10	60	54	35	89	3	4	.253
1987	135	478	132	18	2	12	55	56	26	71	1	3	.276
First Half	73	256	74	10	0	9	34	35	15	35	0	2	.289
Second Half	62	222	58	8	2	3	21	21	11	36	1	1	.261
Vs. RHP		347	94	12	1	8	38	38	16	52	1	1	.271
Vs. LHP		131	38	6	1	4	17	18	10	19	0	2	.290
Home	64	221	73	7	1	7	26	34	12	25	0	1	.330
Road	71	257	59	11	1	5	29	22	14	46	1	2	.230

Dave VALLE, Catcher
Runs Created: 38

	G	AB	Hit	2B	3B	HR	Run	RBI	TBB	SO	SB	CS	Avg
0.99 years		479	121	21	3	18	57	77	24	76	2	0	.253
1987	95	324	83	16	3	12	40	53	15	46	2	0	.256
First Half	47	150	45	11	3	10	26	36	11	17	1	0	.300
Second Half	48	174	38	5	0	2	14	17	4	29	1	0	.218
Vs. RHP		176	38	6	0	5	24	20	6	28	2	0	.216
Vs. LHP		148	45	10	3	7	16	33	9	18	0	0	.304
Home	51	180	44	10	0	8	25	28	8	23	1	0	.244
Road	44	144	39	6	3	4	15	25	7	23	1	0	.271

CHICAGO WHITE SOX

One of the basic differences between a good organization and a poor organization is that a good organization will still get something out of a bad year. Rarely, if ever, have I seen a team get as much out of a bad year as the White Sox did in 1987.

The White Sox opened the 1987 season hoping to contend. "No one in the Western Division scares us," said Larry Himes, who also is not afraid of the Tidy Bowl Man, the Tooth Fairy, or the Keebler elves. "When we left spring training the club had a good attitude. It still thinks it can win." The problem with trying to win with an attitude is that the attitude changes from day to day, but that's another story. Early in the season it became apparent that this was not a year that the Sox would win anything. They played poorly in April and worse in June. By June 28 the White Sox were all but eliminated with a record of 25–46. Catcher Ron Karkovice, projected as a potential star, hit less than a third of his weight and was returned to Hawaii.

Twenty games under (actually, 22) seemed to be a floor for the White Sox, however; they hit that and bounced off for two and a half months. Thirty-nine times between June 27 and September 13 the White Sox hung up another game and checked the standings to find themselves 20 to 22 games under .500—but never once did they drop to 23 under. The Sox did a good job of bouncing back after a loss, but (until September) had trouble following a win with a win. For the season as a whole their winning percentage following a loss (.518) was almost a hundred points higher than their winning percentage following a win (.421).

The Sox team was not as bad as their record during most of this period. While the Sox were 20 under and the Mariners were still over .500 (late June to mid-July) the ratios of runs to opposition runs for the two teams were almost identical, with the Sox' ratio often being better. What that meant is that the won/lost records were something of an illusion, and it was likely that in the second half the won-lost records of the two teams would converge, which is exactly what happened, with the Mariners eventually winding up with 78 wins, the White Sox with 77.

Even this is misleading, for the Sox made real improvement in the second half as well as catching up to where they should have been anyway; at season's end the Sox were still eight games under .500, but had scored more runs than they had allowed (748–746), whereas the World Champion Twins were eight games over .500 despite allowing more than they scored. The Sox record over the first half of the season was 32–49, but over the second half it was 45–36, a pace good enough to win the division if sustained from start to finish.

The stars of the 22–10 record after September 1 were mostly pitchers, Floyd Bannister (6–1, 1.34 ERA in September), Dave LaPoint (4–1, 1.51), Jack McDowell (3–0, 1.93) and Bobby Thigpen (4–1, 1.95). Daryl Boston also

closed strong (again), hitting .377 in September, Harold Baines hit .345 with 20 RBI and Greg Walker .294 with 24 RBI. During one remarkable seven-game stretch (September 24–Oct 1) the White Sox scored only 26 runs (3.7 per game), but won all seven games.

Which, come to think of it, was a general pattern all year. So long as they didn't have too many runs to work with, the White Sox pitchers did a heck of a job. When working with three to five runs, the White Sox won 37 and lost only 30, a .552 percentage, fourth best in baseball. The Sox won six games, which is more than most teams, in which they scored only one or two runs.

But when supported by six or more runs, the Sox lost 15 times. Their .694 winning percentage when working with six or more runs, though it sounds good, was the worst of any major-league team. Finishing just eight games out, those games that they blew when they had enough runs to win, most of which came early in the season, kept them from contending. Ten of those 15 losses were charged to the bullpen, only five to the starting pitcher.

The Sox starting pitching was pretty decent (average game score: 50.5). Their bullpen, particularly when Thigpen was struggling early in the year, was a problem. The White Sox defensive efficiency record, .713, was the best in the major leagues. There is a long complicated formula for that, but what it means is that when a ball was put into play against the Sox defense, they turned that ball into an out 71.3 percent of the time, the best percentage of any major-league team. I've been figuring that for ten years, and just from memory I think this is the first time that a noncontending team has led the majors in that category.

One key to the defense was the addition of Fred Manrique at second base. Jim Fregosi must be given primary credit for giving a shot to Manrique. I wish I had remembered to put Manrique on my Ken Phelps All-Star team in last year's book. I saw Manrique play at Louisville a couple of years ago, when Fregosi was the manager there, and he really impressed me with his agility and reactions in the field. The majors-to-minors translation system showed him to be a capable major-league hitter, expected to do essentially what he did do. I just forgot him when I was drawing up that team. Anyway, I think Manrique will be the American League's next Gold Glove second baseman if he keeps his head in the game. He's really a second shortstop out there, and a good one at that, terrific arm for a second baseman with the quickness and range of a shortstop. The White Sox this year should have their best keystone combination since Fox and Aparicio.

Fregosi used five leadoff men and got excellent production from the leadoff spot, particularly out of Ozzie Guillen, who hit .347 in 55 games as a leadoff man. Redus led off 56 games, Daryl Boston 36, Williams and Royster a few games; on the whole Sox leadoff men hit .291 with 35 doubles, 6 triples, 17 homers, 67 walks, and 44 stolen bases. However, they scored only 102 runs, which also sounds good but isn't; a group of leadoff men who are producing that well ought to score 110 to 115 runs, even for a bad team. The Sox scored only 83 first-inning runs, a very poor number. (Leadoff data courtesy of the *Chicago Baseball Report,* P.O. Box 46074, Chicago, Illinois 60646).

The major media story concerning the Sox was their attempt to enforce petty discipline from the front office. With the team in a slump in June, "at least three players were fined by General Manager Larry Himes for not wearing socks with their dress clothes in the home locker room" (*The Sporting News,* July 20, 1987). Various accounts, which may have been exaggerated, had the Sox posting a flunky in the clubhouse to check these details of appropriate attire. Several Sox players were unhappy about a ban on beer in the clubhouse; Carlton Fisk, for one, sounded off about that, and threatened, apparently in jest, to smuggle beer into his locker. Himes ordered security to check Fisk thoroughly when he came to the park.

Keep that good attitude, Larry, keep that attitude. I certainly wouldn't want to defend Himes for this kind of crap, but I do think it is unfortunate that the attention given to it has obscured some very real accomplishments. The Sox in the second half of the season were the best team in this division. Remarkably, Himes had the self-discipline not to get carried away and start projecting a 1988 pennant. "It's nice to be playing well," he said in September, "but we know where we are."

Where they are is in the talent-collection process. The Sox have been spending the winter body-snatching. If baseball gave points for participating in field events, the White Sox would be legitimate contenders, because they probably have more classic athletes on the roster now than any other team. One of my biggest surprises in compiling the data for this year's book was to note that the White Sox had become the fastest team in the American League, the second fastest in the majors behind the Cardinals (see chart). All of the White Sox speed indicators were above average except the number of stolen-base attempts. The White Sox stolen-base percentage (73 percent) was excellent. Their triples total a little above average. Their double plays grounded into were low. Their runs scored as a percentage of men on base/not home run was above average. Their defensive efficiency record the best in the major leagues.

The addition of Ken Williams to the outfield, along with increased playing time for Darryl Boston, contributed to this. With Baines moving primarily to designated hitter for the season, Ivan Calderon moved into right field; Calderon also runs better than Baines, and of course the big item was that the White Sox left fielder at the start of the 1986 season was Ron Kittle, whereas in 1987 it was Gary Redus. Expect to see the White Sox running more in 1988.

That was 1987; since then they have added a young slugger from New York (Dan Pasqua) and four arms from Kansas City for Bannister. While I admire Himes' ability to resist the delusion that he is on the brink of glory, I think he overdid it a little with respect to the trades. I don't think it is the best approach to bring in young players by the truckload and figure that we'll let them sort themselves out. I think it works a lot better to go through a by-the-numbers problem-solving process:

1) What is our biggest weakness?

2) Who is the one best player that we can get to address that weakness?

3) How can we get him?

I believe in trying to solve one or two specific problems in a year, in other words, rather than simply collecting young players and telling the manager to use the young players to solve the problems. I mean, I love Dan Pasqua as a hitter, but I would rather put Dan Pasqua in a slot (left field or DH) and take my chances with him, rather than making him assert himself from among a crowded outfield cast (Pasqua, Baines, Calderon, Boston, Ken Williams, Redus). I would be happier with an outfield of three of those (four, covering DH) than with all six of them. With six outfielders players get lost, pushed aside, develop attitude problems. With six of them you start trying to do silly things like play Ken Williams at third base. Not satisfied with six outfielders, the Sox are reportedly trying to trade DeLeon—the only starting pitcher they haven't traded yet—for St. Louis' Lance Johnson. Put it this way: having more players than you can put in the lineup inevitably creates inefficient use of resources, which usually creates secondary problems.

But that's a disagreement; it's not a criticism. Collecting lots of good young players may not be the best way to develop a strong team, but if not the best way it's the second-best. I don't think they're lost, like the Dodgers or the Cubs; I just think the road around the mountain is a little longer that way than this way.

The White Sox have no shining third-base candidates, and so in the time-honored tradition they are attempting to move an outfielder in there. This move hardly ever works, but the other Chicago team a year ago tried it and it sort of worked, so the White Sox couldn't resist the temptation. Ken Williams, who has never played a professional game at any position other than the outfield, is being worked out at third; reportedly he resembles a third baseman every bit as much as I resemble Richard Gere. Even in the case where this "works," it doesn't *really* work; in two years the Cubs will need another third baseman, and they'll look back at the Keith Moreland experiment and say "What was the point of that?" The major leagues are not a training ground, and anyway why would you put one of your fastest players at a defensive position that doesn't require speed? I look for Steve Lyons or possibly Donnie Hill to be back at third base by the middle of May.

So what I would have done, had I been in the position the Sox were in at the end of the season, would have been to figure out where the best available young third baseman was (probably Cory Snyder or Eddie Williams from Cleveland), and then I would have attempted to work out a deal to bring in one of those players for a starting pitcher, Dotson or Bannister. With the Indians as desperate for pitching as they are, it's hard to believe that there wasn't a deal there. A few other guys who might have been available: Buechele or Stanley from Texas, Edgar Martinez from Seattle, Rich Schu from Philadelphia, and Chris Brown or Randy Ready from San Diego.

If the Sox had a chance to improve dramatically in

1988, they traded it in for a more distant dream when they traded their starting rotation for a bunch of kids. With Dotson and Bannister gone it will probably take Fregosi until July to establish a starting rotation. Dave LaPoint pitched superb ball late in 1987, but how much can you count on from him, given his up and down career? LaPoint is only 28, and could pitch for several years if his problems are truly behind him. At this writing, the Sox seem to have three starting pitchers—LaPoint, DeLeon, and McDowell. I personally am hoping for a rise in stature by Joel McKeon, or perhaps they'll pull Jim O'Dell out of the low minors or arrange a trade for Randy St. Clair, giving them an unbreakable record of five starting pitchers with ten capital letters; at worst, they should have eight. Other candidates for the rotation include Bill Long, Melido Perez, and Scott Nielsen. McDowell is a Stanford hotshot with a chance to be 1988 Rookie of the Year. Perez pitched briefly with KC last year but looks like he needs a year of AAA. The others are guys who have had chances before and didn't do much with them. Fregosi has his fingers crossed, in other words.

It's not that the White Sox are on the verge of emerging as a good team. They're not, or at least not that I can see. But just one year ago, I thought that Ken Harrelson had emaciated the Sox' talent base to such an extent that the White Sox would not be able to contend for the better part of a decade. I thought that in a couple of years they would be where Atlanta is now. Just to have avoided that fate is a very substantial achievement.

DEFENSIVE EFFICIENCY RECORDS

White Sox	.713
Toronto	.710
Pittsburgh	.708
San Diego	.704
Detroit	.704
California	.702
Philadelphia	.702
Yankees	.701
Minnesota	.698
Texas	.697
Houston	.695
San Francisco	.695
Mets	.695
Baltimore	.694
St. Louis	.694
Cincinnati	.694
Oakland	.693
Montreal	.693
Seattle	.693
Kansas City	.690
Cleveland	.688
Atlanta	.688
Los Angeles	.684
Milwaukee	.677
Cubs	.675
Boston	.672

RUNS SCORED AND ALLOWED WINS AND LOSSES

Wins	482	201	77-0	1.000
Bannister	154	149	19-15	.559
De Leon	141	119	17-14	.548
Blowouts	261	248	21-21	.500
Road Games	354	332	39-42	.481
All Games	748	746	77-85	.475
Pitchers' Duels	82	75	19-21	.475
Home Games	394	414	38-43	.469
One Run Games	140	143	19-22	.463
Dotson	123	146	12-19	.387
Slugfests	373	401	19-32	.373
Losses	266	545	0-85	.000

TEN BEST STARTS

	IP	H	R	ER	BB	SO		
Bannister at Sea, Sep 13	9	1	0	0	0	10	W	95
Long vs. NY, May 5	9	2	0	0	0	5	W	88
Bannister at Bos, May 23	9	2	1	1	1	6	W	84
LaPoint at Oak, Sep 27	9	2	0	0	2	1	W	82
Bannister at Det, July 29	9	5	0	0	2	5	W	80
Dotson at Tor, Aug 15	9	6	0	0	2	6	W	79
Dotson at Cal, June 6	9	5	1	1	2	8	—	79
Long at Cal, June 7	9	7	0	0	0	6	W	79
McDowell at Oak, Sep 25	7	2	0	0	3	7	—	77
DeLeon at Tor, Apr 15	7⅔	3	0	0	6	9	W	76

PITCHERS WHEN SUPPORTED BY THREE TO FIVE RUNS

	G	IP	W-L	Pct	SO	BB	ERA
Dotson	11	82	6-3	.667	45	32	3.51
Bannister	13	84	7-4	.636	53	16	4.48
Long	10	68	3-3	.500	27	10	4.37
DeLeon	18	113	5-6	.455	96	50	3.74

HALL OF FAME WATCH

Could be elected on current accomplishments: Fisk 103.5; **Building credentials but not yet viable candidate:** Fregosi 44; **Working on it:** Baines 20, Dotson 12, Bannister 10; **Long way to go:** Hassey 7, James 6, LaPoint 3, Guillen 2, Calderon 1, D Hill 1, Thigpen 1, G Walker 1. (Fregosi's totals include 29 points as a player, 15 as a manager.)

LOSSES DESPITE SCORING SIX OR MORE RUNS

Toronto	5
Detroit	6
Yankees	6
Cubs	7
Seattle	7
Los Angeles	8
Kansas City	8
Philadelphia	8
Houston	8
Oakland	9
Atlanta	9
San Diego	10
San Francisco	10
Mets	10
Pittsburgh	10
St. Louis	10
Minnesota	11
Montreal	11
Cincinnati	12
Boston	14
Baltimore	14
Milwaukee	14
Cleveland	15
California	15
White Sox	15
Texas	16

TEN WORST STARTS

	IP	H	R	ER	BB	SO		
Bannister at Tex, June 3	3	11	8	8	1	2	L	6
Nielsen vs. Det, Aug 11	1⅔	8	7	7	0	1	L	12
Bannister at KC, Apr 8	3⅔	9	6	6	1	1	L	19
Peterson vs. Sea, Sep 19	4	8	6	6	3	1	—	20
Dotson vs. Sea, June 24	3*	8	6	6	0	2	L	21
Long at Sea, Sep 12	1⅓	7	5	5	0	1	L	21
DeLeon vs. Min, June 14	1⅔	6	5	5	2	0	L	21
Dotson vs. Det, Apr 11	4*	9	6	6	1	2	L	21
Nielsen at NY, July 10	1⅓	6	5	5	1	1	L	22
Bannister vs. Bos, Aug 18	3*	9	5	5	0	1	L	22

Carlton FISK, Catcher
Runs Created: 66

	G	AB	Hit	2B	3B	HR	Run	RBI	TBB	SO	SB	CS	Avg
12.11 years		576	155	28	4	25	88	87	54	89	10	4	.269
1987	135	454	116	22	1	23	68	72	39	72	1	4	.256
First Half	73	254	58	9	1	12	38	42	20	44	0	3	.228
Second Half	62	200	58	13	0	11	30	29	19	28	1	1	.290
Vs. RHP		272	73	12	0	14	37	44	22	46	1	3	.268
Vs. LHP		182	43	10	1	9	31	27	17	26	0	1	.236
Home	68	218	58	13	0	5	30	24	19	36	0	3	.266
Road	67	236	58	9	1	18	38	47	20	36	1	1	.246

Daryl BOSTON, Outfield
Runs Created: 43

	G	AB	Hit	2B	3B	HR	Run	RBI	TBB	SO	SB	CS	Avg
1.78 years		478	116	27	4	10	61	39	36	93	20	10	.243
1987	103	337	87	21	2	10	51	29	25	68	12	6	.258
First Half	73	241	56	14	1	8	34	18	22	50	12	4	.232
Second Half	30	96	31	7	1	2	17	11	3	18	0	2	.323
Vs. RHP		278	69	17	2	10	44	24	24	51	11	6	.248
Vs. LHP		59	18	4	0	0	7	5	1	17	1	0	.305
Home	52	168	54	9	2	5	28	17	12	37	9	4	.321
Road	51	169	33	12	0	5	23	12	13	31	3	2	.195

Greg WALKER, First Base
Runs Created: 93

	G	AB	Hit	2B	3B	HR	Run	RBI	TBB	SO	SB	CS	Avg
4.09 years		542	146	31	4	24	72	91	52	93	4	3	.269
1987	157	566	145	33	2	27	85	94	75	112	2	1	.256
First Half	81	299	72	17	2	17	49	50	36	68	2	0	.241
Second Half	76	267	73	16	0	10	36	44	39	44	0	1	.273
Vs. RHP		356	95	24	2	14	56	51	53	62	0	1	.267
Vs. LHP		210	50	9	0	13	29	43	22	50	2	0	.238
Home	79	273	68	15	1	12	41	50	43	43	1	0	.249
Road	78	293	77	18	1	15	44	44	32	69	1	1	.263

Ken WILLIAMS, Center Field
Runs Created: 50

	G	AB	Hit	2B	3B	HR	Run	RBI	TBB	SO	SB	CS	Avg
0.81 years		521	141	22	2	15	62	63	14	116	27	14	.271
1987	116	391	110	18	2	11	48	50	10	83	21	10	.281
First Half	47	153	43	10	1	4	17	22	4	34	4	5	.281
Second Half	69	238	67	8	1	7	31	28	6	49	17	5	.282
Vs. RHP		232	63	11	1	3	30	28	7	44	11	6	.272
Vs. LHP		159	47	7	1	8	18	22	3	39	10	4	.296
Home	55	193	63	13	1	4	31	27	6	37	11	5	.326
Road	61	198	47	5	1	7	17	23	4	46	10	5	.237

Fred MANRIQUE, Second Base
Runs Created: 33

	G	AB	Hit	2B	3B	HR	Run	RBI	TBB	SO	SB	CS	Avg
0.99 years		369	92	14	4	6	38	33	21	87	6	4	.249
1987	115	298	77	13	3	4	30	29	19	69	5	3	.258
First Half	47	106	23	5	0	1	7	7	3	26	0	1	.217
Second Half	68	192	54	8	3	3	23	22	16	43	5	2	.281
Vs. RHP		154	34	3	0	2	11	20	6	35	5	2	.221
Vs. LHP		144	43	10	3	2	19	9	13	34	0	1	.299
Home	58	141	43	7	3	2	20	19	13	29	3	1	.305
Road	57	157	34	6	0	2	10	10	6	40	2	2	.217

Ivan CALDERON, Right Field
Runs Created: 102

	G	AB	Hit	2B	3B	HR	Run	RBI	TBB	SO	SB	CS	Avg
1.68 years		560	158	37	4	23	88	76	54	118	11	5	.282
1987	144	542	159	38	2	28	93	83	60	109	10	5	.293
First Half	71	275	83	22	1	11	42	39	28	55	8	1	.302
Second Half	73	267	76	16	1	17	51	44	32	54	2	4	.285
Vs. RHP		352	106	27	2	15	56	59	36	69	10	3	.301
Vs. LHP		190	53	11	0	13	37	24	24	40	0	2	.279
Home	71	260	82	20	1	15	53	48	39	47	7	1	.315
Road	73	282	77	18	1	13	40	35	21	62	3	4	.273

Donnie HILL, Infield
Runs Created: 43

	G	AB	Hit	2B	3B	HR	Run	RBI	TBB	SO	SB	CS	Avg
2.89 years		510	134	19	3	7	62	53	29	48	6	3	.263
1987	111	410	98	14	6	9	57	46	30	35	1	0	.239
First Half	52	187	38	7	2	3	22	19	16	18	0		.203
Second Half	59	223	60	7	4	6	35	27	14	17	1	0	.269
Vs. RHP		280	64	11	6	4	38	32	18	22	0	0	.229
Vs.LHP		130	34	3	0	5	19	14	12	13	1	0	.262
Home	56	201	51	11	4	1	29	19	14	11	1	0	.254
Road	55	209	47	3	2	8	28	27	16	24	0	0	.225

Harold BAINES, Designated Hitter
Runs Created: 84

	G	AB	Hit	2B	3B	HR	Run	RBI	TBB	SO	SB	CS	Avg
6.94 years		614	177	30	6	23	79	98	45	89	4	3	.288
1987	132	505	148	26	4	20	59	93	46	82	0	0	.293
First Half	62	239	72	10	2	12	27	49	28	37	0	0	.301
Second Half	70	266	76	16	2	8	32	44	18	45	0	0	.286
Vs. RHP		324	102	18	3	14	39	68	33	37	0	0	.315
Vs. LHP		181	46	8	1	6	20	25	13	45	0	0	.254
Home	66	253	79	15	3	12	35	52	16	37	0	0	.312
Road	66	252	69	11	1	8	24	41	30	45	0	0	.274

Ozzie GUILLEN, Shortstop
Runs Created: 61

	G	AB	Hit	2B	3B	HR	Run	RBI	TBB	SO	SB	CS	Avg
2.83 years		565	151	22	7	2	68	46	16	49	14	6	.267
1987	149	560	156	22	7	2	64	51	22	52	25	8	.279
First Half	84	304	91	13	4	1	33	24	14	27	9	6	.299
Second Half	65	256	65	9	3	1	31	27	8	25	16	2	.254
Vs. RHP		396	123	18	6	2	55	41	16	34	21	6	.311
Vs. LHP		164	33	4	1	0	9	10	6	18	4	2	.201
Home	73	269	85	11	4	2	35	32	17	20	14	1	.316
Road	76	291	71	11	3	0	29	19	5	32	11	7	.244

Gary REDUS, Outfield
Runs Created: 69

	G	AB	Hit	2B	3B	HR	Run	RBI	TBB	SO	SB	CS	Avg
3.64 years		547	134	29	8	15	99	52	79	116	61	16	.245
1987	130	475	112	26	6	12	78	48	69	90	52	11	.236
First Half	70	263	56	12	4	6	43	22	40	62	27	5	.213
Second Half	60	212	56	14	2	6	35	26	29	28	25	6	.264
Vs. RHP		274	58	12	3	5	45	28	34	63	29	4	.212
Vs. LHP		201	54	14	3	7	33	20	35	27	23	7	.269
Home	66	238	58	13	3	4	39	30	34	41	28	5	.244
Road	64	237	54	13	3	8	39	18	35	49	24	6	.228

TEXAS RANGERS

That was some ugly baby. Before the 1987 season Ranger veteran Larry Parrish said that "people expect the labor pains to be over. They expect to see the baby." It was an ugly baby from the first squall. The Rangers lost ten of their first eleven, putting them nine games under .500. Although they didn't fall to ten under until September, the 1987 Rangers never had a winning record. They spent five months on a treadmill, struggling to get above .500 and staying within a week of it. They touched .500 twice, at 1–1 and, on July 27, at 49–49. Then they lost four straight and went back on the treadmill, where they remained until September 20. A 2–11 record after their virtual elimination left them at 75–87.

There is no team in baseball whose failures in 1987 are easier to diagnose, or could be. Texas pitchers walked 760 men. The average American League team walked 558. The Indians were second in the league in walks, 606. The Rangers outdid them by 25 percent.

Forty-four times the Ranger starting pitcher walked five or more men. No other team's starting pitchers walked five men even half as often. Bobby Witt walked five or more men 18 times in 25 starts, but even without those 18 the Rangers would still have led the major leagues in this unenviable accomplishment.

Primarily because of this, the Rangers allowed 849 runs, the most of any team in the division.

That negated a strong offense. Offensively, the Rangers were not much below average at any position. They led the division in runs scored, with 823. They also were not very far above average at any position. Their weakest offensive player in terms of runs created per game was one catcher, Don Slaught (3.62); their best was another catcher, Geno Petralli (6.91). Their softest spot offensively relative to the league was probably third base, where they used six players. Steve Buechele, the most regular, hit just .237, but he did drive in 50 runs in 363 at bats, and then again sometime third baseman Larry Parrish drove in 100. Slaught's figure (3.6) isn't all that bad, and Petralli's (6.9) isn't great. It was a balanced, top-to-bottom offense, with every position contributing and none spectacular.

As a top-to-bottom offense can be, because it doesn't break down going around the corner, the Ranger offense was efficient. The Rangers scored 22 runs more than expected by runs created, (823–801). Their expected runs were still the highest in the West.

With a good offense and awful pitching, the Rangers lost 16 games in which they scored six or more runs, most in the major leagues. Their record when scoring 3–5 runs was 19–33.

In games they won the Rangers scored an average of 7.2 runs, most of any major-league team.

That's it: solid offense top to bottom, young pitching staff undermined by control. The simplest picture of success and failure in the majors.

The pitching staff was not 100 percent at fault in al-lowing those 849 runs. The Rangers are potentially a very good defensive club. First baseman Pete O'Brien is as good at his position as anyone in the league. Second baseman Jerry Browne is quick, smooth, and reliable. Third baseman Steve Buechele has terrific agility. *The Scouting Report: 1987* said of Buechele that he "makes acrobatic plays that remind the Rangers of six-time Gold Glover Buddy Bell. . . . He has a strong arm and can make an accurate throw while off-balance." Shortstop Scott Fletcher, said the same publication, "has good range and a good arm." The Rangers had two center fielders, the wonderfully athletic Oddibe McDowell, and Bob Brower, just as fast and with a better arm. Right fielder Ruben Sierra has one of the best arms in baseball and good speed.

Despite those defensive strengths, the Ranger defense was certainly not good. I didn't mention two positions, catcher and left field. The Rangers had two bombs in the field, the kind of players who can make the whole team look bad. Of their catchers (Porter, Petralli, and Stanley; Slaught's with the Yankees now) none throws extremely well. Ranger opponents stole 205 bases, the most of any major-league team; the next five teams on the list were all National League teams. Pete Incaviglia in left field is possibly the worst defensive outfielder in the American League now that Lonnie Smith is gone. Although Scott Fletcher has played extremely well at shortstop in the past, last year he was having elbow trouble or something and didn't throw well, a relatively essential part of a shortstop's job. Although Steve Buechele is a very capable third baseman, he is not as consistent as he is capable, which Valentine makes worse by shuttling him over to second base once a week so that he can get Larry's Parrish's .918 fielding percentage in the lineup. And although Sierra has all the tools to be a great outfielder, he isn't. Sierra is still young, and he misreads too many balls.

The Rangers committed 151 errors, second most in the league. They turned 148 double plays, a little below average. Their defensive efficiency record, which essentially measures their collective range, was .697, a little above average.

So even when the Rangers got good pitching, they didn't always win. They had 29 quality starts in road games last year, and lost the game 15 times.

Then too, we have to remember that playing behind Bobby Witt is not a fielder's dream. These guys don't throw ground balls to second and deep flies to the gap; they walk people and give up line drives. It has to be frustrating. The average Ranger game last year laster 2 hours, 55 minutes, longest in the American League (the shortest was Seattle at 2:45). Ranger catchers had to chase down 73 passed balls, which doesn't make the defense look very good, not to mention taking the double play out of order a huge number of times. In fact, when you think about the passed balls, the opposition stolen bases, the league-leading 26 balks, an above average wild pitch total and the fact that the Ranger pitchers led the league in strikeouts, the Texas total of 148 double plays seems fairly remarkable.

You probably know that the 73 passed balls by Ranger catchers set an American League record, and I'm sure you know that Charlie Hough was a major reason for that. I haven't studied it, but I would bet that the Texas official scoring had almost as much to do with it.

As I've written before, the silliest distinction in the records is between a passed ball and a wild pitch. The official scorer should be assigned to make a factual record of what happens. He should not be assigned to make a record of his opinions about why it happens. In the case of the wild pitch and passed ball, what happens is precisely the same: a pitch gets away, and a runner advances. Absolutely the only thing that the official scorer has to decide is who is at fault. It is an arbitrary distinction which creates the fiction that Charlie Hough merely happens to be on the mound when the catcher turns butter fingered, but he doesn't have anything to do with it.

The Ranger pitchers, with the wildest staff in memory, were charged with only 61 wild pitches, 7 above average. There is a strong enough correlation between wild pitches and walks that it is very odd for a team to have by far the wildest staff in baseball in terms of walks, but to be in the middle of the pack in wild pitches. That suggests, to me, that in making that arbitrary decision as to who is at fault when a ball gets away, the official scorers have been coming down hard on the catchers—hence a historically high total of passed balls, but a surprisingly low total of wild pitches. The easiest way for that to happen is to have a hometown official scorer who tends to hold the catchers to an unusually high standard. Check, and I'll bet you find that 60 percent of the passed balls were in Texas, but 60 percent of the wild pitches were on the road.

Or perhaps not, because the Ranger catchers have a bad-glove reputation on the road, too. Anyway, this is not the defense it ought to be, and it is not likely to develop into the defense it ought to be until 1) they get a few pitchers who throw strikes; 2) Valentine stops messing around with infielders playing three positions; 3) Larry Parrish stops playing the infield; 4) Pete Incaviglia stops playing the outfield; and 5) the Rangers find a catcher.

I don't see many signs that all those things will happen in 1988. The Rangers haven't traded either Incaviglia or Parrish, who are two of their better hitters. That means that either Incaviglia or Parrish has to be in the field, which means that we're still going to be seeing Buechele at second base some of the time.

Will the Rangers be able to control the running game better? I doubt it. They have traded their best defensive catcher, Don Slaught, and seem to be committed to their worst, Mike Stanley. The Ranger pitchers do such a poor job of holding runners that the catcher has little chance, but Stanley and Petralli are not good defensive catchers. I don't think the Rangers can improve in this area, and I wonder if they can win the pennant if they don't improve.

Over the last five years the Rangers winning percentage on artificial turf is .354, easily the worst in baseball (on grass fields they are at .477, on road grass at .417). Again in 1987, they could not win on plastic, finishing 7–18. I have written too many times that none of us know

what makes a team good or bad on artificial turf to now claim that I understand this phenomenon, but I would suggest that walking five men a game probably doesn't help. Baserunners run faster on turf, which should magnify the advantage of having them.

It is not apparent whether the Rangers are making progress putting together a pitching staff. A year ago (1986) Ranger pitchers walked 736 men, the most in the major leagues in fifteen years, but they could point out that they had a young staff, and one of their competitors, Oakland, had walked almost as many, 667. Last year Oakland cut their walks by 136, to 531. The Rangers went up to 760. Edwin Correa, who won 12 games at age 20 in 1986, was ineffective early in the season. X rays revealed that Correa had a stress fracture of the shoulder blade. He was given the rest of the season off to avoid aggravating the injury, and is expected back strong in 1988. José Guzman, 24, developed back trouble but pitched through it. Charlie Hough is a year older. Bobby Witt was removed from the rotation in May when his control failed to improve, but when he went back into the rotation in late June it was more of the same. For his last eight starts, Witt walked 42 men in 46 innings and had a 5.87 ERA.

There is, in the 1988 strike zone, a ray of hope for the Rangers, for as I wrote in an introductory article, I think the new strike zone will work to the advantage of power pitchers, and in particular power pitchers who have trouble finding the strike zone. The Rangers have more of those than anybody, and thus could be the team most helped by the new strike zone.

But if the new strike zone helps Bobby Witt a little bit, that isn't going to be enough. These guys are so wild that an occasional strike isn't going to do it for them. You can't walk nine men per nine innings and be successful. You can't walk eight men per nine innings and be successful, either.

The Rangers, then, remain the most unpredictable team in the American League, as they have been for three years. I frankly have no idea what to expect of them in 1988. They have a world of young talent. Sometimes you can safely predict that young players will improve. This isn't one of those times. Unless something happens like Bobby Witt suddenly finding the strike zone, I really don't see any of the Ranger's problems getting a whole lot better. I don't see the defense healing itself overnight.

If, for Seattle, you ask the question "Who is likely to make this team better in 1988 than it was in 1987?" the answers are easy—Brantley, Campbell, Mike Moore, Mike Jackson. If you ask the same question for Texas, you get question marks in return: Witt, but will he? Correa, but how much better? Mike Stanley is likely to be the "story," as people discover what a hitter he is, but how much is he really going to help the team, with his defense being what it is?

This season will be a challenge for Valentine. Baseball revolves around control of the strike zone. There is too much talent here to go on losing games by the bushel because the pitching staff doesn't understand that and because you have a couple of positions at which the defense is substandard. A real good manager could win the pennant with this team.

Valentine's handling of his pitching staff has been eccentric. It is unusual for a manager to make a one-way commitment to young pitchers, without regard to the stage of their development. The patience that he has shown with Witt, Williams, Russell, and others is extraordinary. Any other manager in baseball, I think, would have sent Bobby Witt out last year with a diagram of the strike zone in his hip pocket. Sometimes Valentine will go forever with a starting pitcher; other times he will pull him out quickly. He is not by the book. The Rangers had 29 slow hooks, the most in the majors, but they also had 25 quick hooks, well up the list. The total of 54 quick hooks or slow hooks (what you might call nonstandard removals) was by far the highest in the major leagues. Valentine is more or less the opposite of Whitey Herzog in this way, in that Herzog never allows a pitcher to stay in the game and get beat up. Herzog's approach is to put on the field the best defense

he can assemble, and to find pitchers who aren't afraid to use their defenders.

There is nothing wrong with doing things in an original way, and I would never criticize a manager for that. I would never assume that because Bobby was doing things in a way that they are not usually done that he must be doing them wrong. It's not my rule, it's society's rule that is the problem. The rule is that if you are going to do things in your own way you had damn well better make it work. There had better be a payoff there, or you'd better go back to doing things the way everybody else does.

Bobby Valentine has already managed the Rangers longer than anybody else. If the Rangers don't improve, he probably won't be here on October 2. This is the year that we're going to find out exactly how good a manager Bobby Valentine is.

TOTAL OF QUICK HOOKS AND SLOW HOOKS

Texas	54
Baltimore	45
Oakland	45
Yankees	44
San Francisco	40
Seattle	39
Boston	38
California	37
Milwaukee	37
San Diego	36
Cleveland	35
Toronto	35
St. Louis	34
Los Angeles	33
Atlanta	33
Cubs	31
Detroit	30
Minnesota	30
Montreal	28
Mets	28
Philadelphia	25
Cincinnati	25
White Sox	24
Kansas City	22
Houston	21
Pittsburgh	21

RUNS SCORED AND ALLOWED WINS AND LOSSES

Wins	542	260	75-0	1.000
Hough	210	193	22-18	.550
Home Games	426	447	43-38	.531
Witt	110	126	13-12	.520
Blowouts	315	307	25-24	.510
Correa	82	87	7-8	.467
All Games	823	849	75-87	.463
One Run Games	170	173	18-21	.462
Slugfests	495	505	30-37	.448
Guzman	140	155	12-18	.400
Road Games	397	402	32-49	.395
Pitchers' Duels	41	62	10-16	.385
Harris	117	112	7-12	.368
Losses	281	589	0-87	.000

TEN BEST STARTS

	IP	H	R	ER	BB	SO		
Hough vs. Oak, June 14	9	3	1	0	1	8	W	86
Hough at Oak, Sep 8	9	3	1	0	4	9	W	84
Hough vs. Oak, Sep 16	9	3	1	3	7	W		81
Witt vs. Min, June 26	8	1	0	0	6	7	W	81
Hough vs. KC, Aug 18	9	5	1	1	5	13	W	81
Guzman vs. Chi, Aug 20	9	3	1	2	5	W		80
Witt vs. Minn, Sep 30	9	4	1	1	8	11	W	78
Correa vs. NY, Apr 28	7⅔	2	1	0	5	7	W	75
Guzman at Cal, June 16	7⅓	3	1	1	2	9	W	75
Guzman vs. Cal, Sep 18	9	4	1	1	5	5	W	75

PITCHERS WHEN SUPPORTED BY THREE TO FIVE RUNS

	G	IP	W-L	Pct	SO	BB	ERA
Hough	15	107	5-7	.412	90	47	4.13
Guzman	12	78	4-6	.400	60	30	4.14
Witt	11	66	2-4	.333	78	56	4.91

HALL OF FAME WATCH

Building credentials but not yet viable candidate: Porter 62.5; **Working on it:** Hough 26, Parrish 22.5, Howe 11, Paciorek 10.5; **Long way to go:** Valentine 8, Sierra 6, Fletcher 4, Harris 3, McDowell 3, Slaught 3, Petralli 2.5, Incaviglia 2, Mohorcic 2, Mitch Williams 1.

GAMES IN WHICH STARTING PITCHER WALKED FIVE OR MORE MEN

Cincinnati	5
Montreal	5
Boston	5
San Francisco	7
Toronto	7
Milwaukee	8
Yankees	8
St. Louis	8
Seattle	9
Pittsburgh	10
Baltimore	11
White Sox	11
California	12
Oakland	12
Mets	12
Minnesota	15
Philadelphia	15
Los Angeles	16
Atlanta	16
Cubs	17
Houston	17
Cleveland	18
Kansas City	18
Detroit	19
San Diego	21
Texas	44

TEN WORST STARTS

	IP	H	R	ER	BB	SO		
Kilgus at Bal, Aug 7	2*	7	7	7	2	1	L	13
Guzman vs. Mil, Apr 10	⅔	5	7	7	1	0	L	13
Correa vs. Det, May 19	3⅔	8	8	8	4	5	—	14
Guzman vs. Tor, May 8	2⅓	7	7	7	1	1	L	15
Hough vs. Det, Sep 4	1⅓	4	7	7	5	2	L	15
Hough vs. Chi, June 2	1⅔	4	7	7	5	2	L	16
Correa vs. Tor, May 9	1⅔	7	6	6	2	1	L	16
Witt at Oak, Sep 9	1*	6	6	6	2	2	L	17
Witt at Sea, Sep 25	4⅓	7	8	8	3	4	L	18
Witt vs. KC, Aug 19	4⅓	5	8	7	7	5	L	21
Correa at NY, May 14	3⅓	5	7	6	.5	2	L	21

Pete O'BRIEN, First Base
Runs Created: 91

	G	AB	Hit	2B	3B	HR	Run	RBI	TBB	SO	SB	CS	Avg
4.88 years		575	157	28	3	20	74	85	68	61	4	6	.273
1987	159	569	163	26	1	23	84	88	59	61	0	4	.286
First Half	85	312	87	11	0	19	55	57	29	33	0	2	.279
Second Half	74	257	76	15	1	4	29	31	30	28	0	2	.296
Vs. RHP		383	117	18	1	20	64	68	46	31	0	3	.305
Vs. LHP		186	46	8	0	3	20	20	13	30	0	1	.247
Home	78	265	72	14	0	9	35	43	32	28	0	2	.272
Road	81	304	91	12	1	14	49	45	27	33	0	2	.299

Oddibe MCDOWELL, Center Field
Runs Created: 61

	G	AB	Hit	2B	3B	HR	Run	RBI	TBB	SO	SB	CS	Avg
2.43 years		570	143	26	7	21	96	59	63	122	34	10	.251
1987	128	407	98	26	4	14	65	52	51	99	24	2	.241
First Half	67	215	58	17	2	10	40	35	35	56	13	0	.270
Second Half	61	192	40	9	2	4	25	17	16	43	11	2	.208
Vs. RHP		336	82	23	4	12	48	39	34	83	19	1	.244
Vs. LHP		71	16	3	0	2	17	13	17	16	5	1	.225
Home	62	196	49	11	3	5	30	23	19	46	9	2	.250
Road	66	211	49	15	1	9	35	29	32	53	15	0	.232

Jerry BROWNE, Second Base
Runs Created: 59

	G	AB	Hit	2B	3B	HR	Run	RBI	TBB	SO	SB	CS	Avg
0.89 years		537	149	20	7	1	78	46	70	61	30	21	.277
1987	132	454	123	16	6	1	63	38	61	50	27	17	.271
First Half	73	239	60	8	5	0	32	21	37	26	13	11	.251
Second Half	59	215	63	8	1	1	31	17	24	24	14	6	.293
Vs. RHP		335	86	12	3	0	44	22	43	42	16	10	.257
Vs. LHP		119	37	4	3	1	19	16	18	8	11	7	.311
Home	71	245	75	9	3	1	41	22	33	29	15	12	.306
Road	61	209	48	7	3	0	22	16	28	21	12	5	.230

Ruben SIERRA, Right Field
Runs Created: 85

	G	AB	Hit	2B	3B	HR	Run	RBI	TBB	SO	SB	CS	Avg
1.67 years		614	162	29	8	28	88	98	37	107	14	11	.264
1987	158	643	169	35	4	30	97	109	39	114	16	11	.263
First Half	86	344	93	21	3	12	53	51	26	66	9	11	.270
Second Half	72	299	76	14	1	18	44	58	13	48	7	0	.254
Vs. RHP		406	110	24	3	18	65	74	31	82	11	8	.271
Vs. LHP		237	59	11	1	12	32	35	8	32	5	3	.249
Home	77	315	87	18	4	15	52	64	21	54	9	6	.276
Road	81	328	82	17	0	15	45	45	18	60	7	5	.250

Steve BUECHELE, Third Base
Runs Created: 42

	G	AB	Hit	2B	3B	HR	Run	RBI	TBB	SO	SB	CS	Avg
2.21 years		472	111	20	2	17	55	57	35	91	5	5	.235
1987	136	363	86	20	0	13	45	50	28	66	2	2	.237
First Half	79	232	52	15	0	7	28	28	15	43	1	1	.224
Second Half	57	131	34	5	0	6	17	22	13	23	1	1	.260
Vs. RHP		186	35	7	0	5	17	22	16	38	1	1	.188
Vs. LHP		177	51	13	0	8	28	28	12	28	1	1	.288
Home	71	188	47	11	0	6	25	30	18	32	1	1	.250
Road	65	175	39	9	0	7	20	20	10	34	1	0	.223

Larry PARRISH, Designated Hitter
Runs Created: 88

	G	AB	Hit	2B	3B	HR	Run	RBI	TBB	SO	SB	CS	Avg
10.93 years		584	156	32	3	22	75	86	46	114	3	3	.267
1987	152	557	149	22	1	32	79	100	49	154	3	1	.268
First Half	81	299	82	15	0	20	43	60	28	78	1	1	.274
Second Half	71	258	67	7	1	12	36	40	21	76	2	0	.260
Vs. RHP		367	98	17	1	18	48	65	27	94	1	1	.267
Vs. LHP		190	51	5	0	14	31	35	22	60	2	0	.268
Home	75	277	73	11	0	16	41	46	29	69	1	0	.264
Road	77	280	76	11	1	16	38	54	20	85	2	1	.271

Scott FLETCHER, Shortstop
Runs Created: 78

	G	AB	Hit	2B	3B	HR	Run	RBI	TBB	SO	SB	CS	Avg
4.41 years		500	135	23	4	4	68	48	51	56	10	7	.270
1987	156	588	169	28	4	5	82	63	61	66	13	12	.287
First Half	85	333	101	15	4	4	49	39	30	40	7	6	.303
Second Half	71	255	68	13	0	1	33	24	31	26	6	6	.267
Vs. RHP		368	99	19	3	2	52	40	37	48	9	4	.269
Vs. LHP		220	70	9	1	3	30	23	24	18	4	8	.318
Home	78	287	98	17	3	4	54	37	31	25	9	6	.341
Road	78	301	71	11	1	1	28	26	30	41	4	6	.236

Bob BROWER, Center Field
Runs Created: 47

	G	AB	Hit	2B	3B	HR	Run	RBI	TBB	SO	SB	CS	Avg
0.91		343	88	12	3	15	73	51	40	76	18	12	.257
1987	127	303	79	10	3	14	63	46	36	66	15	9	.261
First Half	65	125	31	5	1	6	31	18	22	31	7	4	.248
Second Half	62	178	48	5	2	8	32	28	14	35	8	5	.270
Vs. RHP		127	31	2	2	6	26	25	13	27	7	1	.244
Vs. LHP		176	48	8	1	8	37	21	23	39	8	8	.273
Home	66	155	46	7	2	7	33	20	16	40	4	6	.297
Road	61	148	33	3	1	7	30	26	20	26	11	3	.223

Pete INCAVIGLIA, Left Field
Runs Created: 85

	G	AB	Hit	2B	3B	HR	Run	RBI	TBB	SO	SB	CS	Avg
1.80 years		583	152	26	3	32	93	93	57	196	7	3	.261
1987	139	509	138	26	4	27	85	80	48	168	9	3	.271
First Half	83	315	84	18	3	17	52	50	31	107	8	2	.267
Second Half	56	194	54	8	1	10	33	30	17	61	1	1	.278
Vs. RHP		327	76	14	3	14	52	43	27	114	7	1	.232
Vs. LHP		182	62	12	1	13	33	37	21	54	2	2	.341
Home	71	255	66	12	2	11	38	40	30	85	2	2	.259
Road	68	254	72	14	2	16	47	40	18	83	7	1	.283

CALIFORNIA ANGELS

The California Angels' 1987 season, like a symphony, was performed in three movements. The first movement ended on June 3, with the Angels mired in last place with a record of 22–30. On June 4 Jack Lazorko beat Chicago 3–2, and for two months following the Angels were one of the best teams in baseball, winning 34 of 56 games to reach a record of 56–52, one-half game behind the first place Twins (57–52) and Oakland (56–51). That was the two-thirds point of the season; they had played 108 games, two-thirds of 162. On August 6 and 7 the Mariners battered California 15–4 and 14–0, throwing the Angels into a tailspin which they never pulled out of. The Angels returned to the bottom of the division, finishing tied for last with a record of 75–87.

Since the season divided so neatly into three almost equal parts, I thought I should take a look at what divided it. The Angels, actually, did not start the season playing poorly; they won eight of their first eleven games. What happened then is easy to pinpoint: McCaskill went out. Kirk McCaskill in 1986 was one of the best starting pitchers in baseball. On April 27 McCaskill had surgery to remove bone chips from his elbow; out two months.

The loss of McCaskill left the Angels with a rotation of Witt, Candelaria, Lugo, Sutton, and Fraser. Lugo (0–2, 9.32 ERA) and Sutton (2–6 as of June 3, 5.37 ERA) were losing almost every outing, while no one was winning enough to offset that (Witt was 6–4). Offensively, the Angels were hitting as many home runs as any team in the league except Baltimore, but were near the bottom of the league in runs scored due to low batting averages. In the year of the hitter, early in the season when there are still people battling for .400, the Angels had only one .300 hitter, Brian Downing, and he dropped under .300 in late May. As of June 4 four regulars were hitting below .250, including Doug DeCinces at .216 and Schofield at .213.

With all of that, what may have hurt the team most was the absence of Bob Boone, victimized by the weird rule about not re-signing with your old team in April. The Angels were catching Darrell Miller, who was hitting .189 and not throwing very well. Keep this fact in mind. Anyway, Boone came back in May and began hitting immediately, but for the first two weeks didn't throw nearly as well as he usually does.

The first thing that kicked the team into its midsummer spurt, then, was the return of Boone on May 1, which began to pay dividends when Boone got into top form. The starting rotation was stabilized when Jack Lazorko replaced Urbano Lugo on May 20. Lazorko started on May 20, 25 and 30 and pitched fairly well all three times, but was 0–2. Lazorko's first win on June 4, then, was more than a coincidental turning point for the team, which reached an early-season nadir of eight games under .500, at 22–30. Sutton pitched very well in defeat in his next start (8 6 2 2 0 2, game score 64) then beat Kansas City 12–0 in the start following, and the starting rotation was healthy.

During the second movement of the season, June 4–August 5, the Angels used the same regulars as in the first movement, except that Boone had replaced Miller at catcher. Miller, though still on the roster, all but disappeared. Their team batting average remained low. As of August 5 no Angel was hitting higher than .285, and the team average was 13th in the league. Despite those similarities, the Angels did not play like the Angels of May. In their first 52 games the Angels turned 45 double plays; in the next 56, they turned 65 double plays. The obvious difference was the return of Boone, who all but eliminated the opposition's running game with his remarkable combination of throwing arm, quick release and timely pitchouts, thus keeping the double play in order. Angel opponents on the season stole only 72 bases, 26 less than against any other major league team.

Candelaria started until June 26, when he encountered personal problems; Reuss replaced him in his scheduled start of June 21, and for a while this seemed to make no difference. Candelaria and Reuss are both veteran lefthanders with tremendous control; as of August 5 Candelaria's ERA was 4.40, Reuss's 4.46. McCaskill returned to the rotation on July 16, forcing out Lazorko; the rotation was Witt, Sutton, Fraser, Reuss, and McCaskill.

As for the offense, leading the league in walks and with average numbers of homers and stolen bases, the Angels were scoring runs despite their low batting averages. In the 56 games of the second movement, the Angels scored 293 runs, a little over five per game. They were winning both at home and on the road—in fact, more often on the road. In the first movement the Angels were 11–15 at home and 11–15 on the road; in the second they were 18–13 at home (.581), and 16–9 on the road (.640).

And then what happened? It's a strange story. On July 23 the Red Sox released Bill Buckner; on July 28 he signed with the Angels. "A Fortunate Coincidence for the Angels," said the headline in *The Sporting News* (August 10, 1987). "California's offense landed at the bottom of the American League at the same time Bill Buckner landed on unemployment. It was a coincidence the Angels simply couldn't ignore, and they signed (Buckner) . . . to bolster their sagging attack." Their offense *wasn't* last in the American League, of course; they were last in batting average, but near the league average where it counts, in runs scored.

Anyway, Buckner, with his .150 secondary average, became the Angel DH. Brian Downing was forced into the outfield, with which he was unhappy, which forced Jack Howell from left field to right, putting Devon White in center field and Gary Pettis on the bench. This made no sense, not from any angle. The Angels put Brian Downing in the outfield instead of Gary Pettis, for minimal offensive gain. Although Buckner hit for a higher average than Pettis, their on-base percentages were almost the same. There is little difference in power, since Buckner has no power either, and there is a massive difference in speed. It didn't increase the number of people on base, and it didn't improve their ability to score those who were on.

On August 6, Willie Fraser was hammered by Seattle, leading to a 15–4 defeat. Prior to that start Fraser was 7–7 with a strong 3.76 ERA, but after that he didn't start for ten days, and when he pitched poorly then he was jerked from the rotation. Candelaria returned; the rotation was Witt, McCaskill, Candelaria, Sutton and Reuss, with Witt bumping people back a day to work on three or four days rest, while everybody else had four to six.

The Angels began to struggle. From four games over on August 5 (56–52), they dropped to .500 on August 16 (59–59). Gary Pettis, Gold Glove outfielder, was optioned to Edmonton in the Pacific Coast League. Recalled in his place was Tony Armas, a veteran teammate of Buckner's. Armas has the best of both worlds: he walks as little as Buckner, but strikes out as much as Pettis. For whatever unimaginable reason, however, Armas moved into the Angel outfield. That forced Jack Howell to third base. Veteran Doug DeCinces was released. DeCinces had hit just .234, but with a secondary average near .300. Armas hit .198, with a secondary average of .198.

Mauch had committed himself to a policy that wasn't working. He was abandoning the people who had gotten him into the pennant race, low-average hitters with good defense and good secondary averages, for veterans from other teams. By August 28 the Angels were three games under .500, at 63–66. Mauch charged blindly ahead. On August 29 the Angels acquired second baseman Johnny Ray from Pittsburgh, and immediately another regular, Mark McLemore, hit the bench. McLemore hit .234 but with almost the same secondary average, .233. Ray hit .346—but with a secondary average of .110. Mauch was assembling a lineup for the pennant drive that didn't do anything except hit singles. By August 15 the Angels were eight games under .500, at 68–76. They were dead.

It is easy to see why you would want to have veterans around for a pennant race—in a supporting role. I can understand that. I can's understand this. My feelings about it were summed up by Tracy Ringolsby in the October 10 edition of *Baseball America*. "It's the type of approach," wrote Ringolsby, "that brings back memories of Howser, who watched the Angels make similar moves in a futile effort to beat out the Royals in 1985. 'What they do is tell the kids who got them into contention, "You're good enough to get us here, but not good enough to win,"' Howser said. In other words, the Angels undercut the foundation for the future."

Naturally, General Manager Mike Port didn't see himself as being at fault for making any of these moves. In an interview in the *Riverside Press-Enterprise* of September 14, he blasted his player's desire. "They lack what it takes inside. Some guys have their own interests at heart."

Another critical factor in the collapse should not go unnoticed. Remember early in the season, when Darrell Miller had to fill in for the missing Bob Boone, and didn't do the job? Down the stretch, Mauch worked Bob Boone into the ground. Boone, 39 years old, missed the month of April—and still caught 127 games, third in the American League. Between early August and the Angels elimination Boone caught every game. His batting average as of August 5 was .270. In the season's third movement he hit .196.

Jerry Reuss in the season's third movement was hit hard, driving his ERA well over 5.00. McCaskill also was not sharp.

The Angels wound up 12 games under .500, tied for last at 75–87. The last-place tag is misleading. 1987 was, among other things, the year the American League West essentially caught up with the East. Most people missed this, because the division champion Twins won only 85 games. The fans and media assumed, naturally enough, that the AL East was beating up on the West again. It wasn't. There were no powerhouses in the West, but there were no weaklings, either. It was the most balanced division, from top to bottom, in the history of baseball, with the last-place teams finishing only ten games out of first. The top teams in the AL East weren't beating up on the West, but on the weak sisters of their own division, Baltimore and Cleveland, both far worse than any team in the West. The teams in the West won 48 percent of interdivision games.

In 1985 and 1986 the Angels had a terrific record in one-run games (30–13 in 1985, 28–16 in 1986.) Last year they won only 17 one-run games, the fewest of any major-league team. Their winning percentage in games decided by one or two runs was .429. They played ten one-run games in September, with all those wonderful veterans in the lineup. They lost nine of them.

Angel pinch hitters in 1987 had a tremendous year, hitting .327 with 9 homers and 35 RBI in 147 at bats. The Angel pinch hitters led the league in runs scored, home runs, RBI, batting average, and slugging percentage. Their top pinch hitter was Mark Ryal (10 for 31), who led AL pinch hitters in total bases (19) and slugging percentage (.613) among those with 20 or more tries; he had 3 doubles and 2 homers among his 10 hits. He was aided by George Hendrick (3 home runs), Jack Howell (15 total bases, third in the league) and Ruppert Jones (13 total bases). Angel pinch hitters had a .585 slugging percentage, while only one other team in the league was over .382.

For the second straight season the Angels had an outstanding rookie, this time Devon White. A year ago I didn't think that the Angels' outstanding rookie, Wally Joyner, would be as good the second time around. I was wrong about that; he was better. Undeterred, I'll say the same about Devon White. I thought White would hit .250 to .260 with 10 to 15 homers. On July 2 White was hitting .299 with 17 homers. Over the second half, he lost 36 points and hit only 7 more homers. I frankly don't think that White will sustain the performance indicated by his 1987 season.

Led by White and Pettis, the Angel base stealers were successful when they tried, with a 74 percent success rate just missing the best in the American League. As I mentioned last year, the only people on Mauch's teams who run are the ones who can run; California is the opposite of San Francisco in this way. With Pettis gone the Angels will be light one threat in that category in 1988, although one would guess that Devon White will be running more.

The Angels had another good rookie in DeWayne Buice, a veteran minor leaguer who made the team and surprised the league with 17 saves and 109 strikeouts in 114 innings. Willie Fraser, a rookie pitcher who was a member of that Olympic team, finished 10–10 with a 3.92

ERA, best among the Angel starters; he was returned to the rotation on September 15, when Candelaria went to New York. Yet another rookie was second baseman Mark McLemore, who impressed defensively and wasn't too bad in the box.

Despite having worked into their team these four rookies plus young players like Wally Joyner, Dick Schofield, and Jack Howell, the Angels remained in 1987 the oldest team in the division, although that makes them the oldest team in the youngest division. Much of the age was concentrated in the pitching staff, where the Angels started John Candelaria, Don Sutton, and Reuss, but Bob Boone is three weeks older than Johnny Bench, and Brian Downing is older than he used to be.

Anytime a team finishes within 15 games of first place, they have to be taken seriously as a contender in the following season. The Angels have young players, and they were in the race in 1987. If Kirk McCaskill is able to come back, and one would suppose that he will be, their starting rotation will be much improved. Willie Fraser could improve it further if he continues to develop.

Having said all that, their ability to bounce back in 1988 is somewhat suspect. No player at Edmonton is regarded as a super prospect, with the best being Jim Eppard, a first baseman with no power, and Dante Bichette, an outfielder with no speed. More to the point, this team didn't collapse down the stretch because of bad luck. I've been defending Gene Mauch for 15 years, but there's no defending this performance. There has always been a strain of erratic judgment in this organization. In the last ten years Gene Mauch has helped counteract that. At this point, you've got to be concerned about his ability to continue to do that.

STOLEN BASES ALLOWED

Texas	205
Montreal	201
Houston	199
Atlanta	186
Philadelphia	185
Cubs	169
Minnesota	168
Mets	162
Baltimore	145
Cincinnati	139
Pittsburgh	134
San Francisco	132
San Deigo	124
Kansas City	124
Toronto	123
Los Angeles	120
Milwaukee	119
Oakland	117
Detroit	116
Yankees	114
Seattle	111
Cleveland	111
Boston	109
St. Louis	100
White Sox	98
California	72

RUNS SCORED AND ALLOWED WINS AND LOSSES

Wins	494	224	75-0	1.000
Candelaria	105	96	12-8	.600
Witt	159	154	18-18	.500
Reuss	87	82	8-8	.500
Blowouts	274	297	23-24	.489
Home Games	377	405	38-43	.469
All Games	770	803	75-87	.463
Road Games	393	398	37-44	.457
Pitchers' Duels	55	56	15-18	.455
Sutton	167	146	15-19	.441
Slugfests	443	494	28-37	.431
One Run Games	176	186	17-27	.386
Fraser	108	125	8-15	.348
Losses	276	579	0-87	.000

TEN BEST STARTS

	IP	H	R	ER	BB	SO		
McCaskill at Sea, Apr 15	9	4	0	0	1	9	W	87
Witt vs. Minn, Apr 17	9	3	1	1	1	7	W	83
Fraser at KC, June 13	9	4	0	0	2	5	W	82
Witt vs. Chi, June 6	10	7	1	1	1	8	W	81
Witt at NY, June 1	9	5	2	1	2	11	W	80
Witt at Oak, July 28	9	6	2	2	0	11	W	78
Witt vs. Sea, Apr 7	9	5	1	1	4	8	W	77
Witt at KC, June 12	8	3	1	1	1	6	L	77
Reuss vs. KC, June 21	9	8	0	0	0	6	W	77
Sutton at Mil, May 5	7	2	0	0	1	4	W	76

PITCHERS WHEN SUPPORTED BY THREE TO FIVE RUNS

	G	IP	W-L	Pct	SO	BB	ERA
Witt	12	87	7-4	.636	61	36	3.12
Candelaria	6	34	2-2	.500	26	7	3.93
McCaskill	6	36	2-2	.500	30	14	4.79
Sutton	10	45	3-3	.500	22	10	6.60
Fraser	9	46	3-5	.375	27	22	4.86
Lazorko	7	46	1-4	.200	20	15	4.86

HALL OF FAME WATCH

Fully qualified: Sutton 139; **Could be elected on current accomplishments:** Boone 93; **Building credentials but not yet viable candidate:** Buckner 68.5, Mauch 73, Reuss 45, Armas 38, Candelaria 31; **Working on it:** Hendrick 27, Wynegar 24, Witt 17, Minton 15, Ray 14, Downing 13, DeCinces 12.5, Joyner 11; **Long way to go:** R Jones 9, D Moore 9, McCaskill 4, Lucas 3, Pettis 3, D White 3, Schofield 2.

TEN WORST STARTS

	IP	H	R	ER	BB	SO		
Fraser at Cle, Sep 26	3	8	7	7	2	4	—	17
Candelaria vs. Oak, Aug 15	4	7	8	8	3	4	L	17
Candelaria vs. Cle, June 10	5	11	7	7	1	2	—	18
Candelaria at Det, May 13	2⅔	5	7	7	3	1	L	18
Witt at Oak, Apr 22	3	6	7	6	5	3	L	19
Reuss vs. Bos, July 12	5⅓	11	7	6	1	0	—	19
Witt at Mil, July 17	3⅓	9	6	6	0	1	L	19
Sutton at NY, May 24	2⅔	9	5	5	2	2	—	20
Lugo at Det, May 12	2⅓	8	8	3	1	2	L	20
Sutton at NY, June 3	2⅓	8	5	5	0	0	L	21

ONE-RUN WINS

St. Louis	33
San Francisco	29
Mets	29
Montreal	28
Toronto	27
Philadelphia	27
Cincinnati	27
Detroit	26
Baltimore	25
Houston	25
Milwaukee	24
Yankees	24
Minnesota	24
Atlanta	23
Kansas City	22
Pittsburgh	21
Oakland	20
Cleveland	19
Los Angeles	19
San Diego	19
White Sox	19
Seattle	19
Boston	18
Cubs	18
Texas	18
California	17

Bob BOONE, Catcher
Runs Created: 37

	G	AB	Hit	2B	3B	HR	Run	RBI	TBB	SO	SB	CS	Avg
12.17 years		524	131	22	2	8	49	60	47	44	3	4	.250
1987	128	389	94	18	0	3	42	33	35	36	0	2	.242
First Half	56	179	48	9	0	1	16	19	19	18	0	1	.268
Second Half	72	210	46	9	0	2	26	14	16	18	0	1	.219
Vs. RHP		255	56	13	0	3	29	20	24	28	0	1	.220
Vs. LHP		134	38	5	0	0	13	13	11	8	0	1	.284
Home	62	186	45	7	0	1	23	14	20	19	0	0	.242
Road	66	203	49	11	0	2	19	19	15	17	0	2	.241

Jack HOWELL, Left Field
Runs Created: 70

	G	AB	Hit	2B	3B	HR	Run	RBI	TBB	SO	SB	CS	Avg
1.51 years		488	118	24	5	21	72	68	61	119	5	3	.242
1987	138	449	110	18	5	23	64	64	57	118	4	3	.245
First Half	73	252	66	12	3	15	36	42	36	59	2	3	.262
Second Half	65	197	44	6	2	8	28	22	21	59	2	0	.223
Vs. RHP		376	101	15	3	22	57	52	50	93	4	1	.269
Vs. LHP		73	9	3	2	1	7	12	7	25	0	2	.123
Home	71	230	62	8	3	15	34	40	26	56	2	1	.270
Road	67	219	48	10	2	8	30	24	31	62	2	2	.219

Wally JOYNER, First Base
Runs Created: 111

	G	AB	Hit	2B	3B	HR	Run	RBI	TBB	SO	SB	CS	Avg
1.87 years		619	178	32	2	30	97	116	69	65	7	2	.288
1987	149	564	161	33	1	34	100	117	72	64	8	2	.285
First Half	84	321	89	18	1	20	55	73	48	32	5	2	.277
Second Half	65	243	72	15	0	14	45	44	24	32	3	0	.296
Vs. RHP		363	104	18	1	26	73	78	52	39	7	1	.287
Vs. LHP		201	57	15	0	8	27	39	20	25	1	1	.284
Home	81	307	80	16	1	19	51	57	37	38	3	0	.261
Road	68	257	81	17	0	15	49	60	35	26	5	2	.315

Gary PETTIS, Center Field
Runs Created: 35

	G	AB	Hit	2B	3B	HR	Run	RBI	TBB	SO	SB	CS	Avg
3.60 years		518	125	16	6	4	82	40	69	143	52	13	.241
1987	133	394	82	13	2	1	49	17	52	124	24	5	.208
First Half	87	303	67	12	2	1	36	12	42	93	17	4	.221
Second Half	46	91	15	1	0	0	13	5	10	31	7	1	.165
Vs. RHP		266	60	8	1	0	33	13	39	96	20	4	.226
Vs. LHP		128	22	5	1	1	16	4	13	28	4	1	.172
Home	67	204	45	8	1	0	27	12	23	63	12	2	.221
Road	66	190	37	5	1	0	22	5	29	61	12	3	.195

Mark McLEMORE, Second Base
Runs Created: 45

	G	AB	Hit	2B	3B	HR	Run	RBI	TBB	SO	SB	CS	Avg
0.88 years		497	116	15	3	3	69	47	56	84	28	10	.233
1987	138	433	102	13	3	3	61	41	48	72	25	8	.236
First Half	87	293	64	11	2	1	41	25	32	51	23	5	.218
Second Half	51	140	38	2	1	2	20	16	16	21	2	3	.271
Vs. RHP		307	74	9	2	2	49	31	35	60	24	6	.241
Vs. LHP		126	28	4	1	1	12	10	13	12	1	2	.222
Home	71	213	50	7	1	3	29	24	26	32	13	4	.235
Road	67	220	52	6	2	0	32	17	22	40	12	4	.236

Devon WHITE, Right Field
Runs Created: 87

	G	AB	Hit	2B	3B	HR	Run	RBI	TBB	SO	SB	CS	Avg
1.29 years		540	140	26	5	19	91	70	36	113	32	9	.259
1987	159	639	168	33	5	24	103	87	39	135	32	11	.263
First Half	88	364	104	21	4	17	65	53	20	78	20	5	.286
Second Half	71	275	64	12	1	7	38	34	19	57	12	6	.233
Vs. RHP		440	119	24	3	13	68	61	26	99	24	9	.270
Vs. LHP		199	49	9	2	11	35	26	13	36	8	2	.246
Home	79	314	78	14	3	11	46	39	19	67	21	4	.248
Road	80	325	90	19	2	13	57	48	20	68	11	7	.277

Doug DECINCES, Third Base
Runs Created: 62

	G	AB	Hit	2B	3B	HR	Run	RBI	TBB	SO	SB	CS	Avg
10.18 years		571	148	31	3	23	76	86	61	89	6	5	.259
1987	137	462	108	25	0	16	66	64	70	89	3	4	.234
First Half	81	278	67	12	0	11	43	42	46	55	3	3	.241
Second Half	56	184	41	13	0	5	23	22	24	34	0	1	.223
Vs. RHP		299	62	17	0	9	38	38	34	60	3	2	.207
Vs. LHP		163	46	8	0	7	28	26	36	29	0	2	.282
Home	73	235	64	12	0	10	38	34	40	37	2	3	.272
Road	64	227	44	13	0	6	28	30	30	52	1	1	.194

Brian DOWNING, Designated Hitter
Runs Created: 117

	G	AB	Hit	2B	3B	HR	Run	RBI	TBB	SO	SB	CS	Avg
10.75 years		537	143	25	2	18	81	75	83	75	4	3	.266
1987	155	567	154	29	3	29	110	77	106	85	5	5	.272
First Half	87	327	90	19	3	18	65	47	62	51	2	3	.275
Second Half	68	240	64	10	0	11	45	30	44	34	3	2	.267
Vs. RHP		390	101	19	2	18	76	53	65	50	5	1	.259
Vs. LHP		177	53	10	1	11	34	24	41	35	0	4	.299
Home	76	280	78	18	2	11	51	36	56	43	4	3	.279
Road	79	287	76	11	1	18	59	41	50	42	1	2	.265

Dick SCHOFIELD, Shortstop
Runs Created: 56

	G	AB	Hit	2B	3B	HR	Run	RBI	TBB	SO	SB	CS	Avg
3.59 years		509	116	18	4	10	59	47	44	77	16	4	.228
1987	134	479	120	17	3	9	52	46	37	63	19	3	.251
First Half	89	325	77	9	1	8	37	37	26	40	12	2	.237
Second Half	45	154	43	8	2	1	15	9	11	23	7	1	.279
Vs. RHP		318	77	9	1	7	30	33	23	50	13	1	.242
Vs. LHP		161	43	8	2	2	22	13	14	13	6	2	.267
Home	74	257	66	6	1	4	27	25	21	34	13	3	.257
Road	60	222	54	11	2	5	25	21	16	29	6	0	.243

Bill BUCKNER, Ouch
Runs Created: 51

	G	AB	Hit	2B	3B	HR	Run	RBI	TBB	SO	SB	CS	Avg
14.25 years		624	182	34	3	12	73	80	30	30	12	5	.292
1987	132	469	134	18	2	5	39	74	22	26	2	3	.286
First Half	68	263	72	5	1	2	22	41	9	17	1	3	.274
Second Half	64	206	62	13	1	3	17	33	13	9	1	0	.301
Vs. RHP		350	103	17	1	5	31	58	19	15	1	3	.294
Vs. LHP		119	31	1	1	0	8	16	3	11	1	0	.261
Home	68	238	72	8	2	2	20	42	13	14	1	3	.303
Road	64	231	62	10	0	3	19	32	9	12	1	0	.268

AMERICAN LEAGUE EAST

DETROIT TIGERS

Tweny-two random comments about a remarkable season:

1) The 1984 Detroit Tigers won 26 of their first 30 games, but from then on won 78 of 132, a .591 winning percentage. The 1987 Tigers were 15 games behind that pace by May 11 (11–19) but won 87 of the last 132, a .659 percentage.

2) After that early season sluggishness, I don't know that I have ever seen a team play so well for so long without a torrid stretch. Beginning with the week of May 10 to 16, the Tiger's weekly records were 5–1, 4–2, 5–1, 3–3, 4–2, 4–2, 3–3, 5–2, 5–2, 3–1, 4–2, and 4–2. After a subpar week (3–4—hardly a slump) they picked it up again: 5–2, 5–2, 4–2, 5–2. In 17 weeks their worst week was 3–4, their best 5–1. From mid-September on they were erratic (3–4, 6–0, 2–5, 5–2, 1–0), but in that remarkable 17-week drive they won 71 of 106 games (.670)—without a streak longer than six wins.

3) While the Tigers were struggling early their starting pitching was as strong as at any point in the season. Through 24 games their starting pitchers had a 3.33 ERA and an average game score of 55.2, far better than their final figures of 4.05 and 51.9. They were losing because the offense was struggling and the bullpen was poor.

4) The Tigers tended to put their good hitting and good pitching performances together. When they had a quality start, the team's record was 72–16, an .818 winning percentage, the best of any major-league team.

5) The Tigers won 30 games by five runs or more, most of any major league team. Their first four wins of the season were 9–3, 11–4, 7–1, and 7–1. Later they bombed Kansas City 13–2, battered California 12–4 and 15–2, beat Minnesota 15–7, blasted Cleveland 15–3, pummeled Boston 18–8, kayoed Baltimore 9–0, smashed Milwaukee 11–1, creamed California 12–5, kicked the Yankees 15–4, flattened Minnesota in a three game set 11–2, 7–1, and 8–0, scorched Texas 7–0 and 11–2, and belted Baltimore 12–4, 6–0, and 10–1.

6) When the Tigers scored three to five runs, they were just 30–31. The secret was not that they could win with a fair offense, but that they had few games with no offense and comparatively few bad pitching performances.

7) The Tigers led the majors in runs scored both at home (442) and on the road (454).

8) Their secondary average, .314, was the highest in baseball.

9) Their 88 quality starts were the most in the American League.

10) There were 780 runs scored in Detroit, 851 in Tiger road games, the second straight year that Tiger Stadium has shown as an extreme pitcher's park.

Part of the reason this is thought to be a hitter's park although it isn't seems obvious. Tiger Stadium is short down the lines, but immense in center field. In batting practice hitters can hit home runs at will because they can pull the ball at will, but when the game starts they can't do that. You can't pull most major-league pitchers consistently. So you take batting practice in a dream park, but when the game starts it's back to reality.

Still, this *used to be* a good hitter's park. What has changed is not the park as much as the league; it was a good hitter's park relative to the league. The last five parks added to the American League all have pretty decent hitting characteristics (Minnesota, Seattle, Toronto, Kansas City, Texas), plus there have been changes in several other parks which have improved their offensive characteristics. The parks that used to be the hitter's parks in the AL, Tiger Stadium and Fenway, have been knocked down the list. No Tiger now has led the league in batting average since 1961. Only one Tiger since 1946, Darrell Evans, has led the league in home runs. And no Tiger since Bob Boone's father (1955) has led the league in RBI.

11) When we say that the 1987 Tigers didn't draw well at the gate, we are also making a relative statement; ten years ago 2,061,830 fans would have been quite good. This isn't 1978, and to finish seventh in the league in attendance in a championship year in a city that has traditionally been considered an excellent baseball town is a matter of concern.

A look at the attendance patterns reveals three things. First, their attendance early in the season was even lower than you might have expected. Among their first 28 home dates, their second-largest crowd (after opening day) was 20,993.

Second, after school started their attendance on weeknights dropped sharply despite the pennant race. From August 31 to the end of the season they had 17 home dates. They drew only six crowds as large as 25,000, all on weekends. In the last week of the season they had three crowds under 20,000. You wouldn't see that in Toronto or Kansas City.

Third, the Tigers attendance dropped dramatically against Western division opponents. In 39 dates against division rivals, the Tigers drew an average of 29,017. In 40 dates against the West the average dropped to 23,254, a decline of 19.9 percent. Toronto, by contrast, lost only

79

11.9 percent of their attendance when facing the West, and the Yankees lost less than 2 percent of theirs.

So the Tigers would benefit significantly if the American League would go to playing 20 games a year against their own division and 6 against the other, which would save travel costs and which I think most baseball fans would prefer. Still, if you don't draw when you're not playing well and you don't draw on weeknights when the kids are in school and you don't draw when you're facing a team out of your division—well, that's a lot of negatives. When the Tigers finish last in 1990 or 1991, the attendance picture might be pretty grim.

12) The man who got undue credit for the Tiger offense was Bill Madlock. The Tigers had one outstanding offensive strength (Trammell), and, with Brookens having a solid year, no outstanding weaknesses. In terms of runs created per game, the Tiger regulars were Alan Trammell, 8.94; Darrell Evans, 7.22; Kirk Gibson, 6.97; Chet Lemon, 6.40; Matt Nokes, 6.39; Lou Whitaker, 5.45; Madlock, 4.79; Pat Sheridan, 3.96; and Tom Brookens, 3.67. Madlock also didn't drive in runs as frequently as Trammell, Herndon, Nokes, Gibson, Lemon, or Evans.

13) Sparky Anderson used 213 pinch hitters, the most in the American League. His pinch hitters were not effective, hitting just .227 with one homer. Larry Herndon hit .381 as a pinch hitter (8 for 21), leading the American League, which means that the rest of the Tiger pinch hitters were barely over .200.

14) Sparky removed his pitcher before he had pitched six innings or allowed four runs (a quick hook) only five times, the fewest of any major-league manager. He had 25 slow hooks, fourth-highest in the majors. The ration, five to one, was easily the longest in baseball, and in part because of that Tiger starting pitchers won 74 games, 10 more than any other American League team (Kansas City starters won 64).

If you look at the lists of quick hooks and slow hooks (see charts), it is apparent that the older, more veteran managers tend to congregate on one end of the scale, and the younger managers on the other, with exceptions. Sparky is the slowest hook in the majors, with that 5–25 ratio. Next to him are two other managers who have also been around for a long time, John McNamara (10–28) and Dick Williams (11–28). Behind them was Kansas City (8–14), which was essentially Billy Gardner. Gardner, though he has less major-league experience, is seven years older than Sparky, and has been managing almost as long, only in the minor leagues. (Replacement John Wathan managed 36 games during which he was almost perfectly conventional, with no quick hooks and only one slow hook.) Next up the line was Gene Mauch (16–21), the most veteran manager of all. Tommy Lasorda is a slow hook. Out of baseball last year, Billy Martin may be the slowest hook of all.

Among the men with more quick hooks than slow hooks, you find the younger, less-experienced managers—Jimy Williams, Larry Bowa, Jim Leyland, Dave Johnson, Piniella. Buck Rodgers, closer in age to Larry Bowa than Dick Williams, is on that end. Gene Michael and Pete Rose are relatively quick in going to the pen.

There are two alternative ways to explain this. One is that baseball is still changing in the same way it has been changing for 112 years. For all of that time, starting pitchers have been asked to do less and less. You pick any 10-year period since the 1870s, and you can easily see that at the end of it starting pitchers were expected to do less than at the beginning. In each generation, starters have been asked to start less often and to pitch fewer innings when they started. The fact that the managers now coming into the game go to the bullpen more quickly than the older managers is evidence that this trend is still in motion, and will continue as the older managers pass from the scene.

The alternative explanation would be that experience teaches baseball managers to be patient with their starting pitchers. It would be enormously instructive, I think, to go back to about 1970 and figure quick hooks and slow hooks for that season. First, I think you would be likely to find that the ratio of quick hooks to slow hooks is higher now than it was then, which would tell us how rapidly baseball is changing in this regard. Second, I would want to compare the then-and-now quick hook/slow hook ratios of the managers who span that period—Anderson, Williams, Mauch, McNamara. If their ratios are about the same now as they were 17 years ago, that would suggest that they manage the way they do because that was the way it was done at the time they were learning the job. But if their ratios were higher then, that would suggest that their experience, as managers, has taught them to let the starting pitcher stay in the game.

There are some obvious exceptions. Whitey Herzog, a veteran, was the quickest hook in the majors, with 30 quick hooks, only 4 slow. Roger Craig, who is of the generation of Williams and Anderson but has little managerial experience, is a quick hook. Bobby Valentine, a young manager, is erratic, with high totals in both categories.

15) A puzzling aspect of the Tigers season is the failure of the opposition to exploit the Tigers' weakness against left-handed pitching. The Tigers had a 22–29 record against left-handers, a .431 winning percentage. Against right-handed pitchers their team winning percentage was .685. No other major-league team had anything approaching that 253-point imbalance (Atlanta was second with a 149-point split, see chart). But the Tigers had just 51 decisions against left-handed pitching, an average number (the league average was 51.2).

I can't understand that. Tiger Stadium is widely believed to be a left-handers park, with the right field upper deck hanging out a standing invitation. The lineup obviously lists to the left, with Matt Nokes, Kirk Gibson, Lou Whitaker, and Darrell Evans being left-handers, not to mention Pat Sheridan, who hits the bench against a lefty. Alan Trammell, though right-handed, historically has a very small platoon differential although I haven't seen 1987 data, while Whitaker historically has all kinds of trouble against left-handers (1984–1986 averages of .299 against right-handers, .266 against southpaws). Kirk Gibson over the same three years hit 49 points better against lefties (.296–.247). You would think that the opposition would have worked the left-handers in against Detroit the way they did against New York (62 decisions vs. left-handers) or Baltimore (61).

16) The Tigers over the last five years have the best winning percentage in baseball on grass fields (.587), but have not played particularly well on artificial turf (.504).

On road grass they are at .554, in their home park at .611. This was again true in 1987, when the Tigers were 13–12 on turf.

17) The Tigers took the Angels on the Gary Pettis trade. A position player doesn't have to be a good all-around player to help his team. A guy who can play center field the way Pettis can, can pinch run, pinch hit sometimes, play against left-handers, give Lemon a day off—well, that's a lot of value. Any manager who couldn't find spots in which Gary Pettis can help the team isn't a manager. But if you can't pitch any better than Dan Petry, there's no role for you.

18) Do the Tigers have the fastest outfield in the American League? You don't think of them as having a fast outfield, but who else has four guys who can move like Lemon, Sheridan, Gibson, and Pettis?

19) The Tigers' team speed last year was average (5.2 team speed score), but if they should happen to have a good record on artificial turf this year I guarantee you people will write that the reason for it is that Gary Pettis added speed to what used to be a slow lineup.

20) Detroit in the last five years has used 18 regulars at the nine positions, one of the lowest totals in baseball. Four players (Whitaker, Trammell, Lemon and Gibson) have been regulars throughout that period. They have made just one switch at catcher. Their trouble spots have been first base (Cabell, Barbey, Evans) and third (Brookens, Howard Johnson, Brookens, Coles, Brookens). Brookens is not counted as three players because he has had the job three times.

21) The 1987 Tigers were the oldest team in the American League, with their regulars and top pitchers averaging 31.3 years of age.

22) I will be surprised if this team repeats in 1988. The Tigers in the eighties continue to reenact the story of the Tigers of the sixties, with the 1987 championship being much like the 1972 title except one year earlier in the cycle. That team was put together in the years 1960–1963, with Norm Cash (1960), Dick McAuliffe (1961), Don Wert (1963), Bill Greehan (1963), and Mickey Lolich (1963) joining Kaline, already there, and being joined in 1964 by Willie Horton and Denny McLain. From the beginning of the cycle it took them an awfully long time to get to the top (1968), just as it did this team, which began accumulating players in 1977 and didn't arrive until 1984. By 1972, their second title year, that team was a collection of relics ready to collapse; anyone could have and many people did foresee their last place finish in 1974. This team is not quite to that point, but they're only a year or two away from it.

I see little doubt that one or two of the keys to the stunning 98–64 record of 1987 will drop way off in 1988; top candidates include Evans, Madlock, Lemon, and Trammell. A good team can survive the loss of one or two key players and still contend. The Tigers should stay over .500, and in this rapidly declining division, that might be enough to keep them in contention. But by 1990 and 1991, it is going to be extremely difficult for them to avoid a last-place finish.

ADVANTAGE VERSUS RIGHT-HANDED OR LEFT-HANDED PITCHERS

Detroit	R	.253
Atlanta	L	.149
Boston	L	.131
Kansas City	R	.123
Houston	R	.110
Minnesota	L	.109
Los Angeles	R	.104
Pittsburgh	R	.101
San Diego	L	.093
Toronto	R	.092
Baltimore	R	.085
White Sox	R	.071
Milwaukee	R	.065
Mets	R	.062
Yankees	R	.054
Texas	L	.044
Oakland	L	.041
Philadelphia	L	.038
California	R	.033
Cleveland	R	.029
Seattle	L	.026
St. Louis	R	.007
San Francisco	L	.006
Cincinnati	L	.004
Cubs	L	.002
Montreal	R	.002

RUNS SCORED AND ALLOWED WINS AND LOSSES

Wins	690	308	98-0	1.000
Alexander	64	17	11-0	1.000
Pitchers' Duels	70	51	21-10	.677
Home Games	442	338	54-27	.667
Robinson	120	105	14-7	.667
Blowouts	354	234	30-17	.638
One Run Games	182	172	26-16	.619
Petry	146	123	13-8	.619
Morris	176	128	21-13	.618
All Games	896	735	98-64	.605
Slugfests	582	481	45-30	.600
Tanana	185	164	19-15	.559
Terrell	188	164	19-16	.543
Road Games	454	397	44-37	.543
Losses	206	427	0-64	.000

TEN BEST GAMES

	IP	H	R	ER	BB	SO		
Terrell at Oak, May 1	10	2	1	1	4	8	—	88
Alexander vs. Tex, Aug 30	9	3	0	0	0	6	W	87
Robinson vs. NY, Aug 7	9	5	0	0	0	9	W	86
Alexander at Bos, Sep 23	9	2	0	0	1	3	W	85
Tanana vs. Sea, July 17	9	3	0	0	0	3	W	84
Morris at KC, Aug 13	9	5	1	1	1	11	W	83
Terrell vs. Bal, June 26	9	4	0	0	3	6	W	82
Tanana vs. Tor, Oct 4	9	6	0	0	3	9	W	81
Tanana vs. Tor, June 22	9	5	0	0	2	6	W	81
Morris vs. Bos, Sep 16	9	3	1	0	2	4	W	81

PITCHERS WHEN SUPPORTED BY THREE TO FIVE RUNS

	G	IP	W-L	Pct	SO	BB	ERA
Alexander	6	49	5-0	1.000	25	20	1.82
Morris	14	111	7-4	.636	88	34	3.23
Terrell	14	94	5-5	.500	58	39	4.96
Tanana	8	47	3-4	.429	42	13	4.18
Robinson	11	62	3-4	.429	45	23	5.40
Petry	6	28	0-4	.000	21	15	7.81

HALL OF FAME WATCH

Could be elected on current accomplishments: Sparky Anderson 96, Madlock 70; **Building credentials but not yet viable candidate:** Jack Morris 65, Trammel 59, Whitaker 48.5, W Hernandez 40, Tanana 39, Darrell Evans 38.5; **Working on it:** Lemon 26.5, Petry 19, D Alexander 17; **Long way to go:** Nokes 8, Terrell 6, Grubb 5.5, Herndon 5.5, Thurmond 5, Gibson 3, Morrison 3, Heath 2, Henneman 2, Sheridan 2, Noles 1.

TEN WORST STARTS

	IP	H	R	ER	BB	SO		
Terrell at Mil, July 1	2⅓	6	7	7	2	0	L	15
Terrell at Bal, June 20	1*	6	7	5	2	2	L	17
Petry at Cle, June 1	2⅔	6	7	7	3	2	L	17
Terrell at Chi, Aug 10	5⅔	11	8	7	3	3	L	17
Terrell at KC, Aug 14	4*	8	6	6	5	1	L	18
Robinson at Tor, June 16	3⅔	9	8	6	2	5	L	18
Morris at NY, Apr 20	7⅓	10	8	8	7	2	L	21
Terrell at Bos, June 4	5*	11	6	6	4	4	L	21
Robinson vs. Bal, June 28	3⅔	5	6	6	6	2	—	23
Robinson at Chi, Aug 12	3	7	5	5	3	1	—	23

RATIO OF QUICK HOOKS TO SLOW HOOKS

St. Louis	7.50-1
Toronto	6.00-1
San Diego	4.14-1
San Francisco	4.00-1
Montreal	3.67-1
Pittsburgh	3.20-1
Mets	3.00-1
Oakland	2.21-1
Yankees	1.92-1
Cubs	1.82-1
Cincinnati	1.50-1
Atlanta	1.36-1
Baltimore	1.33-1
Houston	1.33-1
Minnesota	1.31-1
Philadelphia	1.27-1
White Sox	1.18-1
Milwaukee	1.18-1
Los Angeles	1-1.06
Texas	1-1.16
Cleveland	1-1.19
California	1-1.32
Kansas City	1-1.75
Seattle	1-2.55
Boston	1-2.80
Detroit	1-5.00

Matt NOKES, Catcher
Runs Created: 82

	G	AB	Hit	2B	3B	HR	Run	RBI	TBB	SO	SB	CS	Avg
0.99 years		543	154	17	2	35	75	95	37	81	2	1	.284
1987	135	461	133	14	2	32	69	87	35	70	2	1	.289
First Half	72	254	81	9	1	20	46	51	21	37	2	0	.319
Second Half	63	207	52	5	1	12	23	36	14	33	0	1	.251
Vs. RHP		375	115	13	2	28	63	75	27	48	2	1	.307
Vs. LHP		86	18	1	0	4	6	12	8	22	0	0	.209
Home	68	214	66	4	2	14	36	36	19	39	1	0	.308
Road	67	247	67	10	0	18	33	51	16	31	1	1	.271

Kirk GIBSON, Left Field
Runs Created: 95

	G	AB	Hit	2B	3B	HR	Run	RBI	TBB	SO	SB	CS	Avg
5.51 years		583	161	25	6	27	96	91	69	129	30	9	.276
1987	128	487	135	25	3	24	95	79	71	117	26	7	.277
First Half	61	245	69	14	2	11	48	42	29	56	16	4	.282
Second Half	67	242	66	11	1	13	47	37	42	61	10	3	.273
Vs. RHP		309	87	16	3	20	57	59	43	67	18	3	.282
Vs. LHP		178	48	9	0	4	38	20	28	50	8	4	.270
Home	66	240	58	9	2	14	45	44	37	57	13	2	.242
Road	62	247	77	16	1	10	50	35	34	60	13	5	.312

Darrell EVANS, First Base
Runs Created: 103

	G	AB	Hit	2B	3B	HR	Run	RBI	TBB	SO	SB	CS	Avg
15.04 years		549	138	21	2	25	84	83	98	85	6	4	.251
1987	150	499	128	20	0	34	90	99	100	84	6	5	.257
First Half	77	253	65	13	0	19	48	53	53	37	2	3	.257
Second Half	73	246	63	7	0	15	42	46	47	47	4	2	.256
Vs. RHP		351	97	16	0	29	70	79	78	53	6	3	.276
Vs. LHP		148	31	4	0	5	20	20	22	31	0	2	.209
Home	74	246	61	8	0	19	41	49	45	43	2	1	.248
Road	76	253	67	12	0	15	49	50	55	41	4	4	.265

Chet LEMON, Center Field
Runs Created: 86

	G	AB	Hit	2B	3B	HR	Run	RBI	TBB	SO	SB	CS	Avg
9.96 years		564	157	33	5	19	83	74	60	83	5	7	.278
1987	146	470	130	30	3	20	75	75	70	82	0	0	.277
First Half	76	229	62	14	1	11	40	43	37	36	0	0	.271
Second Half	70	241	68	16	2	9	35	32	33	46	0	0	.282
Vs. RHP		290	81	16	2	12	40	51	38	56	0	0	.279
Vs. LHP		180	49	14	1	8	35	24	32	26	0	0	.272
Home	72	223	58	17	0	10	39	34	40	44	0	0	.260
Road	74	247	72	13	3	10	36	41	30	38	0	0	.291

Lou WHITAKER, Second Base
Runs Created: 93

	G	AB	Hit	2B	3B	HR	Run	RBI	TBB	SO	SB	CS	Avg
8.84 years		601	167	27	6	12	94	66	73	77	12	7	.278
1987	149	604	160	38	6	16	110	59	71	108	13	5	.265
First Half	78	311	82	14	2	9	59	31	38	61	8	3	.264
Second Half	71	293	78	24	4	7	51	28	33	47	5	2	.266
Vs. RHP		378	111	29	4	12	80	38	52	61	11	3	.294
Vs. LHP		226	49	9	2	4	30	21	19	47	2	2	.217
Home	72	283	74	17	1	10	53	28	34	50	5	2	.261
Road	77	321	86	21	5	6	57	31	37	58	8	3	.268

Pat SHERIDAN, Right Field
Runs Created: 50

	G	AB	Hit	2B	3B	HR	Run	RBI	TBB	SO	SB	CS	Avg
3.50 years		479	125	21	3	9	64	50	43	97	20	8	.261
1987	141	421	109	19	3	6	57	49	44	90	18	13	.259
First Half	82	269	75	10	2	3	40	32	23	58	10	12	.279
Second Half	59	152	34	9	1	3	17	17	21	32	8	1	.224
Vs. RHP		344	94	16	3	6	47	43	39	66	17	10	.273
Vs. LHP		77	15	3	0	0	10	6	5	24	1	3	.195
Home	66	187	52	11	1	3	26	26	15	45	8	5	.278
Road	75	234	57	8	2	3	31	23	29	45	10	8	.244

Tom BROOKENS, Third Base
Runs Created: 49

	G	AB	Hit	2B	3B	HR	Run	RBI	TBB	SO	SB	CS	Avg
6.60 years		470	116	21	5	9	58	54	32	73	12	8	.247
1987	143	444	107	15	3	13	59	59	33	63	7	4	.241
First Half	81	253	59	11	3	7	33	32	21	33	4	3	.233
Second Half	62	191	48	4	0	6	26	27	12	30	3	1	.251
Vs. RHP		290	70	8	3	6	34	34	17	39	5	3	.241
Vs. LHP		154	37	7	0	7	25	25	16	24	2	1	.240
Home	72	212	48	3	0	6	25	26	18	32	5	1	.226
Road	71	232	59	12	3	7	34	33	15	31	2	3	.254

Bill MADLOCK, Designated Hitter
Runs Created: 56

	G	AB	Hit	2B	3B	HR	Run	RBI	TBB	SO	SB	CS	Avg
11.15 years		591	180	31	3	15	83	77	54	46	16	8	.305
1987	108	387	102	18	0	17	61	57	34	50	4	3	.264
First Half	49	168	41	4	0	11	27	25	13	18	1	1	.244
Second Half	59	219	61	14	0	6	34	32	21	32	3	2	.279
Vs. RHP		215	56	8	0	9	34	29	21	24	3	2	.260
Vs. LHP		172	46	10	0	8	27	28	13	26	1	1	.267
Home	52	180	47	7	0	8	30	28	14	22	2	1	.261
Road	56	207	55	11	0	9	31	29	20	28	2	2	.266

Alan TRAMMELL, Shortstop
Runs Created: 137

	G	AB	Hit	2B	3B	HR	Run	RBI	TBB	SO	SB	CS	Avg
8.89 years		588	169	28	5	13	91	69	62	64	19	9	.287
1987	151	597	205	34	3	28	109	105	60	47	21	2	.343
First Half	76	306	103	15	1	13	54	49	26	33	11	1	.337
Second Half	75	291	102	19	2	15	55	56	34	14	10	1	.351
Vs. RHP		384	129	23	2	17	72	57	36	28	16	2	.336
Vs. LHP		213	76	11	1	11	37	48	24	19	5	0	.357
Home	74	296	103	16	0	13	49	53	27	20	7	1	.348
Road	77	301	102	18	3	15	60	52	33	27	14	1	.339

Mike HEATH, Catcher
Runs Created: 38

	G	AB	Hit	2B	3B	HR	Run	RBI	TBB	SO	SB	CS	Avg
5.84 years		529	133	22	3	11	60	61	36	71	7	6	.251
1987	93	270	76	16	0	8	34	33	21	42	1	5	.281
First Half	51	156	47	12	0	5	21	23	14	24	1	4	.301
Second Half	42	114	29	4	0	3	13	10	7	18	0	1	.254
Vs. RHP		111	28	5	0	3	11	15	9	27	0	0	.252
Vs. LHP		159	48	11	0	5	23	18	12	15	1	5	.302
Home	51	145	43	10	0	8	22	21	12	23	1	3	.297
Road	42	125	33	6	0	0	12	12	9	19	0	2	.264

TORONTO BLUE JAYS

The problem is that you acquire a past. In the beginning, what needs to be done is so clear, so obvious. When you have no players you must acquire the best young players that you can find. When they are ready you put them in the lineup because the people who were there before them are just a holding action, just waiting until the future is warm. When you have no past you have no loyalties, no debts. You know exactly where you are in the cycle. You have a memory of no yesterday's dreams which still might flower tomorrow, and thus there is no confusion of tomorrow with yesterday, plans with dreams or what is right with what is best for the team. On September 20 of 1987 the Toronto Blue Jays had a clean slate. They never will again.

The Blue Jays in the last five years have used only 14 players as regulars, five over the minimum of nine; they have been making a change at only one position a year. Every other major-league team has used at least 18 regulars. (These counts are based on the nine players each year with the most playing time.) Those 14 regulars include Willie Upshaw, Garth Iorg, Rance Mulliniks, Kelly Gruber, Tony Fernandez, George Bell, Jesse Barfield, Lloyd Moseby, and Ernie Whitt, all still on the roster as of the winter meetings. (The five departed are Damasco Garcia, Alfredo Griffin, Dave Collins, Barry Bonnell, and Cliff Johnson.)

Despite that stability, the Blue Jay lineup remains young, with only one key player (Ernie Whitt) being older than 31 in 1987.

They built this team by choosing carefully among the available young talent, and staying with the ones they chose.

Although it will no doubt be remembered that way, the Blue Jays did not lead the American League East from the start until almost the finish. They started 7–7 and trailed the Yankees, Tigers, and even the Brewers for most of the summer. On July 5 they were 45–35, ten games over .500, on July 22 still just 54–40, fourteen over.

Then they got hot. From late July until late September they won almost 70 percent of their games (42/61) to push them to +37. On the first of September the Detroit Tigers were in first place by a game. The Blue Jays went into first on September 7, but the Tigers regained first place on September 9, the Blue Jays on the eleventh, the Tigers on the seventeenth, the Blue Jays on the twentieth. Only after taking three straight from Detroit (September 24–26) did the Blue Jays appear to be in command of the race.

All season, the Blue Jays had avoided losing streaks by bouncing back after losses. The Blue Jays winning percentage following a loss was .631 (41–24), the best in baseball. That's including the last seven games, in which loss followed loss after loss. Before that streak they were 41–18 in games following a loss.

Unfortunately, when it all came down, it came down to winning tight, low-scoring games. Why the Blue Jays could not win that type of game is anybody's guess. They have good starting pitching, an excellent bullpen, excellent team speed. They should be able to win a pitcher's duel.

They couldn't. In slugfests, in games in which more than ten runs were scored, the Blue Jays winning percentage was .685, the best in baseball (37–17). In games in which six to ten runs were scored, the Jays winning percentage was .627, still the best in baseball (42–25). But in pitchers duels, games in which no more than five runs were scored, the Blue Jays winning percentage was .415, one of the worst in baseball (17–24).

The winning percentages of major-league teams in pitcher's duels and slugfests are full of such paradoxes; it often seems studying the data, that the teams that should win pitcher's duels, like Kansas City, actually win slugfests, and the teams that should win slugfests, like Minnesota, actually pick up most of their edge in pitcher's duels. Anyway, the Blue Jays had excellent pitching, good to excellent defense, and a fine bullpen. Let me spit out a few numbers on those:

The Pitching: The Blue Jays led the league in ERA at 3.74.

They were second in the league in strikeouts at 1064.

Although they also were well up the list in walks, there were only seven games in which the Jays' starting pitcher walked five or more men, and the Blue Jays won five of those seven games.

The Bullpen: The Blue Jays through six innings were only a .528 ballclub (they were ahead after six innings 75 times, behind 66 times, tied the other 21). By winning 15 games in which they were behind after six innings and two-thirds of the games in which they were tied after six, the Blue Jays improved their position by ten-and-a-half games in the late innings, up from 85.5 wins (.528) to 96 (.593).

The Defense: Toronto's Defensive Efficiency Record, .710, was the second best in baseball, meaning that when a ball was in play against this defense they did an excellent job of turning that ball into an out.

Blue Jay outfielders threw out 40 baserunners, not the league-leading total this time but one of the top figures, fourth best of the 26 teams.

The Blue Jays had only two games in which they committed more than two errors.

Blue Jay opponents stole 123 bases, about an average number.

With a problem at second base, they did not turn the double play particularly well.

The Blue Jays' weakest point for most of the season was at second base, after veteran Damaso Garcia was traded to Atlanta over the winter. The move seemed safe because 1) the Blue Jays had three young second basemen in the system, 2) Garcia had developed a reputation as a malcontent, and 3) Garcia wasn't that good anyway. The job went first to Mike Sharperson. Sharperson wasn't bad at second but had trouble getting his bat started, and with the Blue Jays struggling they didn't feel free to let him work his way out of it, so he was sent out after just 96 at bats. I think that was a premature decision, but then that's the nature of having three or four candidates to play a position: none of them is going to get a long look if he's not playing well. In the middle of the season Garth Iorg, after years as a platoon third baseman, took over the second base job with help from Manny Lee. Iorg, however, hit .210, and he's the kind of hitter who doesn't help you if he hits .270. Finally Nelson Liriano took over the job and was good, until the last week of the season, at which time, unfortunately, the injury to Fernandez pushed him into the lead-off role.

It would have been better for the Blue Jays not to have wasted time with Iorg at second base. Iorg is 32; his chance of developing into a long-term second baseman is zilch. They had other candidates to look at. If you're going to have to pay the price to break in a new second baseman, why not pay it and get it behind you?

The strongest point of the team, obviously, was the outfield. The three Toronto outfielders in 1987 averaged .285 with 34 homers and 105 RBI apiece, their best year following 1986 averages of .284 with 31 homers and 101 RBI. As far as I know the last time a group of three outfielders to have 300 RBI a year for two straight years was in 1929–1930, when the A's had Bing Miller, Mule Haas, and Al Simmons, and the Cubs had Riggs Stephenson, Hack Wilson, and Kiki Cuyler. Bell, Barfield, and Moseby also scored an average of a hundred runs (102) for the first time. It's very unlikely that they will be able to maintain that pace in 1988. First, they were 27 last year; now they're 28. Almost any group of players will perform better at age 27 than at any other age. Second, the new strike zone will probably cut everybody's numbers. Third, the Blue Jays may not even keep the outfield together. They've had five great years; there's no question but that this is one of the greatest of all outfields. When your average outfielder hits like Dwight Evans, that's an offense.

They have other rookies now trying to break into the outfield. A word about Toronto's rookies. Toronto's AAA team, Syracuse, plays in a very poor hitter's park in a league in which high batting averages are not common. The Blue Jays up to now have played in a very good hitter's park. The result has been that what a player has hit at Syracuse has been a pretty good estimate of what he was going to do in the major leagues, and indeed several Blue Jays (Willie Upshaw, Ernie Whitt, George Bell) have hit much better with Toronto than they ever did with Syracuse. Whereas if a player hits .250 to .270 in another minor-league park you would probably knock off 20 to 50 points and conclude he was marginal as a hitter, or whereas with the Dodgers you would need to knock off nearly a hundred points, if a player hits .250 to .270 at Syracuse, he is probably a .250 to .270 hitter.

With the Blue Jays moving into a new park in a year or so, we don't know whether this relationship will still hold or not. It's a good guess that it will; all of the domed stadiums except the Astrodome have been decent hitter's parks, and the primary variable here—the hitting characteristics of the Syracuse park—haven't changed.

Among the rookies, Sil Campusano has made progress as a hitter, and appears to have moved up close to Lloyd Moseby. Another outfielder, Rob Ducey, is a major-league hitter, but faces the difficult task of dislodging a 40-homer man in left or right. Rumor has it that the Blue Jays would like to move George Bell to designated hitter to make room for Ducey, but that George is not warming up to the notion. The third Syracuse outfielder, Glenallen Hill, is regarded as a prospect but has work to do with the bat.

Catcher Greg Myers is young and big and not a bad hitter. His problem is that he is left-handed. The Blue Jays have a platoon arrangement of a very good left-handed hitting catcher, Ernie Whitt, and a very poor right-handed hitting catcher, Charlie Moore. If Myers were right-handed he would step right into the job; as a left-hander, he may have to wait his turn.

Second baseman Nelson Liriano looks like a .250 to .270 range hitter, but—odd for a middle infielder—with a secondary average higher than his batting average, making him a solid offensive performer.

Over the last five years the Blue Jays have a .599 winning percentage on artificial turf, by far the best in the major leagues (no other team is better than .555), but have played just .517 ball on grass fields. Their 1987 season was essentially typical in this respect, with Toronto having a .616 winning percentage on turf (edging Minnesota as the best in the league) but was just 35–28 on grass fields, still the best of any of the league's four turf teams.

The Blue Jays scored 190 runs more than they allowed (845–655), the best ratio (1.29–1) and the largest positive margin (+190) in the majors. Detroit was at 1.22–1 and +161, second best in both respects. Detroit's ratio would suggest a likely won-lost record of 97–65, which the Tigers beat by one game (98–64). A run/opposition run ratio of 845–655 should lead to a record of 101–61, which the Blue Jays missed by a crucial five games.

Twenty-nine times the Blue Jays beat an opponent by five runs or more, while they lost only 12 such games, a .707 winning percentage in blowouts which was, again, the best in baseball. The Blue Jays may well have been, in truth, the best team in baseball.

What happened? It happened, that's all. It happened like a car wreck or a rape or an aneurism in the brain, an arbitrary punishment selected by an unseen God for an unknown reason, a punishment that could have happened to John or Joe or George Bush or the St. Louis Cardinals just as well, but which sought out the Toronto Blue and sat upon their shoulder with wings of iron. In the last seven games of the season only three Toronto players hit higher than .222 in more than five at bats. Those three were Lloyd Moseby (.379, 2 homers and 6 stolen bases), Rance Mulliniks, .385, and Rick Leach, .250. Cecil Fielder, however, hit .222; Manny Lee, .217; Ernie Whitt, .200; Willie Upshaw, .176; Jesse Barfield, .148; Nelson Liriano, .133; George Bell, .111; and Greg Myers, .111. Garth Iorg went 0-for-9, Juan Beniquez 0-for-15, and Fred McGriff 0-for-7. The pitching was fine; the starting pitchers had an ERA of 3.21. But scoring only 16 runs in the seven games, they needed a win in a close game somewhere. They didn't get it. Of the 15 players who had more than five at bats in the final games, five were rookies or players with very little major-league experience.

A lot of people assume that the Blue Jays' pennant

wreck will make it difficult for them to come back in 1988, that they have to make a trade, stir things up, or the self-doubt from 1987's last week will tear them up. I'm not sure that's true. A sports team's self-confidence is built, in the main, of the confidence of individual players. The Blue Jays collapsed after injuries at the two critical positions, catcher and shortstop. I don't think that experience will shatter the self-confidence of any individual. I wonder if, because of the injuries, the Blue Jays won't feel as if they were cheated of what they had earned, and if the reaction might not be anger, rather than panic. I think it is possible that this team might come out, like the 1986 Mets, determined to prove what they are made of by blowing the league away. And I wouldn't bet that they won't do it.

In many respects the period just ended in Toronto is like the Dick Williams era in Montreal, the years from 1977–1981 when the Expos had the best young team in the National League and, for two or three years, the best combined record in the league, but weren't able to win the close races. When the Expos moved out of that era, they moved into an era of mediocrity, when their pitching staff dissolved, they were unable to hold onto Gary Carter and the farm system stopped producing. While there is no executive in baseball for whom I have more respect than Pat Gillick, one would be foolish not to acknowledge that the same thing could happen here.

But I will be rooting for the Toronto Blue Jays in 1988. I feel like this city and this team and this front office and these fans deserve a World Championship. We have had ten World Champions in ten years, but no team has worked harder, no fans have supported their team any better, no front office has been smarter or more decent. Good luck to 'em.

WINNING PERCENTAGE ON ARTIFICIAL TURF OVER THE LAST FIVE YEARS

Toronto	.599
St. Louis	.555
Houston	.544
Philadelphia	.539
Kansas City	.538
Yankees	.528
Minnesota	.522
Cincinnati	.512
Montreal	.511
Mets	.508
Detroit	.504
Baltimore	.504
California	.488
Atlanta	.466
Pittsburgh	.465
Boston	.459
Seattle	.457
Los Angeles	.452
Oakland	.446
White Sox	.444
San Diego	.419
Cubs	.414
Milwaukee	.403
Cleveland	.401
San Francisco	.390
Texas	.354

RUNS SCORED AND ALLOWED WINS AND LOSSES

Wins	654	281	96-0	1.000
Blowouts	328	179	29-12	.707
Slugfests	460	331	37-17	.685
Key	166	116	24-12	.667
Home Games	425	319	52-29	.642
Cerutti	124	95	13-8	.619
Stieb	185	132	19-12	.613
Clancy	191	136	22-15	.595
All Games	845	655	96-66	.593
Road Games	420	336	44-37	.543
One Run Games	217	214	27-24	.529
Pitchers' Duels	71	92	17-24	.415
Losses	191	374	0-66	.000

TEN BEST GAMES

	IP	H	R	ER	BB	SO		
Clancy at Cal, May 18	9	2	0	0	1	9	W	91
Key vs. KC, May 11	9	4	0	0	0	7	W	86
Stieb vs. KC, July 10	9	4	0	0	2	7	W	84
Flanagan at Det, Oct 3	11	8	2	1	2	9	—	82
Clancy vs. Tex, May 3	8⅓	2	1	1	2	7	W	80
Key vs. KC, July 11	9	3	2	2	2	9	L	80
Clancy at Mil, June 27	9	4	1	1	3	7	W	79
Clancy at Bal, Sep 23	9	5	1	1	1	7	W	79
Clancy at Sea, May 23	9	6	2	1	0	9	W	78
Flanagan vs. Sea, Sep 5	7⅔	4	0	0	1	8	W	78

PITCHERS WHEN SUPPORTED BY THREE TO FIVE RUNS

	G	IP	W-L	Pct	SO	BB	ERA
Cerutti	11	59	5-2	.714	40	16	3.94
Key	18	126	7-3	.700	74	33	3.08
Clancy	14	77	4-6	.400	57	32	4.44
Stieb	8	44	2-3	.400	29	20	4.67

HALL OF FAME

Fully qualified: Phil Niekro 130; **Building credentials but not yet viable candidate:** Bell 40, Flanagan 39, Stieb 34.5; **Working on it:** Fernandez 23, Barfield 20, Henke 14, Moseby 10.5, Key 10; **Long way to go:** Clancy 9, Beniquez 7.5, Mulliniks 6, Whitt, 6, Upshaw 5.5, Jimy Williams 5, Moore 4.5, Eichorn 3, Leach 2.5, Iorg 2.5.

WINNING PERCENTAGE IN GAMES IN WHICH MORE THAN TEN RUNS WERE SCORED

Toronto	.685
Kansas City	.612
Detroit	.600
St. Louis	.600
Mets	.582
Milwaukee	.577
Cincinnati	.547
Minnesota	.541
Houston	.525
San Francisco	.519
Atlanta	.517
Yankees	.515
Oakland	.507
Montreal	.490
Boston	.486
Cubs	.486
Philadelphia	.481
Texas	.448
Seattle	.446
California	.431
Los Angeles	.424
Baltimore	.415
San Diego	.415
Pittsburgh	.415
Cleveland	.387
White Sox	.373

TEN WORST STARTS

	IP	H	R	ER	BB	SO		
Cerutti vs. NY, June 29	1⅓	5	8	8	3	0	—	9
Key at Oak, May 16	3⅓	11	6	6	0	2	L	16
Johnson at KC, May 5	1⅔	7	6	5	0	1	L	20
Clancy at Bos, Apr 12	2⅓	5	6	6	3	1	L	21
Wells at KC, July 4	1⅓	6	5	5	2	2	L	22
Johnson vs. Cle, Apr 9	4	6	7	7	1	1	L	22
Ward vs. Bos, Apr 17	1*	5	5	5	1	0	L	22
Stieb at Mil, June 28	2*	7	6	4	1	2	L	23
Niekro vs. Oak, Aug 29	⅔	4	5	5	2	1	—	23
Stieb vs. Det, Sep 26	2⅓	4	6	6	2	2	—	25

Ernie WHITT, Catcher
Runs Created: 64

	G	AB	Hit	2B	3B	HR	Run	RBI	TBB	SO	SB	CS	Avg
5.99 years		459	115	22	2	18	54	66	49	60	2	3	.251
1987	135	446	120	24	1	19	57	75	44	50	0	1	.269
First Half	68	223	56	15	0	6	30	32	24	27	0	1	.251
Second Half	67	223	64	9	1	13	27	43	20	23	0	0	.287
Vs. RHP		383	105	21	1	19	51	67	38	35	0	1	.274
Vs. LHP		63	15	3	0	0	6	8	6	15	0	0	.238
Home	67	214	56	12	1	11	29	43	25	29	0	1	.262
Road	68	232	64	12	0	8	28	32	19	21	0	0	.276

George BELL, Left Field
Runs Created: 125

	G	AB	Hit	2B	3B	HR	Run	RBI	TBB	SO	SB	CS	Avg
4.51 years		607	177	32	6	31	90	100	35	79	11	4	.292
1987	156	610	188	32	4	47	111	134	39	76	5	1	.308
First Half	85	338	99	14	3	29	62	76	15	48	2	0	.293
Second Half	71	272	89	18	1	18	49	58	24	28	3	1	.327
Vs. RHP		435	128	24	2	31	74	88	27	51	5	1	.294
Vs. LHP		175	60	8	2	16	37	46	12	25	0	0	.343
Home	78	302	88	13	3	19	54	56	23	42	2	1	.291
Road	78	308	100	19	1	28	57	78	16	34	3	0	.325

Willie UPSHAW, First Base
Runs Created: 65

	G	AB	Hit	2B	3B	HR	Run	RBI	TBB	SO	SB	CS	Avg
6.88 years		539	143	26	6	16	78	69	57	84	11	7	.265
1987	150	512	125	22	4	15	68	58	58	78	10	11	.244
First Half	82	303	79	18	3	11	45	41	31	48	8	7	.261
Second Half	68	209	46	4	1	4	23	17	27	30	2	4	.220
Vs. RHP		368	95	16	2	13	50	40	39	48	9	9	.258
Vs. LHP		144	30	6	2	2	18	18	19	30	1	2	.208
Home	73	236	53	9	2	7	39	25	32	36	8	3	.225
Road	77	276	72	13	2	8	29	33	26	42	2	8	.261

Lloyd MOSEBY, Center Field
Runs Created: 106

	G	AB	Hit	2B	3B	HR	Run	RBI	TBB	SO	SB	CS	Avg
6.97 years		595	157	29	7	18	89	81	60	118	29	10	.264
1987	155	592	167	27	4	26	106	96	70	124	39	7	.282
First Half	84	322	83	12	3	14	48	54	36	75	18	6	.258
Second Half	71	270	84	15	1	12	58	42	34	49	21	1	.311
Vs. RHP		394	112	18	2	21	72	70	45	79	32	5	.284
Vs. LHP		198	55	9	2	5	34	26	25	45	7	2	.278
Home	78	298	87	12	3	15	56	49	37	66	19	4	.292
Road	77	294	80	15	1	11	50	47	33	58	20	3	.272

Garth IORG, Second Base
Runs Created: 23

	G	AB	Hit	2B	3B	HR	Run	RBI	TBB	SO	SB	CS	Avg
5.75 years		426	110	22	3	3	44	41	20	52	4	3	.258
1987	122	310	65	11	0	4	35	30	21	52	2	2	.210
First Half	71	169	38	3	0	0	18	18	10	24	0	2	.225
Second Half	51	141	27	8	0	4	17	12	11	28	2	0	.191
Vs. RHP		172	40	8	0	3	24	16	10	34	2	0	.233
Vs. LHP		138	25	3	0	1	11	14	11	18	0	2	.181
Home	60	148	31	5	0	1	15	15	10	26	2	0	.209
Road	62	162	34	6	0	3	20	15	11	26	0	2	.210

Jesse BARFIELD, Right Field
Runs Created: 87

	G	AB	Hit	2B	3B	HR	Run	RBI	TBB	SO	SB	CS	Avg
5.40 years		540	146	25	4	29	85	85	55	133	9	6	.270
1987	159	590	155	25	3	28	89	84	58	141	3	5	.263
First Half	86	322	88	12	1	19	53	51	37	74	2	4	.273
Second Half	73	268	67	13	2	9	36	33	21	67	1	1	.250
Vs. RHP		413	102	16	1	19	61	63	35	98	3	5	.247
Vs. LHP		177	53	9	2	9	28	21	23	43	0	0	.299
Home	80	302	92	18	2	11	43	39	31	59	1	2	.305
Road	79	288	63	7	1	17	46	45	27	82	2	3	.219

Rance MULLINIKS, Third Base
Runs Created: 60

	G	AB	Hit	2B	3B	HR	Run	RBI	TBB	SO	SB	CS	Avg
5.84 years		449	123	30	2	9	57	54	52	68	2	2	.274
1987	124	332	103	28	1	11	37	44	34	55	1	3	.310
First Half	60	155	42	10	0	4	16	12	15	27	1	0	.271
Second Half	64	177	61	18	1	7	21	32	19	28	0	1	.345
Vs. RHP		314	96	26	1	10	33	42	32	51	1	1	.306
Vs. LHP		18	7	2	0	1	4	2	2	4	0	0	.389
Home	61	162	51	15	1	6	19	23	13	32	0	1	.315
Road	63	170	52	13	0	5	18	21	21	23	1	1	.306

Fred MCGRIFF, Designated Hitter
Runs Created: 60

	G	AB	Hit	2B	3B	HR	Run	RBI	TBB	SO	SB	CS	Avg
0.68 years		441	109	24	0	29	87	63	88	156	4	3	.247
1987	107	295	73	16	0	20	58	43	60	104	3	2	.247
First Half	54	147	36	7	0	8	28	20	28	47	3	1	.245
Second Half	53	148	37	9	0	12	30	23	32	57	0	1	.250
Vs. RHP		269	69	14	0	19	53	42	57	90	3	2	.257
Vs. LHP		26	4	2	0	1	5	1	3	14	0	0	.154
Home	54	139	31	11	0	7	27	19	31	52	1	2	.223
Road	53	156	42	5	0	13	31	24	29	52	2	0	.269

Tony FERNANDEZ, Shortstop
Runs Created: 94

	G	AB	Hit	2B	3B	HR	Run	RBI	TBB	SO	SB	CS	Avg
3.54 years		592	179	28	9	6	81	58	40	45	21	11	.302
1987	146	578	186	29	8	5	90	67	51	48	32	12	.322
First Half	86	345	107	19	5	4	54	40	39	28	23	9	.310
Second Half	60	233	79	10	3	1	36	27	12	20	9	3	.339
Vs. RHP		386	129	21	7	3	57	51	30	30	28	8	.334
Vs. LHP		192	57	8	1	2	33	16	21	18	4	4	.297
Home	74	299	90	15	5	1	42	42	27	16	16	2	.301
Road	72	279	96	14	3	4	48	25	24	32	16	10	.344

Kelly GRUBER, Third Base
Runs Created: 37

	G	AB	Hit	2B	3B	HR	Run	RBI	TBB	SO	SB	CS	Avg
1.51 years		340	74	12	3	12	47	36	15	69	9	5	.218
1987	138	341	80	14	3	12	50	36	17	69	12	2	.235
First Half	69	211	59	11	2	6	34	21	9	43	7	1	.280
Second Half	69	130	21	3	1	6	16	15	8	26	5	1	.162
Vs. RHP		189	45	7	0	8	31	20	5	34	10	0	.238
Vs. LHP		152	35	7	3	4	19	16	12	35	2	2	.230
Home	70	144	32	6	2	5	21	19	10	28	3	1	.222
Road	68	197	48	8	1	7	29	17	7	41	9	1	.244

MILWAUKEE BREWERS

One thing that qualifies me to hold this job, I suppose, is a willingness to be wrong. I was wrong about the Milwaukee Brewers last year, and to be frank, I haven't changed my mind. People continue to tell me that this team has oodles of young talent which is in the process of forming a powerhouse. I see a lot of young talent in the minor-league system and some in the majors, but as I see the Brewers they remain a team heavily dependent on one great pitcher and a handful of aging stars.

You know, of course, that the Brewers opened 1987 by winning 20 of their first 23 games. What you may not know is that they did this despite poor starting pitching. With Higuera struggling, the Brewer starters posted a 4.74 ERA during those 23 games. This didn't cost them much, because the Brewers scored 151 runs in the 23 games, an average of almost seven and a half a game, and they won a bunch of high-scoring games by small margins (12–11, 11–8, 8–6, 10–7, 8–7, 10–8). They had only two games among those 20 wins which were extremely well pitched, those two being Nieves' no-hitter and a win by Higuera in the Brewers' next game.

On May 3 the Brewer offense stopped working, and the Brewers then lost 18 of 20, despite starting pitching which was essentially as good as in the 18–3 start. From that point on the Brewer season had three segments: a six-game winning streak (May 30–June 4) propelled by terrific starting pitching, a 35-game stretch (June 5–July 11) during which the Brewers' starters posted a 5.76 ERA and the team dropped under .500 (41–43), and a 78-game stretch from July 12 to the end of the season during which the Brewers, led by Paul Molitor, played consistently well.

The Brewer offense was more explosive than consistent. The Brewers scored six or more runs 77 times, nine more than any other major-league team, although the Tigers scored more runs. If they scored six runs more often than Detroit but scored fewer runs, you know what that means: there were also more days when the offense didn't function. Detroit was held to zero or one run 14 times, Milwaukee 22 times. Since the Milwaukee offense often got to the six-run level where a team most always wins, however, they could win without a good pitching performance. The Brewers won 42 games in which they did not have a quality start, the most of any major league team.

Sometimes they gave up six runs and still won, and then, too, a lot of times they scored six runs and still lost. The Brewers scored more runs in the games they lost (329) than any other major-league team. Supporting the suspect pitching was a suspect defense. They were third in the league in errors. Their defensive efficiency record was one of the poorest in baseball, due to a comparatively slow outfield and an unimpressive infield. Their defense against the running game was average. Their outfielders did not throw well. Having Glenn Braggs in right field is like having him batting third, a tribute to their stubborn evaluation of his potential in the face of his obvious limitations. Braggs has to have the worst arm of any major-league right fielder, not to mention the worst bat.

Terrific offense, poor pitching, poor defense, outstanding bullpen. I couldn't get a line on the manager, Tom Trebelhorn. He was neither a quick hook nor a slow hook. It could be argued that he overused Dan Plesac early in the year, when Plesac was pitching brilliantly. He certainly risked overworking Teddy Higuera, though Higuera showed no ill effects. Milwaukee used only 85 pinch hitters on the year, the fewest of any major league team. They invested 137 outs in first-run strategies, the most of any American-League team.

A Milwaukee farmhand, Lavell Freeman at El Paso, almost hit .400, finishing at .395 with 42 doubles, 24 homers and 70 walks. Despite the stats, *Baseball America* did not name Freeman as one of the ten-top prospects in the league. Freeman should take heart in history. In 1984 Teddy Higuera played at El Paso and led the league in ERA, at 2.60. *Baseball America* didn't name him one of their top-ten prospects, either.

Brewer farmhands top to bottom pile up awesome numbers, in part because they play in great parks for hitters. Several years ago (*1985 Abstract*) I introduced a method for translating minor-league performance into major-league equivalencies. Baseball men generally believe that minor-league batting statistics are not a reliable indicator of how a player will hit in the major leagues. After studying the issue extensively, I concluded that minor-league batting statistics predicted major-league performance with the same accuracy as previous major-league batting statistics. Comparing the minor-league and major-league batting performances of several hundred players, I found only a couple of instances of a player performing in the major leagues in a manner inconsistent with his minor-league performance; I found, in other words, that the chance of a player having a "break" in his record between the minors and majors was no greater than the chance of his having a break in his record as a major league performer.

Since introducing this method I haven't done much with it. I receive letters sometimes telling me that I should present annual charts of major-league equivalent performance for all top minor leaguers. No doubt most people, in writing an annual book, would handle it that way, but I chose not to. To make the minors-to-majors translations requires detailed records on park effects—how each park changes the number of doubles and triples hit, etc.— which are a lot of work to maintain, and a lot of the kind of work that I don't enjoy.

I also believe that you can't expect people to buy the same book year after year; once you've done something, you don't do it again. More than that, I was in this case asserting something which is directly contrary to the prevailing wisdom of baseball. I felt that it would not be advisable to keep pushing the issue, that it would be better simply to say my piece and shut up about it. But it is still my belief that minor-league batting statistics, if properly interpreted, are an extremely reliable indicator of major-league batting ability.

I ran MLEs (major-league equivalencies) for all the Brewers at AAA (Denver) and AA (El Paso). Most of these players figure to hit no better than .240 in the major leagues, as you would expect, but there are some statistics which remain impressive after you let the air out. Steve Stanicek at Denver hit .352 with 25 homers and 106 RBI. The major-league equivalent: .304 with 17 homers, 72 RBI. Teammate Joey Meyer hit .311 with 29 homers and 92 RBI, the equivalent of a .266 with 20 and 62 in the majors; still awfully good for 79 games. Brad Komminsk boils down to .254 with 22 homers, 64 RBI, striking out almost 30 percent of the time—not great but still enough to keep a job. Steve Kiefer in 90 games translates to .282 with 21 homers and 64 RBI. But most stunning is the major-league equivalent for Lavell Freeman: 342 with 33 doubles, 16 homers in 483 at bats.

In the case of the Milwaukee Brewers, there is a second issue—not only "Are minor-league stats meaningful?" but also "Can you make adequate adjustments for people who play in extremely good hitter's parks in the minors?" There is more air than usual to be let out. The system makes adjustments for the number of runs scored in Denver or El Paso by scaling down the offense to the run levels of Milwaukee games; because the Denver team scored 928 runs in 140 games, their statistics are whittled down much more than would be done for almost any other team. But is that enough? Isn't there still a possibility that the park adjustments for some players are inadequate, and the estimates of what people would hit still too optimistic?

It's possible, but I don't see any evidence for it. The Denver team has had more relationships than Liz Taylor; in this decade they have worked for Montreal, Texas, Chicago, and Cincinnati as well as Milwaukee. Denver players have gone to the majors in all of those organizations—Raines and Wallach to Montreal (as well as Dave Hostetler and Terry Francona), O'Brien to Texas, Hulett and Daryl Boston to Chicago, Kal Daniels, Kurt Stillwell, and Eric Davis to Cincinnati. Looking at the major-league equivalencies for all of these players, I find no reason to believe that they are inflated to any extent; there seems to be as much consistency between Denver MLEs and future major-league production as between past and future major-league production.

Speaking of ballparks. Having written for years that Milwaukee County Stadium is *not* a hitter's park, no matter what anybody says, I must now report that it is. I wasn't wrong; this was a pitcher's park from 1953 through 1984. Apparently when they tore down that Bernie Brewer stand in center field—remember the guy who used to dive into a tub of suds?—they substantially improved the visibility for the hitters. For whatever reason, for the last three years this park has tended to slightly favor the hitter—another factor in the upward drift of home run totals. In 1987 the Brewers scored and allowed 860 runs in Milwaukee, as opposed to 819 on the road.

As to why County Stadium was believed to be a hit-ter's park for many years when it clearly was not, a gentleman named John Rickert sent me some fascinating research. Going back to 1971, he studied the number of runs scored in Brewer home and road games by each month of the season. The data showed a clear pattern. In mid-summer, Milwaukee County Stadium shows as a neutral park, with the Brewers scoring and allowing as many runs per game at home as on the road. In the early part of the season and to a lesser extent the late part, County Stadium shows as a pitcher's park. It's not simply that more runs are scored here in mid-summer; more runs are scored everywhere in mid-summer. It is that this pattern particularly affects Milwaukee games, by so much that this may be the essential reason that the park favored the pitchers; the park factor was .90 in April, but 1.01 in July. I think that is a tremendously intriguing finding, and I would like to see similar research done about all the other parks. We'd learn a lot.

Anyway, back to the minors. The same holds for El Paso as Denver; every player who has played at El Paso and has subsequently played in the major leagues has produced essentially similar totals, with two exceptions. The exceptions are Darryl Sconiers, who had personal problems and never played up to his ability in the major leagues, and Dale Sveum. Sveum's season at El Paso doesn't translate as a dramatically better season than he delivered last year, just a substantially different season; his MLE from El Paso 1984 shows .301 with 7 homers, 68 RBI; he played that well but his statistics took an unexpected shape. That leaves Tom Brunansky (1980), Bill Schroeder (1981), Dion James (1982), Randy Ready (1982), Ernest Riles (1983), Mike Felder (1983–1984), Juan Castillo (1983–1984), and Glenn Braggs (1985), all of whom did as major leaguers exactly what their MLEs say that they should have done. The major-league equivalent of Glenn Braggs record at El Paso in 1985: .275, 15 homers, 77 RBI, .446 slugging percentage. His actual performance last season: .269, 13 homers, 77 RBI, .430 slugging.

This is not to say that Stanicek, Meyer, Kiefer, and Freeman are all destined for stardom. I have to say that in some cases, most particularly Kiefer, I remain a little skeptical; I suspect that Kiefer may just have had his best season, like Hostetler in 1981. Joey Meyer is just a hitter, and if the major-league translation of his Denver performance is impressive, the translation of his 1986 performance at Vancouver is not; it shows .240 with 21 homers, 87 RBI. He's going to strike out a lot and hit very few doubles, virtually no triples. Further, remember that 1987 was probably the zenith of a hitter's era; from 1988 on, probably all classes of players are going to have less impressive batting statistics. But I think Meyer could help the Brewers as a DH, I think Steve Stanicek has a very good chance to be the American League's rookie of the year in 1988, and I think the failure of *Baseball America* to consider Lavell Freeman a prospect, given his abilities as a hitter, is preposterous. It's like Dick Stuart said about his 66-homer season. He said he would hear people in the organization raving about some kid who hit 35 homers somewhere, but when he hit 66 homers they couldn't deal with that, so they just discounted it, figured it didn't mean anything. When a guy hits .395 in a good AA league, it's hard to know what to do with that. Take it for what it's worth, but I think that the discounting of Freeman's stats is disproportionate to the real effects of the park. I think the kid can hit.

The MLEs show something else. They show that Glenn Braggs is capable of hitting a lot better than he has yet. Braggs 1987 season is precisely what would be expected from his performance at El Paso—but the equivalent performance for what Braggs did at Vancouver is much, much better than that, well over .300 with the same power ratio. There are other Brewers on the major-league roster who are going to have better years—Surhoff, Sveum, possibly Riles, Nieves, Wegman.

The Brewers had the youngest team in the American League last year. It is in this, and in the Brewers' second half, that their hopes for 1988 are based. Their first half was an amalgam of wild swings, but in a 78-game stretch, half a season, they avoided a losing streak longer than three games, to play at a 104-win pace.

Any team capable of doing that is capable of winning the pennant. If three young players develop significantly the Brewers will be tough to beat. I don't think that's the most likely scenario. The problem is that while the Brewers had young players, it wasn't the young players who were succeeding. The veterans were wonderful—Molitor, Yount, Brock. The younger players were quite unimpressive. The development of younger players is speculative; some develop a great deal from year to year, while many players don't develop at all after age 24. The decline of players after the age of 30 is certain; it happens to everybody. The most likely scenario, I think, is that the sum development of the young players will not offset the decline of the Brewer veterans who were the key to the 1987 season, and that they 1988 season will be disappointing. I don't think that the pitching or the defense of the Brewers is of championship quality. I think they'll win 83 to 88 games.

WINS WITHOUT QUALITY START

Milwaukee	42
Oakland	38
St. Louis	37
San Francisco	36
Texas	34
Toronto	33
Mets	33
Cubs	32
Yankees	31
Montreal	30
Cincinnati	30
Baltimore	28
Atlanta	28
Cleveland	27
California	27
Philadelphia	27
Detroit	26
Minnesota	26
Boston	25
San Diego	24
Kansas City	23
Seattle	23
White Sox	19
Houston	17
Pittsburgh	16
Los Angeles	14

RUNS SCORED AND ALLOWED WINS AND LOSSES

Wins	639	329	91-0	1.000
Higuera	193	155	22-13	.629
Home Games	440	420	48-33	.593
Slugfests	539	502	41-30	.577
Wegman	167	143	19-14	.576
Nieves	190	176	19-14	.576
All Games	862	817	91-71	.562
Blowouts	270	248	23-19	.548
One Run Games	196	192	24-20	.545
Road Games	422	397	43-38	.531
Bosio	99	97	10-9	.526
Pitchers' Duels	38	53	10-14	.417
Losses	223	488	0-71	.000

TEN BEST STARTS

	IP	H	R	ER	BB	SO		
Higuera vs. Cle, Aug 26	10	3	0	0	2	10	W	94
Higuera at KC, Sep 1	9	1	0	0	2	9	W	92
Nieves at Bal, Apr 15	9	0	0	0	5	7	W	89
Bosio vs. Min, Aug 28	9	2	0	0	3	8	W	88
Higuera at Min, Sep 6	9	2	0	0	3	7	W	87
Higuera at Bos, Oct 2	11⅓	6	3	3	3	10	L	81
Higuera vs. Tex, Apr 17	9	5	2	2	2	12	W	79
Higuera vs. Tex, Aug 10	11	5	3	3	4	8	—	79
Higuera vs. Bal, Aug 5	9	6	1	1	3	10	W	78
Bosio at Cal, July 4	8	4	1	1	0	7	W	77

PITCHERS WHEN SUPPORTED BY THREE TO FIVE RUNS

	G	IP	W-L	Pct	SO	BB	ERA
Wegman	10	65	5-0	1.000	29	11	2.89
Higuera	9	69	4-3	.571	65	24	3.50
Nieves	10	55	4-2	.667	50	27	4.77

HALL OF FAME WATCH

Could be elected on current accomplishments: Cooper 95.5, Yount 77; **Building credentials but not yet viable candidate:** Molitor 38.5; **Working on it:** Higuera 17, Barker 12; **Long way to go:** Gantner 7, Plesac 7, Burris 5, Clear 4, Deer 2, Trebelhorn 2, Manning 1, Nieves 1, Riles 1, Surhoff 1, Sveum 1.

NUMBER OF TIMES SCORED SIX OR MORE RUNS

Milwaukee	77
Detroit	68
Boston	68
Texas	67
Toronto	65
Oakland	64
Mets	62
Montreal	61
California	61
Yankees	59
San Francisco	58
St. Louis	58
Kansas City	57
Cincinnati	57
Minnesota	56
Cubs	53
Cleveland	53
Seattle	51
Pittsburgh	50
Atlanta	50
White Sox	49
Baltimore	48
Philadelphia	45
Houston	45
Los Angeles	41
San Diego	41

TEN WORST STARTS

	IP	H	R	ER	BB	SO		
Birkbeck at Min, May 28	⅓	6	6	6	1	0	L	14
Knudson vs. Sea, July 20	4⅓	10	8	6	2	3	—	16
Knudson vs. Oak, July 25	3⅓	10	6	6	0	1	L	17
Nieves at Tex, July 29	2⅓	8	6	6	0	1	—	18
Wegman vs. Bal, Aug 6	3⅓	9	6	5	2	1	—	19
Birkbeck at Sea, May 1	4⅓	10	6	6	2	1	—	20
Wegman at Det, Sep 18	4⅓	7	7	7	3	2	L	20
Higuera at Cle, May 29	6*	11	8	8	1	5	L	22
Higuera vs. Bos, Sep 27	4*	8	6	6	3	3	—	22
Bosio at Chi, Aug 8	7	12	8	7	1	2	L	24

B. J. SURHOFF, Catcher
Runs Created: 56

	G	AB	Hit	2B	3B	HR	Run	RBI	TBB	SO	SB	CS	Avg
0.71 years		556	166	31	4	10	70	96	51	42	15	14	.299
1987	115	395	118	22	3	7	50	68	36	30	11	10	.299
First Half	61	206	55	10	3	5	25	36	15	19	5	5	.267
Second Half	54	189	63	12	0	2	25	32	21	11	6	5	.333
Vs. RHP		310	91	19	3	5	40	51	27	24	10	8	.294
Vs. LHP		85	27	3	0	2	10	17	9	6	1	2	.318
Home	57	194	61	10	2	5	21	41	15	13	5	7	.314
Road	58	201	57	12	1	2	29	27	21	17	6	3	.284

Rob DEER, Left Field
Runs Created: 85

	G	AB	Hit	2B	3B	HR	Run	RBI	TBB	SO	SB	CS	Avg
2.22 years		507	115	17	3	32	78	85	85	201	8	4	.227
1987	134	474	113	15	2	28	78	80	86	186	12	4	.238
First Half	73	262	69	11	2	20	48	49	45	95	10	2	.263
Second Half	61	212	44	4	0	8	23	31	41	91	2	2	.208
Vs. RHP		322	74	9	1	20	49	52	51	138	9	1	.230
Vs. LHP		152	39	6	1	8	22	28	35	48	3	3	.257
Home	65	232	53	7	1	11	28	34	33	94	4	1	.228
Road	69	242	60	8	1	17	43	46	53	92	8	3	.248

Greg BROCK, First Base
Runs Created: 88

	G	AB	Hit	2B	3B	HR	Run	RBI	TBB	SO	SB	CS	Avg
3.93 years		519	130	21	1	21	70	77	69	81	6	3	.250
1987	141	532	159	29	3	13	81	85	57	63	5	4	.299
First Half	68	249	70	12	0	9	31	44	21	28	3	1	.281
Second Half	73	283	89	17	3	4	50	41	36	35	2	3	.314
Vs. RHP		375	114	23	2	10	55	58	43	41	4	3	.304
Vs. LHP		157	45	6	1	3	26	27	14	22	1	1	.287
Home	73	270	81	15	2	5	37	45	26	28	3	2	.300
Road	68	262	78	14	1	8	44	40	31	35	2	2	.298

Robin YOUNT, Center Field
Runs Created: 120

	G	AB	Hit	2B	3B	HR	Run	RBI	TBB	SO	SB	CS	Avg
12.15 years		631	182	33	7	14	94	77	50	72	15	6	.288
1987	158	635	198	25	9	21	99	103	76	94	19	9	.312
First Half	82	326	98	14	4	11	50	45	38	60	6	5	.301
Second Half	76	309	100	11	5	10	49	58	38	34	13	4	.324
Vs. RHP		440	145	16	7	19	74	81	56	66	18	4	.330
Vs. LHP		195	53	9	2	2	25	22	20	28	1	5	.272
Home	79	311	110	13	6	12	54	62	37	47	11	6	.354
Road	79	324	88	12	3	9	45	41	39	47	8	3	.272

Juan CASTILLO, Second Base
Runs Created: 33

	G	AB	Hit	2B	3B	HR	Run	RBI	TBB	SO	SB	CS	Avg
0.88 years		426	92	13	6	3	57	38	43	100	18	9	.216
1987	116	321	72	11	4	3	44	28	33	76	15	7	.224
First Half	62	164	40	6	3	3	25	15	21	41	7	5	.244
Second Half	54	157	32	5	1	0	19	13	12	35	8	2	.204
Vs. RHP		183	42	7	2	2	29	21	31	48	12	6	.230
Vs. LHP		138	30	4	2	1	15	7	2	28	3	1	.217
Home	58	164	43	6	2	3	26	16	16	35	8	5	.262
Road	58	157	29	5	2	0	18	12	17	41	7	2	.185

Glenn BRAGGS, Right Field
Runs Created: 69

	G	AB	Hit	2B	3B	HR	Run	RBI	TBB	SO	SB	CS	Avg
1.17 years		615	160	31	8	15	74	81	50	122	11	5	.260
1987	132	505	136	28	7	13	67	77	47	96	12	5	.269
First Half	70	254	61	13	2	8	35	33	33	57	6	3	.240
Second Half	62	251	75	15	5	5	32	44	14	39	6	2	.299
Vs. RHP		337	90	18	5	11	47	54	29	67	6	3	.267
Vs. LHP		168	46	10	2	2	20	23	18	29	6	2	.274
Home	68	253	66	11	4	4	36	42	25	51	8	3	.261
Road	64	252	70	17	3	9	31	35	22	45	4	2	.278

Paul MOLITOR, Third Base
Runs Created: 125

	G	AB	Hit	2B	3B	HR	Run	RBI	TBB	SO	SB	CS	Avg
6.96 years		661	196	35	7	14	114	67	62	84	40	11	.297
1987	118	465	164	41	5	16	114	75	69	67	45	10	.353
First Half	42	155	50	14	1	4	34	24	19	21	14	6	.323
Second Half	76	310	114	27	4	12	80	51	50	46	31	4	.368
Vs. RHP		320	116	29	5	13	83	62	46	52	32	6	.363
Vs. LHP		145	48	12	0	3	31	13	23	15	13	4	.331
Home	61	231	91	21	4	7	61	38	33	35	23	4	.394
Road	57	234	73	20	1	9	53	37	36	32	22	6	.312

Ernest RILES, Third Base
Runs Created: 33

	G	AB	Hit	2B	3B	HR	Run	RBI	TBB	SO	SB	CS	Avg
2.12 years		589	157	22	5	8	76	61	57	85	6	6	.267
1987	83	276	72	11	1	4	38	38	30	47	3	4	.261
First Half	14	49	12	2	0	1	6	7	4	11	1	0	.245
Second Half	69	227	60	9	1	3	32	31	26	36	2	4	.264
Vs. RHP		219	62	8	1	4	34	33	24	29	3	3	.283
Vs. LHP		57	10	3	0	0	4	5	6	18	0	1	.175
Home	43	133	38	7	1	1	21	17	19	22	0	4	.286
Road	40	143	34	4	0	3	17	21	11	25	3	0	.238

Dale SVEUM, Shortstop
Runs Created: 70

	G	AB	Hit	2B	3B	HR	Run	RBI	TBB	SO	SB	CS	Avg
1.51 years		564	141	26	3	21	80	86	48	130	4	6	.250
1987	153	535	135	27	3	25	86	95	40	133	2	6	.252
First Half	81	271	61	14	0	9	33	43	17	77	2	4	.225
Second Half	72	264	74	13	3	16	53	52	23	56	0	2	.280
Vs. RHP		350	82	16	2	14	55	61	24	87	2	4	.234
Vs. LHP		185	53	11	1	11	31	34	16	46	0	2	.286
Home	76	257	67	14	2	9	46	37	20	68	1	2	.261
Road	77	278	68	13	1	16	40	58	20	65	1	4	.245

Bill SCHROEDER, Catcher
Runs Created: 52

	G	AB	Hit	2B	3B	HR	Run	RBI	TBB	SO	SB	CS	Avg
1.70 years		555	143	25	1	27	71	69	28	149	4	3	.258
1987	75	250	83	12	0	14	35	42	16	56	5	2	.332
First Half	36	119	40	7	0	5	19	15	7	28	2	1	.336
Second Half	39	131	43	5	0	9	16	27	9	28	3	1	.328
Vs. RHP		119	38	9	0	6	22	20	12	18	3	0	.319
Vs. LHP		131	45	3	0	8	13	22	4	38	2	2	.344
Home	36	120	42	7	0	5	16	21	6	28	3	1	.350
Road	39	130	41	5	0	9	19	21	10	28	2	1	.315

MOMENTUM, AD NAUSEUM

As a sports fan you hear a lot about momentum. As a scientist you'll have a hell of a time proving that any such animal exists. I have studied the issue many different ways, trying to isolate something which can be called momentum, and, being unsuccessful, have concluded that that which is called momentum in baseball is not a characteristic of play but a characteristic of the perception of play. When we see a team win 17 of 18 games then start losing with almost equal determination, it becomes irresistible to form a psychic link, momentum, to explain the swings. The position that the swings from high to low are essentially random data patterns probably seems incomprehensible to the average sports fan and announcer, although in fact many baseball people agree with me, and many or perhaps most of my readers.

Anyway, I've studied this a lot of different ways—trying to see whether you can predict wins and losses from who is hot and who is cold, whether a player actually hits better when he is supposed to be on a hot streak, etc. I ran another little study here, since I had daily won-lost logs in the computer for each team. For each team, I asked the computer how many times the team had followed a win with a win or a loss with a loss.

If there were no such thing as momentum (that is, if patterns of winning and losing were random) the average figure for a major-league team in a season would be about 83. You can start out at 81.0 by figuring that, in 162 games, an average team would follow a win with a loss as often as with a win, etc. In 162 games there are only 161 chances to follow up yesterday, so that cuts us to 80.5. The 50 percent figure only works for a .500 team. The Cleveland Indians, losers of 101 games in 162 tries, could be expected to follow a loss with a loss in 38.9% of two-game stretches and a win with a win in 14.2%, and if you work that through you'll figure that in a random pattern they could expect to have 85.4 win/win or lose/lose instances. This figure is the highest of 1987, but 80.5 is as low as you can go. Making adjustments for each team like this, I estimate that a random pattern should yield an average between 82 and 83.

All teams play stretches of home games and stretches of road games and most win more often at home, so this tends to cause the data to cluster to a further extent, albeit a very slight tendency in the normal case. This would drive the 82–83 figure even higher. The fact that a team plays a group of games against one opponent and then a group of games against another should cause further clustering; however, the fact that a different pitcher works each game and that it is impossible for the best pitcher (or the worst) to start several games in a row works against the formation of win/loss clusters, driving the expected number down. Then you got your injuries . . . to allow accurately for all of these factors is damned near impossible, but as best I can estimate one would expect that, given that there were no such thing as momentum, an average team would follow a win with a win or a loss with a loss about 83 times in a season.

The actual average in 1987 was 81.7—below the random expectation. The team in the major leagues most likely to follow a win with a win or a loss with a loss, actually, was not Milwaukee but Baltimore, which followed a win with a win 31 times and a loss with a loss 60 times, a total of 91. Milwaukee was second with 90, while the Cubs were the least "cluster prone," or streaky, team with 71.

This suggests, again, that there is no such thing as momentum in baseball (which is a quote from Dick Howser: "there is no such thing as momentum in baseball") or that if there is such a thing then there must be some countervailing force, which we will call compensation, which is larger. Negative momentum is somewhat stronger than positive momentum.

I think in 30, 40 years, that will be the accepted position. Momentum is one of those superficial concepts that is hard to resist if you don't think it through but hard to conceive of if you follow it through and try to resolve the problems it creates. If a man gets two hits today, how does that make him a better hitter tomorrow? Confidence, of course, but what does the confidence do? Does the confidence make him stronger? Does it give him better eyesight? Does it make his reflexes quicker or his knowledge of the strike zone more comprehensive? And, most importantly, if a hitter's ability changes so dramatically from week to week, how can it remain so much the same from year to year?

The illusion of momentum will in time, I think, be overpowered by its own absurdities. Four years ago, one of the Hirdt brothers wrote an article for the *Village Voice* saying that managers could gain more by platooning hot and cold players than by platooning left-handers and right-handers. But last year the *Elias Analyst* reported that "the evidence we've gathered through an extensive analysis of streaks and slumps shows beyond the shadow of a doubt that the conventional wisdom is completely wrong . . . a player is just as likely to hit well in a game that follows a slump as he is following a week of hot hitting." What's the difference? The difference is that when they tried to prove that hot streaks and slumps were meaningful indicators of future performance, they couldn't. As a small child, I thought that the trees pushed the wind.

NEW YORK YANKEES

The New York Yankees are trapped on a treadmill. Although they have not won anything since 1981, the Yankees have the best winning percentage of any team during the decade, or should I turn that around: although they have the best winning percentage of any team during the eighties, the Yankees have not won anything since 1981. They are acutely aware of this, and so the winter of 1987–1988 was spent in frantic preparations to make the 1988 season the season in which the great nucleus of this team is surrounded by a cast good enough to lift the Yankees off of that 85- to 92-win treadmill, and onto the championship rung. There is an irony in this, for it is exactly this philosophy that creates the treadmill from which the Yankees are so anxious to escape.

To write a comment about the Yankees, you start by piecing together their current roster. This is not easy job. To set up the wild winter trading frenzy, the Yankees used 48 players during 1987, a record for the team. They tried 15 starting pitchers, the most in the majors. As Steinbrenner saw it, the Yankees were doing well until he left them alone. Did you read that story? Steinbrenner says that he went into the Yankee clubhouse in early August, and somebody had cut out of one of the New York papers an article telling George to butt out, that the Yankees could do better if he would just leave them alone. George says that he was deeply hurt by that, and decided that if his involvement wasn't valued he would just pull out and let them fend for themselves. The Yankees, in first place at the time of this incident, drifted out of contention. And, says George, never again. This year the pressure is on, start to finish.

What really happened is that the Yankees started out well in 1987, and remained in first place for much of the summer although not playing terribly well anytime after May. The Yankees in April went 14–7, their second straight outstanding start (they were 14–6 in April of 1986). When Milwaukee faltered the Yanks moved into first place on May 14. By my count the Yankees led the pennant race or shared the lead for 67 days during the summer, the most of any team (Toronto, 54; Milwaukee, 38; Detroit, 33; Baltimore, 2), but during much of that period they were drifting. By May 25 they were 14 games over .500, at 29–15. It was three weeks after that before they reached 15 games over .500, although they had no distinct slump; it was three weeks of win, lose, win, lose. Then, stabilizing a rotation of Rasmussen, Rhoden, Guidry, John, and Tewksbury, the team had another spurt; by July 17 (two days after the All-Star break) they were 23 games over .500, at 57–34. That was the high-water mark; they never got to +24, which means that from then to any other point of the season the Yankees were no better than a .500 team. Their record from May 25 to the end of the season was 60–58, two games over. From July 17 to the end, it was 32–39.

Apart from the obvious stuff like the injuries to Henderson and Randolph and the lack of a catcher or a short-stop, the disintegration of the 1987 Yankees was due to Piniella's inability to establish a solid starting rotation. Despite widespread suspicions that the Yankees did not have the starting pitching they needed, in the early part of the season their starting pitching was terrific. Through May 12 the Yankee starters had an ERA of 3.20. This figure ascended steadily for the rest of the season, to 3.71 by May 30, to 3.93 by June 16, to 3.96 by July 3, to 4.02 by July 22, to 4.19 by August 9, to 4.25 by August 25, to 4.31 by September 15, to 4.37 by the end of the year. The offense, after a point, was not able to overpower the degeneration of the starting rotation.

In those first 32 games Dennis Rasmussen had a 2.89 ERA in 53 innings, with 32 strikeouts and only 12 walks. Tommy John was 2–0 with a 3.81 ERA, Joe Niekro had pitched 25 innings with a 3.20 ERA, Charles Hudson was 4–0 with a 2.08 ERA in 48 innings, and Rick Rhoden was 4–3 with a 3.57 ERA, 45 innings. Only one of those pitchers was there for the duration. Rasmussen and Niekro were traded. Hudson lost effectiveness and was returned to the minors. Rhoden developed stiffness in the upper arm, and was not able to start late in the year. All that was left of the rotation that had projected the Yankees into the race was the 44-year-old Tommy John.

They were often not in the game. Their average margin of defeat was 4.07 runs, the largest in the majors. They lost 26 games by five runs or more.

No pitcher in baseball pitches well from beginning to end, year after year. Look at Jack Morris this year. I guarantee you he'll have a stretch of ten starts with an ERA over 4.50. He always does. The Yankees don't believe in staying with a young pitcher or a young player through the bad stretches; they want everybody to succeed *now*. When a young player goes through a down phase or when a veteran has an off year, the Yankees give up on him. The pressure, the fear of making a mistake and getting shipped immediately to Columbus, inhibits the development of young players, and in many cases flatly destroys them. That means that over a period of time, nobody on the roster is getting better, while some people are getting worse. To keep from slipping back, you have to keep bringing in new talent, players who are at the top of their game. That drives the treadmill. But when the treadmill starts to gain on you, when you start to slip back toward the middle of the pack, what do you do? You turn up the power, of course. You bring in more players who are coming off of good years. You put more pressure on the players. You give up more quickly on the kid who has a couple of bad outings. So then the treadmill runs faster.

In particular, another organization might regret their impatience with Bob Tewksbury. Tewksbury in 1986 finished 9–6 in 23 games, 130 innings, 3.31 ERA. A finesse pitcher with a history of tendinitis, "Tewksbury never gained the confidence of manager Lou Piniella" in 1986 (quote from *The Scouting Report: 1987*). Tewksbury started the 1987 season in the rotation, but after only two starts he was sent to Columbus. At Columbus he was 6–1 with a 2.53 ERA, walking 11 men in 75 innings. Returning to the Yankee rotation on June 21, he had two good starts but then two poor starts, at which point the All-Star break had arrived and it was decided to send Tewksbury to the Cubs as part of the Steve Trout package. Trout bombed, and the Yankees were down another starting pitcher.

The keys to the 1988 Yankees? Number one, Randy Velarde, a young shortstop. Velarde appears to be the best shortstop prospect the Yankees have had in over a decade. If he impresses Billy Martin early, Martin will give him a chance to prove himself. His minor-league record looks like a player—but if he isn't, I doubt that the Yankees can win. The fallback positions (Santana, Meacham, Tolleson, Zuvella, etc.) just aren't very good.

Number two, Al Leiter, a 22-year-old left-handed pitcher. Despite all the things they have done to improve their starting pitching, it just isn't that good unless Righetti is in the rotation or unless somebody is a big surprise. A rotation of Rhoden, Dotson, Candelaria, John, and Guetterman, waiting for Guidry to come off the disabled list, is good enough to win 88 games with a good offense. If Righetti comes out of the bullpen to start, that leaves a weak bullpen. Leiter is important because, while he might be awful, he has the potential to be really good.

Other than Leiter and Velarde, I don't see any Yankee rookies as likely to have an impact. Orestes Destrade obviously is not poised to push Don Mattingly and Jack Clark for playing time, and probably will never reach that level. Roberto Kelly is a decent prospect but doesn't look like anything special.

The third key is Don Slaught. The acquisition of Slaught was an excellent move. He is a solid defensive catcher and I think still capable of surprising us as a hitter; at worst, he's going to out-hit Rick Cerone and Joel Skinner. Slaught is my kind of player, but I worry that he may not be Billy Martin's kind; Billy would probably be happier to have Mike Heath back or something, and could probably get him back if he wasn't with a division rival.

Obviously, it will help if Rickey Henderson stays healthy. I don't see the Jack Clark acquisition as being of any real significance. Yankee designated hitters last year hit .271 with 30 homers, 66 walks, 19 stolen bases; they created 98 runs. Jack Clark cannot play the outfield anymore and isn't likely to push Don Mattingly off first base; he is a designated hitter. It can't be assumed that he is going to have a good year; as a right-handed hitter in Yankee Stadium, he could very well, even if healthy, fail to match the productivity of the Yankees 1987 designated hitters. If he has a good year, how many runs is he going to create? Maybe 120, 125; that would be a heck of a year. Last year the Yankees used the DH spot to get Rickey Henderson's legs in the lineup even when he was hurt; they won't be as able to do that this year.

To be honest, I was appalled to hear people saying that the Yankees had won the pennant on January 5 when they signed Jack Clark. Twelve years ago, at the beginning of the free-agent era, I tried to tell people that a single player just doesn't mean that much in the context of the 30 games or so that separate the best teams from the worst. I wrote articles arguing that a superstar might mean four to six

games a year; that's all. People would say that Andy Messersmith was going to turn the Braves around, and I would try to explain why that was impossible.

I could understand why it was difficult for people to accept at that time. But after we have seen free agents change teams time after time after time without carrying pennants with them, after we have seen Andre Dawson go from Montreal to Chicago without Montreal getting any worse or Chicago getting any better, after we have seen Bruce Sutter leave St. Louis for Atlanta without the Cardinals getting any worse or Atlanta any better, after we have seen Lance Parrish jump from Detroit to Philadelphia without Detroit getting any worse or Philadelphia any better, after we have seen this time and again for twelve years, how can people still think that the *next* free agent is going to be the one who carries the mail? As I see it, Clark improves the Yankees' expectation by maybe a half a game, maybe two games at most. It's no big deal.

George reached a point at which he just had to scratch that free agent itch. Signing a free agent of Jack Clark's age (32) and with his injury history is the ultimate treadmill strategy. Like the Baltimore Orioles (see Baltimore comment), the Yankees are investing in a market that is certain to decline. If you do that at a lower level, as the Orioles have, it's a disastrous strategy. If you buy the very best of the available players, and certainly Jack Clark was that in 1987, it's a defensible strategy, but there is still that undertow, that treadmill, with the inevitable decline of players in their thirties pulling the Yankees away from their goal, while the development of young players in Boston, Cleveland, Milwaukee, and Toronto will be pushing those teams gently forward.

If they hadn't signed Jack Clark, if they hadn't brought back Billy Martin, I would have picked this team to finish about fifth. But if Martin fails to improve the Yankees, it will be the first time. The possibility that I think we really ought to consider is that what Steinbrenner has done with Martin in the eighties actually makes a whole lot of sense; it's non-traditional, and in the sports world that means it's going to be criticized, but it makes sense. Martin's intensity and knowledge of the game make him a tremendous short-term asset to the organization; he can still do more to improve a baseball team overnight than anybody else in the world, including Don Mattingly and Roger Clemens. But his immaturity, his high-pressure tactics, and his mind games over time create so much resentment and hostility that he is a long-term detriment—indeed, he simply can't manage a baseball team for longer than a couple of years, or he will self-destruct. It makes sense, I think, to bring him in, get the benefit of his abilities, and then put him in a cooler somewhere and let things quiet down a bit before you bring him back again.

I think the thing most people don't understand about Billy Martin is how many players have had career years for him. Martin has the insight into the game to see what a player needs to do to improve himself, and the force of personality to convince the player to do that. If you look back at his record you'll find an awful lot of times when Martin has convinced a pitcher to junk the slider and work with the curve and fastball, or has convinced a hitter to stop swinging at bad pitches, or has moved a hitter up on the plate so he could pull the ball better, or has "convinced" a player with an injury history to stay in the lineup, and has seen that player make a sudden, unanticipated improvement in his performance. As likely as not, two years later the player hates him for it, but that comes later.

Perhaps the biggest key to the Yankees chances of winning the pennant is the Toronto Blue Jays. I think the Blue Jays will do one of two things—blow the league apart, or play .500 ball. I don't think they'll be around 90–95 wins. If the Jays play .500 ball, the Yankees are by far the team most likely to move into the breach. If the

Jays play the way they are capable of playing, I doubt that the Yankees will be able to keep up with them.

The problem with the Yankees is that they never want to pay the real price of success. The real price of success in baseball is not the dollars that you come up with for a Jack Clark or a Dave Winfield or an Ed Whitson or a Goose Gossage. It is the patience to work with young players and help them develop. So long as the Yankees are unwilling to pay that price, don't bet on them to win anything.

WINS IN GAMES IN WHICH LESS THAN SIX RUNS WERE SCORED

Yankees	23
Montreal	22
San Diego	22
Detroit	21
Minnesota	20
San Francisco	20
Philadelphia	20
St. Louis	20
Houston	20
White Sox	19
Pittsburgh	18
Toronto	17
Kansas City	17
Baltimore	16
Mets	16
Cincinnati	16
Cubs	15
California	15
Cleveland	14
Oakland	14
Boston	13
Los Angeles	13
Milwaukee	10
Seattle	10
Texas	10
Atlanta	9

RUNS SCORED AND ALLOWED WINS AND LOSSES

Wins	586	259	88-0	1.000
John	192	137	22-11	.667
Home Games	401	346	51-30	.630
Pitchers' Duels	81	55	23-14	.622
Rhoden	117	124	18-11	.621
Rasmussen	146	128	15-10	.600
One-Run Games	174	166	24-16	.600
All Games	788	758	89-73	.549
Slugfests	462	477	34-32	.515
Blowouts	289	312	25-26	.490
Road Games	387	412	38-43	.469
Hudson	85	73	7-9	.438
Guidry	71	75	7-10	.412
Losses	202	499	0-73	.000

TEN BEST STARTS

	IP	H	R	ER	BB	SO		
John at Det, Aug 8	9	2	0	0	1	3	W	85
Rhoden at Chi, May 6	9	2	1	1	3	6	W	82
Hudson vs. Bos, Sep 29	9	4	0	0	1	3	W	81
John at Cle, Apr 26	7	1	0	0	1	4	W	78
Hudson vs. Cle, Apr 13	9	3	3	3	2	10	W	77
Hudson vs. KC, Apr 19	9	7	0	0	3	7	W	77
Guidry at Tor, June 30	7⅔	6	0	0	1	9	W	75
Guidry vs. Min, July 6	9	3	2	2	3	5	L	75
Niekro at Cal, May 23	7⅔	5	0	0	5	5	W	74
Rhoden vs. Tex, July 3	8	5	1	1	0	5	W	73

PITCHERS WHEN SUPPORTED BY THREE TO FIVE RUNS

	G	IP	W-L	Pct	SO	BB	ERA
Rhoden	10	69	7-1	.875	39	21	2.49
Guidry	7	46	3-3	.500	46	15	4.73
John	10	59	2-2	.500	22	17	5.03
Rasmussen	9	45	3-3	.500	24	19	6.40
Hudson	6	29	1-3	.250	16	16	6.44

HALL OF FAME WATCH

Could be elected on current accomplishments: Mattingly 97.5, John 95, Winfield 91.5, Guidry 91.5, B. Martin 80, R. Henderson 72; **Building credentials but not yet viable candidate:** Randolph 47, Righetti 30.5; **Working on it:** Piniella 29, A. Holland 19, Rhoden 15, Easler 13, Kittle 11, T. Stoddard 11; **Long way to go:** C. Washington 8.5, Ward 8.5, Cerone 8, Gullickson 7, Hudson 5, Royster 5, Tolleson 3.5, Salas 3.5, N. Allen 3, Pagliarulo 2, Clements 1, Guante 1, Trout 1. (Martin had 23 points as a player, has 57 as a manager. Piniella had 24 points as a player, has 5 as a manager.)

AVERAGE MARGIN OF DEFEAT

St. Louis	2.70
Toronto	2.77
San Francisco	2.78
San Diego	2.94
Los Angeles	2.96
Mets	2.99
Cincinnati	3.13
Philadelphia	3.27
White Sox	3.28
Houston	3.30
Atlanta	3.32
Detroit	3.45
Oakland	3.47
California	3.48
Pittsburgh	3.48
Boston	3.50
Texas	3.54
Kansas City	3.66
Milwaukee	3.73
Baltimore	3.74
Montreal	3.77
Minnesota	3.86
Seattle	3.89
Cubs	3.92
Cleveland	4.05
Yankees	4.07

TEN WORST STARTS

	IP	H	R	ER	BB	SO		
John vs. Bos, June 26	1⅓	6	8	8	2	0	—	8
Rasmussen at Det, Aug 9	3*	8	8	8	1	3	L	13
Bordi vs. Tex, July 5	3⅓	8	7	7	0	1	L	17
Guidry at Det, Aug 6	2⅓	6	7	7	3	3	L	17
John at Cle, Aug 4	2⅓	6	7	5	3	0	L	18
Rhoden at Det, Aug 7	5⅓	10	8	7	1	3	L	20
Gullickson vs. Bos, Sep 28	4	7	7	7	2	3	—	21
John at Bos, June 20	4⅔	10	6	6	0	1	L	21
Rhoden vs. Tor, June 8	4⅔	7	7	7	2	0	L	22
Rhoden at KC, Apr 10	3⅓	9	5	5	2	3	L	23

Rick CERONE, Catcher
Runs Created: 31

	G	AB	Hit	2B	3B	HR	Run	RBI	TBB	SO	SB	CS	Avg
5.99 years		514	123	23	2	8	49	55	38	56	1	3	.239
1987	113	284	69	12	1	4	28	23	30	46	0	1	.243
First Half	56	141	30	5	0	1	17	14	17	21	0	1	.213
Second Half	57	143	39	7	1	3	11	9	13	25	0	0	.273
Vs. RHP		153	34	6	1	3	16	12	20	26	0	1	.222
Vs. LHP		131	35	6	0	1	12	11	10	20	0	0	.267
Home	57	148	28	4	1	1	12	12	18	26	0	0	.189
Road	56	136	41	8	0	3	16	11	12	20	0	1	.301

Gary WARD, Left Field
Runs Created: 55

	G	AB	Hit	2B	3B	HR	Run	RBI	TBB	SO	SB	CS	Avg
6.03 years		605	171	28	6	18	84	82	45	104	13	4	.283
1987	146	529	131	22	1	16	65	78	33	101	9	1	.248
First Half	85	323	86	15	0	10	45	61	22	64	6	0	.266
Second Half	61	206	45	7	1	6	20	17	11	37	3	1	.218
Vs. RHP		334	76	15	1	12	40	45	21	73	6	0	.228
Vs. LHP		195	55	7	0	4	25	33	12	28	3	1	.282
Home	73	259	73	10	0	7	33	44	15	47	5	1	.282
Road	73	270	58	12	1	9	32	34	18	54	4	0	.215

Don MATTINGLY, First Base
Runs Created: 115

	G	AB	Hit	2B	3B	HR	Run	RBI	TBB	SO	SB	CS	Avg
4.40 years		635	210	45	3	28	100	117	50	41	1	2	.331
1987	141	569	186	38	2	30	93	115	51	38	1	4	.327
First Half	71	283	95	20	2	14	53	60	36	19	0	4	.336
Second Half	70	286	91	18	0	16	40	55	15	19	1	0	.318
Vs. RHP		372	126	29	1	19	60	66	36	23	1	4	.339
Vs. LHP		197	60	9	1	11	33	49	15	15	0	0	.305
Home	70	283	95	14	1	17	51	56	24	25	1	3	.336
Road	71	286	91	24	1	13	42	59	27	13	0	1	.318

Rickey HENDERSON, Center Field
Runs Created: 84

	G	AB	Hit	2B	3B	HR	Run	RBI	TBB	SO	SB	CS	Avg
7.30 years		607	176	28	6	16	129	62	108	84	96	24	.290
1987	95	358	104	17	3	17	78	37	80	52	41	8	.291
First Half	59	226	71	12	2	11	50	23	51	30	25	5	.314
Second Half	36	132	33	5	1	6	28	14	29	22	16	3	.250
Vs. RHP		241	67	10	1	10	51	25	52	38	32	3	.278
Vs. LHP		117	37	7	2	7	27	12	28	14	9	5	.316
Home	44	161	51	8	3	10	41	20	39	25	17	4	.317
Road	51	197	53	9	0	7	37	17	41	27	24	4	.269

Willie RANDOLPH, Second Base
Runs Created: 82

	G	AB	Hit	2B	3B	HR	Run	RBI	TBB	SO	SB	CS	Avg
9.96 years		598	165	24	6	5	100	52	96	48	24	8	.276
1987	120	449	137	24	2	7	96	67	82	25	11	1	.305
First Half	84	317	98	19	2	4	70	47	58	19	9	0	.309
Second Half	36	132	39	5	0	3	26	20	24	6	2	1	.295
Vs. RHP		319	96	16	2	4	63	47	48	18	10	1	.301
Vs. LHP		130	41	8	0	3	33	20	34	7	1	0	.315
Home	68	253	74	14	2	3	56	32	44	12	8	0	.292
Road	52	196	63	10	0	4	40	35	38	13	3	1	.321

Dave WINFIELD, Right Field
Runs Created: 91

	G	AB	Hit	2B	3B	HR	Run	RBI	TBB	SO	SB	CS	Avg
13.09 years		601	171	29	6	25	93	102	66	87	15	6	.285
1987	156	575	158	22	1	27	83	97	76	96	5	6	.275
First Half	85	319	94	13	1	20	58	68	49	52	5	3	.295
Second Half	71	256	64	9	0	7	25	29	27	44	0	3	.250
Vs. RHP		398	97	12	1	14	49	61	41	70	5	5	.244
Vs. LHP		177	61	10	0	13	34	36	35	26	0	1	.345
Home	76	269	76	12	0	11	44	42	41	39	3	4	.283
Road	80	306	82	10	1	16	39	55	35	57	2	2	.268

Mike PAGLIARULO, Third Base
Runs Created: 75

	G	AB	Hit	2B	3B	HR	Run	RBI	TBB	SO	SB	CS	Avg
3.11 years		517	123	26	4	28	73	82	54	117	2	1	.238
1987	150	522	122	26	3	32	76	87	53	111	1	3	.234
First Half	82	279	65	12	2	16	38	46	37	63	1	3	.233
Second Half	68	243	57	14	1	16	38	41	16	48	0	0	.235
Vs. RHP		373	87	19	3	28	63	67	42	69	1	2	.233
Vs. LHP		149	35	7	0	4	13	20	11	42	0	1	.235
Home	74	243	52	10	1	17	36	48	32	56	1	1	.214
Road	76	279	70	16	2	15	40	39	21	55	0	2	.251

Claudell WASHINGTON, Outfield
Runs Created: 46

	G	AB	Hit	2B	3B	HR	Run	RBI	TBB	SO	SB	CS	Avg
10.07 years		576	160	29	6	14	80	70	41	108	28	12	.278
1987	102	312	87	17	0	9	42	44	27	54	10	1	.279
First Half	57	169	48	11	0	5	21	30	17	27	4	1	.284
Second Half	45	143	39	6	0	4	21	14	10	27	6	0	.273
Vs. RHP		254	67	14	0	8	29	41	19	43	8	0	.264
Vs. LHP		58	20	3	0	1	13	3	8	11	2	1	.345
Home	47	144	43	7	0	5	17	21	14	20	6	1	.299
Road	55	168	44	10	0	4	25	23	13	34	4	0	.262

Wayne TOLLESON, Shortstop
Runs Created: 29

	G	AB	Hit	2B	3B	HR	Run	RBI	TBB	SO	SB	CS	Avg
4.25 years		482	120	12	3	2	62	27	44	77	24	9	.249
1987	121	349	77	4	0	1	48	22	43	72	5	3	.221
First Half	86	280	66	4	0	1	42	20	34	55	5	3	.236
Second Half	35	69	11	0	0	0	6	2	9	17	0	0	.159
Vs. RHP		243	56	3	0	1	30	17	25	41	5	3	.230
Vs. LHP		106	21	1	0	0	18	5	18	31	0	0	.198
Home	55	152	32	3	0	1	18	10	23	31	3	1	.211
Road	66	197	45	1	0	1	30	12	20	41	2	2	.228

Dan PASQUA, Outfield
Runs Created: 43

	G	AB	Hit	2B	3B	HR	Run	RBI	TBB	SO	SB	CS	Avg
1.70 years		439	110	16	1	25	61	66	61	126	1	1	.251
1987	113	318	74	7	1	17	42	42	40	99	0	2	.233
First Half	60	169	34	3	0	8	23	23	32	61	0	1	.201
Second Half	53	149	40	4	1	9	19	19	8	38	0	1	.268
Vs. RHP		266	67	6	1	17	40	39	34	81	0	2	.252
Vs. LHP		52	7	1	0	0	2	3	6	18	0	0	.135
Home	54	141	39	1	0	6	19	13	21	43	0	1	.277
Road	59	177	35	6	1	11	23	29	19	56	0	1	.198

PURPLE (WITH RAGE AT) MARTIN

I never thought I'd find myself in the position of defending Billy Martin, but the journalistic response to his latest resurrection seems almost as irrational as the man himself. To read the highly exercised syndicated columnists you would think Martin's every tenure with the Yankees was a one-way journey from Paradise to the depths of the Inferno. In fact, there has never been a time when, under the spell of Martin's sorcery, the Pinstripes have not improved in the standings, on occasion dramatically. In 1975, Bill Virdon had them staggering along at a 53–51 gait before his ouster. By '76, under Martin, they'd moved up to 97–62 and a place in the World Series. When next called upon to practice his alchemy for a full season, in '83, he took a team that had bumbled about under three managers to the tune of 79–83, and brought them up to 91–71 and pennant contention. It was the same story in '85; he inherited a club that failed to come out of the gate for Yogi, and closed with them at 91–54, just missing the division title. The bottom line is that Martin has never, upon taking the Yankee helm early on, won fewer than 90 games. For this, there is widespread gnashing of teeth and rending of flesh?

Yes, I know, it's different this time: the hounds of journalism have already scented Martin preparing a particularly despised heresy for '88—Righetti back in the rotation. All right, he's an excellent closer, but it was only yesterday that he was a first-rate starter, so I certainly consider Martin's position arguable, especially when you consider that the Yankees have gambled for the past two seasons that their lively bats and bullpen would compensate for mediocre starting pitching, and that they've lost both times. Is it so irrational at this point to gamble that an improved rotation with Righetti will compensate for a questionable bullpen? (Sure, I grant that the really rational move would be for Steinbrenner to revert to his free-spending ways and buy a Jack Morris, or a Charley Leibrandt, but at this writing it appears the age of collusion will continue.)

Part of the hostility to Martin this time around, I'm sure, stems from his replacing Lou Piniella, latest of innumerable sainted martyrs broken upon the rack of George Torquemada III. Piniella apparently earned the respect of both his players and the New York press (I wonder sometimes, which of those accomplishments is the more significant?), no easy task, so you have to assume he was doing something right. But the reincarnation of Dick Howser he is not. He's never had enough starting pitching since the day he axed Phil Niekro, and when manna from heaven, in the person of Charles Hudson, unexpectedly 6–0, lands at his feet, he can't wait for him to lose two in a row, which results in a trip to Columbus, with the concomitant boost in confidence. Martin is accused of a compulsive, pernicious impatience, but the the extent that Sweet Lou tolerated, and even encouraged, the ridiculous Bronx–Columbus perpetual motion shuttle that swallowed even Rasmussen and Pasqua, and trapped Henry Cotto as in a revolving door, then he stands indicted as a manager lacking patience every bit as much as his now universally despised successor. The now universally despised successor, though, is more than impatient, he is vindictive. When displeased he tosses accusations about like beanbags. Reggie, Munson, Lee MacPhail, and, of course, George III, all conspire to make his life miserable. Piniella, in sharp contrast, is above such churlishness; when he accuses Rickey Henderson of "jaking it" and rushes him back into the lineup prematurely, he is merely venting his understandable frustration.

Well, I have understandable frustrations also, and now that I've made the best possible case for him, I must confess that I too loathe and despise Billy Martin. The only job I would consider him for is lunatic-asylum keeper—nobody better to provide empathy and compassion for even the most hardened paranoiacs. His continued presence in baseball is, and has always been, a shame and a disgrace. But I don't understand why, in this particular instance, the reaction to his return is so overwhelmingly hostile. Martin now is no more, and no less, than he has ever been. You can bet everything you own that he will get into senseless fights (I guess there is one difference: he's now too old to emerge victorious from out-and-out fisticuffs; twenty years ago Ed Whitson would've turned up in the morgue) and win a lot of ballgames. He always has and he always will. And the across-the-board revulsion at this latest recycling reminds me of nothing so much as the French police captain in *Casablanca*, who is shocked, shocked to discover gambling going on. But he doesn't hesitate to pocket his winnings, and neither will the alienated press, because if Billy Martin confrontation stories aren't the living embodiment of journalistic "winnings," I don't know what are.

—Mike Kopf

BOSTON RED SOX

By 1990, the Boston Red Sox are going to be tough to beat. I figure that in two years the Tigers will be a candidate to lose a hundred games, the Yankees will have lost their war with the treadmill, the Orioles won't be any better than they are now and the Indians still won't have a pitching staff, in addition to which they will still be the Cleveland Indians. That leaves Toronto, Boston, and Milwaukee to fight it out for the future of this division. The Red Sox are going to be a handful.

The question I am asked most often about the 1987 Rod Sox is whether I have ever seen a team with so many outstanding rookies. The answer is no, I don't know that I have. The 1987 team was not a team, exactly, but a collage of three teams—the leftovers from the Red Sox of the past (Rice, Buckner, Stanley), the heralds of the Red Sox of the future (Greenwell, Burks, Marzano, Horn, Benzinger) and three guys off of the Red Sox all-time All-Star team (Evans, Boggs, Clemens). With Clemens not ready to open the season, the Red Sox had to use Bob Stanley as the opening-day starter. They lost, of course, dropped quickly to 0–3 and were able to poke their heads over .500 only one time all year, with an 8–7 record on April 22. By this time they were already five and a half behind Milwaukee, and when they lost their next five games to drop to 8–12, they were effectively out of the race—meaning not that they were in a position from which they couldn't have recovered, but that having fallen into a poor position, they never made any of the kind of faces you make when you're thinking about getting up and putting up a fight. They weren't defeated yet, but they were beaten.

For one thing, they were playing this Godawful catcher. I'm sorry if this is harsh, but there is nepotism here, and as petty as it is, it offends me. The Red Sox in 1979 blew a second-round draft pick on Marc Sullivan, the son of Red Sox then-vice president Haywood Sullivan. After young Marckie hit .203 with one home run in 117 games in the Eastern League (1982), the Red Sox had the effrontery to dress him up in a major-league uniform and foist him off as a major-league player, in two games late the same season. After he went back to the minors and hit .229 and .204, they decided he was ready to play for the major league team. In 1985 and 1986, as a part-timer, Sullivan hit .174 and .193. In 1987 he opened the season as the Red Sox' regular catcher. We should all find our opportunities so abundant.

What I would like to know is, where the hell does Haywood Sullivan get off trying to make his precious little boy an exception to the rules that the rest of the baseball world obeys? The most basic rule of sports is that in the effort to win, you put the team goals ahead of your personal agenda. The public posture of every major-league team is that they expect their players not to play for their own statistics or their own greater glory, but to do what the good of the team demands. They would be appalled if a player stated publicly that he was playing for himself

first and didn't care much whether the Sox won or lost. But Haywood Sullivan wants to add, "Of course, that doesn't apply to me."

And where is the watchdog? What does the press say? They tell us that Marc Sullivan is such a nice kid. Well, who the hell cares if he is a nice kid? Do you have any idea how many nice kids there are in AAA ball? It is not fair to those kids to tell them that Marc Sullivan is playing by a different set of rules than they are. It is not fair to Red Sox fans, and it's not fair to their other players.

I call on Peter Uebberoth to intervene and end to this disgraceful situation. If Uebberoth really cares about the integrity of the game, he should tell Haywood to get Marc Sullivan's sorry ass out of a Red Sox uniform by sundown. Al Campanis's son was a catcher, too; he was about as good as this kid, a lifetime .147 hitter. When Campanis took over the Dodgers his first official act was to trade his own son. He didn't love his son any less than Haywood Sullivan does. He just had the character to say "Son, the rules are just the same for you as they are for anybody else." And if Haywood Sullivan was half a man, he would have done the same thing.

Oh, well . . . what we really need is a good, strong Sports Consumer's Union to deal with this kind of thing. And then Gedman came back, and he was just as bad; Sullivan and Gedman were bad enough to negate, I would say, about 2.5 superstars. The Sox had them. Probably no other team has two players as valuable as Wade Boggs and Roger Clemens. While I am not emotionally committed to the idea that Wade Boggs is the best player in the game, he's hard to argue with. The Sox may have the best player in the game and the best pitcher in the game. Beyond the two guys who are as good as anybody, there's Dwight Evans. The questions you ask about Dwight Evans are not whether he is a good player or whether he can help the team win the pennant, but whether he should be in the Hall of Fame and whether it is in the best interests of the team to keep him at first base, when he is still a fine outfielder.

And beyond Evans, there is Marty Barrett, certainly a fine player, and then there is Bruce Hurst and all of those rookies and now there is Lee Smith. If you think I'm leading up to saying that the Sox should be taken seriously as contenders, I'm sorry to disappoint you.

I have a hard time saying exactly why it is that I don't think the Sox will be in the race on September 15. The most critical problem is that the starting pitching is too thin. In 1987 the gap between their top two starters and the rest of the team was 205 points, the largest in baseball (see chart on Cincinnati charts page). Clemens and Hurst were 35–22, .614; the rest of the team had a winning percentage of .409. A comeback by Oil Can, the development of Jeff Sellers and the addition of Lee Smith could close that gap, but then any team in the league could muster that kind of an argument. Even in saying "Clemens and Hurst," we're giving them the benefit of the doubt on Hurst. Hurst's ERA last year was 4.41, about the league average (4.46), and his career won-lost record is 70–67. Hurst did again last year what he has done all of his career except 1986, when a mid-summer injury gave him some time off: he fell apart down the stretch. From August 15 to the end of the year he had only two good outings.

On another team, the manager probably would not have a guy with a history of blowing out in August leading the league in complete games for most of the year, but then we're dealing with reality here; McNamara isn't going to be fired until the Sox have another year that can be clearly classed a failure. Anyway, so the Sox have one or two good starting pitchers. That's not enough.

There have been other teams that produced a large crop of outstanding rookies in a year or two years; to name a few, the San Francisco Giants in '58, the Royals in '73, the Expos in '77, and the Tigers in '78. Such teams do not usually show up at the top of the standings just one year later. A normal incubation period is three to five years.

Of course, these rookie crops do not ordinarily join a team that already has two or three superstars, so there we are again: in the right circumstances, this team has enough talent to win.

All right, we get back to my real problem: management. Why don't young teams win?

1) Because they don't know how to win. John McNamara isn't the man to teach them.

2) Because young hitters, even those who come into the league and hit .320, normally have to ride the Yo-Yo up and down a few times while learning the league.

3) Because young players don't play team defense.

4) Because young talent has to be sorted out. People have to find their positions. The Red Sox will be leading off Ellis Burks because he's the only guy on the team who can run, but he's obviously not a leadoff hitter. They will be hitting Wade Boggs third, which is another mistake (see other article on Red Sox). I think the Red Sox offensive elements are stronger than their offense will be. Marty Barrett is a solid player, doesn't put a lot of runs on the scoreboard but does the job as well as most of the other guys at his position. The offensive elements are great, but the Sox won't lead the league in runs scored. The Red Sox this year should have some tremendous hot streaks, like Milwaukee last year, but they'll also have slumps. Any time Roger Clemens loses they've got a chance to have a losing streak.

Let's talk about the defense a minute. The 1987 Sox defensive efficiency record, .672, was the worst in the major leagues, meaning that when a ball was put into play against this team it was more likely to put a man on base than against any other team. That is partially a park illusion; let's say it is part ballpark and part first basemen. There are some outs you don't get in Fenway because of the nearness of the stands, and there are quite a few balls that rocket off the wall without any chance to make a play on them. Besides that, though, it just seems like there are always balls that drop in in Fenway. You ever notice that? Ground balls seem to go through the infield rather than at somebody, line drives seem to drop before the outfielder gets to them. I don't know if it's good visibility causing

more hard-hit balls, or what. Anyway, the Blue Jays play in a good hitter's park, too, but they had a DER of .710, almost the best in baseball. The difference was a few guys named Tony Fernandez, Willie Upshaw, and Lloyd Moseby.

Red Sox outfielders in 1987 threw out 47 baserunners, six more than any other major-league team. When you have Dwight Evans playing first base, that's probably an indication that you're not short of outfield arms; Dwight can still throw.

In my opinion, Evans should be in left field. Jim Rice was a great player in his time, but he really hasn't helped the team in three of the last four years. It should be obvious to anybody that he didn't help the team last year, but the question is, did he really help the team in 1985, when he hit .291 and drove in 103 runs, or in 1984, when he hit .280 but drove in 122 runs? I'm sure most people think that if you drive in 122 runs you're a great player no matter what you don't do, but if you put his positive contributions in the context of the enormous number of outs that he makes, I think you'll see that he really wasn't outstanding even then.

The Red Sox average margin of victory in the games they won was almost four runs (3.99), the largest of any major-league team. That statistic will shrink this year because Lee Smith will win them some close games, but in general when they win, the Red Sox will win impressively, just as they did last year. Unfortunately, what counts is not how impressively, but how often.

With a speed score of 4.07, the Red Sox were the slowest team in the major leagues despite the addition of Ellis Burks. With Spike Owen being the second-fastest player in the lineup, that seems like a safe statement; two infielders (Buckner and Boggs) and two outfielders (Rice and Evans) contributed almost nothing to the speed categories. While the Sox not do have one guy who can run, remember that they had five rookies in key roles last year, and the other four don't run. Benzinger and Greenwell are faster than Rice and Evans only because they are younger, Marzano runs like a catcher and Sam Horn runs like an anvil. Shortstop prospect Jody Reed isn't a base stealer. The Sox of the future probably won't run any better than the Sox of recent years. Marc Sullivan, of course, can't run either.

Consistent with his general philosophy of never making a move unless he has to, McNamara used only 91 pinch hitters on the season, the second-lowest total in the majors. McNamara is the father of the minimalist school of managing; his forthcoming book on managerial strategy is sure to be entitled *Let Them Play and See What Happens*. It is appropriate that the most controversial moment of his managerial career came not when he made a move, but when he failed to make one, failing to pinch-run Dave Stapleton for Bill Buckner.

Among the possible 1988 rookies . . . Pat Dodson is now 28, probably a major-league hitter but not going to get a shot unless Horn stops hitting again. I think Jody Reed is going to be a terrific player, far better than Spike Owen. All four starting pitchers at Pawtucket (Curry, Ellsworth, Leister, and Woodward) were decent, although none was brilliant. Again, they would have a better chance of developing one of those guys into a quality starter if they had a better manager.

As to the Lee Smith trade, I'd put my feelings this way: if I were the Sox GM and I had a chance to make the trade, would I make it? You bet. But as an analyst, do I think the trade is going to materially improve the Red Sox? Not really—not by enough, anyway. Lee Smith will mean that the Sox win 88 games instead of 83.

It is not logical, from the standpoint of the universe, for Lee Smith to be with the Boston Red Sox. Smith is 30 years old, carries some extra weight, has bad knees, and has been worked hard for seven years. He's as good a reliever as there is in baseball, but he's probably just got a couple of years left. Logically, he should have gone to a team that has a legitimate shot at the pennant, but needs a relief ace to push them over the hump, like Seattle or California or Kansas City or New York if Righetti is in the rotation. Like Reardon for Minnesota.

Oh, well; if God had intended for this to be a logical universe, he would never have entrusted Jim Frey with a baseball team.

AVERAGE MARGIN OF VICTORY

Boston	3.99
Detroit	3.90
Toronto	3.88
Kansas City	3.77
Texas	3.76
Oakland	3.68
Yankees	3.67
Seattle	3.67
White Sox	3.65
Mets	3.63
California	3.60
San Francisco	3.49
Milwaukee	3.41
San Diego	3.35
Houston	3.34
Cubs	3.32
Pittsburgh	3.30
Cincinnati	3.27
Minnesota	3.26
Atlanta	3.23
Cleveland	3.18
Montreal	3.18
Los Angeles	3.05
Baltimore	3.04
St. Louis	3.01
Philadelphia	2.76

RUNS SCORED AND ALLOWED WINS AND LOSSES

Wins	552	241	78-0	1.000
Home Games	436	383	50-30	.625
Clemens	200	134	22-14	.611
Hurst	158	155	17-16	.515
Blowouts	333	320	26-26	.500
Slugfests	542	543	36-38	.486
All Games	842	825	78-84	.481
One-Run Games	176	179	18-21	.462
Sellers	110	109	10-12	.455
Nipper	166	166	13-17	.433
Pitchers' Duels	56	58	13-17	.433
Stanley	85	118	7-13	.350
Road Games	406	442	28-54	.341
Losses	290	584	0-84	.000

TEN BEST STARTS

	IP	H	R	ER	BB	SO		
Clemens vs. Mil, Oct 4	9	2	0	0	0	12	W	95
Hurst vs. Oak, May 5	9	5	0	0	2	14	W	89
Clemens at Cle, June 17	9	4	0	0	2	12	W	89
Hurst vs. Tor, Apr 10	9	2	0	0	1	6	W	88
Clemens vs. KC, Apr 21	9	3	0	0	1	6	W	86
Hurst vs. Cal, May 10	9	5	0	0	1	9	W	85
Clemens at Bal, Sep 20	9	3	1	0	3	9	W	85
Stanley vs. KC, Apr 22	9	4	0	0	0	7	W	83
Clemens vs. Cle, May 27	9	6	0	0	0	8	W	83
Sellers at Minn, Sep 1	9	5	0	0	2	7	W	82
Schiraldi at Minn, Sep 3	7	3	0	0	0	11	—	82

PITCHERS WHEN SUPPORTED BY THREE TO FIVE RUNS

	G	IP	W-L	Pct	SO	BB	ERA
Clemens	16	134	8-6	.571	118	37	2.88
Hurst	12	84	5-5	.500	70	29	5.70
Nipper	10	59	2-5	.286	28	21	4.91

HALL OF FAME WATCH

Fully qualified: Rice 147.5; **Could be elected on current accomplishments:** Boggs 106; **Building credentials but not yet viable candidate:** Dwight Evans 59, Clemens 55.5, John McNamara 42; **Working ont it:** Stanley 26, Hurst 14; **Long way to go:** Barrett 9.5, Boyd 7, Gedman 7, Crawford 6, Owen 5, Dave Henderson 3, Greenwell 3, Schiraldi 3, Nipper 3.

TEN WORST STARTS

	IP	H	R	ER	BB	SO		
Nipper at Chi, May 31	1⅓	7	9	9	2	1	—	3
Clemens at NY, June 26	2⅓	9	8	8	2	3	—	8
Hurst vs. NY, Sep 7	3⅔	12	7	7	2	3	L	10
Sellers vs. Tor, Aug 12	4*	10	8	8	2	3	L	11
Leister vs. Mil, Oct 3	5*	13	6	6	1	0	L	16
Woodward vs. Det, Sep 22	5⅔	10	8	8	2	1	L	16
Nipper at Det, Sep 15	2⅓	7	6	6	2	1	—	18
Hurst vs. KC, Apr 20	5⅓	9	8	8	2	2	L	19
Leister vs. Cle, May 28	2	6	6	6	1	1	—	20
Stanley at Tor, Apr 17	5	10	7	6	2	1	L	20

TEAM SPEED SCORES FOR 1987

St. Louis	5.93
White Sox	5.72
San Diego	5.56
Mets	5.53
Pittsburgh	5.50
Toronto	5.48
Montreal	5.48
Seattle	5.42
Cincinnati	5.35
California	5.34
Houston	5.30
Detroit	5.24
Milwaukee	5.24
Philadelphia	5.19
Texas	5.12
Cleveland	5.12
Kansas City	5.09
Oakland	5.08
Minnesota	5.05
San Francisco	4.87
Cubs	4.55
Atlanta	4.54
Los Angeles	4.53
Yankees	4.52
Baltimore	4.16
Boston	4.07

Dwight EVANS, First Base
Runs Created: 134

	G	AB	Hit	2B	3B	HR	Run	RBI	TBB	SO	SB	CS	Avg
12.88 years		559	151	31	5	25	92	83	85	108	5	4	.270
1987	154	541	165	37	2	34	109	123	106	98	4	6	.305
First Half	82	288	91	20	1	18	53	69	53	52	4	5	.316
Second Half	72	253	74	17	1	16	56	54	53	46	0	1	.292
Vs. RHP		398	112	27	2	22	78	86	79	82	3	3	.281
Vs. LHP		143	53	10	0	12	31	37	27	16	1	3	.371
Home	73	263	80	23	2	14	45	65	43	44	1	3	.304
Road	81	278	85	14	0	20	64	58	63	54	3	3	.306

Jim RICE, Left Field
Runs Created: 55

	G	AB	Hit	2B	3B	HR	Run	RBI	TBB	SO	SB	CS	Avg
11.72 years		643	194	29	6	31	100	115	52	110	5	3	.302
1987	108	404	112	14	0	13	66	62	45	77	1	1	.277
First Half	69	264	73	13	0	7	45	39	28	52	1	1	.277
Second Half	30	140	39	1	0	6	21	23	17	25	0	0	.279
Vs. RHP		281	77	12	0	9	43	46	29	58	1	1	.274
Vs. LHP		123	35	2	0	4	23	16	16	19	0	0	.285
Home	52	190	58	6	0	7	39	32	24	41	1	1	.305
Road	56	214	54	8	0	6	27	30	21	41	0	0	.252

Marty BARRETT, Second Base
Runs Created: 74

	G	AB	Hit	2B	3B	HR	Run	RBI	TBB	SO	SB	CS	Avg
3.90 years		578	164	29	4	4	74	53	56	37	11	4	.284
1987	137	559	164	23	0	3	72	43	51	38	15	2	.293
First Half	72	286	76	9	0	2	36	23	30	25	8	2	.266
Second Half	65	273	88	14	0	1	36	20	21	13	7	0	.322
Vs. RHP		409	112	18	0	1	48	26	33	34	8	2	.274
Vs. LHP		150	52	5	0	2	24	17	18	4	7	0	.347
Home	68	274	80	15	0	2	39	17	24	18	5	0	.292
Road	69	285	84	8	0	1	33	26	27	20	10	2	.295

Ellis BURKS, Center Field
Runs Created: 85

	G	AB	Hit	2B	3B	HR	Run	RBI	TBB	SO	SB	CS	Avg
0.82 years		680	185	37	2	24	115	72	50	120	33	7	.272
1987	133	558	152	30	2	20	94	59	41	98	27	6	.272
First Half	60	246	62	16	0	13	39	36	16	50	13	2	.252
Second Half	73	312	90	14	2	7	55	23	25	48	14	4	.288
Vs. RHP		409	104	18	2	16	60	41	27	68	17	5	.254
Vs. LHP		149	48	12	0	4	34	18	14	30	10	1	.322
Home	66	256	74	14	1	11	52	30	30	43	13	2	.289
Road	67	302	78	16	1	9	42	29	11	55	14	4	.258

Wade BOGGS, Third Base
Runs Created: 154

	G	AB	Hit	2B	3B	HR	Run	RBI	TBB	SO	SB	CS	Avg
5.38		619	219	41	4	10	108	76	97	47	2	2	.354
1987	147	551	200	40	6	24	108	89	105	48	1	3	.363
First Half	87	333	125	21	4	17	71	55	58	30	0	1	.375
Second Half	60	218	75	19	2	7	37	34	47	18	1	2	.344
Vs. RHP		382	144	29	4	17	76	53	85	34	1	1	.377
Vs. LHP		169	56	11	2	7	32	36	20	14	0	2	.331
Home	75	282	116	28	3	10	60	50	53	24	1	1	.411
Road	72	269	84	12	3	14	48	39	52	24	0	2	.312

Mike GREENWELL, Right Field
Runs Created: 90

	G	AB	Hit	2B	3B	HR	Run	RBI	TBB	SO	SB	CS	Avg
1.07 years		447	146	32	6	21	77	94	40	48	6	4	.327
1987	125	412	135	31	6	19	71	89	35	40	5	4	.328
First Half	59	166	51	14	0	10	27	43	12	17	1	2	.307
Second Half	66	246	84	17	6	9	44	46	23	23	4	2	.341
Vs. RHP		338	107	26	5	18	62	76	31	34	5	4	.317
Vs. LHP		74	28	5	1	1	9	13	4	6	0	0	.378
Home	62	217	71	19	5	8	43	44	19	16	3	2	.327
Road	63	195	64	12	1	11	28	45	16	24	2	2	.328

Spike OWEN, Shortstop
Runs Created: 52

	G	AB	Hit	2B	3B	HR	Run	RBI	TBB	SO	SB	CS	Avg
3.93		548	131	20	8	4	66	49	53	58	13	8	.239
1987	132	437	113	17	7	2	50	48	53	43	11	8	.259
First Half	65	209	53	12	4	0	29	21	26	19	5	3	.254
Second Half	67	228	60	5	3	2	21	27	27	24	6	5	.263
Vs. RHP		305	71	9	5	0	28	29	38	29	6	5	.233
Vs. LHP		132	42	8	2	2	22	19	15	14	5	3	.318
Home	68	224	59	8	5	2	25	28	28	21	5	3	.263
Road	64	213	54	9	2	0	25	20	25	22	6	5	.254

Don BAYLOR, Designated Hitter
Runs Created: 57

	G	AB	Hit	2B	3B	HR	Run	RBI	TBB	SO	SB	CS	Avg
13.58 years		584	153	26	2	24	89	91	57	75	21	9	.262
1987	128	388	95	9	0	16	67	63	45	59	5	3	.245
First Half	86	294	69	7	0	14	55	45	36	38	3	1	.235
Second Half	42	94	26	2	0	2	12	18	9	21	2	2	.277
Vs. RHP		253	59	8	0	10	44	40	33	44	2	1	.233
Vs. LHP		135	36	1	0	6	23	23	12	15	3	2	.267
Home	61	183	49	3	0	10	33	39	17	31	1	0	.268
Road	67	205	46	6	0	6	34	24	28	28	4	3	.224

THE LINEUP

This doesn't have a lot to do with the Boston Red Sox, but before I left the field of sabermetrics I wanted to get it on record. Several years ago, a gentleman named Jeffrey Eby did a study which yielded, among other things, the number of runs scored by each major-league team in each inning. The study found, as you would expect, that the number of runs scored was highest in the first inning, which is the only inning in which you get to decide who will hit, and was lowest in the second inning, when the bottom of the order comes up. After the third inning the number of runs scored leveled off, being almost the same in innings three through seven.

What was surprising, however, was this: If you took the first two innings and added them together, the average was not up from the standard for innings three through seven. It was down. What does that mean? By setting the lineup for the first inning, managers are exercising a degree of effective determination over not one but two innings, the first *and* the second. They accept the cost of a poor second inning in order to get the benefit of a strong first inning—and they lose on the deal! They wind up scoring fewer runs than if they just started the lineup at a random point. Doesn't that imply that they are doing something seriously wrong? If you score fewer runs when you can choose who will hit than you do when you can't choose who will hit, then you must be making a mistake in how you choose, right?

I've been chewing on that for two years now. I will gladly concede that this is the kind of casual inference that in many cases can lead you to an absurd conclusion. There are other factors determining how many runs are scored in each inning, like pitcher fatigue and the number of pinch hitters used, and it is also obvious that there is a degree of determination exercised by the batting order even after the second inning. Nonetheless, I think the argument eventually holds water. There are many reasons why the argument could be wrong, but none of those seems to me to be ultimately as convincing as the argument itself. I guess you'll have to reach your own conclusion about that.

Anyway, when you start thinking about this the natural second question is, "What is the likely mistake that they could be making?" What could managers be doing wrong that could cause the number of runs scored in the second inning to be so low that it offsets the gain from the first inning?

The largest determinant of how many runs are likely to be scored in an inning is whether or not the lead-off man reaches base. If the lead-off man reaches base, the number of runs that will probably be scored in the inning is about three times as high as if the lead-off man is put out. Incredible as it may seem, the number of runs that will probably be scored in an inning is much greater with a man on base and Wayne Tolleson coming up than it is with no one on and Dale Murphy coming up. Now, look at the Red Sox lineup. The one player who is least likely to lead off the second inning is the number-three hitter. For the Red Sox, and indeed for many other teams, the highest on-base percentage belongs to . . . the number-three hitter. Thus, the one player who is most likely to start a successful inning and the one player who is least likely to start the second inning are the same player.

Further, the traditional baseball thinking puts in the fifth spot the slow-moving slugger with the low on-base percentage—the Mike Marshall, the Lance, or Larry Parrish, the Jim Presley or Cory Snyder. Think about it. Who leads off the second inning most often? The first inning ends 1-2-3 a little less than 30 percent of the time. The most common lead-off man for the second inning is the fifth hitter—the one player in all the lineup least suited to be a lead-off hitter!

See, *all* the thinking is focused on creating a perfect first inning; the power hitter is put there to *finish* the first inning. The second inning gets no thought. But the reality is that at least as often as this type of hitter is properly cast in the first inning, he is totally miscast in the second.

Wouldn't it make more sense, I wonder, to put that high on-base percentage, the Wade Boggs or the George Brett or the Dale Murphy, in the fourth spot, and to switch the sluggers with the lower on-base percentages up to the third spot? First of all, if you did that, Wade Boggs would obviously bat more often with men on base. Wouldn't he? The only time Boggs bats in the first but not in the second is when the first two men make out anyway. Boggs would hit in the first inning less often, but all of the difference would be in games that the first two men made out. If you bat him fourth instead of third, you do two things: you give three people a chance to get on base in front of him rather than two, and, if they don't do it, you have him leading off the second inning, and then you've got a chance to score some runs in the second.

I also think there's a similar anomaly in the use of speed in the lead-off spot. When the lead-off hitter attempts to steal a base and is caught, the loss is much larger than when a fifth or sixth hitter attempts to steal a base and is caught. This should be obvious, because when Ellis Burks is caught stealing as a lead-off man, he is taking the bat out of the hands of Dwight Evans or Wade Boggs, whereas if he was hitting lower in the order he would be taking the bat out of the hands of Spike Owen or John Marzano. Conversely, when a lead-off hitter attempts to steal a base and is successful, the gain is less than when a fifth hitter or sixth hitter steals a base. Why? Because the stolen base primarily makes a difference when a single is hit. On an extra base hit, the runner is probably going to score anyway; the advantage is gained when a single is hit, not a double or a homer. Who hits singles more often, Dwight Evans, Mike Greenwell, or Spike Owen? The answer is Spike Owen. Who hit singles more often last year, Wade Boggs or Ed Romero? Yes, he did.

So in the traditional offense, we place the base stealer in the position where the gain of a stolen base is least, and where the cost of a caught stealing is greatest. Further, many managers are so intent upon placing the base stealer in that spot that they will put him there even if he is a power hitter with a low on-base percentage, like Ellis Burks. The Red Sox on base percentages last year included .461 (Boggs), .386 (Greenwell), .417 (Evans), .351 (Barrett), .357 (Rice), .337 (Owen), and .324 (Burks). Who did they lead off? The guy with the .324 on-base percentage—so they can place him in the spot where his base-stealing ability would have the least value.

OK, I know you have to deal with egos. I know you can't fight your players. But I still think, in a strictly logical universe, that the best lineup for the Sox would be something like this:

Vs. Right-Hander	Vs. Left-Hander
Greenwell	Boggs
Evans	Barrett
Horn	Burks
Boggs	Evans
Barrett	Greenwell
Owen	Marzano
Burks	Owen
Marzano	Rice
Rice	Horn

Well, I ought to do a simulation study of this, run games on a computer with a hundred different lineups and see which way they score the most runs. I'm out of the business now, but I might do it anyway.

Several people, maybe a dozen, have done simulation studies of lineups, and have all (as far as I know) reported that it really doesn't make any difference, that one lineup is as good as another. I still don't buy it. For one thing, none of the people who have done these studies have written them up properly. It just isn't good enough to say that "I've studied the issue and found that it doesn't make any difference." That's meaningless. If you expect to convince anybody, you have to give people a chance to evaluate your method, to see what you adjusted for and what you didn't adjust for. Did you adjust for speed? Did you allow for platoon differentials? Did you keep track of runs scored by inning? How many lineup options did you consider? What did you simulate, and what did you not simulate? I've been editing a journal of sabermetric research for six years now, and I've never seen an article on this issue. Unless you give the sabermetric community the opportunity to examine the research, you can't expect your conclusions to be accepted.

In general, the most suspect conclusion in any research is the finding of no effect. If you find no effect, that means that either there is no effect, or you looked in the wrong place. To convince people that there is no effect, you have to demonstrate that you looked everywhere that the effect could reasonably be hiding. There is a very strong presumption that it does make a difference how you arrange your lineup, and until somebody shows me that they have looked everywhere, I'm going to stick with that presumption.

BALTIMORE ORIOLES

In 1984 the Baltimore Orioles had a disappointing season. After winning the World Championship in 1983, the Orioles dropped off in 1984 to 85 wins, 77 losses. By the end of the 1985 season, one year later, the Orioles had changed regulars at five of the nine positions. Looking back on it now, it was a striking passage in the history of the team, one at which the collapse of the Oriole tradition was written large in the Western sky, had we not been too blind to see it.

The Orioles left in place what they saw as the anchors of their team, Ripken and Murray. In making changes at five other positions, they didn't want to risk trying out young, unproven players. In center field, they replaced John Shelby with Fred Lynn, a 33-year-old free agent with an injury catalog in which you could find most anything. At another outfield spot, they replaced Gary Roenicke with Lee Lacy, a 36-year-old free agent. At second base, they replaced Rich Dauer with Alan Wiggins, an established player who was available from San Diego because of drug and personality problems. At third base, they replaced Wayne Gross with Fat Floyd Rayford, a 10-year minor leaguer with a chronic weight problem.

Those changes, rather than fighting off the natural aging process and the natural accumulation of incentive problems which occur within any lineup, made the team immediately older, less well-conditioned, less well-motivated, and more injury-prone. There is no reason why this should not have been known at the time. At only one position, designated hitter, did the Orioles move to give a talented young player a chance to develop (Larry Sheets replacing Ken Singleton).

I noticed this pattern when doing the counts of the number of regulars used over the last five years (see Philadelphia). It is unusual for a team to introduce five new regulars in a season. It is extraordinary for a team to introduce five new regulars in an off-hand way, without making a positive move to restructure the team. Facing what they saw as a disappointing season, they made five individual gambles, apparently without at the time recognizing that there was a pattern.

Then you look at the pitching staff. In 1984 their relief ace, team leader in saves, was Tippy Martinez, who was 34 years old and losing effectiveness. They replaced Tippy—with Don Aase, a 30-year-old veteran who had been on the disabled list every year since the time of Cap Anson.

Then look ahead to 1986, when the Orioles introduced onto their roster one new semi-regular—Juan Beniquez, then 36 years old. Or to 1987, when they introduced two new regulars: Ray Knight and Terry Kennedy. They hoped to make it three, but Rick Burleson didn't pan out.

It has been said that there is no event on record which a competent historian cannot make seem inevitable once it has transpired. I do not want to argue that the dissolution of the Oriole tradition was an inevitable consequence of these decisions. It was not inevitable. It was merely exceedingly probable.

Now, this is so obvious that it embarrasses me to say it, but then I have said it a hundred times before and there is still no general acceptance of it. From the age of 28 on, all groups of players are declining. Almost any group of players will lose 50 percent of their value, as a group, between the ages of 28 and 32. Because some players remain strong into their thirties, and because those who do remain strong remain in the public view, while those who don't disappear from sight, there is a tendency to greatly underestimate the amount of decline that takes place in these years. In 1987, players who were 32 years old as of July 1 included Andre Dawson, Jack Morris, Mike Scott, and Ozzie Smith, but they also included Willie Aikens, Rob Andrews (remember him?), Bobby Brown, John Castino, Julio Cruz, Miguel Dilone, Damaso Garcia, Ruppert Jones, Steve Kemp, Ken Landreaux, Rick Manning, Lee Mazzilli, Broderick Perkins, Gary Roenicke, Billy Sample, Jason Thompson, Ellis Valentine, Claudell Washington, Ross Baumgarten, Jim Beattie, Joe Beckwith, Bobby Castillo, David Clyde, Mark Fidrych, Brian Kingman, Bob Owchinko, Pete Redfern, Sammy Stewart, and Kip Young, not one of whom expected to be where he is at the age of 32 (not to mention an infinite number of such meteorites as Dan Graham, Glenn Gulliver, and Andres Mora, also 32 years old in 1987).

Collectively, ballplayers suffer a tremendous loss of value before age 32. After 32, the rate of decline accelerates rapidly. Between 32 and 36, any group of players is likely to lose 85 percent of its value. So whenever you sign a player over the age of 28, you are buying into a market that is certain to decline. If you see building a baseball team as being a matter of solving 15 problems, then if you make a ten-year solution to each problem you've got to solve one or two problems every year. If you make two-year solutions to your problems, then you have to solve seven or eight problems every year. It isn't easy to find that ten-year solution to a problem, but which do you have a better chance of doing?

The team which resulted in 1987 from three years of these short-end gambles was old, slow, and injury-prone. The strongest points of the team were that 1) they hit home runs, 2) they didn't make errors, and 3) they turned the double play well. The third point is attributable to Cal Ripken and long grass. The other two are the attributes of an old, immobile team, the things that an old player will still do well.

The Orioles had 88 games in which they committed no errors, more than any other major-league team.

They had 16 games in which they turned three or more double plays, as well as any major-league team, and they had 43 games in which they turned two or more double plays.

Their ratio of double plays to errors, 174 to 111, was the best in the major leagues.

On another team, those things might be an asset. On Baltimore, they were a delaying action. Even in the games in which they committed no errors, the Orioles record was

40–48, quite a bit better than their record when they did commit an error (27–47), but still not very good. Their record in those 43 games in which they turned two or more double plays was just 15–28.

The Orioles stolen-base percentage, .605, was the lowest in American League.

The Orioles pitching stats are even uglier. Their starting pitchers pitched only 912 innings, the fewest of any major-league team. The ERA of their starters, for the whole season, was 5.26. That breaks down, for the morbid, as 5.17 in Baltimore, 5.36 on the road.

They broke the record for home runs allowed. In the *Historical Abstract*, I strung through the book a number of times when somebody had predicted that a certain record would never be broken, when it was destined to be broken within a few years. Well, I did it myself this time. On page 44 of the 1986 *Baseball Abstract*, I wrote that the 1964 Kansas City A's "set an all-time record for home runs allowed in a season, with 220. The record will not be broken in the next ten years." The Orioles allowed 226. I did exactly the same thing the people I quoted had done: I underestimated how quickly the game could change.

Obviously you can't defend against the home run, and it is hard to defend a group of pitchers who give up 226 home runs. I still believe, though, that much of what people see as being pitching is in fact defense. The Orioles had no center fielder. They had Fred Lynn in center field, and Ken Gerhardt. They were using left fielders in center. I've got to believe that maybe fifty to a hundred balls fell into the Oriole outfield last year that would have been caught by good defensive outfielders. That makes the pitchers look bad, and that undermines their confidence, and that leads to more homers and more walks. If you took this same group of pitchers and put a good defense behind them, you might be shocked at how much better they would look.

One major disappointment among the pitchers was the performance of Jeff Ballard, who shot through the Oriole system like a bullet, going 37–15 in the two years between signing and reaching the majors. Ballard's major-league stats were almost the same as those of Scott McGregor, which is to say that they were horrible indeed; he gave up a hundred hits in 70 innings, walked more men than he struck out and gave up home runs at an appalling rate. He finished 2–8 with a 6.59 ERA. The opposition batting average against him was .344.

As bad as that sounds, I hope the Orioles don't give up on him. You have to understand that it sometimes takes a control pitcher longer to settle into a major-league job than it does a power pitcher. Look at Scott McGregor's first year, or Mike Flanagan's. They weren't quite this bad, but they were bad, and those guys weren't contending with the 1987 league conditions, which led to a league ERA of 4.46, or with an outfield of two left fielders and a DH. There have been a lot of pitchers like Ballard who, after getting hit hard in their first try at the major leagues, wandered around for five or six years even though they were very good pitchers, just waiting for their second clean shot. Mike Cuellar was one, and Larry Gura another. Maybe I didn't say that exactly right, because power pitchers often come out of the minors and struggle, too, but in a different form. A power pitcher comes up and walks five or six men a game, but then it is obvious what

the problem is. Everybody can see that he's going to be effective once he finds his control. In the case of a finesse pitcher, sometimes it's harder to see that he, too, is just going through a learning process. It looks like he's just getting hammered. Anyway, if the Orioles are smart, they'll hide Ballard in the bullpen or something, try to get his confidence up, and stick with him.

Underlying that comment, I suppose, is that it might be a couple of years before Ballard finds himself, which is probably the last thing the Orioles want to hear. Sometimes failure perpetuates failure. Ballard illustrates the wisdom of one of Earl Weaver's tenets: the best place for a rookie pitcher is in long relief. If the Oriole starting pitching was strong, they would have put Ballard in long relief. Because their starting pitching was so poor, they had to push him into a starting role. Because he was pushed in over his head, his career might be irrevocably damaged.

Well, let me clean up some notes. The Orioles played fairly well following a win (.470 winning percentage in the next game), but did not bounce back after a loss, with a .368 winning percentage following a loss, the worst in baseball.

The Orioles invested only 76 outs in first-run strategies, the fewest of any major-league team, consistent with the Earl Weaver tradition although they no longer have the personnel to make it work. Actually, Earl's first eight Oriole teams, 1968–1975, invested a consistent 120 outs a year in first-run strategies; then, as Earl became more convinced that first-run strategies didn't work, that number began to drop almost yearly, reaching a low of 67 in 1986. The concept of secondary average, when it was invented a few years ago, was a tribute to the traditional Oriole offense, heavily weighted with platoon players who drew walks and hit home runs—the fabled Oriole three-run homers. Last year the Orioles had the lowest secondary average in the American League, .266.

Over the last five years the Orioles home park advantage is only eight and a half games, the smallest in baseball (see charts, Minnesota). Over those five years they are 207–197 at home, 199–206 on the road, and actually have a better winning percentage on artificial turf than on grass fields (see Atlanta comment). Certainly the constant infusion of new players has worked against the development of a home park advantage (see Minnesota comment).

One of the curious features of the Oriole team is their ability to batter the American League West at will. Although the divisions were of almost equal strength last year, the Orioles were an incredible 28 games better against the West (49–35) than against their division rivals (18–60). No other team was remotely comparable. Here, I'll run down the league in order: Oakland was 12 games better against the East (48–36) than against the supposedly weak West (33–45), Milwaukee was also 12 games better against the East, Boston was 5 games better against the East, Cleveland 4 games better against the East, New York even against the two divisions, Detroit 1 game better against the West, Seattle 1 game better against the West, Minnesota 2 games better against the West, Chicago 3 and a half games better against the West, Texas 4 games better against the West, Toronto 5 games better against the West, California 6 games better against the West, Kansas City 8 games better against the West, and Baltimore was *28 games better* against the West. Kind of out of line, don't you think? The Orioles have been fattening up on the West to a disproportionate extent for years. In 1986 the Birds were 14 games better against the West (45–39 vs. 28–50), and in 1985 13½ games better against the West (50–34 vs. 33–44).

There seem to be two good young players in the organization, both of whom are second basemen, Billy Ripken and Pete Stanicek. A reasonable guess would be that Stanicek will be moved to center field, since he is virtually the only person in the organization who can run. I think Stanicek is ahead of Ripken at this point; Billy looks more like the new Rich Dauer than he does like the new Cal Ripken. Actually, there are several good young third basemen in the system, too, but they're further away—Craig Worthington, who needs at least another year of AAA experience, and Leo Gomez, named the number two prospect in the Carolina League by *Baseball America* after hitting .326 with 110 RBI, 95 walks. Jack Voight at Newark in the NY-P league was also a top prospect.

The Orioles remain the only team to have won seven divisional championships, although that distinction will likely be lost within two years. (Oakland, Kansas City, Pittsburgh, Cincinnati, and Los Angeles have all won six. The random probability that one of those teams will win its division in the next two years is 84 percent. The Yankees have won five divisional titles; no team has won four.) To reconstruct this team is going to be a massive undertaking. Many of the humble players they have now—Lynn, Knight, Lacy, Burleson, Dwyer—are going to be gone within a couple of years, leaving gaping holes where now there is marginal production. The Orioles will not be in contention until the next decade is underway.

RATIO OF DOUBLE PLAYS TO ERRORS

Baltimore	174-111
Yankees	155-102
Minnesota	147- 98
White Sox	174-116
St. Louis	172-116
Atlanta	170-116
Boston	158-110
San Francisco	183-129
California	162-117
Toronto	148-111
Seattle	150-122
Detroit	147-122
Pittsburgh	147-123
Cubs	154-130
Kansas City	151-131
Philadelphia	137-121
Milwaukee	155-145
Cincinnati	137-130
Mets	137-137
Texas	148-151
Houston	113-116
Los Angeles	144-155
San Diego	135-147
Oakland	122-142
Cleveland	128-153
Montreal	122-147

RUNS SCORED AND ALLOWED WINS AND LOSSES

Wins	428	224	67-0	1.000
Pitchers' Duels	62	52	16-13	.552
One Run Games	209	205	25-21	.543
Boddicker	140	144	17-16	.515
Flanagan	80	87	8-8	.500
Road Games	378	424	36-44	.450
Slugfests	442	507	27-38	.415
All Games	729	880	67-95	.414
Bell	121	161	12-17	.414
Dixon	79	96	6-9	.400
Home Games	351	456	31-51	.378
Blowouts	177	258	13-23	.361
McGregor	66	86	4-11	.233
Losses	301	656	0-95	.000

TEN BEST STARTS

	IP	H	R	ER	BB	SO		
Schmidt vs. Min, July 12	9	2	0	0	0	7	W	89
Boddicker at KC, Apr 28	9	1	0	0	2	5	W	88
Schmidt vs. NY, June 24	9	3	0	0	0	6	W	87
Boddicker at Sea, May 18	9	3	0	0	2	5	W	84
Bell vs. KC, July 23	9	5	1	1	3	12	W	82
McGregor at Min, May 6	9	3	0	0	3	1	W	79
Bell at KC, July 17	8⅔	6	1	1	0	9	W	77
Habyan at Det, Sep 28	8⅓	5	0	0	1	3	W	75
Flanagan vs. Mil, Aug 15	9	6	1	0	5	7	W	75
Bell at Min, May 5	8⅓	2	3	2	1	7	W	75

PITCHERS WHEN SUPPORTED BY THREE TO FIVE RUNS

	G	IP	W-L	Pct	SO	BB	ERA
Bell	10	58	4-2	.667	45	25	3.86
Schmidt	8	51	3-2	.600	28	9	3.20
Boddicker	17	120	6-6	.500	90	47	4.14
Ballard	7	41	1-4	.200	17	21	5.05
McGregor	7	36	1-4	.200	14	15	7.07
Dixon	6	21	1-4	.200	11	5	9.28
Flanagan	7	42	0-3	.000	18	13	4.75

HALL OF FAME WATCH

Could be elected on current accomplishments: Fred Lynn 82, Eddie Murray 80; **Building credentials but not yet viable candidate:** Cal Ripken, Jr. 66, Scott McGregor 32; **Working on it:** Rick Burleson 23, Terry Kennedy 21.5, Ray Knight 19, Mike Boddicker 19, Lee Lacy 12.5, Don Aase 10; **Long way to go:** Wiggins 7, Doug Corbett 6, Tom Niedenfuer 6, Larry Sheets 4.5, Floyd Rayford 3, Cal Ripken, Sr. 2, Luis DeLeon 2.

ERA BY STARTING PITCHERS

Los Angeles	3.64
Kansas City	3.80
Houston	3.82
Toronto	3.90
Mets	3.92
San Francisco	3.98
St. Louis	4.01
Pittsburgh	4.04
Detroit	4.05
White Sox	4.19
Montreal	4.28
Yankees	4.37
San Diego	4.44
Minnesota	4.47
Boston	4.54
Oakland	4.54
Philadelphia	4.59
Seattle	4.62
Cubs	4.71
California	4.78
Milwaukee	4.79
Atlanta	4.82
Cincinnati	4.87
Texas	4.94
Baltimore	5.26
Cleveland	5.37

TEN WORST STARTS

	IP	H	R	ER	BB	SO		
Dixon at Mil, Apr 25	1*	6	7	7	1	2	L	14
Williamson at Bos, June 30	4⅔	9	8	8	2	2	L	14
Habyan at Bos, Sep 11	3*	10	6	6	1	1	L	15
Ballard vs. Sea, Sep 2	2*	8	6	6	1	0	L	15
McGregor vs. Min, May 11	2⅓	6	7	6	3	0	L	16
Ballard vs. Bos, Sep 18	4*	9	6	6	3	0	L	17
Bell at Oak, Aug 25	4⅔	7	7	7	4	0	L	18
Schmidt at Sea, Aug 22	3⅔	9	6	6	2	2	L	19
Bell vs. Bos, June 10	3⅓	7	6	6	5	2	L	19
McGregor at Mil, Aug 4	3⅓	7	7	7	2	3	—	19

Terry KENNEDY, Catcher
Runs Created: 57

	G	AB	Hit	2B	3B	HR	Run	RBI	TBB	SO	SB	CS	Avg
6.82 years		570	153	28	2	15	58	79	40	99	1	1	.268
1987	143	512	128	13	1	18	51	62	35	112	1	0	.250
First Half	83	303	80	10	1	13	34	42	23	60	1	0	.264
Second Half	60	209	48	3	0	5	17	20	12	52	0	0	.230
Vs. RHP		329	88	9	1	12	31	39	27	61	1	0	.267
Vs. LHP		183	40	4	0	6	20	23	8	51	0	0	.219
Home	73	240	51	6	1	11	26	27	22	59	1	0	.213
Road	70	272	77	7	0	7	25	35	13	53	0	0	.283

Ken GERHART, Left Field
Runs Created: 35

	G	AB	Hit	2B	3B	HR	Run	RBI	TBB	SO	SB	CS	Avg
0.69 years		512	123	17	3	22	65	59	30	103	13	4	.240
1987	92	284	69	10	2	14	41	34	17	53	9	2	.243
First Half	67	196	45	8	2	7	23	18	8	41	6	1	.230
Second Half	25	88	24	2	0	7	18	16	9	12	3	1	.273
Vs. RHP		155	38	6	2	10	25	24	11	29	5	1	.245
Vs. LHP		129	31	4	0	4	16	10	6	24	4	1	.240
Home	44	134	29	6	0	5	16	12	8	24	3	2	.216
Road	48	150	40	4	2	9	25	22	9	29	6	0	.267

Eddie MURRAY, First Base
Runs Created: 103

	G	AB	Hit	2B	3B	HR	Run	RBI	TBB	SO	SB	CS	Avg
10.24 years		610	181	32	2	30	95	108	76	83	5	2	.297
1987	160	618	171	28	3	30	89	91	73	80	1	2	.277
First Half	87	342	95	18	2	20	52	56	35	42	0	0	.278
Second Half	73	276	76	10	1	10	37	35	38	38	1	2	.275
Vs. RHP		397	111	18	2	19	61	56	51	47	0	1	.280
Vs. LHP		221	60	10	1	11	28	35	22	33	1	1	.271
Home	81	300	79	9	0	14	41	37	39	45	1	2	.263
Road	79	318	92	19	3	16	48	54	34	35	0	0	.289

Fred LYNN, Center Field
Runs Created: 58

	G	AB	Hit	2B	3B	HR	Run	RBI	TBB	SO	SB	CS	Avg
10.17 years		588	170	35	4	26	94	97	74	90	7	5	.289
1987	111	396	100	24	0	23	49	60	39	72	3	7	.253
First Half	73	268	67	14	0	14	33	42	31	45	3	7	.250
Second Half	38	128	33	10	0	9	16	18	8	27	0	0	.258
Vs. RHP		271	72	17	0	18	35	49	26	44	2	5	.266
Vs. LHP		125	28	7	0	5	14	11	13	28	1	2	.224
Home	54	191	46	9	0	11	23	28	14	30	2	4	.241
Road	57	205	54	15	0	12	26	32	25	42	1	3	.263

Alan WIGGINS, Second Base
Runs Created: 26

	G	AB	Hit	2B	3B	HR	Run	RBI	TBB	SO	SB	CS	Avg
3.90 years		576	149	16	5	1	89	30	60	49	62	17	.259
1987	85	306	71	4	2	1	37	15	28	34	20	7	.232
First Half	62	238	58	4	2	1	26	11	24	22	18	6	.244
Second Half	23	68	13	0	0	0	11	4	4	12	2	1	.191
Vs. RHP		176	41	2	2	1	23	9	22	19	16	5	.233
Vs. LHP		130	30	2	0	0	14	6	6	15	4	2	.231
Home	34	117	27	2	0	0	12	5	9	13	8	2	.231
Road	51	189	44	2	2	1	25	10	19	21	12	5	.233

Mike YOUNG, Right Field
Runs Created: 48

	G	AB	Hit	2B	3B	HR	Run	RBI	TBB	SO	SB	CS	Avg
3.21 years		505	128	21	2	22	71	67	63	126	7	5	.253
1987	110	363	87	10	1	16	46	39	46	91	10	7	.240
First Half	49	157	40	2	1	9	22	22	25	39	3	4	.255
Second Half	61	206	47	8	0	7	24	17	21	52	7	3	.228
Vs. RHP		219	53	8	1	11	29	25	25	54	7	3	.242
Vs. LHP		144	34	2	0	5	17	14	21	37	3	4	.236
Home	59	190	45	4	1	11	25	26	24	43	5	4	.237
Road	51	173	42	6	0	5	21	13	22	48	5	3	.243

Ray KNIGHT, Third Base
Runs Created: 63

	G	AB	Hit	2B	3B	HR	Run	RBI	TBB	SO	SB	CS	Avg
8.58 years		528	145	30	3	9	53	66	38	64	2	3	.275
1987	150	563	144	24	0	14	46	65	39	90	0	0	.256
First Half	82	314	83	14	0	8	31	34	22	45	0	0	.264
Second Half	68	249	61	10	0	6	15	31	17	45	0	0	.245
Vs. RHP		357	99	20	0	6	27	41	18	56	0	0	.277
Vs. LHP		206	45	4	0	8	19	24	21	34	0	0	.218
Home	73	270	74	13	0	8	26	32	16	42	0	0	.274
Road	77	293	70	11	0	6	20	33	23	48	0	0	.239

Larry SHEETS, Designated Hitter
Runs Created: 90

	G	AB	Hit	2B	3B	HR	Run	RBI	TBB	SO	SB	CS	Avg
2.27 years		507	147	22	0	30	71	91	36	78	1	1	.290
1987	135	469	148	23	0	31	74	94	31	67	1	1	.316
First Half	67	219	70	12	0	15	39	50	17	27	1	0	.320
Second Half	68	250	78	11	0	16	35	44	14	40	0	1	.312
Vs. RHP		324	104	19	0	21	51	65	23	45	1	0	.321
Vs. LHP		145	44	4	0	10	23	29	8	22	0	1	.303
Home	72	241	78	10	0	21	44	57	20	29	1	0	.324
Road	63	228	70	13	0	10	30	37	11	38	0	1	.307

Cal RIPKEN, Shortstop
Runs Created: 90

	G	AB	Hit	2B	3B	HR	Run	RBI	TBB	SO	SB	CS	Avg
6.12 years		626	177	34	4	26	102	93	64	81	2	3	.283
1987	162	624	157	28	3	27	97	98	81	77	3	5	.252
First Half	88	350	94	17	2	17	56	56	41	46	1	3	.269
Second Half	74	274	63	11	1	10	41	42	40	31	2	2	.230
Vs. RHP		413	106	13	1	20	65	74	58	59	2	4	.257
Vs. LHP		211	51	15	2	7	32	24	23	18	1	1	.242
Home	82	310	77	12	2	17	43	50	31	32	1	4	.248
Road	80	314	80	16	1	10	54	48	50	45	2	1	.255

Lee LACY, Outfield
Runs Created: 34

	G	AB	Hit	2B	3B	HR	Run	RBI	TBB	SO	SB	CS	Avg
9.40 years		484	139	22	4	10	69	49	40	70	20	9	.287
1987	87	258	63	13	3	7	35	28	32	49	3	2	.244
First Half	49	152	36	8	2	4	22	19	22	27	2	1	.237
Second Half	38	106	27	5	1	3	13	9	10	22	1	1	.255
Vs. RHP		102	26	3	1	3	17	8	16	25	2	2	.255
Vs. LHP		156	37	10	2	4	18	20	16	24	1	0	.237
Home	47	130	30	7	1	2	17	8	17	32	1	2	.231
Road	40	128	33	6	2	5	18	20	15	17	2	0	.258

CLEVELAND INDIANS

Let me give you what I consider to be the most amazing statistic in the 1988 *Baseball Abstract*. In games in which the Cleveland offense last year scored three to five runs—games in which they had a chance to win if the pitcher did his job, in other words—the Indians record was 14 and 51, a .215 winning percentage. That's assuming that the offense is OK.

As long as the subject is the Cleveland pitching staff, I can keep running amazing numbers at you.

• In the 101 games they lost, Cleveland allowed 748 runs—well over seven runs a game. Only one other major-league team allowed even 600 runs in the games they lost (Baltimore, 656). The average per loss, 7.41, was also easily the highest in the majors.

• The Indians allowed 519 runs in their home park, 63 more than any other major league team.

• The 1961 Yankees, regarded by many as one of the greatest offenses of all time, scored 827 runs. The Indians pitchers allowed 130 runs more than the 1961 Yankees scored.

• Cleveland lost 33 games by five runs or more.

• The Cleveland starting pitcher was knocked out in the first five innings 51 times.

• 30 times the Indians allowed ten or more runs.

• The Indians allowed 957 runs, the most allowed by a major-league team since 1939.

It's a little tough to contend with that kind of pitching; in fact, as I calculate it, to have won the pennant with the pitching staff they had, the Indians would have had to score 1,184 runs, or 7.3 per game. They would have had to have a team batting average, I would guess, about .320 to .325, with maybe 260 to 270 home runs.

The Indians, as I am sure you know, were picked by *Sports Illustrated* as the best team in baseball a year ago. I dasn't twit the magazine too roughly about this, because I make predictions, too, and God knows I don't want to start comparing them; nonetheless, that's a pretty phenomenal accomplishment, the MPE (maximum possible error), picking the very worst team in baseball to be the very best. Deluded by such predictions into believing themselves staring at the lips of glory, the Indians kicked off the campaign by making their annual hair-brained move involving the catching position. A year ago the Indians decided that Andy Allanson was ready to jump from the Eastern League into the starting job, and to put an exclamation mark behind this they released Jerry Willard, who had been their regular catcher the year before and hit .270.

Allanson didn't exactly work out, so last year, as pennant insurance, the Indians signed Rick Dempsey as a free agent, even though this cost them their first round draft pick. A first round draft pick has about a 15 percent chance of being a major-league star. How in the world can you trade a 15 percent chance of getting a star player for the last 5 percent or 10 percent of Rick Dempsey? Then they didn't even have the sense to platoon Dempsey. Dempsey was struggling along with a .177 season until Bo Jackson crunched him at home plate on July 21, put-

ting his season out of its misery. Well, at least it can't get any worse. Indian catchers last year hit .222 (115/517) with 44 RBI. I'm sure the Indians are about ready to try one of those infield-to-catcher conversions; the only question not yet answered is who will be the lucky schnook selected for the effort.

Once play began, it didn't take the Indians long to learn their fate. The Indians lost on opening day, and not only never reached .500, they never reached .400. Through 11 games, 10 of them losses, they had allowed 86 runs. Their starting pitchers had an ERA of 9.07. For a period following that, the starting pitching was actually quite good; for a 19-game stretch (April 19 to May 10) the ERA of Indian starters was 3.20. Their won-lost record peaked at 9–14, a .391 percentage, on May 1. They never got that high again. In the first week of May, despite decent pitching, they lost six straight games to drop to 9–20. On May 26 Greg Swindell, the only Indian starter with a legitimate chance to be outstanding, suffered a broken finger on his glove hand when hit by a line drive. Though he continued to pitch after that, he lost effectiveness, with a 7.36 ERA in his last five starts. It was announced that he had a strained muscle in the shoulder, and then it was changed to a knot on the elbow, and then there were a battery of tests and Swindell was told that the ligament had started to pull away from the bone in the elbow. He was out for the year.

Apart from the fact that the pitching and catching were ghastly, the Indians didn't have a bad team. They had one of the league's best outfields, with Butler, Snyder, and Hall or Carter, and a good infield with Jacoby, Franco, Tabler or Carter, and a second baseman. Another of Pat Corrales' bright ideas was to go without a utility infielder. The Indians until June didn't have a backup shortstop or second baseman on the roster; if they had to make a move they would put Cory Snyder at short. It is likely to be some time before this strategy receives another trial.

The Indians have talent, both in established players and in prospects, but they have very serious problems in talent alignment. The organization is knee-deep in hitters, but desperately short of pitching prospects. The Buffalo pitching staff last year featured Mike Armstrong, Ernie Camacho, Mark Huisman, Bryan Oelkers, Don Schulze, Roy Thomas, Tom Waddell, Frank Wills, and Rich Yett, all of whose names will be familiar to you from their major-league service, but only if you've been paying careful attention. John Farrell, who pitched so brilliantly for the Indians late in the season, was 6–12 with a 5.83 ERA at Buffalo.

Apart from the general problem that the Indians have more of what they don't need and no more of what they desperately need, among the position players the Indians have a left-end buildup, referring to the defensive spectrum. The Indians have six established players who play the "corner" positions—first base, third base, left, and right; those six are Joe Carter, Mel Hall, Brook Jacoby, Carmen Castillo, Cory Snyder, Pat Tabler. That is also where their young players play. So they have to try to force players rightward along the spectrum—Joe Carter into center field, Cory Snyder at shortstop last year. Forced rightward shifts along the defensive spectrum fail the vast majority of the time.

That's what is so critical about Julio Franco, and why this organization has to wake and realize what they have in Franco before they lose him or give him away. Shortstop and catcher can be the hardest positions to fill. When Franco came up he was error-prone, but he's made a lot of progress on that. When he first came up he was a free swinger, but last year his strikeout/walk ratio was one of the best in the league (32/56). His batting averages since he came to Cleveland have gone up every year: .273, .286, .288, .306, .319. After taking criticism for not learning to steal bases, last year Julio turned in his best performance as a base stealer, 32 for 41. The Indians still complain about his being immature, and keep trying to find another shortstop. I hardly know the guy so I guess I shouldn't talk, but I gotta say, if this is immaturity, God bless the immature.

In 1986 Joe Carter obviously was one of the best players in the American League. In 1987, despite the 30/30 accomplishment and the 106 RBI, I really don't think that he helped the team. His batting average, .264, didn't help the team. He took only 27 walks and struck out 105 times. His throwing arm as an outfielder was a problem, and he wound up playing first base, and not very well. What does it mean to hit 32 home runs when you have a team with three players who hit 32 or 33 home runs and you still lose 101 games? His RBI total was good, but RBI are dependant on the context; Carter drove in 105 runs, but batting behind Franco (.389 on-base percentage) and Butler (.399). But after you go through Carter (.304 on-base percentage, 32 homers), Mel Hall (.309 on-base percentage) and Cory Snyder (.273 on-base percentage, 33 homers), the offense is over; there is nobody left on base to continue the offense. Brook Jacoby hit .300 with 32 homers, but only 11 RBI. All right, 69. Anyway, I just don't think you contribute very much to the offense if you drive in runs but don't get yourself on there where the next guy can get his RBI, too. Carter didn't do that.

With Brett Butler gone the Indians are planning to move Carter to the outfield—to center field, specifically, which is necessary because he is the only outfielder they have who approaches center-field speed. I doubt that this will work great; Carter is a good base stealer because he has some speed and is smart, but he's awfully big for a center fielder, and his legs don't seem to have the spring of a center fielder's legs. One suspects that Otis Nixon, now 29, will wind up in center field. I wouldn't be surprised if Nixon would go on to have a pretty good year, hit maybe .265, steal some bases. I would be very surprised if he went on to have a good career.

Brett Butler is a fine player, and the Indians are going to miss him. One spot at which the team should be better this year is at designated hitter. In 1986, with the DH spot split among Pat Tabler, Carmen Castillo and Andre Thornton, Indian designated hackers hit just .249 with 14 home runs. Tabler hit .306 in the role but with no power, and Andre, well past his last leg, hit just .111 in 21 games as a DH. Dave Clark, who spent most of the season at Buffalo (.340 with 30 homers) is a better hitter than that, probably a lot better. There is no guarantee that Clark will make the Indians in 1988, I suppose, but if the Indians send him back out they're dumber than I think they are. Dave Clark would put a hell of a lot more runs on the scoreboard than Pat Tabler will.

There are some other pretty good kids around. Eddie Williams looked to everybody in 1987 as if he was ready to move into a major-league job, prompting the organization's so far unsuccessful efforts to trade Jacoby. The major-league translation of Williams's 1987 season shows a pretty good hitter, but you have to acknowledge the fact that prior to last year his record wasn't very good. He hit .238 at Waterbury in 1986, and his defensive records are consistently awful. The Indians have a couple of potentially pretty-good second basemen. I don't know much about the little guy, Hinzo, but I like what I've seen. Junior Noboa, if healthy, is also in my opinion ready to step into a major-league job. The Indians like shortstop Jay Bell, but unless he was hurt everytime I saw him play he obviously doesn't have a shortstop's arm. The Indians don't need a shortstop, anyway; they need to stop fooling around with Julio Franco's psyche and recognize frankly that they have one of the best players in baseball there. First baseman Don Lovell isn't a bad hitter, but isn't good enough yet to elbow into a team—and league—where first basemen who can hit are plentiful. Outfielder Luis Medina, probably a year away, is a super hitting prospect but faces the same problem as Clark: no place to play in an outfield already stocked with Mel Hall, Cory Snyder, and Joe Carter.

Historically there have been a lot of parallels between the Cleveland Indians and the San Francisco Giants, and one could argue that the Indians 61–101 season in 1987 was a great deal like the Giants 62–100 campaign in 1985; in fact, I would go so far as to argue that the Indians have a better roster now than the Giants did then. This, however, is rather like the comparisons that people make between Bobby Witt and Sandy Koufax at the same age; the whole point about Koufax is not that he was anything special at age 23, but that he later became a great pitcher. The point about the San Francisco Giants is that Al Rosen has done something that is nearly unprecedented in the last two years by making a series of moves which were simultaneously brilliant and lucky. The Cleveland Indians can make immense strides in the next two years, provided only that they commence to make a series of moves which are both brilliant and lucky.

So how good is the organization?

The habit of changing managers in mid-season is one of the ten warning signs of an inept organization. It's a warning sign, I suppose, if you change managers in mid-season to bring in a Dick Williams or a Sparky Anderson or a Jim Fregosi, somebody that you want to be your next manager. If you change managers in mid-season to give the job to a coach who is there primarily because he is a buddy of the previous manager, and then you just leave him there because he seems to be doing all right, that's not a warning sign; that's sufficient for a diagnosis. When you see an organization do that, you know they're just playing it by ear. A team that can't get organized long enough to make a deliberate selection as to who should occupy perhaps their most critical position probably can't get organized enough to plan out a trade or develop a training program or plan an amateur draft, either. Further evidence on this issue was provided over the winter, when the Indians went to Dallas with three third basemen on their roster (Jacoby, Snyder, and Williams) and with third basemen in demand (see Baltimore, Chicago, Detroit, Los Angeles), yet couldn't close a deal for a pitcher; when they came home they still had more third basemen than starting pitchers.

Another of the warning signs of an organization that is lost is the inability to make a mature judgment as to where they are. One can sympathize with the Indian front office for thinking that they were better than they were,

because after all people were telling them that they were a lot better than they were. Still, they made the mistake of believing it.

The Indians will not lose a hundred games again this year. There is too much talent here for that. If Swindell is back and healthy, if Farrell continues to pitch well, if Candiotti can find his rhythm, the starting pitching could be improved enough to push the Indians close to .500. That's a best-case scenario, I think, and there is still the little matter of a bullpen. The Indians should be able to beat the Orioles, but I can't see them finishing higher than fourth.

RUNS ALLOWED IN LOSSES

Cleveland	748
Baltimore	656
San Diego	598
Texas	589
Boston	584
Seattle	583
California	579
Atlanta	575
Cubs	569
White Sox	545
Minnesota	539
Pittsburgh	531
Oakland	530
Philadelphia	503
Yankees	499
Houston	499
Milwaukee	488
Los Angeles	487
Cincinnati	481
Montreal	477
Kansas City	469
Mets	431
Detroit	427
San Francisco	424
St. Louis	387
Toronto	374

RUNS SCORED AND ALLOWED WINS AND LOSSES

Wins	403	209	61-0	1.000
Pitchers' Duels	44	49	14-14	.500
Home Games	373	519	35-46	.432
One-Run Games	202	212	19-29	.396
P Niekro	93	119	9-13	.391
Slugfests	500	631	29-46	.387
Schrom	132	199	11-18	.379
All Games	742	957	61-101	.377
Bailes	85	87	6-11	.353
Swindell	67	94	5-10	.333
Road Games	369	438	26-55	.321
Blowouts	226	382	13-33	.283
Candiotti	118	194	9-23	.281
Losses	339	748	0-101	.000

TEN BEST STARTS

	IP	H	R	ER	BB	SO		
Candiotti vs. NY, Aug 3	9	1	0	0	1	5	W	89
Farrell vs. Mil, Aug 26	9	3	0	0	2	7	—	86
Yett vs. Bos, Aug 29	9	2	1	0	3	5	W	83
Swindell at Bal, Apr 19	9	6	0	0	2	9	W	82
Schrom vs. Chi, Apr 28	9	4	0	0	0	1	W	80
Candiotti vs. Tex, Jul 23	9	4	2	1	1	7	W	79
Candiotti vs. Tor, Apr 21	9	6	0	0	1	3	W	77
Candiotti at Det, Sep 2	8	1	2	1	7	7	L	74
Swindell at Tex, May 5	8⅓	5	2	2	2	10	—	73
Yett at NY, Aug 16	7⅓	4	0	0	2	3	W	71

PITCHERS WHEN SUPPORTED BY THREE TO FIVE RUNS

	G	IP	W-L	Pct	SO	BB	ERA
Bailes	7	39	2-3	.400	15	17	5.49
Candiotti	15	105	4-9	.308	56	44	4.36
Swindell	9	63	2-5	.286	62	26	4.69
Akerfelds	8	45	1-4	.200	27	19	5.64
P Niekro	7	34	0-6	.000	17	15	8.55

HALL OF FAME WATCH

Working on it: Dempsey 29, Carter 20.5, Corrales 19, A Thornton 18.5, Butler 10.5, Franco 10; **Long way to go:** Tabler 8, Jacoby 7.5, Camacho 5, S Stewart 4, Candiotti 2.5, Schrom 2, Snyder 2, Vande Berg 2.

TEN WORST STARTS

	IP	H	R	ER	BB	SO		
Carlton at Chi, July 19	4*	9	9	7	3	1	L	10
Schrom vs. Mil, Aug 20	3	7	8	8	5	2	L	10
Bailes vs. Tex, July 26	2*	8	7	7	1	0	L	11
Niekro vs. Chi, July 5	3*	7	8	8	2	1	L	12
Schrom at Cal, Oct 3	2⅓	8	6	6	0	1	L	18
Niekro vs. Tex, May 11	4*	9	6	6	3	1	L	18
Niekro at Tex, July 10	5*	9	7	7	3	2	L	20
Akerfelds at Tor, Aug 2	1⅔	5	6	6	2	1	L	20
Schrom vs. Det, June 3	1*	6	6	4	0	0	L	21
Bailes vs. Bos, Aug 30	4⅓	10	6	6	1	3	L	21

WINNING PERCENTAGE WHEN SCORING THREE TO FIVE RUNS

St. Louis	45-26,	.634
Kansas City	28-20,	.583
Cincinnati	35-27,	.565
White Sox	37-30,	.552
Houston	32-27,	.542
Los Angeles	37-32,	.536
Montreal	30-26,	.536
Mets	35-31,	.530
Toronto	33-30,	.524
Philadelphia	38-35,	.521
San Francisco	35-33,	.515
Minnesota	32-31,	.508
Pittsburgh	35-35,	.500
Milwaukee	24-24,	.500
Detroit	30-31,	.492
Yankees	30-31,	.492
Cubs	27-30,	.474
California	24-34,	.414
Baltimore	29-43,	.403
Seattle	29-43,	.403
San Diego	28-44,	.389
Oakland	23-38,	.377
Texas	19-33,	.365
Boston	20-36,	.357
Atlanta	23-43,	.348
Cleveland	14-51,	.215

Joe CARTER, First Base
Runs Created: 87

	G	AB	Hit	2B	3B	HR	Run	RBI	TBB	SO	SB	CS	Avg
3.35 years		607	167	29	4	27	87	98	28	102	26	7	.275
1987	149	588	155	27	2	32	83	106	27	105	31	6	.264
First Half	82	329	84	16	2	20	44	67	16	63	19	1	.255
Second Half	67	259	71	11	0	12	39	39	11	42	12	5	.274
Vs. RHP		435	117	22	1	25	63	80	20	77	27	3	.269
Vs. LHP		153	38	5	1	7	20	26	7	28	4	3	.248
Home	72	279	70	15	1	9	28	46	17	43	14	5	.251
Road	77	309	85	12	1	23	55	60	10	62	17	1	.275

Mel HALL, Left Field
Runs Created: 63

	G	AB	Hit	2B	3B	HR	Run	RBI	TBB	SO	SB	CS	Avg
3.59 years		530	149	30	4	18	74	78	43	96	6	4	.281
1987	142	485	136	21	1	18	57	76	20	68	5	4	.280
First Half	78	270	65	7	1	8	31	32	11	43	3	3	.241
Second Half	64	215	71	14	0	10	26	44	9	25	2	1	.330
Vs. RHP		452	124	19	1	17	54	70	17	60	5	4	.274
Vs. LHP		33	12	2	0	1	3	6	3	8	0	0	.364
Home	67	222	64	10	0	8	26	39	10	25	4	2	.288
Road	75	263	72	11	1	10	31	37	10	43	1	2	.274

Tommy HINZO, Second Base
Runs Created: 26

	G	AB	Hit	2B	3B	HR	Run	RBI	TBB	SO	SB	CS	Avg
0.41 years		627	166	22	7	7	76	51	24	115	22	10	.265
1987	67	257	68	9	3	3	31	21	10	47	9	4	.265
First Half	0	0	0	0	0	0	0	0	0	0	0	0	.000
Second Half	67	257	68	9	3	3	31	21	10	47	9	4	.265
Vs. RHP		193	43	5	3	1	18	13	5	42	5	4	.223
Vs. LHP		64	25	4	0	2	13	8	5	5	4	0	.391
Home	32	116	27	5	1	3	15	7	6	25	4	2	.233
Road	35	141	41	4	2	0	16	14	4	22	5	2	.291

Brett BUTLER, Center Field
Runs Created: 97

	G	AB	Hit	2B	3B	HR	Run	RBI	TBB	SO	SB	CS	Avg
5.49 years		586	164	22	11	5	97	44	74	60	42	19	.280
1987	137	522	154	25	8	9	91	41	91	55	33	16	.295
First Half	66	238	66	12	5	1	38	16	45	22	12	5	.277
Second Half	71	284	88	13	3	8	53	25	46	33	21	11	.310
Vs. RHP		376	115	20	8	7	61	26	59	30	29	10	.306
Vs. LHP		146	39	5	0	2	30	15	32	25	4	6	.267
Home	66	246	83	12	7	4	49	16	47	29	22	7	.337
Road	71	276	71	13	1	5	42	25	44	26	11	9	.257

Brook JACOBY, Third Base
Runs Created: 110

	G	AB	Hit	2B	3B	HR	Run	RBI	TBB	SO	SB	CS	Avg
3.80 years		575	162	27	4	20	77	73	56	107	2	2	.282
1987	155	540	162	27	4	32	73	69	75	73	2	3	.300
First Half	86	302	75	11	2	17	35	36	37	46	2	3	.248
Second Half	69	238	87	15	2	15	38	33	38	27	0	0	.366
Vs. RHP		398	125	17	3	27	58	61	47	53	2	3	.314
Vs. LHP		142	37	9	1	5	15	8	28	20	0	0	.261
Home	80	280	78	13	2	21	39	39	38	40	0	2	.279
Road	75	260	84	13	2	11	34	30	37	33	2	1	.323

Cory SNYDER, Right Field
Runs Created: 74

	G	AB	Hit	2B	3B	HR	Run	RBI	TBB	SO	SB	CS	Avg
1.60 years		621	156	28	2	36	83	94	29	181	4	3	.251
1987	157	577	136	24	2	33	74	82	31	166	5	1	.236
First Half	85	313	79	15	1	19	40	52	16	91	3	1	.252
Second Half	72	264	57	9	1	14	34	30	15	75	2	0	.216
Vs. RHP		414	100	12	1	28	55	63	19	111	4	1	.242
Vs. LHP		163	36	12	1	5	19	19	12	55	1	0	.221
Home	78	276	59	12	0	17	35	42	17	76	2	0	.214
Road	79	301	77	12	2	16	39	40	14	90	3	1	.256

Julio FRANCO, Shortstop
Runs Created: 82

	G	AB	Hit	2B	3B	HR	Run	RBI	TBB	SO	SB	CS	Avg
4.70 years		633	186	29	5	7	89	80	46	68	23	10	.294
1987	128	495	158	24	3	8	86	52	57	56	32	9	.319
First Half	87	336	106	16	3	6	59	39	43	36	22	6	.315
Second Half	41	159	52	8	0	2	27	13	14	20	10	3	.327
Vs. RHP		365	118	14	2	4	56	40	39	35	27	6	.323
Vs. LHP		130	40	10	1	4	30	12	18	21	5	3	.308
Home	64	242	75	12	0	5	50	26	28	24	12	4	.310
Road	64	253	83	12	3	3	36	26	29	32	20	5	.328

Pat TABLER, Designated Hitter
Runs Created: 93

	G	AB	Hit	2B	3B	HR	Run	RBI	TBB	SO	SB	CS	Avg
4.48 years		562	164	29	4	9	71	75	51	86	3	3	.292
1987	151	553	170	34	3	11	66	86	51	84	5	2	.307
First Half	87	328	101	24	1	7	43	48	28	48	1	1	.308
Second Half	64	225	69	10	2	4	23	38	23	26	4	1	.307
Vs. RHP		381	107	20	2	5	45	51	38	72	4	2	.281
Vs. LHP		172	63	14	1	6	21	35	13	12	1	0	.366
Home	77	285	95	21	3	5	35	47	27	37	1	1	.333
Road	74	268	75	13	0	6	31	39	24	47	4	1	.280

NATIONAL LEAGUE EAST

ST. LOUIS CARDINALS

There are a number of arguments that are made in favor of the running game as having incidental benefits. As a rule, I don't buy them. In the specific case of the 1987 St. Louis Cardinals, I do.

The stolen base, it is argued, puts pressure on the pitcher, breaks up the infield, and takes the double play out of order. While all of these benefits are real, it is my belief that in general, in the normal case, the hidden benefits of the stolen base are canceled out (sometimes more than canceled out) by hidden costs of the running game. The running game can create a balk, and it can create an error on the pitcher; it can also lead to a runner being picked off first base without being charged with a caught stealing, a hidden cost which doesn't show up in the box score. The running game can distract the pitcher; it can also distract the hitter. Hitters who take pitches to allow the runner to steal often find themselves behind in the count, and for that reason the aggregate batting average of all hitters following a stolen base attempt is awful. The stolen base attempt can break up the infield and allow a hit to get through, but if the runner just stays on first base he'll add 30 points to the batting average of a left-handed hitter by forcing the first baseman to stay close to the bag. If you steal second you give those 30 points back. In general, it's a wash; the negatives and the positives balance out.

But while these things balance overall, they don't balance out for every team in every season. In the particular case of the 1987 St. Louis Cardinals, not the 1986 Cardinals or the 1985 Cardinals, it was not a wash; the Cardinals running game last year did in fact derive very considerable hidden benefits of the running game, and that was in fact one of the central reasons for their success.

The Cardinals speed score, 5.93, was of course the highest in the major leagues. Let me explain something about first-run strategies. The ultimate first-run strategy is the sacrifice bunt, and this is relatively easy to see. A player who executes a sacrifice is giving up his own chance to score a run in order to increase the chance that the man already on will score, and thus it is easy to see that while the successful sacrifice increases the chance that one run will score, it decreases the chance that two or more will score. As Earl Weaver says, if you play for one run that's all you'll get.

This is well understood. What is not understood is that the same applies to a stolen base attempt. If a batter attempts to steal second and is successful, he increases his own chance of scoring a run, but does almost nothing to increase the chance that any other player will score. If he attempts to steal and is thrown out, however, this decreases not only his own chance of scoring but that of every player who will bat in the inning. There is a big, big difference in your chance of scoring a run if you reach first base with no one out or if you reach with one out.

So the runner, in attempting to steal, is doing something to decrease the other players' chance of scoring, and nothing to increase it. Thus the effect of the stolen base attempt, like the sacrifice bunt, is to increase the chance of scoring one run, but to decrease the chance of scoring several runs in an inning.

This is the reason baseball men used to believe that you should not try to steal bases when several runs behind. Announcers are very puzzled by this. "The power hitter doesn't stop trying to hit home runs when you get behind, does he? So why should the base stealer stop trying to steal bases? Why shouldn't you still make the effort to get back in the game?" That's not it, at all; nobody ever believed that when you were behind you shouldn't try to get back in the game. They believed—probably correctly at the time, though not necessarily correctly now—that when you were several runs behind you should not use first-run strategies. They didn't steal bases when they were behind for the same reason that you don't bunt when you are behind. When you need several runs, you shouldn't do things which decrease your chance of having a big inning.

Now, not all runs in a baseball game are equal. The first few runs that you score are crucial. After five runs, each run is, as economists say, of diminishing utility, meaning that it will have less probable impact on the win column. If you score five runs in a game you'll win about 60 percent of the time, but if you score ten you can't win 120 percent of the time, so obviously the second five runs don't mean as much as the first five runs.

One of the possibly legitimate arguments for the running game, then, is that it tends to rearrange runs into more productive groups. A team that uses first-run strategies a lot may tend to score five runs in two games rather than zero in one and ten in the next. A problem with the argument in general is that you will have a heck of a time proving that this benefit actually does accrue to the teams which use first-run strategies.

But, again, in the specific case of the St. Louis Cardinals in 1987, the benefit was there. The Cardinals scored 798 runs, fewer than seven other major-league teams. But they had only 33 games in which they scored fewer than three runs, as few as any major-league team. The offense, while good, was *very* good at getting those one- or two-run innings that avoid a shutout and give the team a chance to win.

And when they had a chance to win, they won. Although the Cardinals team ERA was just 3.91, fifth best in the National League, another measure of a pitching staff is the ability to win with three to five runs, and the Cardinals did that better than anybody. The Cardinals' winning percentage when they scored three to five runs was .634, 51 points better than any other major-league team (see Cleveland charts); particularly remarkable was a 15–9 record when scoring just three runs. Most teams lose almost two-thirds of the time when scoring only three runs, 63 percent actually. With Danny Cox starting and three runs on the scoreboard, the Cardinals were 5–1.

Their starting pitching wasn't overpowering, but it rarely took them out of the game. Cardinal starters had a game score of just 49.4 (average), but they had only 11 starts with a game score under 30, the fewest of any major-league team. Herzog rarely allows a starter to stay out there and get pounded around, giving up six or eight runs before going to the bullpen. Only four times all year did the Cardinals have a slow hook, the fewest of any major-league team. His ratio of quick hooks to slow hooks, 7.5–1, was also the highest in the majors.

The Cardinals won 35 games despite a game score below 50, as many as any major-league team. By contrast, the Mets, trying to catch them and theoretically with a better offense (an offense that scored more runs) could overcome a poor pitching performance only 26 times—a big difference in a race decided by three games.

Their winning percentage without a quality start was .463, the best in the major leagues.

The Cardinals played 60 one-run games, more than any other major league team. They won 51 games by one or two runs, five more than any other major-league team. They played 90 such games, also five more than any other major-league team.

Even when they lost, they didn't lose bad. The Cardinals lost only eleven games by five runs or more, the fewest of any major-league team. Their average margin of defeat, 2.7 runs, was the smallest in the majors.

The Cardinals used only 215 pinch hitters on the year, the fewest in the National League. (Every National League team used more pinch hitters last year than any American League team.) One reason the total of pinch hitters was low is that Herzog makes heavy use of the double switch, bringing in a position player in the middle of an inning when a pitching change is made, so that the pitcher is no longer in the ninth spot. Then the new hitter is in the game, but no one has officially been a pinch hitter.

I think there is a tendency to see the double switch as a novelty item, and that few fans appreciate the real impact of the move. It's not a strategy that a manager will use hundreds of times a year, like a stolen base, a hit and run, or a pinch hitter, but it's impact in the 30 to 50 times a year it is used it can be considerable. Many times you will see a National League manager, with the starter struggling but due to bat in the next inning, leave him out there to try to get out of his trouble. You know that the manager is trying to avoid wasting a reliever for a third of an inning and then having to pinch hit for him, but once in a while while he is trying that, the inning will blow up on the pitcher and the game will get out of hand. I remember once, a long time ago (spring of 1973, I think), I did a study to find out what the ERA of pitchers was in the inning *before* they were removed for a pinch hitter. The answer was, as I recall, a little over 7.00.

Herzog can make the double switch with this team easier than most managers because, with all four infielders playing key offensive roles, he usually has an outfielder hitting seventh or eighth. Most pinch hitters are outfielders. If you have a catcher batting eighth, let's say, then it is hard to make a double switch when the pitcher is due to be the leadoff man, because most teams now only carry two real catchers plus an emergency catcher. If you make a double switch involving the catcher, you may put yourself in danger of having to use the emergency catcher early in the game. Then you won't be able to pinch hit for the new catcher, you won't be able to use the new catcher or the emergency catcher as a pinch hitter, and very often you might stand to lose a platoon advantage, either immediately or later in the game. So if you have a catcher batting eighth, or to a lesser extent a shortstop or second baseman, your opportunities to make the double switch are very limited, whereas if you have an outfielder down there you can almost always do it if you need to.

Anyway, if Herzog uses the double switch 30 times a year, it might keep an inning from exploding on him six or eight times, which would mean that he is in the game and has a chance to win six times when another manager might be out of it. In the world of strategic decisions, where gains and losses are usually measured in hundredths of a win, that is a big item.

A gentleman named Russ Eagle (1212 Park Avenue, Salisbury, NC) has done a thorough statistical analysis of the Cardinal season. A few notes from his work:

• If the season had lasted long enough the Cardinal offense would have been giving runs back. After scoring 6.35 runs per game in May, the Cards slipped to 5.53 runs per game in June, 4.78 in July, 4.76 in August and 3.41 in September. In their first 81 games the Cardinals had an on-base percentage of .359 and scored 460 runs; in the second 81 games they had an on-base percentage of .320 and scored 338 runs.

• The Cardinals came from behind to win 51 times, but from more than three runs behind only three times.

• The Cardinals had an edge of 34 errors on their opponents, commiting 116 while benefitting from 150. Since an average National League team committed 131 errors, the advantage was more in opposition errors (+19) than in their own (+15). Their biggest advantages were at shortstop (38–11) and catcher (22–9).

• The Cardinals scored 110 runs in the fifth inning, their best inning. The Cardinals scored 96 in the first inning and 82 in the second, whereas they scored an average of 94 per inning in innings three through seven. Their opponents scored 84 in the first and 66 in the seconds, whereas they averaged 79 runs in innings three through seven. So both the Cardinals and their opponents followed the general rule, in that they scored fewer runs in innings one and two combined than in a random inning.

• In 1986, when the Cardinals finished last in the league in runs scored, no spot in the batting order totalled more than 80 RBI. Last year the Cardinals got 125 RBI out of the fourth spot, 113 RBI from the fifth spot, 112 RBI from the third spot, 83 RBI from the eighth spot, and 81 RBI from the number-two hitters. Spots one, two, and four also scored over a hundred runs, with the totals being 131, 116, and 111, respectively.

Well, I'd better look ahead a minute and try to finish this off. The Cardinals have three prospects who might contribute to the team in 1988. Lance Johnson, rated the best prospect in the American Association, is obviously ready for a job; he can run, throw, and hit for average. The newspapers have Johnson traded to the White Sox for José DeLeon. I don't think the Cardinals would make that trade; I think if it's made there has got to be more to it than that. Herzog has never been reluctant to slap a player like Johnson in the lineup. In fact, if you asked Whitey Herzog who he would rather have playing for him over the next three seasons, Jack Clark or Lance Johnson, his honest answer might well be Lance Johnson.

Catcher Tom Pagnozzi is in the picture after a fine year at Louisville (.316 with 71 RBI in 320 at bats) while Pena was struggling. In Pagnozzi's nine starts in 1987 the Cardinals went 7–2, their opponents stole only three bases and the staff ERA was slightly better than with either Pena or Lake. The third hot prospect is Steve Peters, a left-handed reliever with sensational stats at both Arkansas and Louisville, who also pitched well in a few games in St. Louis.

For the Cardinals to win in 1988, I think that two young pitchers will have to step forward. That could happen; Magrane, Mathews, and Cox are all capable of having much better years than they had last year, plus Tudor could be there all year. If that doesn't happen, I doubt that the Cardinals can win. The loss of Jack Clark hurts them; the addition of Horner may hurt them worse. I will be surprised if the Cardinals contend in 1988.

WINNING PERCENTAGE WITHOUT QUALITY START

St. Louis	.463
Milwaukee	.452
Toronto	.423
Mets	.418
San Francisco	.409
Oakland	.400
Montreal	.357
Detroit	.351
Cincinnati	.349
Yankees	.344
Texas	.343
Philadelphia	.325
Minnesota	.317
Atlanta	.298
Kansas City	.295
California	.287
Boston	.281
San Diego	.276
Baltimore	.272
Seattle	.258
Cleveland	.257
Cubs	.254
Houston	.246
White Sox	.244
Pittsburgh	.211
Los Angeles	.197

RUNS SCORED AND ALLOWED WINS AND LOSSES

Wins	592	306	95-0	1.000
Tudor	80	54	14-2	.875
Blowouts	213	157	19-11	.633
Cox	151	147	19-12	.613
Home Games	387	339	49-32	.605
Slugfests	414	373	33-22	.600
All Games	798	693	95-67	.586
Road Games	411	354	46-35	.568
Pitchers' Duels	79	73	20-18	.556
One Run Games	252	246	33-27	.550
Magrane	108	111	14-12	.538
Forsch	169	129	16-14	.533
Mathews	131	131	14-18	.438
Losses	206	387	0-67	.000

TEN BEST STARTS

	IP	H	R	ER	BB	SO		
Magrane vs. Mon, Sep 29	9	3	0	0	2	5	W	84
Magrane at SD, May 6	9	4	0	0	3	3	W	82
Mathews vs. Phi, June 25	9	3	0	0	5	5	W	81
Forsch at LA, July 21	9	4	1	1	1	2	W	76
Mathews at Atl, July 5	8⅔	3	1	1	3	4	W	75
Tudor vs. Cin, Aug 31	8	5	0	0	1	4	W	75
Forsch at Mon, Aug 5	8⅔	5	1	1	1	5	—	74
Forsch at Pit, Aug 10	9	7	0	0	1	1	W	73
Mathews vs. Pit, Sep 23	8	5	1	1	0	5	L	73
Cox vs. Mon, Oct 1	9	5	2	2	1	4	W	72

PITCHERS WHEN SUPPORTED BY THREE TO FIVE RUNS

	G	IP	W-L	Pct	SO	BB	ERA
Cox	13	90	8-2	.800	48	37	3.19
Mathews	16	99	8-2	.800	55	38	3.27
Tudor	9	56	6-2	.750	32	15	3.07
Magrane	12	75	4-2	.667	46	28	3.62
Forsch	9	43	1-2	.333	24	11	5.06

HALL OF FAME WATCH

Building credentials but not yet viable candidate: Ozzie 63.5, Herzog 59, McGee 57, Forsch 30; **Working on it:** Pena 29.5, Tudor 29, Clark 25, Herr 24.5, Worrell 22, Cox 19, Coleman 13, Dayley 12; **Long way to go:** Horton 5, Magrane 4, Dawley 4, Driessen 3.5, Pendleton 3, Mathews 3, D Green 2, Tunnell 2.

NUMBER OF TIMES SCORED LESS THAN THREE RUNS

Houston	58
Kansas City	57
Los Angeles	52
Cubs	51
San Diego	49
White Sox	46
Montreal	45
Atlanta	45
Cleveland	44
Philadelphia	44
California	43
Minnesota	43
Texas	43
Cincinnati	43
Baltimore	42
Yankees	42
Pittsburgh	42
Seattle	39
Boston	38
Milwaukee	37
Oakland	37
San Francisco	36
Toronto	34
Mets	34
Detroit	33
St. Louis	33

TEN WORST STARTS

	IP	H	R	ER	BB	SO		
Tunnell at Chi, June 7	3*	11	6	6	1	0	—	12
Forsch at Cin, Aug 22	3*	8	7	7	2	1	—	14
Magrane at Phi, Aug 7	1⅓	4	7	7	3	0	L	15
Cox at Mon, Sep 7	3*	9	7	5	3	1	L	15
Cox vs. Atl, May 25	4⅔	10	7	6	2	2	L	18
Mathews vs. Mon, Apr 14	1*	3	6	6	4	2	L	21
Tudor at Pitt, Apr 12	5⅓	9	6	6	3	2	L	25
Conroy vs. SD, Apr 28	4⅓	7	5	5	3	0	L	26
Forsch vs. Atl, May 26	2*	7	4	4	0	1	—	27
Magrane at Pit, Aug 12	3*	4	6	4	2	0	L	29

115

Tony PENA, Catcher
Runs Created: 30

	G	AB	Hit	2B	3B	HR	Run	RBI	TBB	SO	SB	CS	Avg
5.66 years		575	160	27	3	12	61	68	37	75	8	7	.278
1987	116	384	82	13	4	5	40	44	36	54	6	1	.214
First Half	48	165	42	7	2	1	22	22	17	19	3	1	.255
Second Half	68	219	40	6	2	4	18	22	19	35	3	0	.183
Vs. RHP		247	51	9	4	2	27	27	25	39	2	1	.206
Vs. LHP		137	31	4	0	3	13	17	11	15	4	0	.226
Home	57	187	42	7	3	1	16	21	13	25	2	0	.225
Road	59	197	40	6	1	4	24	23	23	29	4	1	.203

Ozzie SMITH, Shortstop
Runs Created: 102

	G	AB	Hit	2B	3B	HR	Run	RBI	TBB	SO	SB	CS	Avg
9.10 years		587	148	24	5	1	75	49	68	37	38	10	.252
1987	158	600	182	40	4	0	104	75	89	36	43	9	.303
First Half	84	316	95	19	1	0	58	46	52	15	23	4	.301
Second Half	74	284	87	21	3	0	46	29	37	21	20	5	.306
Vs. RHP		380	127	25	4	0	69	45	56	24	31	4	.334
Vs. LHP		220	55	15	0	0	35	30	33	12	12	5	.250
Home	79	286	82	20	2	0	49	36	41	16	26	4	.287
Road	79	314	100	20	2	0	55	39	48	20	17	5	.318

Jack CLARK, First Base
Runs Created: 127

	G	AB	Hit	2B	3B	HR	Run	RBI	TBB	SO	SB	CS	Avg
8.43 years		572	158	31	4	27	94	96	90	100	7	6	.276
1987	131	419	120	23	1	35	93	106	136	139	1	2	.286
First Half	85	293	91	18	1	26	68	86	82	88	1	1	.311
Second Half	46	126	29	5	0	9	25	20	54	51	0	1	.230
Vs. RHP		281	84	14	1	25	58	73	77	94	0	2	.299
Vs. LHP		138	36	9	0	10	35	33	59	45	1	0	.261
Home	65	202	59	10	1	17	49	50	63	66	1	0	.292
Road	66	217	61	13	0	18	44	56	73	73	0	2	.281

Vince COLEMAN, Left Field
Runs Created: 96

	G	AB	Hit	2B	3B	HR	Run	RBI	TBB	SO	SB	CS	Avg
2.81 years		662	174	17	10	1	115	40	64	121	116	22	.263
1987	151	623	180	14	10	3	121	43	70	126	109	22	.289
First Half	78	316	91	3	6	0	66	23	45	69	52	10	.288
Second Half	73	307	89	11	4	3	55	20	25	57	57	12	.290
Vs. RHP		414	124	6	3	0	70	26	41	80	61	15	.300
Vs. LHP		209	56	8	7	3	51	17	29	46	48	7	.268
Home	72	287	79	8	6	3	55	27	29	59	50	12	.275
Road	79	336	101	6	4	0	66	16	41	67	59	10	.301

Tommy HERR, Second Base
Runs Created: 65

	G	AB	Hit	2B	3B	HR	Run	RBI	TBB	SO	SB	CS	Avg
6.26 years		587	161	29	5	3	79	69	68	61	24	8	.274
1987	141	510	134	29	0	2	73	83	68	62	19	4	.263
First Half	70	259	70	14	0	1	46	39	36	33	12	2	.270
Second Half	71	251	64	15	0	1	27	44	32	29	7	2	.255
Vs. RHP		319	77	16	0	0	44	48	39	46	12	3	.241
Vs. LHP		191	57	13	0	2	29	35	29	16	7	1	.298
Home	71	246	69	12	0	1	44	36	34	25	13	2	.280
Road	70	264	65	17	0	1	29	47	34	37	6	2	.246

Willie MCGEE, Center Field
Runs Created: 77

	G	AB	Hit	2B	3B	HR	Run	RBI	TBB	SO	SB	CS	Avg
5.21 years		638	189	26	12	8	87	80	31	95	38	13	.296
1987	153	620	177	37	11	11	76	105	24	90	16	4	.285
First Half	81	324	98	18	6	6	42	69	11	54	6	2	.302
Second Half	72	296	79	19	5	5	34	36	13	36	10	2	.267
Vs. RHP		412	117	21	6	5	54	63	16	55	13	3	.284
Vs. LHP		208	60	16	5	6	22	42	8	35	3	1	.288
Home	76	300	89	20	5	6	41	53	10	45	9	2	.297
Road	77	320	88	17	6	5	35	52	14	45	7	2	.275

Terry PENDLETON, Third Base
Runs Created: 86

	G	AB	Hit	2B	3B	HR	Run	RBI	TBB	SO	SB	CS	Avg
3.30 years		601	159	26	5	6	70	78	48	73	24	11	.265
1987	159	583	167	29	4	12	82	96	70	74	19	12	.286
First Half	85	333	105	16	0	7	54	52	34	39	10	8	.315
Second Half	74	250	62	13	4	5	28	44	36	35	9	4	.248
Vs. RHP		375	97	20	3	8	53	58	52	55	8	7	.259
Vs. LHP		208	70	9	1	4	29	38	18	19	11	5	.337
Home	79	293	78	15	1	5	36	44	28	32	12	6	.266
Road	80	290	89	14	3	7	46	52	42	42	7	6	.307

MANAGEMENT

A manager's job can be divided into three levels of responsibility. The most visible level, and the one which draws the most comment from fans, is what might be called the *game-level* decisions. These are the day-to-day operational questions, such as who should play left field against this pitcher, whether we should bunt now, how long the pitcher should stay in the game, when to pull in the infield, when to pinch hit and who to pinch hit with, how to set up the lineup, etc.

The second level of responsibility, which we will call the *team-level* decisions, involve much larger questions which are much fewer in number. Team-level decisions involve quandaries for the manager like who should be the team's relief ace, whether a young pitcher is ready to start or should be kept in long relief or sent to the minors, whether to choose a regular or use a platoon combination in left field, whether to use a four-man or five-man rotation in April, whether to abandon a player in a slump or stick with him, etc.

The third level of responsibility is that of *personnel management*. Personnel management, in baseball as in everything else, does not revolve around decision making per se, but around characteristics such as courage, honesty, fairness, consistency, maturity, judgment, personality, flexibility, etc.

In this article I want to examine the interplay among these levels of responsibility, focus on a few specific issues, and try to distinguish what I perceive as the critical differences among major-league managers. I have talked for several years about trying to learn to see managers as being not simply "good" or "bad," arranged along a one-dimensional spectrum, but as each making a unique contribution to his own team. This article is a part of the attempt to learn to do that.

A. GAME-LEVEL DECISION MAKING

As best I can estimate, a manager makes about 70 game-level decisions in an average day, or about 11,000 a year. The number obviously can never be determined with any accuracy, for in theory there are many times that many options are presented to a manager, while in practice the number of viable options for some managers in some games may be less than ten.

The first decision for each manager each day presumably is who will be the starting pitcher. This decision, because of it's importance, is worked out for several days at a time and is almost always known at least a couple of days in advance. No other game-level decision has the same importance, but there are eight (or nine) other starters to be named. As a practical matter, every manager probably has at least three of those decisions premade for the entire season depending only upon availability, but for most teams there are three or four decisions to be made each day. When should the catcher be given a day off? Do we want to use a left-handed hitter at first base to gain the platoon advantage, or a right-hander to take advantage of the wind?

Many managers—and I don't particularly endorse this—try to preplan as many as possible of their player utilization patterns so as to minimize the decisions required on this level. This includes not only managers like John McNamara, Billy Gardner, Don Zimmer, Leo Durocher, and Ralph Houk who prefer to use a regular at each position whenever possible, but also rigid platoon managers, like Bobby Cox, who may use two players at a position rather than one, but who still define the roles so firmly that a fan of the team, knowing who was starting for the opposition, could write out the lineup card. All of the managers that I named have had some success, but I feel that the most successful managers, like Earl Weaver, Whitey Herzog, and Sparky Anderson, tend to deliberately keep at least one or two positions open to allow them to make day-to-day realignments. Probably no manager since World War II kept open as many day-to-day options as Casey Stengel.

I think in general that I am suspicious of any manager who tries to eliminate decisions. I always suspect that a manager who reacts in an absolutely predictable way, regardless of the question, is not really thinking about the problem, and may be feeling intimidated by his responsibilities. Managers who use a regular at each position are only using about half of the roster, and often wear out their front-line players, only to find themselves with no bench. Rigid platooning is not as bad, because it does rest half of the roster and tends to create in-game options for the other half.

Once the decision of who to start is made—let's call it four decisions a day, on the average—there arises the question of how to select a batting order. A nine-man batting order can be arranged in 362,880 different ways, but again, at least half of the players are normally fixed in advance. You usually know who your leadoff man is, who your cleanup hitter is; obviously you bat the pitcher ninth. A manager who prefers to use a set regular lineup will, ordinarily, also prefer to lock in the batting order as much as possible. At this moment I have no idea who Don Zimmer will choose to be his leadoff hitter, his number-two hitter, or his number-three hitter, it being unknown if Andre the Home Run Hitter will be back, but nonetheless it is a safe bet that Zimmer will choose a leadoff hitter, a number-two hitter, etc., and will freeze those positions, because that's what Zimmer does.

Anyway, let's say that putting the players in the batting order represents another three or four decisions a day. There are maybe eight or ten moments during an average game in which it is debatable whether the pitcher should come out or stay to face another batter. If you lift the pitcher you have to face the decision of who to bring in. Before you can bring in the reliever you have to make a decision to have him up and warming. These decisions are critical in many ballgames.

In some games there are no viable pinch-hitting options; in other games there might be ten or twelve moments at which a pinch-hitting decision has to be made. Non-obvious decisions about moving the infield in or playing it half-way have to be made two or three times a game, as well as more minor positioning decisions which are probably left to coaches. Decisions about starting or holding the runner or calling for a hit and run are almost continuous throughout the game, requiring response decisions about pitching out, putting on a play, etc. A team averages about 13 baserunners a game, many of whom never run or always run and some of whom will be on in situations where nothing really can be done, but if there is an option the decision has to be made and remade and remade throughout a sequence of pitches, so you can count that at anywhere from 5 to 30 decisions a game.

Reasonable opportunities for a sacrifice bunt probably occur less often than once a game. Hitters who are 3–0 must be told to take or hit away. There are opportunities for defensive substitutes and pinch runners; however, a manager in an average game only makes about three actual substitutions other than pitchers, so it seems to me that one must conclude either that the opportunities for these changes are not numerous, or that most of such opportunities can be easily rejected.

Recognizing, then, that someone else could argue that it was actually 500 decisions a game if he wanted to, I get a reasonable estimate of about 70 decisions that a manager must make during an average game in which he faces multiple viable options. That's more work-related decisions than many of us face in a month. It is, of course, upon this mass of evidence that the merits of various managers are most often debated.

I have always taken the position that I would not try to evaluate managers on this basis. The lifeblood of my work is the attempt to build toward absolute knowledge on specific issues. It has always been my belief, and still is, that with the very rare exception of a case in which a manager does something just really, really stupid, it is impossible to prove objectively that any game-level decision was correct or incorrect. A lot of people like to pretend that they have analyzed these decisions and know how to make them, but what they have really done is weighed out very carefully three or four factors influencing the decision, and ignored the other 15 or 20 factors about which they could not obtain any reliable evidence. I mean, suppose that you analyze a pinch-hitting decision, and you run it through a simulation or whatever and conclude that the run probability is .308 if you make the switch and .246 if you don't, but have you really considered that the statistics representing the hitter in the simulation may not reflect at all his ability to hit this pitcher, that he may be a left-hander and the pitcher a right-hander, and if you have considered that then have you considered that this may be a high-ball pitcher and he may be a high-ball hitter, and if you have considered that have you considered that there may be a wind to right field which might make him 30 percent more likely to hit a home run than he normally would be, and if you have considered those things have you considered that if he is used now he will not be available later when there may or may not be another game situation, and if you have considered all of those things have you considered that the pitcher that he would face later would also be a high-ball pitcher or a low-ball pitcher, and a left-hander or a right-hander, and would tend to pitch inside or outside.

I am not saying that it is not useful to measure and evaluate as many of these factors as we can. By all means, let us measure; let us know what the batter hits against right-handed and left-handed pitchers and high-ball and low-ball pitchers. But we will never know enough, and never be able to build simulations that are complex enough, to tell us with anything remotely approaching reliability whether or not a manager chose the right option. I don't know, you don't know, and in truth the manager doesn't know either. He chooses certain biases by which to make his selection, and he throws his fate to the wind.

If we cannot, then, evaluate objectively a single one of those 11,000 decisions, how must we feel in confronting the entire unrecorded mass of them? Humble, I say, very humble.

People will say that the manager doesn't really have any impact, that he can decide anything he wants but if the players don't execute it isn't going to matter. I can't understand that kind of thinking. There are many systematic differences in the ways that managers resolve these problems. Some managers pinch hit four times as often as other managers. Some managers bunt six or eight times as often as others. Some managers start the runner much more often, or issue intentional walks much more often, or approach the question of when to bring in the reliever in a totally different way. If one man is right 51 percent of the time and another man 49 percent, that's an advantage for the good manager of about 220 decisions a year (2 percent of 11,000 is 220). You mean to tell me that that's not going to show up in the won-lost column? I don't care how much of a knee-jerk manager somebody is; making that many decisions, he's got to make a difference. Nobody could be so much by-the-book that he could make (or refuse to make) 11,000 decisions without having an impact on the results; for one thing, there are too many things that the book doesn't tell you.

But as important as they might be, these decisions are beyond the reach of sabermetrics to evaluate. As a fan I think that John McNamara is a dolt. As an analyst, I try to steer clear of talking about game-level decisions.

B. TEAM-LEVEL DECISION MAKING

Team-level decisions for a manager are few in number but large in impact. A manager probably makes about 10 major and 30 minor team-level decisions in a season. The major team-level decisions facing the Cardinals last year were whether to keep Terry Pendleton at third or try to make a trade, whether to put Joe Magrane in the rotation or in long relief, whether to stick with a catching combination of Lake and LaValliere or to make a trade, etc. The major team-level decisions this year are what to do about Lance Johnson, whether to put José Oquendo at second base instead of Tom Herr, what to do to try to replace Jack Clark, whether to put Steve Peters on the major-league roster or send him to Louisville, whether to make Curt Ford the regular right fielder or to alternate Ford and Morris, etc.

Of course the front office has a great deal of input into team level decisions; it wasn't Whitey Herzog who decided to sign Bob Horner. I think there are at least seven systematic differences among managers in how they make team level decisions. Those are in:

1) Willingness to take a chance on a young player.
2) Decisiveness.
3) Preference for using a regular or a platoon combination.
4) Roster composition.
5) Tendency to prefer offense or defense in selecting a regular.
6) Type of offensive player preferred, and
7) Judgment.

There used to be a difference between managers who preferred a four-man or a five-man rotation, but I don't think anybody uses a four-man rotation anymore.

Perhaps the clearest example of a manager making a strange team level decision in 1987 was Pat Corrales' decision to start the season without a utility infielder on the roster. Corrales had stocked the roster with outfielders and first basemen to use as pinch hitters, but had very few options to use them, because he couldn't pinch hit for an infielder. That's a roster-composition decision; Corrales didn't think through how he was going to use the players he had chosen in game situations.

Roster composition is one of the strengths of Whitey Herzog, and was also a peculiar strength of Earl Weaver. Weaver used to say that the biggest decision he had to make all year was who was the twenty-fifth man on the roster out of spring training. He would turn his roster over and over in his head, looking at question after question. If I have Gary Roenicke in left field to start the game and I have to pinch hit for my shortstop early in the game, will I still have another option later in the game? If it's a 7–4 game in the second inning and we've knocked out their starter but we're still three runs behind and they switch to a left-hander, can I change to a right-handed lineup without ruining my defense? Earl used to drive himself crazy trying to think through all of those things; Corrales, obviously, never really gave it much thought.

It is these decisions, few in number but large in impact, that I think we have a fair opportunity to evaluate. The final category, judgment, might sound subjective by the title, but is in fact rather easy to evaluate. What you're looking at is simple: when this manager made a decision about a player, was he right? Did it work out?

C. PERSONNEL MANAGEMENT AND INSTRUCTION

To evaluate a manager's ability to deal with players, obviously, is the role of a journalist or an insider; what I have as an outsider is only the ability to make a judgment about the information which is relayed to me by those people.

Now, to get to what I was really trying to say, and explain why this really is an article about Whitey Herzog.

In my opinion, to be successful over a period of time, a manager must do two things. First, he must contribute to the team on all three levels. A manager who contributes on any level can be successful for a short period of time, provided that that which he contributes is that which the team needs—but a failure on any level will ultimately undermine his career.

And second, he must integrate the three levels into a consistent whole. The manager must make decisions on all three levels not separately, but all at the same time.

On the first point, take Dick Williams. Williams is a brilliant judge of ballplayers. He has a twenty-year record of making judgments about young players, who can play and who can't, which is just extraordinarily good. It is hard to find a time when he has made a judgment that a young player was ready to move into a major-league job and subsequent events have proven him wrong. That's why his teams have improved so much when he has taken them over.

Williams is also a competent game manager—not a brilliant manager, certainly, but as good as the next guy. But time and again over the last twenty years, Williams has fallen down on the third point. His inability to hold the respect of his players has led to grumbling and dissatisfaction and dissension, and thus ultimately to the failure of the team sufficient to bring about Williams' dismissal. Although Williams has done again in Seattle what he has always been able to do—sort out the talent—the Phil Bradley trade is a sign that the normal Dick Williams process of alienating half the team is underway.

Or take Chuck Tanner. Tanner's strength, in the short run, is in his ability to motivate young players and create a positive clubhouse atmosphere. If you give Tanner a team which has a good deal of talent and which has no incipient attitude problems, Tanner for a couple of years is a heck of a manager.

The problem is that Tanner's record as a judge of horseflesh is just awful. Time and time again throughout the last decade, Tanner has thrust a player into a job, like Omar Moreno in 1986, Jim Acker in 1987, Lee Mazzilli and Marvelle Wynne in 1983, Doug Frobel in 1984, and Joe Orsulak in 1985, only to discover that the guy didn't have anything like the abilities needed to hold the job. So when personnel changes have to be made, Tanner is lost; he just keeps saying that if everybody has a good year we'll win, and the team just keeps losing. Tanner becomes indecisive, sticking people in slots and pulling them out, until ultimately the losing will destroy the atmosphere in the clubhouse. His inability to make team-level decisions consistently gives him few decent options within the game, which undermines his game-level management. The team loses, and the attitude, despite Tanner, will turn sour.

Or take Jim Frey. Frey, like Tanner, is a positive thinker. Unlike Tanner, his record as a judge of ballplayers is pretty decent; he made Dan Quisenberry the bullpen closer at KC in 1980, for example. The problem with Jim Frey is that he is the worst game manager you can imagine. And ultimately, his players will lose confidence in him and confidence in their ability to win, simply because they know that everything that happens in a close game is going to come as a complete surprise to Jim Frey. Then they'll start backbiting, and after about a year the party's over.

Whenever that happens, of course, you know what the local columnist is going to write. He's going to write that the manager (Jim Frey, or Dick Williams, or Chuck) has become a scapegoat for problems which were beyond his control. "If he was such a good manager a year ago," they will always ask, "why isn't he a good manager now? Has he gotten suddenly stupid in the last year?"

My opinion is that most managers are hired for good reasons, and are fired for good reasons. It's not that they get stupid after a couple of years. It is that most managers contribute on one level, or on two levels. By making that contribution, they change the needs of the organization. Once the needs of the organization change, in most cases they are no longer able to contribute.

The prevailing idea about Herzog's success, I think, is that 1) he plays a type of game, with aggressive base-running, tight defense, and constant pressure on the opposition, which keeps his team in the game; and 2) that he is an excellent game manager who is able to exploit any opportunity that such a game presents. That's all true—he does play that type of game, and he is an excellent game manager. That's not why he is successful.

Whitey Herzog has been successful over a long period of time, I believe, because more than any other manager of our time, Whitey makes decisions on all three levels at the same time. I wish I had written down some quotes, but I just know from listening to him over the years that when Herzog explains why he did something, he almost always explains it on at least two levels. If another manager is explaining why an outfielder was sent down, he'll usually say something like, "Well, his batting slump had started to affect him in the field, and we just felt like he'd be better off in Timbuktu where he could play every day and get his confidence up." He's explaining the team-level decision, in other words, strictly on the basis of team-level considerations. Herzog is more likely to say something like "Well, with Charlie Zigafoos playing as well as he's been playing, I didn't really have a role for him, and I didn't want him just sitting around getting edgy." He's explaining why he made the team-level decision, in other words, on the basis of its impact on game-level decisions, and on the basis of how it affects the whole team. If he explains why he made a game decision, he is very likely to explain it on the basis of a prior team-level decision: "I did that because that's his role on the team." I mean, I'm sure that Herzog doesn't think in this particular way, doesn't analyze the decisions as being on three distinct levels, but nonetheless he has the habit of tying together decisions so that they operate on all three levels.

The baserunning? Well, I don't know. It works for Herzog; another manager trying to do the same thing wouldn't have the same luck. There are some very fundamental premises of Herzog's managing which receive very little attention, but which are at least as important as the aggressive baserunning.

1) Never have anybody on your roster that you won't use. If you lose confidence in a player but keep him on the roster, you're making the roster smaller. That inhibits you within the game, and at the same time, you're inviting personnel problems.

2) When a player loses his aggressiveness he loses his value.

3) If a player doesn't want to do the job that you need him to do, get rid of him.

4) Everybody has to play defense. If a player can't play defense it's hard to find an offensive role for him either.

So everything is tied together. Herzog probably makes pitching changes more often than any other manager in baseball with a good team, particularly bringing in a left-hander to face a left-hander and then the right-hander to face the right-hander. Why? Because 1) he truly is not afraid to use anybody on his pitching staff, even if the guy on the mound is going great and the guy he wants to bring in has been hammered in his last three outings; 2) he knows that whoever he brings in is going to have a great defense behind him; 3) if you have a great defense behind you and you're aggressive on the mound and throw strikes you've got a good chance to be successful; and 4) he doesn't have anybody on his team who isn't aggressive and doesn't throw strikes; so 5) you might as well take the platoon advantage anytime you can get it. In explaining one trait, we hit aggressiveness, confidence in the entire roster, and defense. The obsessive base stealing, by itself, is not a very smart strategy, but it's tied in to the whole package. Herzog likes players who are fast because he likes his teams to play great defense (so that he can use any pitcher on the staff, so that he can make a pitching change whenever he wants to to get the left-hander against the left-hander), and most people who can play defense are fast, so if you have them you might as well be aggressive on the bases just like you are aggressive on the mound and just like you are aggressive in the field and just like you are aggressive in attacking personnel problems.

A lot of times in baseball, we use "aggressiveness in the batter's box" as a euphemism for poor judgment. We say that Damaso Garcia is an aggressive hitter, when what we mean is that he is a wild swinger who will chase bad pitches. I think, because of this misuse of the term *aggressiveness* (of which I am as guilty as anybody) that a lot of people assume that Herzog's teams are "aggressive" in the batter's box. They're not, not at all; they're very patient, selective hitters. That's not true aggressiveness, of course, it's just using the word. Anyway, look at the Cardinal walk totals and you'll see that's not the case. Ozzie drew 89 walks, Coleman 70, Pendleton 70, Clark 136, Herr 68. Oquendo in 1983 drew 19 walks; last year, in less playing time, he drew 54. Tony Pena if he'd been healthy would have set a career high in walks. The Cardinals led the league in walks drawn, as they did in 1985, so they have a lot of people on base. The same was true of Herzog's Royals; Otis, Mayberry, Porter, and McRae were all very disciplined hitters, and everybody in the lineup walked some except Frank White.

I suspect, as I reach the end of my project, that Whitey is also reaching the end of his effectiveness in St. Louis. It's been a long run, but people have begun to think that Herzog is magic, that he can solve all of the problems of this team just by sending the baserunners and pulling all the right levers. That's a dangerous sign, I think, a sign that Herzog's run is about over; whenever large numbers of people start saying that you're a genius, you're about to have problems. The signing of Bob Horner, and in particular the way it was handled, with the negotiations underway before Herzog was consulted, clearly signal that Herzog has lost influence in the organization, and may well undermine his authority with the players. There can't be anybody in baseball who is less Whitey Herzog's type of player than Bob Horner. Lance Johnson, who is Herzog's type of player, may be dealt to Chicago.

The Cardinals are not a young team; Pena, Herr, Smith, Forsch, Horner, and Tudor will never see 29 again. Their pitching last year was very suspect, although the defense was so good that it saved them. There are three young pitchers who could develop into a much better staff than the Cardinals had last year, but the other side of that is that if Ozzie Smith gets hurt, the defense could fall apart. The farm system is not one of the best in baseball, although neither is it one of the worst. I suspect that Whitey Herzog may have managed his last championship team in St. Louis.

NEW YORK METS

It took the 1987 Mets too long to get started. With Dwight Gooden and Roger McDowell unavailable to start the season, the Mets lost 20 of their first 36 games. Although they were the best team in the National League once they got things put together, the early problems put them behind in a close race in mid-September. When the race comes down to a having to win a series anything can happen, and what happened was that Ron Darling landed on his thumb and Terry Pendleton hit a home run and the Mets lost.

The role that Dwight Gooden's absence played in putting the Mets behind was obviously important, and obviously has been overstated. During those initial 36 games, when New York dropped 6 games behind the Cardinals, the Mets' starting pitching was as good as any part of the team. During those 36 games the Mets scored only 165 runs, 4.6 per game, well below their ability. They committed 35 errors, a rate that would have led the league had it been sustained. The starters in 36 games pitched 223 innings, struck out 162 men and walked 84, posted a 14–11 won-lost mark and a 4.16 ERA. The bullpen, with McDowell out early and Orosco pitching poorly, was 2–9 and had an ERA around 5.50.

They were already getting things together by Dwight Gooden's return on June 5, the Mets' fifty-first game. Gooden's stats, projected from a 112-game season to a 162-game season: 22–10, 214 strikeouts in 260 innings. The Mets had won nine of 14 games prior to Gooden's return. Among the other things which happened to get the Mets moving: Tim Teufel took over more of the playing time at second base, Terry Leach started for the first time on June 1, McDowell returned on May 14 and regained his effectiveness in a month or so.

There were other things that didn't happen, and because they didn't happen the Mets' progress even after Gooden was back was slow. I admire Davey Johnson. I enjoyed his book, *Bats* (with Peter Golenbock). But to my way of thinking, Davey Johnson in 1987 retreated a substantial distance from the positions which had made him a successful manager in the previous three seasons. To pick a minor thing, in 1986 Johnson ordered only 29 intentional walks, 26 fewer than any other National League team. He was unusual in that respect, and I admired him for it, because the intentional walk in most cases is a knee-jerk reaction that has about as much value as throwing an intentional wild pitch, committing an intentional error, or intentionally striking out as a hitter. But because Johnson is unusual in this respect, he gets second-guessed a lot for not ducking a tough hitter.

Last year, though, Johnson ordered 51 intentional walks, still below average but fairly close to the league norm of 65.

That's a petty thing, but this isn't. When Johnson took over this team, he fought with Frank Cashen to commit the team to youth, to get Cashen to bring Dwight Gooden to the majors, to get a second chance for Wally Backman, and to give up on Ron Hodges or whatever veteran catcher the Mets were using and give a shot to John Gibbons. The young players were essential to the development of his team.

He didn't do that last year. The Mets had two minor-league shortstops, Kevin Elster and Greg Jeffries, who were much better than the guy on the major-league team. The difference between Rafael Santana hitting .220 and Rafael Santana hitting .255 is that when he hits .220 everybody knows he's not contributing. Johnson has to know anyway. Unless he has been struck suddenly stupid, Johnson had to know that Kevin Elster was a better shortstop and a better hitter than Santana. But Johnson either didn't fight for Elster, or he didn't fight hard enough for him.

Frank Cashen's theory is that everybody should spend at least one full year in AAA ball. My theory is that once a player has proven that he can play AAA ball, every extra game that he plays in the minors will make his career less than it would otherwise have been. The best players are those who get to the major leagues when they are young enough to learn major-league skills to the depth of their bones. A player spends an extra year at AAA, he starts to wonder if he's really just a minor-league player. Willie Mays didn't spend a full year at AAA, and Mickey Mantle didn't, and Sandy Koufax didn't and Dwight Gooden didn't and Babe Ruth didn't and Robin Yount didn't and Kirby Puckett didn't and Tony Gwynn didn't and Reggie Jackson didn't and Pete Rose didn't and Andre Dawson didn't and Ozzie Smith didn't and on and on and on.

The position that every player has to play a full season of AAA ball is, I think, intellectually indefensible. The vast majority of the greatest players in baseball history played fewer than 300 games of minor-league ball. Every game you play in professional baseball before you reach the major leagues interferes with the clarity with which you see what happens when you do reach the majors. I think Frank Cashen may have cost the Mets the pennant last year by keeping Kevin Elster at Tidewater. (Actually, if I was running this organization I wouldn't open the season with Elster at shortstop, but with Jeffries, but I realize this is too much to expect from Frank Cashen.)

The managers who are successful over a long period of time tend to become more extreme in their positions as time passes. If you check the charts in this book that focus on managerial decisions, stuff like quick hooks and slow hooks and outs invested in one-run strategies and intentional walks issued and pinch hitters used, you'll find a lot of places where the highest and lowest notches on the chart are occupied by the half-dozen veteran managers who have won several pennants and have very definite ideas on how to do their business: Whitey Herzog, Dick Williams, Sparky Anderson, Tommy Lasorda. They take criticism for doing things in an unusual way, but they take the criticism and keep on doing it. The managers who aren't successful over a period of time will yield to the criticism, and become more conventional.

A related problem (related in the sense of also representing a failure to reevaluate personnel decisions) was the use of Gary Carter in the middle of the batting order. Three years ago Carter was possibly the Mets' best hitter, (.281 with 32 homers and 100 RBI). In 1987 Carter was the Mets' seventh-best offensive regular, nowhere near the hitter that Strawberry or Johnson was, and also clearly behind Hernandez, McReynolds, Teufel, and Dykstra or Wilson. Strawberry created an estimated 132 runs, fourth best in the National League, and third best among right fielders. Other than Carter and Santana (and Backman when he was in the lineup), every Met regular created at least 5.6 runs per game (Strawberry 8.9, Teufel 8.0, HoJo 6.7, Wilson 6.4, Dykstra 6.2, Hernandez 6.0, McReynolds 5.6). Carter was creating 3.7 runs per 27 outs, nowhere near the productivity of the rest of the regulars, and indeed not much better than Santana, at 3.5. In spite of that he continued to hit in the middle of the order most of the year, hitting cleanup a good part of the time until July, and continuing to bat ahead of Johnson even in September, thus depriving Hojo of a 100-RBI season. With a .290 on-base percentage and Frankenstein's knees, Carter represents the typical number-five hitter—the last guy in the league you would pick to lead off an inning, and the guy who most often leads off the second.

Still, the Mets scored 823 runs, 25 more than any other National League team. It wasn't the offense which cost them the title, and thus it wasn't any offensive decision which cost them the title. The Mets as a team had a secondary average of .300, best in the National League. The Mets had more men on base than anyone in the league except St. Louis, lost only 49 runners on stolen base attempts, and still grounded into only 94 double plays, fewest in the league. Adding the two together, they lost only 143 runners by caught stealing or double play, fewer than any other major league team.

I lost the thread there somewhere. The loss of Bobby Ojeda cost the Mets more dearly than missing two months of Dwight Gooden. The last day on which the Mets were under .500 was May 26, at 21–22. On June 26 they were five games over, at 38–33, so that was a decent month, but they still weren't playing like they did in 1986. But again, as at the beginning, once they got the pitching staff put together it took them too long to get started. By July 26 they were only eight games over .500, at 53–45; that month, in its own way, was almost as damaging as May or September. In that period the Mets had a rotation of Fernandez, Gooden, Darling, and sometimes Leach, but didn't gain much ground. They finally got hot then, beginning July 27, and were back in good position by early September, but they needed to get hot about three weeks earlier.

I wrote a year ago that the Mets were an unremarkable defensive team. Last year they were a step below unremarkable:

- Met opponents stole 162 bases, more than the league average of 154.
- Met outfielders threw out only 22 baserunners, fewest in the National League.
- The Mets' fielding percentage, .978, ranked eighth in the league.
- The Mets turned only 137 double plays, nine below average.

- The Mets' defensive efficiency record, .695, was average.

The Met outfielders had tremendous mobility; really, any of the four players could play center field. I don't know whether the low assists total is or is not meaningful; it could have more to do with the type of pitchers the Mets used, or perhaps was just random. Keith Hernandez remains the standard for his position. Several Mets fans told me last year that Hernandez did not play as well in the field as he had in the past, but I wonder if perhaps Hernandez' defensive reputation had not reached the point at which no one, including Hernandez at his best, could have lived up to it. In any case, that is the extent of the Mets' defensive assets. Carter doesn't throw well, and though his effort is unsurpassed his mobility is limited. Neither second baseman, Backman or Teufel, turns the double play particularly well or has exceptional range, in addition to which there is a defensive cost to platooning in the middle of the DP combination. Shortstop Santana was solid but unimpressive. Both third basemen, Johnson and Magadan, are erratic defensive players; Johnson fielded .938 and started only 15 double plays, and most people felt that Magadan, although charged with only two errors, was worse. Johnson, strained at third, played 38 games (or parts of games) at shortstop.

When you lose you second-guess everything, but the trade-off involved in all of these cases was reasonable. Teufel and Johnson were available in large part because they weren't glove wizards; that is part of how the team was put together. They were probably more valuable to the team than light-hitting glove men at the same positions, and I wouldn't urge any changes. But we do have to recognize that the Mets are pushing their luck; another defensive sore spot might be the one which would blow up on them (see Kansas City article).

They finished with 92 wins, and I suppose it isn't fair to regard 92 wins as a failure. I noted last year that the Mets were the only team in the 1980s to win 90 games three straight years. In 1987 the Mets made it four in a row; remarkably enough, the Mets are the only major-league team to have won 90 games in each of the last two seasons. (Incidentally, I erred last year when I stated that the Angels were the only other team with two straight 90+ seasons; the Yankees also had two straight at that time.) The Mets are the only team with four straight 90-win seasons in the eighties; the Mets and Yankees are the only teams with four 90-win seasons, total, the Yankees having crossed that mark in 1980, 1983, 1985, and 1986.

The Mets were somewhat vulnerable to left-handed pitching, finishing 29–26 against lefties (.527), as opposed to .589 against right-handed pitchers. They played badly in day games, finishing 27–29 in daylight (.482) versus 65–41 (.613) in night games. Gooden, of course, continues to have to trouble in day baseball.

What do I think of the 1988 Mets? In additi n to Elster and Jefferies, there are a lot of other you g players here, but there's not much of any place to put them. Tidewater had the best regular-season record in the International League (81–59), and dominated the individual stat accomplishments. Six of the top eight hitters in the league played for Tidewater, led by Randy Milligan (29, 103, .326, major-league equivalent .311 with 26 homers, 82

RBI.) Milligan was picked by *Baseball America* as the number-two prospect in the league, behind Elster. But Keith Hernandez has expressed no particular desire to retire by the end of June, Milligan isn't much of a first baseman and can't even consider the outfield, so what is he going to do? The path is equally well blocked for Terry Blocker, and the Mets might find that they carry on without Mark Carreon. Andre David, .300 with 17 homers at Tidewater, will be 30 in May. Reliever Dewayne Vaughn, league ERA leader at 2.66, would have a better chance to crack the roster if he had a worse ERA and a better fastball, like teammate Reggie Dobie. Dobie is supposed to have a good heat, but frankly I'm suspicious of a 23-year-old power pitcher who strikes out 70 men in 152 innings.

The 1988 Mets need to get Gary Carter out of the middle of the offense. With all the hitters they have, it isn't going to be any big problem for them if their catcher doesn't hit a whole lot. They made it a big deal last year by leaving him in the fourth or fifth spots of the batting order, when he didn't hit a whole lot.

The 1988 Mets probably would be better off to forget about Wally Backman, and give the second base job to Tim Teufel.

Counting on Randy Myers as the left-hander in the bullpen rather than Orosco seems like a positive for the team.

I suspect that the 1988 Mets, like the Mets of 1986, may blow the division apart. While it is well noted that very few teams in the eighties have been able to defend their championships, there have been a number of teams that were able to get back to the top after a hiatus of a year or two—the Dodgers in '81, '83, and '85, the Cardinals in '82, '85, and '87, the Tigers in '84 and '87, etc. I think this remains the most talented team in baseball other than perhaps the Blue Jays, and I expect them to win the division.

WINNING PERCENTAGE IN GAMES DECIDED BY FIVE OR MORE RUNS

Toronto	.707
Mets	.692
Detroit	.638
St. Louis	.633
San Francisco	.615
Kansas City	.553
Milwaukee	.548
Oakland	.543
Atlanta	.538
Montreal	.510
Texas	.510
Boston	.500
White Sox	.500
Cincinnati	.500
Yankees	.490
California	.489
Pittsburgh	.477
Houston	.476
Seattle	.471
Los Angeles	.459
Minnesota	.415
San Diego	.385
Cubs	.383
Philadelphia	.378
Baltimore	.361
Cleveland	.283

RUNS SCORED AND ALLOWED WINS AND LOSSES

Wins	601	267	92-0	1.000
Blowouts	293	181	27-12	.692
Aguilera	94	68	11-6	.647
Home Games	407	335	49-32	.605
Gooden	126	88	15-10	.600
Fernandez	141	116	16-11	.593
Slugfests	425	351	32-23	.582
All Games	823	698	92-70	.568
One-Run Games	213	207	29-23	.558
Pitchers' Duels	56	54	16-13	.552
Darling	161	151	17-15	.531
Road Games	416	363	43-38	.531
Mitchell	91	91	9-10	.474
Losses	222	431	0-70	.000

TEN BEST STARTS

	IP	H	R	ER	BB	SO		
Gooden at Mon, Sep 16	9	3	0	0	2	11	W	90
Leach at Cin, July 2	9	2	0	0	2	3	W	84
Fernandez at SD, May 30	9	5	0	0	4	11	W	84
Darling vs. Chi, Aug 7	9	4	1	1	3	11	W	83
Fernandez vs. StL, Apr 24	9	6	1	1	1	11	W	81
Gooden at SF, Aug 28	9	4	0	0	4	6	W	81
Gooden at Pit, Sep 21	9	7	1	1	0	9	W	78
Gooden vs. Phi, June 20	9	5	2	2	1	7	W	75
Gooden vs. Cin, July 16	9	7	0	0	1	2	W	74
Aguilera vs. Mon, Apr 30	9	3	3	3	2	7	W	74

PITCHERS WHEN SUPPORTED BY THREE TO FIVE RUNS

	G	IP	W-L	Pct	SO	BB	ERA
Aguilera	7	48	4-1	.800	37	12	3.35
Darling	15	94	6-3	.667	73	37	3.45
Gooden	13	96	7-4	.636	83	25	3.76
Fernandez	8	50	4-3	.571	38	23	2.90
Mitchell	6	33	0-2	.000	16	8	4.64

HALL OF FAME WATCH

Could be elected on current accomplishments: Carter 100, Hernandez 92.5, **Building credentials but not yet viable candidate:** Dave Johnson 59, Gooden 50.5, Candelaria 35, **Working on it:** Strawberry 23, Orosco 22, Darling 18, Fernandez 16, Ojeda 15, **Long way to go:** McDowell 9, Backman 8.5, Santana 6, Dykstra 6, Mazzilli 5.5, Almon 4.5, Aguilera 4, McReynolds 3, Sisk 3, Howard Johnson 2, M Wilson 2, Teufel 1. (Dave Johnson had 39 points as a player, has added 20 as a manager.)

RUNNERS LOST BY CAUGHT STEALING AND GROUNDING INTO DOUBLE PLAYS

San Diego	213
Seattle	205
Atlanta	201
St. Louis	198
San Francisco	196
Yankees	193
Minnesota	193
Texas	187
Toronto	186
Los Angeles	185
Baltimore	184
Philadelphia	182
Pittsburgh	179
Milwaukee	178
Oakland	176
Cincinnati	175
Boston	174
Montreal	174
Kansas City	170
White Sox	169
Houston	161
California	159
Detroit	158
Cleveland	157
Chicago	157
Mets	143

TEN WORST STARTS

	IP	H	R	ER	BB	SO		
Cone vs. Hous, Apr 27	5	7	10	7	6	3	L	16
Fernandez at Mon, June 17	4	8	9	7	1	3	L	16
Candelaria at Pitt, Sep 18	1⅓	8	5	5	0	1	—	19
Gooden vs. StL, Sep 12	2	5	6	6	3	1	L	20
Gooden at Cin, July 5	3	9	6	5	0	3	L	22
Schulze at Hous, July 25	5	8	7	7	0	1	L	24
Leach at Chi, Aug 15	4⅔	11	4	4	3	1	L	24
Aguilera at Pit, Apr 20	2⅓	6	4	4	3	1	—	27
Schulze vs. Chi, Aug 8	3⅓	8	4	4	0	0	L	28
Leach at SF, Aug 20	2	6	4	4	1	1	—	28

Gary CARTER, Catcher
Runs Created :58

	G	AB	Hit	2B	3B	HR	Run	RBI	TBB	SO	SB	CS	Avg
11.28 years		584	157	27	2	26	80	96	64	74	3	3	.269
1987	139	523	123	18	2	20	55	83	42	73	0	0	.235
First Half	74	284	67	9	2	11	30	43	25	39	0	0	.236
Second Half	65	239	56	9	0	9	25	40	17	34	0	0	.234
Vs. RHP		340	79	9	2	13	30	56	18	58	0	0	.232
Vs. LHP		183	44	9	0	7	25	27	24	15	0	0	.240
Home	69	255	59	8	1	9	29	42	24	39	0	0	.231
Road	70	268	64	10	1	11	26	41	18	34	0	0	.239

Keith HERNANDEZ, First Base
Runs Created: 98

	G	AB	Hit	2B	3B	HR	Run	RBI	TBB	SO	SB	CS	Avg
11.57 years		577	174	35	5	13	87	89	85	81	5	6	.301
1987	154	587	170	28	2	18	87	89	81	104	0	2	.290
First Half	83	321	92	14	2	10	45	42	39	59	0	2	.287
Second Half	71	266	78	14	0	8	42	47	42	45	0	0	.293
Vs. RHP		335	106	18	1	12	46	58	49	53	0	2	.316
Vs. LHP		252	64	10	1	6	41	31	32	51	0	0	.254
Home	76	281	81	13	1	6	41	38	42	52	0	1	.288
Road	78	306	89	15	1	12	46	51	39	52	0	1	.291

Tim TEUFEL, Second Base
Runs Created: 66

	G	AB	Hit	2B	3B	HR	Run	RBI	TBB	SO	SB	CS	Avg
3.12 years		531	143	35	3	14	75	67	65	79	3	3	.269
1987	97	299	92	29	0	14	55	61	44	53	3	2	.308
First Half	43	130	45	16	0	6	27	27	19	25	2	1	.346
Second Half	54	169	47	13	0	8	28	34	25	28	1	1	.278
Vs. RHP		109	31	7	0	6	16	26	14	26	1	1	.284
Vs. LHP		190	61	22	0	8	39	35	30	27	2	1	.321
Home	47	132	43	16	0	4	20	19	22	18	2	2	.326
Road	50	167	49	13	0	10	35	42	22	35	1	0	.293

Howard JOHNSON, Third Base
Runs Created: 106

	G	AB	Hit	2B	3B	HR	Run	RBI	TBB	SO	SB	CS	Avg
3.51 years		495	127	21	2	22	68	72	60	103	18	7	.257
1987	157	554	147	22	1	36	93	99	83	113	32	10	.265
First Half	83	291	80	11	0	20	48	52	37	64	17	4	.275
Second Half	74	263	67	11	1	16	45	47	46	49	15	6	.255
Vs. RHP		360	91	16	1	21	64	58	57	74	25	6	.253
Vs. LHP		194	56	6	0	15	29	41	26	39	7	4	.289
Home	80	271	71	10	1	13	43	40	42	62	17	4	.262
Road	77	283	76	12	0	23	50	59	41	51	15	6	.269

Rafael SANTANA, Shortstop
Runs Created: 44

	G	AB	Hit	2B	3B	HR	Run	RBI	TBB	SO	SB	CS	Avg
3.17 years		482	120	20	1	3	43	36	33	55	1	2	.249
1987	139	439	112	21	2	5	41	44	29	57	1	1	.255
First Half	73	229	65	10	1	4	24	28	16	35	0	1	.284
Second Half	66	210	47	11	1	1	17	16	13	22	1	0	.224
Vs. RHP		271	68	15	1	2	25	24	15	41	1	0	.251
Vs. LHP		168	44	6	1	3	16	20	14	16	0	1	.262
Home	73	221	54	13	0	2	19	21	17	31	1	0	.244
Road	66	218	58	8	2	3	22	23	12	26	0	1	.266

Kevin MCREYNOLDS, Left Field
Runs Created: 93

	G	AB	Hit	2B	3B	HR	Run	RBI	TBB	SO	SB	CS	Avg
3.98 years		598	159	29	6	24	80	89	49	83	8	4	.266
1987	151	590	163	32	5	29	86	95	39	70	14	1	.276
First Half	82	310	88	20	0	16	44	49	23	35	5	1	.284
Second Half	69	280	75	12	5	13	42	46	16	35	9	0	.268
Vs. RHP		369	99	18	3	17	47	59	28	45	11	1	.268
Vs. LHP		221	64	14	2	12	39	36	11	25	3	0	.290
Home	78	298	82	12	1	18	43	51	22	37	6	0	.275
Road	73	292	81	20	4	11	43	44	17	33	8	1	.277

Lenny DYKSTRA, Center Field
Runs Created: 74

	G	AB	Hit	2B	3B	HR	Run	RBI	TBB	SO	SB	CS	Avg
2.23 years		492	139	33	6	9	91	48	57	65	33	7	.283
1987	132	431	123	37	3	10	86	43	40	67	27	7	.285
First Half	72	232	69	17	2	7	41	21	17	41	11	4	.297
Second Half	60	199	54	20	1	3	45	22	23	26	16	3	.271
Vs. RHP		357	108	31	3	9	75	36	32	54	23	6	.303
Vs. LHP		74	15	6	0	1	11	7	8	13	4	1	.203
Home	67	212	62	17	1	7	46	27	19	27	14	5	.292
Road	65	219	61	20	2	3	40	16	21	40	13	2	.279

Darryl STRAWBERRY, Right Field
Runs Created: 132

	G	AB	Hit	2B	3B	HR	Run	RBI	TBB	SO	SB	CS	Avg
4.14 years		566	150	28	6	36	97	108	88	149	33	12	.265
1987	154	532	151	32	5	39	108	104	97	122	36	12	.284
First Half	84	279	76	17	4	21	51	51	53	68	13	6	.272
Second Half	70	253	75	15	1	18	57	53	44	54	23	6	.296
Vs. RHP		302	94	22	3	23	67	55	72	64	25	8	.311
Vs. LHP		230	57	10	2	16	41	49	25	58	11	4	.248
Home	77	264	85	17	2	20	54	56	40	57	16	7	.322
Road	77	268	66	15	3	19	54	48	57	65	20	5	.246

Wally BACKMAN, Second Base
Runs Created: 28

	G	AB	Hit	2B	3B	HR	Run	RBI	TBB	SO	SB	CS	Avg
4.11 years		505	141	20	3	2	77	36	53	70	24	10	.279
1987	94	300	75	6	1	1	43	23	25	43	11	3	.250
First Half	54	177	45	4	1	0	24	11	12	27	4	2	.254
Second Half	40	123	30	2	0	1	19	12	13	16	7	1	.244
Vs. RHP		265	72	6	1	1	40	21	22	38	11	3	.272
Vs. LHP		35	3	0	0	0	3	2	3	5	0	0	.086
Home	51	169	48	5	0	0	27	15	10	15	7	3	.284
Road	43	131	27	1	1	1	16	8	15	28	4	0	.206

Mookie WILSON, Center Field
Runs Created: 66

	G	AB	Hit	2B	3B	HR	Run	RBI	TBB	SO	SB	CS	Avg
5.70 years		596	166	25	10	9	89	50	36	102	45	14	.279
1987	124	385	115	19	7	9	58	34	35	85	21	6	.299
First Half	69	216	65	11	6	6	31	22	18	48	15	2	.301
Second Half	55	169	50	8	1	3	27	12	17	37	6	4	.296
Vs. RHP		160	54	6	3	6	23	21	16	39	12	1	.338
Vs. LHP		225	61	13	4	3	35	13	19	46	9	5	.271
Home	61	176	47	7	2	5	28	16	18	42	8	2	.267
Road	63	209	68	12	5	4	30	18	17	43	13	4	.325

MONTREAL EXPOS

If I had been eligible to vote for the National League's manager of the year, it would have been an easy choice. As much as I admire Whitey Herzog, and as good a job as Roger Craig did in San Francisco, my man would have had to be Buck Rodgers.

The Expos opened the season among predictions of doom under the dome, widespread speculation that the team would collapse without Andre Dawson. Tim Raines was not available to start the season. The Expos lost their first five games and continued to limp through April. As of May 1 they remained five games under .500, at 8–13. The turning point is spectacularly easy to spot. Tim Raines returned on May 1 and hit a grand slam home run in his first game back. From that point to the end of the season Raines played as well as he has ever played, which is to say that he played as well as anybody in baseball. The Expos, who had scored only 3.7 runs per game through the first 21 games, scored 4.7 per game the rest of the year.

Raines started the offense and keyed the offense, but Tim Wallach drove in 123 runs, Andres Galarraga drove in 90, and Mitch Webster scored 101. On a superficial level, one would think that the Expos had a lot of players having career years. What you must remember, however, is that prior to last year Olympic Stadium was one of the worst hitters parks in baseball, and the stats of the Montreal players were held down by this. In the three years 1984–1986 Tim Wallach hit .246 at home with only 19 home runs, 102 RBI, whereas in road games he hit .248 with 39 homers and 122 RBI; Olympic Stadium was costing him about 7 homers a year, as well as a few points off his batting average. Mitch Webster was even more dramatically effected, hitting just .261 with 5 home runs in Montreal, whereas he hit .307 with 14 home runs on the road. The great Tim Raines hit .317 with 10 home runs in Montreal, but he too was better on the road, hitting .325 with 18 homers in road games. Andre Dawson in those three years hit .251 with 28 homers in Montreal, .272 with 32 homers on the road. All four players also hit more doubles on the road, 56–47 for Raines, 46–37 for Wallach, 55–27 (!) for Dawson and 21–18 for Webster. Dawson's home-road breakdowns earlier in his career were even more dramatic.

With the roof on Olympic Stadium last year, however, the park changed from an extremely poor hitter's park to an extremely good one. The Expos scored and allowed 772 runs in 81 games at home, while they scored and allowed only 689 on the road. Thus in 1987, rather than dragging down the stats of Wallach, Raines, Webster, and Galarraga, Olympic Stadium was pumping them up. So I don't think that the Expos had a lot of players over their heads; I think it was just a change in the level of performance to be expected from these guys.

After Raines got the offense started, the pitching staff continued to struggle for another two weeks. Through 33 games the Expos allowed 169 runs, 5.1 per game. For the rest of the season, they cut that to 4.3. Their staff ERA was tenth in the league through 33 games (4.51); by season's end it had been whittled to 3.92, sixth in the league.

If Buck Rodgers had simply found Dennis Martinez and Pascual Perez, the two pitchers that his team desperately needed to stabilize an injury-rattled rotation, you might say that he was lucky. What happened, though, was that the Expos took a look at every available veteran pitcher who might be able to help them. They opened spring training with Len Barker in their minor-league camp; they gave a few starts early in the season to Lary Sorensen. They tried Charlie Lea. Dennis Martinez and Pascual Perez were the two among many who came through for them. In a sense, the Expos handling of their pitching staff was the exact opposite of the Oakland A's. The A's stocked their major-league roster with high-salaried veterans like Joaquin Andujar and Moose Haas and youngsters with great potential like Plunk and Rijo, and then watched that staff degenerate with injuries and inconsistency. The Expos, rather than confusing the picture by crowding the major-league roster, chose to protect themselves by looking at players at a lower level, pitchers who could be released if they didn't pan out and promoted if they did, but who weren't going to cost a lot either way.

All three of the top contenders in this division, the Cardinals, Mets, and Expos, saw their pitching staffs riddled by injuries in the summer of 1987. The Expos were the best prepared to deal with those injuries, and for that reason their starting pitching got stronger, rather than weaker, over the course of the summer. Montreal pitchers on the season walked only 446 men, the fewest of any major-league team.

The Expos were not a good defensive team. They were eleventh in a twelve-team league in both double plays (122) and fielding percentage (.976); their ratio of double plays to errors was the worst in baseball. Expo opponents stole 201 bases by our count, the highest total in the National League. They have had a problem in that area ever since the Carter trade, and the end of the problem is not on the horizon. Catching at Indianapolis, the Expos' AAA team, were Luis Pujols, Jeff Reed, John Stefero, and Wil Tejada. Tejada is the prospect in the group, so to speak, but with a .247 batting average and no power, he'll have to step up the offense. The inability to stop the running game, of course, takes the double play out of order, but the Expos were playing converted third basemen at both short (Hubie) and second (Vance Law), and neither is particularly good at turning the DP. Actually, Law at second was alternating with Casey Candaele, a part-time outfielder; Candaele was charged with only 3 errors in 68 games at second base, but also turned only 18 double plays.

In a way the Expos are a strange team. Sometimes I like to look at a team as a combination of two rectangles, a "corner rectangle" (first base, third base, left field, and right field) and an "up the middle rectangle" (catcher, second base, shortstop, center field). Many teams concentrate on getting offense at the corner positions and defense at the up the middle positions. The Expos at the corner positions are strong both offensively and defensively; Wallach, Raines, Galarraga, and Webster are not only the Expos' best hitters, but are all four excellent defensive players, although one might wish for a better arm in right. That rectangle is probably the best in the league, although the Mets' is awfully good, too. They do not have a comparable talent player at any up-the-middle position, except possibly Brooks.

One might guess that in that position, the Expos might choose to cement the team with glove wizards up the middle, find a light-hitting catcher or shortstop, and try to beat you with a glove and a bunt and Tim Raines and Tim Wallach. The Expos' defensive rectangle, however, is based around players who are pretty good offensively for the positions they play, but not strong defensively. None of the four regulars (Fitzgerald, Vance Law, Brooks, and Winningham/Candaele) could be considered a good glove. Law and Brooks could be considered a "good bat for a second baseman" and a "good bat for a shortstop," but even at that they don't contribute with the bat the way that the other four players do, although Brooks has had better years. Jeff Reed, perhaps, is the only player on the team who represents the up-the-middle type one might expect to predominate.

That's not a criticism. I'm not suggesting that they would be better off to have the glove men up the middle, only that that is the way most teams would handle it. A team designed that way, strong defensively at all eight positions but with offense at only four, would be trying to win games 2–1 and 1–0. The Expos won more of those games than anybody else, anyway—in fact, the ability to win those games with astonishing consistency was a fundamental key to the Expos' surprising season. Let me cite a few numbers:

• The Expos won 11 games in which they scored less than three runs (that is, 11 games won by the score of 1–0, 2–0, or 2–1). No other major-league team won more than 9 such games. The Cardinals won only two games by those scores.

• The Expos when scoring zero to two runs still managed a winning percentage of .244, easily the best in the major leagues.

• The Expos had a .667 winning percentage in one-run games, 28–14.

• The Expos had a .647 winning percentage (44–24) in games decided by one or two runs, easily the best in the major leagues. The Cardinals were second best in the National League in this respect, at .567.

• The Expos' 24 losses by one or two runs was the fewest of any major-league team. Remarkably enough, every other National League team lost 36 games by one or two runs. The Expos lost only 24.

• The Expos won 22 pitcher's duels (games in which no more than five runs were scored by both teams). This tied for the National League lead.

• The Expos had a .667 winning percentage in pitcher's duels, by far the best in the National League (San Francisco was second at .588).

• The Expos lost only 17 games in which they had a quality start, fewest of any National League team.

All of those statistics reflect one essential fact: the Expos, despite a suspect defense, just did a tremendous job of winning close, low-scoring games. As to why they won those games so consistently, I would cite two things: a tremendous bullpen, and luck. The Expos a year ago traded or gave away Jeff Reardon, their bullpen closer for several seasons, and replaced him with a bullpen-by-committee. The committee was far better than Reardon. Tim Burke, the staff leader in saves with 18, was one of the best-kept secrets in baseball with a 1.19 ERA in 55 games, and other stats consistent with that 1.19 ERA—17 walks in 91 innings, 64 hits given up, only 3 home runs. Probably no player in baseball contributed as much to a contending team as quietly as Tim Burke. Journeyman Andy McGaffigan pitched extremely well, with a 2.39 ERA in 69 games and also good K/W and miscellaneous data. Veteran Bob McClure and Randy St. Claire contributed at a lower level. Expo relievers were second in the major league in saves, 50, and had a .674 winning percentage (29–14), also the second best in the major leagues.

The bullpen, and luck. Because they won the close games, the Expos finished with a won-lost record eight games better than would be predicted by their ratio of runs to opposition runs. The Expos won 91 games with a run/opposition run ratio which would ordinarily produce only 83 wins, the largest such discrepancy in the majors. It has been demonstrated that teams that do this (win more games than predicted by the Pythagorean relationship) tend to decline in the following season by the amount that they have exceeded their expected wins. If this deviation resulted from an ability, it would almost certainly have some carry-over from season to season. Because there is no such carry-over, we assume that it is primarily luck.

Which is one reason I don't think the Expos are likely to contend in 1988, but I have a couple of notes to give you before I get to that.

1) There were only three major-league teams last year that had a winning record but failed to draw two million fans. Those three were Montreal, Milwaukee, and San Francisco. Montreal, with 1,850,324, had the lowest attendance of any team with a winning record.

2) Over the last five years the Expos' record on grass fields (107–102) is better than their record on their native artificial turf. Montreal and Atlanta are the only National League teams to have better records on the kind of surface that they don't have in their home park. The Expos over those five years have a .527 winning percentage, but on the road they have played .512 ball on grass fields, just .479 on artificial turf. The Expos over that period have the smallest home-park advantage in the National League except for Cincinnati.

I use a series of leading indicators to help make a guess about how a team might do in the following season. The indicators for the Expos are the most negative for any National League team except the Cardinals. The one positive indicator is that the team is relatively young, but that's a minor thing because they're not really young, like the Pirates or Padres; all of their key players have reached their prime except Gallaraga and Candaele, and they are 26 and 27, respectively. The three substantial negative indicators are:

1) The Plexiglas principle. Teams that improve sharply in one season tend to decline in the following season. The Expos were up by 12½ games last year.

2) Late season performance. Teams that play well late in the year tend to have a carry-over benefit in the next season. Despite the superb late-season pitching of Pascual Perez, the Expos record over the last two months, 33–28, was not as good as their record early in the year.

3) The Johnson Effect. Teams that have a better won-lost record than is indicated by their runs scored and runs allowed have a strong tendency to decline in the following season.

The Expos' top rookie in 1988 figures to be Johnny Paredes, a right-handed hitting second baseman who hit .312 with 30 stolen bases at Indianapolis (major-league equivalent: .287, 5 homers, and 31 RBI). The failure to give Paredes a look in September is puzzling (did I miss an injury or something here?), but it must be assumed that Paredes was the main reason the Expos didn't make a good offer to Vance Law. Outfielder Alonzo Powell and short-stop Luis Rivera are also well regarded prospects. Powell would break the outfield for quite a few teams, but probably won't find room among Raines, Webster, and Candaele. Rivera hit for the same average at Indianapolis as Paredes (.312) and with the same home-run total (8), but probably will have to wait for Hubie's next injury to get his shot.

Another factor that I think will hurt the Expos next year is the departure of Vice President and General Manager Murray Cook. Cook played a vital role in containing the losses when this organization found that it could no longer afford players like Gary Carter and Andre Dawson. Cook departed last summer under mysterious circumstances; the Expos in the future will have to solve these problems without Cook's help.

Unless Rogers turns in another remarkable managerial performance, I frankly don't think that the Expos can compete again in 1988.

LOSSES BY ONE OR TWO RUNS

Montreal	24
Detroit	28
Milwaukee	30
Minnesota	31
Seattle	32
Baltimore	34
Yankees	35
Pittsburgh	36
Philadelphia	37
Kansas City	38
Mets	38
Cubs	39
Cleveland	39
Toronto	39
Oakland	39
St. Louis	39
Atlanta	39
Cincinnati	39
Boston	40
White Sox	40
Texas	40
San Francisco	41
California	44
Los Angeles	45
Houston	46
San Diego	55

RUNS SCORED AND ALLOWED WINS AND LOSSES

Wins	532	243	91-0	1.000
Martinez	116	73	18-4	.818
One-Run Games	164	150	28-14	.667
Pitchers' Duels	65	50	22-11	.667
Home Games	401	371	48-33	.597
Heaton	154	135	19-13	.592
Youmans	89	108	13-10	.565
All Games	741	720	91-71	.562
Road Games	340	349	43-38	.531
Blowouts	272	274	25-24	.510
B. Smith	135	116	13-13	.500
Slugfests	359	362	25-26	.490
Sebra	90	127	10-17	.370
Losses	209	477	0-71	.000

TEN BEST STARTS

	IP	H	R	ER	BB	SO		
Sebra vs. Chi, July 1	9	3	1	1	1	14	L	90
Heaton at SD, May 23	9	2	0	0	1	5	W	87
Youmans at Hous, July 8	9	1	0	0	2	3	W	86
Martinez vs. Mon, June 15	9	3	0	0	3	6	W	84
Perez at LA, Aug 28	9	3	1	0	0	5	W	84
Sebra at Hous, July 7	9	5	0	0	0	6	W	83
Perez at NY, Sep 17	9	4	1	1	8	W	82
Youmans vs. Cin, July 26	9	6	0	0	0	7	W	82
Perez at Chi, Sep 12	9	5	1	1	2	11	W	82
Sebra vs. StL, June 26	9	6	1	1	0	10	W	81

PITCHERS WHEN SUPPORTED BY THREE TO FIVE RUNS

	G	IP	W-L	Pct	SO	BB	ERA
Heaton	8	50	3-1	.750	27	12	3.75
Martinez	9	61	5-2	.714	36	14	2.95
B. Smith	9	49	3-4	.429	27	13	4.41
Sebra	14	82	4-7	.364	79	32	4.59

HALL OF FAME WATCH

Building credentials but not yet viable candidate: Raines 67; **Working on it:** Bill Campbell 23, Wallach 17, Rodgers 13, D. Martinez 12.5, Brooks 10; **Long way to go:** Lea 9, Sorensen 9, B. Smith 8, McClure 7, P. Perez 5, Burke 4, Webster 4, Engle 3.5, Galarraga 2.5, Youmans 2, Law 2, Hesketh 1, McGaffigan 1.

GAMES WON DESPITE SCORING LESS THAN THREE RUNS

Montreal	11
Cleveland	9
Minnesota	8
San Francsico	7
Houston	7
Detroit	6
San Deigo	6
Yankees	6
White Sox	6
Kansas City	6
California	5
Seattle	5
Texas	5
Mets	5
Philadelphia	5
Pittsburgh	5
Atlanta	5
Boston	4
Baltimore	4
Milwaukee	4
Cincinnati	4
Cubs	3
Los Angeles	3
Toronto	3
Oakland	3
St. Louis	2

TEN WORST STARTS

	IP	H	R	ER	BB	SO		
Sorensen vs. Chi, June 29	2⅓	10	6	6	0	2	L	15
Fischer at Pit, June 24	2*	7	7	7	1	2	L	15
Martinez at Hous, July 6	2⅓	7	6	6	2	3	L	20
Smith vs. Cin, July 23	4⅓	9	7	7	0	3	L	20
Youmans at Cin, Apr 6	3⅓	5	7	7	2	0	L	20
Heaton vs. NY, June 18	4⅔	9	7	7	0	2	L	20
Heredia at NY, May 1	2⅔	8	6	6	1	3	—	20
Sebra at SF, May 31	4⅓	11	5	5	2	3	L	22
Youmans vs. Phi, Apr 23	2⅔	7	5	5	4	2	—	22
Heaton at SD, Aug 25	3	9	5	5	0	3	L	24

Mike FITZGERALD, Catcher
Runs Created: 30

	G	AB	Hit	2B	3B	HR	Run	RBI	TBB	SO	SB	CS	Avg
2.52 years		465	110	18	1	7	39	56	53	87	5	4	.237
1987	107	287	69	11	0	3	32	36	42	54	3	4	.240
First Half	54	157	36	6	0	3	19	21	20	27	2	2	.229
Second Half	53	130	33	5	0	0	13	15	22	27	1	2	.254
Vs. RHP		161	42	7	0	1	22	22	22	24	1	3	.261
Vs. LHP		126	27	4	0	2	10	14	20	30	2	1	.214
Home	62	154	39	8	0	1	19	26	26	25	3	2	.253
Road	45	133	30	3	0	2	13	10	16	29	0	2	.226

Tim RAINES, Left Field
Runs Created: 132

	G	AB	Hit	2B	3B	HR	Run	RBI	TBB	SO	SB	CS	Avg
6.30 years		619	191	34	10	10	115	61	89	68	81	12	.309
1987	139	530	175	34	8	18	123	68	90	52	50	5	.330
First Half	63	246	85	20	1	7	60	37	34	26	25	2	.346
Second Half	76	284	90	14	7	11	63	31	56	26	25	3	.317
Vs. RHP		366	110	21	4	13	81	45	69	34	44	4	.301
Vs. LHP		164	65	13	4	5	42	23	21	18	6	1	.396
Home	74	276	93	15	5	9	65	32	49	29	31	2	.337
Road	65	254	82	19	3	9	58	36	41	23	19	3	.323

Andres GALARRAGA, First Base
Runs Created: 88

	G	AB	Hit	2B	3B	HR	Run	RBI	TBB	SO	SB	CS	Avg
1.70 years		557	158	32	2	15	71	80	44	132	6	4	.284
1987	147	551	168	40	3	13	72	90	41	127	7	10	.305
First Half	79	292	98	28	2	8	45	61	25	62	5	4	.336
Second Half	68	259	70	12	1	5	27	29	16	65	2	6	.270
Vs. RHP		387	115	25	3	6	47	62	24	94	6	8	.297
Vs. LHP		164	53	15	0	7	25	28	17	33	1	2	.323
Home	74	264	83	24	1	7	42	48	24	59	3	7	.314
Road	73	287	85	16	2	6	30	42	17	68	4	3	.296

Herm WINNINGHAM, Center Field
Runs Created: 37

	G	AB	Hit	2B	3B	HR	Run	RBI	TBB	SO	SB	CS	Avg
2.26 years		385	92	15	5	5	41	35	36	88	28	12	.239
1987	137	347	83	20	3	4	34	41	34	68	29	10	.239
First Half	68	171	47	9	3	3	22	27	20	35	15	5	.275
Second Half	69	176	36	11	0	1	12	14	14	33	14	5	.205
Vs. RHP		318	73	17	3	4	28	37	31	59	26	10	.230
Vs. LHP		29	10	3	0	0	6	4	3	9	3	0	.345
Home	69	180	49	9	1	2	20	27	16	38	23	6	.272
Road	68	167	34	11	2	2	14	14	18	30	6	4	.204

Vance LAW, Second Base
Runs Created: 65

	G	AB	Hit	2B	3B	HR	Run	RBI	TBB	SO	SB	CS	Avg
5.29 years		511	129	26	4	10	63	59	56	80	6	4	.252
1987	133	436	119	27	1	12	52	56	51	62	8	5	.273
First Half	77	259	79	18	1	9	34	37	35	40	6	2	.305
Second Half	56	177	40	9	0	3	18	19	16	22	2	3	.226
Vs. RHP		283	75	17	1	9	32	39	27	41	5	1	.265
Vs. LHP		153	44	10	0	3	20	17	24	21	3	4	.288
Home	65	209	56	18	0	3	25	31	24	29	6	2	.268
Road	68	227	63	9	1	9	27	25	27	33	2	3	.278

Mitch WEBSTER, Right Field
Runs Created: 99

	G	AB	Hit	2B	3B	HR	Run	RBI	TBB	SO	SB	CS	Avg
2.60 years		542	153	27	9	13	90	56	57	82	32	13	.282
1987	156	588	165	30	8	15	101	63	70	95	33	10	.281
First Half	82	319	91	19	3	4	52	28	33	42	17	6	.285
Second Half	74	269	74	11	5	11	49	35	37	53	16	4	.275
Vs. RHP		388	108	19	7	8	71	37	53	66	29	5	.278
Vs. LHP		200	57	11	1	7	30	26	17	29	4	5	.285
Home	78	285	76	14	4	9	52	34	36	43	15	6	.267
Road	78	303	89	16	4	6	49	29	34	52	18	4	.294

Tim WALLACH, Third Base
Runs Created: 105

	G	AB	Hit	2B	3B	HR	Run	RBI	TBB	SO	SB	CS	Avg
6.12 years		592	155	32	3	22	70	86	45	93	6	5	.262
1987	153	593	177	42	4	26	89	123	37	98	9	5	.298
First Half	83	317	97	28	1	12	52	73	22	44	5	3	.306
Second Half	70	276	80	14	3	14	37	50	15	54	4	2	.290
Vs. RHP		433	128	25	3	25	63	97	26	70	7	5	.296
Vs. LHP		160	49	17	1	1	26	26	11	28	2	0	.306
Home	78	290	87	26	4	13	47	64	19	45	4	4	.300
Road	75	303	90	16	0	13	42	59	18	53	5	1	.297

Casey CANDAELE, Utility
Runs Created: 51

	G	AB	Hit	2B	3B	HR	Run	RBI	TBB	SO	SB	CS	Avg
1.04 years		532	140	26	5	1	68	28	41	41	10	14	.263
1987	138	449	122	23	4	1	62	23	38	28	7	10	.272
First Half	79	300	84	16	2	0	45	11	28	17	6	5	.280
Second Half	59	149	38	7	2	1	17	12	10	11	1	5	.255
Vs. RHP		336	87	14	3	1	45	20	30	26	5	9	.259
Vs. LHP		113	35	9	1	0	17	3	8	2	2	1	.310
Home	72	244	66	9	3	1	29	12	16	16	2	4	.270
Road	66	205	56	14	1	0	33	11	22	12	5	6	.273

Hubie BROOKS, Shortstop
Runs Created: 54

	G	AB	Hit	2B	3B	HR	Run	RBI	TBB	SO	SB	CS	Avg
5.55 years		610	168	29	5	12	67	81	38	97	6	6	.275
1987	112	430	113	22	3	14	57	72	24	72	4	3	.263
First Half	41	155	44	6	2	7	24	30	8	29	2	0	.284
Second Half	71	275	69	16	1	7	33	42	16	43	2	3	.251
Vs. RHP		309	73	12	2	9	37	38	19	54	3	1	.236
Vs. LHP		121	40	10	1	5	20	34	5	18	1	2	.331
Home	60	228	66	14	1	9	38	37	16	38	2	2	.289
Road	52	202	47	8	2	5	19	35	8	34	2	1	.233

Tom FOLEY, Shortstop
Runs Created: 34

	G	AB	Hit	2B	3B	HR	Run	RBI	TBB	SO	SB	CS	Avg
2.91 years		401	104	20	4	5	41	38	33	56	8	6	.259
1987	106	280	82	18	3	5	35	28	11	40	6	10	.293
First Half	45	109	27	6	1	2	12	10	8	15	4	5	.248
Second Half	61	171	55	12	2	3	23	18	3	25	2	5	.322
Vs. RHP		259	78	17	3	5	35	28	11	35	5	10	.301
Vs. LHP		21	4	1	0	0	0	0	0	5	1	0	.190
Home	54	121	38	7	2	3	18	8	5	21	2	7	.314
Road	52	159	44	11	1	2	17	20	6	19	4	3	.277

PITTSBURGH PIRATES

Gonna let the good times roll. The Pirates stand on the doorstep of a new era. In the long history of a baseball team, it is amazing how few distinct phases there are to a team's performance. The first phase of the modern Pittsburgh Pirates began in 1900, when Honus Wagner was transferred to the Pirates from the dying Louisville franchise. As long as Wagner was at the top of his game (1900–1913), the Pirates were one of the best teams in baseball; as Wagner aged, the team went through a sharp down phase (1914–1917), the nadir of which was a 103-loss season in 1917. In 1918, however, the Pirates put together an interesting team that contained a number of the best managers of the next generation (Billy Southworth, Bill McKechnie, Casey Stengel) and jumped back over .500. The farm systems were just starting then; organizing a sharp network of scouts and farm teams, the Pirates pulled in over the next decade players like Pie Traynor, Paul and Lloyd Waner, Charlie Grimm, Dick Bartell, and Remy Kremer. From 1918 through 1929 the Pirates never finished out of the first division; in 1930, though fifth, they were still 80–74. In the fifteen years following that, 1931–1945, they finished under .500 only four times, and never twice in a row, so really, in the entire period 1918–1945 the Pirates were never seriously out of contention.

In 1946, however, the Pirates collapsed. I don't know what happened, exactly—Frankie Frisch may have been left in charge of the team too long and got grouchy, maybe. Frisch I think was one of those "attitude" guys, wanted to make personnel decisions based on how much he liked the guy. Whatever, the Pirates in 1948 had a good season and seemed to be on the way back, but in 1949 they fell through the ice and drowned. By the early fifties the Pirates had replaced the Browns and Phillies as the worst team in baseball. Branch Rickey was hired to reconstruct the team in the mid-fifties, and by 1958 the Pirates were back in contention.

Although the Pirates did finish under .500 two years in a row (1963–1964) when age and injuries decimated their pitching staff, the Pirates in the years 1958–1983 were anchored in the first division by a handful of stars: Clemente, Stargell, Mazeroski, Oliver. They never had a pitcher of comparable status, but they won many pennants and contended when they didn't win. In 1984 the Pirates again fell upon hard times, and functioned for three plus years as the National League's blocking sled.

What is that, six basic eras? We'll call them the Honus Wagner era (1900–1913), the post-Wagner blues (1914–1917), the McKechnie-Waner era (1918–1945), the Joe Garagiola years (1946–1957), the Clemente-Stargell years (1958–1983), and Tanner's Legacy (1984–1987). That's just six movements in 87 years.

I guess that part of what I am saying here, in a roundabout way, is that when you get to be as bad as the Pirates were in 1985, it's something that can take a hell of a long time to get over, and for that reason if none other we should not be too quick to declare that the good times are

ready to roll in Pittsburgh. *Maybe* the good times are ready to begin. The turning of a page in the history of a team happens maybe once a decade, and as clearly as that moment can be spotted in history it can be awfully hard to recognize when it happens; we can't assume that the Pirate problems are over because they have had two hot months. The Pirates best player last year was Andy Van Slyke, and Van Slyke was very good but somehow I don't really believe that the 1990s in Pittsburgh are going to be called the Van Slyke years.

Well, to look more closely at the 1987 team. The Pirates were the youngest team in baseball, with their regulars and top starters averaging just 24.8 years of age. Coming off of three straight last-place finishes (75–87 in 1984, 57–104 in 1985, 64–98 in 1986) the Pirates stumbled through much of the season as if intent on hanging up another one. Through August 2 the Pirates were at 45–59, deep in last place; they were 19½ games out of first place, and 8½ out of fifth place. Suddenly, at that point, their pitching came together. The Pirates won 35 of their last 58 games (.603), to finish in a fourth-place tie. Working with a rotation of Dunne, Drabek, Fisher, and sometimes Walk, Bielecki, and Palacios, the Pirates starting pitchers over the last two months posted an ERA of 3.60, third best in the major leagues.

The question arises whether the strong late-season performance has any special value in looking ahead to the next season. The only study I have ever done of the question (pages 229–30, 1986 *Baseball Abstract*) compared matched sets of teams which had and had not finished the season strong—that is, a team with a record of 85–77 that had finished the season playing well, and a team with the same record that had finished the season poorly. That study found that there was unquestionably a carryover value; the teams that had finished the season playing well did substantially better in the following seasons than those that had finished the season playing poorly.

The Pirates top offensive player was Andy Van Slyke, who created 108 runs, 6.94 per 27 outs. The Pirates were the only team in the National League East who did not have one of the league's top ten in runs created, although with St. Louis losing Jack Clark they no longer have one either. Actually, part-time outfielder John Cangelosi created 7.33 runs per game; it is generally assumed that he was over his head, but if not, a spot will have to be opened for him. Left field and shortstop were the offensive sore points for the Pirates. The problem in left field seemed to be almost voluntary; the Pirates used R. J. Reynolds, who hit .260 with little power, creating 4.8 runs per 27 outs, while giving little playing time to Cangelosi or Diaz, creating 5.5. Diaz, now 28 years old, has blasted 28 major-league home runs in just 457 major-league at bats. The guy doesn't even strike out a whole lot, 85 times so far (about the same frequency as Andy Van Slyke). That a team desperate for a cleanup hitter can't find 300 at bats a year for a player with that kind of power is a puzzle to everyone except Jim Leyland, who declines to explain it. At shortstop Al Pedrique hit well, .294, and had respectable fielding stats, but he isn't highly regarded after spending two generations in the Mets' farm system, so the Pirates will try to make a kid named Fast Felix Fermin do the job. Fermin hit .268 without a homer in the Eastern League; he seems to be comparable to Rafael Belliard as a hitter.

So the Pirates were solid offensively at catcher, second base, third base, center field, and right field; they were good sometimes and poor sometimes in left field; and they were outright weak at shortstop. At first base was Sid Bream, whose batting was decent relative to the whole league but poor relative to other first basemen; he hit .275 with 13 home runs. He isn't going to have a long career doing that.

The Pirates could not handle left-handers, finishing 32–41 against left-handers (.438), 48–41 (.539) against right-handers. The 73 decisions against lefties was the most in the league, the average being 54. The Pirates as a team hit .270 against right-handers, .257 against lefties. Van Slyke, the Pirates best hitter, was kept from emerging in St. Louis by his difficulties with left-handers, which he continued to have, hitting .334 against right-handers, only .231 against lefties, and also homering only one-fourth as often against left-handers. The Pirates second-best hitter, Barry Bonds, also is a lefty, and also has a good sized platoon differential, .281 with the advantage, .228 without it. The other player acquired in the Pena trade, LaValliere, had a similar discrepancy, .323 against right-handers, .221 against lefties. Although Van Slyke stayed in the lineup against southpaws, LaValliere usually hit the bench, but his replacement Junior Ortiz didn't entirely pick up the slack. First baseman Sid Bream is another left-hander. I haven't seen platoon data for Johnny Ray, a switch-hitter, but Ray also historically has hit much better against left-handers than right-handers. Although several Pirates hit somewhat better against left-handers, no one dominated lefties the way Van Slyke battered right-handers.

The Pirates have two chances to turn that around next year: José Lind and Mike Diaz. Lind, a right-hander, hit .342 against left-handers in his late-season play, which indeed was one of the keys to the Pirates late-season surge, as by that time the Pirates weakness against lefties had become so well known that the Pirates were actually facing as many left-handers as right-handers. Lind hit just .268 at Vancouver, and appears to have been playing over his head in September, although he seems almost certain to hold the second-base job. Diaz last year played most of the time against left-handers and hit 14 of his 16 homers against them, so I'm not sure how much more can be expected of him on that particular count. It seems to me very likely that the Pirates will continue to have trouble against left-handers, and it seems possible that this might significantly undermine the 1988 Pirate season.

The Pirates in recent years have not been able to win on grass fields, with a .386 winning percentage over the last five years. That improved last year, with the Pirates having a respectable 19–23 record on grass fields.

Defensively, the Pirates were pretty good, much improved over recent years. Despite the young staff, they did a better than average job of controlling the running game.

The Pirates' defensive efficiency record, .708, was the best in the National League, due primarily to having two center fielders in the outfield (Bonds and Van Slyke). They were fourth in the league in fielding percentage, average in the number of double plays turned. Their strongest points defensively were at catcher, where Mike LaValliere won the Gold Glove, and in the two outfielders named before; their weakest defensive point, the left side of the infield (third base and shortstop), where they used several players at each position. Bobby Bonilla, a converted outfielder at third base, is a converted outfielder at third base.

Every Pirate farm team finished at or above .500, the first time in the Pirates long history that this had happened (AAA Vancouver 72–72, AA Harrisburg 77–63, Class A Salem 80–59, Class A Macon 73–64, Rookie League Watertown 44–32, and Rookie League Bradenton 33–30). The AAA team is not bursting with prospects; their outfield was Butch (Warm Front) Davis, Benny Distefano, and Tommy Dunbar, three guys who got close to major-league jobs but didn't quite make it. Any of the three could probably help a major-league team in a very limited role. The infielders included U. L. Washington, Slammin' Sammie Khalifa, and Houston Jimenez.

Catcher Mackey Sasser, acquired from the Giants, is a prospect but at a disadvantage in being too much like the incumbent, LaValliere. Both are left-handed-hitting singles hitters with good defensive skills. LaValliere hit .300 with 1 home run in the big show; Sasser hit .318 with 3 homers in the little show. That may keep Sasser, possibly the best player on the Vancouver team, from making the Pirates this year. Pitchers Mike Bielecki and Vicente Palacios definitely have a chance to stick, as does Bob Patterson, who was the Pirates opening-day starter (was too, was too) but wiped out; Patterson at Vancouver was 5–2 with a 2.12 ERA and 92 strikeouts in 89 innings.

At the lower levels there are more prospects, Tommy Gregg at Harrisburg (love him; think he's going to be Rookie of the Year in 1989), Brett Gideon at Harrisburg (canned heat), Tom Prince at Harrisburg (a right-handed Mackey Sasser), Tony Chance at Salem (do-everything outfielder; too early to tell but afraid he might strike out too much), Jeff King at Salem (number-one draft pick in the nation; only impressive asset is power), Mike York at Macon (pitcher; may burn him out by working him too hard at low levels), and Kevin Burdick at Watertown (where's Watertown?).

Can the Pirates move into contention in 1988? I doubt it. I think they have a good chance to finish over .500, but little chance to finish more than a few games over .500. I see two most-likely scenarios for the 1988 Pirates. One is that some of the young pitchers will have trouble getting untracked at the start of the 1988 season, just as Bob Kipper and Bob Patterson had trouble getting untracked at the start of the 1987 season, and will leave the pitching staff hitting on maybe three cylinders. They have so much depth among the young pitchers that when one guy doesn't do it, they can just try another one, but there are two categories of teams: those that are experimenting, and those that are competing. Under such a scenario, the Pirates would probably be put nearly out of the race in May or early June, but would probably get the pitching staff rebuilt in time to finish with 82 to 88 wins. The other likely scenario is that the Pirates will jump into the race with both feet, and could lead the race as late as August 15. After that, however, the underlying weaknesses of the Pirate team and their lack of communal experience are likely to surface, and the Pirates will fade and finish with 84 to 90 wins.

Sam Reich, a friend of mine who is a long-term Pirates fan, reminds me regularly that young pitchers will break your heart. I call it Sam's Law: Young pitchers will break your heart. One can understand how a Pirate fan would come to that position; without any exaggeration and without trying to be funny, I don't think the Pirates have had a pitcher who was a career rotation anchor, a guy who could start 30 times a year for ten or twelve years, since Bob Friend (1951–1965). They've had a lot of guys, from Bob Veale to Steve Blass to John Candelaria to Rick Rhoden, who gave them a few good years.

Anyway, in 1988, Sam's team is a test of Sam's Law. For the Pirates to contend, four out of five young pitchers must continue to pitch well. It can happen, but the odds are against it. Even if they do, the Pirates still have no true cleanup hitter. With the acquisition of Van Slyke and the development of Barry Bonds, they're in better shape there than they were two years ago, when Johnny Ray and Tony Pena sometimes hit 3–4 for them with Sid Bream on deck, but there is still no Darryl Strawberry or Andre Dawson or Jack Clark here to be the first name you write into the lineup card. Mike LaValliere was almost certainly over his head in 1987, and Van Slyke may also have been. I don't see that they have solved their problem with left-handed pitchers. I don't think it's likely that the Pirates can win this thing before 1991.

WINNING PERCENTAGE ON GRASS FIELDS OVER THE LAST FIVE YEARS

Detroit	.587
Mets	.586
Yankees	.567
Boston	.527
Los Angeles	.527
Toronto	.517
Cubs	.514
White Sox	.513
Montreal	.512
San Diego	.512
California	.507
Milwaukee	.502
St. Louis	.502
Baltimore	.501
San Francisco	.497
Oakland	.481
Texas	.477
Cincinnati	.464
Atlanta	.463
Kansas City	.463
Houston	.456
Cleveland	.438
Philadelphia	.424
Seattle	.401
Minnesota	.394
Pittsburgh	.386

RUNS SCORED AND ALLOWED WINS AND LOSSES

Wins	477	213	80-0	1.000
Pitchers' Duels	70	50	18-13	.581
Home Games	404	363	47-34	.580
Dunne	91	84	13-10	.565
Fisher	119	108	14-12	.538
One-Run Games	170	170	21-21	.500
Kipper	89	105	10-10	.500
All Games	723	744	80-82	.494
Reuschel	111	103	12-13	.480
Blowouts	229	244	21-23	.477
Drabek	123	130	12-16	.429
Slugfests	341	394	22-31	.415
Road Games	319	381	33-48	.407
Losses	246	531	0-82	.000

TEN BEST STARTS

	IP	H	R	ER	BB	SO		
Dunne vs. Cin, Aug 25	9	2	0	0	1	7	W	89
Kipper at Chi, Apr 16	9	4	0	0	1	8	W	86
Drabek vs. Hous, Aug 30	9	3	0	0	2	7	W	86
Fisher at StL, Sep 23	9	2	0	0	4	6	W	85
Bielecki vs. Mon, Sep 15	9	3	1	0	0	6	W	85
Reuschel vs. Chi, June 27	9	4	0	0	2	6	W	83
Fisher at Phil, Sep 13	9	5	1	1	2	10	W	81
Dunne vs. Phil, July 30	8	3	0	0	2	7	—	81
Reuschel at SF, July 22	9	5	0	0	1	4	W	80
Reuschel at Atl, June 2	9	2	1	1	4	5	W	80

PITCHERS WHEN SUPPORTED BY THREE TO FIVE RUNS

	G	IP	W-L	Pct	SO	BB	ERA
Reuschel	12	89	5-2	.714	42	24	2.22
Dunne	12	81	6-4	.600	33	29	4.35
Drabek	15	90	6-6	.500	66	22	4.08
Fisher	10	60	3-3	.500	35	31	4.35
Kipper	7	35	3-3	.500	25	18	5.45

AVERAGE AGE OF 1987 REGULARS

Houston	32.1
Detroit	31.3
Yankees	30.4
California	30.1
Atlanta	29.2
San Francisco	29.2
St. Louis	29.0
Kansas City	29.0
Minnesota	28.9
Cubs	28.9
Cincinnati	28.6
Philadelphia	28.2
Baltimore	28.2
Toronto	27.9
Oakland	27.9
Montreal	27.5
Mets	27.5
White Sox	27.4
Boston	27.4
Los Angeles	27.2
Texas	27.1
Cleveland	26.9
Seattle	26.4
Milwaukee	25.7
San Diego	25.6
Pittsburgh	24.8

HALL OF FAME WATCH

Long way to go: U.L. Washington 7, LaValliere 5.5, Leyland 5, Walk 4, Bonilla 2.5, Bream 1, Van Slyke 1, Fisher 1, J. Robinson 1.

TEN WORST STARTS

	IP	H	R	ER	BB	SO		
Dunne at Phil, June 29	5⅓	7	9	9	4	4	L	18
Patterson at SD, May 5	1⅔	5	6	6	3	1	L	19
Kipper vs. NY, Apr 21	3*	7	6	6	3	2	L	20
Dunne at NY, Sep 27	3⅔	8	6	6	3	3	L	21
Fisher vs. NY, Sep 18	2*	4	6	6	2	0	—	22
Dunne vs. Mon, June 25	3⅔	8	5	5	4	2	L	23
Fisher at Atl, June 4	3⅓	7	6	4	4	1	L	23
Patterson vs. NY, Apr 22	4⅔	7	6	6	3	2	L	23
Bielecki vs. NY, Sep 20	5*	9	6	6	2	0	—	23
Kipper at SF, July 21	2⅔	6	5	5	2	0	L	24

Mike LAVALLIERE, Catcher
Runs Created: 50

	G	AB	Hit	2B	3B	HR	Run	RBI	TBB	SO	SB	CS	Avg
1.54 years		444	116	19	1	3	34	47	57	48	0	1	.261
1987	121	340	102	19	0	1	33	36	43	32	0	0	.300
First Half	71	198	58	12	0	0	21	20	28	20	0	0	.293
Second Half	50	142	44	7	0	1	12	16	15	12	0	0	.310
Vs. RHP		263	85	15	0	1	29	30	34	19	0	0	.323
Vs. LHP		77	17	4	0	0	4	6	9	13	0	0	.221
Home	63	174	53	8	0	1	15	21	21	16	0	0	.305
Road	58	166	49	11	0	0	18	15	22	16	0	0	.295

RJ REYNOLDS, Left Field
Runs Created: 46

	G	AB	Hit	2B	3B	HR	Run	RBI	TBB	SO	SB	CS	Avg
2.69 years		509	136	30	4	9	68	65	42	95	22	7	.267
1987	117	335	87	24	1	7	47	51	34	80	14	1	.260
First Half	68	199	58	16	1	4	32	29	19	41	8	1	.291
Second Half	49	136	29	8	0	3	15	22	15	39	6	0	.213
Vs. RHP		278	67	22	1	7	42	41	29	78	14	1	.241
Vs. LHP		57	20	2	0	0	5	10	5	2	0	0	.351
Home	61	172	46	15	1	2	22	23	15	40	7	1	.267
Road	56	163	41	9	0	5	25	28	19	40	7	0	.252

Sid BREAM, First Base
Runs Created: 66

	G	AB	Hit	2B	3B	HR	Run	RBI	TBB	SO	SB	CS	Avg
2.44 years		511	134	30	3	14	64	70	55	73	9	7	.262
1987	149	516	142	25	3	13	64	65	49	69	9	8	.275
First Half	79	280	81	15	3	9	34	32	28	38	5	4	.289
Second Half	70	236	61	10	0	4	30	33	21	31	4	4	.258
Vs. RHP		323	89	16	2	5	42	38	37	40	7	4	.276
Vs. LHP		193	53	9	1	8	22	27	12	29	2	4	.275
Home	75	259	73	14	2	10	38	43	27	28	6	5	.282
Road	74	257	69	11	1	3	26	22	22	41	3	3	.268

Andy VAN SLYKE, Center Field
Runs Created: 108

	G	AB	Hit	2B	3B	HR	Run	RBI	TBB	SO	SB	CS	Avg
4.19 years		495	133	27	8	15	71	68	62	95	33	8	.269
1987	157	564	165	36	11	21	93	82	56	122	34	8	.293
First Half	82	283	83	17	6	13	44	47	27	65	21	6	.293
Second Half	75	281	82	19	5	8	49	35	29	57	13	2	.292
Vs. RHP		335	112	26	6	18	62	56	38	66	21	7	.334
Vs. LHP		229	53	10	5	3	31	26	18	56	13	1	.231
Home	79	278	76	15	4	11	50	46	35	56	17	5	.273
Road	78	286	89	21	7	10	43	36	21	66	17	3	.311

Johnny RAY, Second Base
Runs Created: 71

	G	AB	Hit	2B	3B	HR	Run	RBI	TBB	SO	SB	CS	Avg
5.93 years		616	178	36	4	6	73	68	44	37	11	7	.289
1987	153	599	173	30	3	5	64	69	44	46	4	2	.289
First Half	86	336	89	13	2	4	35	43	29	30	3	1	.265
Second Half	67	263	84	17	1	1	29	26	15	16	1	1	.319
Vs. RHP		361	110	21	3	3	46	49	25	26	3	2	.305
Vs. LHP		238	63	9	0	2	18	20	19	20	1	0	.265
Home	73	275	83	11	1	5	33	41	24	22	0	1	.302
Road	80	324	90	19	2	0	31	28	20	24	4	1	.278

Barry BONDS, Right Field
Runs Created: 93

	G	AB	Hit	2B	3B	HR	Run	RBI	TBB	SO	SB	CS	Avg
1.62 years		595	146	37	7	25	106	66	73	117	42	10	.245
1987	150	551	144	34	9	25	99	59	54	88	32	10	.261
First Half	84	328	82	18	6	13	55	34	35	54	20	5	.250
Second Half	66	223	62	16	3	12	44	25	19	34	12	5	.278
Vs. RHP		345	97	21	4	17	64	38	34	46	21	9	.281
Vs. LHP		206	47	13	5	8	35	21	20	42	11	1	.228
Home	75	268	71	15	6	12	46	31	22	50	12	5	.265
Road	75	283	73	19	3	13	53	28	32	38	20	5	.258

Bobby BONILLA, Third Base?
Runs Created: 78

	G	AB	Hit	2B	3B	HR	Run	RBI	TBB	SO	SB	CS	Avg
1.72 years		519	145	28	4	10	66	70	59	88	6	6	.279
1987	141	466	140	33	3	15	58	77	39	64	3	5	.300
First Half	75	222	65	15	1	7	25	30	15	24	3	3	.293
Second Half	66	244	75	18	2	8	33	47	24	40	0	2	.307
Vs. RHP		232	68	19	1	8	34	36	25	43	1	2	.293
Vs. LHP		234	72	14	2	7	24	41	14	21	2	3	.308
Home	71	223	59	14	1	7	33	33	20	27	2	1	.265
Road	70	243	81	19	2	8	25	44	19	37	1	4	.333

Darnell COLES, Third Base?
Runs Created: 30

	G	AB	Hit	2B	3B	HR	Run	RBI	TBB	SO	SB	CS	Avg
2.08 years		521	125	27	2	15	64	68	54	88	4	5	.240
1987	93	268	54	13	1	10	34	39	34	43	1	4	.201
First Half	44	128	22	5	1	3	11	14	14	19	0	1	.172
Second Half	49	140	32	8	0	7	23	25	20	24	1	3	.229
Vs. RHP		114	23	5	1	2	11	14	12	22	0	1	.202
Vs. LHP		154	31	8	0	8	23	25	22	21	1	3	.201
Home	50	141	33	7	0	8	22	27	19	22	0	1	.234
Road	43	127	21	6	1	2	12	12	15	21	1	3	.165

Al PEDRIQUE, Shortstop
Runs Created: 30

	G	AB	Hit	2B	3B	HR	Run	RBI	TBB	SO	SB	CS	Avg
0.57 years		442	130	18	2	2	42	47	33	51	9	7	.294
1987	93	252	74	10	1	1	24	27	19	29	5	4	.294
First Half	32	64	15	2	1	0	5	4	4	14	2	1	.234
Second Half	61	188	59	8	0	1	19	23	15	15	3	3	.314
Vs. RHP		117	34	6	1	1	12	17	8	17	0	2	.291
Vs. LHP		135	40	4	0	0	12	10	11	12	5	2	.296
Home	49	133	41	5	0	0	16	12	9	14	4	2	.308
Road	44	119	33	5	1	1	8	15	10	15	1	2	.277

Jim MORRISON, Third Base?
Runs Created: 52

	G	AB	Hit	2B	3B	HR	Run	RBI	TBB	SO	SB	CS	Avg
6.26 years		513	135	26	3	18	57	66	32	79	8	5	.263
1987	130	465	116	23	2	13	56	65	29	83	10	6	.249
First Half	81	301	82	21	1	9	36	44	22	50	7	5	.272
Second Half	49	164	34	2	1	4	20	21	7	33	3	1	.207
Vs. RHP		275	64	14	1	7	31	37	7	52	6	1	.233
Vs. LHP		190	52	9	1	6	25	28	22	31	4	5	.274
Home	61	216	57	12	1	7	29	28	15	37	8	2	.264
Road	69	249	59	11	1	6	27	37	14	46	2	4	.237

PHILADELPHIA PHILLIES

In 1987 the Phillies were the only National League team with two players among the top ten in runs created, those being Hayes (113) and Schmidt (111). Samuel just missed the leaders, with 109. In spite of that, the Phillies were ninth in the National League in runs scored.

The Philadelphia offense is a riddle. Does this look like a bad offense, to you? First baseman Von Hayes hit .277 with 21 homers, 121 walks. Second baseman Juan Samuel hit .272 with 28 homers, 100 RBI, and 35 stolen bases, certainly not substandard output for his position. At third base a fellow named Mike Schmidt hit .293 with 35 homers, 113 RBI. Left fielder Chris James hit .294 with 17 homers, 54 RBI in a half-season. He inherited the job from Mike Easler, who had defensive problems but didn't hit all that bad. Center fielder Milt Thompson hit .302 with 42 extra base hits, 46 stolen bases. Right fielder Glenn Wilson hit .264 with 14 homers, 54 RBI, not a good year for him but not all that bad. Catcher Lance Parrish hit 17 homers and drove in 67 runs, among the best figures by a National League catcher. The shortstop didn't hit, but everybody's got one dud. It looks like it should add up to a pretty fair offense.

It didn't. The Phillies scored only 702 runs, 29 below average. What went wrong? Why didn't they score more runs?

I compared each Philadelphia regular to the league average, based on runs created per out. Mike Schmidt, still the Phillies top offensive player, created about 36 runs more than an average NL third baseman with the same number of outs (+36). The four regular infielders put the Phillies about 72 runs ahead of the National League average; relative to the league they were +24 (Hayes), +19 (Samuel), +36 (Schmidt), and −7 (Jeltz), a total of +72.

Philadelphia outfielders, however, were +9 (James), +5 (Thompson), and −32 (Glenn Wilson), a total of −18. This is unfair to Wilson in a way because National League right fielders had a big year (Dawson, Murphy, Parker, Gwynn, Strawberry, Bonds); unfair, but still helpful in an explanatory sense. Part of the Phillies' problem was the lack of big hitting outfielder.

Catcher Lance Parrish was −1, so that cuts the team total to +53. We are still, however, +53 in our totals for a team that actually scored 29 runs less than the NL average. We have an 82-run discrepancy, which is a statistical way of framing the same statement: what should have been a good offense, wasn't.

There is a method irregularity which explains a little bit of the gap. I was comparing only the Phillies regulars to the averages for the whole league, regulars and irregulars. Most irregulars, all over the league, are below average; that's why they're not regulars. By counting only the regulars, we would make an average team above average—or, conversely, by counting the number-two shortstop (Aguayo) and the number-two third baseman (Rich Schu), we would subtract runs from the Phillies. How many? A good estimate would be about 25 for an average team.

The Philly irregulars, however, were highly irregular. In 1986 the Phillies had a good bench. In 1987, it was Greg Gross and pray. Schu didn't have a good year, Aguayo hit .206, Daulton .194, Roenicke .167, Russell .145. Jeff Stone hit .256 with one homer, secondary average below .200. Philadelphia pinch hitters hit .233 and drove in only 21 runs, the fewest of any National League team. Whereas there might have been a 25-run loss for another team when the regulars were out, that loss in the case of Philadelphia might have been more in the range of 40 runs.

Then you get to the Philadelphia pitchers, who at a glance had to be among the worst in the league. Their four starters were Don Carman (.082), Kevin Gross (.190), Shane Rawley (.182), and Bruce Ruffin (.055). Most teams have one starter who can hit a little, like Bob Forsch (.298) or Jamie Moyer (.230) or Rick Aguilera (.225). Batting averages over .200 for a starter are probably more common than those under .100. Even Dan Schatzeder went 2 for 12 last year, all singles. Probable loss compared to other team's pitchers: 5 to 8 runs.

Finally, there is offensive dysfunction. The Phillies "created" 736 runs, but scored only 702.

So that's my solution:

1) The Phillies lacked an outstanding power-hitting outfielder.

2) The Philadelphia bench was awful.

3) Philadelphia pitchers were unusually weak as hitters.

4) There was an offensive dysfunction, a failure of the team to add up to the sum of the parts.

Neither Felske nor Elia ever found a lineup that met the needs of the Philadelphia offense. Felske often had Mike Schmidt batting behind Samuel (on-base percentage of .335), and ahead of Von Hayes (on-base percentage of .404). Elia recognized this problem, and experimented with Hayes batting second. But then Samuel was still hitting ahead of Schmidt, and not much of anybody was hitting fifth, Glenn Wilson or somebody, so that didn't work out. Then Elia moved Hayes into the third spot and batted Juan Samuel leadoff. Now you've got a leadoff man with a .335 on-base percentage and 100-RBI potential. Chris James got hot, so he moved James into the number-three spot, with Schmidt fourth and Hayes fifth. James had an on-base percentage of .344, not much better than Samuel, so that had all the worst features of the other efforts—nobody on base for Schmidt, nobody to drive in Hayes, who was the best man on the team at getting on base. Then Parrish started to hit a little, and they went back to plan R, with Parrish hitting fifth (Samuel/Thompson/Hayes/Schmidt/Parrish). I left out any number of intermediate steps.

In road games, the Phillies scored just 317 runs, missing by just three the lowest total of any major league team.

Phil Bradley has been brought in now to play left field, and there may be additional personnel changes; Steve Jeltz doesn't exactly have a lock on the shortstop job. In the last five years, the Phillies have used 25 players as regulars, more than any other major-league team. (See charts page. In this study, the nine players who had the most plate appearances each season were counted as regulars. If a team used nine new players each year, that would be 45 players; if they used one lineup all five years, that would be 9.) Introducing 16 new players in four years, the Phillies have been adding four new regulars a year, turning over nearly half of the lineup. The 25 players, just to refresh your memory, are first basemen Pete Rose, Len Matuszek, and Von Hayes, second basemen Joe Morgan and Juan Samuel, third basemen Mike Schmidt and Rich Schu, shortstops Ivan DeJesus, Tom Foley, Louis Aguayo, and Steve Jeltz, outfielders Ron Roenicke, Garry Maddox, Chris James, Gary Matthews, Glenn Wilson, Gary Redus, Joe Lefebvre, Sixto Lezcano, Jeff Stone, and Milt Thompson, catchers John Russell, Bo Diaz, Ozzie Virgil, and Lance Parrish. Obviously, the Phillies have been rebuilding in that period, but then so have a lot of other teams.

Anyway, Bradley will now be in left. Even assuming that Von Hayes stays at first base and counting Greg Gross as a pinch hitter, the Phillies have five or six outfield candidates—Milt Thompson, Chris James, Phil Bradley, Jeff Stone, John Russell, and possibly Keith Hughes. Probably James, the surprise of 1987, will take over in right field; perhaps the thinking was that the development of James had made Wilson's one outstanding tool, his throwing arm, less critical to the team, and thus made the player expendable. Keith Hughes had almost the same stats in AAA ball (.294, 17 homers, 54 RBI) that Chris James had in Philadelphia (.293, 17 homers, 54 RBI). Chris James was comparable to Schmidt and Hayes in terms of runs created per out, though he didn't quite match them, and of course he didn't play full time. James tied for the club lead in home runs against left-handed pitchers (9), and just missed leading the team in RBI against lefties with 26 (Schmidt had 27). Hughes and James were teammates in the Northwest League (1982), at Spartanburg in the Southern Atlantic League (1983), and at Reading (1983). They were almost dead even until Hughes went to the Yankees in the Shane Rawley trade, after which his career went awry as the Yankees used him to prove once again that they have equal respect for young ballplayer and box turtles trying to get across the highway. Somehow Hughes wound up back in the Phillie system last year, and has a chance to make the roster after hitting .263 in 76 late-season at bats; however, I thought I saw his name back on the Yankees roster at mid-winter, so maybe he has become a poor man's Ron Hassey or something.

The signing of Lance Parrish as a free agent failed to help the team. I've never been a big fan of Parrish's, which is not to deny that he was the best catcher in the American League for several years. Parrish had three outstanding skills—his home run power, his throwing arm, and his ability to block the plate. The latter two skills, combined with good agility behind the plate, won him three Gold Gloves. He also had some powerful negatives. A combination of low batting averages and few walks gave him a career on-base percentage under .320, which means that in the middle of the order he makes an awful lot of outs for the runs he produces. He doesn't accelerate well, even for a catcher, so he can ground into 20 double plays a year.

Last year he didn't throw well most of the year and had a slugging percentage of .399, one point less than R. J. Reynolds. That left him with one outstanding skill—blocking the plate. The Phillies had a 3.84 ERA with Darren Daulten as the starting catcher (34 games) as opposed to 4.24 with Parrish (123 games).

Parrish probably will have a better year in 1988. I doubt that he is capable of having a big year. Most catchers are destroyed by knee and back injuries. Parrish already has encountered the physical problems which are likely to end his career. In this thirties, with a lot of games already on his knees, his ability to contribute for more than a couple hundred games is very much in question. If the Phillies don't win this year, it becomes almost certain that in time the Phillies will look back at the decision to sign Parrish, and realize that it was costly both in terms of dollars and in terms of the opportunity to develop talent.

I never got a handle of John Felske; when he left, I didn't have any better idea what to expect of him than I did when he was hired. I don't really know why he was hired or why he was fired. The impression was created in the media, whether fairly or unfairly, that Mike Schmidt had undermined Felske's authority by publicly second-guessing him.

A year ago, it appeared to me that the Phillies were on the verge of reemerging as contenders in this division. Despite the additions of Lance Parrish and Phil Bradley, who I feel is a tremendous player, and despite the emergence of Steve Bedrosian as the National League's top relief pitcher, they seem now to be further away than they were then.

The one biggest problem, I think, is the lack of an outstanding starting pitcher. This division is much stronger than the West, so to have a good chance to win the Phillies have to win at least 95 games. It's hard to do that without a rotation anchor, without a pitcher who is ten games or more over .500. Philadelphia starting pitchers in 1987 won just 53 games; they were a collective 53–64 with a 4.59 ERA. Philadelphia starters struck out only 514 men, the fewest of any major-league team. Their bullpen was outstanding, including not only Bedrosian but also Jeff Calhoun (1.48 ERA in 42 games), Kent Tekulve (major league leader with 90 games), and Mike Jackson, and that improved the totals of the Phillie pitchers from very poor to slightly below average, tenth in the league in strikeouts instead of last (877), seventh in the league in ERA instead of tenth or eleventh. Apart from Shane Rawley's 17 wins, the records of the four Philly starters (Carman, Ruffin, Rawley, and Gross), are indistinguishable—4.39 ERA in 35 starts, 4.37 in 33 starts, 4.35 in 35 starts, 4.22 in 35 starts. Among their starting four nobody is a strikeout pitcher. Nobody has serious control problems. Nobody has outstanding control. Rawley won 17 games because the Phillies scored almost five runs a game for him, far more than for the other three guys. It's hard to win a title with a bunch of guys like that.

That's why I think the key to this team in 1988 might be Don Carman. Carman has been working on the Gus Hoefling strength program for a couple of years now, and he may be ready to have an outstanding year. He's had a lot of games in the last year and a half when he was near perfect (see list of best games by Philadelphia starters). He led the Phillies in strikeouts (125) and also had the best control record among the four. He hasn't been consistent enough to make people notice him yet, but he's the only pitcher I see who seems capable of leading the Phillies to the pennant.

In the games they won, the Phillies won by an average of 2.8 runs, the smallest margin of victory in the major leagues. That stat is primarily due to the bullpen, which enabled the Phillies to win a lot of games by narrow margins. The other side of that is that if they aren't as good this year, the Phillies could start losing those games. Bedrosian may have saved the Phillies from having a disastrous season.

Looking ahead to 1988, you have to be concerned about the Phillies' failure to contend in 1987 although so many players were having good to excellent seasons. You also have to believe that this team is capable of playing a lot better than they did last year. With Bradley, Hayes, and Schmidt, the Phillies should have a ton of people on base, although designing a lineup that works remains a challenge. Leaving Mike Jackson and defense out of it, Phil Bradley for Glen Wilson is a terrific trade; it has to make the Philadelphia offense 30 runs better. There is so much talent here that it seems safe to assume that the Phillies will improve offensively relative to the league.

If Carman has a big year, if Schmidt doesn't grow old, if the offense works as well as it ought to, if Bedrosian stays strong, if the Mets don't win 105 games . . . well, sure, the Phillies can win. With the Cardinals and Expos both probably down this year, with the Pirates probably not ready to contend all year, I might go so far as to pick the Phillies second. But there's an awful lot of things that are going to have to go right for them to win it.

NUMBER OF REGULARS USED IN THE LAST FIVE YEARS

Philadelphia	25
San Francisco	24
Pittsburgh	24
Seattle	24
Montreal	22
Milwaukee	22
White Sox	22
Kansas City	22
Baltimore	21
Boston	21
Yankees	21
Oakland	21
Texas	21
Atlanta	21
Cincinnati	20
San Diego	20
Cleveland	19
Mets	19
Los Angeles	19
Detroit	18
Minnesota	18
Cubs	17
Houston	17
St. Louis	17
California	17
Toronto	14

RUNS SCORED AND ALLOWED WINS AND LOSSES

Wins	467	246	80-0	1.000
Rawley	177	153	23-13	.639
One-Run Games	188	182	27-21	.563
Home Games	385	373	43-38	.531
Carman	159	164	18-17	.514
Pitchers' Duels	84	73	20-19	.513
All Games	702	749	80-82	.494
Slugfests	355	385	25-27	.481
Road Games	317	376	37-44	.457
Ruffin	136	160	15-20	.429
K Gross	118	150	14-19	.424
Blowouts	196	246	14-23	.378
Losses	235	503	0-82	.000

TEN BEST STARTS

	IP	H	R	ER	BB	SO		
Carman vs. NY, Sep 29	9	1	0	0	0	5	W	90
Carman vs. SD, May 16	9	3	0	0	1	5	W	85
Carman at StL, Aug 13	9	3	2	0	4	7	—	80
Rawley vs. SF, Aug 26	9	4	2	2	2	10	L	79
Ruffin at Chi, Sep 23	9	6	0	0	1	5	W	79
Jackson vs. Mon, June 7	8⅔	2	1	1	4	6	W	78
Ruffin at Hous, July 19	9	5	1	1	0	3	W	76
Rawley vs. Mon, Apr 29	9	6	0	0	4	4	W	75
Gross at LA, May 30	9	7	0	0	1	3	W	75
Rawley at StL, June 23	8	4	1	1	3	4	W	71

PITCHERS WHEN SUPPORTED BY THREE TO FIVE RUNS

	G	IP	W-L	Pct	SO	BB	ERA
Carman	16	98	8-4	.667	61	34	4.32
Rawley	20	132	11-6	.647	70	47	4.23
Gross	17	102	6-7	.462	56	38	4.85
Ruffin	14	78	4-6	.400	41	24	4.06

HALL OF FAME WATCH

Fully qualified: Mike Schmidt 251; **Building credentials but not yet viable candidate:** Tekulve 60, Parrish 49; **Working on it:** Samuel 25, Bedrosian 19, G Gross 13.5, Hayes 13; **Long way to go:** Wilson 7, Bair 6, Felske 5, Elia 5, Thompson 2.5, K Gross 2, Rawley 2, Carman 1, Cowley 1.

STRIKOUTS BY STARTING PITCHERS

Houston	824
Los Angeles	804
Texas	738
Boston	736
Detroit	724
Milwaukee	694
Kansas City	686
Mets	685
Cubs	656
Minnesota	652
Seattle	647
Montreal	644
Toronto	636
Oakland	635
San Francisco	596
California	588
Pittsburgh	580
White Sox	563
Cincinnati	557
Atlanta	550
Baltimore	540
Yankees	538
San Diego	526
St. Louis	521
Cleveland	520
Philadelphia	514

TEN WORST STARTS

	IP	H	R	ER	BB	SO		
Gross at NY, Aug 5	4*	11	10	10	2	1	L	−1
Rawley at Mon, Sep 19	1	4	8	8	3	0	L	10
Rawley at Mon, June 12	4*	11	7	7	1	1	L	12
Carman vs. StL, June 8	3*	7	7	7	4	0	L	13
Gross at Pit, Oct 3	3*	7	6	6	3	1	L	19
Cowley vs. Chi, Apr 11	⅔	3	7	4	4	0	L	20
Carman vs. Pit, Sep 12	1⅔	4	6	6	3	1	L	21
Ruffin vs. SF, Aug 24	3⅔	9	5	5	2	1	L	22
Carman at Cin, July 7	1⅔	5	5	5	3	0	—	22
Cowley vs. NY, Apr 16	1*	4	5	5	4	1	L	22

Lance PARRISH, Catcher
Runs Created: 53

	G	AB	Hit	2B	3B	HR	Run	RBI	TBB	SO	SB	CS	Avg
7.88 years		601	157	28	3	29	79	97	48	121	3	4	.261
1987	130	466	114	21	0	17	42	67	47	104	0	1	.245
First Half	72	257	60	10	0	9	25	40	21	56	0	0	.233
Second Half	58	209	54	11	0	8	17	27	26	48	0	1	.258
Vs. RHP		328	72	17	0	11	23	51	26	74	0	0	.220
Vs. LHP		138	42	4	0	6	19	16	21	30	0	1	.304
Home	65	234	59	17	0	5	21	34	24	59	0	0	.252
Road	65	232	55	4	0	12	21	33	23	45	0	1	.237

Chris JAMES, Left Field
Runs Created: 66

	G	AB	Hit	2B	3B	HR	Run	RBI	TBB	SO	SB	CS	Avg
0.81 years		499	146	28	7	22	65	73	35	99	4	1	.293
1987	115	358	105	20	6	17	48	54	27	67	3	1	.293
First Half	55	138	43	10	1	7	23	22	9	31	2	0	.312
Second Half	60	220	62	10	5	10	25	32	18	36	1	1	.282
Vs. RHP		209	63	10	3	8	27	28	16	41	3	1	.301
Vs. LHP		149	42	10	3	9	21	26	11	26	0	0	.282
Home	59	172	52	10	3	9	28	31	18	33	2	1	.302
Road	56	186	53	10	3	8	20	23	9	34	1	0	.285

Von HAYES, First Base
Runs Created: 113

	G	AB	Hit	2B	3B	HR	Run	RBI	TBB	SO	SB	CS	Avg
5.78 years		568	157	31	5	16	84	78	70	121	29	11	.276
1987	158	556	154	36	5	21	84	84	84	77	16	7	.277
First Half	82	273	84	21	3	13	47	47	71	39	11	6	.308
Second Half	76	283	70	15	2	8	37	37	50	38	5	1	.247
Vs. RHP		388	115	28	4	18	62	63	86	46	15	6	.296
Vs. LHP		168	39	8	1	3	22	21	35	31	1	1	.232
Home	80	278	70	14	3	14	50	51	71	30	5	3	.252
Road	78	278	84	22	2	7	34	33	50	47	11	4	.302

Milt THOMPSON, Center Field
Runs Created: 85

	G	AB	Hit	2B	3B	HR	Run	RBI	TBB	SO	SB	CS	Avg
2.12 years		522	150	19	6	7	74	36	41	92	42	9	.287
1987	150	527	159	26	9	7	86	43	42	87	46	10	.302
First Half	77	286	76	13	7	3	54	17	24	49	22	5	.266
Second Half	73	241	83	13	2	4	32	26	18	38	24	5	.344
Vs. RHP		443	141	23	9	7	78	41	34	73	45	7	.318
Vs. LHP		84	18	3	0	0	8	2	8	14	1	3	.214
Home	75	270	89	16	7	3	51	24	24	48	26	3	.330
Road	75	257	70	10	2	4	35	19	18	39	20	7	.272

Juan SAMUEL, Second Base
Runs Created: 109

	G	AB	Hit	2B	3B	HR	Run	RBI	TBB	SO	SB	CS	Avg
3.98 years		672	181	35	15	20	106	82	38	158	52	16	.269
1987	160	655	178	37	15	28	113	100	60	162	35	15	.272
First Half	86	340	93	19	6	16	62	57	36	77	21	9	.274
Second Half	74	315	85	18	9	12	51	43	24	85	14	6	.270
Vs. RHP		474	133	28	11	19	83	75	35	115	23	12	.281
Vs. LHP		181	45	9	4	9	30	25	25	47	12	3	.249
Home	81	320	92	22	10	15	63	55	40	73	24	8	.288
Road	79	335	86	15	5	13	50	45	20	89	11	7	.257

Glenn WILSON, Right Field
Runs Created: 62

	G	AB	Hit	2B	3B	HR	Run	RBI	TBB	SO	SB	CS	Avg
5.12 years		572	154	29	4	14	63	72	34	93	5	3	.269
1987	154	569	150	21	2	14	55	54	38	82	3	6	.264
First Half	84	314	92	12	2	12	39	34	21	44	3	4	.293
Second Half	70	255	58	9	0	2	16	20	17	38	0	2	.227
Vs. RHP		414	108	14	2	12	41	42	29	67	3	5	.261
Vs. LHP		155	42	7	0	2	14	12	9	15	0	1	.271
Home	78	278	70	8	1	5	27	28	28	37	1	4	.252
Road	76	291	80	13	1	9	28	26	10	45	2	2	.275

Mike SCHMIDT, Third Base
Runs Created: 111

	G	AB	Hit	2B	3B	HR	Run	RBI	TBB	SO	SB	CS	Avg
13.91 years		562	151	27	4	38	103	108	103	131	12	7	.269
1987	147	522	153	28	0	35	88	113	83	80	2	1	.293
First Half	72	251	73	12	0	19	47	58	41	43	0	1	.291
Second Half	75	271	80	16	0	16	41	55	42	37	2	0	.295
Vs. RHP		389	109	19	0	28	64	86	55	69	2	0	.280
Vs. LHP		133	44	9	0	7	24	27	28	11	0	1	.331
Home	74	260	89	18	0	15	49	67	43	38	2	1	.342
Road	73	262	64	10	0	20	39	46	40	42	0	0	.244

Mike EASLER, Designated Hitter
Runs Created: 34

	G	AB	Hit	2B	3B	HR	Run	RBI	TBB	SO	SB	CS	Avg
7.10 years		518	152	27	4	17	65	74	45	98	3	4	.293
1987	98	277	78	10	0	5	20	31	20	52	1	1	.282
First Half	57	183	51	7	0	1	12	14	14	29	1		.279
Second Half	41	94	27	3	0	4	8	17	6	23	0	0	.287
Vs. RHP		244	73	10	0	5	19	27	15	39	1	1	.299
Vs. LHP		33	5	0	0	0	1	4	5	13	0	0	.152
Home	57	159	50	7	0	3	14	19	12	29	1	0	.314
Road	41	118	28	3	0	2	6	12	8	23	0	1	.237

Steve JELTZ, Shortstop
Runs Created: 28

	G	AB	Hit	2B	3B	HR	Run	RBI	TBB	SO	SB	CS	Avg
2.40 years		418	90	10	5	0	44	28	58	91	4	3	.215
1987	114	293	68	9	6	0	37	12	39	54	1	2	.232
First Half	49	112	20	1	1	0	11	4	16	22	1	1	.179
Second Half	65	181	48	8	5	0	26	8	23	32	0	1	.265
Vs. RHP		213	54	6	4	0	29	5	30	38	1	2	.254
Vs. LHP		80	14	3	2	0	8	7	9	16	0	0	.175
Home	58	163	34	4	3	0	19	9	22	33	1	1	.209
Road	56	130	34	5	3	0	18	3	17	21	0	1	.262

CHICAGO CUBS

There are occasions in your professional life that make you think you're not making any progress. The election of Andre Dawson as the National League's MVP is one of mine. One of the ironies of editing the *Baseball Abstract* is that I am occasionally attacked for placing too much faith in baseball statistics and missing the other elements of the game, the things that "statistics can't measure." The reality is that the essential work of this book is to try to teach people *not* to trust statistics. It was never my idea that we needed to look more carefully at baseball statistics because statistics are the best way to look at baseball. It was my point, rather, that people *do* make judgments about baseball players primarily by statistics, not should but do, and because they do they need a better understanding of what those statistics really mean.

The selection as Most Valuable Player of Andre Dawson, who couldn't have been one of the thirty best players in the National League, is an excellent illustration of this. How did Dawson get to be the MVP? Obviously the decision was primarily based on statistics. Dawson led the National League in home runs and RBI, and the RBI count is the one largest factor in determining who wins the MVP vote. In the twenty years before 1987 (1967–1986), 18 of the 40 MVP Awards were won by players leading the league in RBI, while only seven went to batting champions. Just since 1983 five players have won the MVP Award while leading the league in RBI despite playing for teams which did not finish first. Playing for a championship team is nowhere near as large an aid in winning the MVP Award as is leading the league in RBI.

Now I'm certainly not suggesting that driving in runs is not an important function of a baseball player, or that RBI are not a meaningful statistic. I am suggesting that you would have a better chance to evaluate a player fairly if you looked at the entire statistical package, rather than one or two statistics:

1) Dawson's batting average, .287, was neither a positive nor a negative. Among the 36 regular National League outfielders, Dawson ranked nineteenth in batting average.

2) Dawson's on-base percentage, .328, was a major negative. Dawson drew only 32 walks, while striking out 103 times. His strikeout to walk ratio was one of the worst in baseball.

3) Dawson hit only 24 doubles and only 2 triples, both figures well below average. He stole eleven bases.

4) Despite the 49 homers, Dawson scored only 90 runs, meaning that he scored only 41 runs when not hitting a home run. This is a direct result of his failure to get on base consistently.

The way in which all of these things—the walks, the doubles, the batting average, and the home runs—can be evaluated along a common scale is to look at the impact of each on the number of runs scored by the team. Dawson created an estimated 111 runs, tenth in the National League. He made 463 outs. Of the nine men who created more runs for their team than Dawson, all nine did so while using fewer outs. All of the following people were more productive players, in terms of runs created per out, than Andre Dawson: Mike Aldrete, Jack Clark, Wil Clark, Kal Daniels, Eric Davis, Pedro Guerrero, Tony Gwynn, Von Hayes, Dion James, Chris James, Howard Johnson, John Kruk, Dale Murphy, Tim Raines, Randy Ready, Mike Schmidt, Darryl Strawberry, Tim Teufel, Andy Van Slyke, and Tim Wallach.

Dawson can be given credit for an additional eleven runs because he hit well with men in scoring position. That still wouldn't push him up near Dale Murphy or Tony Gwynn as an offensive player. This, however, is *without* adjusting for illusions of context. After you look at the entire statistical package, you need to look at the illusions that go into making a player's statistics what they are. Some ballparks are much easier to hit in than others. Dawson's statistics were tremendously inflated by playing in Wrigley Field. In Wrigley Field, Dawson hit .332 with 27 home runs. On the road, he hit .246 with 22 homers.

So why did he win the MVP Award? I know what some people will say. It wasn't Dawson's statistics, it was his leadership and his throwing arm. People will say that, but you know it isn't. You don't give an MVP for "leadership" on a last-place team. Half the time, the MVP Award goes to the league leader in RBI. That's not leadership; that's statistics. And if they really understood his statistics, they wouldn't have done it.

Well, enough about the stupid MVP Award. Let me introduce the Cubs with a few notes from the *Chicago Baseball Report* (P.O. Box 46074, Chicago, Illinois 60646):

• The Cubs, for the first time in memory, had a better record in night games (28–28) than in day games.

• Every team in the National League East last year had a winning record against the NL West, ranging from St. Louis (46–26) through the Phillies (38–34). The Cubs were 39–32 against the West, just 37–53 within their own division.

• The Cubs scored only 48 runs in the second inning. They averaged 90 runs per inning in runs 3 through 7, and upped that to 92 in the first inning (+2), then dropped to 48 (−42) in the second inning. Their best inning was the third, in which they scored 102 runs.

• The Cubs' leading hitter in road games was Jerry 20.6Mumphrey, at .379. Their leading hitter against left-handed pitchers was Dernier (.340), against right-handers Mumphrey (.338), in day games Dernier (.336) in night games Mumphrey (.410), with men in scoring position Dawson (.331), in the late innings of close games Dernier (.432).

• Reflecting the characteristics of Andre Dawson, the Cubs versus their opponents were +50 in home runs (209–159), but behind in every other area. They were −49 in hits (1475–1524), −24 in doubles (244–268), −10 in triples (33–43), −124 in walks (504–628), +40 in strikeouts (1064–1024) and −60 in stolen bases (109–169). Because of that, they were −80 in runs scored (720–800).

• With runners on third and less than two out, Cub hitters delivered the run 44 percent of the time; their opponents delivered 50 percent of the time.

• Lee Smith entered the game with a 1-run lead 13 times, and saved the game only 4 times, or 31 percent.

• Left-handed batters facing the Cubs hit .295. Right-handed hitters facing the Cubs hit .260.

• Opposition base stealers were 34 for 45 against Rick Sutcliffe, 34 for 41 when a stolen base attempt was charged, but Sutcliffe picked the runner off first four times. Runners against Ed Lynch were 4 for 11, the same against DiPino.

The Cubs in 1987 were above average at three positions—second base (Sandberg), center field (Martinez and Dernier), and right field (Dawson). They were decent in left field (Mumphrey, Palmeiro, and Dayett) and at catcher (Jody Davis). Keith Moreland at third base wasn't as bad as I thought he'd be, although he did make 28 errors, more than any other major-league player at any position. He got some balls up in the wind again; on the road he hit .244 with 8 homers, but at Wrigley he hit .290 with 19 homers and 55 RBI. The trouble spots were first base, where Leon Durham hit .204 with runners in scoring position, and shortstop. Shawon Dunston was hurt and didn't play particularly well when he wasn't.

Not hitting with men in scoring position was, apart from Dawson, a team-wide problem. The Cubs scored only 720 runs despite offensive totals which should create 789 runs, a massive 69-run shortfall. The Cubs finished fifth in the league in batting average and first in home runs, but eighth in runs scored. No other major-league team had an offensive shortfall remotely approaching that; indeed, if such problems were common, we would have to conclude that runs-created estimates don't work. The primary cause of this was the failure to hit with runners in scoring position. The Cubs as a team hit only .239 with runners in scoring position—Dunston, .234, Sandberg, .233, Moreland, .229, Durham, .204, Davis, .200, Palmeiro, .200, Sundberg, .179. Since the Cubs overall hit .264, they were down 25 points with men in scoring position, which cost them about 47 runs.

The Cubs lack of speed also may have contributed to their failure to score the expected number of runs. They were last in the National League in stolen bases, 109. Their team speed score, 4.4, was the lowest in the National League. It occurs to me in passing that since the Cubs are very low in both stolen bases and walks and missed their runs created by 69, and the Cardinals are very high in categories and overshot their runs created by 53, perhaps we ought to check to see if there is a synergistic value of stolen bases and walks together, not inherent in the value of either. Also due to the lack of speed, the Cubs defensive efficiency record (.675) was the poorest in the National League; there were an estimated 84 hits that dropped in among the Cub players that would probably have been outs on another team.

Traditions die hard in Chicago, even bad ones. When operation Greylord revealed that Chicago courtrooms were still a sewer of bribery and favoritism not much better than when the signed confessions of the Black Sox disappeared from a State Attorney's file cabinet 65 years ago, Studs Terkel complained that these Federal boys were messing around with a Chicago tradition, that this was just how things got done in Chicago. One gets the feeling that the Times-Mirror corporation feels the same way about the Cubs, that they've gotten along fine as losers for all these years so why bother to change anything, heh? It's hard to find anything good to say about an organization that dispatches a fine manager like Gene Michael and hires Mr. Potato Head to be their general manager. Despite their flash of glory, the Cubs have the twenty-third best record in baseball during the decade, and they're burrowing rapidly toward twenty-fourth.

The only thing this organization still has going for it is Harry. Meaningless game in early July, Sutcliffe is throwing repeatedly to first trying to take the lead away from Milt Thompson. All of sudden, early in the move, with the ball still in Sutcliffe's hand, Harry screams "He got him." (I played it back on the video tape several times, and I am certain; the ball is still in Sutcliffe's hand when Harry says the word "him.") Sure enough, Thompson is a tenth of a second late at first base; the ump signals out. So many announcers have no idea when the runner is safe or out even when the tag is made; they'll give you the impression that the umpire just makes a random out call once in awhile. Sure, Harry's had a stroke, he mixes up a player's name now and then—but what other announcer is so into the game that he will know the very instant when the pitcher has the runner by the throat. Bottom of the same inning, ground ball to third. Before the ball even gets to the third baseman, Harry says "they're going to nail the runner at the plate." And they do.

I do not mean to prejudge the abilities of Jim Frey as a general manager. His problems as a manager surface because he has trouble maintaining the respect of his players over a sustained period of time, a function less critical to his new challenge. But the Cubs obviously are not going to win anything with the talent on the 1987 roster. Virtually all of the Cubs' best players of 1987—Mumphrey, Dernier, Dawson, Lee Smith, Sutcliffe, Durham, Moreland, Davis—are well past the point of their careers at which there is any reasonable prospect of their getting better. They're just going to get worse. Sandberg is in his prime. Any improvement the Cubs make is going to have to come from trades, or from the farm system.

The Cubs apparently intend to replace Lee Smith either with Schiraldi or with Drew Hall, who was rated by Baseball America as the best pitching prospect in the American Association despite a 4.48 ERA in 35 games, with 45 walks in 66 innings. Lee Smith had a 4.93 ERA in the Texas League in 1979, too, but he got it straightened out pretty quick after that. I really think that Schiraldi is best suited to be a starter, but there is an immediate need for a relief ace here, and the odds are that Schiraldi will be put to work on it.

The big question about the Lee Smith trade seems to be not whether it was a good idea to trade Lee Smith, but whether the Cubs received value for him. Smith is 30, has worked hard for six years, carries a lot of weight, and has bad knees. A player like that belongs in a pennant race, not burning himself out a mile from where the action is.

But for Al Nipper? Shiraldi might get better, but the best he can do as a reliever is develop into Lee Smith.

So that leaves the farm system. According to *Baseball America,* the top two prospects in the Eastern League were Mark Grace, a first baseman, and Dwight Smith, an outfielder, both of the Cub system. A year ago Grace was regarded as the eighth-best prospect in the Midwest League, where he hit .342 with 15 homers and 95 RBI. Last year he had almost the same stats in AA ball, .333 with 17 and 101 (major-league equivalent .299 with 14 home runs). A teammate in both seasons was Dwight Smith, the Cubs' Ellis Burks. Although not listed as one of the top prospects in either league (he must have some serious defensive problems?), Smith seems to be an even better offensive prospect. In the Midwest League in 1986 he hit .310 (32 points below Grace) but had 11 homers, 11 triples, 59 walks, and 53 stolen bases, an attractive combination. At Pittsfield in 1987 he beat Grace in batting average (.337–.333), home runs (18–17), walks (67–48),

and stolen bases (60–5). He does strike out much more than Grace. Anyway, we can expect to see both of these gentlemen in Cub uniforms within two years, and I expect both to be successful hitters if given a full shot.

No prospect at AAA is of comparable stature; the top men were Palmeiro, who spent half the season in Chicago and belted 14 homers, and Drew Hall, discussed before, who pitched 21 times for the Cubs last year, with a 6.89 ERA. Iowa's double-play combination of Paul Noce and Luis Quinones both played very well, although neither is a highly regarded prospect. At lower levels there are other prospects, including catcher Joe Giradi (A ball) and pitcher Bill Danek (moved to AAA late in the year).

Despite their finishing last in 1987, I suspect that the Cubs have not yet hit bottom. When Grace, Smith and others are ready, the Cubs will have a chance. For the next two years, they will not contend, and they may be hard pressed to avoid a hundred losses.

WINNING PERCENTAGE FOLLOWING A WIN

Detroit	.629
Milwaukee	.604
Mets	.582
St. Louis	.579
Montreal	.571
Toronto	.562
Kansas City	.561
Philadelphia	.538
San Francisco	.528
Minnesota	.518
Boston	.507
Yankees	.506
Cincinnati	.506
Houston	.500
Pittsburgh	.494
California	.493
Texas	.493
Seattle	.481
Baltimore	.470
Los Angeles	.458
Oakland	.457
White Sox	.421
San Diego	.415
Atlanta	.406
Cubs	.405
Cleveland	.317

RUNS SCORED AND ALLOWED WINS AND LOSSES

Wins	433	179	76-0	1.000
Darwin	133	113	18-12	.600
Home Games	334	268	47-34	.580
Scott	132	122	19-17	.528
Slugfests	271	273	21-19	.525
Deshaies	116	108	13-12	.520
Blowouts	213	238	20-22	.476
All Games	648	678	76-86	.469
Pitchers' Duels	79	81	20-23	.465
One-Run Games	195	199	25-29	.463
Knepper	128	165	12-19	.414
Road Games	314	410	29-52	.358
Ryan	114	138	12-22	.353
Losses	215	499	0-86	.000

HALL OF FAME WATCH

Building credentials but not yet viable candidate: Dawson 67.5, Sundberg 67, Sandberg 61, Lee Smith 41, Sutcliffe 32; **Working on it:** Trillo 25, Mumphrey 13.5, J Davis 13; **Long way to go:** Luccesi 9, Moreland 8, Durham 5.5, Michael 5, Dernier 4.5, DiPino 3, Sanderson 2, Dunston 1, Noles 1.

TEN WORST STARTS

	IP	H	R	ER	BB	SO		
Moyer at Atl, Aug 20	5⅓	10	10	10	4	1	L	5
Moyer vs. SD, July 8	3	10	7	7	4	2	L	9
Sanderson vs. NY, June 10	2⅓	9	8	8	0	4	L	11
Trout at NY, June 25	3⅔	9	5	5	5	0	L	18
Lancaster at Phi, Aug 11	4	10	6	6	2	3	—	19
Maddux vs. NY, Aug 16	3⅔	6	7	7	5	4	L	20
Maddux at Phi, Apr 12	3⅓	9	6	6	1	4	—	21
Sanderson at Pit, Oct 1	4⅓	8	6	6	3	1	L	21
Sutcliffe vs. Hous, June 3	5	7	7	7	6	3	W	22
Moyer at Pit, Aug 5	4⅔	6	8	7	4	4	L	22

TEN BEST STARTS

	IP	H	R	ER	BB	SO		
Sutcliffe at StL, Sep 18	9	4	1	1	1	9	W	83
Sutcliffe vs. Mon, Apr 17	9	4	0	0	4	6	W	81
Trout vs. SD, July 6	9	4	0	0	3	5	W	81
Maddux at Mon, July 1	9	4	0	1	2	2	W	80
Trout vs. LA, July 11	9	6	0	0	0	3	W	78
Sutcliffe vs. Mon, Sep 13	9	5	2	1	2	7	W	76
Moyer at Phi, Apr 13	8*	2	2	2	6	12	W	76
Sutcliffe at NY, June 23	8⅔	4	1	1	2	5	W	75
Sanderson at Atl, Aug 19	7⅔	4	1	0	2	7	W	74
Sutcliffe vs. Atl, May 24	8	4	1	1	3	7	—	74

PITCHERS WHEN SUPPORTED BY THREE TO FIVE RUNS

	G	IP	W-L	Pct	SO	BB	ERA
Lancaster	9	57	3-1	.750	36	21	4.11
Stucliffe	14	99	7-3	.700	70	46	2.73
Moyer	12	76	6-3	.667	62	38	4.26
Maddux	8	44	2-4	.333	29	25	5.94
Sanderson	7	36	0-3	.000	23	13	6.19

WALKS BY STARTING PITCHERS

Montreal	266
California	295
Cincinnati	295
San Francisco	299
Yankees	335
Toronto	335
St. Louis	335
Boston	339
Baltimore	343
Milwaukee	345
Pittsburgh	346
Oakland	347
White Sox	351
Houston	352
Mets	358
Seattle	360
Minnesota	371
Philadelphia	381
San Diego	383
Detroit	393
Atlanta	395
Kansas City	398
Los Angeles	407
Cleveland	411
Cubs	418
Texas	520

Jody DAVIS, Catcher
Runs Created: 58

	G	AB	Hit	2B	3B	HR	Run	RBI	TBB	SO	SB	CS	Avg
5.57 years		551	139	27	2	21	59	78	50	107	1	2	.252
1987	125	428	106	12	2	19	57	51	52	91	1	2	.248
First Half	75	263	65	9	2	11	37	30	27	50	1	2	.247
Second Half	50	165	41	3	0	8	20	21	25	41	0	0	.248
Vs. RHP		321	79	10	1	14	41	40	41	72	0	2	.246
Vs. LHP		107	27	2	1	5	16	11	11	19	1	0	.252
Home	61	207	53	9	1	7	30	21	28	41	1	0	.256
Road	64	221	53	3	1	12	27	30	24	50	0	2	.240

Shawon DUNSTON, Shortstop
Runs Created: 32

	G	AB	Hit	2B	3B	HR	Run	RBI	TBB	SO	SB	CS	Avg
1.97 years		597	150	34	5	13	74	55	25	114	18	9	.251
1987	95	346	85	28	3	5	40	22	10	68	12	3	.246
First Half	62	240	62	15	2	5	32	17	6	52	9	1	.258
Second Half	33	106	23	3	1	0	8	5	4	16	3	2	.217
Vs. RHP		268	67	16	2	4	31	19	10	56	11	3	.250
Vs. LHP		78	18	2	1	1	9	3	0	12	1	0	.231
Home	52	181	40	8	2	3	20	15	5	32	9	2	.221
Road	43	165	45	10	1	2	20	7	5	36	3	1	.273

Leon DURHAM, First Base
Runs Created: 79

	G	AB	Hit	2B	3B	HR	Run	RBI	TBB	SO	SB	CS	Avg
6.14 years		562	157	30	6	23	83	85	70	105	17	10	.279
1987	131	439	120	22	1	27	70	63	51	92	2	2	.273
First Half	78	279	82	16	0	15	46	31	31	49	2	1	.294
Second Half	53	160	38	6	1	12	24	32	20	43	0	1	.238
Vs. RHP		365	101	19	1	25	60	55	48	73	2	2	.277
Vs. LHP		74	19	3	0	2	10	8	3	19	0	0	.257
Home	68	236	70	12	0	16	41	41	30	48	0	0	.297
Road	63	203	50	10	1	11	29	22	21	44	2	2	.246

Jerry MUMPHREY, Left Field
Runs Created: 66

	G	AB	Hit	2B	3B	HR	Run	RBI	TBB	SO	SB	CS	Avg
9.40 years		524	152	23	6	7	70	60	50	71	19	9	.290
1987	118	309	103	19	2	13	41	44	35	47	1	1	.333
First Half	64	175	56	9	0	7	22	27	19	26	0	1	.320
Second Half	54	134	47	10	2	6	19	17	16	21	1	1	.351
Vs. RHP		302	102	18	2	13	40	44	34	46	1	1	.338
Vs. LHP		7	1	1	0	0	1	0	1	1	0	0	.143
Home	59	156	45	8	1	7	24	23	19	23	0	0	.288
Road	59	153	58	11	1	6	17	21	16	24	1	1	.379

Ryne SANDBERG, Second Base
Runs Created: 89

	G	AB	Hit	2B	3B	HR	Run	RBI	TBB	SO	SB	CS	Avg
.69 years		645	186	31	7	16	101	71	53	92	36	9	.288
1987	132	523	154	25	2	16	81	59	59	79	21	2	.294
First Half	61	240	69	17	1	12	45	35	32	35	13	1	.288
Second Half	71	283	85	8	1	4	36	24	27	44	8	1	.300
Vs. RHP		409	119	16	2	14	63	46	38	63	16	2	.291
Vs. LHP		114	35	9	0	2	18	13	21	16	5	0	.307
Home	64	257	77	14	2	8	39	33	23	39	8	1	.300
Road	68	266	77	11	0	8	42	26	36	40	13	1	.289

Dave MARTINEZ, Center Field
Runs Created: 75

	G	AB	Hit	2B	3B	HR	Run	RBI	TBB	SO	SB	CS	Avg
1.20 years		473	124	16	8	8	69	36	53	98	17	8	.262
1987	142	459	134	18	8	8	70	36	57	96	16	8	.292
First Half	79	245	75	10	5	3	39	18	36	31	6	4	.306
Second Half	63	214	59	8	3	5	31	18	21	65	10	4	.276
Vs. RHP		436	128	18	8	7	68	35	55	88	16	8	.294
Vs. LHP		23	6	0	0	1	2	1	2	8	0	0	.261
Home	70	231	65	10	5	5	40	17	30	42	4	3	.281
Road	72	228	69	8	3	3	30	19	27	54	12	5	.303

Keith MORELAND, Third Base
Runs Created: 78

	G	AB	Hit	2B	3B	HR	Run	RBI	TBB	SO	SB	CS	Avg
6.42 years		568	160	27	2	17	66	88	52	65	4	4	.282
1987	153	563	150	29	1	27	63	88	39	66	3	3	.266
First Half	86	320	77	12	0	15	32	52	22	39	2	1	.241
Second Half	67	243	73	17	1	12	31	36	17	27	1	2	.300
Vs. RHP		441	114	19	1	24	47	71	24	51	1	2	.259
Vs. LHP		122	36	10	0	3	16	17	15	15	2	1	.295
Home	75	272	79	11	1	19	35	55	22	29	1	3	.290
Road	78	291	71	18	0	8	28	33	17	37	2	0	.244

Andre DAWSON, Right Field
Runs Created: 111

	G	AB	Hit	2B	3B	HR	Run	RBI	TBB	SO	SB	CS	Avg
9.85 years		634	178	32	7	28	93	99	39	101	27	9	.281
1987	153	621	178	24	2	49	90	137	32	103	11	3	.287
First Half	82	331	99	13	2	24	42	74	16	50	7	1	.299
Second Half	71	290	79	11	0	25	48	63	16	53	4	2	.272
Vs. RHP		480	136	19	2	40	69	107	22	81	9	2	.283
Vs. LHP		141	42	5	0	9	21	30	10	22	2	1	.298
Home	74	292	97	13	2	27	45	71	16	47	6	3	.332
Road	79	329	81	11	0	22	45	66	16	56	5	0	.246

Book Reviews

The *Baseball Abstract,* sparing no effort or expense in its determination to bring further enlightenment to the reading public, is for the first time including reviews of some of the past year's most notable baseball books.

Darkness at Noon (The Battle Over Night Baseball at Wrigley Field)
Mike Royko
University of Chicago Press, 286 pages, $19.95 ($14.95 when purchased during daylight hours)

More interesting, these days, than the Cubs performance on the field is the ongoing battle over installation of lights in the friendly confines. This is a controversy, as Royko points out in his inimitable manner, that has torn close-knit Chicago families asunder, much as the Dreyfus affair is said to have done in France. Indeed, police reports for the past two years not an otherwise inexplicable increase in intrafamily homicides, as well as a seemingly endless array of bar wars, the patrons dividing into vitriolic camps of "suns" and "lights." Even teenage gang warfare in the Windy City, it is rumored, has crossed racial and ethnic lines to become a battle between "days" and "nights."

Not surprisingly, Chicago's notoriously corrupt politics has played a major role in the controversy. At first, skittish aldermanic and mayoral candidates tried to straddle the ivy, so to speak, but inevitably were forced to take sides. An already volatile situation was made worse when both pro- and anti-abortion activists jumped into the fray. The anti-abortionists began holding protest marches and labeled themselves "right to lightsers," while the pro-abortionists, predictably, came out in favor of "choice" and called for a Supreme Court ruling. This moved the "right to lightsers" to contemplate a constitutional amendment mandating the installation of lights.

Against this hysteria, even the remnants of the old Democratic machine felt themselves powerless. The late Mayor Washington, after flip-flopping on the issue at least twice, found himself finally vituperated by all factions, and Royko, in his most shocking disclosure, reveals that not everyone in Chicago is convinced that the Mayor died of natural causes: foul play by right to lightsers, who have long threatened a terrorist campaign, is suspected by many. Into this whirlwind stepped a newly appointed Mayor, and as the book went to press, his promise to appoint Jesse Jackson as head of a mediation committee seems at least temporarily to have calmed the storm. But lights or no lights for Wrigley remain one of the most volatile issues of our time, and readers of Royko's book are sure to come away enlightened and yet disheartened, because, as with Catholic versus Protestant in Ireland, or Arab versus Jew in the Middle East, no solution seems on the horizon.

Water Under the Bridge—The Mysterious Death of Ed Delahanty
Mark Lane (Foreword by Senator Edward Kennedy)
Viking Press, 317 pages, $16.95

On the night of July 2, 1903, the Washington Nationals star outfielder Ed Delahanty, in a drunken rage, was forcibly removed from a train near Niagara Falls. The next day he was found drowned, apparently after accidentally falling into the river and being swept over the falls. But was it an accident? Veteran conspiracy theorist Mark Lane (whose previous book, *Rush to Judgment,* created a furor with its claim that the eight Black Sox players were framed by the real villain, Ray Schalk) has reexamined the evidence and reached some surprising conclusions. In digging through old newspaper archives Lane discovered reports that Delahanty was possibly on the verge of being traded to Boston, that year's eventual pennant winner. He then asks, reasonably, who had the most to lose by a star of Delahanty's stature joining the already talented Bean-towners? The obvious answer: Connie Mack and his defending champion Athletics. Sound tenuous? Maybe so, but what then are we to make of the fact, revealed for the first time by Lane, that the bridge tender who supposedly tried to warn Delahanty was a second cousin of Connie Mack's former clubhouse attendant? Want more? Delahanty's jewelry, cash, and clothes were missing when the body was found, in an obvious attempt to simulate robbery, and thus cast suspicion away from the real perpetrators. Why was no autopsy performed? Why was Connie Mack not even questioned?

Though liable, as always, to fits of rhetorical overkill, Lane has marshalled the evidence in an admirable and persuasive manner, one that will likely alter forevermore the reader's perceptions of "The Grand Old Man of Baseball." In a passionate peroration, Lane demands the exhumation of Delahanty's body, and the appointment by Commissioner Ueberroth of a special committee to reexamine the tragedy, a call that this reviewer can only heartily second.

Ate Men Out—A Culinary History of Fat Men in Baseball
Terry Forster (Afterword by Paul Prudhomme)
Simon and Schuster, 999 pages, $49.95

Here is a book that all baseball fans will want to sink their teeth into. The author, old Tub of Goo himself, proves that he has a generous appetite for the lore of the game as seen through the eyes of its most prodigious overeaters. The book is divided into courses rather than chapters, with the first course being a sort of "Glory of Their Times" of gluttons, as the behemoths wax rhapsodic about the toughest meals they ever faced, with Wilbert Robinson achieving particular eloquence as he recalls a post-season barnstorming tour of darkest Africa, in which he was wined and dined by cannibals on only the finest of corn-fed missionary. In the second course, the leaner players describe their adventures as teammates—and opponents—of the corpulent corps. Here Paul Waner earns kudos for recounting how he reduced Fats Fothergill to tearful blubber by forcing him to read, at gunpoint, Kafka's *A Hunger Artist,* and Rogers Hornsby will have you in stitches as he describes taking Jumbo Elliot out for a marathon dusk-to-dawn gorge, and then, that afternoon, laying down bunt after bunt in front of the portly portsider, who finally vomited on the ball while attempting to field it. The third course consists of Forster's somewhat bloated assessment of the contribution of fat men to the national pastime, as well as his "All-Fat" all-star team, which not surprisingly lacks a shortstop and second baseman. As might be expected, this is a weighty tome; too heavy, perhaps, even for your coffee table. (Rumor has it that Forster was the first author ever fined by his publisher for reporting with a grossly overweight manuscript.) Is it too much to hope that possibly a low-calorie paperback edition is in the offing? No matter, *Ate Men Out* is sure to provide nourishing food for thought on the Hot Stove circuit for many years to come.

What, Me Worry?—An Insiders' Account of the '87 Twins
Al Newman
Mad Magazine Press, 249 pages, $15.95

What I like best when a midwestern team wins the World Series is that we are spared all the make-a-quick buck exploitation books that seem to proliferate whenever a New York team wins all the marbles. The Royals' '85 championship produced only Greg Pryor's gripping account of the sixth Series game, *Wallflower at the Iorgy,* and thus far, Al (Fred E.) Newman has produced the only narrative of the Twins' unexpected rise from quasi–Jim Crow cellar dwellers to post-season *wunderkind.* His prose style, while serviceable, does not rival Hemingway's, but it is for his inside nuggets of information that this book is most valuable. He recalls how Steve Carlton, arriving late from Cleveland, and thus witness to feeble performances from both Niekro brothers, lost control in the clubhouse one evening and shouted "all Niekro's stink," almost resulting in a fight to the death with Kirby Puckett, who thought he'd said "negroes." And of course Newman recounts the introduction of the long-awaited Messiah, Don Baylor, whose first address to his new teammates began, "Four score and six years ago, Ban Johnson brought forth upon baseball a new league, conceived in reserve clause, and dedicated to the proposition that the National League was ready to be taken." Remarks Newman drily, "I think leadership had gone to his head."

But the Mad Man is most revealing when he gives his answer to the question that has puzzled all observers: why couldn't the Twins win on the road? To Newman the answer is obvious: AIDS. "Tom Kelly was phobic on the subject," he writes. "Every time we went on the road he'd give an hour lecture on the dangers of contracting AIDS. He painted a graphic picture of what could happen if we ended up in the wrong place, with the wrong person. He said every bar was potentially a gay bar, so watch out. He warned us what a laughingstock the first ballplayer to get AIDS would become, how he'd turn into the butt [I thought his use of that word most inappropriate] of more jokes than even Rock Hudson. Frankly he scared the piss out of most of us. So we just sat around our hotel rooms and got on each other's nerves. You could cut the tension with a knife. No wonder we couldn't play baseball. The '27 Yankees couldn't have won under those circumstances."

Newman goes on to describe how relieved everyone on the team was when the Cardinals defeated the Giants in the NLCS. "Thank God we didn't have to go to San Francisco. Kelly would have gone absolutely out of his mind. We'd have ended up chained to our beds, or allowed out only wearing suits of armor. No way we could've beaten the Giants." And of course, along those same lines, Newman has the answer to why Kelly conspicuously neglected to join the on-field celebration after the final Series out. "Are you kidding? Tom Kelly join a pile-up? With guys hugging and falling all over each other? He might accidentally get somebody's saliva on him. Why do you think you've never seen him go jaw to jaw with an umpire? Not until they start wearing surgical masks."

In sum, this is an engrossing book, and (since Minnesota is not New York) perhaps the only insider's account we will ever have of the ordeal, and eventual triumph, of a team long denounced as too slow, too white, and too lackadaisical. Give it a look.

The Secret Diaries of Shoeless Joe Jackson
Edited by Clifford Irving
McGraw-Hill, 487 pages, $24.95

Every now and again there appears a book that compels us to reexamine some of our most firmly held beliefs about baseball. Barbara Tuchman's *The Gloves of August* was such a book; so was *The Age of the Little Napoleon,* Will and Ariel Durant's classic study of John McGraw and his era. Now comes *The Secret Diaries of Shoeless Joe Jackson,* which will alter forever our perception of this all-time great player, hitherto scorned as an illiterate and a fixer. Jackson obviously lacked formal schooling, but to judge by the quality of the writing in these diaries, he was more than amply self-educated. Here is an excerpt from 1917, in which he ruminates on the character of Charles Comiskey.

> The much esteemed Mr. Comiskey is, I fear, both a liar and a blackguard. He has reneged upon his promise of added pecuniary benefits for next season. The unjust reserve clause hangs about my neck like the Ancient Mariner's albatross, making redress impossible. But of this much I am certain: one day Mr. Comiskey's parsimony, like Marley's Ghost, will return to haunt him, haunt him to eternal damnation. [p. 340]

Sound like the musings of a hick to you?

These diaries, discovered only recently in an attic trunk by the enterprising Mr. Irving, cover only the years of Jackson's major-league career, but they may well come to be accepted as the definitive account of the period. Erudite, anecdotal, philosophical, overflowing with vivid biographical sketches of the luminaries of the era, these diaries are must reading for baseball scholars. The final entry, describing his public humiliation in the wake of the Black Sox scandal, is as searing a portrait of blind justice traduced as we are likely ever to have:

I stood at attention on the mound, in full uniform, my glove and bat in hand. The trumpets blared, the snare drums rolled. The fans, thousands of them, screamed the vilest of epithets, of which "traitor" and "Judas" were the kindest. Comiskey appeared in the dugout, and marched out to face me. First he took my glove and tossed it aside like so much offal. Next he seized hold of my uniform and tore off the precious "Chicago" insignia, letter by letter. Then his evil hands fondled my bat, my favorite bat, which I loved as I love life itself. It had already been sawn-through, so he broke it over his knee as if it were but the frailest twig. Choking back tears of both sorrow and rage, I shouted, "I am innocent! Long live the White Sox! I am innocent! Long live the White Sox!" But the fans drowned out my pleas with their vituperation. [p. 485]

Books Received

(A listing here does not preclude the possibility of a review in the future)

The White Report on Player-Management Intimacy. By Frank White. Hill and Wang, 728 pages, $29.95

The Federal League Papers. Edited by Alexander Hamilton and John Jay. U.S. Governmental Printing Office, 657 pages, $24.95

Jack Clark's Tips for Year Round Health and Fitness. (Foreword by Paul Molitor, afterword by Bob Horner). New American Library, 227 pages, $15.95

Armed and Dangerous. By Pete Gray. Atheneum, 302 pages, $16.95

The Baseball Guide to Insider Trading. By Frank Casken (introduction by Ivan Boesky). Dow Jones Press, 170 pages, $13.95

Nose Candy is Dandy. By Lonnie Smith. Grosset and Dunlap, 295 pages, $17.95

In recent years, Americans have become acutely conscious of past injustices inflicted upon innocent victims. Dr. Samuel Mudd has been exonerated of any complicity in the assassination of Abraham Lincoln. Sacco and Vanzetti have been pardoned by the Governor of Massachusetts, and no one any longer blames Crazy Horse for the carnage at the Little Big Horn. Yet Shoeless Joe Jackson still languishes, his reputation seemingly besmirched beyond repair. Or is it? Surely these long-suppressed diaries will provide the impetus for a reconsideration of the entire Black Sox affair. Is it possible that we may yet turn to the sports section one morning, and gaze upon the words, in large bold type, of a modern day Zola: "I ACCUSE," heralding, at long last, the rehabilitation of an unjustly maligned immortal?

But Liquor is Quicker. By John Candelaria. Henry Holt. 346 pages, $18.95

The Life of Richard Wagner: Vol. I, The Cincinnati Years; Vol. II, The Houston Years. By Ernest Newman. Oxford University Press, 629 and 541 pages, $34.95 each

The Cask of Amalfitano (Joey Amalfitano's Guide to Fine Wines). George Braziller, 250 pages, $16.95

Hoy Polloi (The Autobiography of Dummy Hoy). As told to Dummy Taylor. W. W. Norton, 417 pages, $23.95

Boswell's Life of Walter Johnson. By Thomas Boswell. Doubleday, 372 pages, $21.95

Herzog. By Saul Bellow. Viking Press, 341 pages, $12.95

The Aeneid of Virgil. By Ozzie Virgil and Virgil Trucks. Little, Brown, 197 pages, $14.95

—Mike Kopf

NATIONAL LEAGUE WEST

SAN FRANCISCO GIANTS

I know of no parallel for what has happened here. I know of no other case in the history of baseball where any man has done what Al Rosen has done in San Francisco over the last two years. I would not have believed that it could be done. I would feel that I had failed in my responsibility as an analyst if I did not make you understand this.

To begin with, remember that just two years ago the San Francisco Giants lost a hundred games. In 1986 they improved from 62–100 to 83–79, a giant step for a single season though not a historic one. Teams that take a large step forward, however, usually follow up in the next season with a substantial step backward—just as Cleveland and Texas did in 1987. The Giants, early in the season, seemed likely to hold the ground they had gained in 1986, but no more. Rosen, however, did not accept that condition. He set to work, in the middle of the pennant race, to make the moves he would need to make to push this team over the top.

And he did it.

Now let me give you my prejudices. First, I don't think it is a good idea to restructure your team in the middle of the season. It is hard enough to evaluate the needs and abilities of the team at the end of the season, when everything is at rest, all the numbers are in the book, and the sum of wins and losses that result from those abilities is known; it is hard enough, I say, to understand that mysterious relationship between individual abilities and team performance when nothing is moving. When every player is hot or cold or injured or pouting or trying to prove something to Detroit, it's just too confusing. It's a kaleidoscope, changes every three seconds. It's dangerous to make decisions about that picture; it's a Cleveland Indians strategy. It's too easy to wind up paying through the nose for a pennant that you don't really have a chance to win.

Second, I think it is dangerous to try to build a ballclub too quickly. It is a rule of nature that things which are built too quickly will not endure. A young tree grows a foot a year; if something grows seven feet in one summer, that's a weed. They can slap up a house now in two days, but I would not want to live in any house that was built in less than a couple of months. Any relationship that goes from "What do you do for a living?" to "Do you want to get married?" in less than six months is a good bet to wind up at "What is your lawyer's number?" in another six months. People Express, the airline that went from start-up to being a power in the industry in five years, went belly-up in another five.

Baseball teams illustrate this rule as well. By my count there were 40 major-league teams that lost a hundred games in a season between 1960 and 1985. First of all, most of those teams remained bad in the subsequent years. Only 16 of the 40 teams ever posted a winning record in any of the following three years—in other words, 60% of the 100-game losers followed up the 100-loss season with at least three more losing records. Only 7 out of the 40 teams had winning records one year following their 100-loss campaign.

Look what happened to those 7. The 1961 Phillies (1) were over .500 in 1962 and in contention in 1964, but they were in contention before they were ready to win. They collapsed, and that team never won anything. The 1962 Chicago Cubs (2) jumped over .500 in 1963, but then immediately dropped back under .500, and by 1965 were back to a hundred losses. In 1966 that team jumped from 100 losses to over .500 again (3), but like the 1964 Phillies, found themselves in a pennant race before they were truly a solid team, blew a big lead, and never won anything. The 1973 Texas Rangers (4) lost a hundred games, then jumped to 84–76 under Billy Martin in 1974—but then dropped back under .500, and never won anything. The 1979 Oakland A's (5) lost a hundred games, hired Martin and jumped to 83–79 in 1980. That team did win a divisional title in 1981, with the help of a strike, but then fell completely apart over the following seasons, their pitching staff having been overloaded by Martin to accomplish short-term goals. The 1985 Cleveland Indians (6) lost a hundred games, then jumped to 84–78 and were proclaimed by *Sports Illustrated* as the best team in baseball. They lost 101 games. The 1985 San Francisco Giants are the seventh team. The pattern is as clear as it can be—that when teams are put together too quickly, without being tempered by communal experience at each level, their weaknesses will be exposed and they will disintegrate.

Yet if there is a fundamental weakness underlying the San Francisco success of 1987, if this team was built too quickly or if something was left out of the mix because it was built in motion, I certainly can't see it. Rosen got all the pieces put together. This, ladies and gentlemen, is an excellent ballclub. What do the Giants have?

A) Offense. Despite playing in a poor hitter's park, the Giants scored 783 runs, tied for third in the National League. The Giants have power at six or seven spots in their batting order. Their batting averages are not high because Candlestick Park holds averages down, but with Butler added to Aldrete, Clark, Brenly, and Thompson, the Giants should have a good number of players on base this year.

B) Defense. The Giants led the majors in double

plays. They cut off the running game extremely well, opponents stealing only 132 bases.

C) Pitching. Giant pitchers led the National League in ERA (3.68), and were better than average in strikeouts, walks, and home runs allowed.

Pitching, defense, power, and an attitude you've got to love. The Los Angeles Dodgers, longtime rivals of the Giants, have in recent years developed a reputation as baseball's wimp team, a bunch of guys who get hurt a lot, don't play hard and don't seem to care whether they win or lose. The Giants in the last two years have become the opposite of their rivals, a collection of hard-nosed players who stay in the lineup, fight for every edge and accept defeat with obvious ill will. Will Clark is the clearest example of this, but the rest of the team is much the same— Kevin Mitchell, the kid who doesn't have any flashy talents but shows up at the park before the manager does and takes advantage of whatever the pitcher gives him (what a deal Rosen made in getting him for Chris Brown); Bob Brenly, who converted from third base to catcher after several years in the minors and made the majors at 28, in time to turn in four straight solid years; Jeff Leonard, who sticks out his jaw and shakes his fist in a continuous display of contempt for the opposition. These guys aren't going to give you a thing.

Candlestick Park is similar in its effects on offense to Baltimore's Memorial Stadium—a grass park, a pitcher's park that cuts batting averages—and the style the Giants have developed in response to it is similar to the best of Earl Weaver's teams. A park that cuts batting averages by even a few points seriously interferes with the ability to put together a long inning. To score three runs in an inning without a long ball generally requires six separate acts, singles or stolen bases or runners moving up on an out. If each player's chance of getting on base is cut by 4 percent, a team's chance of getting six straight men on base is cut by 22 percent. If you tried to play "Whitey Ball" in this park, you'd always be up against that.

It's harder to steal bases, of course, on grass fields. Keeping the grass long, the ball moves slower and double plays become more common. The way to overcome these obstacles and win is to have a team that hits home runs, turns the double play very well, avoids the double play on offense, and has pitchers who can keep the ball on the ground and out of the seats. That formula works well anywhere, of course, but it's a formula that a ballpark like this encourages. Although the people who run this organization come from a completely different tradition, they have found the same basic formula.

Two things the great Oriole teams always had that this team hasn't had before were an outstanding defensive center fielder and lots of people on base. They took a step toward adding those things last winter when they signed one of my favorite players, Brett Butler. Butler will strengthen the team defensively and fill the one offensive role at which the Giants were void last year, that of lead-off man and base stealer. He fits with the mold of the Giants. He's a tough player, stays in the lineup 150 games a year, and gives it all he's got every game. He's a pleasure to watch and a championship-quality player as well. Butler's batting average will probably slip a little bit in coming from Cleveland to San Francisco (moving from the wind off the lake to the wind off the bay), but he may hit a few

more home runs. He's 30, but the type of player who will age slowly.

One respect in which Craig is completely different from Earl Weaver is in his handling of his pitchers. Weaver's best teams never had exceptionally strong bullpens; they had terrific four-man starting rotations with a lot of complete games, maybe a thousand innings out of four pitchers. Craig, at least last year, was very quick to go to the bullpen. An interesting contrast between Roger Craig and his old boss Sparky Anderson is that Craig removed his pitcher before the man had pitched six innings and before he had given up four runs 32 times in 1987, the most of any major-league manager. Sparky did it only five times, the fewest of any major-league manager. With the bullpen in the game early, San Francisco relievers were credited with 36 wins, tying St. Louis for the most in the major leagues (Whitey also had 30 quick hooks).

Of course, last year Craig wasn't exactly working with Jim Palmer, Mike Cuellar, and Dave McNally; for most of the year he was starting Kelly Downs and Mark Davis and Mark Grant. This year he'll have Reuschel and Dravecky all year and might have Krukow back; it might be a lot different. Like Anderson, Craig uses a lot of pinch hitters, 309 last year, second-highest total in the major leagues. Giant pinch hitters hit 11 home runs, the most of any major-league team. Their best pinch hitter was Joel Youngblood, 13 for 44 (.295) with 3 home runs. Jeff Leonard hit 2 pinch home runs, six other players hit 1 each. It was the second straight year that the Giants had led the majors in pinch hit home runs, another Oriole trick. 1987 was the third straight fine season for Youngblood as a pinch hitter, putting him in the company of a half-dozen active players who are consistent pinch hitters—Denny Walling, Greg Gross, Thad Bosley, Rance Mulliniks. One other thing that Craig and Anderson have in common: an abiding love of the intentional walk. Sparky ordered 61 intentional walks last year, second-highest total in the American League; Craig ordered 86, tying Philadelphia for the most in the majors.

There is something unusual in the way that Craig chooses to start baserunners, which I haven't been able to diagnose. The Giants' stolen base percentages are awful— 57 percent last year, the worst in the major leagues by a wide margin, and not much better in 1986. Many of the lost baserunners were obviously on hit and run attempts, which is not unusual, but the Giants grounded into only 99 double plays, a very low total for an offense this good (the 1986 figure was even lower). Even the Cardinals, who steal bases much more often and bunt much more often, lost 126 runners to double-play balls. Apparently Craig starts his runners more often early in the inning, or more often with a hitter at the plate who might be likely to ground into a double play, or more often with a ground ball pitcher on the mound, or more often when the hitter is behind in the count, or more often when the second baseman is cheating toward the base, or something. Anyway, the stolen-base percentage is a little misleading because double plays are being avoided, although it is not apparent to me whether there is a net gain or a net loss on the deal. Adding together the caught stealing and the double play balls the Giants still lost 196 runners, fifth-most in the major leagues.

What do I think of the 1988 Giants? Every spring, a

few dozen people will ask me who I think will win the World Championship. I've always ducked the question. I've always said that it was too tough to even speculate about that before the division titles are decided. This spring, I'm not going to duck it. I'm going to tell anybody who asks that I think the Giants are going to win it all.

Oddly, perhaps the most suspect part of the 1988 Giants is also the best part, the starting pitching. In view of the age and injury history of Reuschel and Dravecky, a collapse of the rotation must be seen as a possibility.

Pending injuries and the word on off-season conditioning programs, no Giant rookie figures to make an impact in 1988. The best player at Phoenix most of the year was probably outfielder Jay Reid, who hit .270 with 16 homers and 84 RBI. Late in the year the team was joined by Matt Williams, a third-base prospect with star potential. Williams is supposed to be a good one, but there is no pressure to get him in the lineup, with Mitchell manning third.

Barring a collapse of the rotation, I see no major weaknesses of the team. Their defense up the middle is excellent. They have power. With Butler at the top of the order, they'll have more people on base, and they'll have a better ability to manufacture a run. I have confidence in Craig's ability to handle the pitching staff. This is not an old team of players put together in mid-career, but a young team that developed very suddenly. The Giants face less of a threat within their division than teams in the other three divisions, with only the Reds seemingly strong enough to challenge the Giants.

The San Francisco Giants, three years older than the Minnesota Twins, have never won a World Championship. They'll need to catch some breaks to do it this year. I just believe, watching them play, listening to the things they say, that this is a team of players who hate to lose, and guys who will do what they have to do to win.

WINS BY RELIEVERS

San Francisco	36
St. Louis	36
Cincinnati	32
Toronto	34
Milwaukee	31
Minnesota	30
Montreal	29
Texas	29
Yankees	27
Oakland	27
Philadelphia	27
Baltimore	25
Detroit	24
San Diego	24
California	23
Houston	23
Cleveland	22
Mets	22
Atlanta	22
White Sox	20
Pittsburgh	20
Boston	19
Kansas City	19
Cubs	17
Los Angeles	16
Seattle	16

RUNS SCORED AND ALLOWED WINS AND LOSSES

Wins	559	245	90-0	1.000
Krukow	158	130	18-10	.643
Blowouts	259	167	24-15	.615
Dravecky	85	64	11-7	.611
Pitchers' Duels	66	61	20-14	.588
Home Games	373	312	46-35	.568
One-Run Games	216	210	29-23	.558
All Games	783	669	90-72	.556
Road Games	410	357	44-37	.543
Slugfests	397	334	28-26	.519
Hammaker	131	101	14-13	.519
Downs	112	105	14-14	.500
LaCoss	113	118	12-14	.462
Losses	224	424	0-72	.000

TEN BEST STARTS

	IP	H	R	ER	BB	SO		
Reuschel vs. Hous, Sep 17	9	2	0	0	1	5	W	87
Downs at SD, Apr 15	9	3	0	0	1	7	W	87
LaCoss vs. LA, Aug 16	10	3	0	0	3	4	W	87
Dravecky vs. LA, Aug 15	9	4	0	0	2	7	W	84
Downs vs. Mon, May 31	9	5	0	0	1	7	W	83
Reuschel vs. Phi, Sep 6	9	2	1	1	0	3	W	82
Dravecky vs. Pit, July 21	9	6	0	0	1	4	W	78
Dravecky vs. Mon, Aug 31	9	5	0	0	4	4	W	77
Dravecky vs. Hous, Sep 16	9	4	1	1	1	3	W	77
Downs vs. SD, June 11	9	7	0	0	4	6	W	75

PITCHERS WHEN SUPPORTED BY THREE TO FIVE RUNS

	G	IP	W-L	Pct	SO	BB	ERA
Downs	14	81	5-3	.625	52	26	4.23
LaCoss	12	70	5-5	.500	31	24	3.72
Hammaker	9	55	2-2	.500	39	20	3.79
Dravecky	8	47	2-3	.400	31	13	3.83
Krukow	11	67	2-3	.400	45	16	3.90

HALL OF FAME WATCH

Building credentials but not yet viable candidate: Reuschel 31.5, Roger Craig 30; **Working on it:** Speier 23, DeJesus 15, Krukow 10; **Long way to go:** C Davis 9.5, Dravecky 8, Lefferts 7, Leonard 6.5, Brenly 6, Hammaker 6, Youngblood 5, W. Clark 4.5, D Robinson 4, LaCoss 3, Wilfong 2.5, Aldrete 2.5, Price 2, Uribe 2, Garrelts 1, Mitchell 1, Thompson 1. (Craig had 16 points as a pitcher, and has 14 so far as a manager.)

QUICK HOOKS

San Francisco	32
Oakland	31
Toronto	30
St. Louis	30
San Diego	29
Yankees	29
Texas	25
Baltimore	24
Montreal	22
Mets	21
Cubs	20
Milwaukee	20
Atlanta	19
Minnesota	17
Cleveland	16
Los Angeles	16
California	16
Pittsburgh	16
Cincinnati	15
Philadelphia	14
White Sox	13
Houston	12
Seattle	11
Boston	10
Kansas City	8
Detroit	5

TEN WORST STARTS

	IP	H	R	ER	BB	SO		
LaCoss at LA, Apr 12	3⅓	11	6	6	1	1	L	14
Krukow at NY, May 15	3⅔	9	7	7	2	4	L	17
Hammaker vs. SD, June 13	4⅓	7	8	7	4	4	L	19
Reuschel vs. NY, Aug 30	⅓	5	5	5	1	0	L	20
Hammaker at NY, Aug 18	2*	8	5	5	2	2	L	20
Krukow at Mon, May 20	3⅔	8	6	6	1	2	L	22
Downs at NY, Aug 20	5⅓	11	7	7	1	5	L	22
Downs at Mon, May 18	2⅔	7	5	4	2	1	L	22
Downs vs Hous, June 27	4⅓	9	6	6	1	4	L	24
Downs at Atl, June 16	5⅓	9	7	7	1	4	L	25

Bob BRENLY, Catcher
Runs created: 63

	G	AB	Hit	2B	3B	HR	Run	RBI	TBB	SO	SB	CS	Avg
4.56 years		504	129	23	1	19	65	66	63	82	9	8	.256
1987	123	375	100	19	1	18	55	51	47	85	10	7	.267
First Half	59	168	47	11	1	9	26	23	24	38	6	3	.280
Second Half	64	207	53	8	0	9	29	28	23	47	4	4	.256
Vs. RHP		274	76	12	0	11	42	32	36	63	8	4	.277
Vs. LHP		101	24	7	1	7	13	19	11	22	2	3	.238
Home	62	173	52	10	0	10	27	32	25	31	7	4	.301
Road	61	202	48	9	1	8	28	19	22	54	3	3	.238

Jeff LEONARD, Left Field
Runs Created: 66

	G	AB	Hit	2B	3B	HR	Run	RBI	TBB	SO	SB	CS	Avg
6.13 years		566	155	25	6	16	73	80	39	112	22	8	.274
1987	131	503	141	29	4	19	70	63	21	68	16	7	.280
First Half	85	342	102	25	4	16	51	44	14	46	9	6	.298
Second Half	46	161	39	4	0	3	19	19	7	22	7	1	.242
Vs. RHP		358	109	18	4	14	47	48	15	51	9	5	.279
Vs. LHP		145	41	11	0	5	23	15	6	17	7	2	.283
Home	60	225	63	14	1	9	33	26	11	37	5	5	.280
Road	71	278	78	15	3	10	37	37	10	31	11	2	.281

Will CLARK, First Base
Runs Created: 109

	G	AB	Hit	2B	3B	HR	Run	RBI	TBB	SO	SB	CS	Avg
1.61 years		582	174	35	4	29	96	82	52	108	6	15	.299
1987	150	529	163	29	5	35	89	91	49	98	5	17	.308
First Half	81	290	90	13	4	15	43	40	17	54	3	8	.310
Second Half	69	239	73	16	1	20	46	51	32	44	2	9	.305
Vs. RHP		356	108	13	3	28	63	57	44	65	5	15	.303
Vs. LHP		173	55	16	2	7	26	34	5	33	0	2	.318
Home	77	274	93	17	2	22	49	54	24	46	2	9	.339
Road	73	255	70	12	3	13	40	37	25	52	3	8	.275

Chili DAVIS, Center Field
Runs Created: 78

	G	AB	Hit	2B	3B	HR	Run	RBI	TBB	SO	SB	CS	Avg
5.40 years		583	156	27	4	19	80	77	67	107	18	11	.268
1987	149	500	125	22	1	24	80	76	72	109	16	9	.250
First Half	84	315	79	15	0	14	50	46	37	71	9	5	.251
Second Half	65	185	46	7	1	10	30	30	35	38	7	4	.249
Vs. RHP		317	77	16	0	10	47	42	52	61	15	6	.243
Vs. LHP		183	48	6	1	14	33	34	20	48	1	3	.262
Home	74	223	54	7	1	9	34	28	38	50	5	4	.242
Road	75	277	71	15	0	15	46	48	34	59	11	5	.256

Robbie THOMPSON, Second Base
Runs Created: 58

	G	AB	Hit	2B	3B	HR	Run	RBI	TBB	SO	SB	CS	Avg
1.73 years		560	150	31	5	10	78	53	47	117	16	15	.268
1987	132	420	110	26	5	10	62	44	40	91	16	11	.262
First Half	65	211	52	11	0	7	27	27	18	51	8	4	.246
Second Half	67	209	58	15	5	3	35	17	22	40	8	7	.278
Vs. RHP		291	70	19	3	7	40	28	30	73	10	7	.241
Vs. LHP		129	40	7	2	3	22	16	10	18	6	4	.310
Home	66	205	54	11	3	7	31	25	20	40	6	6	.263
Road	66	215	56	15	2	3	31	19	20	51	10	5	.260

Candy MALDONADO, Right Field
Runs Created: 75

	G	AB	Hit	2B	3B	HR	Run	RBI	TBB	SO	SB	CS	Avg
3.38 years		412	107	24	3	14	50	66	29	72	4	5	.260
1987	118	442	129	28	4	20	69	85	34	78	8	8	.292
First Half	71	277	92	22	2	12	50	48	18	45	7	5	.332
Second Half	47	165	37	6	2	8	19	37	16	33	1	3	.224
Vs. RHP		310	90	19	3	14	48	64	17	57	7	5	.290
Vs. LHP		132	39	9	1	6	21	21	17	21	1	3	.295
Home	62	228	55	9	1	14	29	45	14	44	3	2	.241
Road	56	214	74	19	3	6	40	40	20	34	5	6	.346

Kevin MITCHELL, Third Base
Runs Created: 76

	G	AB	Hit	2B	3B	HR	Run	RBI	TBB	SO	SB	CS	Avg
1.52 years		530	147	28	3	22	78	75	53	100	8	7	.277
1987	131	464	130	20	2	22	68	70	48	88	9	6	.280
First Half	71	235	60	9	1	10	22	36	24	44	0	0	.255
Second Half	60	229	70	11	1	12	46	34	24	44	9	6	.306
Vs. RHP		325	83	9	1	12	39	46	29	68	4	3	.255
Vs. LHP		139	47	11	1	10	29	24	19	20	5	3	.338
Home	66	227	66	11	2	9	35	35	23	43	4	4	.291
Road	65	237	64	9	0	13	33	35	25	45	5	2	.270

Mike ALDRETE, Outfield
Runs Created: 68

	G	AB	Hit	2B	3B	HR	Run	RBI	TBB	SO	SB	CS	Avg
1.30 years		441	131	28	4	8	59	58	58	65	5	2	.297
1987	126	357	116	18	2	9	50	51	43	50	6	0	.325
First Half	60	135	43	6	0	2	19	15	11	21	0	0	.319
Second Half	66	222	73	12	2	7	31	36	32	29	6	0	.329
Vs. RHP		287	94	13	0	9	41	45	40	43	4	0	.328
Vs. LHP		70	22	5	2	0	9	6	3	7	2	0	.314
Home	63	176	59	7	1	7	27	25	26	24	4	0	.335
Road	63	181	57	11	1	2	23	26	17	26	2	0	.315

José URIBE, Shortstop
Runs Created: 48

	G	AB	Hit	2B	3B	HR	Run	RBI	TBB	SO	SB	CS	Avg
2.51 years		501	123	20	4	4	56	41	46	68	17	6	.246
1987	95	309	90	16	5	5	44	30	24	35	12	2	.291
First Half	24	78	22	3	0	1	11	5	6	11	5	0	.282
Second Half	71	231	68	13	5	4	33	25	18	24	7	2	.294
Vs. RHP		213	65	11	5	2	30	17	18	25	11	1	.305
Vs. LHP		96	25	5	0	3	14	13	6	10	1	1	.260
Home	49	155	49	11	3	4	19	18	7	16	5	1	.316
Road	46	154	41	5	2	1	25	12	17	19	7	1	.266

Chris SPEIER, Infield
Runs Created: 43

	G	AB	Hit	2B	3B	HR	Run	RBI	TBB	SO	SB	CS	Avg
13.27 years		524	129	22	4	8	56	53	62	71	3	4	.246
1987	111	317	79	13	0	11	39	39	42	51	4	7	.249
First Half	67	202	52	9	0	8	25	28	25	26	1	5	.257
Second Half	44	115	27	4	0	3	14	11	17	25	3	2	.235
Vs. RHP		225	54	11	0	7	30	26	33	36	3	4	.240
Vs. LHP		92	25	2	0	4	9	13	9	15	1	4	.272
Home	57	159	36	4	0	6	16	17	24	23	2	3	.226
Road	54	158	43	9	0	5	23	22	18	28	2	4	.272

CINCINNATI REDS

The Reds were supposed to win and didn't. I picked them to win. Most everybody picked them to win. What happened?

The pitching wasn't there. The Reds had a 4.24 ERA, ninth in the National League. It was a case of good hitting being negated by bad pitching. Departed pitcher Ted Power, who is an articulate man, said that the Reds problem was that while Pete Rose is very good working with hitters, he doesn't know how to handle a pitching staff very well. In view of the obvious fact that the pitching staff has not come around for Rose, one must attach a certain credibility to that argument, although I would add quickly that I could not identify specifically any mistakes that I thought Rose made in handling his pitchers. The starting pitching never really kept the opposition out of any games. They had only ten games in which the starter posted a game score over 70, the fewest of any major league team.

Rose has shown, to my way of thinking, a very distinct preference for working with control pitchers, and a reluctance to struggle along with pitchers who had the goods but not the finish. Perhaps the most unique major decision that he has made during his managerial tenure was the decision to pull out of the minor leagues and stick into his rotation Guy Hoffman, a finesse pitcher with great control but not much else going for him. In his first year, he also gambled on Tom Browning, 12–10 with a 3.95 ERA with Wichita the year before, 28–29 lifetime in the minor leagues. Browning also has good control, although he has better stuff than Hoffman. The Reds traded for Bill Gullickson, a control pitcher. Rose has never shown, up to now, a willingness to gamble on a power pitcher in the starting rotation.

That's what makes the 1988 trades so interesting. Rijo, Birtsas, and Jackson are the types of pitchers that Rose has not yet worked successfully with, tremendously talented but not fully in command of their talent. It will be very interesting to see whether Rose can convince these young men to be aggressive, to go after the strike zone first and take their chances from there. But I'll say this: you couldn't name a right-handed and left-handed young power pitcher in baseball who have more potential for explosive development than Rijo and Jackson.

While the Reds' starting rotation was awful, their bullpen was terrific. The Cincinnati bullpen had 32 wins and a .681 winning percentage, the best in the major leagues. Unlike the other managers who had strong bullpens and weak starting rotations, Rose didn't seem particularly anxious to get the game to the bullpen. He had only 15 quick hooks, as opposed to 32 for Roger Craig, 30 for Whitey Herzog, and 22 for Buck Rodgers. The Cincinnati bullpen was 19 games over .500; the starting staff was 13 games under .500. Only one other team, Philadelphia, had a similar split. Because of this Cincinnati's top two starters, Gullickson and Power, had a won-lost percentage 88 points worse than the rest of the team, an extraordinary

thing (see chart. The top two starters for the purpose of this chart, as in the special article about the Twins, were defined as the pitchers with the most wins, with the pitcher with fewer losses being used in case of a tie. In this case, the Reds had one pitcher who was 10–11 and two who were 10–13, so it doesn't matter which one you use. I just said Ted Power because he actually pitched better than Browning).

The Reds got into the race, but were not able to make the moves they needed to make to keep pace with San Francisco. After the trade of Reuschel and Robinson to San Francisco, Rose complained publicly that the Pirates lowered the asking price for these pitchers after the Reds talked to them. I suspect that that is not exactly what happened. What I suspect happened, not only in that negotiation but in others, was that the price was higher for the Reds than it was for anybody else. There is a perception that the Reds are just loaded with talented young players, and that they can trade you a Kurt Stillwell or a Kal Daniels or a Jeff Treadway if they decide they want to. If I were negotiating with the Reds, my position would be that if they wanted my pitcher, they were going to have to turn loose of one of those kids. It may seem unfair to the Reds, but it is a perfectly rational negotiating position.

Murray Cook will be up against that now; he was willing and able to make moves, at least. Bill Bergesch was, in a sense, a victim of the brilliant performance by Al Rosen. Can you name another general manager who was fired for being out-maneuvered in a pennant race? I can't. Traditionally, it has always been thought that a general manager's job was essentially done in the off-season, to build the roster up to where it was able to compete. Once the season began, the primary responsibility belonged to the manager, to whip that team into the pennant race. Bergesch, and also Dick Wagner in Houston, suffered by being compared to Rosen, who was able to make a series of in-season moves to push the Giants over the hump.

In Dave Parker, at least the Dave Parker of 1987, the Reds gave up nothing. Parker was taking playing time away from Kal Daniels, Paul O'Neill, and Tracy Jones, all of whom were better hitters than he was (1987 runs created per 27 outs: Kal Daniels 10.43, Paul O'Neill 5.66, Tracy Jones 5.09, Parker 4.51). Daniels and O'Neill are also more than a decade younger than Parker, Jones 9 years and 10 months younger. To have continued to hold on to a declining Dave Parker at the expense of a developing Daniels, O'Neill, and Jones would have made no sense.

There were also charges of "negative leadership" levelled at Dave Parker by Rose and Murray Cook; this seems to be a coming codeword, but what exactly it means could be anything from not showing up at the park on time to not taking an interest in younger players to something more serious. Certainly Rose was not pleased when he wanted Parker to move to first base and Parker wouldn't, and he shouldn't have been pleased with that attitude, in view of the fact that it may have cost the Reds the pennant. Parker is an awful right fielder, slow and unreliable. The Reds seemed to need a first baseman who could put runs on the scoreboard; they played Dave Concepcion at first in 26 games and Terry Francona in 57 games, although Nick Esasky got started and put together his best season over the second half. In any case, I think that to have a key player on any team who won't do what the team needs for him to do for the good of the whole is tremendously damaging. Earl Weaver tells in *It's What You Learn After You Know it All that Counts* that when he was a coach with the Orioles Frank Robinson didn't like to sign baseballs. You know, people are always requesting signed baseballs, and the Orioles (like most organizations) bring boxes of baseballs into the clubhouse for their players to sign. When Weaver took over as manager Frank Robinson came to him and asked what he could do to help Weaver do the job. Earl asked him to sign baseballs. It was symbolic, but it was important, because there was this daily sign that we're all going to pitch in here and do what has to be done. Parker's refusal to move to first base sent the opposite message: my ego is more important than the good of the team.

Creating 10.43 runs/27 outs, Kal Daniels was second in the entire National League, behind Jack Clark at 11.08, Eric Davis was fifth at 9.56, an inch behind Tim Raines and Tony Gwynn, each at 9.57. Daniels' stats, projected to full-time play: 119 runs scored, 39 doubles, 42 homers, 42 stolen bases, .334 average, 104 RBI, 98 walks. No player in baseball history has ever hit 40 homers and stolen 40 bases in the same season, but the Reds had two outfielders who projected to that level had they been playing full time; Davis projected to 46 homers and 63 stolen bases. Daniels projection is a little unrealistic because he really hasn't proven that he can hit left-handers (.197 average against them last year, .188 career vs. left-handers before last year.) However, the way that Davis hits left-handers, the Reds may not see any left-handed starters this year.

I suppose that's an impossible quandary for an opposing manager: would you rather pitch a right-hander and make Kal Daniels a .370 hitter with a home run every 11.7 at bats, or a left-hander and make Eric Davis a .338 hitter with a home run every 8.7 at bats? Four Reds hit over .300 in a hundred or more at bats against left-handers, Concepcion (.345), Davis (.338), Diaz (.350), and Jones (.345); only Daniels hit over .300 against right-handers, but their winning percentages was almost the same either way.

Apart from Eric Davis, the Reds were an unimpressive defensive team. Diaz is a good catcher, and the Reds were a little better than average at stopping the running game. But the team was below average in fielding percentage, below average in double plays, below average in defensive efficiency. Larkin at shortstop was potentially good but not actually all that good; Stillwell was potentially brilliant but actually pretty awful. Buddy Bell as a hitter is as good as he has ever been, but as a third baseman he has lost several steps. Take Davis out of the outfield and the outfield would have been the weakest defensively in the National League.

The Reds have had exactly the same record at home and on the road in each of the last two seasons, 43–38 both places in 1986, 42–39 both places last year. (I would check to see whether this has ever happened before except that I don't care.) Over the last five years the Reds' record at home is only ten and a half games better than on the road, the smallest home park advantage in the National League. Riverfront Stadium is symmetrical and the most nearly neutral park in the league in terms of its impact on runs scored; the Reds, despite a lineup of home-town talent, have not been able to focus on and exploit anything to give them a home field edge.

I think the addition of Jeff Treadway to the lineup will help the team more than most people think. I don't have anything against Ron Oester, but he's one of those guys who doesn't do much to make the other team lose. I mean, he's there, he hits his singles, he doesn't make too many errors, he earns his paycheck, but he doesn't really do much; he doesn't drive in runs or score them. Sort of a National League Jim Gantner. I think Treadway will do more to help the team. Parenthetically, the failure of *Baseball America* to name Treadway among the league's top prospects is puzzling. I mean, would you really rather have Steve Kiefer or Roberto Kelly or Todd Stottlemyre than Treadway?

Apart from Treadway, the famed Cincinnati talent pipeline seems to be . . . well, not empty, certainly, but without any more Eric Davises within a year of the majors. The best pitcher at Nashville was Pat Pacillo, who didn't pitch well in 12 National League games, but remains a good prospect. The best regulars were catcher Terry McGriff and third baseman Chris Sabo. McGriff isn't going to dislodge Diaz, but Sabo does appear to be in line for a shot at a third-base job sooner or later. At AA (Vermont, Eastern League) the Reds have prospects at the same positions—catcher Joe Oliver, third baseman Marty Brown, starting pitchers Rob Lopez and Steve Oliverio. Their minor-league stats are not impressive, but the Reds' current AAA and AA teams both play in very poor hitter's park. When their minor-league hitters move to the majors, they move to a situation that is tougher in terms of quality, but easier in another way, with better parks to hit in. These players are going to hit nearly as well in the majors, then, as they did in the minors—as you will find if you look back at the players who have played for Vermont in the past. Kal Daniels at Vermont hit .313 with 17 homers, 62 RBI. Barry Larkin there hit .267 with one home run in 72 games, and Paul O'Neill hit .265 with a .453 slugging percentage; all have had similar major-league performance. So stats that wouldn't say "prospect" in another organization are good stats here. Dan Boever hit .301 with 14 homers, 61 RBI; the major league equivalent would be .289 with 12 homers, 57 RBI.

I think the Reds will have a good year. The offense obviously is of championship quality. With fewer runs being scored this year they may not score more than the 783 runs they scored last year, but relative to the league I think the offense will improve in 1988. Giving playing time to O'Neill, Jones and Daniels rather than Parker will help the offense. Treadway will help the offense. Larkin probably will have a better year. The three offensive trouble spots could be third base and catcher (because of age) and first base (because of inconsistency), but they're reasonably well backed up at all of those. If Esasky doesn't hit, Bell can be moved to first, with Sabo at third.

The offense should be better, and the pitching should be better. I remain Danny Jackson's biggest fan; I think that at worst he'll be good and at best he'll be great. A rotation of Jackson, Rasmussen, Browning, and Rijo, Hoffman, or Pacillo could be good enough to get the team to the bullpen five or ten games over .500, and with this bullpen that could be good enough.

I don't know Pete Rose; have never met him. My reading of him is that he has a native intelligence that focuses on a challenge. To this point he hasn't done a very good job of building his rotation, but I suspect that this year he will focus on that as a challenge. I think that just as Rose used to ask himself between at bats what adjustments he needed to make to build a better staff. If he does that, and if he finds the right answers, the Reds should be very much in the race in 1988.

Is Jackson, Rasmussen, Browning, Hoffman, and Rijo really a championship quality rotation? It could be, but you certainly couldn't predict it to be. If this wasn't a championship quality defense last year, why would it be in 1988? Given the other strengths of the team, I think the Reds will win around 90 games. I doubt that that will be enough to beat the Giants.

WINNING PERCENTAGE OF BULLPEN

Team	Pct
Cincinnati	.681
Montreal	.674
Milwaukee	.608
Toronto	.607
San Francisco	.600
Philadelphia	.600
Kansas City	.592
Yankees	.587
St. Louis	.581
Detroit	.571
Minnesota	.566
Texas	.547
Oakland	.540
Houston	.523
Seattle	.516
Baltimore	.500
San Diego	.480
Cleveland	.458
Mets	.458
White Sox	.455
California	.451
Atlanta	.449
Boston	.442
Los Angeles	.432
Pittsburgh	.426
Cubs	.415

RUNS SCORED AND ALLOWED WINS AND LOSSES

Wins	546	271	84-0	1.000
Browning	133	136	18-13	.581
R Robinson	110	77	10-8	.556
Slugfests	417	376	29-24	.547
One-Run Games	212	208	27-23	.540
Power	153	141	18-16	.529
All Games	783	752	84-78	.519
Home Games	396	401	42-39	.519
Road Games	387	351	42-39	.519
Gullickson	127	130	14-13	.519
Blowouts	254	238	19-19	.500
Pitchers' Duels	67	73	16-18	.471
Hoffman	109	106	10-12	.455
Losses	237	481	0-78	.000

HALL OF FAME WATCH

Fully qualified: Pete Rose 317; **Could be elected on current accomplishments:** Parker 107, Concepcion 101.5; **Building credentials but not yet viable candidate:** B. Bell 60; **Working on it:** Soto 24, Franco 14, Diaz 13, E. Davis 12; **Long way to go** D. Collins 8.5, Rasmussen 6, Browning 6, Hume 5 Power 5, Scherrer 4, K. Daniels 2.5, F Williams 2. (Rose had 309 points as a player, and has 8 so far as a manager.)

TEN WORST STARTS

	IP	H	R	ER	BB	SO		
Gullickson vs. StL, Aug 23	4⅔	10	8	8	5	3	L	10
Hoffman vs. SD, July 30	4*	8	7	7	4	1	L	15
Gullickson at Atl, June 20	2⅓	6	7	7	2	1	L	16
Reuss at StL, May 17	4⅔	10	7	7	2	2	L	16
Power vs. Phi, July 6	5	9	8	8	3	3	L	17
Reuss vs. NY, May 12	1⅓	7	6	5	1	1	L	18
Hoffman vs. Phi, July 8	4⅓	9	7	7	0	2	L	19
Hoffman at SD, Aug 14	2⅔	7	6	6	2	2	L	20
Reuss vs. LA, June 7	2⅔	8	5	5	1	0	L	21
Browning vs. SF, June 8	3	6	6	6	1	0	—	22

TEN BEST GAMES

	IP	H	R	ER	BB	SO		
Browning vs. LA, Sep 9	9	2	1	1	2	8	W	85
Gullickson vs. Hous, Apr 18	9	4	0	0	4	W		83
Power at SD, Aug 14	8*	3	0	0	2	6	W	80
Robinson at SD, Aug 16	7	2	0	0	1	8	W	80
Power at NY, May 5	8⅓	6	0	0	2	9	W	78
Browning vs. Chi, Aug 29	9	5	1	1	2	6	W	77
Power vs. LA, June 6	9	3	2	2	2	6	W	77
Power at Hous, Apr 25	7⅓	2	0	0	1	3	—	76
Power at LA, June 26	9	7	0	0	1	3	W	75
Gullickson at Chi, May 20	9	7	2	2	2	9	W	72

PITCHERS WHEN SUPPORTED BY THREE TO FIVE RUNS

	G	IP	W-L	Pct	SO	BB	ERA
Hoffman	7	44	1-0	1.000	31	12	3.25
Browning	18	111	7-6	.538	73	33	3.89
Robinson	8	47	2-2	.500	24	14	2.11
Gullickson	7	43	2-2	.500	27	9	5.02
Power	12	78	3-5	.375	49	32	4.02

1987 GAP BETWEEN TOP TWO STARTERS AND REST OF STAFF

Team	Gap
Boston	.205
Oakland	.182
Baltimore	.165
Houston	.165
Pittsburgh	.160
Kansas City	.160
Los Angeles	.157
Atlanta	.145
Yankees	.132
Texas	.125
Philadelphia	.122
Milwaukee	.113
San Diego	.113
Cubs	.111
Minnesota	.102
Mets	.101
White Sox	.094
Montreal	.091
California	.083
Cleveland	.083
Toronto	.051
Seattle	.043
Detroit	.031
San Francisco	.017
St. Louis	−.010
Cincinnati	−.088

Bo DIAZ, Catcher
Runs Created: 59

	G	AB	Hit	2B	3B	HR	Run	RBI	TBB	SO	SB	CS	Avg
5.30 years		533	139	28	1	14	56	77	35	72	2	2	.261
1987	140	496	134	28	1	15	49	82	19	73	1	0	.270
First Half	82	295	86	20	1	7	29	53	13	46	1	0	.292
Second Half	58	201	48	8	0	8	20	29	6	27	0	0	.239
Vs. RHP		358	85	16	1	11	34	58	12	53	0	0	.237
Vs. LHP		138	49	12	0	4	15	24	7	20	1	0	.355
Home	73	252	77	20	1	8	31	52	10	34	1	0	.306
Road	67	244	57	8	0	7	18	30	9	39	0	0	.234

Kal DANIELS, Left Field
Runs Created: 100

	G	AB	Hit	2B	3B	HR	Run	RBI	TBB	SO	SB	CS	Avg
1.12 years		490	162	30	4	29	96	78	73	82	37	9	.331
1987	108	368	123	24	1	26	73	64	60	62	26	8	.334
First Half	68	228	72	15	1	17	51	37	35	41	16	7	.316
Second Half	40	140	51	9	0	9	22	27	25	21	10	1	.364
Vs. RHP		292	108	20	1	25	62	58	51	45	25	6	.370
Vs. LHP		76	15	4	0	1	11	6	9	17	1	2	.197
Home	53	175	54	12	0	13	32	29	25	29	10	2	.309
Road	55	193	69	12	1	13	41	35	35	33	16	6	.358

Nick ESASKY, First Base
Runs Created: 57

	G	AB	Hit	2B	3B	HR	Run	RBI	TBB	SO	SB	CS	Avg
3.24 years		529	130	24	4	24	66	79	60	147	3	3	.246
1987	100	346	94	19	2	22	48	59	29	76	0	0	.272
First Half	35	108	27	4	1	11	18	29	10	24	0	0	.250
Second Half	65	238	67	15	1	11	30	30	19	52	0	0	.282
Vs. RHP		255	71	14	2	16	34	44	12	54	0	0	.278
Vs. LHP		91	23	5	0	6	14	15	17	22	0	0	.253
Home	56	191	47	9	1	10	23	31	19	42	0	0	.246
Road	44	155	47	10	1	12	25	28	10	34	0	0	.303

Eric DAVIS, Center Field
Runs Created: 124

	G	AB	Hit	2B	3B	HR	Run	RBI	TBB	SO	SB	CS	Avg
2.31 years		513	140	22	5	35	119	95	79	139	68	10	.273
1987	129	474	139	23	4	37	120	100	84	134	50	6	.293
First Half	74	271	87	16	2	27	75	68	43	72	33	3	.321
Second Half	55	203	52	7	2	10	45	32	41	62	17	3	.256
Vs. RHP		327	89	15	4	20	75	61	57	98	29	4	.272
Vs. LHP		147	50	8	0	17	45	39	27	36	21	2	.340
Home	65	232	65	10	2	17	62	42	44	64	29	2	.280
Road	64	242	74	13	2	20	58	58	40	70	21	4	.306

Kurt STILWELL, Infield
Runs Created: 46

	G	AB	Hit	2B	3B	HR	Run	RBI	TBB	SO	SB	CS	Avg
1.45 years		465	114	18	6	3	59	41	43	67	7	6	.245
1987	131	395	102	20	7	4	54	33	32	50	4	6	.258
First Half	74	230	59	9	3	3	29	24	17	29	2	5	.257
Second Half	57	165	43	11	4	1	25	9	15	21	2	1	.261
Vs. RHP		298	80	18	5	4	45	24	26	34	4	6	.268
Vs. LHP		97	22	2	2	0	9	9	6	16	0	0	.227
Home	62	150	39	9	4	3	22	12	14	22	2	2	.260
Road	69	245	63	11	3	1	32	21	18	28	2	4	.257

Dave PARKER, Right Field
Runs Created: 77

	G	AB	Hit	2B	3B	HR	Run	RBI	TBB	SO	SB	CS	Avg
11.93 years		613	182	36	6	23	88	100	45	99	12	9	.297
1987	153	589	149	28	0	26	77	97	44	104	7	3	.253
First Half	87	343	93	17	0	19	54	56	27	65	7	0	.271
Second Half	66	246	56	11	0	7	23	41	17	39	0	3	.228
Vs. RHP		384	100	17	0	18	48	54	35	59	5	3	.260
Vs. LHP		205	49	11	0	8	29	43	9	45	2	0	.239
Home	78	291	82	15	0	14	45	53	23	38	4	2	.282
Road	75	298	67	13	0	12	32	44	21	66	3	1	.225

Buddy BELL, Third Base
Runs Created: 84

	G	AB	Hit	2B	3B	HR	Run	RBI	TBB	SO	SB	CS	Avg
14.05 years		611	172	29	4	14	80	76	57	52	4	6	.282
1987	143	522	148	19	2	17	74	70	71	39	4	1	.284
First Half	72	256	75	14	1	6	40	33	30	21	2	0	.285
Second Half	71	266	75	5	1	11	34	37	41	18	2	1	.282
Vs. RHP		380	111	16	2	10	50	52	47	27	4	1	.292
Vs. LHP		142	37	3	0	7	24	18	24	12	0	0	.261
Home	73	262	78	10	1	8	41	40	41	10	2	0	.298
Road	70	260	70	9	1	9	33	30	30	29	2	1	.269

Tracy JONES, Outfield
Runs Created: 52

	G	AB	Hit	2B	3B	HR	Run	RBI	TBB	SO	SB	CS	Avg
1.01 years		441	133	20	3	12	68	53	32	45	38	9	.302
1987	117	359	104	17	3	10	53	44	23	40	31	8	.290
First Half	68	230	69	13	2	10	34	30	15	24	19	6	.300
Second Half	49	129	35	4	1	0	19	14	8	16	12	2	.271
Vs. RHP		190	45	7	1	5	21	23	6	23	12	2	.237
Vs. LHP		169	59	10	2	5	32	21	17	17	19	6	.349
Home	56	160	48	9	2	4	27	13	14	10	17	2	.300
Road	61	199	56	8	1	6	26	31	9	30	14	6	.281

Barry LARKIN, Shortstop
Runs Created: 52

	G	AB	Hit	2B	3B	HR	Run	RBI	TBB	SO	SB	CS	Avg
1.02 years		586	149	20	5	15	89	61	44	72	28	6	.254
1987	125	439	107	16	2	12	64	43	36	52	21	6	.244
First Half	55	187	39	9	0	6	28	19	14	25	8	2	.209
Second Half	70	252	68	7	2	6	36	24	22	27	13	4	.270
Vs. RHP		308	71	12	0	7	43	27	22	40	12	4	.231
Vs. LHP		131	36	4	2	5	21	16	14	12	9	2	.275
Home	67	241	57	9	0	6	37	27	24	32	13	3	.237
Road	58	198	50	7	2	6	27	16	12	20	8	3	.253

Dave CONCEPCION, Infield
Runs Created: 39

	G	AB	Hit	2B	3B	HR	Run	RBI	TBB	SO	SB	CS	Avg
14.84 years		575	154	26	3	7	66	63	48	78	21	7	.268
1987	104	279	89	15	0	1	32	33	28	24	4	3	.319
First Half	62	167	52	8	0	0	21	17	17	11	2	2	.311
Second Half	42	112	37	7	0	1	11	16	11	13	2	1	.330
Vs. RHP		129	38	6	0	0	16	16	14	13	3	2	.295
Vs. LHP		150	51	9	0	1	16	17	14	11	1	1	.340
Home	47	133	42	9	0	1	14	14	10	7	2	3	.316
Road	57	146	47	6	0	0	18	19	18	17	2	0	.322

YOUR NEW PITCHER

When it comes to bad luck, Danny Jackson has taxed the limits of credibility. A year ago, Danny was picked by *Sports Illustrated* as the best candidate to win the American League Cy Young Award. Their reasoning, one supposes, was that Danny's tough luck had to run out sooner or later. In 1985 Jackson posted a good 3.42 ERA, but finished just 14–12 because he had the poorest offensive support of any Royal starter. In 1986 he cut his ERA to 3.20, but finished just 11–12 due to the poorest offensive support of any major league pitcher. Surely, we all figured, this can't continue in 1987?

In 1987 Jackson's ERA was 4.02, still almost half a run a game better than the league average. His ERA was as good as or better than that of Bruce Hurst (15–13), Mike Witt (16–14), Walt Terrell (17–10), Bert Blyleven (15–12), Tommie John (13–6), Curt Young (13–7), Jose Guzman (14–14) or Dave Stieb (13–9). Jackson finished 9–18.

At this point, the willingness of people to believe that Danny was just simply unlucky has been stretched—stretched, for most people, well beyond the breaking point. "Jackson had chances to win games last year, and he didn't do it," is a common refrain in the KC area. "If he had a good ERA and didn't win in one year, then maybe you'd say he was unlucky. But year after year? It can't be bad luck year after year. Jackson just doesn't have the composure to pitch well when he needs to pitch well."

The fact that Danny had chances to win games and didn't do it, by itself, means little. Every pitcher in baseball last year had chances to win games and didn't do it at least a few times. Roger Clemens on June 26 had a 9–0 lead after two innings—and he blew it. The Red Sox lost the game. Danny in his whole career has never done anything like that. Jack Morris last year had nine games in which the Tigers scored three runs or more, and yet he failed to win. Clemens had thirteen such games. He had the luxury of kicking away thirteen opportunities for a victory, because he had 32 such chances. Danny didn't.

As to his composure . . . well, I saw most of Jackson's starts last year. He was my "draw." You know how that works—every year, if you go to 20 home games a year, you're going to run into the same starting pitcher 15 times. Danny was the one I kept running into in 1987. I didn't see a pitcher losing his composure. I thought, on some occasions, that he showed considerable restraint in not losing his temper during what must have been an astonishingly frustrating season, going in dreaming of a Cy Young season and finding himself, on August 1, saddled with a 4–13 record despite a pretty good ERA. I saw a pitcher losing a lot of games 2–0 and 3–2.

But that's just the point, would reply the other side. Jackson has pitched just well enough to lose. If he gets two runs, he allows three. If he gets three, he allows four or five. But he hasn't done what he has to do to win.

But, of course, he does win sometimes—he has won 34 games over the last three years, which is a lot more

than, say, Gene Nelson or Dan Schatzeder. He has won a lot of close games, even last year. On May 3, when the Royals scored just 2 runs, he pitched a four-hitter to beat Cleveland 2–1, the one run being unearned. When the Royals scored just two runs on June 19, Jackson shut out California (one of the key teams the Royals had to beat) for a 2–0 win. When the Royals scored just three runs against Minnesota, *the* team the Royals had to beat, on June 29, Jackson beat the Twins 3–2. When the Royals scored just three runs on August 26, Jackson shut out Texas for a 3–0 win.

The question is, can he—or can *anybody*—be expected to win games consistently with two or three runs? He was shut out last year five times, more than some American League teams. He had two runs or less eighteen (!) times. Could any pitcher, other than Sandy Koufax, win consistently with that kind of offensive support? Sure, he hasn't taken advantage of 100 percent of his opportunities, but that's not realistic. The question is, what advantage has he taken of his opportunities? How do you balance it?

Before I can let go of Danny, as a Royals' fan, I felt I just had to resolve this once and for all. I entered into a computer file the data on all of Jackson's major-league starts. As a comparison, I also entered all the appearances over the last three years for Walt Terrell of the Tigers. Terrell's ERAs over the last three years have never been as good as Jacksons:

```
1985   Jackson:   3.42   Terrell:   3.85
1986   Jackson:   3.20   Terrell:   4.56
1987   Jackson:   4.02   Terrell:   4.05
```

But his won/lost records have been better:

```
1985   Terrell:   15–10   Jackson:   14–12
1986   Terrell:   15–12   Jackson:   11–12
1987   Terrell:   17–10   Jackson:    9–18
```

The inevitable conclusion that people will draw is that Terrell has pitched well when he has had to pitch well to win.

The first thing I looked at was how many times each pitcher had been supported by each number of runs. This includes all starts of his major league career for Jackson (111 starts) and all starts, 1985–1987, for Terrell (103 starts), in both cases including post-season play. The runs breakdown shows a dramatic difference in pattern:

NUMBER OF TIMES SUPPORTED BY X RUNS

X =	0	1	2	3	4	5	6	7	8	9	10 or more
Jackson	9	16	22	19	11	10	10	8	3	2	1
Terrell	1	7	13	14	16	15	9	10	7	6	5

Jackson has been shut out nine times, Terrell only once. Jackson has had 25 games with zero or one run; Terrell has had 8. Jackson has had 66 games with 0–3 runs. Terrell has had barely half as many, 35. But Terrell has a 68–45 advantage in the games that starting pitchers usually win, the games with four runs of support or more, and

Terrell has an 18–6 edge in the "automatic wins" category, the games in which the teams scored eight or more runs. Altogether, Terrell has been supported by 509 runs, or 4.94 per game. Jackson has been supported by 379 runs, or 3.41 per game. Jackson has had the support of 130 less runs in eight more games.

The new question is, however, "When Jackson had the runs, did he win?" When Terrell had one run, how often did he win? When Jackson had one run, how often did he win? Given the same number of runs to work with, how often did each pitcher win?

Obviously, neither pitcher won at all when the team scored no runs, this being impossible. Jackson was 0–8 in such games, Terrell 0–1. Why don't I do the chart first, and then discuss it:

Working With	Jackson		Terrell		Edge To
0 Runs	0–8	.00	0–1	.00	None
1 Runs	1–14	.07	0–6	.00	Jackson
2 Runs	7–11	.389	5–8	.385	Jackson
3 Runs	5–10	.33	9–4	.69	Terrell
4 Runs	6–3	.67	5–6	.45	Jackson
5 Runs	6–2	.75	5–6	.45	Jackson
6 Runs	5–1	.83	2–1	.67	Jackson
7 Runs	4–1	.80	7–0	1.00	Terrell
8 Runs	2–0	1.00	7–0	1.00	None
9 Runs	1–0	1.00	4–0	1.00	None
10 Or More	1–0	1.00	3–0	1.00	None

The first thing that strikes me here is that Jackson is 1–22 in games in which his team had no runs or only one run. Those games are virtually always losses, of course—Jackson had one 1–0 victory, Terrell none. But those 22 losses account for almost half of Jackson's 50 career defeats.

Given three runs to work with, Terrell has, in fact, pitched better than Jackson. These are their records in games in which their team scored three runs:

	GS	IP	W	L	Pct.	SO	BB	ERA
Terrell	14	103.1	9	4	.692	58	38	2.87
Jackson	19	112	5	10	.333	62	41	4.18

Given three runs, Terrell pitched well enough to win consistently; Jackson did not. Incidentally, a normal record for an American League pitcher given three runs would be 6–9. Terrell's record in these games is exceptional, Jackson's a little below average.

But this is the *only* level at which this happens. In games in which the team scored two runs, Jackson's record is truly exceptional, 7–11. Terrell's is odd, in that he also has a very good won-lost record (5–8) but a high ERA:

	GS	IP	W	L	Pct.	SO	BB	ERA
Jackson	22	154	7	11	.389	93	75	2.86
Terrell	13	84.1	5	8	.385	53	38	4.80

I doubt that any major-league pitcher, other than perhaps Gooden or Clemens, has a won-lost record when working with only two runs significantly better than Danny Jackson's. Two runs gives the pitcher a chance to win, but only if he pitches extremely well.

Given four runs and a decent chance to win, Jackson has out-pitched Terrell by a wide margin:

	GS	IP	W	L	Pct.	SO	BB	ERA
Jackson	11	83	6	3	.667	65	27	3.14
Terrell	16	102.2	5	6	.455	58	36	5.08

Given five runs to work with, Jackson has won routinely, while Terrell has had a terrible time:

	GS	IP	W	L	Pct.	SO	BB	ERA
Jackson	10	66.1	6	2	.750	54	24	3.93
Terrell	15	96.1	5	6	.455	46	47	5.61

The record of Jackson's teams with five runs is excellent, 8–2. The Tigers record when they score five runs and throw Terrell at the opposition is 6–9. Combining the two, when his teams score four or five runs, Jackson is 12–5 and his teams are 15–6. When his teams score four or five, Terrell is 10–12 and his teams are 12–19.

Even given six runs, Terrell has had trouble winning consistently. Terrell has posted a 4.97 ERA, and the Tigers with six runs have lost five of nine games:

	GS	IP	W	L	Pct.	SO	BB	ERA
Jackson	10	59.1	5	1	.833	31	30	4.25
Terrell	9	58	2	1	.667	32	27	4.97

Jackson's team in these games is 7–3; Terrell's, 4–5.

With seven or more runs, Jackson has lost once in his career and Terrell has never lost. That offsets the one-nothing games, where Jackson has one victory and Terrell has none.

You can, if you want, put these together in a formal way by projecting Jackson's won-lost record at each level of offensive support onto Terrell's number of opportunities. For example, Jackson in 19 starts with three runs was 5–10. Project that onto Terrell's number of opportunities at that level (14), and you get a probable record of 3.7 wins and 7.4 losses. Repeat this procedure at every stop, and you conclude that given Terrell's pattern of offensive support, Jackson's record would probably be about 48–30—a game and a half better than Terrell's record of 47–32.

Ordinarily, I would compare their records on the road to remove the possibility of a park bias, but given Terrell's well known home-road disparity (over the three years he was 32–8 at home, 15–24 on the road) that obviously would be unfair to Terrell. But the pattern, I think, is very clear. Given almost any level of offensive support, Jackson has been more consistent in delivering a victory than has Terrell. Terrell's superior won-lost record is simply and totally created by his superior offensive support. It is the ERA, not the won-lost record, which indicates how well the two men have pitched.

HOUSTON ASTROS

Superficially at least, Houston's starting pitchers may have had the best credentials of any major-league team:

• Astro starting pitchers struck out 824 men, most in the major leagues.

• Astro starting pitchers made 93 quality starts, the most of any major-league team.

• Houston had 32 starts with game scores of 70 or better, the most of any major-league team.

• They had only 19 games with game scores under 30, fifth-fewest of any team.

• Their average game score, 53.4, was the best of any major-league team.

• The Astros' record when scoring three to five runs was 32–27, third best in the National League.

• The Houston starting pitcher lasted less than five innings only 24 times, second-best in the major leagues.

• In the games they won, the Astros allowed an average of just 2.36 runs, the fewest of any major-league team.

• Astro starters posted an ERA of 3.82, third best in the major leagues. The staff ERA, 3.84, was fourth in the majors.

Unfortunately, it was all done in one park. In the Astrodome, the Astros' pitching starts were terrific. In the Astrodome the Astros allowed only 268 runs, 38 fewer than any other major-league team. But in road games they allowed 410 runs, missing by just two the highest total in the National League (the Cubs allowed 412). All of those starts were, to one extent or another, strictly a park illusion.

The Astro offense didn't work anywhere. The Astro offense ranked twenty-fifth among the 26 teams in runs scored in their home park. In road games they ranked twenty-sixth.

Since neither the offense nor the defense worked on the road, the Astros on the road had a record of 29–52.

The 1987 Astros, defending champions, began the season well. The Astros won their first six games, all of them at home. They went on the road on April 13. They lost. From that point on the season was a roller coaster ride, ascending regularly to about five games over .500, then dipping down again, each time dipping lower than the time before. Holding at five games over .500 until May 14 (19–14), the Astros then lost eight of nine to drop two games under .500 (22–22). They rallied strongly over the following month; by June 27 they were back to seven games over, at 40–33. A prolonged slump cut them back under .500 by July 19, to three games under .500 by August 1, to four games under .500 by August 13. Winning ten of eleven in mid-August, the Astros vaulted back into the race by August 24; they were 65–60. They were one-half game out of first; the Giants were 66–60.

And then they fell apart. They lost seven straight games. Over the last six weeks their record was 11–26. What went wrong?

In 1986, when Hal Lanier was the toast of the town,

he said that the most important thing that he learned from working with Whitey Herzog was how to run a pitching staff. Last year, however, Lanier did something that Whitey Herzog has never done in his whole career, something the avoidance of which is one of the small secrets of his success: Lanier rode his horse too hard. Through the first 16 starts of the season, Mike Scott was perhaps even better than he had been in his Cy Young 1986 season; he was 9–3 with 125 strikeouts in 111 innings, only 68 hits allowed and a 2.10 ERA. His average game score was 67.6. For the rest of the season, however, Scott was a very ordinary pitcher—a 7–10 record, a 4.16 ERA, 131 hits allowed in 136 innings, average game score of 53.3. We don't know that this decline could have been avoided, but we do know that during those first 16 starts, Scott worked awfully hard.

If you look back at Whitey Herzog's career, you'll find that he has essentially always had excellent team ERAs, but that he has never had Cy Young winners or even really Cy Young candidates. The Royals led the league in ERA in 1977, missed by a tiny margin in 1976 and finished third in 1978. The Cardinals were third in the league in ERA in '82, second in '85, above average the rest of the time—yet no Herzog pitcher has won the Cy Young Award. Why? Because he doesn't manage that way. If his starting pitcher is tired, he gets him out of there and puts in a reliever. The pitcher may win 15 rather than 22, but he'll be there next year. There just aren't very many pitchers who can complete game after game after game, year after year; there aren't, and never have been. The Houston fans must pray that Scott's arm will snap back over the winter, and maybe it will, but that was strike one in the degeneration of the 1987 Astros.

There is a second moment, equally clear, at which the Astros season started to go sour. It was the moment at which Ken Caminiti went into the lineup. At the All-Star break the Astros were one game over .500, 44–43. Caminiti was called up from Columbus (Southern League, AA) over the break; he had hit .325 at Columbus with 15 homers, 69 RBI in 95 games. In his first few games with the Astros Caminiti was the second coming of George Brett. In his first game he hit a triple and a home run, scoring both runs of a 2–1 win; in his second game he added two more hits, in his third game two more hits, one of them a double, in his fourth game he hit a home run. After one oh-fur, he added a 2-for-4 and a 2-for-5. Then he didn't do a damn thing the rest of the year. Through his first seven games he hit .407 (11/27) with a .741 slugging percentage; the rest of the season he hit .222 with 1 homer and 19 RBI in 56 games—but, because he had played so well through those first seven games, he stayed in the lineup. What may be worse than the fact that he stayed in the lineup was that he was taking playing time away from Denny Walling, one of the Astros' best hitters during their championship 1986 season. Walling, hitting .299 at the All-Star break, batted only 131 times over the second half of the season. The Astros scored 4.16 runs per game over the first half of the season, 3.81 the second half.

Strike three was Jim Deshaies. Deshaies was 10–4 on August 24 despite a 19-day stay on the disabled list with what was believed to be tendinitis in his shoulder. He had an ERA of 7.27 in his last seven starts, and was found at the conclusion of the season to have "a slight tear in the left rotator cuff. . . . 'It sounds a lot worse than it is,' said Deshaies." (October 26, 1987, *The Sporting News*.)

Relief ace Dave Smith had to be nursed through the season because of a tender elbow. Through August 24, Smith had pitched 51 innings, giving up only 25 hits and 6 earned runs, a 1.06 ERA. Over the last 37 games he pitched only 9 innings, giving up 14 hits and 5 earned runs.

The inability to use Smith forced Lanier to use his number-two and -three men in the bullpen down the stretch. Rookie Rocky Childress, who had a 1.72 ERA in 20 appearances through August 20, pitched 12 more times, with an ERA of 5.29 ERA. Journeyman Larry Andersen, with a 2.86 ERA in 52 games through August 20, pitched 15 more times with an ERA of 5.48.

On August 31 Danny Darwin had to leave the game after one inning because of a pulled muscle in his left side. He didn't start again until September 17.

Mike Scott pitched 62 innings over the period with a 4.06 ERA, about as well as he had been pitching since June. Three pitchers pitched well over the period—Heathcock, Agosto, and Nolan Ryan.

Shortstop Craig Reynolds during the last six weeks hit .198.

Catcher Alan Ashby hit .200.

Billy Hatcher, suspended early in the period for using an illegal bat, had a .311 batting average at the time. He hit only .203 when he returned.

Two outfielders, Kevin Bass and Gerald Young, continued to hit well during the collapse.

The Astros defensively were a combination of strong points and soft points. No Astro won a Gold Glove, but second baseman Billy Doran and all three second-half outfielders (Young, Hatcher, and Bass) are excellent defensive players. The other three infielders (Davis, Caminiti, and Reynolds) were at best average on defense. The big defensive problem was at catcher. Astro opponents stole 199 bases, third-highest total in the major leagues. That, combined with a major-league leading 1,137 strikeouts, took the double play away from them; the Astros turned only 113 double plays, lowest total in the major leagues.

In last year's *Baseball Abstract,* I wrote that "I foresee a difficult two- or three-year period ahead for the Astros." I cited seven reasons for this: fat pitchers, a question about whether or not Mike Scott could repeat his 1986 season, the fact that the Astros had loaded up for the 1986 stretch drive with veterans like Dave Lopes, Matt Keough and Aurelio Lopez, who would not contribute in 1987, the age of a few key performers, the lack of a catcher, improved competition from Cincinnati and Los Angeles, and the inability of Dick Wagner to work successfully with talented subordinates. One of those factors was irrelevant or even dead wrong; the competition was not improved. But all of the other factors did combine to destroy the Astros' 1987 season. The Astros "got through" a few of those problems,

put them behind them, but the others in my opinion will continue to make life difficult for the Astros in the next year or two.

1) Fat Pitchers. Kerfeld, Lopez, Smith, possibly Knepper. They were way down last year, and they dragged the team down with them. That's behind them in one sense, since the Astros won't be counting on most of these guys in the future, but still ahead of them in another, since they must still rebuild the staff to championship quality.

2) A question about Mike Scott's ability to pitch at a high level. That question remains.

3) The veterans who joined the team for the 1986 stretch drive have extracted their cost and have been dispatched.

4) The age of key performers. The average age of the Astro regulars in 1987 (eight position players, four starting pitchers, and the relief ace) was 32.1 years, making them the oldest team in the major leagues (see Pittsburgh charts). Most of the age was concentrated among the pitchers—Nolan Ryan (40), Bob Knepper (33), Mike Scott (32), Danny Darwin (31) and Dave Smith (32). Those are 1987 ages; add one for 1988. Shortstop Reynolds and catcher Alan Ashby also contributed to driving the age up. They made a little progress on this late in the season, in replacing the Garner/Walling combination with Ken Caminiti and replacing Jose Cruz with rookie sensation Gerald Young. The problem essentially remains to be solved.

5) The lack of a catcher. The Astros last year again used their first-round draft pick on a catcher, and this time they seem to have done a better job. First-round pick Craig Biggio went to Asheville, where he hit .375 with 49 RBI in 64 games, not to mention 31 stolen bases. The problem can't be considered solved.

6) The Dick Wagner era. The catching problem—the failure to trade for a usable catcher—was one of the bones of contention between Hal Lanier and Dick Wagner, which led to an early surfacing of the inevitable problems created by having Dick Wagner run your organization. Wagner was fired, and that's behind them now.

7) The quality of the opposition. Although the NL West had a very poor season in 1987, I think the division will be much stronger, and the NL East much weaker, in 1988. If not this year, then it will in 1989.

The Astros' signing of Joaquin Andujar this winter reminds me that one of the distinguishing marks of a quality organization is that a quality organization is never content to pick up the odds and ends of a player's career. If you think of a player's career as a watermelon, a juicy delicious center surrounded by good but less tasty parts surrounded by the somewhat bitter parts near the rind surrounded by the rind itself, which must be thrown away; it is all called by the same name, watermelon, and it's parts are not clearly marked, but when you look at the player's career as a whole one of the critical questions is who ate the heart of it. The Cincinnati Reds paid for Joaquin Andujar's minor-league instruction. The Astros struggled with him in his early years in the majors. The Oakland A's and now the Astros again must pick up the tab to acquire a pitcher with a big name and a big rep. But the Cardinals ate the heart of his career, employing him for four and a half years during which he went 68–53 and was never overpaid. A lot of people think that the Cardinals must be wailing and gnashing their teeth over the departure of Jack Clark, but in a few years you'll see that they did the same thing there—the Giants paid to school him and put up with him in his early years, the Yankees picked up the tab for his near-MVP campaign in 1987, and in two years somebody else will pay him another million in the hopes that he can show another flash of brilliance, but the Cardinals ate the heart of his career. Milwaukee trained Darrell Porter, the Cardinals and then the Rangers paid the most money for him—but the Royals ate the heart of his career. The Andujar gamble isn't an awful one; Joaquin's arm is sound as of now and if his arm is sound he can pitch. But he'll never win 41 games in a two-year stretch again. The Astros have settled to clean up the rind of his career and to get a few bites of the bitter part near the rind. No way I would have signed him.

Another thing that was being written a year ago, when the Astros were on top of the world, was that Hal Lanier had turned the Astros around by concentrating on moving baserunners, hitting behind the runner, etc. I wrote then that "my opinion is that, as an offensive manager, Hal Lanier did a very poor job . . . in spite of the fact that the number of runs scored was up around the rest of the league, the Astros dropped from 693 runs scored to 654." Last year the number of runs scored by the league was up by another 675 runs (56 per team). The number scored by the Astros was down another six runs.

The Astros have a core of good young talent, in Bass, Davis, Young, Doran, Deshaies, maybe Hatcher. They're not going to win in 1988, and if they keep signing people like Joaquin Andujar to get them over the hump, it could be a long time before that core of talent forms into a ballclub.

AVERAGE GAME SCORE

Houston	53.4
Los Angeles	53.3
Detroit	51.9
Toronto	51.9
Kansas City	51.8
Mets	51.6
Pittsburgh	50.9
White Sox	50.5
San Francisco	50.1
Montreal	50.0
Boston	49.6
St. Louis	49.4
Minnesota	49.2
Oakland	49.0
Yankees	48.8
San Diego	48.6
Milwaukee	48.5
Seattle	48.3
California	47.7
Texas	47.6
Cubs	47.4
Cincinnati	47.2
Philadelphia	47.1
Atlanta	46.2
Baltimore	45.4
Cleveland	44.6

RUNS SCORED AND ALLOWED WINS AND LOSSES

Wins	433	179	76-0	1.000
Darwin	133	113	18-12	.600
Home Games	334	268	47-34	.580
Scott	132	122	19-17	.528
Slugfests	271	273	21-19	.525
Deshaies	116	108	13-12	.520
Blowouts	213	238	20-22	.476
All Games	648	678	76-86	.469
Pitchers' Duels	79	81	20-23	.465
One-Run Games	195	199	25-29	.463
Knepper	128	165	12-19	.414
Road Games	314	410	29-52	.358
Ryan	114	138	12-22	.353
Losses	215	499	0-86	.000

TEN BEST STARTS

	IP	H	R	ER	BB	SO		
Scott at LA, Apr 15	9	1	0	0	1	10	W	94
Scott at Mon, May 8	9	2	0	0	2	12	W	93
Scott at Mon, July 22	9	4	0	0	3	10	W	86
Ryan vs. Cin, Apr 25	8	3	0	0	2	11	—	85
Darwin at LA, June 14	9	2	1	1	1	6	W	84
Scott at Pit, May 18	9	3	1	1	2	8	W	83
Ryan vs. SD, Sep 19	9	5	1	1	1	11	—	83
Scott vs. Cin, June 15	8*	7	0	0	0	14	W	82
Scott vs. SF, June 5	7	2	1	1	1	13	W	81
Scott vs. LA, June 20	9	3	2	2	1	9	W	81

PITCHERS WHEN SUPPORTED BY THREE TO FIVE RUNS

	G	IP	W-L	Pct	SO	BB	ERA
Scott	14	110	8-2	.800	111	20	2.46
Ryan	11	71	4-3	.571	107	23	2.28
Darwin	12	77	4-3	.571	44	23	2.93
Knepper	11	64	3-6	.333	31	15	4.81
Deshaies	10	57	1-3	.250	43	22	5.81

HALL OF FAME WATCH

Fully qualified: Nolan Ryan 152.5; **Building credentials but not yet viable candidate:** D. Lopes 42, M. Scott 38; **Working on it:** D. Smith 26, Jose Cruz 24, Knepper 15, Ashby 15, A. Lopez 12 **Long way to go:** C. Reynolds 9, G. Davis 9, Lanier 8, Thon 8, Bass 5.5, Doran 5, Puhl 3.5, Walling 3.5, Andersen 3, Darwin 1, B. Hatcher 1, Kerfeld 1. (All of Lanier's points are as a manager.)

TEN WORST STARTS

	IP	H	R	ER	BB	SO		
Knepper at Chi, June 3	1	7	9	9	2	1	L	2
Scott at SD, Sep 11	2	6	7	7	5	0	L	11
Scott at SF, Aug 12	6⅔	12	8	8	3	3	L	18
DeShaies at SD, Sep 13	4⅓	9	8	7	2	6	L	19
Knepper at Cin, Apr 17	4*	9	7	5	1	2	L	21
Scott vs. StL, May 24	1⅓	2	7	5	6	1	L	21
Knepper vs. Cin, Apr 26	5	12	5	5	1	3	L	25
Mallicot vs. Cin, Oct 2	1⅔	5	4	4	4	0	—	25
Ryan at Chi, June 2	2*	6	5	5	1	3	L	26
Scott at Atl, July 28	4	9	5	5	2	4	L	26

RUNS SCORED ON THE ROAD

Detroit	454
Oakland	443
Milwaukee	422
Toronto	420
Mets	416
St. Louis	411
San Francisco	410
Boston	406
Texas	397
California	393
Yankees	387
Cincinnati	387
Baltimore	378
Minnesota	375
Cleveland	369
Seattle	357
Los Angeles	355
White Sox	354
Montreal	340
Kansas City	340
Cubs	339
San Diego	330
Atlanta	326
Pittsburgh	319
Philadelphia	317
Houston	314

Alan ASHBY, Catcher
Runs created: 61

	G	AB	Hit	2B	3B	HR	Run	RBI	TBB	SO	SB	CS	Avg
7.87 years		487	120	22	2	11	48	61	54	73	1	1	.246
1987	125	386	111	16	0	14	53	63	50	52	0	1	.288
First Half	69	206	63	13	0	8	28	34	30	24	0	0	.306
Second Half	56	180	48	3	0	6	25	29	20	28	0	1	.267
Vs. RHP		245	75	13	0	14	39	53	37	40	0	0	.306
Vs. LHP		141	36	3	0	0	14	10	13	12	0	1	.255
Home	63	200	67	8	0	8	33	40	26	29	0	0	.335
Road	62	186	44	8	0	6	20	23	24	23	0	1	.237

Billy HATCHER, Outfield
Runs Created: 89

	G	AB	Hit	2B	3B	HR	Run	RBI	TBB	SO	SB	CS	Avg
2.03 years		569	156	27	4	9	87	54	36	66	47	13	.274
1987	141	564	167	28	3	11	96	63	42	70	53	9	.296
First Half	80	320	101	16	2	7	54	38	27	46	33	3	.316
Second Half	61	244	66	12	1	4	42	25	15	24	20	6	.270
Vs. RHP		362	111	16	2	7	63	37	25	41	32	5	.307
Vs. LHP		202	56	12	1	4	33	26	17	29	21	4	.277
Home	65	259	79	11	0	3	46	27	20	43	26	3	.305
Road	76	305	88	17	3	8	50	36	22	27	27	6	.289

Glenn DAVIS, First Base
Runs Created: 80

	G	AB	Hit	2B	3B	HR	Run	RBI	TBB	SO	SB	CS	Avg
2.64 years		592	153	31	2	30	83	101	54	89	3	1	.258
1987	151	578	145	35	2	27	70	93	47	84	4	1	.251
First Half	82	324	89	22	1	15	39	49	25	50	2	1	.275
Second Half	69	254	56	13	1	12	31	44	22	34	2	0	.220
Vs. RHP		385	98	22	1	17	42	65	27	54	3	1	.255
Vs. LHP		193	47	13	1	10	28	28	20	30	1	0	.244
Home	76	285	71	16	1	12	34	45	24	41	3	1	.249
Road	75	293	74	19	1	15	36	48	23	43	1	0	.253

Gerald YOUNG, Center Field
Runs Created: 44

	G	AB	Hit	2B	3B	HR	Run	RBI	TBB	SO	SB	CS	Avg
0.44 years		623	200	20	5	2	100	34	59	61	59	20	.321
1987	71	274	88	9	2	1	44	15	26	27	26	9	.321
First Half	5	21	4	1	0	0	3	1	3	3	4	0	.190
Second Half	66	253	84	8	2	1	41	14	23	24	22	9	.332
Vs. RHP		169	47	4	2	0	28	8	20	15	17	6	.278
Vs. LHP		105	41	5	0	1	16	7	6	12	9	3	.390
Home	37	145	52	8	2	0	24	8	16	14	11	7	.359
Road	34	129	36	1	0	1	20	7	10	13	15	2	.279

Billy DORAN, Second Base
Runs Created: 99

	G	AB	Hit	2B	3B	HR	Run	RBI	TBB	SO	SB	CS	Avg
4.83 years		607	168	24	6	10	89	54	81	70	28	14	.277
1987	162	625	177	23	3	16	82	79	82	64	31	11	.283
First Half	87	348	95	11	1	12	49	40	41	44	15	7	.273
Second Half	75	277	82	12	2	4	33	39	41	20	16	4	.296
Vs. RHP		402	112	18	2	9	53	46	43	45	23	6	.279
Vs. LHP		223	65	5	1	7	29	33	39	19	8	5	.291
Home	81	292	89	9	1	7	45	36	55	31	19	8	.305
Road	81	333	88	14	2	9	37	43	27	33	12	3	.264

Kevin BASS, Right Field
Runs Created: 90

	G	AB	Hit	2B	3B	HR	Run	RBI	TBB	SO	SB	CS	Avg
4.34 years		526	145	26	5	14	70	65	31	70	16	8	.276
1987	157	592	168	31	5	19	83	85	53	77	21	8	.284
First Half	86	330	93	18	5	9	47	49	29	44	10	7	.282
Second Half	71	262	75	13	0	10	36	36	24	33	11	1	.286
Vs. RHP		365	104	18	1	9	53	50	43	46	12	3	.285
Vs. LHP		227	64	13	4	10	30	35	10	31	9	5	.282
Home	79	302	86	17	2	10	48	52	30	45	13	2	.285
Road	78	290	82	14	3	9	35	33	23	32	8	6	.283

Denny WALLING, Third Base
Runs Created: 50

	G	AB	Hit	2B	3B	HR	Run	RBI	TBB	SO	SB	CS	Avg
6.25 years		393	110	19	4	7	53	52	43	41	7	3	.280
1987	110	325	92	21	4	5	45	33	39	37	5	1	.283
First Half	60	194	58	13	1	3	29	19	17	22	4	1	.299
Second Half	50	131	34	8	3	2	16	14	22	15	1	0	.260
Vs. RHP		290	85	20	4	4	40	30	38	27	5	1	.293
Vs. LHP		35	7	1	0	1	5	3	1	10	0	0	.200
Home	52	156	45	7	0	2	22	19	19	18	3	1	.288
Road	58	169	47	14	4	3	23	14	20	19	2	0	.278

José CRUZ, Goodbye
Runs Created: 47

	G	AB	Hit	2B	3B	HR	Run	RBI	TBB	SO	SB	CS	Avg
14.29 years		548	156	27	7	11	72	75	62	72	22	9	.285
1987	126	365	88	17	4	11	47	38	36	65	4	1	.241
First Half	77	266	67	15	2	8	38	29	24	46	2	0	.252
Second Half	49	99	21	2	2	3	9	9	12	19	2	1	.212
Vs. RHP		237	59	14	3	7	37	25	28	40	3	1	.249
Vs. LHP		128	29	3	1	4	10	13	8	25	1	0	.227
Home	60	180	48	10	2	6	20	22	15	31	4	1	.267
Road	66	185	40	7	2	5	27	16	21	34	0	0	.216

Craig REYNOLDS, Shortstop
Runs Created: 42

	G	AB	Hit	2B	3B	HR	Run	RBI	TBB	SO	SB	CS	Avg
8.10 years		508	131	16	8	5	55	43	25	45	7	4	.258
1987	135	374	95	17	3	4	35	28	30	44	5	1	.254
First Half	68	193	51	10	1	2	19	20	13	19	4	1	.264
Second Half	67	181	44	7	2	2	16	8	17	25	1	0	.243
Vs. RHP		331	89	17	3	4	31	28	27	34	4	1	.269
Vs. LHP		43	6	0	0	0	4	0	3	10	1	0	.140
Home	69	189	49	8	2	0	15	10	17	19	1	1	.259
Road	66	185	46	9	1	4	20	18	13	25	4	0	.249

CHEAP WINS, TOUGH LOSSES

When you have data in a computer, you start thinking about things you can do with it. This is totally the wrong way to approach sabermetrics; nothing of interest has ever been developed by starting with the numbers and figuring out what you can do with them. All the good stuff comes from starting with a question and trying to assemble the evidence that relates to it.

Anywho, as Wade West used to say, I had on computer a record of every start by each major-league pitcher in 1987, when somebody said to me that Eric Show had to be the unluckiest pitcher in the major leagues, and ticked off a handful of games in which Show had pitched well, but been charged with a defeat. Granted, I thought, Show was pretty unlucky, finishing 8–16 with a better-than-league ERA, but was he the *most* unlucky pitcher? What about Danny Jackson, or Fernando, or Nolan Ryan, or Tom Candiotti?

I decided to define and count two categories of performance related to this issue: Cheap Wins and Tough Losses. A cheap win is any game in which the starting pitcher is credited with a win despite a game score below 50. A tough loss is any game in which a starting pitcher is charged with a defeat despite a game score of 50 or above.

The first thing I discovered is that there are more tough losses than cheap wins. There are a couple of technical reasons for this—the average game score last year was 49.4 rather than 50.0, and I defined the midpoint (50) as being a potential tough loss, rather than a potential cheap win—but those things explain only a small part of the disparity. One thing that contributes to the imbalance is that you can be charged with a loss if you pitch only two innings, while you can't get a win—and thus can't get a cheap win—if you are out before five. To balance the scales, you'd need a rule that said that a starting pitcher couldn't be charged with a loss unless he allowed at least three runs, or something. There were, in the major leagues last year, 234 cheap wins and 369 tough losses. For each 100 games played, there were 11 cheap wins and 18 tough losses.

The unluckiest pitcher, by far, was Nolan Ryan. Ryan was credited with no cheap wins. He was charged with 11 tough losses. These are the major-league pitchers who were charged with five or more tough losses:

Nolan Ryan	11
Mark Gubicza	7
Tom Candiotti	6
Jack Morris	6
Mike Witt	6
Orel Hershiser	6
Kevin Gross	6

Mike Witt and Kevin Gross were credited with two cheap wins; none of the rest of these pitchers had more than one. Ryan's record was 8–16; had he been credited with a win every time he pitched well and got a decision, and been charged with a defeat whenever he pitched poorly and had a decision, his record would have been 19–5. Ryan, you know, spoke out saying that he should have been considered for the Cy Young Award despite his won-lost record, and certainly there is something to that; I have been trying to tell people for more than a decade that single-season won-lost records are not a reliable guage of how well a man has pitched. Ryan in 1987 was 0–5 when he didn't pitch well, and 8–11 when he did pitch well.

Ryan's "adjusted" record, 19–5, certainly would have had him in the running for a Cy Young Award, but if the same were done for other pitchers, there would be other impressive records. Adjusted records would include: Tom Candiotti, 12–13 rather than 7–18; Jack Morris, 24–5 rather than 18–11 (Morris had six tough losses, no cheap wins); Jimmie Key, 21–4 rather than 17–8; Mike Witt, 20–10 rather than 16–14; Danny Jackson, 14–13 rather than 9–18; Mark Gubicza, 19–12 rather than 13–18; Frank Viola, 21–6 rather than 17–10; Orel Hershiser, 21–11 rather than 16–16; Fernando Valenzuela, 19–9 rather than 14–14; Eric Show, 12–12 rather than 8–16; Bob Sebra, 10–11 rather than 6–15; Kevin Gross, 13–12 rather than 9–16; and Mike Scott, 20–9 rather than 16–13. The pitchers I listed were those who gain four games or more in the adjustment, and thus that is, in effect, a list of the unluckiest pitchers of 1987.

The major-league pitcher with the most cheap wins was Ron Darling of New York, who had five. Oddly, Darling was regarded for most of the season as a very unlucky pitcher, but between July 22 and August 16 he had three games in which he picked up wins despite so-so pitching, including a win in a 23–10 game at Wrigley on August 16. No pitcher was "lucky" to the extent that Ryan or Morris was "unlucky"; Darling had five cheap wins but three tough losses, so his record in a fair universe would have been 10–10, rather than 12–8. A 10–10 record would have been consistent with his 4.29 ERA. The major-league pitchers who had four cheap wins were Richard Dotson, Curt Young, Dave Stewart, Rick Sutcliffe, Les Lancaster, and Shane Rawley. Most of those pitchers had about as many tough losses as cheap wins, but Lancaster had four cheap wins, no tough losses, so his record would adjust from 8–3 to 4–7. The adjusted records of other pitchers who would lose two or more games: Eric Bell, 8–15 rather than 10–13; Dan Petry, 7–9 rather than 9–7; Juan Nieves, 12–10 rather than 14–8; Mike Smithson, 2–9 rather than 4–7; Lee Guetterman, 9–6 rather than 11–4; Scott Sanderson, 6–11 rather than 8–9; Rick Augilera, 8–6 rather than 11–3; Shane Rawley, 15–13 rather than 17–11; Bruce Ruffin, 9–16 rather than 11–14; Floyd Youmans, 6–11 rather than 9–8; Brian Fisher, 9–11 rather than 11–9; Bob Forsch, 9–9 rather than 11–7; Zane Smith, 13–12 rather than 15–10; Randy O'Neal, 1–5 rather than 4–2; Doyle Alexander, 11–13 rather than 14–10; Mario Soto, 0–5 rather than 3–2; and Jim Deshaies, 9–8 rather than 11–6.

If you look at those lists of names and records, you will learn something. The list of the unluckiest pitchers in the major leagues includes many of the best pitchers in baseball: Mike Scott, Jack Morris, Nolan Ryan, Mike Witt, Orel Hershiser, Fernando, Jimmie Key, Frank Viola. All of these actually deserved better records than they posted. Roger Clemens just missed the list; he should have finished 23–6 rather than 20–9. The list of the luckiest pitchers is, for the most part, a list of guys who are going to be out of the league in three years. From this we learn, or in this we can see, that luck is a levelling factor in won-lost records. The difference between the best pitchers and the worst pitchers is much greater than is reflected in one-season won-lost records.

In these lists, however, we can also see where the method breaks down. Many of the pitchers who are listed as most "unlucky" pitched in pitcher's parks, in consequence of which they pitched in a lot of games in which neither team was able to score many runs. Houston, Los Angeles, and Kansas City all had two pitchers on the "unlucky" list; the Cubs, Braves, and Red Sox didn't have any. Was Zane Smith, who "should have finished" 13–12 rather than 15–10, actually a "lucky" pitcher? Hardly. He just posted lower game scores because of pitching in Atlanta. The Cubs' starters had 17 cheap wins, only 11 tough losses; Houston had 6 and 22, and Los Angeles had

2 and 24. That detail overstates the problem, which is not systematically that extreme. Even in road games, LA pitchers had many fewer cheap wins and more tough losses than did the Cubs. Six of Nolan Ryan's 11 tough losses were on the road, so he would have led the majors in tough losses even if he'd only had two in the Astrodome. But it is a problem that you'd have to deal with if you were going to put a lot of weight on this method.

In closing I was going to run a list of Ryan's tough losses. In the eleven games Ryan pitched 69 innings, struck out 89 men, gave up 50 hits and had a 3.16 ERA. Houston's offense, however, scored only 17 runs in the 11 games (1.55 per game), and the bullpen allowed 21 runs in 25⅓ innings (7.46 per nine innings), so Ryan got stuck with an 0–11 record:

	IP	H	R	ER	BB	SO	Game Score	Outcome
April 13 at LA	6	4	3	3	5	9	56	Lost, 4–2
April 18 at Cin	4⅔	2	1	1	2	6	60	Lost, 8–10
May 16 vs Chi	6	5	2	2	2	9	61	Lost, 2–1
May 22 vs StL	6⅔	5	3	3	6	11	57	Lost, 7–5
June 23 at SD	6	4	4	3	2	4	52	Lost, 4–1
July 3 at Phi	7	7	2	2	3	10	62	Lost, 2–1
July 8 vs. Cin	7	4	1	1	3	9	71	Lost, 1–0
July 29 at Atl	5⅓	2	4	1	4	5	55	Lost, 5–3
Aug 29 at Pit	6	4	2	2	6	7	57	Lost, 8–2
Sep 29 vs LA	7	6	4	4	3	9	55	Lost, 6–1
Oct 4 vs Cin	7	7	2	2	1	10	64	Lost, 2–1

LOS ANGELES DODGERS

That which has ailed the Los Angeles Dodgers in recent years is, I think, essentially what plagued the Disney company in the years following the death of Walt Disney. Disney developed for his company a set of practices, guidelines, ethics, and operating procedures which pumped out success after success. He did not do things the way they were done in the rest of the entertainment business, but his formula worked for him because he knew what all of the elements of his product were, where to find them and how to combine them. He created a self-contained industry within the industry, and for 30 years during which the world and the industry changed enormously he went on succeeding because he knew what his basic principles were and how to adapt his product without compromising those principles.

Following his death, however, the world kept changing, and his company no longer knew how to adapt. Lacking the self-confidence to ask "What needs to be done here, in this new and unique situation," they tried instead to ask "What would Walt Disney have done here?" This was the wrong question not because Walt would not have known what to do, but because his successors couldn't really predict his thinking in his absence. They couldn't reach any consensus. Each understood his own place within the world that Walt had built, but no one felt confident enough to command the whole world or to guide it into the future. They got the conservative element of his thinking, but without the spark of genius that drove it.

So too the Dodgers, with the phenomenal stability of the Dodgers, with the Dodger way of doing everything, which unfortunately no longer works. In my 27 years as a baseball fan, I don't know that I have ever seen a team put together such an awesome collection of cast-offs, failed prospects, one-dimensional talents, and burnt-out minor players. All of the following men played for the 1987 Dodgers: Ron Davis, Phil Garner, Mickey Hatcher, Brad Havens, Danny Heep, Glenn Hoffman, Bill Krueger, Tito Landrum, Tim Leary, Len Matuszek, Orlando Mercado, Tom Niedenfuer, Alex Trevino, Brad Wellman, and Matt Young. This doesn't even count the guys, like Jerry Reuss and Bill Madlock, who were a legitimate part of the team in the past and were still hanging around as the season started. Is this how you guys think you're going to build a team?

The impression that one gets is that the Dodgers can no longer recognize a prospect when they see one. They certainly can't find them in the draft anymore. The Dodgers have a young third baseman named Jeff Hamilton who is a fine hitter and regarded as a decent glove. The Dodgers keep piddling around with him, giving him a few at bats, a few games. He hasn't hit well yet, but who else do they have to play third base? Pedro Guerrero? Bill Madlock? Phil Garner? Mickey Hatcher? Steve Sax? They're talking about playing Steve Sax there this year. Makes a lot of sense, doesn't it; a guy has trouble playing second base because his throws are off target, so you move him to third.

While they won't make a commitment to a legitimate prospect in Hamilton, the Dodgers continue to insist that Chris Gwynn, who is a fourth-line prospect, is going to be a major-league star, and that sooner or later José Gonzalez is going to learn to hit. If the organization can't evaluate the players who are right in front of them 200 days a year, you wonder what chance they have in a trade. In 1986 Mike Devereaux and Mike Ramsey were teammates at San Antonio. Devereaux hit .302 with 10 homers, 53 RBI and 30 stolen bases; Ramsey hit .283 with 2 homers, 37 RBI and 21 stolen bases while playing in four more games. Devereaux walked 45 percent more often and struck out barely over half as much. Almost everyone in the league thought that Devereaux was a better player—but the Dodgers started the 1987 season with Mike Ramsey in center field, and Devereaux in double-A.

You can get by with that kind of crap, if you're right. If you know more than the stats, and more than the common opinion, you can throw the stats out the window and base your decisions on your own reading of the players. But the other side is, if you're going to ignore what everybody else can see and base your decision on your instincts, you had damn well better be right. Ramsey couldn't do the job in any respect.

Anyway, Hamilton is a good player if they'll stick with him. José Gonzalez isn't ready but has made some progress, and Chris Gwynn is a bad joke (do they really expect us to believe that a guy who hits .279 at Albuquerque with 5 homers and 5 stolen bases is a major-league player?). The development of Shawn Hillegas enabled the Dodgers to trade a starter, a liberty which bounced off their foot out of bounds when they traded Welch for Griffin.

One element of the Houston comment also applies to the Dodgers, to a lesser extent. The Dodger pitching stats, and in particular the stats for their starting pitchers, are impressive. Dodger starting pitchers pitched 1,076 innings, most in the National League (see Kansas City charts). Dodger starters had an ERA of 3.64, best in the majors, struck out 804 men, second best in the majors, had 91 quality starts, second best in the majors, and 97 starts with game scores of 50 or better, best in the majors. Dodger starters had 31 starts with game scores over 70, second highest in the majors, and only 12 starts under 30, second fewest; the ratio between those two was easily the best in the major leagues. Their average game score just missed being the best in the major leagues, 53.3 to Houston's 53.4. They were over .500 (37–32) when they scored three to five runs. Only 18 times all year was a Dodger starting pitcher knocked out in the first five innings; only Houston (24 times) was close in this regard.

But remember, this is Dodger Stadium; on the road, they weren't that terrific. At home they allowed only 306 runs, but also scored only 280. On the road they scored

355, but also allowed 369. If they traded a pitcher for a hitter every winter they would still have better pitching stats than hitting stats. Incidentally, the 280 runs scored by the Dodgers at home was 54 runs fewer—almost 20 percent fewer—than any other major-league team scored in its home park.

Tommy Lasorda has been quoted as saying something this winter about the Dodgers in 1988 playing a lot of 11–10 games. That will never happen in Dodger Stadium, regardless of how poor the defense or how strong the offense. The Dodgers play fewer high-scoring games than any other major-league team. Last year the Dodgers had only 33 games in which more than ten runs were scored by the two teams. The Astros had 40 such games, and every other major-league team had at least 49 such games. So you can see that the Dodgers have a long way to go before they even get up to having a normal number of high-scoring games, and it's just incomprehensible that they could actually play a lot of such games.

The critical failure of the Dodgers in 1987 was a stunning inability to win the type of games that they play most often. Despite the impressive credentials of the starting pitchers, the Dodgers simply could not win a pitcher's duel. I consider any game in which no more than five runs are scored by both teams to be a pitcher's duel. The Dodgers played 41 pitchers duels, one of the highest totals of any major league team, as you would expect them to with a good pitching staff and a poor offense. But they won only 13 of those games, a .317 winning percentage—by far the worst of any major-league team.

Obviously, if you can't win the type of games that you specialize in playing, you can't win.

Playing a lot of low-scoring games means playing a lot of close games. The Dodgers played 85 games which were decided by one or two runs, most in the major leagues other than St. Louis.

Probably due to playing so many close games, Lasorda used 338 pinch hitters, about 10 percent more than any other major-league team. His pinch hitters were awful, hitting .165, which is to be expected in view of who they were, the same collection of roughnecks and roustabouts listed before. Mickey Hatcher went 1 for 16 (.063) as a pinch hitter during the season, on the heels of a 1986 pinch hitting performance of 6 for 38 (.158); GM Fred Claire announced at the time of his re-signing for 1988 that Hatcher was a good pinch hitter. Danny Heep was 5 for 35 as a pinch hitter (.143), Ralph Bryant 6 for 29 (.207), Ken Landreaux 10 for 50 (.200), Len Matuszek 0 for 13, Alex Trevino 7 for 33 (.212), Reggie Williams 0 for 9. Fernando and Orel were used as pinch hitters a few times, plus Landrum and Garner when they were acquired, plus Scioscia when he was available, Sax, Guerrero, Anderson, Duncan, and Marshall on occasion. I wonder if they have considered reactivating Manny Mota?

The Dodgers last year committed "only" 155 errors, their best total since 1982. It was still the worst total in the major leagues, but it was an improvement of 26 errors over 1986, when they committed 181. It was the third straight time the Dodgers led the National League in errors. They were charged with only 67 errors in Los Angeles, 88 on the road.

I did a little study which convinced me that way too much was being made of the defensive problems as an element of the Dodger failures in recent years. Oh, I grant you; it's an awful defense. The question is, if it was a good defense, would they win?

I had a summary of every Dodger game in the computer, and I wrote a program to select 162 games in which the Dodgers turned more double plays and committed fewer errors. Their true ratio was 144/155 (144 double plays, 155 errors), and they finished 73–89.

What if you selected 162 games in which their ratio was normal? The league norm was 146/131. I selected 162 games in which the Dodgers turned 146 double plays and committed only 131 errors; of course, you have to select some games twice, and ignore some other games. The Dodgers' record in the 162 games selected was just 74–88, an improvement of one game.

What if you selected for a good ratio, 160/120? I get 75–87. What about an exceptional ratio, 185/100? At that level they would lead the National League in both double plays and fielding percentage. The record selected was 79–83. To get the Dodgers over .500, you have to select games in which their ratio of double plays to errors would be the best in major league history. To get them to challenge the Giants, you have to select games in which they turn 240 double plays and commit only 70 errors.

Sure, I see the limitations of the method as clearly as you do. I know there's more to "defense" than turning double plays and not committing errors. The fact remains that the reason people talk about the Dodger defense is that they commit so many errors, and if they stopped committing all those damned errors people would stop talking about it.

Think about the conclusion, and you realize it makes sense. The Dodgers last year scored only 635 runs, the fewest of any major-league team. Their bullpen was awful, a nightmare. If they had an average defense, what would they have? They'd have exceptional starting pitching, an average defense, the worst offense in the major leagues and the worst bullpen in the major leagues. That sure sounds to me like a team that would have a heck of a time winning more than 75 games. The importance of the defense is that the defensive shortcomings interfered with the Dodgers' ability to win the pitcher's duels.

The Dodgers could not win, even with a good starting performance. Thirty-five times the Dodgers had a game score of 50 or better from their starting pitcher, but still lost, the most of any major-league team. By contrast, the Dodgers won only 11 times with a game score below 50, the fewest of any major-league team. Every other team won at least 16 times with a sub-par pitching performance.

I'm doing some late editing here, after late roster changes. How much of this still applies, after a winter of frantic shuffling? I think most of it does; what the Dodgers have done this winter is the same thing they have been doing, only at a higher level. Although Griffin is a very popular player with the fans and respected by his teammates, the reality is that he didn't help Cleveland, he didn't help Toronto, he didn't help Oakland, and he's not going to help Los Angeles. He does bring the Dodgers some things that they needed. He is aggressive on the bases. He'll stay in the lineup. He plays a position they needed to have filled. In view of his age (31), his condition, body type and habits, it is a reasonable guess that he will have several years left. He's not worth Bob Welch.

Bob Welch is a fine pitcher—not a great pitcher, but a staff-stabilizing 220-inning a year rotation anchor. He's a more valuable property than Alfredo Griffin. The Dodgers last year had a team secondary average of .223, by far the worst in baseball (Houston was next to last at .246). They are trying to build innings with singles, and without very many of those. Alfredo Griffin, with a career secondary average of .157, is not the man to set that right.

Well, what bout the free agents, Mike Davis and Kirk Gibson? Davis is a traditional Dodger, in the tradition of the last six years: a superb athlete, but just a fair player. To help a team win, he's got to be surrounded by superior talents. Gibson I like a lot because of his intensity and diverse skills, which I think the Dodgers need, but you've got to face some realities: he'll be 31 in May, he gets hurt a lot, and he's not going to hit in Dodger Stadium, over a period of years, the way he hit in Detroit.

If Hillegas and Belcher both turn out to be pitchers, if they win 30 games between them, you've got to admit that there is a chance the 1988 Dodgers could have a big year. I think it more likely that the year won't be big enough. The Dodgers, I think, are still two or three years away from reaching the point at which the Baltimore Orioles have finally arrived, the point of realizing that they have a bad team and that the infusion of established veterans in the class of Ray Knight, Terry Kennedy, and Alfredo Griffin is just delaying the work that has to be done. Kirk Gibson, I think, is the Dodgers' Fred Lynn.

WINNING PERCENTAGE WHEN SCORING LESS THAN THREE RUNS

Montreal	.244
Cleveland	.205
San Francisco	.194
Minnesota	.186
Detroit	.182
Mets	.147
Yankees	.143
White Sox	.130
Seattle	.128
San Diego	.122
Houston	.121
Pittsburgh	.119
California	.116
Texas	.116
Philadelphia	.114
Atlanta	.111
Milwaukee	.108
Kansas City	.105
Boston	.105
Baltimore	.095
Cincinnati	.093
Toronto	.088
Oakland	.081
St. Louis	.061
Cubs	.059
Los Angeles	.058

RUNS SCORED AND ALLOWED WINS AND LOSSES

Wins	411	188	73-0	1.000
Welch	165	116	22-13	.629
Home Games	280	306	40-41	.494
Hershiser	142	130	17-18	.486
Valenzuela	137	139	16-18	.471
Blowouts	171	186	17-20	.459
All Games	635	675	73-89	.451
Slugfests	226	247	14-19	.424
Road Games	355	369	33-48	.407
One-Run Games	184	197	19-32	.373
Pitchers' Duels	60	96	13-28	.317
Honeycutt	52	109	3-17	.150
Losses	224	487	0-89	.000

TEN BEST STARTS

	IP	H	R	ER	BB	SO		
Welch vs. SF, Oct 1	9	1	0	0	1	7	W	91
Welch vs. Phi, May 29	9	3	0	0	2	7	W	86
Welch vs. SD, Apr 24	9	4	0	0	2	8	W	85
Honeycutt vs. Chi, May 12	9	4	0	0	1	6	W	84
Welch at Chi, July 12	9	4	0	0	1	5	W	83
Welch at Pit, Apr 29	7	1	0	0	1	8	W	82
Valenzuela at NY, Aug 25	9	4	1	1	8	13	W	80
Hershiser vs. SD, June 30	9	7	0	0	1	7	W	79
Welch vs. SD, Sep 26	9	6	1	1	1	8	W	78
Hershiser vs. SF, Apr 11	9	7	1	1	1	9	W	77

PITCHERS WHEN SUPPORTED BY THREE TO FIVE RUNS

	G	IP	W-L	Pct	SO	BB	ERA
Welch	12	87	6-2	.750	70	27	2.47
Valenzuela	18	142	8-6	.571	118	70	3.68
Hershiser	14	103	7-6	.538	74	30	3.51
Honeycutt	6	28	0-2	.000	27	10	4.18

HALL OF FAME WATCH

Building credentials but not yet viable candidate: Valenzuela 55.5, Lasorda 55, Guerrero 33; **Working on it:** Sax 25.5, Ron Davis 24, Welch 19, Garner 18, Hershiser 16, Landreaux 12.5; **Long way to go:** Scioscia 9, Niedenfuer 6, Hatcher 6, Shelby 5, Pena 5, M. Young 3, Duncan 2.

NUMBER OF PINCH HITTERS USED:

Los Angeles	338
San Francisco	309
Cubs	301
Houston	298
Philadelphia	298
Cincinnati	291
Pittsburgh	288
San Diego	257
Montreal	254
Mets	251
Atlanta	236
St. Louis	215
Detroit	213
Toronto	205
Texas	184
Yankees	180
California	164
Minnesota	157
Cleveland	140
Kansas City	137
Oakland	134
Seattle	106
White Sox	105
Baltimore	103
Boston	91
Milwaukee	85

TEN WORST STARTS

	IP	H	R	ER	BB	SO		
Hershiser at Hous, Sep 28	5⅓	10	9	9	3	5	L	14
Honeycutt at Chi, July 9	2*	8	6	6	1	2	L	17
Leary at Chi, July 11	2⅓	8	6	5	1	1	L	19
Welch at Mon, May 16	4*	8	7	6	4	3	L	19
Welch vs. SF, Apr 9	4⅔	9	7	7	2	3	L	19
Honeycutt vs. SF, July 29	2⅓	5	6	6	2	1	L	22
Valenzuela vs. Chi, July 26	5⅓	9	6	6	3	1	—	24
Welch at Atl, Sep 12	6⅔	9	8	8	2	3	—	25
Hillegas vs. Hous, Sep 14	4*	9	6	4	1	2	L	25
Howell at Atl, Aug 2	3⅓	7	5	4	4	2	L	26

Mike SCIOSCIA, Catcher
Runs Created: 58

	G	AB	Hit	2B	3B	HR	Run	RBI	TBB	SO	SB	CS	Avg
4.98 years		488	129	23	1	6	45	48	69	31	4	3	.264
1987	142	461	122	26	1	6	44	38	55	23	7	4	.265
First Half	71	232	60	14	0	3	22	19	32	14	4	2	.259
Second Half	71	229	62	12	1	3	22	19	23	9	3	2	.271
Vs. RHP		329	86	18	0	6	33	28	39	12	4	2	.261
Vs. LHP		132	36	8	1	0	11	10	16	11	3	2	.273
Home	69	219	57	6	0	2	21	16	29	5	3	3	.260
Road	73	242	65	20	1	4	23	22	26	18	4	1	.269

Pedro GUERRERO, Left Field
Runs Created: 121

	G	AB	Hit	2B	3B	HR	Run	RBI	TBB	SO	SB	CS	Avg
6.03 years		562	174	27	4	28	89	91	65	96	14	7	.310
1987	152	545	184	25	2	27	89	89	74	85	9	7	.338
First Half	85	306	98	11	2	19	54	54	38	58	4	4	.320
Second Half	67	239	86	14	0	8	35	35	36	27	5	3	.360
Vs. RHP		378	123	18	0	19	57	63	47	64	5	6	.325
Vs. LHP		167	61	7	2	8	32	26	27	21	4	1	.365
Home	77	275	89	11	0	12	39	43	34	44	7	3	.324
Road	75	270	95	14	2	15	50	46	40	41	2	4	.352

Franklin STUBBS, First Base
Runs Created: 47

	G	AB	Hit	2B	3B	HR	Run	RBI	TBB	SO	SB	CS	Avg
2.21 years		467	104	13	3	21	57	58	42	117	8	2	.223
1987	129	386	90	16	3	16	48	52	31	85	8	1	.233
First Half	84	272	72	14	2	12	34	38	22	63	5	1	.265
Second Half	45	114	18	2	1	4	14	14	9	22	3	0	.158
Vs. RHP		300	74	16	3	16	47	47	30	63	6	1	.247
Vs. LHP		86	16	0	0	0	1	5	1	22	2	0	.186
Home	69	209	35	7	0	6	20	21	14	49	3	0	.167
Road	60	177	55	9	3	10	28	31	17	36	5	1	.311

John SHELBY, Center Field
Runs Created: 71

	G	AB	Hit	2B	3B	HR	Run	RBI	TBB	SO	SB	CS	Avg
3.90 years		477	119	19	3	13	65	53	24	95	17	5	.249
1987	141	508	138	26	0	22	65	72	32	110	16	7	.272
First Half	69	234	61	14	0	11	28	30	15	49	7	2	.261
Second Half	72	274	77	12	0	11	37	42	17	61	9	5	.281
Vs. RHP		333	82	15	0	11	43	39	21	72	11	3	.246
Vs. LHP		175	56	11	0	11	22	33	11	38	5	4	.320
Home	74	260	61	8	0	8	27	34	16	57	8	4	.235
Road	67	248	77	18	0	14	38	38	16	53	8	3	.310

Steve SAX, Second Base
Runs Created: 76

	G	AB	Hit	2B	3B	HR	Run	RBI	TBB	SO	SB	CS	Avg
5.75 years		640	181	24	5	4	88	48	55	62	43	20	.283
1987	157	610	171	22	7	6	84	46	44	61	37	11	.280
First Half	88	340	88	11	4	3	43	26	26	39	20	7	.259
Second Half	69	270	83	11	3	3	41	20	18	22	17	4	.307
Vs. RHP		405	114	12	5	4	54	31	29	47	22	9	.281
Vs. LHP		205	57	10	2	2	30	15	15	14	15	2	.278
Home	77	289	75	9	2	2	35	15	19	28	18	6	.260
Road	80	321	96	13	5	4	49	31	25	33	19	5	.299

Mike MARSHALL, Right Field
Runs Created: 55

	G	AB	Hit	2B	3B	HR	Run	RBI	TBB	SO	SB	CS	Avg
4.19 years		556	151	26	1	25	69	86	43	132	5	6	.272
1987	104	402	118	19	0	16	45	72	18	79	0	5	.294
First Half	60	229	66	11	0	9	26	36	9	51	0	5	.288
Second Half	44	173	52	8	0	7	19	36	9	28	0	0	.301
Vs. RHP		277	83	11	0	11	28	54	13	59	0	4	.300
Vs. LHP		125	35	8	0	5	17	18	5	20	0	1	.280
Home	51	183	52	7	0	5	21	24	10	34	0	3	.284
Road	53	219	66	12	0	11	24	48	8	45	0	2	.301

Mickey HATCHER, Handyman
Runs Created: 39

	G	AB	Hit	2B	3B	HR	Run	RBI	TBB	SO	SB	CS	Avg
5.33 years		531	149	29	3	7	56	59	26	38	2	2	.281
1987	101	287	81	19	1	7	27	42	20	19	2	3	.282
First Half	57	160	53	13	1	4	17	23	8	8	1	1	.331
Second Half	44	127	28	6	0	3	10	19	12	11	1	2	.220
Vs. RHP		162	40	6	1	3	10	21	8	13	1	3	.247
Vs. LHP		125	41	13	0	4	17	21	12	6	1	0	.328
Home	49	137	35	8	0	4	12	22	8	8	1	2	.255
Road	52	150	46	11	1	3	15	20	12	11	1	1	.307

Dave ANDERSON, Utility
Runs Created: 26

	G	AB	Hit	2B	3B	HR	Run	RBI	TBB	SO	SB	CS	Avg
2.83 years		421	96	17	2	4	53	29	49	69	14	6	.228
1987	108	265	62	12	3	1	32	13	24	43	9	5	.234
First Half	66	162	40	8	3	1	19	8	10	21	5	3	.247
Second Half	42	103	22	4	0	0	13	5	14	22	4	2	.214
Vs. RHP		193	44	10	1	1	25	7	17	35	8	4	.228
Vs. LHP		72	18	2	2	0	7	6	7	8	1	1	.250
Home	56	140	35	6	2	0	16	6	14	24	7	4	.250
Road	52	125	27	6	1	1	16	7	10	19	2	1	.216

Mariano DUNCAN, Shortshop
Runs Created: 24

	G	AB	Hit	2B	3B	HR	Run	RBI	TBB	SO	SB	CS	Avg
2.02 years		609	142	19	3	10	75	43	42	125	48	11	.233
1987	76	261	56	8	1	6	31	18	17	62	11	1	.215
First Half	60	215	46	6	1	4	27	14	13	55	8	1	.214
Second Half	16	46	10	2	0	2	4	4	4	7	3	0	.217
Vs. RHP		170	31	4	1	2	20	9	13	43	8	1	.182
Vs. LHP		91	25	4	0	4	11	9	4	19	3	0	.275
Home	35	110	25	3	0	3	11	9	7	27	5	1	.227
Road	41	151	31	5	1	3	20	9	10	35	6	0	.205

SQ, IQ

A year ago, in the second comment for the St. Louis Cardinals, I introduced a method of evaluating a player's speed by looking at a variety of speed-related categories—triples, stolen bases, stolen base percentage, double plays, range factor, runs scored as a percentage of times on base/not home run. If I used those kinds of names I guess I would probably have called it "SQ", speed quotient. There are two things I wanted to do here. The first is to update you on a some refinements in several ways, three of which are important enough to discuss briefly.

First, I decided to base them on two-year, rather than one-year, stats. This is important because several categories involving speed—triples, grounded into double plays, stolen bases, and stolen-base percentage—have relatively small single-season norms, and thus are subject to more fluctuation than is desirable.

Second, whereas in the first effort I had evaluated triples on a straight-line scale, I changed that to a sliding scale. The problem there was that many players hit triples more than twice as often as the league average, which is fewer than 4 triples per player per season, so if you establish an average triples rate at 5.0, there are going to be many players who max out that scale at 10.0. If you don't understand that don't worry about it; it's not important.

Third, I decided to base the speed score on only five of the six categories, ignoring one. This was possible because I had intended for the average to be about 5.0, but in practice the average player came out to about 4.7 or 4.8. When I changed the triples scale the average dipped even lower, to about 4.5. Another problem with the system is that it could penalize a player for certain things which didn't necessarily mean that he lacked speed—for example, if a player is fast but just doesn't happen to be a base stealer, or if he is fast and steals bases but just happens to play first base—then the low score on that scale would distort his speed score. Then I realized that I could solve both problems at the same time—restore the average to about 5.0, and "forgive" a player for one indication that he lacked speed—by basing the speed score on five of the six categories, ignoring the lowest one.

I don't have speed scores for all players for 1988, so I don't know if Vince Coleman retained his title as the fastest man in baseball or not. Maybe I'll get them done and run that in a comment in Section III. Anyway, at the time I wrote that essay, I wrote that speed is "the only [characteristic] you can use both on offense and defense, [and so] probably the only characteristic of a player that you can evaluate by looking at so many different areas of play."

Later, however, I realized that there is another characteristic of a player that is useful both on offense and on defense. You know what it is? It's called "intelligence." Sometimes athletes like to lecture us on the importance of intelligence in baseball, and will go so far as to assert that that is what sports are really all about, that everything revolves around intelligence. They sometimes prefer to be-

lieve this, of course, because it suits them to believe that they are successful athletes not because they can run fast and throw hard and react quickly, but because they are smarter than the rest of us. I used to have a drill sergeant who would scream at us about lacking the "physical intelligence" to accomplish some task. I always wanted to ask for a definition of physical intelligence, but I thought I'd probably get a physical definition.

Anyway, while sports obviously do not revolve primarily around intelligence, quite certainly intelligence is important to an athlete, and is reflected in his play in many different ways. Could we make an inventory of those, I wondered?

Probably not, but what the hell, I can't get shot for trying. It seems to me that there are five characteristics that one would naturally tend to associate with intelligence in a baseball player. Those are:

1) The tendency not to make errors. One would expect that an intelligent athlete would be a better judge of his abilities and of the conditions, and would have less tendency to commit errors than a stupid athlete.

2) Command of the strike zone. The strike zone is "learned." One may be born with good speed or good eyes or strong arms, but you're not born knowing the strike zone.

3) Effective baserunning relative to speed. One would tend to think that given two players of the same speed, the more intelligent player would have a better stolen-base percentage, that he would be a better judge of when he could steal and when he couldn't, that he would learn how to read the pitchers and get a jump more quickly.

4) Consistency. One would tend to assume that wild swings in performance are not indicative of quick adjustments to a problem, that an intelligent player would get more out of his ability, and thus be more consistent at approaching his best performances.

5) Growth. One might tend to think, absent other evidence, that an intelligent player would learn more about the league than the league would learn about him, and that for that reason he would grow and develop as a player from the point at which he entered the league, whereas a stupid player might tend to find that, after his initial impact, the league tends to catch up with him.

Now, I'm not assuming that any of this is absolutely true. But if it is true, then in the same way that we can evaluate speed, one could evaluate a player's intelligence by searching for patterns among fielding percentages (relative to league norms), strikeout to walk ratios, stolen-base percentages (relative to speed), consistency as a hitter and fielder, and growth in value over the years.

Now, you know I can't do this. I can't do it because a) saying that a player is stupid is a very personal thing to say, and b) I can't independently support it. The speed scores can be independently verified by watching players run; anyone can see that Vince Coleman is fast and Alan Ashby is slow. I can't say that somebody is stupid unless

I can support it, and I can't support it in any other way. If I figured a hundred baseball IQs, probably five of them would be completely out-in-leftfield-wrong, and I'd be doing those people an injustice, not that that's ever stopped me before. You can figure player IQs, in the privacy of your own home, but I can't.

What struck me, though, is that if you did figure intelligence scores, you know who would probably score as the dumbest player in baseball? The new Dodger, Alfredo. Well, not the very dumbest; I guess Luis Salazar would get the very lowest score, but Alfredo would be way down there. Look:

1) Error prone. Alfredo's led the league in errors four times, just missed by one error of leading last year.

2) Poor command of the strike zone. One year he had 33 strikeouts and 4 walks, career ratio is about 2–1.

3) Extremely poor stolen base percentages in view of his excellent speed. Griffin has 161 career stolen bases with 114 times caught stealing, an amazingly bad ratio for a man with his speed.

4) Inconsistency. Griffin in his first four years in the league hit .287, .254, .209, .241.

5) Lack of growth. The best year Griffin has ever had was his rookie season, 1979, when he took 40 walks and hit .287. He's never matched his rookie performance in batting average, hits, runs scored, walks.

In spite of this, Griffin is *not* regarded by those who know him as stupid, not at all—in fact, dramatically not so. He is regarded as being extremely bright, particularly about money, level-headed, and sharp as a tack. A lot of people who know him have an almost mythic respect for him.

So what can you say? He may be smart, but he doesn't play smart. He takes foolish chances as a player; anybody who has seen him has to know that. I should add that while his PIQ (playing IQ) would still be low, it would be much higher now than it would have been four or five years ago. He has improved his play in almost all of the relevant aspects.

Who would be at the other extreme? Probably the highest-rated player in baseball, if evaluated in these five areas, would be Ozzie Smith. Smith makes extremely few errors, has tremendous strikeout/walk ratios (among the best in baseball), is a very good percentage base stealer, and *if* you don't look at his rookie year, has shown an almost perfect pattern of consistency and growth as a hitter. His rookie year, which was better than any of the three years that followed it, kind of throws the pattern off there, but Smith has just shown remarkable development as a hitter over the last nine years, getting a tiny bit better almost every year than the year before.

A few of the other players who would be evaluated by this method as among the smartest in the game: Tim Raines, Carlton Fisk, Mike Schmidt, Tony Gwynn, Keith Hernandez, Phil Bradley, Brian Downing, Don Mattingly, Eddie Murray, Ryne Sandberg. A few of those who wouldn't score so well: Rick Manning, Juan Samuel, Dave Parker, Tim Wallach, Shawon Dunston, Joel Skinner, Cory Snyder, Marvelle Wynne.

The odd thing here is—the other odd thing, I suppose—that a lot of people, casual baseball fans, tend to see Alfredo and Ozzie as being similar players. They're both shortstops, similar in size and build, with some superficial similarities in batting statistics. Alfredo is regarded as a guy who will make some spectacular plays if not quite being Ozzie. I'm sure that a lot of Dodger fans think that they're getting an Ozzie Smith–type shortstop. Ozzie is one of my favorite players, while I don't have a lot of use for Griffin, precisely because in my opinion he doesn't play a good percentage game. He doesn't exploit the advantages that make a team a winner.

ATLANTA BRAVES

Twenty-two random notes about a team lost at sea:

1) Atlanta had only 51 games in which they turned no double plays, the fewest of any-major league team.

2) There is an intriguing comparison between the Braves and the Twins. In slugfests, in games in which eleven or more runs were scored, the two teams had similar records (Atlanta 31–29, Minnesota 33–28). In games in which six to ten runs were scored, Minnesota did a little bit better but not a lot (Atlanta 29–48, Minnesota 32–40). But in pitchers' duels, games in which no more than five runs were scored, Minnesota was the best team in baseball, with a record of 20–9. Atlanta was the second-worst, with a record 9–15.

3) Even in the games they won, Atlanta allowed an average of 3.68 runs, more than any other team.

4) In recent years I have been arguing that what might be called the common conception of what type of team plays well on artificial turf—a speedy outfield, a quick infield, strong throwing arms, an offense of players who make contact—is not founded in any research or any particularly compelling logic. It's just sort of made up out of air; there is no real reason to believe that that is the real model for success on artificial turf, and indeed if you look at who actually wins and who actually loses in grass and turf games, there is no support for that model.

At the end of the 1987 season I did a five-year breakdown of records by all teams on grass fields and artificial turf. As you would expect because of the home field advantage, 23 of the 26 teams have done better on the type of surface of their home park. One turf team, Montreal, has a better winning percentage on grass fields than on artificial turf, albeit by an infinitesimal margin (.5120 to .5117). Two teams which play at home on grass fields have managed anyway to have better records on artificial turf than on grass fields. The two teams? Baltimore and Atlanta. OK, it's a tiny margin (each team is .003 better on turf), but you tell me why that happens. I submit that you could not name any other two organizations which over the last few years have fit the profile of a turf team any worse. Both teams are slow, both teams are desperately short of agile, acrobatic infielders and outfielders with powerful throwing arms, and both offenses have been based completely around power hitters. Yet over the last five years, Atlanta's winning percentages are .493 at home, .402 on road grass and .466 on road turf. Baltimore's winning percentages are .512 at home, .486 on road grass and .504 on road turf. That's over five years, meaning that all samples involve at least 120 games. If the common idea of what type of team does well on artificial turf is correct, then you tell me why that has happened.

5) The Braves played well against left-handed pitchers (28–25), but without a left-handed power threat in the lineup dropped off to 41–67 against right-handers, the largest left/right differential in the National League. Murphy and Virgil, who hit 71 homers between them, are both right-handed; their top left-handed home run hitter was Ken Griffey's father with 14.

6) The Braves' AAA farm club, Richmond, was beyond belief. They finished 56–83. Their leading home run hitter was John Rabb with 20; Rabb, however, hit just .226 and drove in 50 runs. Their leading RBI man was Darryl Motley, with 58 (13, 58, .254). First baseman Dave Griffin hit .248 with 15 homers and 57 RBI. Their leading hitter was veteran catcher John Mizerock, who hit a mighty .279 with two home runs. Their leading base stealer was Trench Davis, long-term minor leaguer who swiped 44 bases but had a .256 average and 3 homers. He's an outfielder. Their shortstop was Mike Fischlin. Is this a bad team, or what? Their best chance to get a player off that team would seem to be José Alvarez, a pitcher with a 9–13 record and a 4.34 ERA, but who did have good K/W data.

The AA team, Greenville, wasn't quite as bad, but doesn't have anybody obvious who has got a chance to be a star. Their best prospect is a bit pitcher named Tommy Greene who will be in Atlanta uniform later this summer if he doesn't start walking everybody in sight.

7) I wrote a year ago that if Dale Murphy got hurt, this team had a chance to lose a hundred games. Dale Murphy was an MVP candidate, and the Braves still lost 92 games. It now seems likely that even Murphy's magnificent play cannot keep the Braves from soon encountering that fate. As bad as this team is, I believe that they're going to get substantially worse in the next few years. Murphy is 32; he'll be around for eight or ten years, but he's entering the period of probable decline. The young players they think are going to get better (Perry and James) probably won't, although Dion James has a chance to develop a little more. Ken Griffey and Ozzie Virgil will have a tough time repeating their 1987 seasons. The loss of David Palmer, the departure of Doyle Alexander and Gene Garber leaves them with all the opportunity in the world for young pitchers, because they've only got one pitcher, Zane Smith. Nobody in this organization has shown that he knows how to put together a ballclub.

8) Dale Murphy led the National League in runs created, 143. Actually, although I never present them that way because the idea of a player creating a hundredth of a run is a little absurd, the runs created estimate for Murphy was 142.52, while that for Tony Gwynn of San Diego was 142.51; Gwynn created more runs per out.

9) I looked up the Braves first-round draft picks over the last ten years; the list is 1978—Bob Horner; 1979—Brad Komminsk; 1980—Ken Dayley; 1981—Jay Roberts; 1982—Duane Ward; 1983—No pick, gave it up to sign Pete Falcone; 1984—Drew Denson; 1985—Tommy Greene; 1986—Kent Mercker; 1987—Derek Lilliquist.

The first three (Horner, Komminsk, and Roberts) are around, albeit not with the Braves.

I don't know what happened to Jay Roberts; can't find a record of him.

Duane Ward made seven stops in the Atlanta farm system and never had an ERA below 4.29 anywhere, which didn't keep him from reaching the Braves in 1986. After ten appearances and a 7.31 ERA, he was traded to Toronto for Doyle Alexander, and has continued to pitch poorly for Syracuse and Toronto.

Drew Denson, a first baseman, hit .219 with 14 homers at Greenville, 33 walks and 95 strikeouts; he seems to have little chance to play in the majors.

Tommy Greene I mentioned before; he pitched well at Greenville.

Kent Mercker must have arm trouble or something; he pitched 3 times for Durham (0–1, 5.40 ERA) but that seems to have been his only activity in 1988, unless he was farmed out to a co-op team or something.

Derek Lilliquist, *Baseball America*'s 1987 College Pitcher of the Year and the Braves 1987 pick, signed and pitched twice in the Gulf Coast League, striking out 16 men while giving up only 3 hits and no runs; he then moved on to Durham, where he was almost as brilliant in 3 outings, 2–1, 29 Ks and only 13 hits allowed in 25 innings. He's a left-hander who will be in Atlanta any day now if he keeps pitching that way.

You all may remember that Bill Lucas died suddenly at the age of 43 in 1979. Lucas was the Braves' farm director and later General Manager during the period when they scouted, signed, and developed Murphy, Horner, Glenn Hubbard, Brook Jacoby, and Brett Butler. At his death the Braves were left in the hands of General Manager John Mullen, with Henry Aaron as Vice-President and Director of Player Development. What happened, obviously, is that the team of Mullen and Aaron didn't get the job done. The team continued to improve for a couple of years, but began to decline in 1983 when the system stopped producing talent. The early returns on the performance of Bobby Cox as GM are somewhat more encouraging.

10) The Braves turned 79 double plays in road games last year, 91 at home. The league double-play average is 146, so they would have been well above that had they only matched their road total at home.

11) In Fulton County Stadium the Braves scored 421 runs and allowed 450; on the road (in 80 games) they scored 326 and allowed 379. The park factor for the year, then, was 1.22, meaning that to adjust for their offensive totals you need to divide the hitters' runs/created game by 1.11 and divide their pitcher's ERAs by the same. Actually, you have to make an adjustment for the fact that the Braves don't have County Stadium among their road parks, so the correct figure is 1.1, not 1.11.

The Braves scored 747 runs last year, fifth in the league, but allowed 829, most in the league. The appearance is created that they have the league's fifth-best offense, but worst pitching and defense. With park adjustments, however, their runs scored drop to 679, tenth in the league, and their runs allowed drop to 754, also tenth in the league. Their offense, in fact, is as bad as their pitching.

12) Brave starting pitchers had an ERA last year of 4.47 in road games, but 5.16 in Atlanta.

13) Unlike any other team that I noticed, the Braves played better when they committed multiple errors. In games in which they committed two errors the Braves were 13–11; when committing more than two, they were 4–3.

14) The Braves' defense last year was a little better than either their hitting or their pitching. Their ratio of double plays to errors (170 to 116) was one of the best in baseball. Virgil did a little better job of stopping the running game than the Braves had done in the past; opponents still stole 186 bases, but that was tenth in the league, rather than last. Their defensive efficiency record, .688, was also tenth in the league.

15) Runs created/27 outs for the Braves: Dale Murphy, 9.14; Dion James, 7.07; Albert Hall, 5.64; Ken Griffey, 5.39; Glenn Hubbard, 5.25; Ozzie Virgil, 4.92; Ted Simmons, 4.86; Gerald Perry, 4.35; Ken Oberkfell, 4.34; Jeff Blauser, 3.95; Rafael Ramirez, 3.49; Graig Nettles, 3.28; Ron Gant, 2.94; Ron Roenicke, 2.73; Andres Thomas, 2.59. Based on that, both changes around second—Thomas and Gant instead of Ramirez and Hubbard—seem likely to weaken the Braves even further. With park adjustments, all of the 1988 Braves would appear to be below league norms except the three outfielders—Murphy, James, and Griffey.

The Braves' strongest point offensively was that they did get a good many people on base. Their on-base percentages included Dale Murphy at .417, Dion James at .397, Glenn Hubbard at .378 and Albert Hall at .369. This was an improvement over recent years.

What they did least-well offensively was hit home runs. Their home run total, 152, was the National League average—and in this park, that's awful.

16) The Braves had 29 home crowds last year under 10,000.

17) The Braves started the season playing well, and, perhaps more surprisingly, recovered well from their first big slump. The Braves jumped off to a 4–1 start and then to 6–3. By April 26 they were 7–11, but rallied and spent most of May over .500. The last date at which they were over .500 was June 20, with a record of 34–33. For the rest of the season they were 35–59. The Braves record by months: April, 9–12; May, 16–12; June, 11–16; July, 9–17; August, 11–17; September, 12–15; October, 1–3.

In May, the Braves' best month, the Braves scored 169 runs in 28 games, 6.04 per game. Despite an ERA during the month of 5.03 by their starting pitchers, the Braves had a winning record both at home (9–6) and on the road (7–6).

The ERA of Braves starters from August 1 to the end of the season was 5.44.

18) The Braves runs scored, 754, was essentially the same as their runs created, 747.

19) The Braves were the third-slowest team in the National League, with a team speed score of 4.48; the bottom three were almost equal, and far below any other team. The bottom three are Atlanta, 4.48, Los Angeles, 4.43 and Chicago 4.36. Everybody else was at least 4.87. The Braves tied for the league lead in grounding into double plays, with 133.

20) Although only a few players remain with the Braves, almost everybody who played on the Braves' 1982 Championship team is still active. Bob Horner hit .327 for the Yakult Swallows, with 31 homers, 73 RBI. Claudell Washington hit .279 with 9 homers, 44 RBI for the Yankees. Rufino Linares hit .389 for the Mexico City Reds, with 20 homers and 93 RBI; he was second in the league in hitting, and in my opinion could definitely play major-league ball at some level. Jerry Royster hit .265 in the American League, with 7 homers and 27 RBI in just 196

at bats. Brett Butler hit .295 for Cleveland, with 9 homers, 41 RBI, 91 walks, and 33 stolen bases. Phil Niekro was an itinerant laborer, including one outing with the Braves at the end of the year. Bob Walk, who was the number-two starter on that team, was 8–2 with a 3.31 ERA for the Pirates. Steve Bedrosian won the National League Cy Young Award. Ken Dayley had a 9–5 record and a 2.66 ERA for the Cardinals. Pascual Perez went 7–0 with a 2.30 ERA for the Expos. Donnie Moore was hurt most of the year, but had a 2.70 ERA and 5 saves for the Angels. Joe Cowley started the year with the Phillies. Hubbard, Ramirez, Murphy, Benedict, Mahler, and Garber were still with the Braves. The only players with significant playing time for that team (50 innings or 200 plate appearances) who are retired are Rick Camp and Chris Chambliss. Unless Rick Camp is pitching in Venezuela . . .

21) Bruce Benedict of the Braves had a slugging percentage last year of .189; Bob Forsch had a slugging percentage of .509. This was the fifth consecutive year that Forsch had posted a better slugging percentage than Benedict, beginning in 1983 when Benedict played in the National League All-Star game. The margins have been .352–.348, .313–.297, .400–.231, .329–.300 and .509–.189.

22) Most of the teams that have moved list as their team records only their records after moving. The Braves don't; they include records in Boston and Milwaukee among their team records, which puts most of them out of reach. If they just listed Atlanta, though, Dale Murphy would not be annexing them wholesale. Murphy has 310 home runs for Atlanta; Henry Aaron had 335 here. The Braves really haven't had many career regulars here. They've traded away most of the people who have started good careers here, like Darrell Evans, Brett Butler and Dusty Baker. Evans was traded for four players, all of whom have been gone from Atlanta for more than a decade.

GAMES IN WHICH TURNED NO DOUBLE PLAYS

Atlanta	51
Baltimore	52
White Sox	53
Cubs	56
California	56
Boston	57
Yankees	58
San Francisco	59
Milwaukee	61
St. Louis	61
Toronto	62
Kansas City	62
Texas	62
San Diego	63
Seattle	63
Mets	63
Philadelphia	65
Pittsburgh	65
Cleveland	66
Detroit	66
Los Angeles	68
Cincinnati	68
Minnesota	69
Montreal	76
Oakland	80
Houston	84

RUNS SCORED AND ALLOWED WINS AND LOSSES

Wins	477	254	69-0	1.000
Z Smith	188	158	22-14	.611
Blowouts	255	257	21-18	.538
Home Games	421	450	42-39	.519
Slugfests	440	431	31-29	.517
One-Run Games	217	220	23-26	.469
Palmer	139	157	12-16	.429
All Games	747	829	69-92	.429
Alexander	57	70	6-10	.375
Pitchers' Duels	35	51	9-15	.375
Mahler	125	162	10-18	.357
Road Games	326	379	27-53	.338
Puleo	60	77	5-11	.313
Losses	270	575	0-92	.000

HALL OF FAME WATCH

Could be elected on current accomplishments: Dale Murphy 111.5, Ted Simmons 110.5, Graig Nettles 90; **Building credentials but not yet viable candidate:** Tanner 55, Griffey 32; **Working on it:** Oberkfell 10; **Long way to go:** Benedict 9, Virgil 7, Hubbard 5, D. James 3.5, McWilliams 3, Z Smith 2, Motley 2, R Mahler 2, Ramirez 2, Assenmacher 1, Dedmon 1, D Palmer 1.

TEN WORST STARTS

	IP	H	R	ER	BB	SO		
Glavine at Hous, Aug 17	3⅔	10	6	6	5	1	L	13
Mahler at StL, May 28	4*	10	7	6	2	2	L	16
Mahler vs. SD, June 7	3⅔	8	7	7	3	2	—	16
Mahler at Phil, July 24	2⅔	7	7	5	4	2	L	18
Mahler at Hous, Aug 15	2⅔	7	6	6	2	1	L	19
Glavine vs. SD, Sep 7	5	8	7	7	4	2	L	21
P. Niekro vs. SF, Sep 27	3*	6	5	5	6	0	—	21
O'Neal at Mon, May 11	3	6	6	6	2	1	—	22
Palmer vs. Cin, June 18	3*	8	5	5	2	1	L	22
O'Neal at NY, July 20	1⅔	4	5	5	5	0	L	22
Dedmon at Chi, Aug 27	⅓	4	5	5	1	0	—	22

TEN BEST STARTS

	IP	H	R	ER	BB	SO		
Z. Smith at Pit, Sep 1	9	4	0	0	0	8	W	87
Z. Smith at SF, Apr 17	9	4	0	0	0	8	W	87
Mahler vs. Phi, Apr 7	9	3	0	0	4	2	W	79
Z. Smith at SF, June 29	9	5	0	0	0	2	W	79
Alexander vs. LA, June 10	9	4	1	1	1	4	W	78
Palmer at SF, Apr 18	7	2	0	0	2	6	—	77
Alexander vs. SF, June 16	9	5	2	2	1	7	W	75
Alexander vs. Chi, May 31	9	5	1	1	2	3	—	74
Z. Smith at SD, Aug 12	9	6	1	1	4	5	W	72
Alexander at NY, July 21	9	4	3	2	1	3	W	71

PITCHERS WHEN SUPPORTED BY THREE TO FIVE RUNS

	G	IP	W-L	Pct	SO	BB	ERA
Z. Smith	16	112	7-3	.700	66	49	3.53
Puleo	6	36	3-2	.600	24	11	4.29
Mahler	15	87	3-8	.273	44	42	5.61
Palmer	11	64	2-6	.250	42	24	5.37

AVERAGE RUNS ALLOWED IN WINS

Houston	2.36
San Diego	2.54
Los Angeles	2.58
White Sox	2.61
Pittsburgh	2.66
Montreal	2.67
Kansas City	2.67
San Francisco	2.72
Seattle	2.79
Mets	2.90
Yankees	2.91
Toronto	2.93
California	2.99
Cubs	3.05
Philadelphia	3.08
Boston	3.09
Minnesota	3.14
Detroit	3.14
Oakland	3.20
St. Louis	3.22
Cincinnati	3.23
Baltimore	3.34
Cleveland	3.43
Texas	3.47
Milwaukee	3.62
Atlanta	3.68

Ozzie VIRGIL, Catcher
Runs created: 63

	G	AB	Hit	2B	3B	HR	Run	RBI	TBB	SO	SB	CS	Avg
3.83 years		502	121	19	2	23	61	72	58	103	1	1	.241
1987	123	429	106	13	1	27	57	72	47	81	0	1	.247
First Half	71	246	57	6	0	20	34	43	27	49	0	1	.232
Second Half	52	183	49	7	1	7	23	29	20	32	0	0	.268
Vs. RHP		319	82	11	1	20	41	54	31	61	0	1	.257
Vs. LHP		110	24	2	0	7	16	18	16	20	0	0	.218
Home	62	213	55	8	1	15	33	44	29	38	0	0	.258
Road	61	216	51	5	0	12	24	28	18	43	0	1	.236

Ken GRIFFEY, Left Field
Runs Created: 62

	G	AB	Hit	2B	3B	HR	Run	RBI	TBB	SO	SB	CS	Avg
11.11 years		587	176	31	7	12	94	69	58	72	17	7	.300
1987	122	399	114	24	1	14	65	64	46	54	4	7	.286
First Half	67	242	73	14	1	11	38	45	25	30	2	6	.302
Second Half	55	157	41	10	0	3	27	19	21	24	2	1	.261
Vs. RHP		312	92	22	1	12	50	53	40	45	3	6	.295
Vs. LHP		87	22	2	0	2	15	11	6	9	1	1	.253
Home	64	223	65	15	1	8	39	39	24	30	2	4	.291
Road	58	176	49	9	0	6	26	25	22	24	2	3	.278

Gerald PERRY, First Base
Runs Created: 69

	G	AB	Hit	2B	3B	HR	Run	RBI	TBB	SO	SB	CS	Avg
2.65 years		463	121	21	2	9	61	57	55	52	25	13	.261
1987	142	533	144	35	2	12	77	74	48	63	42	16	.270
First Half	71	260	66	12	1	4	34	36	24	37	14	4	.254
Second Half	71	273	78	23	1	8	43	38	24	26	28	12	.286
Vs. RHP		408	112	24	1	7	54	57	37	42	30	14	.275
Vs. LHP		125	32	11	1	5	23	17	11	21	12	2	.256
Home	71	255	66	20	1	2	39	32	28	23	20	9	.259
Road	71	278	78	15	1	10	38	42	20	40	22	7	.281

Dion JAMES, Center Field
Runs Created: 95

	G	AB	Hit	2B	3B	HR	Run	RBI	TBB	SO	SB	CS	Avg
1.80 years		528	156	32	6	6	77	53	61	62	12	10	.295
1987	134	494	154	37	6	10	80	61	70	63	10	8	.312
First Half	70	258	75	20	3	5	49	26	51	42	4	4	.291
Second Half	64	236	79	17	3	5	31	35	19	21	6	4	.335
Vs. RHP		405	127	30	5	9	68	47	48	49	9	6	.314
Vs. LHP		89	27	7	1	1	12	14	22	14	1	2	.303
Home	65	237	89	21	4	5	44	35	39	20	6	3	.376
Road	69	257	65	16	2	5	36	26	31	43	4	5	.253

Glenn HUBBARD, Second Base
Runs Created: 67

	G	AB	Hit	2B	3B	HR	Run	RBI	TBB	SO	SB	CS	Avg
7.38 years		544	133	27	3	9	67	55	66	77	4	4	.244
1987	141	443	117	33	2	5	69	38	77	57	1	1	.264
First Half	81	260	76	20	2	5	45	29	56	31	0	1	.292
Second Half	60	183	41	13	0	0	24	9	21	26	1	0	.224
Vs. RHP		339	87	24	2	3	46	26	53	45	1	1	.257
Vs. LHP		104	30	9	0	2	23	12	24	12	0	0	.288
Home	69	220	55	12	2	3	39	19	45	31	1	1	.250
Road	72	223	62	21	0	2	30	19	32	26	0	0	.278

Dale MURPHY, Right Field
Runs Created: 143

	G	AB	Hit	2B	3B	HR	Run	RBI	TBB	SO	SB	CS	Avg
9.38 years		595	166	26	4	33	99	99	78	131	15	6	.279
1987	159	566	167	27	1	44	115	105	115	136	16	6	.295
First Half	87	317	98	16	1	25	66	61	71	78	10	4	.309
Second Half	72	249	69	11	0	19	49	44	44	58	6	2	.277
Vs. RHP		416	119	19	1	30	73	75	55	104	6	4	.286
Vs. LHP		150	48	8	0	14	42	30	60	32	10	2	.320
Home	81	269	93	11	1	25	65	61	77	52	13	3	.346
Road	78	297	74	16	0	19	50	44	38	84	3	3	.249

Ken OBERKFELL, Third Base
Runs Created: 63

	G	AB	Hit	2B	3B	HR	Run	RBI	TBB	SO	SB	CS	Avg
7.37 years		533	151	27	5	3	63	48	63	38	8	5	.283
1987	135	508	142	29	2	3	59	48	48	29	3	3	.280
First Half	68	259	81	20	2	0	37	27	26	11	1	3	.313
Second Half	67	249	61	9	0	3	22	21	22	18	2	0	.245
Vs. RHP		366	98	18	0	3	42	31	40	19	3	2	.268
Vs. LHP		142	44	11	2	0	17	17	8	10	0	1	.310
Home	68	259	76	15	1	2	39	30	29	13	0	2	.293
Road	67	249	66	14	1	1	20	18	19	16	3	1	.265

Albert HALL, Outfield
Runs Created: 48

	G	AB	Hit	2B	3B	HR	Run	RBI	TBB	SO	SB	CS	Avg
1.67 years		324	83	17	4	2	56	22	39	45	29	11	.256
1987	92	292	83	20	4	3	54	24	38	36	33	10	.284
First Half	44	141	38	11	2	1	26	13	23	15	15	6	.270
Second Half	48	151	45	9	2	2	28	11	15	21	18	4	.298
Vs. RHP		170	48	12	4	2	28	15	25	20	21	5	.282
Vs. LHP		122	35	8	0	1	26	9	13	16	12	5	.287
Home	47	136	40	7	2	3	30	13	23	19	13	6	.294
Road	45	156	43	13	2	0	24	11	15	17	20	4	.276

Andres THOMAS, Shortstop
Runs Created: 25

	G	AB	Hit	2B	3B	HR	Run	RBI	TBB	SO	SB	CS	Avg
1.23 years		541	131	23	2	9	50	59	18	82	8	9	.242
1987	82	324	75	11	0	5	29	39	14	50	6	5	.231
First Half	60	236	59	10	0	4	23	29	13	35	4	3	.250
Second Half	22	88	16	1	0	1	6	10	1	15	2	2	.182
Vs. RHP		228	53	7	0	4	21	30	11	42	5	4	.232
Vs. LHP		96	22	4	0	1	8	9	3	8	1	1	.229
Home	43	174	45	4	0	4	18	22	5	29	4	0	.259
Road	39	150	30	7	0	1	11	17	9	21	2	5	.200

SAN DIEGO PADRES

For several years I wrote team comments which dealt not with the team, but with some issue related to the team. Last year I wrote detailed articles about each team which were actually about the team. I just intended it as a one-shot thing, but the articles were so popular with my readers that I hardly dared not to do it again this year.

But since this is the last team comment that I will ever write for the *Baseball Abstract*, and since I really don't know a damn thing about the San Diego Padres anyway, I wondered if you would mind if I reverted to my old form here, and talked about something else. I mean, I'm sure I could kick up some obscure statistical accomplishments about the Padres (did you know San Diego's winning percentage when they had a quality start was only .547, by far the lowest of any major league team?), but all that there really is to say about the Padres is that 1) Tony Gwynn is Gweat, 2) the Padres are terrible, 3) the Padres are young, 4) the Padres are almost certain to be somewhat better this year, but 5) they're not going to win anything until at least 1991. That's all I could tell you about the Padres if I took eleventy-seven thousand words.

What I wanted to write about instead is a very basic question. Of all of the studies I have done over the last twelve years, what have I learned? What is the relevance of sabermetric knowledge to the decision-making processes of a team? If I were employed by a major-league team, what are the basic things that I know from the research I have done which would be of use to me in helping that team?

I'm going to try to list, in true *Baseball Digest* form, the ten things that I have learned which I feel would have the most significance for a ball club:

1. Minor-league batting statistics will predict major league batting performance with essentially the same reliability as previous major-league statistics.

It is important to understand this for several reasons, first of all because the opposite is widely believed to be true. That gives you a potential edge on the competition. If you're talking about trading for a minor-league prospect and you have his major-league equivalencies, that gives you a big advantage: you *know* what kind of a hitter the player is, while the other guy doesn't know and believes that you don't know.

Second, knowing what a player is likely to hit in the major leagues—with the same margin of doubt you have for anybody else—opens up to you a range of players who are more or less available, some of whom can hit. I would not want to give the impression that there are a huge number of available AAA players who are good major-league hitters. We're not talking about players who are going to win triple crowns. It's just that there is an occasional player out there, like Randy Ready and Dion James a year ago, who can be picked up for almost nothing, can step into a job and help the team. A couple of guys who are decent major league hitters if they ever get a shot: Wade Rowdon and Andre David. There is a third reason this is important, which we will discuss in a moment.

2. Talent in baseball is not normally distributed. It is a pyramid. For every player who is 10 percent above than the average player, there are probably 20 players who are 10 percent below average.

The import of understanding this is that it alters your attitude toward potential lineup changes. If you believe that talent is scarce, then you are reluctant to make changes. You perceive yourself as hanging over an abyss, a talent void. That puts you in a position of weakness in dealing with your players. If a player stops hitting, you stay with him longer. If a player becomes demanding and obstreperous, you give in to him. If a player gets hurt, you force him back into the lineup sooner than you ought to, or sometimes you'll make a trade you shouldn't make to "plug the gap."

A corrollary of this is that the true cost of losing a superstar is stunningly small—three, four games a year in most cases. No player carries a team. The ability of most teams to sustain an injury or a free agent loss and continue to compete is far greater than most fans believe—so long as the team believes in themselves. So long as they don't panic, but just keep putting out the effort, most teams can sustain major injuries and continue to play at substantially the same level. A team loses a Lance Parrish, an Andre Dawson, a John Tudor, a Jack Clark, a Bruce Sutter, and a good many of the fans will always slap their heads and say, "That's it. We're dead now." But the history of almost any season shows that that isn't true, that you can promote a Matt Nokes, put together a platoon combination, form a bullpen-by-committee, give another player the chance he's been waiting for, and eight times in ten come out of it not losing very much.

This is also the third reason it is important to understand that minor-league batting statistics can be translated into meaningful major-league equivalents. Knowing what minor-league batting stats mean puts you in touch with that replacement-level talent. You won't panic when you lose a valuable player if you are able to evaluate the possible replacements. It doesn't mean you're always right, of course. I was wrong about Matt Nokes last year, but I was wrong because I didn't look carefully enough at the minor-league stats, didn't realize that when he had a .491 slugging percentage in AA ball in 1985, he had done that at Shreveport, one of the worst places in the world to hit. By the way, a kid named Ty Dabney had a big year there in 1987, and should turn out to be a major-league hitter if he ever gets a shot.

3. What a player hits in one ballpark may be radically different from what he would hit in another.

I have hammered on this one so much over the years that to repeat it now would be of little value, but certainly there is still an inadequate understanding of this in many front offices. Andre Dawson still wins the MVP Award for his Wrigley Field stats. People still think that Kirk Gibson is going to hit in Dodger Stadium the way he did in Detroit. You have to remind people that everything has to be park-adjusted to have meaning.

4. Ballplayers, as a group, reach their peak value much earlier and decline much more rapidly than many people believe.

The biggest study of this issue was published in the 1982 *Abstract*, the first published by Ballantine. That study found, examining all players born during the 1930s, that between the ages of 30 and 35:

- Superstars lost 25 percent of their value.
- Star players lost 50 percent of their value.
- Good ballplayers and marginal regulars lost 84 percent of their value.

This data is a little different in the 1980s because long-term contracts keep around players who would otherwise have been released, but still, players reach their peak as a group at 27 and decline after that at an accelerating rate. That's why building a team with players in their thirties, as the Dodgers are now trying to do, virtually always fails. Over the next four years Gibson, Mike Davis, and Alfredo Griffin will probably lose 60–70 percent of their value. They'll get hurt more, hit less, decline as fielders. Am I picking on the Dodgers again? Sorry. Anyway, adding a 33-year-old player to a team that needs to put some quality in a spot to get them over the hump in a defensible strategy, as for example with Garvey in San Diego, but even then you've got to understand that you're going to pay a price for it in later years.

5. Players taken in the June draft coming out of college (or with at least two years of college) perform dramatically better than players drafted out of high school.

This result was reported in a study of the draft which was the first special issue of the newsletter I ran for a couple of years. The study compared players drafted out of high school and college—for example, comparing high school players drafted in spots 6 through 10 of the first round to college players drafted in spots 6 through 10 of the draft. The study found that in every category (top-five draft picks, second-five, second-ten, etc.) the players drafted out of college were more likely to become major-league players, more likely to become regulars, more likely to play in an All-Star game, more likely to become superstars. The players coming out of college were clearly undervalued as draft prospects, and the players out of high school overvalued.

The study was published in 1984, and was able to evaluate fairly well the drafts up to 1979 or 1980. Since then there has been a shift in draft priorities. In the early years most of the top ten draft picks were made up of high school kids; now very few high school kids are drafted 1 through 10. The teams were finding through experience the same thing I found in the study. We can assume that the overvaluing of high school players is now much less dramatic than it was at that time. However, examining the last four or five drafts, the pattern appears to persist. Most of the really good players coming out of the high rounds of the draft are drafted out of college. The Mets are an exception; they've drafted Gooden, Strawberry, and Jeffries out of high school.

6. The chance of getting a good player with a high draft pick is substantial enough that is clearly a disastrous strategy to give up a first-round draft pick to sign a player like Rick Dempsey, Pete Falcone, or Bill Stein.

Teams have a tendency to assume that a first round draft pick doesn't mean that much anyway, so they'll take the risk. This would have been a bad gamble in the old days, when 10–20 percent of high draft picks panned out, because you'd be trading a ten percent chance of getting a good player for 10 percent of the career of a mediocre player. But the scouting is so much better now, and the players are drafted out of college when they are much closer to the majors, that the percentage of high draft picks who become good players is much higher, and the idea of giving up a high draft pick, a potential star, for a player of this ilk is just flat insanity. There have been some pretty awful de facto trades made by teams that gave up a draft pick to sign a marginal free agent, when the draft pick went on to become vastly more valuable than the free agent. A few of them:

In order to sign Don Baylor as a free agent, the Yankees gave the California Angels a third-round draft pick. Baylor gave the Yankees three undistinguished seasons. The draft pick: Wally Joyner.

In order to sign Tim Stoddard as a free agent, the San Diego Padres gave a first-round draft pick to the Cubs. Stoddard pitched a year and a half for the Padres, very ineffectively. The player picked: Rafael Palmeiro.

In order to sign Frank Tanana as a free agent, the Texas Rangers gave the Boston Red Sox their first-round draft pick in 1982. Tanana went 31–49 for the Rangers. The player picked by Boston: Sam Horn.

7. A power pitcher has a dramatically higher expectation for future wins than does a finesse pitcher of the same age and ability.

Take two pitchers of roughly the same age and ability, but one of whom is a strikeout pitcher and the other of whom is not. The odds are that the strikeout pitcher will pitch much longer and will win more games in the future than the finesse pitcher.

I discovered this in the late seventies, and it's been an extremely useful piece of information to me. Look at the non-strikeout pitchers who have won the Cy Young Award in the last ten years—Steve Stone, Lamarr Hoyt, Pete Vuckovich, John Denny. They're all gone; none of them can pitch anymore. Look at the list of the pitchers who won *The Sporting News* Rookie Pitcher of the Year Award from 1980 through 1985. Craig McMurtry went 15–9 with a 3.08 ERA in Atlanta in 1983, but struck out only 105 men. Where is he now? Tom Browning won 20 as a rookie for Cincinnati in 1985, but struck out only 155 men. The guys who won that award and went on to be really good were Righetti, Valenzuela, Bedrosian, Langston, Gooden—the guys who throw hard. It's easy to say now that McMurtry and Browning were never that good, but the teams that had them sure as hell thought they were good. Those kind of pitchers are rarely consistent over a period of years.

8. Single-season won-lost records have almost no value as an indicator of a pitcher's contribution to a team.

A related point. You still see trades made (Danny Jackson, Lee Guetterman) and salaries established based on the assumption that the won-lost record indicates how well the man has pitched. Ordinarily nothing predicts future performance in a statistical category as well as past performance in the same category, but ERA is a far better predictor of future winning percentage than is winning percentage itself.

9. The largest variable determining how many runs a team will score is how times they get their leadoff man on.

You might think this would be higher, and maybe it should be; God knows I have run the idea that on-base percentage is the key to an offense into the ground. On-base percentage is one of the keys to evaluating production, but the key thing for a club to understand is not how a player performed for somebody else, but how he might perform for us. A player might have a .370 on-base percentage for another team, but if he's 32 years old and we're playing in a pitcher's park and we acquire him, he might have a .320 on-base percentage over the next three years for us. Then what good was it to know that he was a good player where he was? So I think that, to a baseball team, the factors that enable you to adjust performance—how this player will perform in our park, at this level, at this age, etc.—are more important than those that enable you to evaluate performance.

10. Any one of the following:

A great deal of what is perceived as being pitching is in fact defense.

True shortages of talent almost never occur at the left end of the defensive spectrum.

Rightward shifts along the defensive spectrum almost never work.

Our idea of what makes a team good on artificial turf is not supported by any research.

When a team improves sharply in one season, they will almost always decline in the next.

The platoon differential is real and virtually universal.

WINNING PERCENTAGE IN GAMES DECIDED BY ONE OR TWO RUNS

Montreal	.647
Milwaukee	.605
Detroit	.600
Minnesota	.575
St. Louis	.567
Philadelphia	.538
Toronto	.524
Mets	.519
Seattle	.515
Pittsburgh	.514
San Francisco	.506
Baltimore	.500
Yankees	.500
Cincinnati	.500
Cubs	.494
Texas	.481
Cleveland	.480
Atlanta	.473
Los Angeles	.471
Oakland	.466
Kansas City	.465
White Sox	.444
Houston	.432
California	.429
Boston	.412
San Diego	.337

RUNS SCORED AND ALLOWED WINS AND LOSSES

Wins	383	165	65-0	1.000
Whitson	151	146	17-17	.500
Pitchers' Duels	83	75	22-22	.500
Grant	65	73	8-9	.471
Home Games	338	357	37-44	.457
Jones	110	109	10-12	.455
Slugfests	360	406	22-31	.415
All Games	668	763	65-97	.401
Blowouts	208	279	15-24	.385
Show	134	158	13-21	.383
One-Run Games	189	204	19-34	.358
Hawkins	98	116	7-13	.350
Road Games	330	406	28-53	.346
Losses	285	598	0-97	.000

TEN BEST STARTS

	IP	H	R	ER	BB	SO		
Grant vs. Atl, Sep 16	9	2	0	0	3	9	W	89
Jones vs. Atl, Aug 10	9	2	0	0	1	4	W	86
Whitson at SF, June 12	9	4	0	0	6	6	W	85
Show at LA, Apr 26	9	3	0	0	0	4	W	85
Show vs. Hous, Sep 11	9	4	0	0	4	8	W	83
Whitson at Hous, Sep 19	9	6	1	0	0	7	—	80
Whitson vs. Hous, June 23	9	2	1	1	5	6	W	80
Show at LA, July 1	9	4	0	0	1	2	W	80
Nolte vs. Phi, Aug 29	9	4	1	1	4	7	W	78
Dravecky at SF, June 14	9	5	1	1	2	6	W	77

PITCHERS WHEN SUPPORTED BY THREE TO FIVE RUNS

	G	IP	W-L	Pct	SO	BB	ERA
Grant	12	76	5-5	.500	42	42	3.39
Show	18	107	4-5	.444	57	44	3.54
Whitson	17	99	5-8	.385	81	33	5.10
S Davis	6	22	1-3	.250	18	16	7.07
Hawkins	6	32	1-4	.200	10	15	6.69

HALL OF FAME WATCH

Fully qualified: Steve Garvey 130.5; **Could be elected on current accomplishments:** Goose Gossage 95, Larry Bowa 78.5, Tony Gwynn 72; **Building credentials but not yet viable candidate:** Templeton 42.5; **Long way to go:** Hawkins 9, Show 6, Brown 5.5, Kruk 5, Santiago 4.5, Ready 2.5, Salazar 2.5, Flannery 2, Whitson 2, McCullers 1, M Davis 1. (Bowa had 76.5 points as a player, has 2 as a manager.)

OUTS INVESTED IN FIRST-RUN STRATEGIES

San Diego	172
St. Louis	156
Atlanta	154
San Francisco	152
Los Angeles	141
Milwaukee	137
Montreal	131
Pittsburgh	129
Mets	119
California	114
Oakland	113
Texas	113
Minnesota	112
Philadelphia	112
Seattle	111
Cubs	107
White Sox	106
Houston	104
Cincinnati	103
Cleveland	98
Boston	97
Detroit	89
Yankees	81
Toronto	80
Kansas City	77
Baltimore	76

TEN WORST STARTS

	IP	H	R	ER	BB	SO		
Jones at Phi, May 16	3⅔	7	8	7	5	2	L	14
Show at Cin, July 29	2⅓	8	6	6	1	2	L	18
Whitson vs. StL, July 16	3⅔	7	7	7	4	4	—	19
Hawkins vs. Pitt, July 25	1⅔	5	6	6	3	1	L	19
Jones at Cin, July 30	5*	11	6	6	3	1	W	19
Grant at Hous, Aug 2	2*	9	5	5	1	2	L	19
Nolte at SF, Sep 15	2⅓	6	6	6	1	1	L	21
Hawkins vs. StL, May 7	3⅔	6	6	6	2	0	L	23
Dravecky vs. Mon, May 23	2⅓	7	5	5	1	1	L	23
Show at Atl, Aug 4	5	9	7	7	2	4	L	23

Benito SANTIAGO, Catcher
Runs Created: 77

	G	AB	Hit	2B	3B	HR	Run	RBI	TBB	SO	SB	CS	Avg
1.01 years		602	180	35	2	21	73	84	18	123	21	13	.299
1987	146	546	164	33	2	18	64	79	16	112	21	12	.300
First Half	76	279	79	12	1	7	26	32	7	66	10	6	.283
Second Half	70	267	85	21	1	11	38	47	9	46	11	6	.318
Vs. RHP		364	102	16	1	10	37	50	10	80	19	8	.280
Vs. LHP		182	62	17	1	8	27	29	6	32	2	4	.341
Home	76	274	77	17	1	11	29	45	10	50	8	4	.281
Road	70	272	87	16	1	7	35	34	6	62	13	8	.320

Carmelo MARTINEZ, Left Field
Runs Created: 73

	G	AB	Hit	2B	3B	HR	Run	RBI	TBB	SO	SB	CS	Avg
3.58 years		498	127	25	1	18	62	70	74	87	2	4	.255
1987	139	447	122	21	2	15	59	70	70	82	5	5	.273
First Half	74	235	63	10	1	9	27	42	38	42	4	2	.268
Second Half	65	212	59	11	1	6	32	28	32	40	1	3	.278
Vs. RHP		263	72	10	2	6	30	38	33	52	4	3	.274
Vs. LHP		184	50	11	0	9	29	32	37	30	1	2	.272
Home	70	216	61	8	1	10	31	42	37	40	4	2	.282
Road	69	231	61	13	1	5	28	28	33	42	1	3	.264

John KRUK, First Base
Runs Created: 92

	G	AB	Hit	2B	3B	HR	Run	RBI	TBB	SO	SB	CS	Avg
1.60 years		453	141	19	3	15	66	81	74	94	13	9	.311
1987	138	447	140	14	2	20	72	91	73	93	18	10	.313
First Half	72	216	73	7	1	10	37	40	42	45	6	3	.338
Second Half	66	231	67	7	1	10	35	51	31	48	12	7	.290
Vs. RHP		310	105	11	1	16	55	63	57	55	17	6	.339
Vs. LHP		137	35	3	1	4	17	28	16	38	1	4	.255
Home	71	215	64	6	0	8	38	41	45	51	11	4	.298
Road	67	232	76	8	2	12	34	50	28	42	7	6	.328

Stan JEFFERSON, Center Field
Runs Created: 45

	G	AB	Hit	2B	3B	HR	Run	RBI	TBB	SO	SB	CS	Avg
0.80 years		558	128	11	9	11	81	40	51	125	43	14	.229
1987	116	422	97	8	7	8	59	29	39	92	34	11	.230
First Half	48	175	42	5	3	2	24	11	23	47	16	6	.240
Second Half	68	247	55	3	4	6	35	18	16	45	18	5	.223
Vs. RHP		268	60	6	7	7	39	25	24	62	23	7	.224
Vs. LHP		154	37	2	0	1	20	4	15	30	11	4	.240
Home	62	213	45	5	3	5	32	17	25	59	20	5	.211
Road	54	209	52	3	4	3	27	12	14	33	14	6	.249

Tim FLANNERY, Second Base
Runs Created: 25

	G	AB	Hit	2B	3B	HR	Run	RBI	TBB	SO	SB	CS	Avg
5.06 years		429	110	13	4	2	45	36	47	48	3	4	.256
1987	106	276	63	5	1	0	23	20	42	30	2	4	.228
First Half	55	139	34	2	1	0	15	9	21	10	2	3	.245
Second Half	51	137	29	3	0	0	8	11	21	20	0	1	.212
Vs. RHP		235	53	4	1	0	20	18	38	26	2	3	.226
Vs. LHP		41	10	1	0	0	3	2	4	4	0	1	.244
Home	50	122	30	3	0	0	15	10	21	9	0	3	.246
Road	56	154	33	2	1	0	8	10	21	21	2	1	.214

Tony GWYNN, Right Field
Runs Created: 143

	G	AB	Hit	2B	3B	HR	Run	RBI	TBB	SO	SB	CS	Avg
4.75 years		622	208	30	8	7	99	60	58	34	33	12	.334
1987	157	589	218	36	13	7	119	54	82	35	56	12	.370
First Half	85	316	117	20	7	5	62	34	41	17	29	6	.370
Second Half	72	273	101	16	6	2	57	20	41	18	27	6	.370
Vs. RHP		340	128	24	10	4	74	34	52	25	40	4	.376
Vs. LHP		249	90	12	3	3	45	20	30	10	16	8	.361
Home	79	282	110	15	11	5	69	25	44	19	26	4	.390
Road	78	307	108	21	2	2	50	29	38	16	30	8	.352

Chris BROWN, Third Base
Runs Created: 30

	G	AB	Hit	2B	3B	HR	Run	RBI	TBB	SO	SB	CS	Avg
2.17 years		562	157	24	3	17	68	74	46	86	10	8	.279
1987	82	287	68	9	0	12	34	40	20	46	4	4	.237
First Half	45	161	38	6	0	7	20	21	10	21	2	3	.236
Second Half	37	126	30	3	0	5	14	19	10	25	2	1	.238
Vs. RHP		189	42	6	0	7	20	26	10	32	2	3	.222
Vs. LHP		98	26	3	0	5	14	14	10	14	2	1	.265
Home	40	137	30	6	0	5	17	18	10	20	1	1	.219
Road	42	150	38	3	0	7	17	22	10	26	3	3	.253

Randy READY, Infield
Runs Created: 81

	G	AB	Hit	2B	3B	HR	Run	RBI	TBB	SO	SB	CS	Avg
1.51 years		512	138	32	9	12	84	65	73	65	6	3	.270
1987	124	350	108	26	6	12	69	54	67	44	7	3	.309
First Half	64	175	54	15	1	1	31	22	29	22	5	2	.309
Second Half	60	175	54	11	5	11	38	32	38	22	2	1	.309
Vs. RHP		175	50	11	2	6	23	28	21	26	0	2	.286
Vs. LHP		175	58	15	4	6	46	26	46	18	7	1	.331
Home	63	171	58	12	4	7	29	34	30	20	3	1	.339
Road	61	179	50	14	2	5	40	20	37	24	4	2	.279

Garry TEMPLETON, Shortstop
Runs Created: 42

	G	AB	Hit	2B	3B	HR	Run	RBI	TBB	SO	SB	CS	Avg
9.70 years		626	174	26	9	5	77	58	31	89	24	12	.278
1987	148	510	113	13	5	5	42	48	42	92	14	3	.222
First Half	80	265	58	7	3	2	19	18	24	49	5	3	.219
Second Half	68	245	55	6	2	3	23	30	18	43	9	0	.224
Vs. RHP		321	69	7	4	3	25	27	28	59	11	2	.215
Vs. LHP		189	44	6	1	2	17	21	14	33	3	1	.233
Home	73	250	51	7	4	2	22	22	21	52	5	3	.204
Road	75	260	62	6	1	3	20	26	21	40	9	0	.238

DEAR BASEBALL ABBY

The reader will be pleased to learn that the phenomenal success and increasing influence of *The Baseball Abstract* has not been lost on the men who play and manage major-league baseball. Increasingly, they have written to *The Abstract* (or *Baseball Abby* in their felicitous shorthand) soliciting counsel on all manner of baseball-related subjects. *Baseball Abby* is more than eager to assist the the men who, after all, make our great national pastime what it is today. The following is a random sampling of the sage advice dispensed over the past year by *Baseball Abby.*

Dear *Baseball Abby,*

I am a recently discharged manager, looking for another job, but not disposed toward taking anything run-of-the-mill. You see, in my first two managerial stints, I won the division title at the outset, something few, if any, have ever accomplished. I'm rather proud of that achievement, and want to stand a decent chance of making it three in a row if and when I manage again. Which brings me to my problem: I've been offered the reins of the Twins for '87. It's very tempting; I like the city, and the money is good, but I wonder, can they contend? I really want to extend my streak, and worry that I cannot do so with Minnesota. What do you suggest?

OUT OF THE FREYING PAN

Dear Freying Pan,
So you want to finish first in '87, do you? Well, take my advice and forget about the Twins. They're going absolutely nowhere. They have no rotation, no team speed, and Andy MacPhail is still wet behind the ears. Not to mention that their fans (such as exist) are the depths—they sit on their hands as though they're at a funeral, which they will be, yours, if you're foolish enough to take the job. I suggest you wait for a vacancy to open in Atlanta— now there's a team that's going places.

Dear *Baseball Abby,*

I am a rookie outfielder who, as I write—late June— is leading his team in homers and RBIs. I know, you're already asking yourself, what's the problem, why isn't he satisfied? Well, you see, the trouble is that, no matter how hard I try, I can't forget my first love, which is football, and which I stupidly gave up for this new relationship. I realize that baseball cares for me a lot; it didn't even make me go to the minors for more than a few weeks, but just recently I found out that football wants me back desperately, and doesn't even care whether I give up baseball or not. So now I am torn, and don't know which way to turn, as I love them both, and don't want to abandon either. What should I do?

DESPERATE IN KANSAS CITY

Dear Desperate,
Why are you so worried that no one will accept you for what you are in spite of your emotional ambivalence? Simply tell baseball how you feel about football, and how you need to spend some quality time with both in order to resolve your conflicts. Don't concern yourself about people being judgmental; I'm sure they'll be, almost to a man, warm and supportive, especially the veteran players and the fans. Besides, once you have your feelings out in the open, and are free of all repression, your performance on the diamond is bound to improve. So take my advice and go for it all.

Dear *Baseball Abby,*

I don't mean to brag, but it is arguable that I am the most valuable player in baseball. I hit for average, draw walks, steal bases, am durable, and still in my twenties. The problem? I don't earn as much money as players with half my talent. I'm eligible for free agency at the end of '86, but given the owner's indifference to high-priced players after the '85 season, wonder if that is the way to go? Also I like the city in which I play, and feel a sense of loyalty to my teammates. I'm totally in a quandary. What do you suggest?

IT NEVER RAINES BUT IT POURS

Dear Never Raines,
You may be a valuable player, but you certainly lack a valuable backbone. Of course you should opt for free agency. The owners are bluffing; they're scared shitless of a possible collusion rap; they'll be falling all over themselves to bid for your services. And even if they're not, so what? The worst that can happen will be for you to re-sign with your present team on May 1. I know, you're worried about missing the first twenty games, but what if you do? Your team is hopeless, no way they can contend; so they lose three or four they might have won with you in the lineup, will it matter over the long haul? Forget your wimpy scruples, grab for the bucks.

Dear *Baseball Abby,*

I have just received my unconditional release, and in spite of my age, my lack of speed and range, not to mention my wretched OBP and SA, other teams—contending teams—are interested in me. I've narrowed my choices to the Angels and the Twins, but cannot make up my mind between the two. I am desperate to return to the World Series and shed the goathorns that were unfairly hung upon me last year, and I know of no one to turn to but you. I beg you, please help me avoid going down in history as another Fred Snodgrass. Your advice is my command.

THE BUCKS STOPS WHERE?

Dear Bucks Stops,
Are you kidding? It's an open and shut case. Who do you want on your side in the heat of a pennant race—the battle-tested Gene Mauch and warriors like DeCinces, Downing, Sutton, and Boone, or the rookie manager with no personality and a bunch of Twinkies who go cream-

filling up at the thought of a road game? This is the biggest opportunity of your life, not everyone gets a second chance. Your only course is to call Mike Port and tell him "California Here I Come." Looking forward to seeing you once again in the Fall Classic.

Dear *Baseball Abby,*

I am the General Manager of a contending team, and as the stretch drive beckons you'd think I'd be happy. But in fact my life has been made a constant misery. The trouble is my manager—I personally elevated him from the coaching ranks, but is he grateful? No, all he does is bitch and moan, publicly, that I'm not getting him the right players. You think quality ball players are growing on trees? To hear him talk, all I have to do is wave my magic wand and here's a Rick Reuschel, there's a Don Baylor. Well, I don't have to tell you, Abby, that it's not that simple. I could easily ignore the creep, or even fire him, except that he seems to have the ear of the owner, not to mention the support of many fans and journalists. I'm frankly at my wit's end, and desperate enough to make any kind of deal if only it will relieve the pressure on me. What do you suggest?

WAGNERIAN SOAP OPERA

Dear Wagnerian Soap,

Abby applauds your course of action. It's silly to waste your time salivating over unobtainable players like Reuschel and Baylor. It is said that Mike Flanagan is available, but everyone knows his arm is dead. There is, however, one blockbuster deal you might be able to make. You need help at shortstop, and rumor has it that the Royals are shopping their most popular player, a legitimate World Series hero to boot. If this is so, do not hesitate—grab him at all cost. Not only will you strengthen your infield and get the manager off your back, but the fans are sure to respond to this player's undeniable charisma. In short (no puns intended), you'll be back in everyone's good graces in no time, and probably back in the playoffs. So forget about your carping critics; you'll have the last laugh at this year's Winter Meetings.

Dear *Baseball Abby,*

As if I didn't have enough problems, there's this female reporter covering my team who is making my life a living hell. She's all the time unnerving me with stupid questions like "why does your average continue to plummet?" and "why don't you draw walks anymore?" and "why do you have such a rotten personality?" I tell you, Abby, I can't take much more. I know I have to do something, but I fear the power of the press, as well as the wrath of management. I feel as if I'm trapped in a maze. What can I do?

IF I WERE KONG

Dear Kong,

You have every right to file a grievance charging undue harassment, even by a member of the fourth estate. But you must make your feelings known, otherwise everyone will ignore you. So your only option is to tell the world how you've been mistreated. Blow the whistle on the bitch. Rat on her.

Dear *Baseball Abby,*

I had the best season of my career in '86, but does my general manager show any appreciation? Not a bit, he refuses to even consider giving me a raise. I'm not a greedy man, and I certainly don't expect a long-term contract at my age, but I think I'm entitled to some acknowledgement that the team couldn't have gone all the way without me. But the GM is adamant, so I can either swallow my pride and accept the same salary, or become a free agent. There's a team in the American League that has made me an offer: it's for less money, but at least they do want me. My present team just doesn't seem to care. Tell me, Abby, which way should I go?

THE MORNING AFTER THE KNIGHT BEFORE

Dear Knight Before,

Verily it is written that man does not live by bread alone. Your present team is trying to destroy your self-esteem; can you honestly take that lying down, no matter how much money is at stake? This is no time for shrewd calculation; if they don't show you the proper respect, show them your middle finger. Besides, revenge is sweet, and when the '87 season begins and they realize they have no competent replacement for you, you'll have the pleasure of saying "I told you so." And not only that, the AL team you mentioned is sure to be much-improved by your acquisition, and could easily be in the thick of things come September. So make the move, and remember he who laughs last laughs best.

Dear *Baseball Abby,*

I am a General Manager with a proven track record— in '84 I took my team to the play-offs for the first time in almost forty years—but believe it or not, I think I'm going to be forced to resign. I keep hearing reports that the owners will veto my selection for new manager, and then what choice will I have? Even worse, rumors abound that they have already picked my successor, none other than—but no, this is beyond the bounds of reason—Jim Frey. Oh, Abby, am I going mad? I keep praying that this is a nightmare from which I will soon awake, and yet how can it be a nightmare if I can't even sleep from worry? Please help me, there is no one else I can turn to.

CHICAGO DOES DALLAS

Dear Dallas,

I'm not surprised the owners are thinking of forcing you out, you're so blatantly paranoid. Jim Frey as General Manager? Anybody who believes that is beyond the help of Abby, and needs rather to be fitted for a straitjacket. How long have you exhibited these symptoms? Soon I suppose you'll be telling me that when Frey gets your job, his first act will be to hire Don Zimmer as manager, and his next to trade your best pitcher for two mediocrities. But I don't mean to belittle; you are obviously in serious need of treatment. Have you considered a medical leave of absence?

—Mike Kopf

PLAYER RATINGS
AND COMMENTS

INTRODUCTION TO PLAYER RATINGS

The players in this year's *Baseball Abstract* will be rated by subjective judgment. Mine. For the past couple of years I've rated players by a poll of the members of Project Scoresheet, but this year I just decided to do it myself.

The form is new; the rankings and comments have been separated. On pages 179–83 the players are listed in the order in which I rank them. Beginning on page 184, there are comments about players in alphabetical order.

I know what a lot of people are going to say—you'd rather have comments about everybody. This is a central part of why I'm not doing the book after this year. Comedian George Carlin has observed that when he looks at the tapes of Ed Sullivan shows from twenty years ago, he can't believe the kind of material he was getting by with back then. George used to do the hippy-dippy weather man, who was a kind of spaced-out character who would say things like "Hey man. They're talking about Snoooww out there." The idea of a weather man taking a cavalier approach to the weather was incongruous, and people would laugh, but looking back on it the material could have been a lot better, and the idea that he created his reputation by doing this sort of thing seems, to Carlin, rather astonishing.

When I started rating players, there wasn't nearly as much information available as there is now. When I look back on the comments I had about players in 1982 (hit .306 against left-handed pitching . . . last two years has hit 21 and 26 points better on the road than in Oakland) I am astonished that I got by with it, much less that I built my reputation by doing it. About 70 percent of the comments were just one or two sentences. It was all right at the time because the information wasn't available anywhere else and nobody else was doing it, but the world has changed, and I'm still trapped in that same form, trying to find some piece of objective information to pass along about each player that isn't already available. It becomes harder every year to do that, and at the same time I expect more and more of myself.

So you have to get away from the form. You have to stop doing the hippy-dippy weatherman, have to move on and find something else that's better and more interesting now. The time has come for me to do that.

CATCHERS

1. Mike Scioscia, Los Angeles
2. Benito Santiago, San Diego
3. Gary Carter, Mets
4. B. J. Surhoff, Milwaukee
5. Bob Brenly, San Francisco
6. Matt Nokes, Detroit
7. Bo Diaz, Cincinnati
8. Mike LaValliere, Pittsburgh
9. Ernie Whitt, Toronto
10. Terry Steinbach, Oakland
11. Scott Bradley, Seattle
12. Carlton Fisk, White Sox
13. Terry Kennedy, Baltimore
14. Tony Pena, St. Louis
15. John Marzano, Boston
16. Alan Ashby, Houston
17. Lance Parrish, Philadelphia
18. Bob Boone, California
19. Jody Davis, Cubs
20. Ozzie Virgil, Atlanta
21. Don Slaught, Texas
22. Jamie Quirk, Kansas City
23. Tim Laudner, Minnesota
24. Mike Fitzgerald, Montreal
25. Rick Cerone, Yankees
26. Chris Bando, Cleveland

FIRST BASEMEN

1. Don Mattingly, Yankees
2. Dwight Evans, Boston
3. Keith Hernandez, Mets
4. Eddie Murray, Baltimore
5. Will Clark, San Francisco
6. George Brett, Kansas City
7. Pete O'Brien, Texas
8. Kent Hrbek, Minnesota
9. Wally Joyner, California
10. Mark McGwire, Oakland
11. Jack Clark, St. Louis
12. Glenn Davis, Houston
13. Von Hayes, Philadelphia
14. John Kruk, San Diego
15. Alvin Davis, Seattle
16. Greg Walker, White Sox
17. Darrell Evans, Detroit
18. Andres Galarraga, Montreal
19. Leon Durham, Cubs
20. Pat Tabler, Cleveland
21. Gerald Perry, Atlanta
22. Greg Brock, Milwaukee
23. Nick Esasky, Cincinnati
24. Willie Upshaw, Toronto
25. Sid Bream, Pittsburgh
26. Franklin Stubbs, Los Angeles

SECOND BASEMEN

1. Ryne Sandberg, Cubs
2. Billy Doran, Houston
3. Lou Whitaker, Detroit
4. Juan Samuel, Philadelphia
5. Willie Randolph, Yankees
6. Frank White, Kansas City
7. Rob Thompson, San Francisco
8. Marty Barrett, Boston
9. Tommie Herr, St. Louis
10. Steve Sax, Los Angeles
11. Harold Reynolds, Seattle
12. Jerry Browne, Texas
13. Tim Teufel, Mets
14. Glenn Hubbard, Atlanta
15. Vance Law, Montreal
16. Nelson Liriano, Toronto
17. Jeff Treadway, Cincinnati
18. Steve Lombardozzi, Minnesota
19. Johnny Ray, Pittsburgh
20. Fred Manrique, White Sox
21. Tony Bernazard, Oakland
22. Tommy Hinzo, Cleveland
23. Mark McLemore, California
24. Joey Cora, San Diego
25. Billy Ripken, Baltimore
26. Juan Castillo, Milwaukee

THIRD BASEMEN

1. Wade Boggs, Boston
2. Mike Schmidt, Philadelphia
3. Tim Wallach, Montreal
4. Gary Gaetti, Minnesota
5. Terry Pendleton, St. Louis
6. Paul Molitor, Milwaukee
7. Kevin Seitzer, Kansas City
8. Howard Johnson, Mets
9. Brook Jacoby, Cleveland
10. Kevin Mitchell, San Francisco
11. Buddy Bell, Cincinnati
12. Mike Pagliarulo, Yankees
13. Jim Presley, Seattle
14. Rance Mulliniks, Toronto
15. Carney Lansford, Oakland
16. Keith Moreland, Cubs
17. Bobby Bonilla, Pittsburgh
18. Ray Knight, Baltimore
19. Steve Buechele, Texas
20. Ken Oberkfell, Atlanta
21. Chris Brown, San Diego
22. Tom Brookens, Detroit
23. Doug DeCinces, California
24. Ken Caminiti, Houston
Los Angeles (Vacant)
White Sox (Vacant)

SHORTSTOPS

1. Ozzie Smith, St. Louis
2. Tony Fernandez, Toronto
3. Alan Trammell, Detroit
4. Cal Ripken, Baltimore
5. Julio Franco, Cleveland
6. Dick Schofield, California
7. José Uribe, San Francisco
8. Ozzie Guillen, White Sox
9. Scott Fletcher, Texas
10. Alfredo Griffin, Oakland
11. Hubie Brooks, Montreal
12. Rey Quiñones, Seattle
13. Spike Owen, Boston
14. Dale Sveum, Milwaukee
15. Greg Gagne, Minnesota
16. Barry Larkin, Cincinnati
17. Shawon Dunston, Cubs
18. Al Pedrique, Pittsburgh
19. Angel Salazar, Kansas City
20. Steve Jeltz, Philadelphia
21. Rafael Santana, Mets
22. Garry Templeton, San Diego
23. Craig Reynolds, Houston
24. Mariano Duncan, Los Angeles
25. Wayne Tolleson, Yankees
26. Andres Thomas, Atlanta

LEFT FIELDERS

1. Tim Raines, Montreal
2. George Bell, Toronto
3. Pedro Guerrero, Los Angeles
4. Phil Bradley, Seattle
5. Kirk Gibson, Detroit
6. Vince Coleman, St. Louis
7. José Canseco, Oakland
8. Joe Carter, Cleveland
9. Kal Daniels, Cincinnati
10. Kevin McReynolds, Mets
11. Billy Hatcher, Houston
12. Gary Redus, White Sox
13. Jack Howell, California
14. Pete Incaviglia, Texas
15. Ken Griffey, Atlanta
16. Jim Rice, Boston
17. Chris James, Philadelphia
18. Rafael Palmeiro, Cubs
19. Rob Deer, Milwaukee
20. Carmello Martinez, San Diego
21. Jeff Leonard, San Francisco
22. Dan Gladden, Minnesota
23. Gary Ward, Yankees
24. Ken Gerhardt, Baltimore
25. Bo Jackson, Kansas City
26. R. J. Reynolds, Pittsburgh

CENTER FIELDERS

1. Kirby Puckett, Minnesota
2. Eric Davis, Cincinnati
3. Rickey Henderson, Yankees
4. Brett Butler, Cleveland
5. Lloyd Moseby, Toronto
6. Robin Yount, Milwaukee
7. Andy Van Slyke, Pittsburgh
8. Willie McGee, St. Louis
9. Len Dykstra, Mets
10. Chili Davis, San Francisco
11. Ellis Burks, Boston
12. Dion James, Atlanta
13. Milt Thompson, Philadelphia
14. Mickey Brantley, Seattle
15. Oddibe McDowell, Texas
16. David Martinez, Cubs
17. Chet Lemon, Detroit
18. Gerald Young, Houston
19. Ken Williams, White Sox
20. Dwayne Murphy, Oakland
21. Willie Wilson, Kansas City
22. Gary Pettis, California
23. Fred Lynn, Baltimore
24. John Shelby, Los Angeles
25. Stan Jefferson, San Diego
26. Herm Winningham, Montreal

RIGHT FIELDERS

1. Tony Gwynn, San Diego
2. Dale Murphy, Atlanta
3. Darryl Strawberry, Mets
4. Jesse Barfield, Toronto
5. Andre Dawson, Cubs
6. Danny Tartabull, Kansas City
7. Barry Bonds, Pittsburgh
8. Ivan Calderon, White Sox
9. Kevin Bass, Houston
10. Tom Brunansky, Minnesota
11. Dave Winfield, Yankees
12. Mike Greenwell, Boston
13. Larry Sheets, Baltimore
14. Mitch Webster, Montreal
15. Ruben Sierra, Texas
16. Devon White, California
17. Cory Snyder, Cleveland
18. Candy Maldonado, San Francisco
19. Mike Davis, Oakland
20. Mike Marshall, Los Angeles
21. Dave Parker, Cincinnati
22. Mike Kingery, Seattle
23. Glenn Wilson, Philadelphia
24. Glenn Braggs, Milwaukee
25. Curt Ford, St. Louis
26. Pat Sheridan, Detroit

DESIGNATED HITTERS

1. Ken Phelps, Seattle
2. Brian Downing, California
3. Larry Parrish, Texas
4. Harold Baines, Chicago
5. Sam Horn, Boston
6. Mel Hall, Cleveland
7. Fred McGriff, Toronto
8. Bill Madlock, Detroit
9. Steve Balboni, Kansas City
10. Claudell Washington, New York
11. Roy Smalley, Minnesota
12. Mike Young, Baltimore
13. Reggie Jackson, Oakland
14. Cecil Cooper, Milwaukee

RIGHT-HANDED STARTERS

1. Roger Clemens, Boston
2. Jack Morris, Detroit
3. Dwight Gooden, Mets
4. Mike Scott, Houston
5. Mike Witt, California
6. Orel Hershiser, Los Angeles
7. Bret Saberhagen, Kansas City
8. Rick Sutcliffe, Cubs
9. Nolan Ryan, Houston
10. Charlie Hough, Texas
11. Rick Rhoden, Yankees
12. Dave Stewart, Oakland
13. Bob Welch, Los Angeles
14. Rick Reuschel, San Francisco
15. Bert Blyleven, Minnesota
16. Jim Clancy, Toronto
17. Dave Stieb, Toronto
18. Danny Cox, St. Louis
19. Ron Darling, Mets
20. Walt Terrell, Detroit
21. Doyle Alexander, Detroit
22. Mike Dunne, Pittsburgh
23. Doug Drabek, Pittsburgh
24. José DeLeon, White Sox
25. Mark Gubicza, Kansas City

26. Richard Dotson, White Sox
27. José Guzman, Texas
28. Eric Show, San Diego
29. Kelly Downs, San Francisco
30. Bill Wegman, Milwaukee
31. Juan Nieves, Milwaukee
32. Danny Darwin, Houston
33. Bob Forsch, St. Louis
34. Mike Krukow, San Francisco
35. Mike LaCoss, San Francisco
36. Mike Boddicker, Baltimore
37. Dennis Martinez, Montreal
38. Willie Fraser, California
39. Mike Moore, Seattle
40. Floyd Youmans, Montreal
41. Ted Power, Cincinnati
42. David Palmer, Atlanta
43. Bob Sebra, Montreal
44. Bryn Smith, Montreal
45. Jim Jones, San Diego
46. Les Straker, Minnesota
47. Kevin Gross, Philadelphia
48. Brian Fisher, Pittsburgh
49. Scott Bankhead, Seattle
50. Mark Grant, San Diego
51. Tom Candiotti, Cleveland

52. Don Sutton, California
53. Bill Long, White Sox
54. Scott Sanderson, Cubs

55. Bill Gullickson, Yankees
56. Mike Morgan, Seattle
57. Jeff Sellers, Boston
58. Ed Whitson, San Diego
59. Bob Stanley, Boston
60. Bobby Witt, Texas
61. Jeff Robinson, Detroit
62. Al Nipper, Boston
63. Mike Smithson, Minnesota
64. Dan Petry, Detroit
65. Joe Niekro, Minnesota
66. Rick Mahler, Atlanta
67. Andy Hawkins, San Diego
68. Greg Maddux, Philadelphia
69. Ken Schrom, Cleveland
70. Phil Niekro, Retired

LEFT-HANDED STARTERS

1. Teddy Higuera, Milwaukee
2. Frank Viola, Minnesota
3. Jimmie Key, Toronto
4. Charlie Leibrandt, Kansas City
5. Mark Langston, Seattle
6. Dave Dravecky, San Francisco
7. Floyd Bannister, White Sox
8. Zane Smith, Atlanta
9. Curt Young, Oakland
10. Frank Tanana, Detroit
11. Fernando Valenzuela, Los Angeles
12. Bruce Hurst, Boston
13. Danny Jackson, Kansas City
14. Sid Fernandez, Mets
15. Don Carman, Philadelphia
16. Shane Rawley, Philadelphia
17. Tommie John, Yankees
18. Greg Mathews, St. Louis
19. Dennis Rasmussen, Cincinnati
20. Joe Magrane, St. Louis
21. Atlee Hammaker, San Francisco
22. Bruce Ruffin, Philadelphia
23. Jamie Moyer, Cubs
24. Neal Heaton, Montreal
25. Steve Ontiveros, Oakland
26. Jim Deshaies, Houston
27. Mike Flanagan, Toronto
28. Eric Bell, Baltimore
29. Guy Hoffman, Cincinnati
30. Rick Honeycutt, Oakland
31. John Cerutti, Toronto
32. John Candelaria, Mets
33. Tom Browning, Cincinnati
34. Bob Knepper, Houston
35. Bob Kipper, Pittsburgh
36. Steve Carlton, Minnesota
37. Jerry Reuss, California

RELIEF ACES

1. Tom Henke, Toronto
2. Steve Bedrosian, Philadelphia
3. Todd Worrell, St. Louis
4. Lee Smith, Cubs
5. Tim Burke, Montreal
6. John Franco, Cincinnati
7. Dan Plesac, Milwaukee
8. Dave Righetti, Yankees
9. Dennis Eckersley, Oakland
10. Dave Smith, Houston
11. Jeff Reardon, Minnesota
12. Don Buice, California
13. Doug Henneman, Detroit
14. Jeff Robinson, Pittsburgh
15. Roger McDowell, Mets
16. Bobby Thigpen, White Sox
17. Dale Mohorcic, Texas
18. Lance McCullers, San Diego
19. Don Robinson, San Francisco
20. Dan Quisenberry, Kansas City
21. Edwin Nuñez, Seattle
22. Alejandro Peña, Los Angeles
23. Jim Acker, Atlanta
24. Wes Gardner, Boston
25. Doug Jones, Cleveland
26. Tom Niedenfuer, Baltimore

ALAN ASHBY

Hitting for Average:	B	
Hitting for Power:	B	
Plate Discipline:	B	
Baserunning:	D –	
OVERALL OFFENSE:		B
Reliability:	B +	
Arm:	D –	
Handling of Staff:	A	
OVERALL DEFENSE:		C –
Consistency:	B	
Durability:	C	
OVERALL VALUE:		C +
In a Word: **Slow**		

JESSE BARFIELD

Hitting for Average:	B	
Hitting for Power:	A –	
Plate Discipline:	B –	
Baserunning:	C –	
OVERALL OFFENSE:		B
Defensive Range:	B –	
Reliability:	A	
Arm:	A +	
OVERALL DEFENSE:		A
Consistency:	B +	
Durability:	A	
OVERALL VALUE:		B +
In a Word: **Cannon**		

STEVE BEDROSIAN

Fastball:	A –	
Curve or Slider:	C +	
Other Pitches:	C	
Control:	B +	
OVERALL STUFF:		B +
Delivery:	B +	
Holding Runners:	D –	
Fielding/Hitting:	C –	
OVERALL MECHANICS:		C +
Composure:	A –	
Consistency:	B +	
Durability:	B +	
OVERALL VALUE:		B +
In a Word: **Closer**		

Turning 36 in July, Alan Ashby had his best year yet as a hitter. When Ashby reached the major leagues in the mid-seventies he was regarded as a defensive catcher who didn't hit much. In his first 3 years Ashby never hit higher than .239, with only 11 home runs in over 300 games in the 3 years. In 1978 he had his first good year with the bat, .261 with 9 homers in 81 games. In 1981 he upped the average to .271. In 1982 he hit 12 home runs. In 1985 he hit .280. In 1987 he set career highs in homers (14), RBI (63) and batting average (.288). A switch hitter, Ashby as a young player would hit .260 as a left-handed hitter but almost nothing, below .200, as a right-hander. He's improved a lot both ways.

While his offense has grown and grown, his defense has waned. Ashby hasn't thrown very well for several years. I do note, however, that over the last 3 years the Astros ERA with Ashby as the starting catcher has been much better than with other catchers—3.44 in 1985, 3.10 in 1986 and 3.47 in 1987 as opposed to 4.18, 3.21 and 4.52 when he was out of the lineup.

In my first estimate of speed scores, last year, I figured Alan Ashby to be the slowest player in baseball, with a speed score of 1.7. The speed scores are a little higher under the refined method, but among the players I figured (see Vince Coleman), Ashby remains apparently the slowest, with a speed score of 2.1. He was followed by LaValliere, 2.7, Al Davis, 2.7, Gary Carter, 2.7, Matt Nokes, 2.9 and Keith Hernandez, 3.1.

Neil Munro has been looking carefully at Jesse's fielding statistics. He reports that if you want to compare outfield assists totals, you have to draw a line at 1946 or before, or comparisons have no meaning, since all of the all-time leaders in career assists began their careers before 1920.

Anyway, 1946 to the present involves a substantial number of outfielders. Among all outfielders from 1946 to the present, Barfield is already among the top ten in career double plays. He has doubled off 34 runners, tied with Carl Furillo and Johnny Callison for the tenth spot. The number-one man is Willie Mays, with 60. Of the other players in the top ten, all played at least 1,675 major-league games—at least. Barfield has joined the list in 839 games, half as many. Mays, the career leader, average 3.4 double players per 162 games in the outfield. Barfield is averaging 6.6.

In career assists, the top man post-war by far is Clemente, with 266; he is followed by Hank Aaron, 201, Carl Yastrzemski, 195, and Willie Mays, 195. The top ten extend down to Carl Furillo, with 151; Barfield is about three years away from that list, with 101.

Clemente averaged 18.2 assists/ 162 games; no one else in the top ten averaged more than 16.0 (Johnny Callison). Barfield is averaging, to date, 19.5 assists per 162 games. "Unless it is Al Kaline's outfield stats for 1955–1958 or Johnny Callison's for 1962–1966," writes Munro, "I have never seen figures to compare with the ones Jesse has accumulated in right field during the last three years."

Here's another testimony to the genius of the Atlanta Braves. Bedrosian in 1984 had a 2.37 ERA as a reliever for the Braves, struck out 81 men in 84 innings. They worked him too hard (70 games, 120 innings in 1983, headed for similar totals in 1984) so he started to have arm troubles. The Braves decided, to save his arm, to make him a starter. As a starting pitcher in 1985, Bedrosian was 7–15 with a 3.83 ERA—almost the same record Goose Gossage had when they made him a starter (9–17, 3.94 ERA). This was only about the fortieth time I've seen this mistake made; pitchers like this (one-pitch fire-ballers who come out and throw as hard as they can for as long as they can) almost never make it as starting pitchers. Todd Worrell was a starting pitcher in the Texas League in 1984; he went 3–10 with a 4.49 ERA. If they'd left him in a starting role he would probably still be in the Texas League.

Another reason for trying Bedrock in the starting rotation was that the Braves had signed Bruce Sutter for the 1985 season. Sutter, however, was ineffective (4.48 ERA) and hurt, so obviously you move Bedrosian back to the bullpen, right?

Not a chance. While his value was down, the Braves traded him for Ozzie Virgil. Does this organization have its stuff together, or what?

GEORGE BELL

Hitting for Average:	A−	
Hitting for Power:	A	
Plate Discipline:	D	
Baserunning:	C−	
OVERALL OFFENSE:		A−
Defensive Range:	B	
Reliability:	D	
Arm:	B−	
OVERALL DEFENSE:		B−
Consistency:	A	
Durability:	A	
OVERALL VALUE:		B+

In a Word: **Slugger**

I can recite George Bell's career statistics in my sleep. This comes from having helped prepare arbitration cases for him three years in a row. The cases are never heard, mind you—the Blue Jays always start coughing up money 20 minutes before the case is supposed to be heard—but we know very well that we have to prepare them on the assumption that they are certain to be heard, so we do. A few things I know about George from doing these cases:

• George makes quite a few errors, but over the last 2 seasons he has never really made an error that cost the Blue Jays anything. Last year he made 11 errors in 11 different games, but the Blue Jays won 9 of those games (in large part because Bell himself hit like Babe Ruth's older brother in those games), and in the other 2 games the errors were just overthrows that didn't lead to any unearned runs.

• On August 30, 1987, the Blue Jays were a game behind the Tigers, at 76–53. The Blue Jays from then until September 26 won 20 of 26 games to move to 96–59, 3½ games ahead. During those 26 games Bell hit .373 with 7 doubles, a triple and 8 homers for a .707 slugging percentage; he drove in 24 runs and scored 20. During a 20-game stretch beginning September 6, Bell hit .413 with 18 RBI, and had streaks of 5 games and 6 games in which he drove in a run every game. He drove in runs in 14 of the 20 games, and in the 6 games in which he didn't drive in runs he hit .389 (7/18) and scored 3 runs.

• George has thrown out more baserunners in the last 4 years than any outfielder except Jesse Barfield and Glenn Wilson.

WADE BOGGS

Hitting for Average:	A+	
Hitting for Power:	B−	
Plate Discipline:	A	
Baserunning:	D+	
OVERALL OFFENSE:		A
Defensive Range:	C	
Reliability:	C+	
Arm:	B−	
OVERALL DEFENSE:		C+
Consistency:	A	
Durability:	B+	
OVERALL VALUE:		A−

In a Word: **Offense**

I have a system for evaluating what I call "trade value," or estimated future value. The top ten list for 1987, consisting of still-young players who have extremely high proven value, consists of George Bell, Wade Boggs, Tony Fernandez, Tony Gwynn, Rickey Henderson, Don Mattingly, Kirby Puckett, Tim Raines, Cal Ripken, and Alan Trammell—nine American Leaguers and Tim Raines. Whereas in the past I have based trade value on the combination of age and approximate value in the most recent season, this time I used age and established value, which causes the list to have players a year or two older. Had I used approximate value in 1987, I would probably have had Mark McGwire, Eric Davis, and Danny Tartabull on the list rather than Henderson, Ripken, and one of the 29-year-olds, Boggs or Trammell.

Just how hard it is to get to 3000 hits with a late start can be seen in part by comparing Boggs hit totals to Rickey Henderson and Alan Trammell. Boggs, Henderson, and Trammell were all born in 1958, Trammell in February, Boggs in June, and Henderson in December. By the time Boggs reached the majors Trammell already had 524 hits, Henderson 410. Despite his phenomenal hit totals—1060 hits in five years—he has yet to catch either of them. He has been gaining on Henderson at a rate of 50 hits a year, so at current rates he can expect to catch Henderson in 1990 (Henderson still has him by 108). He has been gaining on Trammell, however, by an average of only 33 hits a year, though, so at the rate he is going he won't catch Trammell until 1997. They'll be 39 years old before he makes up for that late start.

GEORGE BRETT

Hitting for Average:	A−	
Hitting for Power:	B+	
Plate Discipline:	B+	
Baserunning:	C+	
OVERALL OFFENSE:		A−
Defensive Range:	B	
Reliability:	C−	
Arm:	B+	
OVERALL DEFENSE:		C+
Consistency:	C−	
Durability:	D	
OVERALL VALUE:		B

In a Word: **Ballplayer**

George's brother Ken was quoted last summer as saying that he didn't think George would make the Hall of Fame unless he got 3000 hits. I have to say, as an analyst, that there is no question that Ken is wrong about that. There has never been a player of Brett's accomplishments who has been left out of the Hall of Fame, and with the charisma that Brett has, the many celebrated things he has done that are not included in the formal summary of his career accomplishments, it seems extremely unlikely that he will be the first player of this calibre to be denied. I mean, it may seem intuitively that 3000 hits is the Hall of Fame standard for a great hitter, but think about it. There are almost 200 players in the Hall of Fame. There are only 16 people who have had 3000 career hits. Obviously, the Hall of Fame can't expect 3000 hits from everybody. Three thousand hits is the highest standard required of a candidate, the standard demanded of a long-term player who doesn't have many other things going for him, like Al Oliver or Vada Pinson. It's not a standard that is required for a Duke Snider, a George Sisler, an Ernie Banks, or a George Brett.

Al Oliver drove in 100 runs only twice, never scored 100 runs, never won a Gold Glove or an MVP award, played in 7 All-Star games, and led the league in 7 offensive categories. Brett has driven in or scored 100 runs seven times, has won a Gold Glove and an MVP, has played in 9 All-Star games and has led the league in 17 offensive categories. That puts him in a whole different class. You'd have a hard time to begin with just finding somebody who played in nine All-Star games and isn't in the Hall of Fame.

I say that with some reluctance, as

it may be that Ken said what he did in an attempt to get George to focus on the goal of 3000 hits, so as to get him to do a better job of off-season conditioning. I don't want to undermine the effort. My method for estimating such things shows George with only a 12 percent chance of getting 3000 career hits. Being in and out of the lineup with injuries, Brett's established hit level is just 135. He needs another 781 hits, and he'll be 35 in May. The method figures that he's six years away from 3000 hits, and you just can't expect a 35-year-old player to maintain the same level of productivity until he's 40. To get 3000 hits, then, Brett needs to stay in the lineup more over the next two or three years.

Despite the method, I think he probably will do it. If he plays until he's 41, he'll have to average 112 hits a year. If he were to get 170 hits this year, that average would drop to 102. If he were to get 160 hits the year after that, the average would drop to 90. Given the quality of hitter that he is, I don't think that (when healthy) he'll have any trouble staying in the lineup as long as he needs to stay in the lineup, within reason. I think that, if he focuses on the goal, if he can dodge an injury once in a while, he can clear 3000 hits with room to spare.

GARY CARTER

Hitting for Average:	D+	
Hitting for Power:	C	
Plate Discipline:	C−	
Baserunning:	D	
OVERALL OFFENSE:		C−
Reliability:	B	
Arm:	D	
Handling of Staff:	A	
OVERALL DEFENSE:		B−
Consistency:	B+	
Durability:	B+	
OVERALL VALUE:		C+
In a Word: **Fading**		

This was the first time since I began doing player ratings in 1980, based on the 1979 season, that Gary Carter has failed to rank first at his position. The reasons for this should be pretty obvious, and if they are not obvious now they will probably be obvious by this time next year. Berra, the other most consistent year-in, year-out catcher in history, was able to bounce back with the bat somewhat when the Yankees got more catching help for him and could give him 30 games a year in the outfield. With four outfielders already, that's going to be hard to do for Carter. The Mets for the last two seasons have played as well without Carter in the lineup as with him. I wouldn't suggest that this makes him totally expendable, but certainly he is no longer one of the key figures on the team.

Analytical stat notes on Carter . . . Carter's career offensive winning percentage is now .630, which is almost the same as that of the other great catchers of history—Bench (.621), Berra (.643), Lombardi (.610), Campanella (.602), Dickey (.626), Hartnett (.654), and Schang (.607). Carlton Fisk is close to that group (.590) . . . His career approximate value, which I switched to calling "gross value" in the revised version of the *Historical Abstract*, is 172, the third-highest of any catcher in history behind Bench (190) and Berra (182), and just ahead of Dickey (171) . . . It is estimated that 57 percent of his career value is offensive, 43 percent defensive.

RICK CERONE

Hitting for Average:	D	
Hitting for Power:	D	
Plate Discipline:	C	
Baserunning:	D	
OVERALL OFFENSE:		D
Reliability:	B+	
Arm:	C+	
Handling of Staff:	D	
OVERALL DEFENSE:		C
Consistency:	C	
Durability:	C+	
OVERALL VALUE:		D
In a Word: **Mistake**		

Did I read this winter that the Yankees had given Cerone a contract for 1988? What does this guy have to do to play himself out of the league? Cerone broke the World's record for "Longest Career Milked out of One Good Year" several years ago, and just goes on running up the tab; it was previously held by Elliott Maddox.

Cerone had the one good year with the bat, 1980, and got four years out of that while people waited for him to repeat. By that time, people figured that since he'd been around for all these years with a career .230-something batting average and no other offensive assets, he must be a hell of a defensive catcher. The problem with this theory is, if he's such a good defensive catcher, why do his teams have poor records and higher Earned Run Averages when he is in the lineup than when he's out? Last year the Yankees had a 4.46 ERA and a 46–40 (.535) record with Cerone catching, as opposed to 4.24 and 43–33 (.566) without him. This was his best year in this respect in three years (see catcher's stats). In 1986 the Brewers had an ugly 4.68 ERA with Cerone catching, as opposed to 3.54 without him. In 1985 the Braves had a 4.61 ERA with Cerone as the starting catcher, 3.81 without him; they were 26–52 with Cerone in the starting lineup, 40–44 without him. I will grant that one season of this wouldn't mean much, but after a few years you have to wonder. The team was about 19 runs worse with Cerone catching last year, 75 runs worse with him in 1986, and 62 runs worse with him in 1985. That's 156 runs. Doesn't that strike you as quite a few runs to wave off as an anomaly?

JACK CLARK

Hitting for Average:	B	
Hitting for Power:	A−	
Plate Discipline:	A	
Baserunning:	D−	
OVERALL OFFENSE:		A−
Defensive Range:	D	
Reliability:	C	
Arm:	B	
OVERALL DEFENSE:		C
Consistency:	D+	
Durability:	D−	
OVERALL VALUE:		C+
In a Word: **Fragile**		

I believe that something has gone seriously wrong in the Cardinal front office in the last fourteen to sixteen months, and that the costs of this will become evident either in 1988 or in 1989. There have been at least a dozen signals that tell me this, which I obviously don't have time to recount in detail, but let me hit the highlights:

1) The mishandling of Clark's free agency. Clark left the Cardinals because they didn't communicate to him that they wanted to keep him. Phone calls from Clark and his agent apparently were not returned. Clark apparently wanted to talk to Herzog, but the message didn't get through.

2) The bungled signing of Bob Horner. The Cardinal front office told the media that they were interested in signing Horner before they told their own manager. Herzog when he heard about it expressed the opinion that Horner couldn't play.

3) The signing of Horner in and of itself. Bob Horner is not a good player, and he's not the right type of player for this team or this park. He gets hurt a lot, his conditioning is poor, he's not young; his only real asset is power, and in St. Louis? Herzog was right about him.

4) The trade of Lance Johnson and Ricky Horton for José DeLeon. Incredibly bad trade. It's not that it can't work—DeLeon has a great arm, and might turn in a big year with the support of the Cardinal offense and defense. But you just don't trade a kid who has got a chance to be a big star for a 27-year-old pitcher with a lifetime record of 32–55. Not to mention that they threw in a pitcher, Horton, who might have a better year than DeLeon.

Parenthetically, I edited the comments on the NL East for *The Great American Baseball Stat Book*. The guy who wrote the comment on Horton speculated that Horton might become a 20-game winner when he got traded and got a chance to pitch. I used the comment because it was well written, the best thing I had about Horton, but I don't think that's likely. I like Horton a great deal, but I think he's a pitcher who needs a great defense behind him to be successful, that it's very questionable if he can pitch 220 innings a year and somewhat questionable if he will be effective the second time through the order. Anyway,

5) In retrospect, the trade of Mike Dunne, Andy Van Slyke, and Mike LaValliere for Tony Pena. I didn't criticize the trade at the time so I can't second-guess the logic of it now, but the obvious fact is that the Cardinals traded three players, all of whom were very good, for one player who wasn't very good.

6) The re-signing of Tony Pena to a two-year, $2.2 million contract extension in September despite his poor performance. Was it a sound business judgment, that Pena despite two off years in three, was going to come back strong, or was it done to cover their ass, to avoid allowing Pena to become a free agent and expose the fact that the Cardinals made a bad trade?

As to what, specifically, has gone wrong, what has led to this series of blunders and inexplicable decisions, I honestly don't know. It may be that there are some executives who are jealous of the fact that Herzog has gotten so much of the credit for the Cardinals success, or it may simply be that somebody is in over his head. I don't deal with personalities, but with decisions. There is a line of bad decisions here.

WILL CLARK

Hitting for Average:	A−	
Hitting for Power:	A−	
Plate Discipline:	C	
Baserunning:	D+	
OVERALL OFFENSE:		B+
Defensive Range:	A−	
Reliability:	B	
Arm:	B+	
OVERALL DEFENSE:		B+
Consistency:		
Durability:	B	
OVERALL VALUE:		B+
In a Word: **Aggressive**		

Will Clark be a great player, or won't he? If Gary Ward were a basketball player, would that make him a Ward of the Court? Can Vance Law ever be repealed? Why didn't Danny Darwin ever evolve into the pitcher people thought he would be? Can Rick Honeycutt the mustard anymore? Is Dale's horse any better today? How about Moose's Haas? What does Ron Cey about being retired? Do you think that this will be the year Billy Beane sprouts?

Last year *The Scouting Report: 1987* put on it's back cover that in the previous year they had written that Roger Clemens had the ability to be a 25-game winner. Which of the following quotes do you think is most likely to appear on the back cover in 1988? About Kevin Seitzer: "Seitzer is capable of hitting .300 with 15–18 homers and 75–80 RBIs. He just may be the biggest surprise on the Royals' team this year."

About Will Clark: "Clark will probably never be a big home run hitter, but he has alley power . . . Clark is a potential .300 hitter who has the eye to hit nearly 20 home runs in a season."

About Mark McGwire: "The excitement about McGwire was already in recession at the end of the season. By September, it was known that the holes in McGwire's bat and glove still might be too big for the big leagues . . . (after) Oakland's acquisition of Ron Cey, McGwire will be hard-pressed to make the early April party."

Hey, guys, I love the book. It's just that you're my only chance to get even, all right?

ROGER CLEMENS

Fastball:	A
Curve or Slider:	A−
Other Pitches:	A
Control:	B+
OVERALL STUFF:	A
Delivery:	B+
Holding Runners:	A−
Fielding/Hitting:	B+
OVERALL MECHANICS:	A−
Composure:	A
Consistency:	A
Durability:	A−
OVERALL VALUE:	A
In a Word:	**Excellence**

Let's look at the contest for the Cy Young Award in terms of average game score. Among American League pitchers with ten or more starts, the highest average game scores belonged to:

1. Doyle Alexander   66.45
2. Roger Clemens   61.28
3. Jimmie Key   59.44
4. Jack Morris   58.62
5. Frank Viola   58.17

Followed in order by Bret Saberhagen, Mark Langston, Teddy Higuera, Dave Stewart, and Charlie Hough. Obviously, however, there would be a problem with simply voting the players in this order, that being that Roger Clemens had 36 games of 61.3, and Doyle Alexander had only 11 games of 66.4, hardly an equivalent accomplishment.

We could adjust for this by crediting the player with one point for each game score point that he is over 50.000 on the season—that is, multiplying the number of starts for each pitcher times his margin over 50. This would produce:

1. Roger Clemens   +406
2. Jimmie Key   +340
3. Frank Viola   +294
4. Jack Morris   +293
5. Bret Saberhagen   +243

Followed in order by Langston, Higuera, Stewart, Alexander (+181), and Hough. Alexander's feat of placing among the ten best pitchers in the league despite starting only 11 times remains impressive. This method would be the equivalent of Pete Palmer's method—comparing each pitcher to an average pitcher, and mea-suring his value by what he does to move the team over or under average.

Clemens is about +400, which is to say that he is as valuable as he would have been had he been an exactly average pitcher for 28 starts and pitched eight "Perfect 100s," eight no-hitters with lots of strikeouts. That's a pretty substantial margin of performance over the average guy.

I have problems with that method, as you may know, because it assumes that an average pitcher has no value when obviously he does. I mean, if you can start 30 times a year and be an average pitcher, you'll make $500,000 to $600,000 a year, maybe more. What counts is how far you are above a replacement-level pitcher. A replacement-level pitcher might have an average game score about 44, 45. Same method, only comparing each pitcher to 45.00 per game rather than 50.00:

1. Roger Clemens   +586
2. Jimmie Key   +520
3. Frank Viola   +474
4. Jack Morris   +463
5. Mark Langston   +415

If the game score method were perfect, if there were no problems with park illusions and no miscellaneous considerations like the impact on a pennant race, that would be the method I would use. I think in 1987 Clemens was obviously the best pitcher in the league, just as he was the year before.

VINCE COLEMAN

Hitting for Average:	B	
Hitting for Power:	D−	
Plate Discipline:	C+	
Baserunning:	A+	
OVERALL OFFENSE:		B−
Defensive Range:	B+	
Reliability:	D+	
Arm:	B	
OVERALL DEFENSE:		B
Consistency:	B	
Durability:	B+	
OVERALL VALUE:		B
In a Word:	**Improved**	

I ran a player analysis package for a group of about 100 players, who could be loosely described as 90 of the 100 best players in baseball, plus 10 miscellaneous other players. The top ten speed scores were Vince Coleman, 9.0, Eric Davis, 8.6, Brett Butler, 8.2, Barry Bonds, 8.1, Willie Wilson, Rickey Henderson, and Tim Raines, all 8.0, Ellis Burks and Andy Van Slyke, 7.9, and Juan Samuel, 7.8.

Last summer I did a study of the accuracy of career projection systems, like the Brock system I introduced several years ago. In doing that I discovered that the accuracy of projections based on three full years of data (after a player had been in the majors for three full years) was substantially better than the projections based on a player's first two years, to a surprising extent. There were several players in the study whose third season was the first true indicator of their ability, in most cases the first time they played as well as they were capable of (Johnny Callison, Lou Brock, Roy White, Pete Rose) but also in a few cases the season in which they revealed that they weren't as good as they looked (Joe Pepitone).

The Vince Coleman of 1985–1986 didn't impress me much; he was a wild swinger whose inability to get on base consistently essentially negated his strength. But last year he jumped from .232 to .289, and with 70 walks as well he had an on-base percentage of .363. I take the improvement to be real, and as long as it is, I'll take the player.

KAL DANIELS

Hitting for Average:	A	
Hitting for Power:	A –	
Plate Discipline:	A –	
Baserunning:	A –	
OVERALL OFFENSE:		A
Defensive Range:	B	
Reliability:	D	
Arm:	D +	
OVERALL DEFENSE:		C –
Consistency:	?	
Durability:	?	
OVERALL VALUE:		B
In a Word: **IF**		

ERIC DAVIS

Hitting for Average:	B	
Hitting for Power:	A	
Plate Discipline:	A	
Baserunning:	A	
OVERALL OFFENSE:		A –
Defensive Range:	A	
Reliability:	B +	
Arm:	B +	
OVERALL DEFENSE:		A –
Consistency:	C	
Durability:	C	
OVERALL VALUE:		B +
In a Word: **Dynamite**		

MARIANO DUNCAN

Hitting for Average:	C –	
Hitting for Power:	D +	
Plate Discipline:	D	
Baserunning:	B +	
OVERALL OFFENSE:		D +
Defensive Range:	B	
Reliability:	D –	
Arm:	C –	
OVERALL DEFENSE:		C –
Consistency:	D	
Durability:	D	
OVERALL VALUE:		D +
In a Word: **Floundering**		

If he can hit left-handers. If he can stay healthy. If his glovework isn't too bad.

In the estimates of the percentage of career value which was offensive (see Ozzie Smith), Kal Daniels was on the other end; 91 percent of his value so far has been with the bat. The top ten were Ken Phelps (95 percent offense, 5 percent defense), Daniels, Mark McGwire (89–11), Don Mattingly (86–14), Incaviglia (85–15), Kent Hrbek (84–16), Wally Joyner (82–18), Will Clark (82–18), Reggie (81–19), and Pedro Guerrero (81–19).

I may be a minority of one, but I like this kid better than Eric Davis. Kal Daniels just might be the best hitter of the 1990s. He was awesome last year, producing at a rate 119 runs scored, 39 doubles, 42 homers and 42 stolen bases, 98 walks, 104 RBI, .334 average. When he was 20 years old at Vermont in 1984, he had a season that was equivalent to over .300 in the major leagues, with doubles, homers, walks, and stolen bases. He's done nothing since that is any less impressive, including hitting .371 and slugging .674 in 42 games at Denver. A projection based on his 1986 season is almost as stunning—.320 average, extra base hit totals of 33–13–20, 73 walks, 50 stolen bases. He's a year younger than Eric Davis, and in my opinion well ahead of him as a hitter.

Daniels will never become the defensive player that Eric Davis is, and last year had a lot of trouble with left-handed pitching. But as a hitter, he's got it.

Eric Davis in 1981 in the Northwest league scored 67 runs in 62 games, hitting .322 with a .561 slugging percentage. In the 62 games he stole 40 bases and drew 57 walks, a secondary average of .692. From that point it only took the Reds five years to get him in the regular lineup. Tony Gwynn was in the Northwest league that year; he was a major-league regular by the end of the next season. Phil Bradley was in the league; he hit .301 with one home run. He was a regular in the majors in three years.

What would you think of a stat that gave outfielders credit for catching a ball that would otherwise have been a home run? HRS—Home Runs Saved . . . I doubt that Eric will ever be a consistent .300 hitter. He struck out last year 134 times in 474 at bats, even worse in 1986. To do that and hit .293 is a remarkable accomplishment; it means you have to hit over .400 when not striking out. I don't think Davis can hit .300 more than once or twice unless he cuts down significantly on the strikeouts.

Davis last year had a Power/Speed number of 42.5, an all-time record, breaking the 42.4 set by Rickey Henderson in 1986. There have now been four seasons of 40.0—Bobby Bonds in 1973 (39 HR, 43 SB), Rickey Henderson in 1986 (28 HR, 87 SB), Eric Davis in 1986 (27 HR, 80 SB), and Eric Davis in 1987 (37 HR, 50 SB). We're still waiting for our first 40/40 season . . . The Reds have no obvious leadoff man, no one with a high run element ratio. Davis and Daniels have run elements ratios near one; almost everyone else is under one . . . .

When doing the study of platoon differentials that appears in the first section of the book, I noticed that there were many switch hitters who had enormous platoon differentials—in fact, I would bet that the average platoon differential for switch hitters was far larger than the norm for either right-handers or left-handers. That's rather extraordinary, isn't it? Why do players switch hit? Obviously, the reason they switch hit is to avoid hitting with a platoon disadvantage. If you switch hit to avoid the platoon differential and you wind up with a huge platoon differential, it isn't working, is it?

The players who were switch hitters but had large platoon differentials included Alan Ashby, Wally Backman, Kevin Bass, Julio Cruz, Mariano Duncan, Jerry Mumphrey, Gary Pettis, Tony Phillips, Johnny Ray, R. J. Reynolds, Alan Wiggins, and Mitch Webster. Some of those players may be true switch hitters who just happen to be stronger from one side, and others, like Wally Backman, may just be desperation switch hitters who move to the right side because they can't hit left-handers. My concern is not with either of those groups of players.

My concern is with what we might call the "forced switch hitters," the right-handed hitters who are told when they enter professional baseball to become switch hitters so that they can "take advantage of their speed." Once in a while, I suppose, this strategy works, usually when the player makes the decision to do it on his own, like Maury Wills or Eddie Murray. In the great majority of cases, I wonder if the attempt to become a switch hitter isn't a recipe for professional disaster. It's not simply that these players don't become as good with the bat from the left side as they are from the right; that might be more than one could expect. What concerns me is that they fail even to reach the level at which they would probably perform with a normal platoon differential. Look at a few of them:

• Mariano Duncan in his career has batted 446 times as a right-handed hitter. As a right-handed hitter he has hit .274 (.273 prior to 1987, .275 in 1987) with 12 home runs for a slugging percentage of .401. Given a normal platoon disadvantage, he would probably hit, as a right-hander facing right-handers, about .250–.260 with somewhat reduced power, slugging percentage around .360; that would make him, overall, about a .260–.265 hitter with a slugging percentage around .375.

Instead, trying to switch hit, Duncan has hit .209 as a left-handed batter, (.217 prior to 1987, .182 in 1987), and with sharply reduced power, just 8 home runs in 784 at bats. His slugging percentage as a left-handed hitter is .281, leading to a career average of .233 with a slugging percentage of .324.

• Tony Phillips over the last four years has batted 473 times as a right-handed hitter, and in that role has hit .313 with a slugging percentage of .427. Given a normal "platoon drag," he would have an average over that period in the neighborhood of .300, with a slugging percentage around .400.

Instead, batting 959 times as a left-hander, Phillips has hit just .230 left-handed with a .340 slugging percentage, dragging him down to an overall .258 with a slugging percentage of .369. As a right-handed hitter Phillips has more walks than strikeouts (67–58); as a left-hander he has struck out almost twice as often as he has walked (121–220).

• Mitch Webster over the last four years has batted 490 times as a right-handed hitter, hitting .314 with 30 doubles and 18 homers in 490 AB, a .502 slugging percentage. Though he has remained respectable enough as a left-handed hitter to stay in the league (.266 with a .407 slugging percentage), Webster still is not the hitter he probably would be if he weren't trying to switch hit. Few right-handed hitters who hit as well as Webster does against lefties hit as poorly as he does against right handers.

Two of the worst examples of this I have seen were Julio Cruz and U. L. Washington, both natural right-handed hitters who were forced switch hitters. Both of these guys had some real pop in their bats batting right-handed, sometimes compiling slugging percentages right-handed up around .500.

Batting left-handed, they were singles hitters, and bad singles hitters. I never saw Cruz in a locker room, but Washington is a big, muscular guy in the upper body, tremendously strong arms. Batting his natural way in 1982, he hit .323 with 9 homers in 155 at bats, a .561 slugging percentage; in 1980 he hit .300 against lefties with a .447 slugging percentage. It seemed obvious to me that if he had been a right-handed hitter all the way, he would have hit enough to be a major-league third baseman. But he had been forced into this dumb experiment with switch hitting, and by the time it was apparent that it was killing his career, it was too late to undo it. He hadn't faced a right-handed pitcher batting right-handed for seven years.

What the Dodgers are doing in pressuring young kids to switch hit, of course, is precisely the same thing they are doing in shuffling people around to unfamiliar fielding positions. They look at Pedro Guerrero and say, well, he's agile, got good reflexes, and he can throw, so why can't we just put him at third base? They look at Mariano Duncan as an athlete, and they say well, he's a great athlete and fast and he can hit right-handed, so why don't we have him hit left-handed and pick up some extra hits? And it doesn't work, because *baseball is harder than that.* You don't learn to play third base by going to the instructional league. It takes years. You don't learn to hit at a major-league level in two or three years. You cannot teach a player to hit.

Part of the problem is that people are not normally ambidextrous, and the extent to which we are not varies enormously. I'm getting a little off the subject here, but the whole concept of batting "right-handed" or "left-handed" is somewhat misleading, because you're not really hitting with your left hand or your right hand; you hit with both, and your eyes and your legs and your mind. "Right-handed" and "left-handed" are just the names we give to the position in the batter's box, not a literal description of how the player hits. But most of us, as well as being right-handed, are right-eyed, as I'm sure most of you know. You don't use both eyes equally. If you think about it, when you take what is called a "right-handed" stance in the batter's box, which eye are you in position to use? The left one, of course, which for most of us is the weaker eye. That, I suspect, is one of the contributing reasons for the comparative dominance in baseball of left-handed hitters—because they are set up to use their good eye.

And yet, ironically, that "advan-

tage" for a left-handed hitter may be exactly why it is so difficult for most players to learn to switch hit. Great hitters have an exceptional ability to track a moving object in flight. I suspect that it's very difficult, unless you start doing it early in life, to learn two distinct eye patterns for tracking a baseball.

Whatever. What I'm really saying here is that, for whatever reason, it usually doesn't work. I'll tell you what would be interesting. Remember Les Cain, the Tiger pitcher? The Tigers forced him to work with a sore arm in 1972, and he ruined his arm. He filed a workman's comp action against the Tigers, claiming they had damaged his career by making him pitch hurt, and he collected a couple of years' salary, which at that time wasn't much but if it happened now a team would be looking at a million dollar loss. After that, teams got a lot more careful about asking a pitcher to work hurt.

It would be real interesting if one of the guys who the Dodgers pressured into switch hitting were to find out that it didn't work, and then sue the Dodgers for ruining his career. He would say, in proper legalese, "Look, you forced me to switch hit, and I worked on it as hard as I could, and I wound up hitting 75 points less left-handed than I do right-handed. Nobody who just lives with the normal platoon disadvantage hits 75 points less against right-handed hitters. You forced me to do something that destroyed my career." What would the club say? That's your tough luck? Until that happens, the Dodgers will probably just go on ruining player's careers with their silly theories.

MARK EICHORN

Fastball:	C	
Curve or Slider:	B	
Other Pitches:	A	
Control:	B	
OVERALL STUFF:		B
Delivery:	B	
Holding Runners:	C+	
Fielding/Hitting:	C	
OVERALL MECHANICS:		C+
Composure:	B+	
Consistency:	B	
Durability:	A−	
OVERALL VALUE:		B
In a Word:	**Intriguing**	

The "B" grade for his delivery is based on a mix of feelings—on the one hand, it's a deceptive delivery, and a delivery that is tough on a right-handed hitter, but on the other it's a jerky, off-balance delivery that isn't a great asset for his defense and doesn't figure to be a great asset to his durability. Let's put it this way: It ain't pretty, but it seems to work.

Eichorn is a unique player, a man whose career was going nowhere until he adopted the oddball motion a few years ago—a sidearm, almost underhand motion that he completes by hopping toward base. I wonder if you would mind if I used Eichorn to make series of points which are only vaguely related.

In the very early history of baseball, the pitchers threw underhanded. It has been my belief for many years that at some point in future baseball history, throwing underhanded or low sidearm will return, and will again become the dominant mode. There are several reasons for thinking this, the most basic of which is one which has been cited many times before, that being that it is a more natural motion, and therefore a motion which puts less strain on the arm. While that is merely an arguable advantage, not extensively tested in experience, there are other reasons for suggesting this:

1) There have been more successful underarm pitchers in baseball history than most of you probably think. Carl Mays, a brilliant pitcher of Babe Ruth's time, stood upright on the mound and threw straight underarm. Eldon Auker, who won 130 games in the American League in the thirties and early forties, was a submariner. Ted Abernathy, who saved 28 games with a 1.27 ERA for the Reds in the sixties sometimes scraped his knuckles on the pitching mound. In our own time, of course, Kent Tekulve and Dan Quisenberry have turned under good careers.

2) These pitchers have surprisingly little in common other than the underhand status. Mays threw like a softball pitcher but had a blazing, frightening fastball that exploded past hitters. Auker's delivery was a little bit like a tether ball spinning around at a 20-degree angle to the pole; his stock in trade as I understand it was a very heavy forward rotation on the ball, which tended to cause anything that was hit off of him to burrow into the ground. Abernathy twisted his torso so that his arm was almost perpendicular to the ground, but he was actually throwing sidearm, upper body bent severely to the right. Tekulve throws low sidearm, sort of flying his arm like a flag. Quisenberry is similar to Tekulve but faces the hitter more and throws with less body motion; he also threw a sidearm knuckleball for a couple of years.

This diversity suggests, to me, that an underarm motion is not simply a trick or a novelty, but an alternative that will support a variety of motions and pitches—just like throwing overhand.

3) Those pitchers who have thrown underhand have been disproportionately successful for their numbers. Abernathy, Quisenberry, and Tekulve among them must have all had seasons in which they pitched a lot of innings with ERAs in the ones. They have shown, as a group, exceptional career longevity.

4) With the exception of Abernathy with his control motion, all of the successful underhand pitchers have had very good control. Quisenberry's control record is probably the best of any pitcher of the lively ball era.

5) These pitchers were, as a group, the most marginal of talents. They were, like Eichorn, pitchers whose careers were going nowhere until they got down and dirty. Abernathy as an overhand pitcher had ERAs of 5.96, 4.15, 6.78 and 12.00. As an underhand pitcher, he had a career ERA of 2.77. Only Carl Mays among them was regarded as a real athlete.

That much success from *that little* talent has got to be trying to tell us something. If you had a group of marginal hitters—let's say, Angel Salazar, Mario Mendoza, and Rafael Belliard—and if there were something they could do (lets say, start using the bottle bat) which would turn them into .300 hitters, wouldn't you think that would be of considerable interest among marginal talents?

6) Let's say that it is true that one can throw harder overhanded than underhanded. I don't know that that is inevitably true, but let's say that it is generally true. But let's say that one can manage better control underhanded than overhanded, a proposition for which there is good evidence. Which is more important to quality pitching: Power or Control?

Baseball men love to tell you, of course, that it is control—yet there is a great reluctance to follow up on that wich actions. No serious person doubts, I think that a soft tosser must overcome a tremendous prejudice to earn a chance in the major leagues.

7) Quite apart from control, I believe that the natural trajectory of an underhanded throw is an advantage for the submariner—or, at the least, an alternative which has advantages. An overhanded throw is naturally thrown on a line, descending from shoulder height (plus the mound) into the region of the batter's knees-to-navel. An underhanded toss can both rise and fall, meaning that an underhanded pitch can be thrown with an amount of topspin which would make an overhanded pitch uncontrollable. In my opinion, that is potentially a tremendous aid to an underhand pitcher.

Now, having said those things, I have been somewhat surprised that the underhanded motion has not shown more signs of catching on than it has. I would have thought that the success of Quisenberry and Tekulve, among others, would tend to light a brush fire among pitchers whose careers were endangered. The spark hasn't shown signs of catching—yet neither has it gone out. Counting Eichorn, we've got three pitchers now who sometimes throw underhanded, the most we have had in my memory. It is easy to see how, in time, that three could become 20, and the 20 could become 50 and the 50 grow to 200. But it hasn't happened.

DARRELL EVANS

Hitting for Average:	C	
Hitting for Power:	B+	
Plate Discipline:	A	
Baserunning:	D+	
OVERALL OFFENSE:		B−
Defensive Range:	C	
Reliability:	B+	
Arm:	C	
OVERALL DEFENSE:		B−
Durability:	A−	
Consistency:	B−	
OVERALL PLAY:		B−
In a Word: **Efficient**		

In the December, 1985 edition of the *Baseball Analyst,* I published a study entitled "Changes in Productivity as Players Age." There had been some published comments to the effect that players do not predictably decline as hitters as they age, which seemed very strange to me. The study focused on all players who had 200 plate appearances in a season at the age of 37 from 1960 to 1980, and compared their productivity as hitters in their prime years (25–29) and in their later years (35–39). The study found, as most of you would expect, that the great majority of the players (31 of 37) were more effective hitters at 25–29 than at 35–39.

Of the players who apparently improved their offensive productivity as they got older, all six had something in common with Darrell Evans. They all played in much better hitters parks in their later years than they did in their prime years. The implication, of course, is that it may be that no player, with an extremely rare exception, is truly a better offensive player after age 35 than before. Some players, like Evans, seem to improve their productivity, but in large part that is a statistical illusion created by moving to a better park. Evans is a true anomaly, of course, showing remarkable retention of his skills, and he is not actually helped by playing in Tiger Stadium. But in what might have been his best years, his stats were hurt by playing in Candlestick. Evans was probably the best defensive third baseman of the seventies other than Schmidt, Nettles, and Aurelio Rodriguez.

CARLTON FISK

Hitting for Average:	D+	
Hitting for Power:	B−	
Plate Discipline:	D+	
Baserunning:	D	
OVERALL OFFENSE:		C−
Reliability:	B	
Arm:	B	
Handling of Staff:	A	
OVERALL DEFENSE:		B+
Consistency:	C	
Durability:	B	
OVERALL VALUE:		B−
In a Word: **Forty**		

I developed an experimental formula to estimate a player's chance of having a better year next year than last year. I won't detail the formula because it is complex and untested, but the elements are:

1) Age. A player's chance of having a better year is assumed to be high if he is younger than 27, to be level at 27–30, and to decline after that.

2) The relationship between the last year (1987 in this case) and the player's previously established value. A player who plays better than he had in the past is assumed to be likely to decline, while a player who plays less well than in the past is likely to improve.

3) The relationship of the last year to the group norms. Everybody tends to be drawn toward the center. A player who has a superb season, like George Bell or Alan Trammell, will tend to decline in the following season.

In addition, I created penalties for catchers who have caught more than 1200 career games, and for players whose performance was such that they were unlikely to hold their jobs in 1988, although almost none of those were among the 100 or so players studied. The ten players who were estimated to have the poorest chance to improve their 1987 performance in 1988 were, in order, Carlton Fisk (19 percent), Mike Schmidt (26 percent), Ozzie Smith (32 percent), Alan Ashby (35 percent), Alan Trammell (37 percent), Brian Downing (37 percent), Gary Carter (37 percent), Dave Parker (38 percent), Frank White (38 percent), and Wade Boggs (38 percent).

ANDRES GALLARAGA

Hitting for Average:	B+	
Hitting for Power:	C+	
Plate Discipline:	D	
Baserunning:	D	
OVERALL OFFENSE:		C+
Defensive Range:	B+	
Reliability:	A−	
Arm:	C	
OVERALL DEFENSE:		B+
Consistency:	C	
Durability:	C	
OVERALL VALUE:		C+
In a Word: **Suspect**		

I know the Montreal fans are going to be horrified that I have this guy rated so low, but I'm really not sold on him. He hit .305 last year but with 127 strikeouts and 28 walks, not counting intentional. That's an unstable combination of accomplishments. Over time, he'll either improve the K/W ratio, or the batting average will go down. He didn't hit for average in the minors, although he did hit for more power. He hit .336 through the All-Star break last year, but then hit .270 the second half, with less than half as many RBI (61 before, 29 after).

I'm not saying he's not going to make it, but if he does I think he's going to have to start hitting some homers. The Montreal fans think he is the new Keith Hernandez (.300 hitter, line drive power, Gold Glove), but when Hernandez was Gallaraga's age he'd been a regular for five and a half years, had an MVP year behind him (1979) and was coming off a .321 year (1980) with 16 homers, 99 RBI, led the league in runs scored. Hernandez walked more than he struck out. Whereas Hernandez at ages 25–26 was 26 for 39 (67 percent) as a base stealer, Gallaraga was 13 for 28 (46 percent). With his size (over 200 pounds) and history of knee injuries, Andres will slow down fast. Hernandez is a left-handed hitter, and has the platoon advantage working in his favor most of the time; Gallaraga, who has shown a substantial platoon differential, is a right-handed hitter who will have that working against him most of the time. I just don't think Gallaraga will ultimately succeed as a Hernandez-type player. I think he's going to have to hit 30 homers a year to be much of a player.

KIRK GIBSON

Hitting for Average:	B	
Hitting for Power:	B+	
Plate Discipline:	B	
Baserunning:	A−	
OVERALL OFFENSE:		B+
Defensive Range:	A−	
Reliability:	D+	
Arm:	D−	
OVERALL DEFENSE:		C
Durability:	C	
Consistency:	B+	
OVERALL PLAY:		B+
In a Word:	**Intense**	

You have probably heard sometime that bit about Christ that goes "He lived to be only 33 years old. He never traveled more than a hundred miles from his home. He never wrote a book or held an office. He never married, and he left no family. He made no major inventions or discoveries of science. He never put his name on a line of designer swimwear. Yet he changed the world forever . . ." I was thinking about that when trying to chart Kirk Gibson's progress as a Hall of Fame candidate. Someplace here I was talking about "Hall of Fame seasons," .300 years with 30 homers and 100 RBI. Gibson has never done all of those things in one season. In fact, he's never done any of those things in any season—never hit .300 or hit 30 homers or driven in 100 runs. He's never scored a hundred runs. He has never led the league in any offensive category. He has never led the league in anything except errors. He has never had 200 hits. He has never won an MVP Award; indeed, he has never even made the All-Star team. He has never won any major regular-season award—not Rookie of the Year, Comeback Player of the Year, Gold Glove, or Silver Slugger. He has never been named to the *Sporting News* post-season American League All-Star team. He has never thrown out a baserunner (OK, he has thrown out a baserunner, but almost never).

Gibson has collected only three Hall of Fame markers, an absurdly low total for a player of his ability. The system ordinarily works extremely well; if the player does anything which characterizes a great player, he'll get credit for it. Whitaker, Morris, and Trammell are all in the range of 48 to 65—not Hall of Famers yet, but making consistent progress, on the way toward the

Hall of Fame if they keep performing. Gibson has three. Even Matt Nokes picked up eight for his one season—a couple of points for hitting 30 home runs, three points for making the All-Star team, a point for having a good offensive season while playing a key defensive position, a couple of points for playing a key defensive position on a division champion team. Even Pat Sheridan has two points, Jim Morrison three, John Grubb five and a half, and Mark Thurmond five. Gibson's only markers are a point for hitting more than 35 doubles in 1985 and a couple of points for being a regular on a World Champion team in 1984.

My ordinary response to discovering that the Hall of Fame system didn't seem to work for a player would be to try to figure out what he player did that stamped him as an outstanding performer, and then design some way to reflect this in the system. You could do this, I suppose, for Gibson—give him a couple of points for each season of 20 homers and 20 stolen bases, give him one point for a 90-RBI season. I don't want to do too many things like that, though, because they throw off all of the previous calculations. You have to go back and re-figure every player who drove in 90 runs or had a 20/20 year and make sure that you're not altering those estimates so that somebody who is obviously not a Hall of Famer shows up as qualified.

First, I just don't think that accomplishments of that nature ordinarily stamp a player as destined for immortality. Second, in the case of Gibson they would probably be inadequate, anyway, moving him from 3 points to 14 or something. Third, while we might tend to assume that Gibson is in fact making some progress toward recognition as a great player, this is merely an assumption, and should not be treated as a fact. A "reputation" is the most unreliable element of a player's credentials. In twenty years, Gibson's statistics through 1987 will be exactly the same as they are now—but the memory of these years will be very different, colored by events as yet unknown. And fourth, if Gibson has an MVP season and a career long enough to start picking up points for career accomplishments, then the Hall of Fame system will probably recognize these things, and if he doesn't he's probably not going to make it anyway.

And yet, he is who he is. I'm not saying this to put him down (put him down? James, you were comparing him to *Christ*. And he thought being compared to Mickey Mantle was pressure . . .) but just to point out the oddity of it. Gibson has never done, really, any of the things that ordinarily characterize a great player—and yet he is, probably, the central player on a talented and important team. By dint of intensity, athletic ability, and a not inconsiderable measure of production, he has created a persona that tends to dwarf his statistics.

DWIGHT GOODEN

Fastball:	A	
Curve or Slider:	A	
Other Pitches:	B+	
Control:	B+	
OVERALL STUFF:		A
Delivery:	B+	
Holding Runners:	D−	
Fielding/Hitting:	B−	
OVERALL MECHANICS:		C+
Composure:	A	
Consistency:	C	
Durability:	A	
OVERALL VALUE:		A−

In a Word: **Recovering**

TONY GWYNN

Hitting for Average:	A+	
Hitting for Power:	D	
Plate Discipline:	A−	
Baserunning:	A−	
OVERALL OFFENSE:		A−
Defensive Range:	B+	
Reliability:	B	
Arm:	B	
OVERALL DEFENSE:		B+
Consistency:	A	
Durability:	A	
OVERALL VALUE:		A−

In a Word: **Golden**

RICKEY HENDERSON

Hitting for Average:	B	
Hitting for Power:	B	
Plate Discipline:	A−	
Baserunning:	A	
OVERALL OFFENSE:		A−
Defensive Range:	B+	
Reliability:	B	
Arm:	B−	
OVERALL DEFENSE:		B
Consistency:	C	
Durability:	D+	
OVERALL VALUE:		B

In a Word: **Electric**

If you want an early favorite for the 1988 National League MVP, Dwight Gooden would seem to be the man. Whether Gooden pitched as well in 1987 as in 1986 is debatable. His ERA was up 37 points, but the league ERA was up 36 points, and Gooden in 1987 won 60 percent of his starts, as opposed to 52 percent in 1986. No other major-league pitcher won 60 percent of his starts (20 or more). He wasn't the Dwight Gooden of 1985, but that he came through his problems and pitched as well as he did as often as he did should send him into the winter with the confidence he needs to get himself ready for 1988. With the Mets poised to take the division, with the rules giving the high strike . . . well, he should be ready to have a year.

Did you ever think of Strawberry and Gooden as the Whitey and Mickey of the eighties? Well, think about it . . . the great young outfielder, held up always to impossible comparisons, the great pitcher, the best of friends, in New York City, on the best team in baseball. Of course, Strawberry and Gooden are always getting into some kind of trouble, while Whitey and Mickey were choir boys. I'd like to think that in thirty years we will look back on this time and remember them fondly, warts and all but with the warts not put under such a magnifying glass and blown up to be as big as a house. I would hope that Dwight and Darryl will grow old and respectable and write books full of wild stories about the things that happened to them when they were young rogues and had the world by the tail. Keith Hernandez will play Phil Rizzuto (the classy veteran, looking on with a bemused expression). Yogi appears to be as yet uncast, but we're looking carefully at Mookie.

There are six players who have a currently established chance of getting 4000 career hits. Those six are Don Mattingly (7 percent), Tony Gwynn (5 percent), Kirby Puckett (5 percent), Tony Fernandez (4 percent), Robin Yount (3 percent), and Tim Raines (1 percent). The chance that one of those players will get 4000 career hits is 23 percent; the chance that two will is 2 percent . . . The 1987 season was by far the best of Gwynn's career, with 143 runs created (previous high: 113) and an offensive winning percentage of .825 (previous high: .731) . . .

Tony batted second or third almost all of last year, but still drew 26 intentional walks. That's a pretty amazing number; intentional walks usually happen in the bottom part of the batting order, where the hitters are getting progressively weaker, with a number-eight hitter often leading the league in intentional walks. There were several things that contributed to it: 1) Gwynn obviously was a far better hitter than anyone else on the team, even though he batted second, 2) Gwynn, a left-handed hitter, was usually followed to the plate by Carmello Martinez, a right-hander, so that a platoon advantage was often to be gained, and 3) Bowa bunts a lot. If the pitcher bunts for the first out and the leadoff man makes an out, that puts Gwynn at the plate with two out and a base empty . . .

The Padre offense should be one of the most improved in baseball this year, relative to the league at least. With Gwynn, Ready, Kruk, Santiago and Martinez they really shouldn't be tenth in the league in runs scored . . .

I wanted to talk a minute about the concept of run element ratio. Run element ratio divides the parts of secondary average into that which is valuable early in the inning, valuable for scoring runs (walks and stolen bases) and that which is valuable late in the inning, or valuable for driving in runs (power). The formula is $(SB + BB)/(TB − H)$. If a player is over 1.00, then generally speaking you want him up early in the inning. If he is under 1.00, then he is more valuable later in the inning. Vince Coleman's career run element ratio is 4.4, meaning that he has little use except as a leadoff man; Don Mattingly's is .38, meaning that he is much more valuable later in the inning.

The highest run elements ratios that I found (these are career figures) are for Vince Coleman (4.4–1), Gary Pettis (3.8), Ozzie Smith (3.22), Willie Randolph (2.44), Rickey Henderson (2.29), Steve Sax (2.04), Brett Butler (2.00), Tim Raines (1.99), Mike La-Valliere (1.91), Billy Doran (1.64), and Mike Scioscia (1.59). These are all players who are much better at starting trouble than finishing it.

I think there are two types of players who are awkward to position properly in an offense. Those are 1) players who have no speed but still have high run element ratios, like Mike Scioscia and Mike LaValliere; and 2) players who have extremely low run element ratios. A player like Scioscia is difficult to position offensively because he is much more valuable early in the inning than late in the inning, but managers are reluctant to use him early in the inning because of his lack of speed. I'll discuss the second problem in discussing Cory Snyder.

TOM HENKE

Fastball:	A	
Curve or Slider:	D+	
Other Pitches:	B+	
Control:	B+	
OVERALL STUFF:		A−
Delivery:	A−	
Holding Runners:	D	
Fielding/Hitting:	C−	
OVERALL MECHANICS:		C+
Composure:	A−	
Consistency:	A−	
Durability:	A−	
OVERALL VALUE:		B+
In a Word: **Bullets**		

Henke in the last two years has struck out 246 men in 185 innings, 11.95 per 9 innings. Gossage at his more fearsome hit 10K per 9 innings only one time, 10.2 in 1977. Dick Radatz, The Monster, was over 10.00 his first three years, reaching a peak of 11.02 in 1963. Bruce Sutter hit 10K only once, 10.85 in 1977. Righetti and Bedrosian have never been near 10, or Worrell either. Lee Smith has hit 10 twice, 10.32 in 1985 and 10.33 last year. The only one of those pitchers who could match Henke's control record (only 25 walks last year) was Sutter. Ryne Duren reached 12 once, but in a season when he pitched only 49 innings. So the question I would ask is, has there ever been a reliever who could come in and blow people away the way Henke can? I wonder. If he gets the high strike this year, I'm not sure what he might do.

Henke, Bedrosian, and Lee Smith were all born in the same month, December of 1957. They turned 30 this winter. Also born that month: Bob Ojeda, Eduardo Romero, Pat Sheridan.

An interesting sabermetric study would be to check the effectiveness of Henke in games in which he did and did not follow Eichorn. A lot of people think that Henke is made especially overpowering when he comes to the mound after a couple of innings of Eichorn floating the ball up to the plate. The theory makes intuitive sense but who knows? I doubt that you'd find a dramatic difference.

KEITH HERNANDEZ

Hitting for Average:	A−	
Hitting for Power:	C	
Plate Discipline:	A−	
Baserunning:	D	
OVERALL OFFENSE:		B
Defensive Range:	A	
Reliability:	A	
Arm:	A−	
OVERALL DEFENSE:		A
Consistency:	A+	
Durability:	A	
OVERALL VALUE:		A−
In a Word: **Dependability**		

Keith's offensive winning percentage dropped below .700 last year for the first time since 1978, and it was well below .700 although he remained a productive offensive player (.623 winning percentage). His runs created since 1982: 101, 98, 108, 100, 106, 98. His approximate values over the same years: 13, 13, 14, 13, 14, 13. Has anybody else, even Eddie Murray or Willie Randolph, been as consistent?

That's what makes the dip in offensive winning percentage of more interest: It seems more likely to establish a new level of ability, rather than to represent just a fluctuation. He was down slightly in batting average, walks, and doubles, while runs scored around the league were up.

Hernandez is a few months younger than George Brett and Jim Rice, all born in 1953. Rice has 2275 hits, Brett 2219, Hernandez 2010. In 1988, with runs scored probably down sharply, all three will begin the serious business of trying to hang onto as many of their skills as they can, and seeing how long they can stay on the horse. Probably just one of them will make it to 3000. My money would be on Brett because I think he's the best hitter of the three, and as you age your bat determines your longevity more than anything else, but that could be just a Royals' fans view of it. At the moment, Hernandez retains an estimated 95 percent of his peak value, as contrasted with 70 percent for Brett and 68 percent for Rice.

Hernandez' speed scores: 1979, 5.9; 1980, 5.9; 1981, 5.6; 1982, 5.4; 1983, 5.5; 1984, 4.3; 1985, 3.6; 1986, 3.5; 1987, 3.1.

TEDDY HIGUERA

Fastball:	B+	
Curve or Slider:	B	
Other Pitches:	B	
Control:	B+	
OVERALL STUFF:		B+
Delivery:	A	
Holding Runners:	B+	
Fielding/Hitting:	A−	
OVERALL MECHANICS:		A−
Composure:	A	
Consistency:	A−	
Durability:	A	
OVERALL VALUE:		A−
In a Word: **Sharp**		

Higuera was up and down last year, brilliant in stretches and struggling in stretches. Higuera I suspect is one of the half-dozen pitchers in our generation who can work 8 to 10 innings a start without being destroyed by it. The way that managers have tested the limits of starting pitchers for the last century is quite a bit like the way they used to test for witches, by pond dunking. You ever read about that? If a woman (or a person, usually a woman) was suspected of being a witch, they'd tie her to a pole and dunk her in the pond. If she survived for several minutes under water, then she was a witch and should be stoned or burned at the stake or whatever. If she drowned, then you knew she was innocent. Of course, the woman was dead, but at least you knew she wasn't a witch.

That's how managers used to test starting pitchers, and to some extent still do—just throw them out there and let them pitch. In each generation there are a handful of pitchers who can start 35, 40 times a year and pitch 7 or more innings a start. If you try that and it ruins the pitcher's arm then you know he's not one of those pitchers. Managers establish as a normal workload the workload that Jack Morris and Teddy Higuera are capable of handling, but which destroys most pitchers in a year or two. They're a little better about it now, but there are still an awful lot of young pitchers whose arms are ruined by managers who are under pressure to win now, and who don't see any point in building a pitcher up gradually.

KENT HRBEK

Hitting for Average:	B	
Hitting for Power:	B+	
Plate Discipline:	B+	
Baserunning:	D	
OVERALL OFFENSE:		B+
Defensive Range:	D	
Reliability:	B+	
Arm:	B	
OVERALL DEFENSE:		B−
Consistency:	B	
Durability:	B+	
OVERALL PLAY:		B+
In a Word: **Productive**		

GLENN HUBBARD

Hitting for Average:	D+	
Hitting for Power:	C	
Plate Discipline:	B+	
Baserunning:	D	
OVERALL OFFENSE:		C+
Defensive Range:	C+	
Reliability:	B	
DP Pivot:	A	
OVERALL DEFENSE:		B
Consistency:	B	
Durability:	B	
OVERALL VALUE:		B−
In a Word: **Gritty**		

BROOK JACOBY

Hitting for Average:	B+	
Hitting for Power:	B+	
Plate Discipline	B	
Baserunning:	D+	
OVERALL OFFENSE:		B+
Defensive Range:	C+	
Reliability:	C−	
Arm:	C	
OVERALL DEFENSE:		C
Consistency:	B	
Durability:	A−	
OVERALL VALUE:		B−
In a Word: **Buried**		

The biggest joke in post-season play last year was Tom Kelly telling the media that Kent Hrbek was the best defensive first baseman in the American League, and the broadcasters parroting this as if it was reasonable. It's ridiculous. I mean, we got Don Mattingly, Pete O'Brien, Eddie Murray, Wally Joyner, and Willie Upshaw in the league, and he's going to have us believe that this moose is our best defensive first baseman? Sure, he's got a pretty good arm and soft hands, but his mobility is poor at best and he just pulls rocks sometimes. In twelve post-season games he made six distinct misplays. I'm not faulting Kelly for lying to the media—that is, after all, a part of his job, to build up his players—but when there's a huge discrepancy between what you see on the field and what people are telling you, guys, you really ought to notice.

Hrbek's a fine player, though—defense a little above average, but he rings up the scoreboard.

What the hell is it with this organization? Oakland, I mean. At the moment the A's have three second basemen on their roster—Hubbard, Bernazard, and Phillips. The funny thing is that I like all three players. They have different strengths. Bernazard is a good offensive player, with more power than usual at the position, good secondary average, but not much of a defensive players. Phillips I think would have been one of the best in the league if he could just have stayed healthy, as he has most of Bernazard's strengths and much better range at second. Hubbard is a hustling player, very quick on the DP, hits doubles and walks. But why do you need all three of them? I know they'll get rid of one of them before the season starts, but how does signing Hubbard help the team?

Same thing in the outfield—if you've got McGwire and Canseco, what do you want with Dave Parker? He's just more of the same, except he's left-handed. Why wouldn't you rather add—oh, I don't know, a Mike Young, a Mike Kingery, maybe. And it's the same thing I wrote about on the pitching staff. They seem determined to collect as many guys as they can like Rick Honeycutt and Moose Haas. I mean, they're all right, but why do the A's think they'll be better off with eight of these guys rather than four?

Hubbard will move the A's from 122 double plays, last in the league, up toward the middle of the league; if they keep Honeycutt he'll move them up even higher. But Parker's 37, Honeycutt's 33, Hubbard's 30, and they just duplicate the skills of younger players. Do they really think that's how you put together a championship team?

There's a remarkable contrast between the RBI counts for Jacoby and National League third baseman Tim Wallach, who in fact is a very similar player. Jacoby hit for a better average than Wallach (.300–.298) and hit more home runs (32–26), but Wallach drove in 123 runs while Jacoby drove in only 69! Sixty-nine RBI to begin with has to be a record low for a guy who hits .300 with 30 homers; I can't believe anybody's ever done that before. Although I have not yet seen the counts of how many times each player batted with runners in scoring position, when there is a contrast that extreme in RBI counts it quite certainly has to be a product of multiple factors—in other words, Wallach hit many more times with runners on base *and* did a better job in those situations, not just one factor or the other. Neither factor operating by itself could create a discrepancy like that; it would have to be both. Since Wallach batted behind the great Tim Raines and the good Mitch Webster, he probably batted, at a guess, maybe 160–170 times with men in scoring position, and probably 300 times with men on base. Since Jacoby batted behind Joe Carter, Cory Snyder, and Mel Hall, who only reach base when they hit home runs, he may have batted only 110–120 times with men in scoring position, and maybe 240 times with men on base. You can check what the real figures are in the spring. Obviously, Wallach also had a good year with men in scoring position, and obviously Jacoby didn't.

Is that a function of clutch ability, or luck? It's just luck. Certainly there is such a thing as clutch performance; in any given year some players are going to do very well in key situations, and others won't. But that has no predictive significance. Over a period of years, both Wallach and Jacoby will—and have—hit about as well with men on base and in scoring position as in other situations. Over the three years before 1987, Jacoby hit .276 overall, Wallach .247. With men on base, both players went up a little—Jacoby up 17 points to .293, Wallach up 11 points to .258. The advantage in both cases was with runners on first base only, the situation which forces the first baseman to hold on the runner. In that situation Jacoby hit .321, Wallach .274. With men in scoring position, both players were within three hits of their overall averages, Wallach at .248 and Jacoby at .268. Both players had essentially identical slugging percentages with the bases empty, with men on base and overall. With the bases empty: Wallach, .398, Jacoby, .396. With men on base: Wallach, .433, Jacoby, .432. Overall: Jacoby, .416, Wallach, .414. The only "clutch" difference between the players in the years 1984–1986 was that Jacoby hit much better in the late innings of close games, .286–231.

I rate Wallach higher than Jacoby because 1) he's a better defensive player, and 2) clutch performance deserves a certain degree of respect, even though it is not a function of ability. There could be a carryover effect of the Jacoby's remarkable 69-RBI season, if he spends the winter worrying about it. If he were to get it in his head that he couldn't hit with men in scoring position, which will happen once in a great while, then in time that would undermine his whole game—offense, defense, everything. There have been players who started drinking heavily after having seasons like this. But in all likelihood, as time passes their clutch performance will even out again.

JIMMIE KEY

Fastball:	C+	
Curve or Slider:	B	
Other Pitches:	B –	
Control:	A –	
OVERALL STUFF:		B
Delivery:	B+	
Holding Runners:	B	
Fielding/Hitting:	A	
OVERALL MECHANICS:		B+
Composure:	A	
Consistency:	A	
Durability:	A	
OVERALL VALUE:		A –
In a Word: **Command**		

Jimmie has to be the most consistent pitcher in the majors in terms of giving a solid performance every time he takes the mound. With 36 starts last year he had 29 game scores that were over 50, which I think is the highest percentage in the major leagues. With the exception of the first month of the 1986 season, he has been like that for three years, turning in one solid performance after another after another. Even among his seven below-average outings last year, most scored in the 40s, which means that they weren't far below average. Other notes on the same theme:

• In his 17 wins last year, Key pitched 128 innings, posted a 2.11 ERA. That's nothing special—almost any pitcher would be that effective in the games that he won, and many would be much more effective.

• In his 11 no-decisions, Key pitched 75 innings (almost 7 per outing) and posted an ERA of 3.00. The Blue Jays won 7 of the 11 games despite scoring less than 4 runs per game. That's a very good performance, far better than typical performance in no-decisions.

• In his 8 losses, Key pitched 58 innings (over 7 per start). He struck out 36 men and walked only 11—even when losing. His ERA in those games was 3.88. That's truly exceptional.

• Only once during the season (May 16 at Oakland) was Key knocked out of the box in the first 5 innings.

• Only twice all year, April 26 at Chicago and September 6 vs. Seattle in Toronto, did Key walk more than three men—and he won both of those games, allowing only two runs each time.

DON MATTINGLY

Hitting for Average:	A	
Hitting for Power:	B+	
Plate Discipline:	C	
Baserunning:	D	
OVERALL OFFENSE:		A –
Defensive Range:	B+	
Reliability:	A –	
Arm:	B	
OVERALL DEFENSE:		B+
Consistency:	A	
Durability:	B+	
OVERALL VALUE:		A
In a Word: **Hitter**		

Don Mattingly has now had three straight seasons in which he hit .300 with 30 homers and 100 RBI. That's a Hall of Fame season, a season characteristic of the greatest power hitters ever.

I thought I would count how many times this has been done. Did the *Baseball Digest* already do this? There have been 195 "Hall of Fame seasons," turned in by 78 different players. The players who did it five times or more were Babe Ruth (12 times), Lou Gehrig (10), Jimmie Foxx (9), Hank Aaron (7), Joe DiMaggio (7), Willie Mays (7), Ted Williams (7), Stan Musial (6), Mel Ott (6), Hank Greenberg (5), and Frank Robinson (5). All are in the Hall of Fame.

Among players who are eligible for the Hall of Fame, there are 28 players who turned in one such season. Only 5 of those 28, or 18 percent, are in the Hall of Fame. Seven eligible Hall of Famers did it twice, and 3 of those 7 have been elected. Twelve players did it 3 or 4 times, and 10 of those 12 (83 percent) are in the Hall of Fame. As mentioned, players who did it 5 or more times are all Hall of Famers, 11 of 11. All together, 29 of the 58 players who are eligible for the Hall of Fame (exactly half) are in the Hall of Fame; that figure will rise as time passes.

There are 13 active players who have had Hall of Fame seasons. Those are Jim Rice (4 times), Don Mattingly (3), Eddie Murray (3), Dave Parker (2), Cecil Cooper (2), Dale Murphy (2), George Bell (2), and Fred Lynn, Dave Winfield, Pedro Guerrero, George Brett, Dwight Evans, and Danny Tartabull. Reggie Jackson, also active in 1987, did it once.

ODDIBE MC DOWELL

Hitting for Average:	C−	
Hitting for Power:	C+	
Plate Discipline:	B	
Baserunning:	B+	
OVERALL OFFENSE:		B−
Defensive Range:	B	
Reliability:	B+	
Arm:	C−	
OVERALL DEFENSE:		B−
Consistency:	C	
Durability:	B	
OVERALL VALUE		B−
In a Word: **Struggling**		

A superficial look at the stats would show that Oddibe McDowell had a disappointing 1987 season (.241, 14 homers, 52 RBI), while Texas right fielder Ruben Sierra had an outstanding year in his first full season (.263, 30, 109). The runs created method shows McDowell as creating more runs per 27 outs (5.06) than Sierra (4.45).

This calls for a closer look. Why did McDowell create more runs?

1. Despite the difference in batting average, McDowell was on base more often. McDowell walked 97 percent more frequently (.110 of plate appearances) than Sierra (.056).

2. McDowell stole 24 bases in 26 attempts, while Sierra was 16 for 27 as a base stealer. Because of that, McDowell was not only on base more often, but in scoring position more often. And with an adjustment for the caught stealing, the difference in the number of times they were on base is even larger.

3. The difference in their power is not enormous. Although Sierra homered more often, per plate appearance it was only 43 percent more often. McDowell hit more doubles per plate appearance and more triples.

4. Sierra grounded into double plays 50 percent more frequently.

So adding all of those things together, almost any analytical method would show McDowell to be the superior offensive player, in terms of runs or bases in relation to outs made. McDowell in his three years has improved substantially as a base stealer and in terms of plate discipline.

MARK MCGWIRE

Hitting for Average:	B	
Hitting for Power:	A	
Plate Discipline:	B−	
Baserunning:	D	
OVERALL OFFENSE:		B+
Defensive Range:	C	
Reliability:	D+	
Arm:	D	
OVERALL DEFENSE:		C−
Durability:	—	
Consistency:	—	
OVERALL PLAY:		B
In a Word: **Powerful**		

It seemed to me that a lot of the problem the pitchers were having with McGwire stemmed from the unusual fact that he has two distinct power zones. On a pitch up and in, almost where you might throw to jam a hitter, he'll flick the bat with his wrists and just muscle it out of the park. On a pitch down and away he'll extend them monstrous arms, take a long, sweeping swing, and drive the ball—a different swing, looks like a completely different hitter, but the same result. If you visualize the strike zone as an oval, you're not ordinarily going to throw down the middle, and then if you take a chunk out of the top and a chunk out of the bottom that doesn't leave much. Pitchers say that there are a few hitters that you have to pitch belt-high, and maybe McGwire will turn out to be one of them, but there's an understandable reluctance to try that.

It was written a lot last summer that the old AL rookie home run record was 37, by Al Rosen. Rosen said that he didn't know that he had the record, and he guessed there just wasn't any publicity about it at the time. Well, the reason there wasn't any publicity about it at the time is that he wasn't considered a rookie at the time. This record was very well known when I was kid. The record was 31, by Ted Williams, and there was quite a bit of publicity about it when Bob Allison hit 30 in 1959, and there was publicity again when Jimmie Hall broke it in 1963 (33) and again when Tony Oliva almost broke it in 1964 (32). I was amazed to discover last summer that all of that had been forgotten.

KEVIN MITCHELL

Hitting for Average:	B	
Hitting for Power:	B	
Plate Discipline:	C+	
Baserunning:	C+	
OVERALL OFFENSE:		B
Defensive Range:	B−	
Reliability:	C	
Arm:	B	
OVERALL DEFENSE:		B−
Consistency:	C	
Durability:	C	
OVERALL VALUE:		B−
In a Word: **Worker**		

This kid is becoming one of my favorite players. I don't know if I mentioned this a year ago, but when I did the rookie studies in the 1987 *Abstract,* I think the most-similar rookie to Kevin Mitchell was Lee May. Although May was a first baseman and Mitchell a third baseman, they were the same age as rookies (24) and hit about the same—Mitchell .277 with extra base hit totals of 22–2–12, May .265 with 29–2–12. Mitchell had better strikeout and walk data.

While most of the 1986 rookies split from their most-comparable partners in 1987, Mitchell continued to track Lee May as a hitter. May in his second year as a hitter hit .290 with 22 homers, 80 RBI; Mitchell hit .280 with 22 homers, 70 RBI. This is good news, because if Mitchell could play third base and continue to hit like Lee May, that would make him a hell of a player; May in his third season hit 38 homers and drove in 110 runs. Mitchell won't likely continue to hit like May. May's second season was 1968, the nadir of a pitcher's era; Mitchell's second season was the best hitter's year in 30 years or more. May's 1968 season, in the context of it's time, was a better season, and in addition to that Mitchell will have to work on his defense as well as his hitting. (Lee May didn't play much defense.) Still, if Mitchell doesn't hit like Lee May, he could still develop as a hitter like, say, the guy who played high school basketball with his Daddy, Graig Nettles. If he does that, that will be good enough.

JACK MORRIS

Fastball:	B+	
Curve or Slider:	A−	
Other Pitches:	A−	
Control:	B−	
OVERALL STUFF:		A−
Delivery:	A	
Holding Runners:	D+	
Fielding/Hitting:	A−	
OVERALL MECHANICS:		B−
Composure:	B	
Consistency:	A	
Durability:	A+	
OVERALL VALUE:		A−
In a Word: **Ace**		

For the ninth straight year, Jack Morris last year did a few things that would be characteristic of a Hall of Fame pitcher. He won 18 games. He struck out over 200. He pitched in the All-Star game. He pitched in the Championship Series.

With 162 career wins, Morris has now entered the range in which his career totals start to help him get toward getting in the Hall of Fame. Trivia question: which two Hall of Fame pitchers has Jack Morris already passed in career wins (not counting guys who are in more as managers or something)? The answers are Hoyt Wilhelm, 143, and Dizzy Dean, 150. Sandy Koufax is just three wins away, at 165.

Morris is now 138 wins away from 300. He has established a performance level of 18.7 wins per year, so he is 7.4 years away from the goal. Turning 33 years old early in the season, it remains unlikely that he will get there. He is within five years of 250 wins.

One thing in Morris' record that you don't see very often is that he has become a strikeout pitcher after being a successful starter. Morris won 64 games from 1979 to 1982, while striking only about one man per two innings (457 Ks in 912 innings). The two years after that he won 39 and struck out 6.4 per nine innings, and in the two following that won 37 and struck out 7.1 per nine innings. It is more common for a young pitcher to get his strikeouts, but negate them with walks. Morris has shown the ability to adjust in many ways.

DALE MURPHY

Hitting for Average:	B+	
Hitting for Power:	A	
Plate Discipline:	A	
Baserunning:	B	
OVERALL OFFENSE:		A
Defensive Range:	C+	
Reliability:	B	
Arm:	B+	
OVERALL DEFENSE:		B
Consistency:	A	
Durability:	A+	
OVERALL VALUE:		A−
In a Word **Cooperstown**		

Some people are real hard to educate. I've been trying to tell people for ten years that the theory that Bob Horner made Dale Murphy a better hitter was obvious nonsense, that the stats showing the opposite were just bogus small samples, that overall Dale Murphy hit no better with Bob Horner in the lineup than out of the lineup. When Horner left the team last year I must have told a thousand people that no, this was not going to hurt Dale Murphy at all. I've collected and published about a dozen quotes, from ballplayers like Eddie Murray and Dwight Evans, saying that no, having a great hitter coming up behind them doesn't make any difference in the pitches they see.

So last year Horner left the Braves, and Murphy went on to have possibly his best season. I thought "that's it; we'll never hear again about Bob Horner making Dale Murphy a better hitter." So I turned on a Braves game in early September, and what do you think? The announcer was telling us that it was amazing that Murphy could have this kind of a year without even having Horner coming up behind him, and what kind of a year do you think he would have had if Horner was still here? Eiccshh!!

Perhaps because of the loss of Horner, Murphy did lead the majors in intentional walks, with 29. What would you think of a rule allowing a player to turn down a walk if he wanted? Not just an intentional walk, but theoretically any walk. Did I write about this before? It is probably the most major change in the rules that I could support. Think about it: why was the walk rule adopted? The rule about four balls being a walk was adopted to force the pitcher to pitch to the batter, not to dodge him by throwing balls out of reach.

The rule accomplishes this, ordinarily, by creating a penalty for not pitching to the hitter—he gets a free pass. The problem is that in some game situations the penalty is so weak that the rule does not work, and is actually stood on its head: the pitcher takes the very rule that was adopted to force him to pitch to the hitter—and uses it to avoid facing a tough hitter. It's directly contrary to the intent of the rule, and for that reason I think its totally consistent with the rules for the hitter to be given an option as to whether or not he wants to walk.

The rule could be adopted in several forms, but the essential idea is that if you walk a hitter and he turns down the walk and you walk him again, he goes to second base, and everybody else advances by at least one base. The rule could be written so that if the walk was refused the count would revert to 0–0, or, in the weaker form, so that the strikes would carry over but the balls would revert to zero. In the latter case, the effective rule would be that if you wanted to intentionally walk a hitter you would have to give him at least one strike, since it is unlikely that a hitter would often turn down a free pass in order to hit behind in the count.

Some of my friends have objected that the rule would take strategy out of the game, but I just think that's completely wrong. What it would do is create an option for a strategic response, and thus create strategy, rather than avoid it. It gives the offensive manager an extra option—do I take this free base and express my confidence in the on deck hitter as well as my opinion that the other guy's action doesn't make any sense, or do I invoke my right to make him pitch to Dale Murphy? It exposes directly conflicts of opinion between managers, for if one manager chooses to give the intentional walk and the other one chooses to accept it, then clearly the two men disagree about the correctness of the strategy.

I just think in general that it is in the best interests of the game to allow the Dale Murphys and Tony Gwynns to hit with men on base. I know the rule seems radical now, but if it had been thought of in 1887 I think they'd have adopted it. Let's correct their oversight, and give Dale Murphy another 10–15 RBI a season.

EDDIE MURRAY

Hitting for Average:	B	
Hitting for Power:	B	
Plate Discipline:	B+	
Baserunning:	C	
OVERALL OFFENSE:		B
Defensive Range:	B	
Reliability:	B	
Arm:	B+	
OVERALL DEFENSE:		B+
Consistency:	A	
Durability:	B+	
OVERALL VALUE:		B
In a Word: **Consistent**		

It will be interesting to see whether Eddie, entering the decline phase of his career within a couple of years if he hasn't already, will be able to focus on career goals and pursue them. It was always Eddie's reputation that he played as well as he needed to play, in the best sense, that when the game was close and late, when there were runners on base, he rose to the challenge, but the rest of the time he didn't play with the same intensity, so that his stats were not quite the equal of some other players. The problem last year may have been, in part, that it never mattered. The Orioles were out of it early, were out of a lot of games, didn't have many people on base, and all there was to play for was the stuff that never inspired him—his own stats.

Eddie was born an Oriole and seemed likely to die an Oriole, but one wonders now if it makes any sense for them to keep him. The Orioles probably won't be back in the pennant race for several years. Eddie is 32 and has a huge contract, and he is still a fine player even at the level of 1987, which one figures he is still capable of exceeding. The Oriole farm system is not burgeoning with prospects, and the ballclub has many needs. As it stands right now, they're going to be paying Eddie millions of dollars to lead them to a .500 season. One would think that if the Orioles could get a young pitcher and a legit prospect for Eddie from a team that was trying to get over the top—say, Greg Mathews and Todd Zeile from the Cardinals— they'd almost have to take it.

GARY PETTIS

Hitting for Average:	C−	
Hitting for Power:	D	
Plate Discipline:	B	
Baserunning:	A	
OVERALL OFFENSE:		C+
Defensive Range:	A	
Reliability:	A−	
Arm:	B+	
OVERALL DEFENSE:		A
Consistency:	B	
Durability:	A	
OVERALL VALUE:		B−
In a Word: **Useful**		

As much as I admire Gene Mauch, I think that he just completely missed the boat with this guy. You know that expression about "playing within yourself," which I guess a lot of people think is a cliché, but cliché or not there aren't very many good ballplayers who don't know what they can do and what they can't do. The managerial equivalent of that is playing within the limits of your ballclub, not asking people to do what they're not capable of doing. "You've got your mules, and you've got your race horses," Billy Martin says, "and you can kick a mule in the ass all you want to and he's not going to be a racehorse." Gene Mauch is constantly credited by the media with not asking players to do what they're not capable of doing—but in this case, that's just what he did. Gene Mauch could never accept that Gary Pettis is what he is.

Pettis strikes out a lot. He's not a bad player, the best in baseball in center field and a decent offensive player as well, because his on-base percentages are pretty fair, in the .340 range. He gets on base more often than Willie Wilson, let's say. Mauch could never accept that. He wanted him to be a different type of player—a contact hitter, a guy who would choke up on the bat and slap the ball to the opposite field. I mean, I agree that it would be wonderful if he was that type of player, but he simply isn't. As a 26-year-old rookie in 1984, he struck out in 29 percent of his at bats. You simply cannot tell a man at that age to stop doing one thing and start doing another, and teach him to be a successful major-league hitter. I submit that there has never in the history of baseball been a player who learned how to hit at the age of 27. The example people always give who believe you can remake a hitter in the

middle of his career is Matty Alou, who hit .231 with the Giants in 1965, then won the National League batting title in 1966 after joining Harry Walker. But what that ignores is Matty Alou's batting averages in his first two major-league seasons: .310, and .292. The Giants had him pinch hitting a lot, and over three seasons he had gone 13-for-94 as a pinch hitter, a .138 average, which was dragging him down, and he'd had a couple of off years—but he rarely struck out, even in 1965, and he could hit. I've seen players who pushed themselves to higher and higher levels over a period of years, like Brian Downing, Alan Ashby, and Frank White, but I've never seen a player just learn to hit, or learn a hitting style, after the age of 25. I submit that it can't be done, that the game is too hard for that.

Gene Mauch, however, was determined that Gary Pettis was going to be the first. Pettis is an excellent number-nine hitter, perfectly designed for the spot—decent on-base percentage, extremely high run element ratio (3.8–1). Just the man to give the one to four hitters in the offense a head start. The thing to do with him was to put him in the nine spot, see if he could move up from 65 walks a year to 85, see how many bases he could steal, see if he could push the .250 batting average to .270. Forget about the damn strike-outs; they don't matter, anyway. Not good enough for Mauch; Mauch wanted him to stop striking out, hit .300 and become a lead-off hitter. And he worried about that, and he worried about it, until he pushed Pettis back to AAA.

KEN PHELPS

Hitting for Average:	C	
Hitting for Power:	A	
Plate Discipline:	A	
Baserunning:	D	
OVERALL OFFENSE:		B+
Defensive Range:	D	
Reliability:	C	
Arm:	D	
OVERALL DEFENSE:		D
Consistency:	B+	
Durability:	B	
OVERALL VALUE:		B-
In a Word: **Deadly**		

KIRBY PUCKETT

Hitting for Average:	A	
Hitting for Power:	B+	
Plate Discipline:	D	
Baserunning:	B-	
OVERALL OFFENSE:		B+
Defensive Range:	A	
Reliability:	B+	
Arm:	A	
OVERALL DEFENSE:		A-
Consistency:	B	
Durability:	A	
OVERALL VALUE:		B+
In a Word: **Adorable**		

TIM RAINES

Hitting for Average:	A	
Hitting for Power:	B	
Plate Discipline:	B+	
Baserunning:	A	
OVERALL OFFENSE:		A
Defensive Range:	A	
Reliability:	B+	
Arm:	C+	
OVERALL DEFENSE:		B+
Consistency:	A	
Durability:	A	
OVERALL VALUE:		A-
In a Word: **Brilliant**		

Phelps had his best year yet in 1987, still gaining slowly on a regular job at the age of 33. He had .756 offensive winning percentage last year, beating his best of .742 in 1986, beating his .734 in 1984. His career batting average is just .241, but per 550 at bats he has hit 40 home runs and drawn 118 walks, leading to 99 RBI and 96 runs scored per 550.

Seven active players (1000 or more at bats) have career secondary averages over .400; those seven are Eric Davis (.555), Ken Phelps (.488), Rickey Henderson (.483), Darryl Strawberry (.473), Mike Schmidt (.472), Tim Raines (.412), and Barry Bonds (.409). Rounding out the top ten are Reggie Jackson (.391), Jack Clark (.382), and Kirk Gibson (.376). Two young players also are over .400 in less than a thousand at bats, Kal Daniels and Mark McGwire.

Phelps in 1987 had a better year against left-handed pitching, which has historically given him trouble. There have been some calls to get him in the lineup against left-handed pitching, but the Mariners record against lefties (24–24) actually was somethat better than their record against right handers. Gary Matthews didn't do much of a job as the right-handed DH, and I don't really understand why they wanted Matthews anyway rather than Dave Hengel, a power-hitting outfield who has been at Calgary for a couple of years. Hengel isn't Ken Phelps but he's a better hitter than Matthews.

Probably no player in any city is as popular as Kirby is in Minnesota. They just love the guy up there—children, teammates, bankers, and bureaucrats. He's hard not to love. What other major-league superstar would let his teammates rub his head for luck? Who else would say, when asked what he would wish for by *USA Today,* that he would like to have a body like Glenn Braggs? Is his phone number still in the book?

Young players are often bathed in a transcendant innocence which makes them attractive. Then they start doing commercials, trading on that attraction, and we know it's just a matter of time until they are caught trying to capture some chemicals or are hit with a paternity suit and start fighting with the club over money. Willie Mays played stickball in the streets of Harlem only for one year. When he came out of the army in '54 he didn't have time for that anymore, and yet we remember that as a central part of his identity; even more, as an image of the era. Willie played stickball in the heart of the McCarthy era with America at war. We use that image to scrub up our memory of the time, to make it simpler and more innocent. Part of the charm of Kirby is that his skin of innocence seems thicker than usual, and seems to be wearing off more slowly.

In 1986 the Twins had Kirby leading off most of the year, with a run element ratio of .409. In retrospect, it's no wonder they finished sixth . . . Kirby has an estimated 30 percent chance of getting 3000 hits, 15 percent chance of getting 3500, 5 percent chance of getting 4000. He is one of the players with the best chance of getting an impressive career total, and is 250 hits ahead of Wade Boggs at the same age.

Dear Bill:

You asked me to send you a brief summary of my remarks concerning the comparison of Tim Raines and Wade Boggs that I mentioned during supper in Chicago.

Over the last five years, Wade Boggs has reached base an average of 311 times per season, for a team which has scored an average of 794 runs. Tim Raines has reached base an average of 275 times (36 less) for a team which has scored an average of only 656 runs. In spite of that, Raines has scored 37 runs more than has Boggs.

During the 1986 season, I made a point of watching Boggs on the basepaths as much as possible, to try and get some idea of why he scores so few runs (that is, so few for a player who is on base so often and has very good hitters coming up behind him.) I get to see Tim Raines play quite often (on TV, anyway) as our English channel has one Expo game per week and our French channel usually has two Expo games per week. While it is true that I do not see Boggs in more than ten games per season, he is on base so often that it is possible to get an idea of how he runs the basepaths if you concentrate on that feature of the game. Statistically, Boggs career SB–CS record of 10 and 13 pretty well describes him accurately running the bases as far as I can tell. He is not a very fast runner in any case, but is also slow to accelerate to top speed. While on base, he watches batted balls hit by his teammates until they are by a fielder before he begins to take off for the next base. He looks awkward while he runs, and displays a great deal of hesitation.

Raines, on the other hand, is like a cat on the bases. He is in motion as the ball leaves the bat, and seems to have an instant for whether the ball will be caught or drop in for a hit. He is extremely fast at getting his speed up quickly. As a base stealer, he has simply the highest stolen-base percentage in history (for players with 300 or more SB), with a SB–CS record of 511–74.

Don't get me wrong when I am critical of Boggs—I would take him for my ball club any day, even if he had to bat from a wheelchair. It is just that in looking for the fine details that might separate these two stars, you must give some consideration to Raines' overall athletic skills. I also believe that the choice for the best player in the game today (if we say that McGwire and Davis have not yet played enough to be considered) comes down to these two. The only other player that might be considered is Rickey Henderson, but if consistency counts for much, then he has to be rated behind Raines and Boggs.

Whether I have been fair in judging Boggs from a few games or not can be seen by examining the statistics that relate to baserunning. While Boggs is on base an average of 36 more times per season, he scores 7 or 8 fewer runs per year. Also, he does this while playing in a park that may be the best for scoring runs in the majors, while Raines works in the one that was probably the worst until they completed the roof. There is little doubt that Boggs has had better hitters coming up behind him during the period in question, for even if Dawson and Carter might have produced like Rice and Evans had they played in Fenway Park, they did not do so in Montreal.

The 1985 season provides a good comparison of these two players. Raines managed to score 115 runs while getting on base 268 times (he has scored more in other years), while Boggs managed "just" 107 runs while reaching base 340 times. That figure of 340 times on base also happens to be the seventh best mark in this century! Ruth had years of 352 (1921), 379 (1923), and 346 (1924), Williams got 345 (1947) and 358 (1949), while Gehrig had 342 in 1936. As a team, Boston outscored the Expos by 167 runs in 1985. Boggs was followed by players like Rice (103 RBI in 140 games), Buckner (110 RBI), Armas (64 RBI in 385 at bats), Gedman (80 RBI), and Easler (74 RBI). Dwight Evans batted leadoff much of the year, but he sometimes hit behind Dawson also. Raines was followed in the lineup by Brooks (100 RBI), Dawson (91 RBI), and Wallach (81 RBI).

Raines gets in scoring position more often than does Boggs, because he usually steals 50 to 70 more bases than the Bosox third baseman.

Again, it is hard to be critical of either Raines or Boggs as fine ball players. However, Raines will almost certainly outlast Boggs as a regular, and there can be little doubt that he will still be playing in the outfield long after Boggs has moved from third base to first, or becomes a DH. If Raines could have signed as a free agent with a club like Detroit, Boston, Toronto, or New York this past season (and thus began playing on opening day) he surely would have scored over 150 runs. Through the 1987 season, Boggs had a career on-base average and slugging percentage about 40 points better than Raines, but I have no doubt that if they both played in the same park, Raines would advance at least 30 points in each category. While Boggs is a better third baseman than most observers want to give him credit for, Raines is also a fine fielder. As a consequence, if you rate them pretty much even even as hitters (with park adjustments) and fielders, you must give the nod to Raines for his baserunning ability.

Best Regards,
Neil Munro

RANDY READY

Hitting for Average:	B+	
Hitting for Power:	B	
Plate Discipline:	A	
Baserunning:	B	
OVERALL OFFENSE:		A–
Defensive Range:	Where?	
Reliability:	C	
Arm:	C	
OVERALL DEFENSE:		D
Consistency:	?	
Durability:	?	
OVERALL VALUE:		B–
In a Word: **Productive**		

Offensively, Randy Ready was everything the Padres could have asked for and more, truly one of the best offensive players in baseball in terms of productivity per at bat. It's not just that he hit .309, but that he hit .309 with 40 percent of his hits for extra bases, got on base constantly with walks (.423 on base percentage) and swiped 7 bases in 10 attempts. He had more extra base hits than Gary Carter did with 50 percent more at bats, and drew more walks than eight of the league's 12 leadoff men—without even playing regularly. Projected to full-time play he would show 41 doubles, 9 triples, 19 homers, 108 runs scored, 85 RBI, 11 stolen bases, 105 walks. Pretty terrific year.

He hasn't found a spot yet; he played second and third, and doesn't seem to be either the Padres' second baseman of the future (Joe Cora?) or third baseman of the future (Chris Brown). But if he keeps hitting, they're going to find a place for him.

Ready was the big star off of last year's Ken Phelps All-Star team. The Ken Phelps All-Star team was a team of players who are considered fringe players, available players, but who I believe in. Two of the players on the original Ken Phelps All Stars got a chance to play a good bit, and both played well, those being Randy Ready and Brian Dayett. Ron Roenicke, center fielder on the team, spent the year pinch hitting for Philadelphia, not very well. At catcher I suggested a combination chosen from five players, four of whom were in the majors in 1987 (Steve Lake, Jamie Quirk, Geno Petralli, and Dave Engle) and three of whom played well (Lake, Quirk, and Petralli). Pitcher Tim Conroy started the season with St. Louis, but bombed, and pitcher Brad Havens pitched for

Los Angeles, decently but unimpressively. Relief ace Mark Huisman struck out 38 men and walked only 12, but pitched his way out of the league anyway. Pitcher Dan Schatzeder went 6–2 in long relief, but pitched poorly in both leagues. The rest of the members of the team spent the season in the minor leagues.

On balance, the Ken Phelps All Stars did about as well as could have been expected; my biggest regret is that I forgot to include Freddie Manrique on the team, although I knew he could play. I thought I'd try it again, albeit not at the same length. The second annual Ken Phelps All Star team:

Catcher:	John Gibbons
First Base:	Mike Laga
Second Base:	Junior Noboa
Third Base:	Wade Rowdon
Shortstop:	Luis Quinones
Left Field:	Duane Walker
Center Field:	Nick Capra
Right Field:	Brad Komminsk
DH:	Scotti Madison
Starter:	Ray Krawczyk
Starter:	Pete Filson
Starter:	Bob Tewksbury
Starter:	Bob Walk
Relief Ace:	Jay Baller

Other good candidates for the team: Kevin Romine, Dave Meier, Mike Stenhouse, Jim Traber, Jim Weaver, Dave Hengle, Nelson Simmons.

CAL RIPKEN

Hitting for Average:	C+	
Hitting for Power:	B	
Plate Discipline:	B+	
Baserunning:	D	
OVERALL OFFENSE:		B
Defensive Range:	C	
Reliability:	B+	
Arm:	B	
OVERALL DEFENSE:		C+
Consistency:	A	
Durability:	A+	
OVERALL VALUE:		B
In a Word: **Regular**		

Ripken's chance of breaking Lou Gehrig's consecutive-game streak would seem to be something between 5 and 25 percent, depending on your assumptions. Ripken at the moment is 7.4 seasons away from 2130. If we assume that Ripken has an 80 percent chance of playing in every game next year and that that figure will hold steady, Ripken's chance of breaking the record would be about 20 percent. If we assume that his chance is 80 percent next year and will decline over time by 5 percent per year, the chance would be about 6 percent.

I don't think the record is as unbreakable as people would have you believe. You hear people say that Gehrig's record will never be broken because today's players don't have the kind of dedication that it would require to stay in the lineup for 14 years, which is obviously a pretty silly argument. I don't think that human nature changes very much from generation to generation; certainly the sportswriters of Gehrig's time said the same things about players then that are often written now. But even assuming that it has, it still seems obvious that if the record were to be broken, it would be broken not by an ordinary individual, whose attitude and approach to his work was the norm for his time, but by an exceptional individual like Gehrig, Ripken, Dale Murphy, or Billy Williams. I would tend to stand that argument on it's head, and argue that the record is vulnerable precisely because human characteristics like determination and the ability to play with pain can be applied to breaking it. I mean, DiMaggio's streak is going to be hard to break because determination is almost irrelevant to it; you can't manufacture a hit by being determined. I expect Gehrig's record to be broken in my lifetime.

ANGEL SALAZAR

Hitting for Average:	D–	
Hitting for Power:	D–	
Plate Discipline:	F	
Baserunning:	C–	
OVERALL OFFENSE:		F
Defensive Range:	C+	
Reliability:	A	
Arm:	A+	
OVERALL DEFENSE:		B+
Durability:	B	
Consistency:	B	
OVERALL PLAY:		D
In a Word: **Borderline**		

Last fall Carmen Corrica was telling me what a wretched offensive season Wayne Tolleson was having. I told him I'd bet Angel Salazar was worse than Tolleson, but Carmen said "How can you be worse than a .220 hitter who hasn't had an extra base hit in two months?" So I compared them, and actually Tolleson was *nowhere near* as bad as Salazar. Tolleson had less power (7 extra bases on hits during the season as opposed to 13) but Tolleson beats him easily in batting average (16 point edge), picks up an edge as a baserunner and wallops him 43–6 in walks drawn, giving him an 87-point edge in on-base percentage. So Angel was, beyond doubt, the worst-hitting regular of 1987.

Unlike Tolleson, though, Salazar is a legitimate shortstop. His glove almost kept him in the lineup last year, bad as he was at bat. I've been watching Kansas City shortstops since Dick Howser in '61, and Angel had the best arm we've ever had there. Every throw is a carbon copy of the last one, comes in about eight inches over the first baseman's eyes, on a line. He can make the throw from the hole as well as anybody.

Angel is not an acrobatic shortstop. He has rather slow feet and doesn't like to dive for a ball. He's not a "turf" shortstop, like Ozzie; he's more of an old-time grass shortstop, like Roy McMillan. In 1986 he was very deliberate afield, losing plays by taking his time, but he was more aggressive last year. While he was in Montreal there were complaints about his attitude, but that never came up in KC.

JUAN SAMUEL

Hitting for Average:	C+	
Hitting for Power:	B+	
Plate Discipline:	D+	
Baserunning:	B+	
OVERALL OFFENSE:		B
Defensive Range:	A−	
Reliability:	C	
DP Pivot:	D+	
OVERALL DEFENSE:		C+
Consistency:	A	
Durability:	B+	
OVERALL VALUE:		B−
In a Word: **Mercurial**		

You know the concept of power/speed number? The formula is

$$(2*HR*SB)/(HR + SB).$$

Juan's power/speed number is outstanding (31.1), but that's not what I wanted to talk about. The concept of joining two statistics into one and giving credit for balance between the two can be applied to identify the most excellent combinations in a variety of different topics other than power and speed—the number of wins by two pitchers, for example (the Perry brothers wound up at 255.2, while the Niekro brothers are at 260.0), or the wins by a right-hander and a left-hander on the same staff (Koufax and Drysdale were at 24.4 in 1965), or doubles and home runs by the same hitter (remember Willie Stargell having 40 of each), or home runs by teammates (Mantle and Maris post an incomprehensible 57.3).

That's not what I wanted to talk about, either. For several years, I've been trying to find some way to tie three numbers together in the same way, so that a player had to do all three things to rate high. The characteristics of the power/speed form are that 1) a player who has 30 of each will rate at 30.0; 2) a player who has the same total but not the same balance will rate lower; 3) the result cannot exceed the average of the two figures.

I finally figured it out last summer. I'll make the three elements to be joined here doubles, triples, and homers, which are joined into one "extra base hit number." The formula is:

$$((2B*3B) + (2B*HR) + (3B*HR))/ (2B + 3B + HR)$$

Which makes sense once you figure it out—it's really a form of the same thing. Took me forever to find the thing, though.

Juan Samuel, as you would expect, had the highest extra base hit number in the majors in 1987, 25.1:

$$((37*15) + (37*28) + (15*28))/(37 + 15 + 28)$$

I looked up the highest extra base hit numbers of all time, but I lost the lists, which I think in retrospect is just as well. This is the kind of thing that's fun to figure for yourself if you have the formula, but if somebody just gives you the list it's kind of a "so what?" I think the highest single-season figure in history was by Lou Gehrig in 1927 (52 doubles, 18 triples, 47 homers, XBH number of 36.1), and that the highest career figure may have been by Musial (404.3), but that's just from memory, and could be wrong.

I believe the second-highest extra base hit number in the majors in 1987 belonged to George Bell (32−4−47, 21.9), followed in order by Mark McGwire, Andy Van Slyke, and Barry Bonds.

RYNE SANDBERG

Hitting for Average:	B	
Hitting for Power:	B−	
Plate Discipline:	B	
Baserunning:	A−	
OVERALL OFFENSE:		B+
Defensive Range:	B+	
Reliability:	A−	
DP Pivot:	B+	
OVERALL DEFENSE:		A−
Consistency	B	
Durability	B	
OVERALL VALUE:		B+
In a Word: **Complete**		

Complete, but unspectacular. I always wonder whether if you switched Ryne Sandberg and Billy Doran, Doran might not be the bigger star. They're awfully similar players, although Doran playing in the Astrodome is never going to be able to compile the batting stats that Sandberg can in Wrigley. Both players are graceful, hustling, consistent, not flashy; both steal bases, have some power, make the plays they are supposed to make and a few extras.

In my newsletter about three years ago I took a look at the career records of all players who had played at least 1300 career games and were no longer active—I think it was 443 players. One question I asked about each player is in how many categories was he above the group norms. There were nine categories plus defensive position was considered a tenth, so that a player who was above average in everything—batting average, frequency of doubles, triples, and homers, walks drawn, stolen bases, slugging average, frequency of runs scored, RBI—and who also played a key defensive position (catcher, second base, shortstop, or center field) would be a perfect "10," above average in all respects. I found that among the 443 players there were two players who were perfect 10s, those being Willie Mays and a 1920s infielder named George Grantham, who also started his career as a second baseman for the Cubs.

Sandberg, I suspect, might be the third. If he's going to wind up his career below average in anything I don't know what it would be. He's probably the only non-pitcher in baseball who doesn't grade below a "B" in any area.

BENITO SANTIAGO

Hitting for Average:	A−	
Hitting for Power:	C	
Plate Discipline:	F	
Baserunning:	B	
OVERALL OFFENSE:		B−
Reliability:	D−	
Arm:	B+	
Handling of Staff:	D	
OVERALL DEFENSE:		C
Consistency:	?	
Durability:	?	
OVERALL VALUE:		C+

In a Word: **Scintillating**

When I first sketched the rankings for the catchers, I had Santiago in the top spot. When I did the point-by-point evaluation, I realized that, as brilliant a talent as he is, that wouldn't wash. Santiago's frontline strengths—hitting for average, power, and throwing—are clearly the best in the game, and in a couple of years he will probably be the number-one catcher. But last year Santiago was charged with 22 errors, 10 more than any other National League catcher, and was charged with 22 passed balls, while no other NL catcher let by more than 15. The total of 44 defensive mistakes is the highest in the majors, with only one catcher over 25 (Geno Petralli, 37). Santiago also walked only 16 times, so his on-base percentage was poor despite the high average.

Santiago's season was much better than the major-league equivalency of his 1986 performance at Las Vegas. He hit .286 at Vegas, equivalent to about .255 at San Diego. But he is very young, just 21 last year, and at that age, a player often makes large strides as a hitter from year to year. The question now is how much power he is going to add. People think of Santiago as a Manny Sanguillen type, but his 18 home runs as a rookie are 3 more than Johnny Bench hit, and 6 more than Sanguillen's career high. It's unlikely that Santiago will add power the way Bench did, for four reasons—1) he's a year older; 2) Bench as a rookie hit 40 doubles, an indication of additional power; 3) Bench had shown more power in the minors than Santiago; and 4) power hitters are almost always selective hitters. But Santiago is certainly the most impressive young catcher since Gary Carter.

MIKE SCHMIDT

Hitting for Average:	B+	
Hitting for Power:	A−	
Plate Discipline:	A−	
Baserunning:	D+	
OVERALL OFFENSE:		A−
Defensive Range:	B+	
Reliability:	B+	
Arm:	B	
OVERALL DEFENSE:		B+
Consistency:	A	
Durability:	A	
OVERALL VALUE:		A−

In a Word: **Immortal**

All ballplayers, as a group, retain 11 percent of their peak value at the age of 37. Superstars maintain 49 percent of their peak value at the age of 37. Mike Schmidt retains 91 percent of his peak value at the age of 37.

I made estimates of the percentage of peak value retained by most of the best players in the game. The formula is 1987 established value, divided by the highest established value the player has had at any point in his career. These are a few of the figures:

Born 1955: Jack Clark, .97; Robin Yount, .84; Jeff Leonard, .75

Born 1954: Ozzie Smith, 1.00; Andre Dawson, .90; Gary Carter, .81.

Born 1953: Keith Hernandez, .95; George Brett, .70; Jim Rice, .68.

Born 1952: Fred Lynn, .54; Darrell Porter, .22.

Born 1951: Alan Ashby: 1.00; Dave Winfield, .88; Dave Parker, .77.

Born 1950: Brian Downing, .99; Frank White, .93.

Born 1949: Mike Schmidt, .91; Don Baylor, .48.

Born 1948: (No one in study)

Born 1947: Carlton Fisk, .70.

Born 1946: Reggie Jackson, .43.

The players studied were mostly outstanding players, so these figures are far above group norms. Other players born in 1949 include Dusty Baker, Steve Brye, Bill Buckner, Enos Cabell, Cecil Cooper, Oscar Gamble, Phil Garner, Bobby Grich, Mike Hargrove, George Hendrick, Enzo Hernandez, Ron Hodges, Fred Kendall, Larry Lintz, Garry Maddox, Jerry Martin, Bake McBride, John Milner, Jerry Morales, Greg Pryor, Lenny Randle, Ted Simmons, Frank Taveras, Andre Thornton, John Wathan, John Wockenfuss, and Richie Zisk.

MIKE SCIOSCIA

Hitting for Average:	B−	
Hitting for Power:	D+	
Plate Discipline:	B+	
Baserunning:	D+	
OVERALL OFFENSE:		C+
Reliability:	B	
Arm:	B+	
Handling of Staff:	A−	
OVERALL DEFENSE:		B+
Consistency:	B+	
Durability:	C	
OVERALL VALUE:		B

In a Word: **Tough**

I don't know that I have ever seen a position at which the players were harder to rank than the catchers are this year. Ordinarily you can begin by sorting out three or four players who are outstanding and an equal number who awful, five or six more who are clearly above average and several more who below average, and then you have a middle group left and your only problem is putting people in order within those groups. Among the 1987 catchers there aren't any groups. Nobody is outstanding, but there are only five or six teams that are truly weak; everybody is just sort of OK, like the American League West last year.

The catchers who had the best years in 1987 (Benito Santiago, Matt Nokes, Mike LaValliere, B. J. Surhoff) haven't done anything in the past, and the players who have performed well in the past (Gary Carter, Lance Parrish, Tony Pena) didn't do much last year. The players who had the best years with the bat (Santiago, Nokes, Alan Ashby, Terry Kennedy) aren't good defensive players, and the best defensive catchers (Bob Boone, Pena) don't hit or at least didn't hit in 1987. Most of the players who hit for average (Surhoff, LaValliere, Scott Bradley) didn't hit for power, and the ones who hit for power (Carter, Bob Brenly, Parrish, Tim Laudner) didn't hit for average. Many of the best catchers—in fact, almost all of them—are platoon players (Brenly, Surhoff, Nokes, Whitt, Steinbach, Bradley), and most of the guys who did play regularly (Ozzie Virgil, Jody Davis, Parrish) weren't all that terrific. The players who play in the best hitters' parks (Virgil, Davis, Marzano) aren't the best hitters, and the guys who play in the best pitchers' parks (Ashby, Steinbach) aren't the best fielders. Almost everybody was either a rookie (Santiago, Surhoff, Nokes, Steinbach, Marzano), having his first good year (LaValliere), or at an age where you wonder if he was having his last good year (Carter, Whitt, Fisk, Pena, Parrish, Boone, Ashby). There are only three players that you can say are just bad (Fitzgerald, Cerone, and Bando), and there's nobody who is just all-around good.

Granting that there isn't much difference between being number one in this lot and being number twenty, I decided to go with Mike Scioscia as the best. I think the best catching situation in the majors was in Seattle, where the Mariners had a platoon of two guys (Dave Valle and Scott Bradley) who are both pretty good. Scioscia historically has four outstanding strengths (one of the best strikeout/walk ratios in baseball, good arm, excellent ability to block the plate, strong ability to work with pitchers) and four outstanding weaknesses (slow, no power, doesn't hit left-handers, gets hurt a lot). Two of those weaknesses have gone away. He improved against left-handers in 1986 (.234) and hit very well against them in 1987, actually better than he hit right-handers. He hasn't been seriously hurt now in the last four years, and in the last three years has probably played almost as much as any catcher (142 games last year, 138 as a catcher). His lack of power is dramatically overstated by playing in Dodger Stadium; he has hit three times as many home runs in his career on the road (24) as in L.A. (8). Dodger Stadium hurts all of his offensive totals, and keeps people from realizing that he is as good a hitter as he is (in the last two years, for example, he has hit 31 doubles on the road, but only 13 in L.A.). And as to his speed, it's something you can live with for a catcher, plus he stole 7 bases in 11 tries.

So I don't see Scioscia as having, at this point, any real glaring weaknesses, and he's the only catcher whom you can say that about. Lasorda starting hitting him second last September, which I think is where he should have been all along. When some of the 1987 rookies develop and their production stabilizes, Scioscia won't be able to hold the top spot. But I think that right now, talking about currently proven ability, he's the best catcher in the game.

MIKE SCOTT

Fastball:	A
Curve or Slider:	C
Other Pitches:	A
Control:	B+
OVERALL STUFF:	A
Delivery:	C
Holding Runners:	D−
Fielding/Hitting:	C
OVERALL MECHANICS:	C−
Composure:	B
Consistency:	B
Durability:	?
OVERALL VALUE:	B+
In a Word: **Overpowering**	

Scott is heading into the option year of his contract, and will have considerable incentive to have a big year. The last time he was in this position he jumped from 5–11 to 18–8. I figure that if he makes a comparable leap forward again next year, Dwight Gooden in the future will be competing for the Mike Scott Award.

Scott's stats in the early part of last season look like the kind of stats you see when somebody takes a number one draft pick with four years of college ball and sends him to the Appalachian League, where he goes 6–0 with an ERA about the size of Ed Meece's IQ. In his third start his game line was 9 1 0 0 1 10, game score 94. In his eighth start was 9 2 0 0 2 12. Then there was the start that was 7 2 1 1 1 13, and the one that went 8 7 0 0 0 14, and the game after that that went 9 3 2 2 1 9. That was his sixteenth start; he was 9–3 with 125 strikeouts in 111 innings, had allowed only 68 hits.

For the rest of the season he was an ordinary pitcher, so we'll see if he can bounce back. I would bet that he can; I'd bet on him to have not necessarily his best season this year, but probably his best win total.

KEVIN SEITZER

Hitting for Average:	A
Hitting for Power:	B−
Plate Discipline:	B+
Baserunning:	B−
OVERALL OFFENSE:	A−
Defensive Range:	B+
Reliability:	C
Arm:	B
OVERALL DEFENSE:	B
Consistency:	?
Durability:	?
OVERALL VALUE:	B+
In a Word: **Slasher**	

There are some arguments that I am, as a Royals' fan, not allowed to make. Mark McGwire was a unanimous American League Rookie of the Year; no voter disagreed. As a Royals' fan, I have zero chance of convincing anybody that Seitzer was a better player.

McGwire won the award because what he did was a) unprecedented, and b) highly publicized. But since the award obviously should be based on value, not uniqueness, and since what Seitzer did was also extremely rare (first rookie in 23 years to get 200 hits), that seems to me almost totally irrelevant to who deserved the honor.

Offensively, McGwire led Seitzer in two categories—home runs (49–15) and RBI (118–83). Thirty-four homers are a very important advantage, certainly, but then so are 46 hits. Seitzer beat him in everything else—runs scored (105–97), hits (207–161), doubles (33–28), triples (8–4), walks (80–71), strikeouts (Seitzer struck out 85 times, McGwire 131), and stolen bases (12–1). Still, McGwire was a slightly superior offensive player. Seitzer created an estimated 120 runs, or 7.03 per game (27 outs); McGwire created an estimated 131 runs or 8.61 per game. Their offensive winning percentages were .754 for McGwire, .724 for Seitzer. McGwire was better, but it was close.

Defensively, Seitzer has a big edge. McGwire was expected to open the season as the third baseman, but when put at third base was so obviously inept that he was moved to first in April, and will never be moved back. Seitzer was expected to play left field or first base, but when George Brett was out for a while Seitzer stepped in and played third so well that Brett will never get the third base job back. Seitzer finished seventh in the league in games at third base (141), but sixth in putouts (105), third in assists (292), second in total chances (419), and third in double plays (32).

My argument would be, shouldn't defense count for something? Is a first baseman who creates 131 runs really more valuable than a third baseman who creates 120? Wouldn't it have been worth a few runs if McGwire could have played third base?

A couple of things hurt Seitzer. One was a note that *USA Today* ran, in late August or early September, a picture of Seitzer with a caption like "Defensive Problems" or something. I don't know what they were thinking of. He was playing terrific at third base. Another was that he has an odd throwing motion, straight overhand with the ball gripped sideways, and it worries you because you think he's going to throw it away, but he doesn't, no more often than the next guy. If I'd had a Rookie of the Year vote, I'd have given it to Seitzer. Whether that is an argument for Seitzer or an argument that I shouldn't be allowed to vote, you'll have to decide.

JOHN SHELBY

Hitting for Average:	C −	
Hitting for Power:	C	
Plate Discipline:	D	
Baserunning:	B	
OVERALL OFFENSE:		C −
Defensive Range:	B +	
Reliability:	C	
Arm:	B	
OVERALL DEFENSE:		B
Consistency:	D −	
Durability:	B	
OVERALL VALUE:		C −
In a Word: **Fluke**		

If Shelby can repeat his 1987 season in 1988, he'll move way up the list among center fielders. Until that happens, he seems like the most obvious fluke of 1987, a player whose season was, and will remain, out of the context of his career. Shelby is 30 years old now, had had several chances to win the regular center field job in Baltimore but could never hold onto it. When he came to the National League he was fired up, and apparently the book on him wasn't too good, as he started hitting home runs at an unprecedented pace.

Looking ahead to 1988, Shelby's whole career has been on a yoyo. Even last year, hitting as well as he did, he struck out three times as often as he walked. With the strike zone being larger next year, I figure the best that can be expected of him is that he'll hit in the .240 range with 15–20 homers. What's more likely is that he'll hit in the .240 range without 15–20 homers.

RUBEN SIERRA

Hitting for Average:	C +	
Hitting for Power:	B	
Plate Discipline:	D	
Baserunning:	C +	
OVERALL OFFENSE:		C +
Defensive Range:	B +	
Reliability:	D	
Arm:	A	
OVERALL DEFENSE:		B
Durability:	A −	
Consistency:	B	
OVERALL PLAY:		B −
In a Word: **Ascending**		

It is a story often told that Ruben Sierra as a kid idolized Roberto Clemente, modeled himself after Clemente, and indeed if you see him hitting right-handed you can't miss the similarities. He has many of the same mannerisms and even the same talents, that odd ability to swing late on an outside pitch and slap it out of the catcher's mitt and into right-center. Physically he is very different than Clemente, bigger in the upper body, a bigger bone structure. Sierra is listed as weighing 175 pounds, same as Clemente, but looks bigger. It is worthy of note that at the age of 21 he has already exceeded Clemente's career high in home runs. Clemente didn't drive in a hundred runs until he was 31 years old.

Anyway, what has always struck me as odd about this is the timing. Sierra was born in October 1965. Clemente died in December 1972. Sierra was seven. How, then, did Sierra manage to study Clemente's mannerisms? Videotape? Film? It's hard to imagine a 14-year-old Puerto Rican kid owning a VCR, but obviously I'm missing something.

As you can see, I don't think Sierra is a great player yet. His power, which is his strongest offensive asset, isn't outstanding. He homered less often than teammates Incaviglia and Parrish and no more often than Brower. His batting average was just about the league average, and his on-base percentage was poor (.302). He hasn't made any offensive use of his speed, and he's a sometimes brilliant but erratic outfielder.

DARRYL STRAWBERRY

Hitting for Average:	B+
Hitting for Power:	A−
Plate Discipline:	B+
Baserunning:	B+
OVERALL OFFENSE:	A−
Defensive Range:	B+
Reliability:	D+
Arm:	B
OVERALL DEFENSE:	C+
Consistency:	A
Durability:	B
OVERALL VALUE:	B+
In a Word:	**Graceful**

Among the players of our generation, Strawberry is the best positioned to hit a really impressive number of home runs. Darryl has 147 career home runs, an established home run level over 30, and might well turn out to be younger than the 1988 Rookie of the Year (he is 26). To hit 400 home runs, he would need to play until age 35 and average 25 home runs a year, which doesn't seem too tough. To hit 500 home runs, he would need to play until age 37 and average 29 to 30 home runs a year, which still seems extremely realistic, although the estimated chance of it is only 35 percent. To hit 600 home runs, he would need to play until age 39 and average 32 home runs a year, which would be tough (estimated 16 percent chance). To get 700 home runs, he would need to play until he was 41 and average 35 home runs a year, which would be extremely tough (estimated 4 percent chance.) To break Aaron's record, he would need to average 38 homers a year from now until age 41, which would be almost impossible (no established chance). Strawberry is 32 home runs behind Aaron at the same age, and as I've observed before, Aaron will be almost impossible to catch from behind.

Strawberry's 35 percent chance of hitting 500 career homers is the best of any young player at the moment; Dale Murphy is ahead of him in time. Like the list of 3000-hit candidates (see Yount) is a list of young players waiting to be sorted out. It appears that about four active players will later clear 500 home runs, as the sum of the established chances is 3.92. The leading candidate to get 600 home runs is Mike Schmidt (41 percent), followed by Murphy (20 percent), Mark Mc-Gwire (18 percent), Strawberry (16 percent), and George Bell (15 percent).

Strawberry last year had, for the first time, a good year hitting in Shea Stadium, hitting over .300 there and with 20 of his 39 home runs at home; he still has career totals of 84 home runs on the road, only 63 at home. Having competed to this point under a home field disadvantage also gives him a chance to improve his stats in the future.

Despite the enormous attention he receives as a number-one draft pick and a New York player, I think few fans appreciate what a great offensive player this guy is. His combination of power, speed, walks, and a decent batting average put a tremendous number of runs on the scoreboard. Strawberry's offensive winning percentage's beginning in his rookie 1983 season are .716, .659, .794, .711, and .782. His career figure, .730, is better than Andre Dawson's career high, which occurred in 1980. Don Mattingly's career offensive winning percentage is .713, which is a slightly misleading comparison because Mattingly competes in a nine-man offense, while Strawberry is in an eight-man. Still, comparing the two carefully, Mattingly makes more outs a season than Strawberry (career average of 456 outs/162 games for Mattingly, 441 for Strawberry) with very comparable run production (career averages of 100 runs and 117 RBI/season for Mattingly, 97 runs and 108 RBI for Strawberry). They're close.

PLAYERS WHO HAVE AN ESTABLISHED CHANCE OF HITTING 500 HOME RUNS

Dale Murphy	.58
Darryl Strawberry	.35
Mark McGwire	.34
George Bell	.33
Jesse Barfield	.22
Eddie Murray	.22
Tom Brunansky	.21
Don Mattingly	.19
Andre Dawson	.18
Jose Canseco	.18
Kent Hrbek	.17
Cal Ripken	.15
Eric Davis	.12
Gary Gaetti	.10
Will Clark	.09
Jim Presley	.06
Ruben Sierra	.06
Danny Tartabull	.06
Pete Incaviglia	.04
Glenn Davis	.04
Mike Pagliarulo	.04
Cory Snyder	.04
Joe Carter	.03
Howard Johnson	.03
Matt Nokes	.03
Rob Deer	.02
Dwight Evans	.02
Wally Joyner	.02

OZZIE SMITH

Hitting for Average:	B	
Hitting for Power:	D	
Plate Discipline:	A–	
Baserunning:	B+	
OVERALL OFFENSE:		B
Defensive Range:	A	
Reliability:	A	
Arm:	B+	
OVERALL DEFENSE:		A
Consistency:	A	
Durability:	A	
OVERALL VALUE:		A–
In a Word: **Wizard**		

When analyzing the careers of about a hundred players, I tried to estimate the percentage of their career value which was offensive, and the percentage which was defensive. These estimates were based on the Value Approximation Method. The Value Approximation Method is a way of just "counting" the positive things the player does—if you hit .250, that's a point, if you hit .275, that's another point, if you steal 20 bases, that's a point, if you turn 90 double plays, that's a point, etc. It's an intuitive system, based on attempting to evaluate players in the same way that they are evaluated for awards, trades, etc., and the results of this experiment should not be taken more seriously than is justified by the method. What I did this time was just keep track, in essence, of how many points I was counting for offensive achievements, and how many for defensive achievements, and then find the ratio between the two.

Ozzie, as you might expect, had the highest percentage of his value in defensive achievements, 64 percent. There were six players in the study whose value was at least 50 percent defensive (in at least 500 games); those six were Ozzie, 36–64, Jim Sundberg, 42–58, Alan Ashby, 47–53, Mike Scioscia, 49–51, Frank White, 49–51, and Gary Pettis, 50–50. Ashby I suppose is a surprise, but he spent a lot of years as a defensive catcher. The norm for shortstops seemed to be a little over 50 percent offense (Julio Franco, 53 percent; Tony Fernandez, 54 percent), but the study focused on quality players, so you might get very different results if you included a bunch of guys named "Rafael" in the study. Santana might be 70 percent defensive or more.

CORY SNYDER

Hitting for Average:	D	
Hitting for Power:	B+	
Plate Discipline:	F	
Baserunning:	C	
OVERALL OFFENSE:		C–
Defensive Range:	C	
Reliability:	D+	
Arm:	B+	
OVERALL DEFENSE:		C+
Consistency:	?	
Durability:	A	
OVERALL VALUE:		C
In a Word: **Spotty**		

In discussing Rickey Henderson, I was talking about the concept of run element ratio. The lowest run element ratios that I found were for Cory Snyder (.225), Matt Nokes (.310), Jim Presley (.319), Don Mattingly (.381), Benito Santiago (.382), Mark McGwire (.394), Jim Rice (.420), Harold Baines (.438), Will Clark (.442), Glenn Davis (.447), and Joe Carter (.467). These are all players who are much better at finishing trouble than at starting it. This list is not exhaustive; there could be other players who have equally low ratios.

One of the things I think I have found, just in the last year, is that one problem in the design of an offense is the use of players with extremely low run element ratios in the four and five spots, who often lead off the second inning, leading to extremely few runs scored in the second inning. If you look at the list above, you'll see that many of these players, who are the least suited in baseball to lead off an inning, usually bat in the spot where they often lead off the second inning. I think you should try to avoid that.

If the player is an outstanding hitter, like Don Mattingly or Harold Baines or Mark McGwire or Will Clark or Jim Rice at his best or Matt Nokes last year, you can avoid this problem by placing the player in the number three spot. In the case of Nokes, for example, you can move Kirk Gibson or Alan Trammell, whose run element ratios are about 1.00 and who therefore are as valuable at one part of the inning as at another, to the fourth and fifth spots, and use Nokes at third; that way you'll score just as many runs in the first inning (I think) and more in the second.

The harder case is when you have a player who has a very low run ele-

ment ratio, but who isn't really a good enough hitter to be put in the number-three spot, like Cory Snyder or Jim Presley. In my opinion, these people logically should hit eighth. The eighth spot is the end of the cycle of the offense, either in the NL, where the pitcher bats ninth, or in the AL, where the ninth spot is ideally filled by a player who doesn't get on base enough to be a lead-off man, but who still has a high run element ratio—thus starting off the next offensive cycle. But that creates a problem, too, because if you put an undisciplined hitter batting ahead of the pitcher he won't get any pitches to hit, and his strikeouts will usually go through the roof.

So Cory Snyder is a hard player to use offensively—wherever you put him, you create one problem or another. Somebody last summer described Brook Jacoby as the "American League Leon Durham." Actually, by the end of the year he was worse off than Durham in terms of RBI productivity. But what do the two players have in common? Durham batted after Andre Dawson, whose run element ratio was .246; Jacoby batted after Snyder. That's why RBI aren't what people try to make them out to be, a measure of a hitter's "productivity," and part of why Andre Dawson wasn't anything like the Most Valuable Player in the National League. If you drive in runs but don't do anything to carry on the offense, that's going to show up in the RBI count of the next two or three players.

A large part of the Indians trouble last year is that they had not one, but several players consecutively with very low run element ratios—Joe Carter, then Mel Hall, then Snyder. By that time the offense is dry; there's nothing left. That's also part of the problem that the Oakland A's are going to have this year, when they have McGwire, Canseco, and Parker; they think it's going to be an explosive offense, but it isn't. They've got three straight players with very low run element ratios, and that just isn't going to work.

I don't mean to hammer on this, but it's an awfully important point, and before I leave this field I wanted to make a clear exposition on it. Let me put it this way. Suppose that you have an offense of nine average players, which in the American League last year would mean nine guys who hit .265, slug .425 and have on-base percentages of .333. If you trade at one position for a man who has the same on-base percentage but drives in more runs, you have improved the ability to capitalize on opportunities, but in so doing you have reduced the number of opportunities remaining. For that reason, if you make the exact same substitution again, the second substitution will be less effective than the first.

If, however, you trade at one position for a player who has a higher on-base percentage, you have improved the ability to capitalize on opportunities, and in so doing you have also increased the number of remaining opportunities. For that reason, if you make the exact same substitution again, the second substitution will be more effective than the first. Understand? An RBI man helps the offense in one way but hurts it in the other; a player who sets the table helps the offense in both ways. That is why the St. Louis Cardinal offense works so well—an offense of eight leadoff men, or eight guys with high run element ratios, is a perfectly workable offense, because so long as people keep getting on base, runs are going to keep scoring. But an offense that strings together several people with low run element ratios is not workable.

So that creates a paradox, and it also defines one of the limitations of the runs created method. Who is a better offensive player: Kevin McReynolds or Vince Coleman? Kevin McReynolds—in the context of an ordinary offense. But which would score more runs, an offense of eight Vince Colemans, or an offense of eight Kevin McReynoldses? An offense of eight Vince Colemans. It's a perfectly valid paradox, and one that Whitey Herzog has exploited brilliantly.

WALT TERRELL

Fastball:	C+	
Curve or Slider:	B+	
Other Pitches:	D	
Control:	C	
OVERALL STUFF:		C
Delivery:	B+	
Holding Runners:	A	
Fielding/Hitting:	B	
OVERALL MECHANICS:		B+
Composure:	A−	
Consistency:	B+	
Durability:	A	
OVERALL VALUE:		B−
In a Word: **Solid**		

The book *The Scouting Report: 1987* says that "opponents can bunt on Terrell, an offensive weapon that he detests." Well, sacrifice hits allowed happens to be an official stat, so I checked how many bunts Terrell had actually allowed. Last year, in 245 innings, he allowed 3 sac bunts; in 1986 he allowed only 2 in 217 innings. So obviously, you can't bunt on him; maybe you think you can, but nobody makes it work.

The same book said about Terrell's ability to hold runners that "his hold is average. However, a short leg kick during his delivery makes him difficult to steal against." This isn't totally inaccurate, I suppose, but a more accurate synopsis would be that "If you try to steal bases against this guy, you ought to have your brain replaced." According to the *Great American Baseball Stat Book,* opponents in 1986 stole exactly two bases against Terrell, two bases in eight attempts. Over a three-year period opponents were 17 for 44 trying to steal against him, which is about six runs worse than not trying to steal at all.

Except, not necessarily against Terrell. Terrell, you see, throws a heavy, sinking fastball, a pitch that generates ground balls. Against a pitcher like that, you need to be able to steal, and you need to be able to bunt; if you can't, you can't avoid the double play. So the key to understanding Terrell is to realize that he does, in fact, do all of the things that he needs to do to support his central skill, which is throwing that sinker.

ALAN TRAMMELL

Hitting for Average:	B+	
Hitting for Power:	B	
Plate Discipline:	C+	
Baserunning:	B+	
OVERALL OFFENSE:		B+
Defensive Range:	C	
Reliability:	B	
Arm:	C−	
OVERALL DEFENSE:		C+
Consistency:	C	
Durability:	B+	
OVERALL VALUE:		B
In a Word: **Homely**		

Just for the heck of it, I checked the number of double plays turned by each American League team over the last ten years, the ten years of Trammell and Whitaker. The Tigers in that period rank eighth in the league in double plays, 1566, although they are a little over the league average of 1534. The fourteen teams in order of DP are California (1623), Seattle, Baltimore, Boston, Minnesota, Milwaukee, Toronto, Detroit, New York, Chicago, Kansas City, Texas, Cleveland, and Oakland. Oakland, with 2305, is more than a hundred behind any other team. I don't see any particular patterns there, other than that the three bottom teams (Texas, Cleveland, and Oakland) haven't done very well.

Double plays around the league have been declining over the ten-year period, from more than 2300 in 1979–1980 down to the 2200s in 1982–1983, to 2179 in 1984, 2159 in 1986, and 2119 in 1987. In Trammell and Whitaker's first five years the Tigers turned 800 double plays, sixth in the league; in the last five years they have turned 766, tenth in the league. Minnesota led in DP over the first five years with 831 (Gene Mauch's influence), but dropped to twelfth the second five years, with the Angels taking over the top spot with 880 (Gene Mauch again). Oakland was last in both periods. The Tigers led the league in DP in 1978, Trammell and Whitaker's first year, but have not led since, being succeeded by Minnesota (1979), Toronto/Boston (1980), Milwaukee (1981–1982), California (1983, 1985), New York (1984), Seattle (1986) and Baltimore/Chicago (1987). Three teams (Kansas City, Detroit, and New York) have kept one second baseman all ten years, while only Detroit has kept one shortstop.

FRANK VIOLA

Fastball:	B+	
Curve or Slider:	B+	
Other Pitches:	B+	
Control:	B	
OVERALL STUFF:		B+
Delivery:	A	
Holding Runners:	A	
Fielding/Hitting:	C+	
OVERALL MECHANICS:		A−
Composure:	A	
Consistency:	A	
Durability:	A	
OVERALL VALUE:		A−
In a Word: **Sweet**		

Can we get a All-Musical Instruments team? We can if you count Bells. We got Frank Viola, Steve Sax, Sam Horn, Kevin Bass, Tim Drummond. If you use Bells, though, you've got George, Buddy, Terry, Eric . . . . God knows who all. You could use Jeff, Jerry, and Jody Reed.

The Twins scored just 155 runs for Viola last year (4.3 per start), but won 22 of 36 games, a .611 percentage. They were 23–14 with Blyleven starting, but that was with five runs a game . . . With Viola starting in the Metrodome the Twins were 15–4 (.789); on the road, they were 7–10 (.412). Viola had 20 starts with a game score over 60, the same as Roger Clemens (20 of 36), so he would have won 20 games with any kind of offensive support. Dave Stewart had only 15 starts with game scores over 60 (15/37 as opposed to 20/36), and that was in a pitcher's park. Saberhagen had 16 game scores over 60, almost all of them early in the year (16/33) . . . counting post-season play, Viola started 41 times in 1987 and was 20–10 . . . we had Viola rated way too low last year, ranked as the seventeenth best starting pitcher in the league . . . I was wondering who was the closest thing to a contemporary Warren Spahn, and decided it was obviously Viola—left hander, durable, consistent, cuts off the running game, good K/W data. Viola is a loosey-goosey pitcher, looks like he's double-jointed. His limbs swing free in his motion, which should immensely reduce the strain on his arm, and enable him to pitch a long time. Then I got to wondering: was Spahn like that? Anybody remember his motion that clearly? By the time I remember him he was 40 . . .

TIM WALLACH

Hitting for Average:	B−	
Hitting for Power:	B	
Plate Discipline:	D+	
Baserunning:	C+	
OVERALL OFFENSE:		B
Defensive Range:	B+	
Reliability:	B	
Arm:	A	
OVERALL DEFENSE:		B+
Consistency:	D	
Durability:	B+	
OVERALL VALUE:		B+
In a Word: **Rugged**		

Wallach last year hit .300 with 13 homers at home, and .300 with 13 homers on the road. One might infer from this that the new roof on the Metrodome had nothing to do with Wallach's improvement, in which case you would be completely wrong, not only because Wallach had 26 doubles and 4 triples at home (.552 slugging percentage) as opposed to 16 and none on the road (.482 slugging), but also because prior to last year Wallach was distinctly hurt by playing in Montreal, hitting almost two-thirds of his career home runs on the road.

Before last year Wallach was the most consistent fade-out in baseball. Over the three previous years he had hit .314 in April, .259 or better in each of the first three months, but no higher than .234 in July, August, or September, finishing with a .199 average in September. Part of the reason for this was that Wallach stayed in the lineup with injuries, sometimes serious injuries, which got worse rather than better.

The other split in Wallach's record is that he hits finesse pitchers, control-type pitchers, far better than he hits power pitchers. For that reason, and also because his command of the strike zone is not very good, he may have difficulty adjusting to the 1988 strike zone.

LOU WHITAKER

Hitting for Average:	C+	
Hitting for Power:	C−	
Plate Discipline:	B	
Baserunning:	B−	
OVERALL OFFENSE:		B−
Defensive Range:	B−	
Reliability:	B	
DP Pivot:	B+	
OVERALL DEFENSE:		B
Consistency:	A−	
Durability:	A	
OVERALL VALUE:		B
In a Word: **Anchor**		

For people who believe that we are manufacturing platoon players by assigning people to platoon roles, please consider the case of Alan Trammell and Lou Whitaker. These two guys have been facing the same pitchers every day almost since they entered baseball. As hitters they have been as comparable as any two men could be; I'm sure you've seen those comparisons showing that their career stats cross every couple of seasons and for a moment are almost identical. And yet, Trammell (a right-handed hitter) consistently hits with more power against left-handed pitching (and slightly better averages), while Whitaker (a left-handed hitter) just has all kinds of trouble with left-handed pitching. Why? Same pitchers. Same experiences. Each of them is as familiar with left-handed pitching as the other. It's just harder for a left-handed hitter to hit a left-handed pitcher.

The favorite toy, my method of estimating a player's chance of getting 3000 hits, shows Trammell with a 30 percent chance of getting 3000 hits, Whitaker only a 13 percent chance. In view of the long-term similarity of their records, that distinction hardly seems reasonable, although I guess time will tell. Whitaker is a year older than Trammell, and so at the moment has three disadvantages—one less year, 25 fewer hits, and a lower established hit level. Those things combine to make it appear less likely that he can get to 3000 hits.

MIKE WITT

Fastball:	B+
Curve or Slider:	A−
Other Pitches:	C+
Control:	B
OVERALL STUFF:	B+
Delivery:	B
Holding Runners:	B+
Fielding/Hitting:	C
OVERALL MECHANICS:	B
Composure:	B+
Consistency:	A
Durability:	A
OVERALL VALUE:	B+
In a Word: **Lanky**	

Witt had a heck of a year for a guy who started slowly and faded badly. In April, with Bob Boone not there to catch him, Witt finished 2–2 with a 5.18 ERA. By the end of July he was 13–6 and seemed on target for his first 20-win season, but he faded badly in August and September, along with the rest of the team; after August 1 he was 3–8 with an ERA of 4.64. He pitched three times during the season on three days rest, with a 2–1 record, 2.70 ERA. With four days rest, he was 12–8 with a 4.15 ERA. With five days rest, he was 1–4 with an ERA of 5.50.

The Scouting Report: 1987 says that "Gene Mauch hates to relieve him: Mauch reasons that his stuff is so outstanding that hitters are always elated to see him go." That one's dead on; the Angels had 21 slow hooks last year—9 for Mike Witt, no more than 3 for anybody else. Seven of the nine games were lost, so the value of leaving him in is questionable.

ROBIN YOUNT

Hitting for Average:	A−
Hitting for Power:	C+
Plate Discipline:	B
Baserunning:	B
OVERALL OFFENSE:	B+
Defensive Range:	B−
Reliability:	B+
Arm:	D
OVERALL DEFENSE:	C+
Consistency:	B+
Durability:	B
OVERALL VALUE:	B
In a Word: **Classy**	

As he has been for several years, Robin remains the one player with the best current shot at 3000 hits. With 198 hits last year Yount now has 2217; he is essentially five years away from 3000 hits. He could make it in four years, but that's very unlikely, would require 193 hits a season. Anyway, being only 32 years old and five years away from 3000 hits, he is in excellent shape; my method for evaluating these things shows him as having a 71 percent chance of getting 3000 hits. He is the only player who is more likely to get 3000 hits than not, but there is a group of young hitters emerging behind Yount who are well positioned early in the game—Mattingly, Gwynn, Puckett, Boggs, Raines. In another four years some of those players, the ones who continue to have good years, will be up at 50 to 70 percent, while the others will have dropped down or even out. Fifteen active players have at least a 20 percent chance of getting 3000 hits, which is more than normal, probably due to the high offensive totals of recent years. This chart suggests that seven active players will probably get 3000 hits, which is not unprecedented. Eight players active in the late sixties later cleared 3000 hits, and another group is now forming for a charge.

Yount also has the best established shot at 3500 hits, a 21 percent chance; he is followed on that chart by Mattingly (18 percent), Gwynn (15 percent), Puckett (15 percent), Raines (12 percent), and Trammell (10 percent).

PLAYERS WHO HAVE AN ESTABLISHED CHANCE OF GETTING 3000 HITS

Robin Yount	71%
Don Mattingly	34%
Tony Gwynn	30%
Alan Trammell	30%
Kirby Puckett	30%
Tim Raines	29%
Eddie Murray	28%
Tony Fernandez	28%
Wade Boggs	24%
Jim Rice	24%
Cal Ripken	24%
Keith Hernandez	23%
Julio Franco	22%
Steve Sax	21%
Bill Buckner	20%
Ryne Sanderg	17%
George Bell	17%
Willie Wilson	17%
Harold Baines	16%
Lloyd Moseby	15%
Lou Whitaker	14%
Juan Samuel	13%
Dale Murphy	13%
Dave Winfield	12%
George Brett	12%
Buddy Bell	11%
Paul Molitor	11%
Carney Lansford	10%
Willie McGee	10%
Rickey Henderson	7%
Alvin Davis	6%
Tom Brunansky	5%
Kent Hrbek	5%
Phil Bradley	4%
Andre Dawson	4%
Brook Jacoby	4%
Danny Tartabull	4%
Ruben Sierra	3%
José Canseco	2%
Terry Pendleton	2%
Kevin Bass	1%
Darryl Strawberry	1%

SECTION
IV

STATS

In 1988 a company run by some friends of mine (Dick Cramer and John Dewan) plans to collect a pitch-by-pitch, play-by-play database for every game played during the season. The database will be updated daily, and to make this run, obviously they will need a network of scorers in every city where major-league baseball is played.

First of all, I should distinguish this operation from Project Scoresheet. Project Scoresheet is a not-for-profit group that collects scoresheets from every game for the benefit of its members. STATS (Sports Team Analysis & Tracking Systems, Inc.), is a profit-making (or deficit-showing, as the case may be) private company. I founded Project Scoresheet but am no longer associated with them, although I'll still do anything I can to help them too. John Dewan, who once ran Project Scoresheet, has left that position and now works with STATS. I should also note here that I own about 5 percent of the stock in the company, although that's not why I'm doing this; you all know that it has always been my policy to try to help anybody who wanted to do anything worthwhile in this field.

The scoring of games will be done at the ballpark or off the TV. After the game, scorers will send the information by a modem to a central computer, where the stats will be compiled. For this reason the primary scorers will be required to own or have access to an IBM-compatible computer for the scoring.

STATS, being a business, will of course pay for the scoresheets; how much I don't know. They are also planning a profit sharing plan for scorers, and they may be able to make available tickets to games. In addition, the scorers will have access by computer to the stats which are compiled; a scorer as I understand it would be able to make a daily check on batting averages against left-handed and right-handed pitching, etc. of the players on his own team (so long as he didn't try to resell the information). This is hard for me to believe; ten years ago, when I started trying to collect platoon breakdowns, it took me several weeks of letter-writing and telephoning to collect stats from about half the teams. How much access you will have will depend apparently on how many games you have scored or something.

At the moment, some of the directors of Project Scoresheet and STATS tend to see themselves as being competitors and are engaged in some stupid squabbling over absolutely nothing. There is no fundamental reason why both groups cannot succeed, or why any individual cannot or should not send scoresheets to both. My effort in this field has been to break the Elias monopoly, and to insure for the fans permanent access to the records of the games. I support both groups because I think we're better off with two independant sources for public access, rather than one; indeed, if there were a third credible effort I'd support that, too. But you've got to remember, guys, that Elias is still there and still wants desperately to deny everybody else access to the scoresheets. Nothing would make them happier than for you two to push each other over into insolvency. Watch your ass, OK?

If you are interested in being a part of the STATS scoring network, write to

STATS
7250 N. Cicero
Suite LL 3
Lincolnwood, Illinois 60646

or call 312-676-3322. Good luck.

DISCOVERY

I wanted to do a very quick report here on a discovery that was made a little over a year ago by a man named Dick O'Brien, which I have been intending to get into the book somewhere but never have.

Sabermetricians have been interested for several years in the question of how much of an impact on offense, on the "carry" of the ball, might be associated with differences in park elevation. It is well know that the dimensions of Fulton County Stadium in Atlanta, one of the best home run parks in baseball, are almost identical to those of Busch Stadium in St. Louis, one of the worst. There has never been a consensus as to what caused this odd phenomenon, apart from a general consensus that the people who want to ascribe it to "psychological factors" probably have a screw that needs to be tightened in their scientific machine, but one of the theories that has been put forward is that the effect of altitude on the carry of the ball may have been underestimated. Fulton County Stadium is about 1000 feet above sea level—not tremendously high, but one of the highest parks in the National League—while Busch Stadium is only 455 feet above sea level.

This theory, if true, might explain a good many other phenomena—for example, the fact that the ball doesn't travel in Florida. I'm sure you've seen those letters to the editor; baseball men are always saying that the ball doesn't travel well in the "moist, heavy air" in Florida, and there's a physicist somewhere who has a conniption fit every time he sees that and fires off a "How many times do I have to tell you" letter repeating vociferously that a baseball actually travels better, not worse, in moist air. Phoenix is the other side—hot, dry air, and the ball travels well.

All of Florida, of course, is near sea level, while Phoenix rests on a plateau. It might well be that the real explanation for the fact that the ball doesn't carry well in Florida and does in Phoenix is simply the elevation.

Anyway, let me get to the point. In the June 1986 issue of the *Baseball Analyst,* a small publication which I edit, Dick O'Brien reported on a study of the effects of ballpark elevation and humidity as factors in home run production. O'Brien made a marvelous discovery. It's called the Texas League. Living in El Paso, O'Brien noticed that all of the parks in the Texas League over the last decade have nearly the same dimensions. The dimensions in Beaumont are a few feet shorter, but basically every park in the league is 330–395–335, or thereabouts.

Since all of the parks are in the same general area, there is minimal variation among them in temperature conditions. It happens, however, that there is a huge difference among the parks in elevation (and therefore in humidity). The park in Beaumont, which is now out of the league, was only 20 feet above sea level, and three other parks in the league were less than 300 feet above sea level. Two parks, however, were about 800 feet above sea level, while one park (Midland) is 2780 feet above sea level, and one park (El Paso) is 3700 feet above sea level.

The basic theoretical condition of science is "other things being equal." Well, here is a case in which the other things happen to be equal. And guess what? When O'Brien looked at the number of home runs hit by the teams that play in each of these parks over a period of years, he found an almost perfect relationship: the higher the altitude of the park (and therefore incidentally the drier the air), the more home runs the team which played there would hit.

Another thing that makes this finding convincing is that minor-league teams turn over their personnel so completely from year to year. If a major-league team hit a lot of home runs consistently over a ten-year period, you might ascribe that to the talent—but in the Texas League, you're talking about ten completely different teams.

O'Brien's study, to me, is absolutely compelling evidence that the elevation of a park is, in fact, a major determinant of the number of home runs hit there—and is, in all likelihood, the primary explanation for the difference in home runs hit in St. Louis and Atlanta.

A fascinating study, I thought. O'Brien himself is an interesting duck, a retired army officer who has corresponded with me for several years and written articles for the *Baseball Analyst,* with great humor. Suddenly in the summer of '86 he began popping out these brilliant little insights. I haven't heard from him in a while now, but I think that if he does nothing else, he should have a paragraph in the history of sabermetrics for his massive contribution to unraveling that mystery.

WINNING PERCENTAGE WITH QUALITY STARTS

Detroit	.818
Yankees	.806
Montreal	.782
Seattle	.753
Toronto	.750
Pittsburgh	.744
Minnesota	.738
San Francisco	.730
Boston	.726
Kansas City	.714
Mets	.711
Cincinnati	.711
Milwaukee	.710
St. Louis	.707
California	.706
White Sox	.690
Philadelphia	.671
Baltimore	.661
Texas	.651
Los Angeles	.648
Oakland	.642
Cubs	.638
Houston	.634
Atlanta	.612
Cleveland	.596
San Diego	.547

LOSSES DESPITE QUALITY START

Yankees	14
Detroit	16
Montreal	17
Seattle	18
Boston	20
Baltimore	20
Milwaukee	20
San Francisco	20
California	20
Minnesota	21
Toronto	21
Texas	22
Pittsburgh	22
Cincinnati	22
Cleveland	23
Kansas City	24
Oakland	24
Mets	24
St. Louis	24
Cubs	25
White Sox	26
Philadelphia	26
Atlanta	26
Los Angeles	32
Houston	34
San Diego	34

WINS BY ONE OR TWO RUNS

St. Louis	51
Milwaukee	46
Montreal	44
Toronto	43
Philadelphia	43
Detroit	42
San Francisco	42
Minnesota	42
Mets	41
Los Angeles	40
Cincinnati	39
Cubs	38
Pittsburgh	38
Texas	37
Cleveland	36
Yankees	35
Atlanta	35
Houston	35
Baltimore	34
Oakland	34
Seattle	34
California	33
Kansas City	33
White Sox	32
Boston	28
San Diego	28

ONE-RUN GAMES

St. Louis	60
Houston	54
San Diego	53
San Francisco	52
Mets	52
Los Angeles	51
Toronto	51
Cincinnati	50
Atlanta	49
Cleveland	48
Philadelphia	48
Oakland	47
Baltimore	46
Minnesota	46
Milwaukee	44
California	44
Cubs	43
Kansas City	43
Montreal	42
Detroit	42
Pittsburgh	42
White Sox	41
Yankees	40
Boston	39
Texas	39
Seattle	34

WINS BY FIVE OR MORE RUNS

Detroit	30
Toronto	29
Mets	27
Kansas City	26
Montreal	25
Boston	25
Yankees	25
Oakland	25
Texas	25
San Francisco	24
Seattle	24
Milwaukee	23
California	23
Minnesota	22
White Sox	21
Pittsburgh	21
Atlanta	21
Houston	20
St. Louis	19
Cincinnati	19
Cubs	18
Los Angeles	17
San Diego	15
Philadelphia	14
Baltimore	13
Cleveland	13

LOSSES BY FIVE OR MORE RUNS

St. Louis	11
Toronto	12
Mets	12
San Francisco	15
Detroit	17
Atlanta	18
Milwaukee	19
Cincinnati	19
Los Angeles	20
White Sox	21
Kansas City	21
Oakland	21
Houston	22
Baltimore	23
Philadelphia	23
Pittsburgh	23
Montreal	24
San Diego	24
California	24
Texas	24
Boston	25
Yankees	26
Seattle	27
Cubs	29
Minnesota	31
Cleveland	33

CLOSE GAMES (ONE OR TWO RUNS)

St. Louis	90
Los Angeles	85
San Diego	83
San Francisco	83
Toronto	82
Houston	81
Philadelphia	80
Mets	79
Cincinnati	78
Cubs	77
California	77
Texas	77
Milwaukee	76
Cleveland	75
Pittsburgh	74
Atlanta	74
Minnesota	73
Oakland	73
White Sox	72
Kansas City	71
Detroit	70
Yankees	70
Montreal	68
Boston	68
Baltimore	68
Seattle	66

WINNING PERCENTAGE IN ONE-RUN GAMES

Montreal	.667
Detroit	.619
Yankees	.600
Philadelphia	.563
Seattle	.559
San Francisco	.558
Mets	.558
St. Louis	.550
Milwaukee	.545
Baltimore	.543
Cincinnati	.540
Toronto	.529
Minnesota	.522
Kansas City	.512
Pittsburgh	.500
Atlanta	.469
White Sox	.463
Houston	.463
Boston	.462
Texas	.462
Oakland	.426
Cubs	.419
Cleveland	.396
California	.386
Los Angeles	.373
San Diego	.358

WINS BY STARTING PITCHERS

Detroit	74
Mets	70
Kansas City	64
Montreal	62
Yankees	62
Toronto	62
Seattle	62
Milwaukee	60
Pittsburgh	60
Boston	59
Cubs	59
St. Louis	59
Los Angeles	57
White Sox	57
Minnesota	55
San Francisco	54
Oakland	54
Philadelphia	53
Houston	53
California	52
Cincinnati	52
Atlanta	47
Texas	46
Baltimore	42
San Diego	41
Cleveland	39

AVERAGE RUNS ALLOWED IN LOSSES

Los Angeles	5.47
Toronto	5.67
St. Louis	5.78
Houston	5.80
San Francisco	5.89
Kansas City	5.94
Philadelphia	6.13
Mets	6.16
San Diego	6.16
Cincinnati	6.17
Atlanta	6.25
White Sox	6.41
Pittsburgh	6.48
Oakland	6.54
California	6.66
Detroit	6.67
Cubs	6.69
Montreal	6.72
Texas	6.77
Yankees	6.84
Milwaukee	6.87
Baltimore	6.91
Seattle	6.94
Boston	6.95
Minnesota	7.00
Cleveland	7.41

RUNS SCORED AT HOME

Detroit	442
Milwaukee	440
Boston	436
Texas	426
Toronto	425
Atlanta	421
Minnesota	411
Mets	407
Pittsburgh	404
Seattle	403
Montreal	401
Yankees	401
Cincinnati	396
White Sox	394
St. Louis	387
Philadelphia	385
Cubs	381
California	377
Kansas City	375
Cleveland	373
San Francisco	373
Oakland	363
Baltimore	351
San Diego	338
Houston	334
Los Angeles	280

GAMES IN WHICH STARTING PITCHER PITCHED LESS THAN FIVE INNINGS

Los Angeles	18
Houston	24
Mets	29
Seattle	30
Pittsburgh	30
Kansas City	31
St. Louis	31
Atlanta	31
Detroit	32
White Sox	32
Cincinnati	32
Boston	33
Cubs	34
Milwaukee	35
Montreal	35
Minnesota	36
San Diego	40
Texas	41
Yankees	42
Toronto	43
California	43
Oakland	43
San Francisco	45
Baltimore	47
Philadelphia	47
Cleveland	51

GAMES IN WHICH MORE THAN TEN RUNS WERE SCORED

Detroit	75
Boston	74
Milwaukee	71
Toronto	67
Texas	67
Yankees	66
Baltimore	65
Oakland	65
California	64
Minnesota	61
Atlanta	60
Cleveland	59
Seattle	56
Cubs	55
Mets	55
St. Louis	55
San Francisco	54
San Diego	53
Pittsburgh	53
Cincinnati	53
Philadelphia	52
Montreal	51
White Sox	51
Kansas City	49
Houston	40
Los Angeles	33

STARTS WITH GAME SCORE UNDER 30

St. Louis	11
Los Angeles	12
Mets	16
Pittsburgh	18
Toronto	19
Houston	19
San Francisco	20
Minnesota	21
Kansas City	22
Oakland	22
Yankees	23
Atlanta	23
Montreal	24
San Diego	24
White Sox	24
Seattle	24
Philadelphia	24
Cincinnati	24
Boston	25
Texas	25
Detroit	26
California	27
Milwaukee	28
Cubs	29
Baltimore	34
Cleveland	36

RUNS ALLOWED AT HOME

Houston	268
Los Angeles	306
San Francisco	312
Toronto	319
Mets	335
Detroit	338
St. Louis	339
Yankees	346
Minnesota	348
Kansas City	349
Oakland	351
San Diego	357
Pittsburgh	363
Montreal	371
Philadelphia	373
Boston	383
Cubs	389
Seattle	400
Cincinnati	401
California	405
White Sox	414
Milwaukee	420
Texas	447
Atlanta	450
Baltimore	456
Cleveland	519

RUNS ALLOWED ON THE ROAD

White Sox	332
Toronto	336
Kansas City	342
Montreal	349
Cincinnati	351
St. Louis	354
San Francisco	357
Mets	363
Los Angeles	369
Philadelphia	376
Atlanta	379
Pittsburgh	381
Detroit	397
Milwaukee	397
California	398
Seattle	401
Texas	402
San Diego	406
Houston	410
Cubs	412
Yankees	412
Baltimore	424
Cleveland	438
Oakland	438
Boston	442
Minnesota	458

STARTS WITH GAME SCORE OVER 70

Houston	32
Los Angeles	31
Kansas City	31
Detroit	29
Toronto	29
Boston	25
White Sox	24
Mets	24
Seattle	23
Montreal	20
Pittsburgh	20
San Francisco	19
California	19
Yankees	18
Minnesota	18
Cubs	17
San Diego	17
Oakland	17
Milwaukee	16
Philadelphia	16
Texas	15
St. Louis	14
Atlanta	14
Baltimore	13
Cleveland	13
Cincinnati	10

RUNS SCORED IN LOSSES

Cleveland	339
Baltimore	301
Boston	290
San Diego	285
Texas	281
California	276
Atlanta	270
White Sox	266
Seattle	256
Oakland	249
Pittsburgh	246
Minnesota	242
Cincinnati	237
Cubs	236
Philadelphia	235
Los Angeles	224
San Francisco	224
Milwaukee	223
Mets	222
Houston	215
Montreal	209
Detroit	206
St. Louis	206
Yankees	202
Toronto	191
Kansas City	180

WINNING PERCENTAGE FOLLOWING A LOSS

Toronto	.631
Yankees	.597
St. Louis	.591
San Francisco	.583
Detroit	.578
Montreal	.557
Oakland	.550
Mets	.543
Minnesota	.526
Cincinnati	.526
Cubs	.523
White Sox	.518
Milwaukee	.500
Pittsburgh	.500
Seattle	.488
Kansas City	.468
Boston	.464
Philadelphia	.457
Los Angeles	.449
Texas	.442
Atlanta	.440
Houston	.435
California	.430
Cleveland	.416
San Diego	.396
Baltimore	.368

AVERAGE RUNS SCORED IN WINS

Texas	7.23
Boston	7.08
Detroit	7.04
Milwaukee	7.02
Atlanta	6.91
Oakland	6.88
Toronto	6.81
Cleveland	6.61
California	6.59
Yankees	6.58
Mets	6.53
Cincinnati	6.50
Seattle	6.46
Kansas City	6.45
Minnesota	6.40
Baltimore	6.39
Cubs	6.37
White Sox	6.26
St. Louis	6.23
San Francisco	6.21
Pittsburgh	5.96
San Diego	5.89
Montreal	5.85
Philadelphia	5.84
Houston	5.70
Los Angeles	5.63

WINS DESPITE GAME SCORE BELOW 50

Milwaukee	35
St. Louis	35
Yankees	29
Philadelphia	29
San Francisco	28
Texas	28
Atlanta	28
Cubs	28
Toronto	27
Oakland	27
Mets	26
Cincinnati	26
Minnesota	25
Montreal	25
Cleveland	25
California	24
Baltimore	23
Boston	23
Detroit	22
San Diego	19
White Sox	19
Kansas City	19
Seattle	18
Pittsburgh	18
Houston	16
Los Angeles	11

WINNING PERCENTAGE WHEN SCORING SIX OR MORE RUNS

Toronto	.923
Detroit	.912
Yankees	.898
Montreal	.870
Cubs	.868
Seattle	.863
Kansas City	.860
Oakland	.859
Mets	.839
San Francisco	.828
Milwaukee	.828
St. Louis	.828
Philadelphia	.822
Houston	.822
Atlanta	.820
Los Angeles	.805
Minnesota	.804
Pittsburgh	.800
Boston	.794
Cincinnati	.789
Texas	.761
San Diego	.756
California	.754
Cleveland	.717
Baltimore	.708
White Sox	.694

SLOW HOOKS

Texas	29
Boston	28
Seattle	28
Detroit	25
Baltimore	21
California	21
Cleveland	19
Los Angeles	17
Milwaukee	17
Yankees	15
Kansas City	14
Oakland	14
Atlanta	14
Minnesota	13
Cubs	11
White Sox	11
Philadelphia	11
Cincinnati	10
Houston	9
San Francisco	8
San Diego	7
Mets	7
Montreal	6
Pittsburgh	5
Toronto	5
St. Louis	4

STARTS WITH GAME SCORE OVER 50

Los Angeles	97
Detroit	96
Houston	94
Toronto	92
Mets	91
Kansas City	89
White Sox	87
San Francisco	86
Pittsburgh	86
Montreal	84
Minnesota	84
St. Louis	81
Boston	79
Yankees	78
Seattle	78
Milwaukee	77
Oakland	77
Cincinnati	77
San Diego	75
California	75
Texas	75
Cubs	74
Philadelphia	72
Atlanta	66
Baltimore	65
Cleveland	61

INTRODUCTION TO CATCHERS' STATS

The following charts about catchers contain nine columns of information about each catcher who started a major-league game in 1987. Those categories are:

GS—The number of games he started as a catcher.

OSB—The number of bases stolen by the opposition in those games.

Avg—Ah, gee, guys, you can figure that out.

Inn—The number of defensive innings (or innings pitched) in those games (regardless of whether the catcher stayed in the game).

ER—The number of Earned Runs allowed by the catcher's team in games that he started.

W—The number of games won by the team with this starting catcher.

L—The number of games lost by the team with this starting catcher.

ERA—The Earned Run Average of the team in games started by this catcher.

(TmERA)—The ERA of the team for the season.

Troy AFENIR

Year	Team / Lg	GS	OSB	Avg.	Inn	ER	W	L	ERA	(TmERA)
1987	Hous N	5	8	1.60	43.0	27	1	4	5.65	3.84

Andy ALLANSON

Year	Team / Lg	GS	OSB	Avg.	Inn	ER	W	L	ERA	(TmERA)
1986	Cle A	92	66	.72	813.1	408	49	43	4.51	4.58
1987	Cle A	48	26	.54	432.1	232	20	28	4.83	5.28
2 Years		140	92	.66	1245.2	640	69	71	4.63	4.82

Alan ASHBY

Year	Team / Lg	GS	OSB	Avg.	Inn	ER	W	L	ERA	(TmERA)
1975	Cle A	82	64	.78						
1976	Cle A	73	75	1.03						
1977	Tor A	121	67	.56						
1978	Tor A	79	51	.65						
1979	Hous N	103	70	.68						
1980	Hous N	105	100	.95						
1981	Hous N	74	59	.80						
1982	Hous N	90	104	1.16	803.2	335	40	50	3.75	3.42
1983	Hous N	79	82	1.04	715.0	269	39	40	3.39	3.45
1984	Hous N	54	63	1.17	478.2	196	21	33	3.69	3.32
1985	Hous N	55	60	1.09	500.2	191	24	31	3.44	3.66
1986	Hous N	87	94	1.08	785.0	270	60	27	3.10	3.15
1987	Hous N	105	122	1.16	940.2	362	54	51	3.47	3.84
13 Years		1107	1011	.91	4221.8	1623	238	232	3.46	3.49

Mark BAILEY

Year	Team / Lg	GS	OSB	Avg.	Inn	ER	W	L	ERA	(TmERA)
1984	Hous N	102	112	1.10	919.2	313	58	44	3.06	3.32
1985	Hous N	96	70	.73	859.0	349	55	41	3.66	3.66
1986	Hous N	44	50	1.14	396.2	133	22	22	3.02	3.15
1987	Hous N	14	15	1.07	120.0	89	5	9	6.67	3.84
4 years		256	247	.96	2295.1	884	140	116	3.47	3.45

Chris BANDO

Year	Team / Lg	GS	OSB	Avg.	Inn	ER	W	L	ERA	(TmERA)
1981	Cle A	8	4	.50						
1982	Cle A	49	24	.49	436.1	217	21	28	4.48	4.11
1983	Cle A	34	17	.50	302.0	160	14	20	4.77	4.43
1984	Cle A	59	28	.47	528.1	230	33	26	3.92	4.26
1985	Cle A	57	53	.93	495.1	297	15	42	5.40	4.91
1986	Cle A	71	44	.62	634.1	328	35	35	4.65	4.58
1987	Cle A	63	46	.73	542.2	339	22	41	5.63	5.28
7 Years		341	216	.63	2939.0	15.71	140	192	4.81	4.63

Bruce BENEDICT

Year	Team / Lg	GS	OSB	Avg.	Inn	ER	W	L	ERA	(TmERA)
1978	Atl N	16	15	.94						
1979	Atl N	69	64	.93						
1980	Atl N	111	81	.73						
1981	Atl N	86	83	.97						
1982	Atl N	111	96	.86	1001.1	403	67	43	3.62	3.82
1983	Atl N	129	128	.99	1146.0	476	70	59	3.74	3.67
1984	Atl N	96	84	.88	860.2	335	44	52	3.50	3.57
1985	Atl N	65	71	1.09	572.1	246	28	37	3.87	4.19
1986	Atl N	49	27	.55	426.0	194	20	29	4.10	3.97
1987	Atl N	28	33	1.18	246.0	131	10	18	4.79	4.63
10 Years		760	682	.90	4252.1	1785	239	238	3.78	3.84

Damon BERRYHILL

Year	Team / Lg	GS	OSB	Avg.	Inn	ER	W	L	ERA	(TmERA)
1987	Chi N	7	8	1.14	60.0	47	2	5	7.05	4.55

Bruce BOCHY

Year	Team / Lg	GS	OSB	Avg.	Inn	ER	W	L	ERA	(TmERA)
1978	Hous N	45	46	1.02						
1979	Hous N	37	40	1.08						
1980	Hous N	2	1	.50						
1982	NY N	16	16	1.00	140.1	48	5	11	3.08	3.88
1983	SD N	8	4	.50	70.1	45	4	4	5.76	3.62
1984	SD N	20	18	.90	185.1	67	12	8	3.25	3.48
1985	SD N	27	30	1.11	244.1	97	13	14	3.58	3.40
1986	SD N	30	36	1.20	268.0	124	13	17	4.16	3.99
1987	SD N	18	19	1.06	157.1	70	11	7	4.01	4.27
9 Years		203	210	1.03	1066.0	451	58	61	3.81	3.77

Bob BOONE

Year	Team / Lg	GS	OSB	Avg.	Inn	ER	W	L	ERA	(TmERA)
1975	Phil N	81	31	.38						
1976	Phil N	97	79	.57						
1977	Phil N	119	79	.56						
1978	Phil N	117	68	.58						
1979	Phil N	110	54	.49*						
1980	Phil N	130	123	.95						
1981	Phil N	64	77	1.20						
1982	Cal A	138	48	.35*	1260.0	532	84	55	3.80	3.82
1983	Cal A	135	65	.48	1222.2	587	60	75	4.32	4.31
1984	Cal A	133	54	.41	1202.0	506	69	64	3.79	3.96
1985	Cal A	136	57	.42*	1230.1	534	75	61	3.91	3.91
1986	Cal A	137	44	.32*	1241.0	509	84	53	3.69	3.84
1987	Cal A	118	46	.39*	1063.0	515	52	66	4.36	4.38
13 Years		1515	825	.54	7219.0	3183	424	374	3.97	4.03

Scott BRADLEY

Year	Team / Lg	GS	OSB	Avg.	Inn	ER	W	L	ERA	(TmERA)
1985	NY A	3	3	1.00	25.0	11	0	3	3.96	3.69
1986	Sea A	49	32	.65	436.1	203	21	28	4.19	4.65
1987	Sea A	77	68	.88	671.0	363	36	41	4.87	4.49
3 Years		129	103	.80	1132.1	577	57	72	4.59	4.53

Bob BRENLY

Year	Team / Lg	GS	OSB	Avg.	Inn	ER	W	L	ERA	(TmERA)
1981	SF N	10	7	.70						
1982	SF N	48	53	1.10	429.0	179	24	24	3.76	3.64
1983	SF N	75	56	.75	657.2	262	33	42	3.59	3.70
1984	SF N	114	101	.89	1030.1	486	49	66	4.25	4.39
1985	SF N	102	85	.83	911.2	354	37	65	3.50	3.61
1986	SF N	78	56	.72	693.2	256	40	38	3.32	3.33
1987	SF N	100	83	.83	905.2	357	54	46	3.55	3.68
7 Years		527	441	.84	4628.0	1894	237	281	3.68	3.77

Sal BUTERA

Year	Team / Lg	GS	OSB	Avg.	Inn	ER	W	L	ERA	(TmERA)
1980	Minn A	28	16	.57						
1981	Minn A	51	23	.45						
1982	Minn A	42	29	.69	369.1	201	12	30	4.90	4.72
1983	Det A	1	1	1.00	11.0	4	1	0	3.27	3.80
1984	Mon N	1	1	1.00	8.0	4	0	1	4.50	3.31
1985	Mon N	40	42	1.05	351.2	164	19	21	4.20	3.55
1986	Cin N	33	30	.91	298.0	119	20	13	3.59	3.91
1987	Cin-Min A	43	51	1.19	364.2	227	16	27	5.61	4.62
8 years		239	193	.81	1402.2	719	68	92	4.61	4.22

Gary CARTER

Year	Team / Lg	GS	OSB	Avg.	Inn	ER	W	L	ERA	(TmERA)
1975	Mon N	55	21	.38						
1976	Mon N	54	27	.50						
1977	Mon N	142	110	.77						
1978	Mon N	147	80	.54*						
1979	Mon N	135	75	.56						
1980	Mon N	146	94	.64*						
1981	Mon N	99	53	.54*						
1982	Mon N	154	106	.69	1364.2	475	82	69	3.13	3.31
1983	Mon N	140	89	.64	1273.0	492	71	69	3.48	3.58
1984	Mon N	135	103	.76	1200.0	417	69	66	3.13	3.31
1985	Ny N	139	100	.72	1282.0	439	85	54	3.08	3.11
1986	NY N	119	115	.97	1091.0	371	77	42	3.06	3.11
1987	NY N	132	120	.91	1177.1	507	75	57	3.88	3.84
13 Years		1597	1093	8.62	7388.0	2701	459	357	3.29	3.38

Rick CERONE

Year	Team / Lg	GS	OSB	Avg.	Inn	ER	W	L	ERA	(TmERA)
1975	Cle A	3	2	.67						
1976	Cle A	4	4	1.00						
1977	Tor A	28	10	.36						
1978	Tor A	79	48	.61						
1979	Tor A	133	69	.52						
1980	NY A	146	56	.38*						
1981	NY A	65	34	.52						
1982	NY A	86	55	.64	787.2	330	41	46	3.77	3.99
1983	NY A	70	45	.67	624.0	292	38	32	4.21	3.86
1984	NY A	36	16	.44	318.1	131	19	17	3.70	3.78
1985	Atl N	78	64	.82	703.0	360	26	52	4.61	4.19
1986	Mil A	66	39	.59	594.2	309	32	34	4.68	4.02
1987	NY A	86	60	.70	775.1	384	46	40	4.46	4.36
13 Years		880	502	.57	3803.0	1806	202	221	4.28	4.07

Darren DAULTON

Year	Team / Lg	GS	OSB	Avg.	Inn	ER	W	L	ERA	(TmERA)
1983	Phil N	1	2	2.00	9.0	1	1	0	1.00	3.34
1985	Phil N	27	25	.93	238.2	120	11	16	4.53	3.68
1986	Phil N	45	54	1.20	397.1	187	22	23	4.24	3.85
1987	Phil N	34	34	1.00	300.0	128	17	17	3.84	4.18
4 Years		107	115	1.07	945.0	436	51	56	4.16	3.91

Jody DAVIS

Year	Team / Lg	GS	OSB	Avg.	Inn	ER	W	L	ERA	(TmERA)
1981	Chi N	53	38	.72						
1982	Chi N	120	93	.78	1074.2	489	56	64	4.10	3.92
1983	Chi N	140	129	.92	1232.1	567	59	81	4.14	4.08
1984	Chi N	141	119	.84	1257.2	510	88	53	3.65	3.75
1985	Chi N	129	120	.93	1147.1	544	63-65-1		4.27	4.16
1986	Chi N	142	98	.69	1274.0	636	59	82	4.49	4.49
1987	Chi N	119	124	1.04	1067.1	534	60	59	4.50	4.55
7 Years		844	721	.85	7053.1	3280	385	404	4.19	4.15

Jeffrey DeWILLIS

Year	Team / Lg	GS	OSB	Avg.	Inn	ER	W	L	ERA	(TmERA)
1987	Tor A	10	4	.40	87.2	32	5	5	3.29	3.74

Rick DEMPSEY

Year	Team / Lg	GS	OSB	Avg.	Inn	ER	W	L	ERA	(TmERA)
1975	NY A	11	8	.73						
1976	NY-Bal	59	27	.46						
1977	Bal A	84	30	.36						
1978	Bal A	130	62	.48*						
1979	Bal A	113	47	.42*						
1980	Bal A	95	50	.53						
1981	Bal A	72	32	.44						
1982	Bal A	101	46	.46	914.1	389	61	40	3.83	3.99
1983	Bal A	109	65	.60	980.0	383	68	41	3.52	3.63
1984	Bal A	104	57	.55	918.0	379	58	46	3.72	3.71
1985	Bal A	111	80	.72	985.1	498	56	55	4.55	4.38
1986	Bal A	99	68	.69	897.2	381	52	47	3.82	4.30
1987	Cle A	49	35	.71	430.2	246	19	30	5.14	5.28
13 Years		1137	607	.53	5126.0	2276	314	259	4.00	4.11

Bo DIAZ

Year	Team / Lg	GS	OSB	Avg.	Inn	ER	W	L	ERA	(TmERA)
1978	Cle A	39	23	.59						
1979	Cle A	11	11	1.00						
1980	Cle A	52	40	.77						
1981	Cle A	42	20	.48						
1982	Phil N	135	115	.85	1213.1	454	77	58	3.37	3.61
1983	Phil N	127	110	.87	1141.1	398	73-53-1		3.14	3.34
1984	Phil N	22	20	.91	194.1	63	13	9	2.92	3.62
1985	Phil-Cin	67	54	.85	607.0	239	34	33	3.54	3.70
1986	Cin N	127	103	.81	1152.0	513	65	62	4.01	3.91
1987	Cin N	130	106	.82	1166.0	534	67	63	4.12	4.24
10 Years		752	602	.80	5474.0	2201	329	278	3.62	3.76

Brian DORSETT

Year	Team / Lg	GS	OSB	Avg.	Inn	ER	W	L	ERA	(TmERA)
1987	Cle A	2	4	2.00	17.0	17	0	2	9.00	5.28

Jack FIMPLE

Year	Team / Lg	GS	OSB	Avg.	Inn	ER	W	L	ERA	(TmERA)
1983	LA N	48	34	.71	429.2	149	28-19-1		3.12	3.10
1984	La N	7	8	1.14	63.0	22	3	4	3.14	3.17
1986	LA N	4	3	.75	35.0	12	2	2	3.09	3.76
1987	Cal A	2	1	.50	16.0	10	0	2	5.62	4.38
4 Years		61	46	.75	543.2	193	33	27	3.19	3.19

Carlton FISK

Year	Team / Lg	GS	OSB	Avg.	Inn	ER	W	L	ERA	(TmERA)
1975	BOS A	68	34	.50						
1976	BOS A	130	89	.68*						
1977	BOS A	149	61	.41						
1978	Bos A	150	102	.68						
1979	Box A	34	24	.71						
1980	Box A	112	73	.65						
1981	Chi A	89	64	.72						
1982	Chi A	129	79	.61	1142.1	498	70	59	3.92	3.87
1983	Chi A	123	73	.59	1099.1	452	78	45	3.70	3.67
1984	Chi A	82	50	.61	751.1	342	36	46	4.10	4.13
1985	Chi A	119	84	.71	1064.1	459	63	53	3.88	4.07
1986	Chi A	64	54	.84	569.1	247	29	35	3.90	3.94
1987	Chi A	102	68	.67	905.1	418	51	51	4.16	4.30
13 Years		1351	855	.63	5532.0	2416	327	289	3.93	3.98

Mike FITZGERALD

Year	Team / Lg	GS	OSB	Avg.	Inn	ER	W	L	ERA	(TmERA)
1983	NY N	7	12	1.71	61.0	20	2	5	2.95	3.68
1984	NY N	101	88	.87	903.0	341	56	45	3.40	3.60
1985	Mon N	93	107	1.15	853.1	281	55	38	2.96	3.55
1986	Mon N	61	82	1.34	546.0	226	37	24	3.73	3.78
1987	Mon N	87	115	1.32	768.1	340	47	40	3.98	3.92
5 Years		349	404	1.16	3131.2	1208	197	152	3.47	3.70

Rich GEDMAN

Year	Team / Lg	GS	OSB	Avg.	Inn	ER	W	L	ERA	(TmERA)
1980	Bos A	2	2	1.00						
1981	Bos A	57	51	.89						
1982	Bos A	74	60	.81	679.2	338	37	39	4.48	4.03
1983	Box A	52	70	1.35	463.0	240	24	28	4.67	4.34
1984	Bos A	115	77	.67	1033.0	461	66	49	4.02	4.18
1985	Bos A	129	67	.52	1153.1	505	67	62	3.94	4.06
1986	Bos A	123	56	.46	1095.1	471	72	51	3.87	3.93
1987	Bos A	41	24	.59	368.1	201	19	22	4.91	4.77
8 Years		593	407	.69	4792.2	2216	285	251	4.16	4.13

Ron HASSEY

Year	Team / Lg	GS	OSB	Avg.	Inn	ER	W	L	ERA	(TmERA)
1978	Cle A	23	18	.78						
1979	Cle A	61	50	.82						
1980	Cle A	103	77	.75						
1981	Cle A	53	23	.43						
1982	Cle A	91	85	.93	837.1	342	49	42	3.68	4.11
1983	Cle A	96	62	.66	853.2	422	40	56	4.45	4.43
1984	Cle-Chi	40	29	.73	371.1	179	14	25	4.34	4.22
1985	NY A	65	51	.78	576.0	260	41	24	4.06	3.69
1986	NY-Chi	55	33	.60	489.2	213	33	22	3.92	4.03
1987	Chi A	24	23	.96	212.0	109	14	10	4.63	4.30
10 Years		611	451	.74	3340.0	1525	191	179	4.11	4.13

Mike HEATH

Year	Team / Lg	GS	OSB	Avg.	Inn	ER	W	L	ERA	(TmERA)
1978	NY A	23	12	.52						
1979	Oak A	18	13	.72						
1980	Oak A	43	23	.53						
1981	Oak A	76	34	.45						
1982	Oak A	77	37	.48	689.0	323	34	43	4.22	4.54
1983	Oak A	69	43	.62	619.1	301	33	36	4.37	4.34
1984	Oak A	95	54	.57	835.0	443	44	51	4.77	4.48
1985	Oak A	94	44	.47	829.1	470	40	54	5.10	4.41
1986	StL N	51	35	.69	478.2	195	21	30	3.67	3.37
1986	StL N	27	13	.48	237.2	107	17	10	4.05	4.02
1987	Det A	54	35	.65	484.2	223	34	20	4.14	4.02
10 Years		627	343	.55	4173.2	2062	223	244	4.45	4.25

Ed HEARN

Year	Team / Lg	GS	OSB	Avg.	Inn	ER	W	L	ERA	(TmERA)
1986	NY N	36	33	.92	328.0	130	24	12	3.57	3.11
1987	KC A	5	3	.60	44.1	11	3	2	2.24	3.86
2 Years		41	36	.88	372.1	141	27	14	3.41	3.20

Ron KARKOVICE

Year	Team / Lg	GS	OSB	Avg.	Inn	ER	W	L	ERA	(TmERA)
1986	Chi A	36	26	.74	313.1	112	17	19	3.22	3.94
1987	Chi A	31	6	.19	285.1	149	10	21	4.70	4.30
2 Years		67	32	.48	598.2	261	27	40	3.92	4.11

Bob KEARNEY

Year	Team / Lg	GS	OSB	Avg.	Inn	ER	W	L	ERA	(TmERA)
1982	Oak A	20	12	.60	180.2	89	8	12	4.43	4.54
1983	Oak A	89	46	.52	799.0	379	41	48	4.27	4.34
1984	Sea A	127	67	.53	1129.2	553	55	72	4.41	4.31
1985	Sea A	94	54	.57	831.0	451	41	53	4.88	4.68
1986	Sea A	60	39	.65	530.2	268	24	36	4.55	4.65
1987	Sea A	13	2	.15	116.0	49	8	5	3.80	4.49
6 Years		403	220	.55	3587.0	1789	177	226	4.49	4.47

Terry KENNEDY

Year	Team / Lg	GS	OSB	Avg.	Inn	ER	W	L	ERA	(TmERA)
1978	StL N	9	5	.56						
1979	StL N	27	21	.78						
1980	StL N	38	50	1.32						
1981	SD N	97	84	.87						
1982	SD N	133	102	.77	1228.1	467	70	64	3.42	3.52
1983	SD N	141	139	.99	1278.1	512	67	74	3.60	3.62
1984	SD N	141	105	.74	1266.0	492	80	61	3.50	3.48
1985	SD N	135	109	.81	1208.0	452	70	65	3.37	3.40
1986	SD N	114	102	.89	1014.1	430	54	60	3.82	3.99
1987	Balt A	135	111	.82	1201.2	676	58	77	5.06	5.01
10 Years		970	828	.85	7196.2	3029	399	401	3.79	3.83

Steve LAKE

Year	Team / Lg	GS	OSB	Avg.	Inn	ER	W	L	ERA	(TmERA)
1983	Chi N	22	23	1.05	196.1	94	12	10	4.31	4.08
1984	Chi N	15	10	.67	132.2	55	8	7	3.73	3.75
1985	Chi N	33	17	.52	295.0	124	14	19	3.78	4.16
1986	Chi N	4	8	2.00	37.0	27	3	1	6.57	4.49
1986	StL N	14	4	.29	121.2	56	7	7	4.14	3.37
1987	StL N	51	25	.49	466.1	210	32	19	4.05	3.91
5 Years		139	87	.63	1249.0	566	76	63	4.08	3.94

Tim LAUDNER

Year	Team / Lg	GS	OSB	Avg.	Inn	ER	W	L	ERA	(TmERA)
1981	Minn A	10	6	.60						
1982	Minn A	89	74	.83	790.1	421	34	55	4.79	4.72
1983	Minn A	47	53	1.13	415.2	236	18	29	5.11	4.66
1984	Minn A	75	36	.48	665.1	284	42	33	3.84	3.85
1985	Minn A	53	34	.64	466.0	240	21	32	4.64	4.48
1986	Minn A	57	32	.56	503.0	247	31	26	4.42	4.77
1987	Minn A	76	68	.89	678.1	310	47	29	4.11	4.63
7 Years		407	303	.74	3518.2	1738	193	204	4.45	4.51

Mike LAVALLIERE

Year	Team / Lg	GS	OSB	Avg.	Inn	ER	W	L	ERA	(TmERA)
1984	Phil N	2	0	.00	20.1	5	0	2	2.21	3.62
1985	StL N	11	5	.45	96.0	34	6	5	3.19	3.10
1986	StL N	93	50	.54	838.0	289	50	43	3.10	3.37
1987	Pitt N	99	70	.71	885.1	386	53	46	3.92	4.20
4 Years		205	125	.61	1839.2	714	109	96	3.49	3.77

William LINDSEY

Year	Team / Lg	GS	OSB	Avg.	Inn	ER	W	L	ERA	(TmERA)
1987	Chi A	5	1	.20	45.0	15	2	3	3.00	4.30

Dwight LOWRY

Year	Team / Lg	GS	OSB	Avg.	Inn	ER	W	L	ERA	(TmERA)
1984	Det A	11	8	.73	98.0	34	9	2	3.12	3.49
1986	Det A	45	30	.67	402.2	190	22	23	4.25	4.02
1987	Det A	6	8	1.33	52.0	16	4	2	2.77	4.02
3 Years		62	46	.74	552.2	240	35	27	3.91	3.93

Barry LYONS

Year	Team / Lg	GS	OSB	Avg.	Inn	ER	W	L	ERA	(TmERA)
1986	NY N	2	6	3.00	18.0	1	2	0	0.50	4.11
1987	NY N	30	41	1.37	276.2	114	17	13	3.71	3.84
2 Years		32	47	1.47	294.2	115	19	13	3.51	3.86

Scotti MADISON

Year	Team / Lg	GS	OSB	Avg.	Inn	ER	W	L	ERA	(TmERA)
1987	KC A	3	5	1.67	27.0	7	3	0	2.33	3.86

Kurt MANWARING

Year	Team / Lg	GS	OSB	Avg.	Inn	ER	W	L	ERA	(TmERA)
1987	SF N	1	1	1.00	9.0	3	1	0	3.00	3.68

John MARZANO

Year	Team / Lg	GS	OSB	Avg.	Inn	ER	W	L	ERA	(TmERA)
1987	Bos A	48	32	.67	421.2	183	27	21	3.91	4.77

Lloyd McCLENDON

Year	Team / Lg	GS	OSB	Avg.	Inn	ER	W	L	ERA	(TmERA)
1987	Cin A	6	5	.83	54.0	48	2	4	8.00	4.24

Mike MACFARLANE

Year	Team / Lg	GS	OSB	Avg.	Inn	ER	W	L	ERA	(TmERA)
1987	KC A	7	4	.57	60.0	18	2	5	2.70	3.86

Terry McGRIFF

Year	Team / Lg	GS	OSB	Avg.	Inn	ER	W	L	ERA	(TmERA)
1987	Cin A	23	23	1.00	206.1	86	13	10	3.75	4.24

Bob MELVIN

Year	Team / Lg	GS	OSB	Avg.	Inn	ER	W	L	ERA	(TmERA)
1985	Det A	25	19	.76	226.1	83	12	13	3.30	3.78
1986	SF N	76	68	.89	688.2	263	39	37	3.44	3.33
1987	SF N	60	48	.80	547.1	239	35	25	3.93	3.68
3 Years		161	135	.84	1462.1	585	86	75	3.60	3.53

Darrell MILLER

Year	Team / Lg	GS	OSB	Avg.	Inn	ER	W	L	ERA	(TmERA)
1986	Cal A	3	4	1.33	25.0	16	1	2	5.76	3.84
1987	Cal A	17	7	.41	152.0	101	6	11	5.98	4.38
2 Years		20	11	.55	177.0	117	7	13	5.95	4.30

Orlando MERCADO

Year	Team / Lg	GS	OSB	Avg.	Inn	ER	W	L	ERA	(TmERA)
1982	Sea A	5	3	.60	43.0	17	3	2	3.56	3.88
1983	Sea A	59	54	.92	523.1	254	23	36	4.37	4.12
1984	Sea A	21	13	.62	185.1	85	9	12	4.13	4.31
1986	Tex A	31	25	.81	284.1	100	21	10	3.17	4.11
1987	Det A	8	5	.62	73.1	35	0	8	4.30	4.02
1987	LA N	1	1	1.00	9.0	3	1	0	3.00	3.72
5 Years		125	101	.81	1118.1	494	57	68	3.98	4.13

Charlie MOORE

Year	Team / Lg	GS	OSB	Avg.	Inn	ER	W	L	ERA	(TmERA)
1975	Mil A	40	29	.72						
1976	Mil A	46	44	.96						
1977	Mil A	118	81	.69						
1978	Mil A	74	36	.49						
1979	Mil A	89	61	.69						
1980	Mil A	78	39	.50						
1981	Mil A	29	18	.62						
1982	Mil A	17	5	.29	139.0	61	9	6	3.95	3.98
1984	Mil A	4	6	1.50	36.0	21	1	3	5.25	4.06
1985	Mil A	96	58	.60	861.0	413	43	53	4.32	4.39
1986	Mil A	63	31	.49	551.1	204	33	30	3.33	4.02
1987	Tor A	34	31	.91	304.2	155	14	20	4.58	3.74
12 Years		688	439	.64	1892.0	854	100	112	4.06	4.14

Greg MYERS

Year	Team / Lg	GS	OSB	Avg.	Inn	ER	W	L	ERA	(TmERA)
1987	Tor A	2	0	0.00	19.1	4	0	2	1.88	3.74

Jerry NARRON

Year	Team / Lg	GS	OSB	Avg.	Inn	ER	W	L	ERA	(TmERA)
1979	NY A	29	18	.62						
1980	Sea A	29	20	.69						
1981	Sea A	58	45	.78						
1983	Cal A	3	3	1.00	28.0	3	1	2	0.96	4.31
1984	Cal A	29	17	.59	256.0	135	12	17	4.75	3.96
1985	Cal A	26	17	.65	227.0	99	15	11	3.93	3.91
1986	Cal A	22	13	.59	190.0	96	7	13	4.55	3.84
1987	Sea A	2	3	1.50	18.0	7	2	0	3.50	4.49
8 Years		198	136	.69	719.0	340	37	43	4.26	3.94

Carl NICHOLS

Year	Team / Lg	GS	OSB	Avg.	Inn	ER	W	L	ERA	(TmERA)
1986	Bal A	2	2	1.00	17.0	7	1	1	3.71	4.30
1987	Bal A	7	8	1.14	60.2	26	3	4	3.86	5.01
2 Years		9	10	1.11	77.2	33	4	5	3.82	4.85

Tom NIETO

Year	Team / Lg	GS	OSB	Avg.	Inn	ER	W	L	ERA	(TmERA)
1984	StL N	28	20	.71	248.1	101	12	16	3.66	3.58
1985	StL N	83	58	.70	751.1	263	53	30	3.15	3.10
1986	Mon N	20	35	1.75	1.82.2	83	8	12	4.09	3.78
1987	Minn A	36	38	1.06	320.2	157	19	17	4.41	4.63
4 Years		167	151	.90	1503.0	604	92	75	3.62	3.59

Matt NOKES

Year	Team / Lg	GS	OSB	Avg.	Inn	ER	W	L	ERA	(TmERA)
1985	SF N	13	21	1.62	117.1	59	4	9	4.53	3.61
1986	Det A	7	3	.43	62.0	24	3	4	3.48	4.02
1987	Det A	94	68	.72	846.0	377	60	34	4.01	4.02
3 Years		114	92	.81	1025.1	460	67	47	4.04	3.97

Charlie O'BRIEN

Year	Team / Lg	GS	OSB	Avg.	Inn	ER	W	L	ERA	(TmERA)
1985	Oak A	2	0	0.00	22.0	6	1	1	2.45	4.41
1987	Mil A	10	5	.50	91.2	46	0	10	4.54	4.62
2 Years		12	5	.42	113.2	52	1	11	4.12	4.59

Junior ORTIZ

Year	Team / Lg	GS	OSB	Avg.	Inn	ER	W	L	ERA	(TmERA)
1982	Pitt N	4	2	.50	38.0	15	2	2	3.55	3.81
1983	Pitt-NY	58	68	1.17	520.1	226	27	31	3.91	3.67
1984	NY N	25	26	1.04	226.0	77	16	9	3.07	3.60
1985	Pitt N	23	19	.83	198.1	128	5	18	5.82	3.97
1986	Pitt N	29	28	.97	261.2	109	12	17	3.75	3.90
1987	Pitt N	55	55	1.00	490.1	258	23	32	4.74	4.20
6 Years		194	198	1.02	1734.2	813	85	109	4.22	3.89

Larry OWEN

Year	Team / Lg	GS	OSB	Avg.	Inn	ER	W	L	ERA	(TmERA)
1981	Atl N	5	8	1.60						
1983	Atl N	2	1	.50						
1985	Atl N	19	22	1.16	182.0	73	12	7	3.61	4.19
1987	KC A	59	34	.58	516.1	231	27	32	4.03	3.86
4 Years		85	65	.76	698.1	304	39	39	3.92	3.94

Tom PAGNOZZI

Year	Team / Lg	GS	OSB	Avg.	Inn	ER	W	L	ERA	(TmERA)
1987	StL N	9	3	.33	80.0	34	7	2	3.83	3.91

Mark PARENT

Year	Team / Lg	GS	OSB	Avg.	Inn	ER	W	L	ERA	(TmERA)
1986	SD N	3	8	2.67	26.1	12	0	3	4.10	3.99
1987	SD N	4	1	.25	34.1	13	1	3	3.41	4.27
2 Years		7	9	1.29	60.2	25	1	6	3.71	4.15

Lance PARRISH

Year	Team / Lg	GS	OSB	Avg.	Inn	ER	W	L	ERA	(TmERA)
1978	Det A	74	31	.42						
1979	Det A	135	71	.53						
1980	Det A	114	56	.49						
1981	Det A	88	44	.50						
1982	Det A	127	51	.40	1133.0	493	61	66	3.92	3.80
1983	Det A	125	56	.45*	1112.2	480	68	57	3.88	3.80
1984	Det A	124	44	.35*	1127.0	415	83	41	3.31	3.49
1985	Det A	118	61	.52	1071.2	465	66	52	3.91	3.78
1986	Det A	82	40	.49	733.1	316	45	37	3.88	4.02
1987	Phil N	123	139	1.13	1103.1	520	61	62	4.24	4.18
10 Years		1110	593	.53	6281.0	2689	384	315	3.85	3.83

Tony PENA

Year	Team / Lg	GS	OSB	Avg.	Inn	ER	W	L	ERA	(TmERA)
1980	Pitt N	5	6	1.20						
1981	Pitt N	54	28	.52						
1982	Pitt N	127	78	.61	1143.2	501	67	59	3.94	3.81
1983	Pitt N	144	116	.81	1303.1	478	80	64	3.30	3.55
1984	Pitt N	139	97	.70	1262.0	428	65	74	3.05	3.11
1985	Pitt N	138	86	.62	1247.0	510	52	86	3.68	3.97
1986	Pitt N	132	108	.82	1181.0	512	52	80	3.90	3.90
1987	StL N	102	71	.70	919.2	398	56	46	3.89	3.91
8 Years		841	590	.70	7056.2	2827	372	409	3.61	3.69

Geno PETRALLI

Year	Team / Lg	GS	OSB	Avg.	Inn	ER	W	L	ERA	(TmERA)
1982	Tor A	9	6	.67	83.0	34	6	3	3.69	3.95
1985	Tex A	32	32	1.00	280.2	177	8	24	5.68	4.56
1986	Tex A	22	18	.82	195.1	93	14	8	4.28	4.11
1987	Tex A	50	65	1.30	436.2	217	21	29	4.47	4.63
4 Years		112	121	3.87	995.2	521	49	64	4.71	4.45

Darrell PORTER

Year	Team / Lg	GS	OSB	Avg.	Inn	ER	W	L	ERA	(TmERA)
1975	Mil A	120	86	.72						
1976	Mil A	105	87	.83						
1977	KC A	121	60	.50						
1978	KC A	141	76	.53						
1979	KC A	141	64	.45						
1980	KC A	80	39	.49						
1981	StL N	51	41	.80						
1982	StL N	108	94	.87	980.1	366	62	46	3.36	3.37
1983	StL N	121	63	.62*	1093.2	476	58	63	3.92	3.79
1984	StL N	116	94	.81	1045.1	429	63	53	3.69	3.58
1985	StL N	65	39	.60	590.2	197	41	24	3.00	3.10
1986	Tex A	22	32	1.45	201.0	89	10	12	3.99	4.11
1987	Tex A	1	1	1.00	9.0	6	1	0	6.00	4.63
13 Years		1192	776	.65	3920.1	1563	235	198	3.59	3.54

Tom PRINCE

Year	Team / Lg	GS	OSB	Avg.	Inn	ER	W	L	ERA	(TmERA)
1987	Pitt N	3	3	1.00	25.1	9	1	2	3.20	4.20

Jamie QUIRK

Year	Team / Lg	GS	OSB	Avg.	Inn	ER	W	L	ERA	(TmERA)
1979	KC A	2	1	.50						
1980	KC A	11	13	1.18						
1981	KC A	15	13	.87						
1982	KC A	14	11	.79	125.0	62	6	8	4.46	4.08
1983	StL N	16	23	1.44	142.0	66	6	10	4.18	3.79
1985	KC A	15	11	.73	134.0	52	9	6	3.49	3.49
1986	KC A	38	16	.42	339.2	132	20	18	3.50	3.82
1987	KC A	88	77	.88	776.1	344	48	40	3.99	3.86
8 Years		199	165	.83	1517.0	656	89	82	3.89	3.83

Floyd RAYFORD

Year	Team / Lg	GS	OSB	Avg.	Inn	ER	W	L	ERA	(TmERA)
1984	Bal A	50	35	.70	453.1	178	25	25	3.53	3.71
1985	Bal A	23	18	.78	201.1	76	12	11	3.40	4.38
1986	Bal A	5	5	1.00	44.0	29	4	1	5.93	4.30
1987	Bal A	13	15	1.15	115.1	67	4	9	5.23	5.01
4 Years		91	73	.80	814.0	350	45	46	3.87	4.10

Jeff REED

Year	Team / Lg	GS	OSB	Avg.	Inn	ER	W	L	ERA	(TmERA)
1984	Minn A	7	6	.86	60.0	31	3	4	4.65	3.85
1985	Minn A	2	2	1.00	17.0	3	1	1	1.59	4.48
1986	Minn A	49	36	.73	440.2	239	20	29	4.88	4.77
1987	Mon A	61	68	1.11	558.0	231	37	24	3.73	3.92
4 Years		119	112	.94	1075.2	504	61	58	4.22	4.28

Ronn REYNOLDS

Year	Team / Lg	GS	OSB	Avg.	Inn	ER	W	L	ERA	(TmERA)
1982	NY N	2	1	.50	17.0	7	0	2	3.71	3.88
1983	NY N	23	28	1.22	200.0	80	8	15	3.60	3.68
1985	NY N	11	8	.73	102.0	36	7	4	3.18	3.11
1986	Phil N	35	47	1.34	305.0	112	20	15	3.30	3.85
1987	Hous N	30	40	1.33	268.2	114	13	17	3.82	3.84
5 Years		101	124	1.23	892.2	349	48	53	3.52	3.73

John RUSSELL

Year	Team / Lg	GS	OSB	Avg.	Inn	ER	W	L	ERA	(TmERA)
1986	Phil N	81	115	1.42	749.1	322	44	37	3.87	3.85
1987	Phil N	5	11	2.20	45.0	25	2	3	5.00	4.18
2 Years		86	126	1.47	794.1	347	46	40	3.93	3.87

Mark SALAS

Year	Team / Lg	GS	OSB	Avg.	Inn	ER	W	L	ERA	(TmERA)
1984	StL N	2	4	2.00	17.0	4	1	1	2.12	3.58
1985	Minn A	95	58	.61	839.1	424	48	47	4.55	4.48
1986	Minn A	56	42	.75	489.0	273	20	36	5.02	4.77
1987	NY-Minn	40	39	.97	353.0	198	21	19	5.05	4.44
4 Years		193	143	.74	1698.1	899	90	103	4.76	4.55

Benito SANTIAGO

Year	Team / Lg	GS	OSB	Avg.	Inn	ER	W	L	ERA	(TmERA)
1986	SD N	15	11	.73	134.2	74	7	8	4.95	3.99
1987	SD N	140	103	.74	1241.2	599	53	87	4.43	4.27
2 Years		155	114	.74	1376.1	673	60	95	4.40	4.24

Mackey SASSER

Year	Team / Lg	GS	OSB	Avg.	Inn	ER	W	L	ERA	(TmERA)
1987	Pitt-SF	4	3	.75	36.0	16	3	1	4.00	3.94

Bill SCHROEDER

Year	Team / Lg	GS	OSB	Avg.	Inn	ER	W	L	ERA	(TmERA)
1983	Mil A	22	17	.77	203.0	85	15	7	3.77	4.02
1984	Mil A	58	50	.86	512.1	239	26	32	4.20	4.06
1985	Mil A	46	39	.85	407.0	194	19	27	4.29	4.39
1986	Mil A	32	25	.78	285.2	126	12	20	3.97	4.02
1987	Mil A	63	50	.79	562.2	311	37	26	4.97	4.62
5 Years		221	181	.82	1970.2	955	109	112	4.36	4.28

Mike SCIOSCIA

Year	Team / Lg	GS	OSB	Avg.	Inn	ER	W	L	ERA	(TmERA)
1980	LA N	44	49	1.11						
1981	LA N	87	64	.74						
1982	LA N	107	84	.79	984.0	371	57	50	3.39	3.26
1983	LA N	10	3	.30	93.2	34	8	2	3.27	3.10
1984	LA N	101	75	.74	914.2	300	55	46	2.95	3.17
1985	LA N	130	81	.62	1178.0	380	78	52	2.90	2.96
1986	LA N	108	79	.73	970.0	403	51	57	3.74	3.76
1987	LA N	128	94	.73	1156.0	451	61	67	3.51	3.72
8 Years		715	529	.74	5296.1	1939	310	274	3.30	3.37

Danny SHEAFER

Year	Team / Lg	GS	OSB	Avg.	Inn	ER	W	L	ERA	(TmERA)
1987	Bos A	19	15	.79	173.0	87	7	12	4.53	4.77

Ted SIMMONS

Year	Team / Lg	GS	OSB	Avg.	Inn	ER	W	L	ERA	(TmERA)
1975	StL N	148	99	.67						
1976	StL N	107	62	.58						
1977	StL N	139	96	.69						
1978	StL N	119	120	1.01						
1979	StL N	118	100	.85						
1980	StL N	121	116	.96						
1981	Mil A	73	47	.64						
1982	Mil A	119	94	.79	1077.1	456	72	47	3.81	3.98
1983	Mil A	84	84	1.00	749.1	321	41	43	3.86	4.02
1985	Mil A	11	8	.73	100.0	57	6	5	5.13	4.39
1986	Atl N	5	13	2.60	45.0	28	1	4	5.60	3.97
1987	Atl N	14	15	1.07	123.0	49	9	5	3.59	4.63
12 Years		1058	854	.81	2094.2	911	129	104	3.91	4.05

Joel SKINNER

Year	Team / Lg	GS	OSB	Avg.	Inn	ER	W	L	ERA	(TmERA)
1983	Chi A	2	2	1.00	18.0	0	2	0	0.00	3.67
1984	Chi A	23	19	.83	201.1	76	12	11	3.40	4.13
1985	Chi A	15	11	.73	132.1	59	8	7	4.01	4.07
1986	Chi A	49	30	.61	444.1	216	21	28	4.38	3.94
1986	NY A	52	24	.46	461.1	203	28	24	3.96	4.11
1987	NY A	46	32	.70	407.2	175	27	19	3.86	4.36
5 Years		187	118	.63	1665.0	729	98	89	3.94	4.05

Don SLAUGHT

Year	Team / Lg	GS	OSB	Avg.	Inn	ER	W	L	ERA	(TmERA)
1982	KC A	32	12	.38	285.2	141	15	17	4.44	4.08
1983	KC A	73	48	.66	646.1	307	37	36	4.27	4.25
1984	KC A	112	65	.58	1007.2	426	60	52	3.80	3.92
1985	Tex A	97	55	.57	852.1	412	38	59	4.35	4.56
1986	Tex A	85	89	1.05	751.2	369	42	43	4.42	4.11
1987	Tex A	55	64	1.16	505.1	245	26	29	4.36	4.63
6 Years		454	333	.73	4049.0	1900	218	236	4.22	4.24

Mike STANLEY

Year	Team / Lg	GS	OSB	Avg.	Inn	ER	W	L	ERA	(TmERA)
1986	Tex A	2	1	.50	18.0	11	0	2	5.50	4.11
1987	Tex A	56	75	1.34	493.1	275	27	29	5.02	4.63
2 Years		58	76	1.31	511.1	286	27	31	5.03	4.61

Matt STARK

Year	Team / Lg	GS	OSB	Avg.	Inn	ER	W	L	ERA	(TmERA)
1987	Tor A	3	6	2.00	30.0	6	2	1	1.80	3.74

John STEFARO

Year	Team / Lg	GS	OSB	Avg.	Inn	ER	W	L	ERA	(TmERA)
1983	Bal A	1	0	0.00	9.0	8	0	1	8.00	3.63
1986	Bal A	41	36	.88	343.0	189	10	31	4.96	4.30
1987	Mon N	14	17	1.21	124.0	59	7	7	4.28	3.92
3 Years		56	53	.95	476.0	256	17	39	4.84	4.19

Terry STEINBACH

Year	Team / Lg	GS	OSB	Avg.	Inn	ER	W	L	ERA	(TmERA)
1987	Oak A	97	62	.64	863.2	446	46	51	4.65	4.32

Marc SULLIVAN

Year	Team / Lg	GS	OSB	Avg.	Inn	ER	W	L	ERA	(TmERA)
1984	Bos A	2	1	.50	17.0	18	1	1	9.53	4.18
1985	Bos A	23	13	.57	211.2	113	9	13	4.80	4.06
1986	Bos A	36	22	.61	316.1	148	22	14	4.21	3.93
1987	Bos A	54	38	.70	473.0	290	25	29	5.52	4.77
4 Years		114	74	.65	1018.0	569	57	57	5.03	4.35

Jim SUNDBERG

Year	Team / Lg	GS	OSB	Avg.	Inn	ER	W	L	ERA	(TmERA)
1975	Tex A	149	78	.52						
1976	Tex A	134	98	.73						
1977	Tex A	136	47	.35*						
1978	Tex A	146	74	.51						
1979	Tex A	144	74	.51						
1980	Tex A	147	101	.69						
1981	Tex A	97	40	.41*						
1982	Tex A	129	74	.57	1137.2	554	49	80	4.38	4.28
1983	Tex A	118	78	.66	1063.0	395	54	63	3.34	3.31
1984	Mil A	99	40	.40	885.0	386	40	59	3.93	4.06
1985	KC A	107	60	.56	969.1	372	61	46	3.45	3.49
1986	KC A	124	70	.56	1101.0	480	56	68	3.92	3.82
1987	CHI N	35	37	1.06	307.1	147	14	21	4.30	4.55
13 Years		1565	871	.56	5463.1	2334	274	337	3.84	3.84

B. J. SURHOFF

Year	Team / Lg	GS	OSB	Avg.	Inn	ER	W	L	ERA	(TmERA)
1987	Mil A	89	64	.72	809.2	393	54	35	4.37	4.62

Mickey TETTLETON

Year	Team / Lg	GS	OSB	Avg.	Inn	ER	W	L	ERA	(TmERA)
1984	Oak A	22	8	.36	198.0	86	10	12	3.91	4.48
1985	Oak A	66	60	.91	601.2	236	36	30	3.53	4.41
1986	Oak A	75	57	.76	660.0	293	36	39	4.00	4.31
1987	Oak A	65	54	.83	582.0	260	35	30	4.02	4.32
4 Years		228	179	.79	2041.2	875	117	111	3.86	4.36

Alejandro TREVINO

Year	Team / Lg	GS	OSB	Avg.	Inn	ER	W	L	ERA	(TmERA)
1978	NY N	3	0	.00						
1979	NY N	33	22	.67						
1980	NY N	78	58	.74						
1981	NY N	37	17	.46						
1982	Cin N	103	89	.86	936.1	346	44	59	3.33	3.66
1983	Cin N	51	40	.78	458.2	186	24	27	3.65	3.98
1984	Atl N	65	68	1.05	577.1	238	35	30	3.71	3.57
1985	SF N	47	37	.79	419.0	170	22	25	3.65	3.61
1986	LA N	50	39	.78	449.1	193	20	30	3.87	3.76
1987	LA N	33	24	.73	290.0	147	11	22	4.56	3.72
10 Years		500	394	.79	3130.2	1280	156	193	3.68	3.70

Dave VALLE

Year	Team / Lg	GS	OSB	Avg.	Inn	ER	W	L	ERA	(TmERA)
1984	Sea A	7	3	.42	65.0	16	6	1	2.22	4.31
1985	Sea A	19	15	.79	162.0	100	7	12	5.56	4.68
1986	Sea A	9	6	.67	80.0	55	3	6	6.19	4.65
1987	Sea A	70	40	.57	625.2	294	32	38	4.23	4.49
4 Years		105	64	.61	932.2	465	48	57	4.49	4.53

David VAN GORDER

Year	Team / Lg	GS	OSB	Avg.	Inn	ER	W	L	ERA	(TmERA)
1982	Cin N	45	50	1.11	397.0	181	14	31	4.10	3.66
1984	Cin N	31	29	.94	271.2	136	6	25	4.51	4.16
1985	Cin N	42	29	.69	379.2	172	24	18	4.08	3.71
1986	Cin N	2	2	1.00	18.0	6	1	1	3.00	3.91
1987	Bal A	7	11	1.57	62.0	32	2	5	4.65	5.01
5 Years		127	121	.95	1128.1	527	47	80	4.20	3.88

Ozzie VIRGIL

Year	Team / Lg	GS	OSB	Avg.	Inn	ER	W	L	ERA	(TmERA)
1982	Phil N	26	32	1.23	234.0	130	11	15	5.00	3.61
1983	Phil N	35	53	1.51	311.1	145	16	19	4.19	3.34
1984	Phil N	124	105	.85	1108.2	452	64	60	3.67	3.62
1985	Phil N	115	118	1.03	1024.1	397	57	58	3.49	3.68
1986	Atl N	107	137	1.28	953.2	407	51	56	3.84	3.97
1987	Atl N	119	137	1.15	1058.2	555	50	69	4.72	4.63
6 Years		526	582	1.11	4690.2	2086	249	277	4.00	3.91

Ernie WHITT

Year	Team / Lg	GS	OSB	Avg.	Inn	ER	W	L	ERA	(TmERA)
1978	Tor A	1	0	0						
1979	Tor A	92	73	.79						
1981	Tor A	60	28	.47						
1982	Tor A	74	43	.58	674.0	301	37	39	4.02	3.95
1983	Tor A	95	51	.54	854.0	406	53	42	4.28	4.12
1984	Tor A	97	51	.53	885.0	402	51	46	4.09	3.86
1985	Tor A	113	55	.49	1015.2	363	73	40	3.22	3.31
1986	Tor A	109	62	.57	985.0	449	60	49	4.10	4.08
1987	Tor A	113	81	.72	1012.1	408	75	38	3.63	3.74
9 Years		754	444	.59	5426.0	2329	349	254	3.86	3.83

Robbie WINE

Year	Team / Lg	GS	OSB	Avg.	Inn	ER	W	L	ERA	(TmERA)
1986	Hous N	1	2	2.00	9.0	0	1	0	0.00	3.15
1987	Hous N	8	11	1.38	69.0	24	3	5	3.13	3.84
2 Years		9	13	1.44	78.0	24	4	5	2.77	3.76

Butch WYNEGAR

Year	Team / Lg	GS	OSB	Avg.	Inn	ER	W	L	ERA	(TmERA)
1976	Minn A	133	124	.93						
1977	Minn A	138	80	.58						
1978	Minn A	121	72	.6						
1979	Minn A	141	60	.43						
1980	Minn A	133	60	.45						
1981	Minn A	36	29	.81						
1982	Minn-NY	82	57	.70	722.1	360	40	42	4.49	4.18
1983	NY A	84	59	.70	759.2	301	48	36	3.57	3.86
1984	NY A	117	69	.59	1054.2	437	65	52	3.73	3.78
1985	NY A	90	54	.50	813.1	310	54	36	3.43	3.69
1986	NY A	52	35	.67	465.2	225	27	25	4.35	4.11
1987	Cal A	25	17	.68	226.1	83	17	8	3.30	4.38
12 Years		1152	716	.62	4042	1716	251	199	3.82	3.92

A GLOSSARY OF TERMS IN USE IN SABERMETRICS

Adjusted Range Factor

The number of plays made by a player per estimated nine innings of defensive play.

Approximate Value

A crude integer estimate of the value of a given season, ranging from 0 for ineffective, part-time play up to an average of 9 or 10 for a regular player, 16 to 20 for an MVP-type season.

Award Share

The total MVP Award vote drawn by a player over the course of his career, stated in constant terms with 1.00 representing the potential vote for one season. (Award Shares could also be calculated for a few other awards, such as the Cy Young.)

Base-Out Percentage

A method developed by Barry Codell for the evaluation of offensive statistics; quite similar to total average.

Brock System

Any of a series of systems which involve a complex set of several hundred interlocking formulas, designed to project a player's final career totals on the basis of his accomplishments to this point of his career.

Career Value

The value of a player to his team over the course of his entire career; also called Gross Value.

Cheap Win

Any game in which the starting pitcher is credited with a victory despite a game score below 50.

Defensive Efficiency Record

A mathematical attempt to answer this question: Of all balls put into play against this team, what percentage did the defense succeed in turning into outs?

Defensive Spectrum

An arrangement of defensive positions according to raw abilities needed to learn to play each. The spectrum has shifted at times throughout history, but generally reads "designated hitter, first base, left field, right field, third base, center field, second base, shortstop." Catcher is not a part of the spectrum.

Defensive Winning Percentage

A technique of evaluation of defensive statistics by a series of charts, resulting in a two-digit percentage estimate. An average defensive player should have a defensive winning percentage of .50.

Established Performance Levels

A player's Established Performance Level is the level of performance in an area which the player has clearly established the ability to maintain.

Estimated Runs Produced

A method developed by Paul Johnson to estimate the number of runs resulting from any combination of offensive incidents. Closely parallels runs created.

Expected Remaining Future Value

Also called "Trade Value."

The Favorite Toy

A method used to estimate the chance that a player, at a given point in his career, will reach some standard of career excellence (such as 3000 hits, 500 home runs).

Game Scores

A method used to evaluate each start by a pitcher on a scale of zero to a hundred, thus focusing on the pitcher's best and worst starts.

Gross Value

The sum of the approximate values for a player over the course of his career.

Hall of Fame Assessment System

A method used to evaluate whether a player is doing or has done the things which characterize Hall of Famers.

Indicated ERA

A method of guessing what pitcher's ERA might be based on the two categories for which he is wholly responsible—home runs allowed and walks.

Isolated Power

The difference between batting average and slugging percentage.

Johnson Effect

The tendency of teams that exceed their Pythagorean projection for wins in one season to relapse in the following season. Parallel effects have also been established for the tendency of teams that violate the normal relationship between offensive incidents and runs resulting; these are also sometimes referred to as Johnson Effects.

Linear Weights

A common mathematical tool used to derive the value of each element within a data set, and thus produce formulas that can combine those values. Commonly used by Pete Palmer in analyzing baseball.

Major-League Equivalency

The major-league performance that is equivalent to a given performance in the minor leagues.

Offensive Earned Run Average

A method developed by Thomas Cover to estimate the number of earned runs created by each player per 27 outs.

Offensive Losses

An estimate of the number of team losses that would result from a player's offensive production.

Offensive Winning Percentage

A mathematical answer to this question: If every player on a team hit the same way that this player hits, and the team allowed an average number of runs to score, what would the team's winning percentage be?

Offensive Wins

An estimate of the number of team wins that would result from a player's offensive production.

On-Base Percentage

If you don't know what on-base percentage is you shouldn't be reading this book.

Overall Wining Percentage

A combination of offensive and defensive winning percentages.

Palmer Method

The collective analytical procedures developed by Pete Palmer.

Park Adjustment

Any of a number of methods used to adjust offensive or defensive statistics for park illusions.

Park Illusion

The distortion of offensive or defensive abilities as reflected in statistics due to the characteristics of a given park.

Peak Value

The value of a player to his team at his highest clearly established level of performance.

Power/Speed Number

A combination of home runs and stolen bases into a single number, so designed that a player who hits 30 home runs and steals 30 bases will have a power/speed number of 30.0.

Project Scoresheet

A volunteer organization that collects and distributes scoresheets of all major-league games for the public.

Pythagorean Method

The practical application of the Pythagorean theory to derive conclusions or state relationships.

Pythagorean Theory

The name given to a known property of any baseball team, that being that the ratio between their wins and their losses will be similar to the relationship between the square of their runs scored and the square of their runs allowed.

Quality Starts

The number of starts in which a pitcher pitches six innings or more and gives up three runs or less.

Quick Hook

Any game in which a starting pitcher is removed before pitching six innings or allowing four runs.

Rachel McCarthy James

One incredibly sweet little girl.

Range Factor

The average number of plays per game successfully made by a fielder (that is, total chances per game minus errors per game).

RBI Importance

That portion of a player's runs batted which are counted as victory-important.

RBI Value

A method of assessing the value of each run batted in, developed by Tim Mulligan.

Reservoir Estimation Technique

The process of comparing a team's talent resources by figuring the "trade value" of all players on the roster.

Runs Created

An estimate of the number of team runs that would result from a player's offensive statistics; can be derived by any of a number of formulas.

Run Element Ratio

The ratio between the things a hitter does which are of use early in the inning (walks and stolen bases) and those which are more useful later in the inning (power). The formula is $(BB+SB)/(TB-H)$.

Sabermetrics

The search for objective knowledge about baseball.

SABR

The Society For American Baseball Research.

Secondary Average

The sum of a player extra bases on hits, walks and stolen bases, expressed as a percentage of at bats.

Signature Significance

The existence, rare but occasionally seen, of significant evidence about the ability of a player that can be seen in a very small sample of his work.

Similarity Scores

A method used for evaluating the "degree of resemblance" between two players or two teams.

Slow Hook

Any game in which the starting pitcher pitches more than nine innings, allows seven or more runs, or has a combination of innings pitched and runs allowed totalling 13 or more.

Speed Score

A method of evaluating a player's speed on a ten-point scaled based on his performance in six speed-related categories.

Star Value

A method of counting and weighting the star-type accomplishments of a player, such as the number of times he has had 200 hits or 100 RBI or 20 wins as a starting pitcher.

Total Average

A method developed by Thomas Boswell for the evaluation of offensive statistics.

Tough Loss

Any game in which the starting pitcher is charged with a loss despite a game score of 50 or above.

Trade Value

An estimate of the approximate value that a player will have in the rest of his career.

Victory-Important RBI (VI-RBI)

An attempt to measure the number of a player's runs which are contributions to victory.

APPENDIX

Approximate Value
and the
Value Approximation Method

The Traditional Value Approximation Method has 13 rules for non-pitchers, 5 rules for pitchers. These are:

Non-Pitchers:

1) Award 1 point if the player has played at least 10 games, 2 if 50 games, 3 if 100 games, 4 if 130 games or more.

2) Award 1 point if the player has hit .250 or better, 2 if .275, 3 if .300 . . . 7 if .400 or better.

3) Award 1 point if the player's slugging percentage is above .300, 2 if above .400 . . . 6 if above .800.

4) Award 1 point if the player has a home run percentage (home runs divided by at bats) of 2.5 or more, 2 if 5.0 or more, 3 if 7.5 or more, 4 if 10.0 or more.

5) Award 1 point if the player walks one time for each 10 official at bats, 2 if twice for each 10 at bats, 3 if three times for each ten at bats.

6) Award 1 point if the player steals 20 bases, 2 if 50 bases, 3 if 80 bases.

7) Award 1 point if the player drives in 70 runs while slugging less than .400, 1 point if he drives in 100 runs while slugging less than .500, or 1 if he drives in 130 while slugging less than .600.

8) Award 1 point if the player's primary defensive position (the position at which he plays the most games) is second base, third base, or center field; 2 if it is shortstop. For catchers, award 1 point if the player catches ten games, 2 if he catches 80, 3 if he catches 150.

9) Award 1 point if the player's range factor is above the league average at his position. Catchers and first basemen have no range factors; first basemen get 1 point if they have 100 assists.

10) Award 1 point if the player's fielding average is above the league average at his position.

On points nine and ten, if you are figuring a player over the course of his career, you will probably want to establish period norms for fielding average and range at the position, rather than trying to figure the league average for each season separately.

11) Award 1 point to a shortstop or second baseman who participates in 90 or more double plays, 2 for 120 or more, 3 for 150 or more. Award 1 point to an outfielder who has 12 or more assists plus double plays. Award 1 to a catcher who is better than the league average in opposition stolen bases per game.

12) Award 1 point if the player has 200 hits. Award 1 point if the player leads the league in RBI.

13) Reduce all points awarded on rules one through 12 for players who have fewer than 500 at bats and fewer than 550 plate appearances. Reduce by at bats divided by 500 or plate appearances divided by 550, whichever is better for the player.

Pitchers:

1) Award 1 point if the pitcher has pitched in 30 or more games, 2 if 55 or more, 3 if 80 or more.

2) Award 1 point if the pitcher has pitched 40 innings, 2 if 90 innings, 3 if 140 innings . . . 7 if 340 innings.

3) Figure for the pitcher his total of 2 (wins + saves) minus losses. Award 1 point if the pitcher's total is 6 or more, 2 if 14 or more, 3 if 24 or more, 4 if 36 or more, 5 if 50 or more, 6 if 66 or more, and 7 if 84 or more.

4) Award 1 point if the pitcher has won 18 or more games. Award 1 point if the pitcher led the league in ERA. Award 1 point if the pitcher led the league in saves.

5) Establish a mark 1.00 run above the league ERA. Subtract the pitcher's ERA from this, and multiply that by the number of decisions that the pitcher has had. Divide by 13. (What you are doing here is giving credit for a low ERA. If the pitcher's ERA is more than a run above the league average, this will result in a negative figure, a subtraction. A pitcher's approximate value can be reduced by this factor, but no player's approximate value can be reduced below zero.)

The outcome of this point-count system is called approximate value.

Brock2 System

A full account of the Brock2 system can be found on pages 301–5 of the 1985 *Baseball Abstract*.

Defensive Efficiency Record

A Defensive Efficiency Record is a team statistic, intended to estimate the percentage of all balls in play that a team has turned into outs.

To figure DER, you begin by making two estimates of the number of times that a team's defense has turned a batted ball into an out. The first is:

$$PO - K - DP - 2(TP) - OCS - A \text{ (of)}$$

This assumes that a batted ball has been turned into an out every time a putout is recorded unless 1) the putout was a strikeout, 2) two or three putouts were recorded on the same play, or 3) a runner has been thrown out on the bases. OCS is opponents caught stealing, and A (of) is outfielder's assists, both of which can be found on the division sheets.

The second estimate is:

$$TBF - K - H - W - HBP - .71 \text{ Errors}$$

This assumes that every batter facing the team's pitchers has been put out by the fielders unless 1) he strikes out, 2) he gets a hit, 3) he walks, 4) he is hit by the pitch, or 5) he reaches base on an error.

These two estimates will almost always be within 1 percent of one another, usually within .5 percent. You then take the average of the two, which is called Plays Made (PM).

DER is Plays Made divided by Plays Made Plus Plays NOT Made:

$$\frac{PM}{PM + H - HR + .71 \text{ Errors}}$$

An average defensive efficiency record is about .695. Almost all successful teams will be above average.

Defensive Winning Percentage

The exact method for deriving a defensive winning percentage is explained in the appendix to the 1983 and 1984 *Baseball Abstracts*.

Expected Remaining Approximate Value
also known as
Trade Value

Trade Value is used to assess the size of a team's talent pool, by comparing the "apparent futures" that a team has (see Minnesota comment).

The formula for this has two stages. First of all, you find the player's "Y Score" by the formula 24 − .6 (Age):

$$Y = 24 - .6 (Age)$$

The Y score and the player's approximate value are then put together by the following formula:

$$(AV - Y)^2 \times \frac{(Y + 1) \times AV}{190} + \frac{AV (Y)^2}{13}$$

The Favorite Toy

The Favorite Toy is a method that is used to estimate a player's chance of getting to a specific goal—let us say, 3000 hits.

Four things are considered in this matter. Those are:

1) The Need Hits—the number of hits needed to reach the goal. (This, of course, could also be "Need Home Runs" or "Need Doubles"—Whatever.)

2) The Years Remaining. The number of years remaining to reach the goal is estimated by the formula 24 − .6 (age). This formula assigns a 20-year-old player 12.0 remaining seasons, a 25-year-old player 9.0 remaining seasons, a 30-year-old player 6.0 remaining seasons, and a 35-year-old player 3.0 remaining seasons. Any player who is still playing regularly is assumed to have at least 1.5 seasons remaining, regardless of his age.

3) The Established Hit Level. For 1984, the established hit level would be found by adding 1982 hits, two times 1983 hits, and three times 1984 hits, and dividing by six. However, a player cannot have an established performance level that is less than three-fourths or his most recent performance—that is, a player who had 200 hits in 1984 cannot have an established hit level below 150.00.

4) The Projected Remaining Hits. This is found by multiplying the second number, the years remaining, by the third, the established hit level.

Once you get the projected remaining hits, the chance of getting to the goal is figured by (projected remaining hits) divided by (need hits), minus .5. By this method, if your "need hits" and your "projected remaining hits" are the same, your chance of reaching the goal is 50 percent. If your projected remaining hits are 20 percent more than your need hits, the chance of reaching the goal is 70 percent.

Two special rules:

1) A player's chance of continuing to progress toward a goal cannot exceed .97 per year. (This rule prevents a player from figuring to have a 148% chance of reaching a goal.)

2) If a player's offensive winning percentage is below .500, his chance of continuing to progress toward the goal cannot exceed .75 per season. (That is, if a below-average hitter is two years away from reaching a goal, his chance of reaching that goal cannot be shown as better than nine-sixteenths, or three-fourths times three-fourths, regardless of his age.)

Game Score

To figure a pitcher's game score in a game:
1) Start with 50.
2) Add 1 point for each out recorded by the starting pitcher.
3) Add 2 points for each inning the pitcher completes after the fourth inning.
4) Add 1 point for each strikeout.

5) Subtract 2 points for each hit given up.
6) Subtract 4 points for each earned run allowed.
7) Subtract 2 points for an unearned run.
8) Subtract 1 point for each walk.

Runs Created

There are three forms of the runs created formula. All three have an A factor, a B factor, and a C factor; in all cases the formula is assembled by (A times B) divided by C. These are the three versions:

1. Basic Runs Created

   A   Hits Plus Walks
       (H + W)
   B   Total Bases
       (TB)
   C   At Bats Plus Walks
       (AB + W)

2. Stolen Base Version

   A   Hits Plus Walks Minus Caught Stealing
       (H + W − CS)
   B   Total Bases Plus (.55 times Stolen Bases)
       (TB + .55SB)
   C   At Bats Plus Walks
       (AB + W)

3. Technical Version

   A   Hits Plus Walks and Hit Batsmen Minus Caught Stealing and Grounded Into Double Plays
       (H + W + HBP − CS − GIDP)
   B   Total Bases Plus .26 Times Hit Batsmen and Unintentional Walks Plus .52 Times Sacrifice Hits, Sacrifice Flies, And Stolen Bases
       (TB + .26 (TBB − IBB + HBP) + .52 (SH + SF + SB))
   C   At Bats Plus Walks Plus Hit Batsmen Plus Sacrifice Hits Plus Sacrifice Flies
       (AB + TBB + HBP + SH + SF)

Offensive Winning Percentage

To figure offensive winning percentage:
1) Figure runs created per 27 outs.
2) Divide by the league average of runs per game.
3) Square the result.
4) Divide that figure by one plus itself.

If done for a league, this will produce a figure above .500. If done for a player who is average in every respect, it will produce a figure of .500. If done for a player who is above average, it will produce a figure above .500.

Speed Scores

To figure speed scores, start with the player's record over the last two seasons combined. With that record, you figure six elements of the speed score:

1) The stolen base percentage. Figure the score here as $((SB+3)/(SB+CS+7) - .4) * 20$.

2) The frequency of stolen base attempts. Figure the score here as $(SB+CS)/(Singles+BB+HBP)$. Take the square root of that, and divide that by .07. If a player attempts to steal one-tenth of the time when he is on first base, you take the square root of .10 (.316) and divide that by .07, yielding a speed score of 4.52.

3) Triples. Figure the player's triples as a percentage of balls

in play $(3B)/(AB - HR - SO)$. From this assign an integer from 0 to 10, based on the following chart:

Less than .001	0
.001–.0023	1
.0023–.0039	2
.0039–.0058	3
.0058–.0080	4
.0080–.0105	5
.0105–.013	6
.013–.0158	7
.0158–.0189	8
.0189–.0223	9
.0223 or higher	10

4) The number of runs scores as a percentage of times on base. Figure first the percentage as $(R - HR)/(H + HBP + BB - HR)$. From this subtract .1, and then divide by .04. Thus, if a player has 150 hits, 5 hit by pitch and 95 walks, hits 30 home runs and scores 100 runs, you would figure $(100 - 30)/(150 + 5 + 95 - 30)$, or $^{70}\!/_{220}$, which is .318. Subtract .1, and you have .218. Divide by .04, and his speed score on this point would be 5.45.

5) The frequency of grounding into double play. The formula here is $((.055 - (gdp/(ab - hr - so))/.005)$.

6) Range factor. If the player is a catcher, his speed score on this point is 1; if a first baseman, 2; if a designated hitter, 1.5. If he plays second base, then his speed score element six is 1.25 times his range factor; if third base, 1.51 times his range factor; if shortstop, 1.52 times his range factor; if the outfield, 3 times his range factor. Remember to figure range factors over a two-year period.

If any speed score is over 10.00, then move it down to 10; if it is less than zero, move it up to zero. No element can be outside the 0 to 10 range.

When you have the six elements of the speed score, throw out the lowest one. The player's speed score is the average of the other five.

BREAKIN' THE WAND

Well, it's time for me to go. The *Baseball Abstract* has been good to me. Starting this project twelve years ago was a casual decision. I had written some articles for the *Baseball Digest*, wrote a regular column for a publication called the *Baseball Bulletin*. When *The Sporting News* said something that got a reaction from me, I'd write them a letter, and sometimes they'd publish it. I didn't have any trouble getting published, but none of that seemed to be going anywhere.

What was frustrating to me about this stage of my career was that the articles that I could sell were just formula articles; note the elements of the form, assemble such elements, produce the package. The articles that I thought were really good, the articles that made a contribution toward one's understanding of the subject would not sell. The stolen-base revolution was just getting rolling then, and no baseball broadcast was complete without a comment to the effect that you don't steal on the catcher, you steal on the pitcher. Ted Simmons was in his prime, and there were people who thought that Simmons was as valuable a player as Johnny Bench. What was missing from these discussions was obvious: no one knew how many bases were stolen against Ted Simmons, or against Johnny Bench, or against Steve Carlton or against Jim Palmer.

So I counted 'em. I collected all *The Sporting News* for a season, and I couldn't count stolen bases against the specific pitcher or catcher, so I did the best I could: I counted the bases stolen in the games started by Steve Carlton, and the games started by Jim Palmer, and the games started by each pitcher and each catcher.

It was obvious from doing this that both the pitcher and the catcher had a role to play in determining how many bases were stolen. It was obvious that the difference between Johnny Bench catching and Ted Simmons was at least 50 stolen bases a year. I felt that, from doing the research, I had learned something worth knowing.

I wrote up an article, and I sent it around. Nobody wanted to publish it. I couldn't understand that. If people liked to discuss the role of the pitcher and the catcher in preventing the stolen base, then how could they not want to have the information that bore directly on the issue? It made no sense. I felt that the editors who lay between me and the public were simply wrong in rejecting the article.

There were other articles like this that I wanted to write, but knew that I could not get to the public. So I decided to write them up, bind them into my own book, and sell that book directly to the public.

In retrospect, it is fortunate that I had not the foggiest idea what I was up against. I had no idea how difficult it would be to produce that book. I had no idea how difficult it would be, once I had written the book, to turn it into a commercial product. I had no idea how difficult it would be to market that project once it existed. I am certain that I could never have begun the project if I had known.

I began with a list of about 20 projects that I intended to complete and make into a book. I started in January. About the middle of April I had completed four of these projects. Well, not really completed them; I had done a lot of work on four of the projects. At that point, I began to pull in the reins, and trim the projects down to a manageable size.

The first book was very far from being what I wanted it to be. I did the second book because I knew that I could do a better job than I had done on the first. In the first effort I had compiled data, but had not had the time—or, indeed, the self-confidence—to write about the material. I think I was probably a better writer then than I am now. I think I wrote as well when I was in college as now. It seems to me that in the last ten years I haven't learned much about writing, and probably have forgotten some of the things I used to know. But at that time, I didn't have the confidence to do it. I was obsessed with the idea that since I was charging money directly to the consumer, I had to provide pure information, free of opinion or interpretation. The public, I had decided, wasn't going to pay money for my opinions; they wanted the facts.

In the years 1977–1981 I produced the book every year out of my home. I wrote articles about teams and players, and typed them up and had them photocopied and stapled together, and we sold them. Susie undertook the main responsibility for handling of sales, taxes, preparation of the manuscript, even doing some of the research work and editing. We never sold very many copies—about 2200 tops, I think—but good things happened as a consequence of doing the book:

• Dan Okrent, who was well connected in the publishing world, saw a copy of the book, and took it upon himself to help me. Dan recommended me to *Esquire* magazine, and I began to write annual preseason baseball pieces for them.

• Alan Hendricks, an agent for ballplayers, saw a copy of the book, and recommended me to his associates—his brothers—to help them in the preparation of arbitration cases.

• Although the number of people who read the book was not what you might call an economic number, my relationship with my readers was tremendously satisfying. Of those 2200 people, maybe 300 would write to me in a year, and I would write back. They were very kind letters, from people who were happy to have discovered the *Abstract,* and felt that it was a sort of small private treasure, known only to a few select people. Some of my correspondents in this period, men like Dallas Adams and Pete Palmer, contributed tremendously to helping me clarify my thinking about the issues that I wrote about. Many of these people disagreed with me, you understand, but they would disagree to a purpose, to point out an alternative that I might not have thought of or an approach I had discarded too hastily.

Perhaps more than any of this, what made me certain that I was onto something was the reaction I got from what might be called casual contacts—people I would meet at a wedding, on the bus, at work, or at a ballgame—who were genuinely interested in talking about the same things that I wrote about. Although I never tried to sell the book to a publisher, several times one or another of my readers would become an unpaid advocate of the book, and would send it to someone they knew who worked in the publishing world, urging them to publish it nationally. The response was always that there was no market for such a book. Sports books don't sell, they would say, and a sports book like this, involving long, technical analysis—well, it didn't have a chance. But you couldn't tell me that the public was not interested in my work, when I would meet so many people just in the ordinary course of living who were interested.

It is a wonderful thing to know that you are right and the world is wrong; would God that I might have that feeling again before I die. I was developing, in those days, a technique of listening very carefully to the things that baseball people said, and then asking the question: If this is true, what would be the consequences of it? If it was false, what would be the consequences of that? Where would I find those consequences? To most people it no doubt seemed that I was writing about statistics, but I wasn't, not ever; in the years I've been doing this book I have written no more than a couple of articles about baseball statistics. The secret of the success of the book was that I was dead in the center of the discussion. I was writing about exactly the same issues that everybody else was talking about, only in a different way. I would check. If somebody said that the DH rule was making it easier for American League pitchers to win twenty games, I would check to see if the consequences of that statement were in place. If someone said that the Milwaukee Brewers were winning a lot of ballgames in the late innings, I would check. When someone said that the Philadelphia Phillies would collapse because they were getting old, I figured the average age of the starting eight on every major-league team since 1920 to find out what the relationship was between aging and predictable decline.

It happens that the consequences of these statements are usually found in the statistics, and that even when they are not ("average age" is not a statistic in the traditional sense) they must usually be expressed as numbers. Because of this association I was thought of, by people who knew about my work but didn't understand it, as a sta-

stician, even though I never figured very many statistics, and wasn't very good at it when I had to do it. As I saw it, baseball had two distinct mountains of material. On the one hand, there was a mountain of traditional wisdom, things that people said over and over again. On the other hand, there was a mountain of statistics. My work was to build a bridge between those two mountains. A statistician is concerned with what baseball statistics *are.* I had no concern with what they are. I didn't care, and don't care, whether Mike Schmidt hit .306 or .296 against left-handed pitching. I was concerned with what the statistics *mean.*

Sportswriters, in my opinion, almost never use baseball statistics to try to understand baseball. They use statistic to decorate their articles. They use statistics as a club in the battle for what they believe intuitively to be correct. That is why sportswriters often believe that you can prove anything with statistics, an obscene and ludicrous position, but one which is a natural outgrowth of the way that they themselves try to use statistics. What I wanted to do was to teach people instead to use statistics as a sword to cut toward the truth.

I was doing this for several years when no one else was, and by 1980 I was years ahead of anyone else in the field. A large part of the charm of the book in that time, I think, was that it assumed an intelligent audience. They kept telling me that the public wasn't interested, and I kept saying, yes, *the* public isn't interested, but there is *a* public that is. It isn't *The Sporting News* public. It isn't *The Baseball Digest* public. It isn't the public that is happy to be told that to a hitter like Rod Carew it doesn't make any difference whether the pitcher is left-handed or right-handed.

It is, instead, an informed public, a public that already knows those things, and wants to know more. It is an educated public, a public that recognizes an opinion and a fact, distinguishes between a cliché and a theory. It is, simply, an audience that wants more.

That approach, I think, caused people to react positively to the early books. The books had, in retrospect, many flaws; the writing was spotty, the research often shallow. The key was that it was written to an intelligent audience. If you think of the public as a pyramid—a lowest common denominator of perhaps 40 million baseball fans, with a second level of perhaps 5 million hard-core baseball fans, and another level of perhaps 300,000 hardcore baseball fans who are educated and intelligent and tolerant. Well, forget the levels; just get the idea of a pyramid of baseball fans, getting more serious and more intelligent toward the top. I was aiming at the top of the pyramid.

Journalism, by its nature, *must* appeal to the lowest common denominator, the lowest level of the pyramid. It must not assume any knowledge. The rule is that if you refer to Babe Ruth, you have to explain who Babe Ruth was; otherwise, some portion of the potential audience will be lost. To reach the largest possible audience, you must write to the lowest common denominator—but if you write to the lowest common denominator, almost all of the audience will feel that they are being patronized, and will regard you with a certain contempt. If you assume the highest possible level of knowledge, you lose people and you wind up with a small audience—but an audience that is flattered. By assuming an intelligent audience, I developed a small audience, but an audience with which I had a wonderful relationship.

In 1981, Dan Okrent wrote an article about me and my work for *Sports Illustrated*. After that several publishing companies were interested in distributing the book. I signed with Ballantine Books, and we (Susie and I) began working with them in 1982. We made a few minor changes in the form of the book, but it was essentially the same. Peter Gethers, then an editor at Ballantine, did a terrific job of selling the book within the company, giving it a chance to find its audience.

The first edition of the book sold well. The second edition sold better. The third edition sold better. This remains true; I don't think we've ever had a year when the sales didn't increase. It became the best-selling baseball book of each season. The irony was that by abjuring the goal of trying to write to a large audience and focusing instead on serving a small audience—I had stumbled, quite by accident, onto a large audience.

This accident of marketing has a couple of things to tell us about the publishing business. Remember that people used to say that sports books don't sell? After John Feinstein, it will be a long time before anybody says that again, but why is it that sports books often don't sell?

The answer is, because they're terrible. Most books about baseball are terrible. They're written to the lowest common denominator and the lowest common denominator doesn't buy books.

You see, most baseball fans don't like this book. That's the truth. The book is too hard to understand, and there are too many statistics and there's too much math and who cares what James thinks, anyway? And that doesn't matter a whit, because I'm not writing to those people. I don't care what they think. I'm not writing to them, I'm writing to you.

Look, you can't write a book that everybody likes. Everybody doesn't like Shakespeare. Everybody doesn't like the Bible. It would be foolish for me to think that everybody is going to like Bill James. A book can't survive by being innocuous. To find a niche, a book has to exert a positive attraction to *somebody*.

Fortunately, there are 40 million baseball fans in this country. If 99 percent of them hate the book, that's no problem; that leaves 400,000 potential buyers. If one-fourth of those who don't hate the book will buy it, you're on the best seller list.

After the book became successful, there was a period of years in which it was not rational for me even to consider whether I wanted to keep doing it. Having written the book for several years for almost no money, I couldn't walk away from it the minute it began to pay off. The process of writing this book is so exhausting that since 1978, I have never finished one book without swearing that I could never do it again. I mean it. Every year since 1978, I have told Susie in the spring that this would be the last year of the *Abstract*. I was quite serious when I said it, so wrung out from putting the book together that I did not believe I could ever do it again. When I had a yearly contract, I always thought I'd have to find a way to get out of the contract.

I made it to the end of this contract, and the time has come to consider whether or not I should sign another. I have decided not to.

I think that some of the things that have been accomplished by the success of the *Abstract* are positive. I think that a few things are known now, known by the entire baseball world, that were not known ten years ago and likely would not have been known were it not for my having done this. I very often hear people, baseball people and baseball fans, say things in the context of discussion that I know they would never have known ten years ago.

I mentioned somewhere in this book that I had made up a file that had almost all the career appearances of Sandy Koufax. In analyzing that file, I discovered something really astonishing. You know the tremendous leap forward that Sandy Koufax made in 1962? From 1958 through 1961, Koufax's ERAs were 4.48, 4.05, 3.91, and 3.51—making slow improvement, but nothing special. From 1962 through 1966, Koufax led the league in ERA every year, with an aggregate ERA under 2.00.

But you know what? He didn't make a great leap forward in 1962. What happened was that in 1962 he moved from a park that was absolutely terrible for him—the Los Angeles Coliseum, with its 251-foot left field line—to a park that was great for him, Dodger Stadium.

• In 1960 in road games, Koufax had an ERA of 3.00, and struck out 126 men in 105 innings; he was 7–6. His problem was that in Los Angeles, his home park, he went 1–7 with an ERA of 5.27.

• In 1961 in road games, Koufax was 9–6 with an ERA of 2.78. His problem was that in Los Angeles, though his record was almost as good (9–7), his ERA was 4.29, pushing him to an overall mark of 3.52.

• Koufax's career ERA in the Coliseum was 4.40, with a 17–23 record. In the same years, his record on the road was 28–21 with an ERA of 3.46 (all figures include World Series play).

• In 1962, Koufax's ERA on the road was 3.53, his worst in several years. But by posting an ERA in Dodger Stadium of 1.75, he cut his overall ERA to 2.54—and led the league for the first time.

• In 1963, Koufax's ERA on the road was 2.30. At Dodger Stadium, it was 1.36.

In 1964, Koufax's ERA on the road was 2.93. At Dodger Stadium, it was 0.85. He allowed 12 earned runs in 127.2 innings in L.A.

• In 1965, Koufax's greatest year, he pitched 25 times on the road with a 2.54 ERA, 13–6 record (still including World Series), struck out 193 men in 180.2 innings. In Dodger Stadium, he pitched 21 times, finished 15–3 with a 1.31 ERA and 218 strikeouts in 179 innings.

The point is certainly not that Koufax wasn't a great pitcher. The point is that nobody knew. Did you? I was a consumptive baseball fan in those years. I don't think I ever heard anyone say that what had happened to Koufax in 1962 was not that he learned to throw his curve ball behind in the count, but that he went from a park that added 75 points a year to his ERA to one that cut 60 points a year off of it.

If that happened today, we would know. We would know that, just as we know that Dwight Gooden doesn't pitch well in day baseball, just as we know that Bob Horner has hit two-thirds of his career home runs in Atlanta and that Wade Boggs one year hit .390 with two strikes on him and that Pat Tabler has been terrific with the bases loaded. I have helped create the conditions by which these things are known, and I am proud of that.

But if there has been a growth in the access to and understanding of meaningful baseball statistics, there has been an unchecked explosion in access to meaningless ones. The idea has taken hold that the public is just endlessly fascinated by any baseball statistic you can find, without regard to whether it means anything. The success of the *Baseball Abstract* proves that, doesn't it? The fact that this book appeals to perhaps one-quarter of one percent of the nation's baseball fans is lost; what sticks in the mind is that it is the best-selling book about baseball. The fact that the book is obsessively concerned with seeing through the illusions of baseball statistics, trying to understand what they really mean . . . this fact, I say, is lost; what sticks in the mind is that there are a whole lot of numbers here.

I would like to pretend that the invasion of statistical gremlins crawling at random all over the telecast of damn near every baseball game is irrelevant to me, that I really have nothing to do with it. It just happened.

I know better. I didn't create this mess, but I helped.

Every success in the publishing industry spawns immediate imitators, and the *Abstract* certainly has not been an exception to that. As once publishing people assured themselves that sports books don't sell, they later assumed that the public had a limitless capacity to consume baseball statistics. The fallout of that assumption was a Chernobyl of statistics, polluting nearly every discussion. As valuable as statistics can be in the context of an analysis, they are equally out of place in the middle of an at bat—the difference, to paraphrase Roger Miller, between sugar in your candy and sugar in your soup.

So saturated has the world become with this type of research that I question whether anything I discovered now would have a real impact, no matter what it was. In the early years of the *Abstract* there were a few basic things we learned—that the number of runs scored was a predictable consequence of the individual offensive incidents, that ballparks had a huge impact in shaping batting statistics—which permanently colored the way in which people who read the book saw the game. Many people told me that because they read the *Abstract,* they saw a baseball game through different eyes.

I wonder if it would be possible for anything I found to have the same impact now. I wonder if we haven't become so numbed by all of these numbers that we are no longer capable of truly assimilating any knowledge which might result from them.

It was such a casual decision to start the *Abstract,* and it is such a gut-wrenching decision to stop it. I suppose there is a law of nature there; it is a casual decision to ask for a date, a gut-wrenching decision to ask for a divorce. But the nature of my relationship with my audience has also changed tremendously in the last few years, and again, I am not pleased with the changes. My readers were once one of my greatest sources of pleasure; they were so pleased to find me, and I so pleased to find them, that for six or seven years it was a virtual love feast.

I still have many of those readers, and I still get many letters during the course of a year that are a great pleasure to me. But as time goes by, I get more and more letters that irritate the living hell out of me. People have started

assuming that I am a goddamn public utility or something. I get letters from people telling me that I do this well but that I shouldn't do that and I should do more of that and less of this and try some of the other. If they irritate me enough, I write back "Dear Jackass: I am not your employee. It is not my function to write about what you are interested in. I write about what I am interested in. If you want to read it, read it. If you don't, don't. But DON'T TELL ME WHAT TO WRITE ABOUT."

While it is not necessarily expressed in a hostile voice, that idea has always been fundamental to my work, a relic of my sixties youth. It also explains how I got into doing this. I wouldn't let editors, twelve years ago, tell me what I should write about and what I shouldn't. It's my time and my talent and my life, and these are three of my most precious possessions. Why should I let you tell me what to do with them?

The emphasis on this could easily be taken out of context, for as I say, most of my letters are still very intelligent, thoughtful, constructive. But whereas I used to write one "Dear Jackass" letter a year, I now write maybe thirty. Thirty letters, out of the hundreds I write in a year, isn't a very large percentage. But is it, in three years, going to be a hundred? I hate to say it and I hope you're not one of them, but I am encountering more and more of my own readers that I don't even like, nitwits who glom onto something superficial in the book and misunderstand its underlying message. I think that whenever a writer finds that he is beginning to dislike his own readers, it's a very clear sign that he's heading down the wrong road.

I have met a lot of wonderful people in the years since the *Abstract* went national, including not only colleagues like Craig Wright and John Dewan and Don Zminda, but just readers who would write once in a while or do a good piece of research. Let me give you one more reason for my quitting. It may be in the best interest of sabermetrics for me to step aside.

In the years that I have been doing this, I have done everything I possibly could to further not my own career, but the field of sabermetrics. In these pages I have written articles in praise of and passed along the address of anybody who wrote anything worthwhile about sabermetrics. I have tried to share the spotlight. Whenever a reporter called me and wanted to talk about my work, I've told him he should call Pete Palmer or Craig Wright or John Dewan or Dick Cramer, too. When economic opportunities have come my way, I have always asked first whether they could be converted for the benefit of the whole field of sabermetrics. I have hired people to do piece work, to write articles for me or help me on arbitration cases, not because I needed the help but because I figured they could use the opportunities. I have included in these pages articles by and letters from my readers, sometimes paying them a little money for it and sometimes not but still giving their work and their name a little bit of exposure. I have put countless hours into editing small publications and organizing projects for the sabermetric community, like Project Scoresheet. I have loaned my name out to other people's newsletters and other publications like the *Great American Baseball Stat Book,* without asking or accepting a cent in return. I have critiqued research for other people, analyzed their work, and recommended changes. I have suggested ideas for research. I have written letters of recommendation and letters of support. I have written glowing reviews of competitor's books, and given more cover quotes than I can remember. I have arranged contacts with my agent and my editor and anybody else I know. I've got a lot of black marks in my ledger, I know, but I can say with a clear conscience that I could not have done more than I have done to try to help the other people who want to work in sabermetrics, and that I have never knowingly passed up an opportunity to help a potential competitor who wasn't trying to establish a monopoly.

I have done this, in a way, because I thought it was the right thing to do, and because it was a way of paying back Dan Okrent for his efforts to help me when I was starting out, and because I always knew that I was going to get out of the field anyway, so I wasn't threatened by what anybody else was doing. I believe that, because I did these things, I leave sabermetrics in good hands; there are a lot of people out there doing good work.

I wonder if the best thing for those people now isn't for me to step out of the field, go on and do something else. There aren't jobs available for an infinite number of sabermetricians. I wonder if, try as I might to avoid it, my being here isn't getting in the way of other people's ability to develop a reputation. Not only that, but I am by nature a controversial cuss. I can't avoid saying things that make some people mad, and that's really not what science is about. I wonder if maybe it would be in the best interest of sabermetrics if the loudest voice in the choir belonged to someone who was a little more restrained, a little more considered, like Craig Wright or Don Zminda.

I've also got to say, guys, that having done this, I've now done all I can do. I can't help you any more. The field is maturing, and as it is there are more signs of greed and unchecked ambition, and the point at which that stuff starts to appear is the point at which I start to lose sympathy for your cause. Sabermetrics is best served not by its members behaving like economic competitors, but by adopting the ethics of an academic discipline supporting baseball in the way that the College of Agriculture supports farming.

I'm going to bury this comment in the middle of a long article, but I do believe that the *Abstract* will carry on next year, under someone else's direction. I do believe that there will be a *1989 Baseball Abstract,* but I don't know who will edit it or what it will be like. I'm not even sure there will be one, but if there is, it will be done on a very small scale, like the early *Abstracts*—desktop publishing, as it is called now. There will not be a nationally distributed *Abstract,* at least for a few years. If I decide to do it, I'll try to find the most qualified person, and turn the whole thing over to him. If you would like to receive information about the *1989 Baseball Abstract,* please write to *1989 Baseball Abstract,* c/o Bill James, Winchester, Ks. 66097. Letters sent to this address will be put in a shoebox and unopened until next October or something, and I swear to God if you send a check or money order to this address I'm going to keep the money and not give you anything in return.

Of the other books about sabermetrics, much as I hate to say it, the *Elias Analyst* has become the best. The first *Analyst* I didn't think much of; they imitated the superficial form of the *Abstract,* but what they poured into that form was just a lot of reference material, with no real analytical content. The second year they tried imitating my silly headlines and random comments. Last year, though, there were signs that whichever one of the Hirdt boys it is that does this stuff was actually beginning to get the hang of it. They've imitated my work so meticulously that they're actually showing some signs of understanding it.

As I'm sure you know if you read both books, the *Elias Analyst* has ripped off my methods and my research so closely that many passages fall just short of plagiarism. They use methods that are nearly identical to my methods, repeat research that is virtually identical to my research and sometimes write it up in phrases that vary only slightly from my phrases—without giving me any credit. In the publishing industry, this is accepted competitive behavior. In an academic discipline, it is reprehensible misconduct. The sad part is that they're not hurting me. I mean, we sell probably two and a half or three times as many books as they do, and the growth in our sales over the period of their "competition" is probably greater than their total sales. They're not hurting me; they're hurting themselves. The public isn't stupid. The public recognizes a ripoff. If they would lay aside this self-defeating and small-mindedness and adopt the ethic of the field, they'd gain a lot of respect and wind up selling more books.

They can't do that, because Seymour Siwoff controlled a monopoly for more than twenty years, and he can't give up the surly vision that he can regain control of the field. I think what a lot of people don't understand is that I have attacked the Elias Bureau for exactly the same reason that I have worked so hard to help everyone else in the field: that I want people who want to work in sabermetrics to have that opportunity, and the Elias Bureau wants to prevent them from having that opportunity.

Well, they're there anyway; I leave the field to whoever is playing on it. Because four months a year of cyclical depression has gotten to be too much for me. Because I am no longer certain that the effects of my doing this kind of research are in the best interests of the average baseball fan. Because I wonder if anything I found now could have any real impact on the game. Because I have been repaid for my years of doing this book in anonymity, and no longer have any claim to go on drawing paychecks from it. Because while I have enjoyed doing this book, I have only one lifetime and many dreams. Because I have confidence that I will make a living one way or another. Because I feel that I am on a collision course with my own audience. Because I suspect that my leaving the field may be in the best interests of sabermetrics.

Because it is time to go, friends. I'm breakin' the wand, exit stage right. I hereby release any and all of my formulas, theories, and other systems of analysis to any other analyst who wishes to use them and to call them by name (runs created, value approximation method, etc.) either for private or economic use, even by Elias should they so desire. I'll be doing other things, writing other books. I won't be hard to find. I hope that some of you will enjoy those other books. I know that some of you won't, and that's all right, too. It's been good.

Bill James
Sabermetrician, Retired
February 1988